Paradise Poisoned
Learning about Conflict, Terrorism and Development from Sri Lanka's Civil Wars

John Richardson

Paradise Poisoned
Learning about Conflict, Terrorism and Development from Sri Lanka's Civil Wars

John Richardson

International Center for Ethnic Studies
Kandy, Sri Lanka

© International Centre for Ethnic Studies (ICES), 2005
ISBN 955-580-094-4

Enquiries should be addressed to the publisher.

First published 2005

The International Centre for Ethnic Studies
554/6A, Peradeniya Road
Kandy, Sri Lanka

Printed by
Karunaratne & Sons
67, UDA Industrial Estate
Katuwana Road, Homagama
Sri Lanka.
+94 (11) 2 855 520, +94 (11) 5 551 965

To

Kingsley M. de Silva
and
Louis W. Goodman

Foreword

It is both a pleasure and a privilege to write this foreword to Professor John Richardson's thorough and exhaustive study *Paradise Poisoned* that examines the complex relationship between "Conflict, Terrorism and Development" using Sri Lanka as a case study. This is the result of over seventeen years of dedicated scholarship. There are foreign scholars who write books on developing countries with nothing more than a casual acquaintance of the country concerned and then declare themselves "experts" on that country. What the reader will find between the covers of this book is a work of a very different nature and calibre.

Professor Richardson's first visit to Sri Lanka was in 1987. On that occasion he also participated in an international conference of the ICES where I met him for the first time. Over the next seventeen years he frequently visited the island that he has virtually come to consider as his second home. In those numerous visits he has spent varying periods of time including lengthy sabbaticals teaching and researching. Over the years I saw Professor Richardson painstakingly gather data on Sri Lanka—talking to people, reading primary and secondary sources, collecting statistics, and observing events. His mission was to understand why this island nation that showed remarkable stability and promise in the early years of independence not only failed to realise its full development potential but gradually moved towards producing one of the most violent and protracted internal wars in the world. The readers will find his answer to that question provided in this book.

The three themes *Conflict, Terrorism and Development* that he brings together in his analysis are perhaps the three major challenges that the world confronts at the beginning of the new millennium. Improving the living standards of over one billion people who live on less than one dollar a day and another 1.7 billion who live on less than two dollars a day is the major development challenge of our time. Resolving conflict without violence and defeating terrorism have become the major issues of governance of our time. Professor Richardson's work analyses the complex links that exist between these two major issues. But as the book's sub-title *Learning about Conflict, Terrorism and Development from Sri Lanka's Civil Wars* makes clear his study is not a mere treatise for academe. He also provides some very practical policy suggestions to make the world a better and more peaceful place.

The ICES is delighted to have had this opportunity to publish Professor Richardson's work. It is all the more satisfying because this is one way of showing our appreciation to him for the services he has rendered to the Centre in the last several years as a member of the board of directors. He had offers from publishers in USA. But he felt that publishing it in the West would price it beyond the reach of many Sri Lankan readers. He did not want that to happen because he strongly felt that his first duty was to make his work accessible to the people whose problems he chose to study. We sincerely hope that the Sri Lankan readers of this book would find Professor Richardson's insights helpful to understand our country better and to find a lasting and peaceful solution to the nation's problems. As the author persuasively argues Sri Lanka holds some very valuable lessons in governance and development that have wider applicability that we believe the book's international readership will find interesting and useful.

S W R de A Samarasinghe
Director
International Centre for Ethnic Studies
554/6A, Peradeniya Road
Kandy
Sri Lanka

November 17, 2004

Contents

Part III
Symptoms of Infection and Immune System Responses:
How Sri Lanka's United Front Government Coped with a Violent
Insurrection and Shortcomings of its Marxist Development Model

Part IV
Failure of Radical Therapies:
How Sri Lanka's 'Open Economy' Development Model and
Strengthened Presidential Authority Failed to Prevent
Conflict and Terrorism from Escalating Out of Control

Part V

Diagnosis, Treatment and Prevention:
Why Deadly Conflict and Terrorism are not only
Predictable, but Preventable

dgements

...ninates a project that began, as described
...st visited Sri Lanka in 1987. Our brief
...stay, in 1988, when I taught in Colombo
...ogram and my wife, Emily, helped initiate
...nil Women in Jaffna District, under the
... Much of the basic conflict events and
...his period, with able assistance of a team
...n, Neluka Silva, Manjula de Silva, Sham-
..., Indrani Illaperuma, Danika Umagiliya,
...hi Gnanaselvem and H.M Jayewardena.
...ousekeeper and administrative assistant.
...sergeant in the 'Ceylon Army' not only
...our first teacher of Sri Lankan customs,
...es, including that of Mr. Peiris, these ini-
...d into lasting friendships that have been
...s to Sri Lanka.

1987 also marked the beginning of my long association with one of the
world's unique research institutions, the International Centre for Ethnic Studies, with offices in Kandy and Colombo and with and two of its founding
directors, Professors Kingsley M. de Silva and S.W.R. de A. Samarasinghe. Professor de Silva's *History of Sri Lanka* (1981) and *Managing Ethnic Tensions in a
Multi-Ethnic Society* (1986) were among the first books I read about Sri Lanka.
The fact that twenty-one of Kingsley's publications appear in the bibliography
of this volume is but one small measure of his contributions to my own work.
Later I also came to know the Colombo ICES Directors, Radhika Coomaras-
wami and the late Neelan Tiruchelvam and benefited from their lifetimes of
experience as committed scholar-activists in Sri Lanka. I was deeply honoured,
when some years later I was invited to become a board member of the ICES.
The fine libraries of the ICES Kandy and Colombo Offices, ably managed by
Ms. Kanthi Gamage and Mr. Ponundurai Thambirajah have been invaluable
resources for me and many other Sri Lankan scholars over the years.

My colleagues at the University of Colombo most graciously accepted a
putative Sri Lankan researcher/scholar, with only superficial knowledge, into

their midst. Among those who willingly joined in numerous conversations touching on my research and helped to educate me, Shelton Kodikara, Stanley Wijesundera and Newton Gunasinghe, are now deceased, as is another mentor, the distinguished journalist and long-time *Lanka Guardian* editor, Mervyn de Silva. Other University of Colombo colleagues who have been patient recipients of my queries and, in some cases, reviewers of draft chapters include Jayadeva Uyangoda, A.R. Ariaratne, W.D. Lakshman, Amal Jayewardene, Sri Hettege, Tressie Leitan, Arjuna Parakrama. and Dayan Jayatileke.

I must also acknowledge the hospitality of the University of Colombo, accorded to me by several Vice Chancellors, that permitted me to occupy the 'Vice Chancellor's Lodge' at Number 5 Bagatelle Terrace on numerous visits. Those visits were made more comfortable and convenient by the hard work of Colombo University's caretaker for the entire period, Mr. B.G.T. Bandara.

Dr. G.P.S.H. de Silva, then Director of Sri Lanka's National Archives, not only gave my researchers access to the Archives' newspaper files, over many months, but gifted me one of my most valuable sources, his *A Statistical Survey of Elections to the Legislatures of Sri Lanka, 1911-1977* (1979). Without this remarkably detailed compilation, published in the days before personal computers and spreadsheets, my grasp of Sri Lanka legislative and electoral politics, especially in the early post-independence years would have been fragmentary, at best. A comparably valuable volume, also painstakingly compiled in the pre-personal computer era, was Patrick Peebles *Sri Lanka: A Handbook of Historical Statistics* (1982). Later, I became acquainted with Professor Peebles, which enabled me to not only to acknowledge his *Handbook,* but more fully appreciate the depth of his knowledge about Sri Lanka.

Many Sri Lankan friends and acquaintances have been unfailingly supportive while patiently awaiting publication of a book that they may, increasingly, have thought would never appear in print. They have invited me to their homes on many occasions, answered questions, introduced me to friends, read draft chapters and educated me in innumerable discussions of Sri Lankan history, culture, politics and economics. Among them are Sita Peiris, Bena Peiris, Joe Karunaratne, Charmane Karunaratne, Bradman Weerakoon, Tissa Jayatileka, Willie Mendis, Douglas Umagiliya, Chandra Jayaratne, Rohanna Jayaratne, Sister Bernard Vas, Lucien Mellawa, Kanthi Mellawa, Tilak Ranaviraja, Sunethra Ranaviraja, Ranjan Amerasinghe and Wimila Amerisinghe. Sita and Bena Pieris, Joe Karunaratne and Tilak Ranaviraja were particularly helpful in providing detailed comments on draft chapters. Sita's invitation to deliver the G.C. Mendis Memorial Lecture, honouring her father, motivated me to produce a first iteration of what appears in this book as the 'development and deadly conflict system' model. I have not accepted the suggestions of these friends in every case, but hope they will not interpret this as meaning that I have not valued their contributions and willingness to help.

In 2001, at an important juncture, I had the good fortune to be selected as one of the first resident scholars at the incomparable Pemberley International Centre for Scholars, founded by Dr. Brendon Gooneratne. My Pemberley residence made possible the completion of critical writing tasks, but an unexpected value-added was the nightly dinners that Dr. Gooneratne and I took together. He is deeply steeped in Sri Lankan history and was most generous with his views and experiences. Later, I became acquainted with his wife, Dr. Jasmine Gooneratne, one of Sri Lanka's finest writers, whose book *Relative Merits: A Personal Memoir of the Bandaranaike Family of Sri Lanka*, played such an important role in shaping my early views of Sri Lankan society.

There have also been many collaborators and supporters on the American side. First on the list would have to be the many research assistants, most provided by American University's School of International Service, who worked on the project. These included Deborah Furlong, Jianxin Wang, Shinjinee Sen, Gillian Barnes, Jan Rubenstein, Sarah Johnson, Christina Melhorn Landi, Kenneth Friesen, Burcu Akan, Naren Kumarakulasingam, Kristine Herrmann, Ramzi Nemo, Ravinatha Aryasinha, Mark Hamilton and Jessica Roach. Christina, Kenneth, and Jianxin were critical team members as well as scholarly collaborators during the data collection stage, while Kristine copyedited one iteration of the entire manuscript. Mark Hamilton was responsible for the accuracy and completeness of the footnotes, compensating with meticulous attention to detail for my omissions, oversights and inconsistencies. Jessica Roach, an experienced NGO administrator, recreated herself as a book designer/compositor and was responsible for preparing camera ready copy. Wesley Schauble, the Centre for Teaching Excellence's creative and technically skilled staff designer, created the book cover, with pictures provided by one of Sri Lanka's premier photographers, Dominic Sansoni. The unique community of colleagues that is American University's International Development Program patiently encouraged me to complete the project, but never asked why it was taking so long. Deborah Brautigam and Vidya Samarasinghe were helpful in providing substantive comments and, in Vidya's case, many nuanced translations of Sri Lankan phrases. Among the U.S. community of Sri Lankan scholars, I am particularly grateful to Ambassador (and Professor) Howard Wriggins. We became acquainted rather late in the project, but his encouragement has been unstinting, and he has contributed many valuable comments. Nicholas Onuf and his wife Sandi, our predecessors in the Link Program, first welcomed us to number 5 Bagatelle Terrace and introduced us to Sri Lanka. Nick has been a supportive colleague and thoughtful commentator throughout the project. Donella Meadows, my collaborator on several previous books, contributed encouragement and helpful ideas before her untimely death, as did Elizabeth Cowan Neeld, also a collaborator on a previous book, and my sister-in-law, Edith Bingham.

Funding for the project included a research grant from the School of International Service that was used to support my field research in Sri Lanka and a grant from the U.S. Institute of Peace that provided partial course relief for a year as an initial draft of the case study portion of the manuscript was taking shape. There was also partial support from the Pemberley International Centre for Scholars for my time in residence. Over the project's life, additional time for writing was provided by three Sabbatical leaves. Academic professionals accept this time off – one year out of every seven – as a right, but such an entitlement is unknown, of course, in most professions. I consider this tradition to be a great privilege and am grateful that the Trustees of American University continue to sustain it.

Inevitably, book writing intermingles with family life. This is especially true when the project spans seventeen years. My marriage to Emily Richardson and my work on *Paradise Poisoned* commenced almost simultaneously. The book has been an unanticipated, perpetual, living presence in our lives. I never imagined, and certainly Emily did not, that a small South Asian nation on the opposite side of the world and a writing project of this magnitude would become my major professional preoccupation for a seemingly indefinite period. During this time Emily did not choose to be the wifely collaborator that is extolled, truthfully or not, by some scholars in book prefaces. She has had her own goals, priorities and a significant professional career that partly grew out of her remarkable public health work in Jaffna district, literally in the midst of conflict. Over these past seventeen years I have gained deep respect for her independence, strength, and courage. She has accepted this consuming project, not of her own choosing, as part of our lives, while continuing to be true to herself. There has been much to learn from her example. The lessons have been valuable and I am grateful for them.

Paradise Poisoned is dedicated to two scholars with whom my relationship, too, has been more or less coincident with the project. In very different ways, each has served as mentor and role model. The name of Kingsley de Silva, Sri Lanka's premier historian for many years, will be familiar to many readers. In nominating Kingsley for the Fukuoka prize several years ago, I described his career as 'characterised by prolific scholarship, meticulously high standards, prescience and originality. ... It is the breadth of his contributions,' I continued, 'as well as the high quality in each arena where he has made his mark that makes Kingsley de Silva truly exceptional.' When writing about Sri Lanka, Kingsley has been the 'audience' who has been present on the other side of my computer screen. Kingsley is not accepting of foreign scholars who write about Sri Lanka but have not done their homework. But to me, he has been an affirming role model. He has challenged me to do my best and has motivated me do to *my* homework. No mentor could do more. *Paradise Poisoned* is my best effort to live up to Kingsley's high standards.

Louis Goodman, a Latin American scholar, may be less well known to readers. But as Dean of American University's School of International Service he has established himself as one of the world's most effective leaders in International Relations higher education. A measure of his leadership is the ability to demand that faculty meet high standards, while empowering them to follow their own intellectual lights. It is an exceptional Dean who would accept, without grumbling, the decision of a senior scholar to embark on a new field of inquiry for which he had, essentially, no qualifications. Sri Lanka was not an area where big research grants were to be found; where mainstream books were to be written; where wealthy fee-paying students could be attracted to American University. Lou not only hasn't grumbled; he has been unconditionally supportive these many years. *Paradise Poisoned* is my best effort to justify that support.

'Preface and acknowledgements' sections typically end with a routine reminder that while those acknowledged have made contributions, the statements and conclusions found in a volume are the author's sole responsibility. In this instance the reminder needs to be more than routine.

Many of the issues addressed in *Paradise Poisoned* are not only sensitive but unresolved. Though my case study mostly ends in 1988 and major protagonists have mostly passed from the scene, their families, supporters and opponents live on. For many, events about which I have written remain present realities. The issues are contemporary. Thus, it is particularly important to emphasise that positions taken and conclusions reached in *Paradise Poisoned* are solely my own. Among my Sri Lankan friends and mentors, I am certain that there are those who would disavow, perhaps strongly, some of what I have written. In particular I wish to emphasise that members of my Sri Lankan research team (they were mostly students then and are all adults now) played no role in producing the final product. They simply collected data and assembled materials for my subsequent use, often several years later. I did not seek their opinions on controversial issues and they did not proffer them.

In the 'preface' to his classic, *Ceylon: Dilemmas of a New Nation* (1961), my friend Howard Wriggins wrote something that I have carried with me throughout this project. After acknowledging many who had helped him, Howard said, 'I am deeply in their debt and trust that anything said in the following pages will not deter them from giving similarly to Ceylonese and other scholars who may be piqued by the lacunae in this study to correct and improve upon it.'

Ceylon: Dilemmas of a New Nation was written in simpler, less controversial times. But Howard's wish is mine, as well. When *Paradise Poisoned* has appeared in print, I pray that my Sri Lankan friends will not regret our relationship and that I will still be welcomed, both in their homes and in their beautiful land.

John Richardson
Washington, D.C.
2 September 2004

Prologue

I have long believed that a book's central message should come first and be given in a few words. Why must readers and reviewers struggle to learn what an author believes is fundamentally important?

Paradise Poisoned is the principal product of a seventeen year project, devoted to understanding linkages between deadly conflict, terrorism and development, by viewing them through the lens of Sri Lanka's post-independence history, from 1948 through 1988. After a period of relative tranquility, escalating conflict and terrorism engulfed this beautiful island nation. Coping with two civil wars became the principal preoccupation of Sri Lanka's government and people. Explaining how tranquility was supplanted by all-encompassing violent conflict and terrorism became the focal point of my inquiries.

What have I learned about preventing deadly conflict and terrorism from Sri Lanka's civil wars?

What I have learned, of fundamental importance, from Sri Lanka's civil wars, is this. **We know more than enough to choose policies that will help prevent protracted deadly conflict and terrorism. We also know more than enough to avoid policies that will cause protracted deadly conflict and terrorism.** Our state of knowledge is analogous to our knowledge about the relationship between cigarette smoking and lung cancer. We know that smoking is a principal cause of lung cancer, though there are other causes. We know that refraining from smoking is the best way of avoiding lung cancer, though some abstainers may still contract the disease.

A promising, proactive strategy for preventing deadly conflict and terrorism can be summarized in ten imperatives. Their relevance extends well beyond Sri Lanka, to Kosovo, Kashmir, Palestine, the Sudan, Afghanistan and, in particular, Iraq. Chapter 22 discusses these imperatives in detail. The intervening chapters provide context and supporting evidence.

The ten imperatives are these:

1. Maintaining public order and preventing social turbulence from escalating into protracted deadly conflict are prerequisite to the success of all other development policies.

2. Polarising political rhetoric and tactics must be forgone, however tempting their short-term benefits may seem. Like mustard gas, which had to be abandoned as a weapon in World War I, this strategy has a tendency to 'blow back' upon the user.[1]

3. Meeting the needs and aspirations of fighting age young men should be the first priority of national development polices and of programs funded by international donors.

4. Developing countries should have internal security forces (police and paramilitary) that are generously funded, professional, apolitical and trained to meet the complex challenges of maintaining public order in a changing society.

5. Development policies that meet human beings' common aspirations – to feel good about their lives, the circumstances in which they live and future prospects for themselves and their children – will contribute most effectively to keeping violent conflict and terrorism within acceptable bounds.

6. Those who frame development policies should seek a middle path between capitalism's efficient, but Darwinian precepts, and socialism's egalitarian, but stultifying precepts.

7. Good governance and democratisation must be part of the 'successful development' mix. Most important are governance institutions that are open to 'bad news' and self-correcting.

8. Multinational corporations, businesses and businessmen's organisations[2] should play a more active role in supporting successful development policies.

9. Successful development requires a long-term view. Giving sufficient weight to the long-term requires institutional mechanisms and discourses that extend beyond the next election and term in office of political leaders presently in power.

10. There must be realistic, rigorous, opportunity-costs analyses of military options, versus *equivalent expenditures* for non military options, before proceeding down the slippery slope of 'military solutions' to complex development problems.

'We know our people'

Some readers want to know more than the typical preface provides about the context out of which a book grew and why the author considers it distinctive. This section is for such readers.

The story begins when, some years ago, a picture of Iran's former Prime Minister, Amir Abbas Hoveyda, an expression of fear and bewilderment on his face, appeared on the front page of my *Washington Post.* He had been imprisoned by Islamic revolutionary guards for months, while awaiting 'trial.' Soon after the picture was taken, revolutionary judges held a brief hearing and sentenced him to death. Guards immediately hustled him from the hearing room to an outdoor courtyard and carried out the sentence with shots to the back of his head.

I had known the Prime Minister in happier times. As a young systems engineering consultant, I had helped develop computerised simulation models to aid senior policy makers affiliated with Iran's Plan and Budget Organisation in their long-term development planning work. Our two-year project culminated with a three-hour 'on-line' demonstration of the models, exclusively for cabinet ministers and senior military officers. An elegant luncheon followed our demonstration.

The luncheon gave me an opportunity to speak personally with Dr. Hoveyda and I gathered my courage to pose a troubling question. As tactfully as possible, I asked if he was not concerned that social-economic disruptions created by Iran's accelerated industrialisation and urbanisation might be politically destabilising. In the rare opportunities that an intense work schedule gave me to walk about Teheran, these disruptions were evident, even to someone not schooled in Iran's culture. The Prime Minister responded confidently that I need not concern myself with such matters. 'We know our people,' he emphasised. Looking at the *Post* photograph, I recalled the conversation and wondered what Dr. Hoveyda's thoughts might have been during his imprisonment and in the moments before his execution.

In ensuing years, I worried about unintended contributions of my work to the draconian scenario that followed Mohammed Reza Shah Pahlavi's abdication. By then, I had co-authored a widely read book on ending world hunger[3] and joined a faculty that trained international development professionals. I knew that even before the Cold War ended, violent conflict was endemic in many developing nations. Yet neither the book on hunger, nor our graduate curriculum, nor the international development professional literature generally, had much to say about linkages between development, deadly conflict and terrorism. Development practitioners are, by and large, idealistic individuals who believe their work contributes to human well-being, especially the well-being of individuals who seem powerless to help themselves. 'How probable was it that some elements of international development practice were more likely to produce deadly conflict than enhanced well-being?' I wondered.

The subject of *Paradise Poisoned* – identifying the causes of deadly conflict and terrorism so that these pathologies could be prevented – became a major professional preoccupation. In the late 1980s, my colleagues among development professionals expressed little interest. 'Internal security' matters were viewed as the domain of politicians, police and military professionals.

Events in the 1990s changed this. Devastating outbreaks of deadly conflict and terrorism – especially the internationally riveting Rwandan genocide – spurred creation of the Carnegie Commission on Preventing Deadly Conflict, charged with answering the question 'what might have been done at an early stage [of potential deadly conflicts] to avert mass violence and achieve a just outcome?' The events of September 11, 2001 made 'preventing terrorism' a global preoccupation. More recently, unfolding scenarios in Afghanistan and Iraq have reminded policy makers that military intervention is not a sufficient conflict prevention strategy. There must be a long-term development strategy as well.

The Carnegie Commission's landmark report, *Preventing Deadly Conflict*[4], gave weight to the idea of development and deadly conflict linkages by identifying 'structural prevention – or peace building' – as a cost-effective conflict prevention strategy. Important elements of structural prevention, according to the report, were the development, by individual states, of 'mechanisms to ensure bedrock security, well-being and justice for their citizens... [and] meeting people's basic economic, social, cultural and humanitarian needs...'[5] 'The costs of prevention are miniscule,' *Preventing Deadly Conflict* concluded, 'when compared with the costs of deadly conflict and the rebuilding and psychological healing in its aftermath.'[6]

Like the Carnegie Commission report, *Paradise Poisoned* identifies causes of deadly conflicts and explains why they are so difficult to resolve. It points to early warning indicators of conflict outbreaks and proposes structural prevention strategies. Thus it is intended to reach the same professional audiences as the report. Now that the 'war on terrorism' has become a global concern, general readers in both developed and developing countries will also find the book to be of interest. Clearly the cost-effective way to fight terrorism is by preventing groups like *Al Qa'eda* from forming in this first place or, when they have formed, to cut off their pool of potential recruits.

Paradise Poisoned differs from the Carnegie Commission Report in five respects that make it a useful complement as well as a stride forward on the terrain mapped out by *Preventing Deadly Conflict*:

- It argues that the early warnings envisioned by the Carnegie Commission do not come early enough. High-leverage, cost-effective interventions should, whenever possible, come before what the Report calls 'symptoms [of] states at risk' become apparent.

- It shows how the relationship between relatively minor incidents of violent conflict and failed development strategies can provide timely early warning indicators. Recognizing the significance of these early warning indicators can trigger remedial measures focusing – as appropriate – on economic policy, governance, democratisation and security.

- It compiles 'political conflict incidents' in graphically compelling 'fever charts' that map the escalation of violent conflict in Sri Lanka over a 40-year time horizon. It compares types of incidents to show how the pathogens created by militant movements can infect a country like a disease.

- It uses an explicit systems analysis methodology to represent the *development and deadly conflict system* as a structure of interlocking feedback loops, synthesising relevant development and conflict theories. Coupled with contextually rich descriptions, this structure provides a basis for showing linkages between development failures and topologies of rising conflict intensity exhibited in the 'fever charts.'

- Rather than generalising from a number of conflicts, *Paradise Poisoned* describes in some detail, over a long time period, one of the most perplexing escalations of deadly conflict and terrorism in the post-World War II era.

- *Paradise Poisoned* combines political history with economic analysis, grounded in a comprehensive economic data base that was created especially for this book. (My commitment to combine political and economic perspectives, in the classic political economy tradition using systems analysis as an integrating framework, mostly explains why the book is so long.)

Why this particular case? Sri Lanka, once a prototype of successful development, had long been discussed by development practitioners as a puzzling example of development failure. My interest in linking deadly conflict, terrorism, and development highlighted it as an interesting subject for study. The choice was partly serendipitous. American University's 'Link' program with Colombo University gave me the opportunity to live and work there. As I learned more, it became clear that Sri Lanka's post-independence experience provided a setting for considering linkages between terrorism, conflict and an unusually diverse range of development scenarios.

Paradise Poisoned is not about current events in Sri Lanka. Most of the political leaders about whom I write are, like Prime Minister Hoveda, dead. By distancing from current events, I hope to free readers from viewing my conclusions as commentaries on contemporary political debates and maneuverings. In the case of Sri Lankan readers, this is probably unrealistic, but *Paradise Poisoned* is not written primarily for Sri Lankans. It is written so that others can take heed and learn from their experiences.

Part I

Anatomy and Physiology:
Linkages Between Deadly Conflict,
Terrorism and Development

1
'How Could We Have Come To This?'

Fear is the Key. A creeping 'insurgency' with hardly a shot fired has Colombo encircled, reducing the administration to an all-too-visible condition of helplessness.'
- Mervyn de Silva, editor, Lanka Guardian

'How could we have come to this?'

I first heard this question while participating in a seminar on 'Sri Lanka's Ethnic Conflict' one humid Colombo afternoon in June 1987. Sri Lankans posed such questions because they had witnessed the transformation of their island nation from development 'success story' to often-cited example of protracted, deadly civil conflict's devastation.[1] During 1988, when my wife and I lived in Sri Lanka for an extended period, its murder rate was one of the world's highest, more than 50,000 Indian troops fought Tamil rebels in the island's North, and Colombo itself was threatened by a shadowy guerrilla movement of radical Sinhalese youth. Subsequently, bombs felled Sri Lanka's Defence Minister, President and leading opposition presidential candidate. Still later, Tamil suicide bombers blew up an explosive-packed vehicle in the heart of Colombo's business and tourist district, killing 89, injuring more than 1,338. The international airport was infiltrated by suicide bombers who destroyed three Sri Lankan Airlines' jumbo jets and damaged three others, terrorising hundreds of passengers waiting in airport lounges.[2]

Sri Lanka was still fighting guerrilla attacks and urban terrorism when I visited in September-October 2001. Forbidding barriers and military checkpoints impeded some downtown Colombo streets. Businesses that once catered to tourists were shuttered. Colourfully uniformed ceremonial sentries who once guarded 'Temple Trees', the gracious residence of Sri Lanka's Prime Ministers, had been replaced by fatigue-clad elite cadres who manned their posts, automatic weapons at the ready, in sand-bagged bunkers. Deadly conflict was frightening away tourists, fuelling inflation, discouraging investment, motivating capital flight (human as well as financial) and nurturing a culture of violence.

'If it's all supposed to work out like the economists think, can someone tell me why Sri Lanka has not worked out?' The questioner was a professional from the United Nations High Commission for Refugees (UNHCR), attending a Washington, DC seminar in early 2001.[3]   For years, Sri Lanka was viewed as a model developing nation. It gained independence peacefully and sustained one of the few authentically competitive democratic systems in the Global South. When economic historian Morris W. Morris devised his Physical Quality of Life Index in 1977, to capture non-economic aspects of development success, he discovered that Sri Lanka's 'quality of life' compared favourably with European nations such as Portugal and Yugoslavia, though its per-capita GNP ranked it among the world's poorest.[4]   In 1977, Sri Lanka became, via a general election, one of the world's first nations to replace Marxist economic planning with relatively free trade, deregulation and privatisation. An economic boom followed. The outbreak of two civil insurrections and subsequent intractability of the conflict with Tamil militants not only bewildered many Sri Lankan politicians and citizens, but also perplexed policy analysts and scholars who had been citing the island nation as a political and economic development success story.

In 1988, deadly conflicts in developing nations did not concern most international development practitioners, though scholars such as Donald Horowitz, Cynthia Enloe and Myron Weiner had identified 'ethnic conflicts' as generic phenomena deserving study.[5] The devastating communal massacres that followed British India's partition were 'ancient history.' Most civil wars (with ethnic overtones or not) were viewed through the prism of Cold War politics, and in many the contending factions were sustained by aid from the rival superpowers.

Possible relationships between development policies and outbreaks of violent conflict had been explored even less. My employment as an engineering consultant for Iran's Plan and Budget Organisation, prior to the Islamic revolution, raised questions in my mind about such relationships. What role, I wondered, had the work of 'experts' such as myself played in the violent events of the late 1970s and the subsequent shape of Iran's Islamic Republic? When I later sought information on development-conflict linkages, personally contacting officials in the World Bank, the U.S. Agency for International Development and other development agencies, my inquiries elicited little interest.[6]

The end of the Cold War changed this. A period of global optimism that followed the Soviet Union's collapse was short lived. *'From Cold War to deadly peace'*: the Carnegie Commission on Preventing Deadly Conflict so characterised the early 1990s.[7]   In the Commission's landmark report, a world map identified 37 'Major Conflicts of the 1990s' as splashes of crimson. Fifteen were in Africa, five in Latin America, six in Asia, four in the Middle East, and seven in former communist nations. Of these, all but two were deadly civil conflicts, though in many of these, one or more contending factions had at least some international support.[8]

The Commission and many other studies have highlighted civil conflicts' brutality, costliness and pervasiveness.[9] In some conflicts, 90 per cent of those killed were non-combatants; more than 40 per cent of Rwanda's population was either killed or displaced as a result of genocidal attacks and the civil war that followed. Civil war caused nearly 80 per cent of Angola's agricultural land to be abandoned. In Mozambique 480,000 children died from war-related causes and 200,000 were orphaned or abandoned by adults. In a growing number of conflicts, many of the most unrestrained combatants are themselves child soldiers who have known no other life than war. Sierra Leone's Revolutionary United Front used random amputations on men, women and children as a form of punishment and intimidation in a war that displaced nearly half the nation's population. Thousands have lost limbs to land mines in many other developing nations. Swelling refugee populations are one consequence of civil wars that impose heavy burdens on neighbouring countries and the international community. Using conservative estimates, the UNHCR identified a population of refugees and internally displaced persons numbering more than 16.5 million in 1998. 4.8 million of these were in Africa, 6.7 million in Asia and 3.9 million in Europe.[10]

The difficulty of resolving civil wars should make protagonists think more than twice before initiating them. Civil wars, writes I. William Zartman, 'rise and fall in intensity, start and drag in negotiation, sometimes reach a temporary and artificial 'settlement' only to burst out later on.'[11]   Among many instances of unresolved, protracted conflicts he gives as examples (with the date of the first violent outbreak in parentheses) Eritrea-Ethiopia (1952), Sudan (1955), Cyprus (1964), Angola (1975), Afghanistan (1979),[12] and one might add to the list, Israel-Palestine (1947) and India-Pakistan (1947). Indeed, measured against these cases, the 26-year conflict between Tamil militants and Sri Lanka's government seems a relative newcomer on the world scene.[13] 'Internal conflicts last a long time,' Zartman concludes, 'because negotiations are as hard to produce as victories. Mutually satisfactory, second best settlements are unattractive to parties playing for ultimate stakes.'[14]

Closely linked to the intractability of deadly civil conflicts are the cost and uncertainty of post-conflict reconstruction. Problems of recreating the devastated physical and economic structures are compounded by less-well-recognised problems of recreating a viable social infrastructure. Many of a nation's most talented individuals will have been killed or fled the country. The men, women and children who remain, even those who have escaped physical injury, are often traumatised, frustrated, distrustful and fearful of the future. Communal ties, so essential to the resiliency of a developing society, are fractured. Restoring basic services and restarting the engine of economic production will be costly and time-consuming. Most individuals are likely to be worse off than when the conflict began. In this fragile climate, conflicts over scarce resources are inevitable and the danger that protagonists may once again choose violence as a means for resolving their differences is high. Theda Skocpol and her students have found that regimes coming to power after violent revolutions are often more repressive than their predecessors.[15]

Deadly civil conflicts may be the most tragic social pathology of the post-Cold War era. I say 'the most tragic' because they impede so greatly the amelioration of other social pathologies: poverty, famine and chronic hunger, illiteracy, ecological degradation, AIDS and other epidemic diseases. Their pervasiveness, brutality, costliness, and intractability as well as the uncertainties of post-conflict reconstruction amply justify further case studies posing the question that begins this chapter—and further: *What could we have done to prevent the conflict that has killed our family members and friends, devastated our lives, destroyed what was being so painstakingly developed? What can we learn and share from our experiences that may help others to avoid following a similar path? How can we share what we have learned most powerfully and effectively?* The 'we' of these questions are, principally, political leaders and citizens of the nations, from Angola to Zaire, that have been victimised by civil war. There is another group of individuals, too, who must continue to pose questions about the causes and prevention of civil wars. Foreign political leaders, multilateral and non-governmental organisation leaders, leaders in the private sector and development practitioners share in the responsibility for causing civil wars, though they bear few of the costs.

The need for conflict prevention, then, is a more than sufficient motivation for detailed study of circumstances leading to one the most perplexing civil wars of the post- World War II era. But focusing on conflict prevention defines our inquiry's scope too narrowly.

Needed: early warning systems and conflict prevention strategies

What the Carnegie Commission calls 'structural prevention – or peace building' is the most cost-effective way of preventing deadly conflict.[16] Structural prevention is implementing 'strategies to address the root causes of deadly conflict, so as to ensure that crises do not arise in the first place or if they do, they do not recur'.[17] Such strategies are of two broad types. First, 'the development of international regimes to manage the interaction of states and the development by individual states (with the help of outsiders if necessary) of mechanisms to ensure bedrock security, well-being, and justice for their citizens.'[18]

This book focuses primarily on the second: issues relating to 'meeting people's basic economic, social, cultural and humanitarian needs...' This type of structural prevention can equally be called 'successful, sustainable development.'[19]

The Carnegie Commission writes further: 'Too often in the past [development] activities have been given less attention than they deserve, partly because their conflict prevention significance has been less than fully appreciated'.[20] This is a convoluted way of stating what is widely recognised, but not adequately taken into account: that people whose economic, social, cultural and humanitarian needs are unmet and who see themselves as victims of injustice are prime candidates for violent behaviour, un-organised or organised.

A voluminous 'conflict theory' literature reminds us that matters are not quite that simple. Human suffering does always evoke violent behaviour. Who will behave violently, when specific incidents of conflict will erupt and when multiple incidents will metastasise into longer-term deadly conflict may be difficult to predict, with certainty. But we know at least as much about the relationship between social pathologies and violent conflict as we do about the relationship between heavy smoking and the diseases it causes – lung cancer in particular. We may not be able to predict who, specifically, will contract lung cancer, when the symptoms will become manifest or how many cigarettes must be smoked to cause the disease. Nonetheless, we can confidently advise individuals who are concerned about contracting lung cancer to refrain from smoking cigarettes. So, too, we can advise political leaders who are concerned about catalyzing civil war to implement policies that address material and psychic needs of their people and refrain from oppressing them.

Promoting effective development surfaced as a global concern following World War II, but it would be wrong to say that it has ever been a top global priority. The United Nations Development Program (UNDP) has chronicled and measured the state of human development in its *Human Development Reports* for more than a decade. Its 2001 report warned of 'serious setbacks and reversals' in the 1990s, a period when many of the world's richest nations experienced record levels of economic growth. Among the setbacks reported were 20 nations that lost ground in areas measured by the UNDP *Human Development Index* (HDI) a composite of longevity, educational attainment and per-capita income.[21] In Sub-Saharan Africa, more than 20 countries experienced drops in life expectancy, primarily due to HIV/AIDS. A 77-country study, covering 82 per cent of the world's people, showed that inequality rose in 45 countries, while only falling in 16.[22] 'Inequality,' the UNDP report noted, 'is likely to erode social capital, including a sense of trust and citizen responsibility that is key to the foundation and sustainability of sound public institutions.'[23]

While many developing nations experienced setbacks and reversals, most of the world's aid-giving nations, members of the Development Assistance Community (DAC) of the OECD were enjoying a decade of unprecedented economic growth and relief from Cold War military pressures. These improved circumstances were not reflected in stronger commitments to human development, quite the opposite. Between 1990 and 1999, 12 DAC nations reduced their levels of development assistance as a percentage of GNP, for a total reduction of nearly 30 per cent. The United States was the second largest donor, but (along with Luxembourg) gave the smallest percentage of GNP (.21 per cent) and reduced its per cent contribution the most, by more than 50 per cent. Every DAC nation but one reduced the percentage of GNP that it gave to Global South countries.[24]

Perhaps this will change with a growing awareness of the link between violent political conflict and development failure – the failure of a nation to meet its people's basic economic, social, cultural and humanitarian needs. Calls for 'early warning systems' to anticipate outbreaks of deadly conflict point in the direction of what is needed, but fall short. The Rwandan genocide, in which more than 800,000 were slaughtered, created uncountable numbers of refugees and has destabilised much of central Africa, exhibited the potential cost-effectiveness of early warning systems with unusual clarity.

The Carnegie Commission writes:

> Since 1994, many knowledgeable people, including the commander of UNAMIR (United Nations Assistance Mission for Rwanda) at the time have maintained that even a small trained force, rapidly deployed at the outset, could have largely prevented the Rwandan genocide. But neither the force nor the will to deploy it existed at the time. When concerned governments finally turned to the United Nations and to the Security Council, there was neither a credible rapid reaction force ready to deploy nor the moral authority or will to assemble it quickly enough.[25]

Some months later, however, the conflict had reached such catastrophic proportions that it could not be ignored. Putting human costs aside, international expenditures for relief and reconstruction over the next three years exceeded two billion dollars. The costs of a preventive intervention might well have been only one third of this amount.[26] The Commission concludes: 'Prevention entails action, action entails costs and costs demand trade-offs. *The costs of prevention, however, are miniscule when compared with the costs of deadly conflict and the rebuilding and psychological healing in its aftermath'*.[27] This proposition applies equally to the conflicts in Israel-Palestine, Bosnia, Sudan, Liberia, Ethiopia-Eritrea, Zaire, Sierra Leone, Nicaragua, and Colombia, as well as the focus of this book, Sri Lanka, and many others. Moreover early warning is feasible, because 'the circumstances that give rise to violent conflict can usually be foreseen'[28] even if the specific event that will trigger the escalation of violence cannot be identified.

The Carnegie Commission is to be applauded for connecting conflict prevention with effective development more strongly than heretofore; however the early warnings envisioned in *Preventing Deadly Conflict* do not come early enough. The high-leverage, cost-effective point for intervention is much earlier in the unfolding of events through which conflict becomes violent and metastasises into full-scale civil war. But what warning signals should trigger this very early intervention? How are local leaders and potential external players to know where and when to intervene and by what means? How can they be motivated to do so? Seeking answers to these questions, using the unfolding of violent conflict in Sri Lanka as a case in point, is one purpose of this book.

Why deadly conflict outbreaks signal development failure

The Carnegie Commission's *Preventing Deadly Conflict* points us towards answers. Two contributions to a growing literature on state capacity and weak states provided Commissioners with a list of 'indicators' or 'symptoms' of 'states at risk.' The list is illuminating: [29]

- Demographic pressures: high infant mortality, rapid changes in population, including massive refugee movements, high population density, youth bulge, insufficient food or access to safe water; complications resulting from two or more ethnic groups sharing and being emotionally attached to the same land (territory) and needing to draw sustenance from the same physical ecosystem.
- A lack of democratic practices: criminalisation or delegitimisation of the state, or human rights violations.
- Regimes of short duration.
- Ethnic composition of the ruling elite differing from the population at large.
- Deterioration or elimination of public services.
- Sharp and severe economic distress: uneven economic development along ethnic lines and a lack of trade openness.
- A legacy of vengeance-seeking group grievance.
- Massive, chronic or sustained human flight.

International development scholars would agree that these indicators warned of deadly conflict, but also view them as signalling development failure. They would argue, further, that the time for cost-effective intervention is long before events have unfolded to produce a critical mass of symptoms indicating that an eruption of deadly civil conflict is imminent. But often there us little agreement about early indications of development failure and necessary remedial measures until long after the fact (and sometimes not even then). This complicates the task of designing an 'early warning system' and makes funding early interventions difficult to justify. How can we know that development trends are tending toward a critical mass of conflict evoking symptoms before it is too late?

Civil wars do not erupt like a thunder squall that suddenly shatters the tranquillity of a peaceful summer afternoon. Rather, they culminate trends of intensifying violent political conflict incidents, including violent counter-measures by state security forces intended to maintain or restore public order. Such trends are warning signals that conflict may metastasise out of control. As *Preventing Deadly Conflict* makes clear, social pathologies increase the potential for protracted deadly conflict. Social pathologies are a primary target of development programs just as epidemic diseases are a primary goal of public health programs. When development succeeds, social pathologies are reduced or eliminated. When development fails, social pathologies and their adverse human impacts are, like diseases and their symptoms, more evident. Thus an intensifying trend of violent incidents is an indication of development failure as well as an early warning that protracted conflict may be on the horizon. By recognising this connection, we can look toward mapping country-level effects of social pathologies in much the same way a pathologist charts the spread of a disease and a public health practitioner charts the spread of an epidemic. Such mappings can provide timely warnings of the need to alter development policies and programs.

The pathology metaphor is not original. Historian Crane Brinton used it in his classic, *The Anatomy of a Revolution*, suggesting that it might be useful to 'regard revolutions as a kind of fever.' A revolution's onset, he suggests, can be tracked on a 'fever chart' in much the same way a nurse charts periodic temperature readings at the foot of her patient's bed.[30] While Brinton's revolutions differ from some deadly conflicts that concern us, the idea of using a fever chart to measure intensifying violence fits well with our focus on relationships between development failures, social pathologies and intensifying violent conflict trends.

The first of many fever charts to be presented (Figure 1.1) illustrates how Brinton's metaphor has been applied to Sri Lanka's post-independence history from 1948 through 1988.

The variable plotted against time is *intensity of political conflict incidents*, which to avoid cumbersomeness, I often abbreviate as *political conflict intensity*. Vertical lines mark the dates of elections that changed Sri Lanka's dominant ruling party.[31] They are important markers because changes in the ruling party also meant significant changes in governance philosophy and economic policy.

A technical description of the political conflict index will be provided later (interested readers can turn to chapter 4 now if they wish), but a brief preview may be useful before considering what a chart like this might tell us. I define a

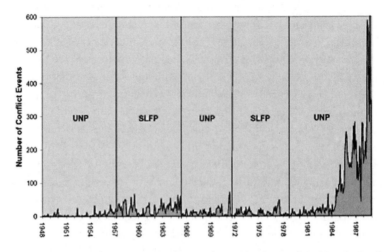

Sri Lanka's dominant parties were the United National Party (UNP) and the Sri Lanka Freedom Party (SLFP). Often they governed as the dominant party in a larger coalition.

Figure 1.1 Fever Chart of Violent Political Conflict 1948-1988

'political conflict incident,' as an expression of protest against or conflict with the government in power or the established political order that typically (but not always) involves violence. Intensity refers to the incident's level of violence, which can be none.[32]   Inclusion of some non-violent incidents is important because non-violent protest marches, demonstrations and general strikes (*hartals*) are a common political tactic in Sri Lanka and other South Asian nations.[33] For example, typical incidents include:

- Demonstrations or riots with political overtones (including ethnically motivated riots)
- Politically motivated strikes
- Assassinations of government or party officials; assassinations of individuals identified as 'traitors' by a militant group
- Attacks on or destruction of government property (military installations, police stations, administrative offices, trains and buses).

My multiethnic Sri Lankan research team[34] compiled written descriptions of more than 6,500 incidents covering the 40-year period of the study.

Descriptions might comprise only a short paragraph, but sometimes ran to a page or more. We then scored the intensity of each event using a composite index adapted from the work of Russian sociologist Pitrim Sorokin. Sorokin designed his index to measure what he called the 'fluctuation of internal disturbances' in nations over very long time periods.[35] The numbers plotted on the 'fever chart' are the sum of conflict event intensities for each month. What they depict is quite consistent with Brinton's metaphor: a qualitative, topological representation of relative conflict intensities over a long-time period.

Viewing the chart from this perspective, what patterns reveal themselves? A sharp increase in conflict intensity after 1984 is most striking. If the chart plotted infection in a biological organism, the period prior to 1984 could be labelled 'relatively good health.' The organism seems resilient. When infections occur, they run their course quickly, either because they are not virulent, because the immune system responds effectively or because appropriate treatment is provided. After 1983, there is a qualitative change. This period might be labelled 'chronic illness.' High levels of infection are the normal state. Reduced levels are transient remissions. By 1988, an ominous pattern of cancerous growth is apparent. The disease appears to be life threatening. The obvious, qualitative change after 1983 raises questions for the diagnostician. What distinguishes the new virulent strain? Has the organism experienced fundamental change? What happened during the transition period –1982 through 1984 – from 'good health' to 'chronic illness?'

Closer examination of the 'good health' period reminds us that episodes of political conflict are not entirely absent from Sri Lanka, even when sojourners were describing the island as a paradise. Noticeable increases in conflict intensity occurred during the period from 1956 through 1965. This decade was far more turbulent than the years that immediately preceded and followed it. A severe outbreak also occurred in 1971, but quickly subsided. What produced these outbreaks? What prevented them from metastasising into protracted civil war? The chart is more interesting for the questions it raises than the answers it provides.

Seeking answers to these questions must be postponed, briefly, because this book is not written primarily for Sri Lankan readers and scholars. The basic facts of Sri Lanka's geography (including its location), its rich cultural traditions, its multifaceted ethnoreligious composition and its turbulent political history are not matters of general knowledge. Few are aware that the evolution of Sri Lanka's political economy after independence, along with its class and ethnic civil wars, make it a uniquely interesting subject for those concerned with development-conflict linkages. Some basic background information on these matters should be provided before proceeding further.

The isle of Serendib and its people

Sri Lanka long has been described as a 'paradise' by travellers. Marco Polo called it 'undoubtedly the finest island of its size in the world' [36] Arab seafarers named the island 'Serendib,' which was what an eighteenth-century English writer had in mind when he coined the word 'serendipity,' the 'facility of making happy and unexpected discoveries by accident.'[37] *Lanka* means 'the resplendent' in Sinhala.

Few places on earth have such geographical variety in such a small area. The island is only 270 miles long and 140 miles across at its widest point (Figure 1.2) – smaller than Ireland and only slightly larger than the American state of West Virginia. A flat plain makes up the entire northern half of the island and continues around the entire coastline. Until the 1930s, a heavy belt of forests north of the ancient capital, Anuradhapura, formed a natural barrier between the Sinhalese and Tamil peoples. Later, Sinhalese migrants cleared much of this, but the area around Vavuniya remains heavily forested and has served as a hideout and training area for Tamil Tiger guerrillas. The island's south-central region is hilly and mountainous, ranging from 3,000 to 7,000 feet above sea level. The western and southern coasts have beautiful and relatively unspoiled surfing beaches that have been a major attraction for tourists.[38] The climate is tropical, with temperatures averaging 27°C and sometimes exceeding 38°C, especially in the cities and on the northwest coast. There are two monsoons. In good years, the southwest monsoon provides heavy rains from April to June; the northeast monsoon, less heavy and less reliable, visits from mid-October through February.

Sri Lanka is still a largely rural and agricultural nation. In 1987, agriculture contributed more than 25 per cent to the GDP and employed nearly 50 per cent of the labour force.[39] A Sri Lankan ideal is to own and farm a plot of land that includes a house, a garden and, perhaps, one or two coconut trees. Many attain this. Perhaps because of smallholder agriculture dominance and relatively equitable land distribution, rural-urban migration has been less than in many Global South countries.

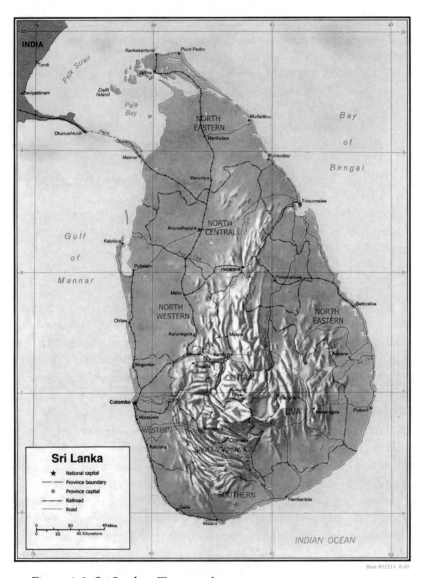

Figure 1.2 Sri Lanka: Topography
Source: The General Libraries, The University of Texas at Austin

Geographers divide the island into three climactic zones – wet, intermediate and dry. Dry and intermediate zone lands, in the island's northeast, receive only one monsoon each year and that can be uncertain. The dry zone is dotted with massive irrigation 'tanks' (artificial lakes) built by Sinhalese kingdoms that dominated the region up until the fourteenth century. Many tanks had fallen into disuse, but a massive irrigation and hydroelectric project, the Mahaweli development scheme, has revitalised Sri Lanka's tradition as one of the world's great hydraulic civilisations, making it possible to grow rice and some mixed vegetable crops on thousands of previously uncultivable acres.

The wet zone generally has no water shortage but inaccessibility and hilly terrain limit the amount of land that can be used for cultivation.[40] Most of Sri Lanka's cash crops are grown in this region. Coconuts, along with rice and garden crops are grown in the lowlands. Rubber is grown in the lowlands and intermediate highlands.[41] Plantations that produce some of the world's finest tea dominate the 'up-country' highland districts.[42]

Ethnoreligious groupings: the Sinhalese

Data from the 1981 census, showed the ethnic composition of Sri Lanka's 16 million inhabitants to be about 74 per cent Sinhalese, 12.6 per cent Sri Lankan Tamil, 5.6 per cent Indian Tamil and 7.1 per cent Muslim. History, language, culture and religion have combined to give each of these groups a separate identity and a distinct role in the island's political life. Figure 1.3 shows their respective geographic concentrations, which significantly influence Sri Lankan political life.

The majority Sinhalese began migrating to the Island from North India in about 500 B.C. and settled in the northeastern or dry zone. Buddhism came to the island in the third century B.C., and became an integral part of Sinhalese culture. Sri Lanka became 'the island of the Dhamma' (*Dhammadipa*) a place of special sanctity for Buddhism.[43] A revered giant Bhodi tree in the ancient capital of Anuradhapura is said to be from a sapling of the original tree under which the Buddha obtained enlightenment, more than 2,500 years ago.[44] Sinhalese identity, Buddhism and 'the island of the Sinhalese people' (*Sinhadipa*) remain inextricably linked in Sinhalese traditions, even though some Sinhalese are Christians. For many Sinhalese, Sri Lankan 'national identity' is part of this mix as well. This makes defining a national identity that embraces non-Sinhalese Sri Lankan citizens more difficult.

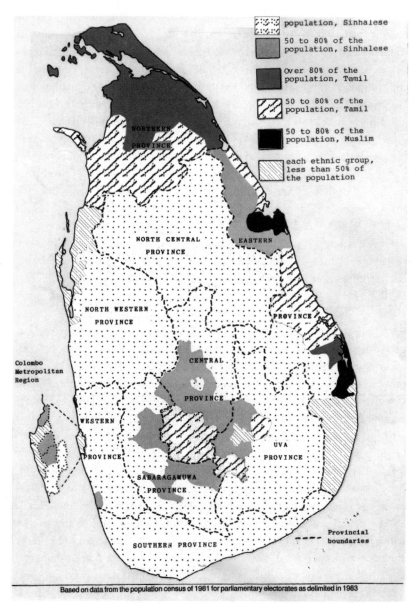

Figure 1.3 Geographic Concentration of Sri Lanka's Major Ethnic Groups

Deeply rooted identification with the island as a whole persisted despite invasions from Tamil Nadu that left it divided, politically. Eventually, the seat of Sinhalese government was established in Kandy, located in the central highlands, while Tamils controlled the north and east. Protected by mountains, the Kandyan kingdom retained its independence during the early colonial period, when Portuguese and Dutch forces conquered the island's periphery, but fell to the British in 1815. Thus, Kandyan Sinhalese in the highlands were free of colonial domination for nearly 200 years during which lowland Sinhalese were subject to Portuguese, Dutch and then British rulers. Kandyans still represent a conservative force in Sri Lankan politics and regard themselves as protectors of Sinhalese-Buddhist traditions against modernising encroachments, not only from foreigners and Tamils, but also from the more cosmopolitan lowland Sinhalese.

The Sinhalese caste system, a product of interchanges with India, has declined in importance, but still influences social mobility and politics.[45] The *Goyigama* (farming) caste, comprising nearly half of the Sinhalese, is atop the hierarchy. The *Karava* (fisherfolk), *Durava* (toddy tappers) and *Salagama* (cinnamon peelers) are also large caste groupings with influential members in business, politics and government service.[46] Classified advertisements for suitable marriage partners in the Sri Lankan newspapers often mention caste, along with religion and (in the case of women) the size of the dowry. Sri Lanka's chief executives – Prime ministers and, more recently, executive presidents – have always been Sinhalese, as have cabinet ministers.[47] All but one chief executive, Ranasinghe Premadasa, have been from the *Goyigama* caste.[48]

Prior to 1956 the Sinhalese-dominated government's pro-Sinhalese political agenda was relatively low key. In the early 1950s, however, the charismatic S.W.R.D. Bandaranaike altered Sri Lanka's political landscape forever by beginning to vocally advocate an overtly populist, pro-Sinhalese and pro-Buddhist political agenda. Campaigning on a platform to make Sinhala the only official language 'within 24 hours' after becoming Prime Minister, and to give preferential treatment to Sinhalese in education and employment, he swept to power in the general election of April 1956. Bandaranaike was felled by an assassin's bullet in 1959, but his policies were continued by his widow, Sirimavo Bandaranaike, who served as Prime Minister from 1960 through 1965 and again from 1970 through 1977.[49] A new and more turbulent era in Sri Lankan politics had begun. Having opened the Pandora's Box of race-based politics, Sinhalese politicians could not close it. When opportunities offered themselves, leaders of both major parities have sought political advantage by making populist appeals to Sinhalese-Buddhist nationalism and they continue to do so.

Appeals to this 'ethnic' ideology are effective because they call forth deeply rooted identities and fears in the Sinhalese community. In addition to its sacrosanct status in Theravada Buddhist beliefs,[50] the island of Sri Lanka is the only home of the Sinhalese race. While the Sinhalese are a majority on their island, they are, as historian Kingsley M. de Silva has noted, a majority with a minority complex.[51] For many, the epic struggles of Sinhalese heroes against Tamil invaders from the north are more than ancient history – they are living realities.[52]

The Sri Lanka Tamils

Contrasting them with the Sinhalese, K.M. de Silva characterises Sri Lanka Tamils as a minority with a majority complex.[53] Their demands have been for 'equal status' and, more recently, for hegemony over one-fourth of the island's land area and nearly half its coastline.

There were Tamil migrants in Sri Lanka as early as the third century B.C. Sinhalese Prince Dutthagamini's triumph over the Tamil King Elara, taught as an epic to virtually all Sinhalese schoolchildren, is said to have occurred about 137 B.C.,[54] however many Tamil settlements remained. During the fifth and sixth centuries, militant Hinduism supplanted Buddhism in South India. Leaders of powerful, aggressive Indian states began to cast covetous eyes on the productive irrigated lands and flourishing civilisation of the Anuradhapura Kingdom and to mount invasions. By the thirteenth century, a permanent Tamil Kingdom had been established in the island's north.[55]

The period of independent Tamil rule was short-lived. In the early sixteenth century, Portuguese traders landed on the southwest coast and by 1600 had established political control over the north and the southwest littoral. With the Portuguese came Roman Catholic missionaries who proselytised aggressively and successfully. The Portuguese soon were supplanted by the Dutch, who were replaced by the British in 1796. Both the Dutch and British introduced administrative systems that identified Tamils as a distinct community and emphasised their differences from Sinhalese.

The Tamils' colonial-era status differed from Sinhalese in two respects that tended to motivate their outstanding young men towards careers in government service and professions. First, Tamils benefited from a superior system of primary and secondary education, established by Christian missionaries, which emphasised high-quality English language instruction. Second, as the North's population grew, opportunities to make a traditional living in agriculture became limited; commercial development in the North also offered limited opportunities. Young Tamils with ambition and talent competed successfully for limited openings in the university faculties of Law, Science and Engineering and passed civil service examinations with high marks. As the colonial period drew to a close and during the early years of independence, Tamils were disproportionately represented in professions and government (though less so than many Sinhalese believe). The capital city was now populated by a large contingent of talented 'Colombo Tamils' who conversed in English, were more cosmopolitan than their Jaffna counterparts, and played influential roles in the capital city's society.[56]

Historically, caste divisions were rigid among the Tamils, especially in Jaffna society, though years of political conflict have eroded them. As in India, *Brahmins*, members of the priestly class, are regarded as the highest. Next come the *Vellala* or farming caste (corresponding to the Sinhalese *Goyigama*) followed by craftsmen such as goldsmiths, carpenters and blacksmiths. Traditionally, there was a sharp division between these 'clean' castes and 'unclean' castes such as fishermen, toddy-tappers, barbers and drumbeaters. During the colonial period and up to the 1980s, the *Vellala* caste used its dominant position and rules prohibiting intermarriage between castes to exclude other Tamils from the economic and social opportunities that modernisation provided. This may explain why militant youth are predominantly lower caste in contrast to the more traditional Tamil politicians who are mostly *Vellala*. Some argue that the rebelliousness of Tamil youth is as much a reaction to Jaffna's rigid caste system as to discriminatory policies imposed by Sinhalese dominated governments.[57]

Long before S.W.R.D. Bandaranaike elevated Sinhalese nationalism as a political agenda, Tamil politicians were concerned about protecting their rights. They were the first to form a communally oriented political party. They pressed for retention of communally oriented representation schemes that would give them power to block major constitutional changes. When these tactics failed, they attempted to form political coalitions that would forestall preferential treatment for the Sinhalese in the areas of language, religion, government employment, university admissions and national symbols. When Sinhalese electoral majorities overwhelmed them and coalition building failed, they resorted to

Gandhian tactics of *satyagraha* (peaceful non-co-operation), then to demonstrations and strikes. These tactics also failed.

The history of post-independence Sri Lanka, from a Sri Lankan Tamil perspective, is a history of lost privileges, intensifying discrimination, failure of democratic institutions to protect their rights and, finally, coercion by an overwhelmingly Sinhalese security establishment. While moderate Tamil politicians continued to work within the political process of campaigns, parliamentary representation, negotiation and compromise, repeated failures to advance their community's agendas gradually discredited them and their tactics. The initiative passed to a more militant group of youth with little use for a country whose flag featured the Lion of the Sinhalese Kings and the leaves of the sacred Bodhi tree, holy of holies to Theravada Buddhists. Inspired by Marxist revolutionary ideologies, these young men formed and enrolled in groups such as the Eelam Revolutionary Organisation of Students (EROS), the People's Liberation Organisation of Tamil Eelam (PLOTE), the Tamil Eelam Liberation Organisation (TELO), the Eelam Peoples Revolutionary Liberation Front (EPRLF) and the most militant, disciplined and ferocious of them all, the Liberation Tigers of Tamil Eelam (LTTE). Their goal – an independent Tamil nation of Eelam – was an outcome Sinhalese could never accept. The militants' principal tactics were terrorism and, increasingly, guerrilla warfare, directed at both Sinhalese and moderate Tamils who opposed them.

The Indian Tamils

'Indian Tamils'[58] are largely concentrated in the tea growing areas of the Central Province, with much smaller concentrations in the north. Most have little in common with Sri Lanka Tamils, although they share the same language and religion. They began migrating from South India to Sri Lanka in the second half of the nineteenth century when infestations of leaf fungus and failing markets caused Sri Lanka's coffee plantations to be replanted in tea and, to a much lesser extent, in rubber. Tea growing required a disciplined labour force, willing to live on the plantations permanently and work for low wages. Plantation work, while arduous, was superior to anything available in India. Tamil migrants were recruited in large numbers and settled permanently in 'lines' (small adjacent huts) on plantation lands or in small rural enclaves. By independence, the number resident in Sri Lanka exceeded 800,000.[59]

This influx, coupled with the expansion of plantation lands, bred resentment among conservative Kandyan Sinhalese. As voting rights were extended and alternative formulas for representation began to be debated, the possible political role of Indian Tamils (many now resident in Sri Lanka for a generation or more) became a matter of concern to Sinhalese pro-independence leaders.[60] Were they to be given voting rights, their numbers would overwhelm Sinhalese in some key districts. Indian Tamil voters, Sinhalese leaders feared, would be receptive to appeals of leftist political parties or open to manipulation by plantation owners.[61]

Sri Lanka's first Prime Minister, D.S. Senanayake, solved this problem shortly after independence, by having parliament pass laws that excluded most Indian Tamils from Sri Lankan citizenship and removed them from the electoral roles. Interestingly, many Sri Lankan Tamil politicians did not oppose this. Senanayake's government envisioned repatriation, but India's Prime Minister Nehru would now allow the Indian Tamils, many of whom had lived in Sri Lanka for decades, to return. Thus, the consequence of Senanayake's legislation was to make them stateless persons. Indian Tamils' status was the subject of nearly continual negotiations between the Sri Lankan and Indian governments for the next 15 years. The matter was finally resolved, in 1964, by an agreement between Sri Lankan Prime Minister Sirimavo Bandaranaike and Nehru's successor, Lal Bahadur Shastri. The agreement provided for repatriating 525,000 Indians and granting Sri Lankan citizenship to 300,000. The remaining 150,000 were to be the subject of future negotiations. These dragged on into the 1980s with increasingly favourable outcomes for the Indian Tamils as their political power increased.[62]

To a superficial observer, the lives of tea pickers and plantation factory workers might seem little changed from 50 years ago. In fact, their situation is quite different. This partly explains why relatively few have made common cause with militant Sri Lankan Tamils. Beginning in 1965, Indian Tamil political leader Savumiamoorthy Thondaman began strengthening his ties with the Sinhalese party that controlled the government from 1965 though 1970, and again from 1977 through 1994 (the United National Party or UNP). This alliance was mutually beneficial. The UNP strengthened its position in parliament while the wages, education, and medical care on plantations improved substantially. Now, Indian Tamils' family incomes compare favourably with those of many Sinhalese, Sri Lanka Tamils and Muslims,[63] although levels of health and education still tend to be lower. Paradoxically, these recent immigrants to the island, formerly marginalised, appear to have found a more secure place in the Sri Lankan social and political order than the Sri Lankan Tamils.[64]

The Muslims

Like the Indian Tamils, members of Sri Lanka's Muslim community have largely avoided direct confrontation with pro-Sinhalese political agendas. A majority, called Moors, are descended from Arab traders who settled on the island during the eighth century. Additional Muslims from India (sometimes called 'Coast Moors') migrated during the British period. Moors typically speak Tamil but many speak Sinhala as well and some use it as their primary language. A smaller group of migrants from the South Pacific, the Malays, live mostly in the South and speak their own language. Religion, rather than language or ethnic origins, binds Muslims together.[65]

K.M. de Silva labels Muslim leaders' political strategy 'pragmatic adaptation'.[66] Characteristics of the Muslim community that distinguish it sharply from the Sri Lanka Tamils have necessitated this strategy and contributed to its effectiveness. Unlike the Tamils, Muslims are distributed geographically throughout the island. In all but the Eastern Province districts of Trincomalee and Ampara, they make up less than 10 per cent of the population. Only in Ampara are they the largest ethnic group, with nearly 42 per cent of the population.[67]

In the electoral system established after 1935, based on single member districts, it was clear that few Muslim candidates, campaigning as Muslims, were likely to win seats. Alternatives to a communally based political strategy would need to be devised. Muslim occupational patterns were also distinctive. Some, particularly in eastern districts, were cultivators, but a disproportionate number engaged in trade and commerce. It was these fields that upwardly mobile young men typically chose for careers. Relatively few Muslims sought university education or competed for positions in the government service. Policies of 'favouritism' toward Sinhalese in these areas, which infuriated Tamil youth, had little impact on Muslims.

Muslims did have a post-independence communal agenda, but Sinhalese did not view it as threatening. During the colonial era, they had successfully sought government support for separate legal procedures, applicable to Muslims only, governing marriage, divorce, and inheritance. They wanted to safeguard and strengthen these protections for their unique cultural identity. In education, also, they wanted special provisions for training in Arabic, recognition of the Muslim calendar, and flexibility for Muslim students in choosing a language of instruction.[68] None of these goals were seen as competing with Sinhalese political agendas.

That the Muslims would eschew communal politics was not clear during the last years of British rule. Anti-Muslim riots in 1915 had aroused Muslim fears and stimulated a hitherto dormant political consciousness. Drawn together by a common language, Muslims and Tamils formed an unsuccessful coalition that advocated communally weighted voting schemes and constitutional protections for minority rights. However, a clear turning point came in 1946 when key Muslim leaders decided to ally with the newly created United National Party (UNP). Later, they became active in the rival Sri Lanka Freedom Party (SLFP) as well. Now Muslims do have a communal party, the Sri Lanka Muslim Congress (SLMC), but they are also active in other parties and continue to pursue relatively non-confrontational communal goals with considerable success.

The English-speaking elite

An important non-ethnoreligious group prior to independence, and for many years afterwards, was the small English-speaking elite that dominated Sri Lankan society. Members included all the island's races and religions. They held assets in all spheres of economic activity. They occupied top positions in universities, the civil service and all of Sri Lanka's competing political parties. An intricate network of family ties, which sometimes crossed party lines, tied many together. Most who preserve these traditions are now in their early sixties or older. Some of their children have remained on the island and are attempting to follow in their parents' footsteps, but their education and upbringing in a more modern, egalitarian and turbulent Sri Lanka have been quite different. Many younger elite Sri Lankans, especially young Tamils, have capitalised on foreign university credentials and their parents' dwindling wealth to escape from the daily stress and tragedy of life on the island. They have begun new lives and are raising their children in Britain, Canada, Australia and the United States.[69]

To spend an evening with the older generation of Sri Lanka's elite is to be reminded of the formality, elegance and contradictions of upper-class Victorian England. The men played cricket and rugby together and prepared for their Advanced Level Examinations (London) at English-style public schools like Royal, St. Thomas, and Trinity.[70] Many graduated from Oxford or Cambridge; others from Sri Lanka's version of those hallowed institutions, Peradeniya. They debated Sri Lanka's future and engaged in endless political discussions over whiskeys at clubs modelled on British counterparts. They led the country peacefully to independence as a secular, multi-ethnic and multi-religious society. They played interlocking roles as top government officials, business leaders and university dons. For many of the elite, during the early years of independence, life in Ceylon was, indeed, life in paradise. And, like the Victorians whose culture they modelled, many of these 'leaders' had little empathy with their people they governed or understanding of the forces that would transform their lives.

In the 1950s, they lived through the turbulence of the 'Sinhala only' language policy. Most lost lands and assets in the Marxist experiments of the early 1970s. Some adapted; others were destroyed, not only financially, but also personally. Many rejoiced when the centrist United National Party, with its platform of economic liberalism, triumphed in the late 1970s, though some continued their support for the more populist Sri Lanka Freedom Party. They viewed militant leaders like the Tamil Tigers' Velupillai Prabhakaran and the People's Liberation Front's (JVP) Rohana Wijeweera with a mixture of incomprehension and contempt.[71] Now, authentic members of Sri Lanka's traditional elite are an endangered species, facing extinction. Sri Lanka's present leaders, whatever their antecedents, are very different.

Experiencing Sri Lanka's civil wars

I need to add something of the personal context from which this book has been written. In 1987, my brief description of Sri Lanka and its people would have been as new to me as it now is to some readers. I had written a brief piece on Sri Lanka's development policies[72] and built computer simulation models showing how flawed development policies might lead to deadly conflict. But I knew that academic research in the United States was different than experiencing a culture and having 'violent political conflict incidents' be part of daily life. I wanted to *ground* my analytical work in personal experience. When a visiting professorship in Colombo University's Department of Modern History and Political Science became available in 1988,[73] I proposed a one-year stay that would combine teaching with research and was given the appointment. This section recounts brief vignettes that are intended to convey what it was like, for my wife Emily and me, to live our lives amidst the day-to-day circumstances of Sri Lanka's deadly conflicts.[74]

We first visited Sri Lanka for three weeks in June 1987. Our trip was a combined honeymoon and reconnaissance for the more extended stay that was to begin the following January. A few weeks prior to our departure, stories in the *New York Times* and *Washington Post* described the bombing of Colombo's main bus station, also mentioning earlier political assassinations and a bloody massacre by Tamil rebels at the nation's most sacred religious shrine. Feature stories spoke of Sri Lanka's 'disintegration,' however we decided not to cancel our plans. Later, when I spoke at a sparsely attended international conference in Colombo – press reports had caused most participants to cancel their plans – Sri Lankan participants seemed pleased that we had come and amused to learn that it was our honeymoon. During our visit, we felt no danger walking Colombo streets and travelling by train to 'safe' parts of the country.[75]

In July, two weeks after we returned to the United States, the political situation deteriorated. Under pressure, Sri Lankan President J.R. Jayewardene accepted the introduction of a large Indian army contingent, dubbed 'The Indian Peace Keeping Force' (IPKF), to pacify Tamil rebels in the islands' northeast.[76] Soon, more than 50,000 Indian troops were bogged down in a full-fledged guerrilla war with a tenacious, elusive enemy.

Adding to Jayewardene's problems, the Indians' arrival rekindled Sri Lanka's second civil war, a class conflict between rural Sinhalese youth and the nation's elite ruling establishment.[77] Shadowy cadres of the JVP began murdering politicians and administrators. Their strategy was to weaken the economy, polarise the society and reduce the capacity of the government to govern. Countermeasures by government security forces were reported to be both brutal and ineffective.

Deadly conflicts continued in the north and south throughout the fall of 1987, but we decided to return for my teaching assignment anyway. In January 1988, we settled into a spacious colonial-era 'bungalow' a few miles south of Colombo's central business district and within walking distance of the university. While I introduced my students to quantitative social science and collected political conflict data, Emily experienced the Tamil insurgency and Indian intervention first hand, managing a community health training program in several rural areas of Sri Lanka's strife-torn Northern Province.

'Small problems…'

English speaking Sri Lankans often used the word 'problem', or sometimes 'a small problem', to refer to the demonstrations, strikes, incidents of sabotage, bombings and killings that increasingly disrupted normal patterns of life. By now, such problems were normal front-page fare in *The Island* and *The Daily News*,[78] which I read regularly each morning. They were duly recorded in my database as political conflict incidents.

During the early months of our stay, what surprised me most was not the frequency of problems, but the resiliency of everyday life in the face of their disruptions. Friends who lived in Beirut during bad times there have shared similar impressions. Colombo, in particular, seemed insulated. The ubiquity of machine-gun toting soldiers, obligatory searches before entering commercial buildings and occasional disruptions of electricity and running water were an accepted and manageable part of daily routines. (Emily said she always used pencil to write in her appointment calendar, because the future was never certain.) Drawn by bargain prices, middle class European and Asian tour-groups continued to populate resort hotels in southern coastal towns, enjoying the island's warm sunshine and gorgeous beaches. In the ancient capitals of Kandy, Anuradhapura and Polonnaruwa, tourists waited patiently in line to view relics of the island's 2,000 year-old civilisation.

Even in the Tamil City of Jaffna, with Indian troops bivouacked in the town's centre and major intersections watched by machine-gun nests, most people seemed to be engaged in everyday activities most of the time. But here, one also had a sense of impermanence and tension. Apart from military vehicles, bicycles and an occasional patched-together Austin A-4 were the only means of transportation. Cordon and search operations, curfews and cuts in basic services frequently disrupted daily living. Sabotage, guerrilla actions, firefights and reprisals killed non-combatants randomly.

Historian Barbara Tuchman, describing fourteenth century France, pictures conditions similar to those we encountered in Sri Lanka. She writes:

> Charles [V] reigned in a time of havoc, but in all such times there are unaffected places filled with beauty and games, music and dancing, love and work. While clouds of smoke by day and the glow of flames by night mark burning towns, the sky over the neighbouring vicinity is clear; where the screams of tortured prisoners are heard in one place, bankers count their money and peasants plough behind placid oxen somewhere else. Havoc in a given period does not cover all the people all the time, and though its effect is cumulative, the decline it drags behind takes time before it is recognised.[79]

In the fall of 1988, Colombo residents began to personally face conditions that Sri Lankans living elsewhere on the island had been experiencing for months and even years.

'Your plane ticket receipts can be used as curfew passes'

Emily and I returned to Colombo in November 1988, after a month's stay in New Zealand and Singapore. During our trip, we heard little news of Sri Lanka. Airport ground staff who welcomed us said nothing about any problems. A 30 per cent increase in the taxi fare to Colombo was the first intimation of a deteriorated security situation. Our taxi driver justified the increase by explaining that petrol was scarce and a curfew was in force. I knew that during curfews, driven vehicles and individuals walking outside of their homes or workplaces were required to carry passes issued by the security forces. Individuals without passes could be detained or even summarily shot. Our airline ticket receipts would serve as curfew passes at army roadblocks on the road to Colombo, the driver explained.[80]

Driving through familiar streets of a city normally bustling with life, but now silent and empty, was an eerie experience. Occasionally street lamps provided some illumination but shops were dark and barricaded. An occasional armed sentry, official vehicle, stray dog or homeless person, were the only life on the streets. People whose 'home' was the street were apparently unofficial exceptions to curfew regulations. We passed several lying under building alcoves with blankets and saris pulled over their heads. I wondered if some were People's Liberation Front (JVP) guerrillas in disguise. Passage through normally traffic-clogged streets was swift. Heavily armed soldiers accepted our ticket stubs as passes without question at four checkpoints including two on the normally busy sea coast road to Kollupitiya district where we lived.

The next day, anecdotes from staff and friends, plus a month of accumulated newspapers helped us form a clearer picture of recent events in Sri Lanka. Nightly curfews in Colombo, it became apparent, were just one indicator of a deteriorating situation. During November, activities of JVP guerrillas had intensified, eroding the authority of President J.R. Jayewardene's government. Within 10 miles of the city, bus service was sporadic and under army escort. Bus drivers and passengers who ignored JVP posters warning them to stay home had been shot and killed. Colombo's normally bustling central rail station was shuttered and empty except for a protective cordon of security guards. Emily observed that Colombo residents were now experiencing conditions that were commonplace for Tamils living in the island's Northern and Eastern Provinces.

The JVP claimed to represent Sri Lanka's 'masses' against the ruling elite. But killings, sabotage, general strikes and curfews hurt poor people most. 'Casual labourers,' who received their wages at the end of each day, had no money to buy food for their families. Payment of other workers was delayed because of closed offices and banks. In rural areas, offices of the government-run 'People's Bank' had been burned. There were long lines for food and water, long waits for a few crowded buses. People were threatened, intimidated, robbed and killed in their homes by JVP hit squads and by pro-government death squads. Sometimes the assailants were just gangs of ordinary thugs, hired by an enemy to settle some score. Police were widely viewed as ineffective or corrupt. Poor people avoided contact with them, if at all possible. Rumours circulated that lower police ranks had been infiltrated by JVP sympathisers who were fingering informants for execution.

As late as 6 November, Sri Lanka's *Times* quoted optimistic projections for the peak November-April season from tourist industry representatives, who cited advance hotel bookings of 50 to 80 per cent occupancy. However, two days later the resurgent tourist industry received a crippling blow. Hotel employees in the prime resort areas south of Colombo received threats, purportedly from the JVP. Many stayed home from work. In some hotels, guests went without food while in others, JVP messengers ordered kitchen staffs to serve only Sri Lankan curries. Several tourist coaches, ferrying new arrivals from Katunayake airport[81] to the south were unable to refuel and stalled on the road. On 9 November, following an emergency meeting of tour operators and Tourist Board members with President Jayewardene, a nervous government ordered the evacuation of foreign tourists from resort hotels. Within a few days virtually all had left the island, after chaotic airport scenes. Charter flights from Europe to Sri Lanka were cancelled.[82] On the streets of downtown Colombo, filled with jewellery, craft and antique shops, foreigners became a rare sight. In Colombo's six five-star hotels, a scattering of businessmen and development consultants were the only foreigners to be seen. Prospects for business or development seemed unpromising. 'Fear is the Key,' wrote *Lanka Guardian* editor Mervyn de Silva: 'A creeping 'insurgency' with hardly a shot fired [has] Colombo encircled, reducing the administration to an all-too visible condition of helplessness.'[83]

Saying 'farewell...'

Some weeks later, as Sri Lanka prepared for its sixteenth Presidential election in December, we bid farewells to many friends, packed household goods and prepared for our return to the United States. Sri Lankan parties could often last until the small hours of the morning, but our farewell socialising ended early – Colombo's nightly curfew was 9:00 PM. The evening before our departure we took the now customary precaution of engaging a hotel room close to the airport. This made it less likely that a curfew, roadblock or terrorist attack would cause a missed flight. Space was readily available; there were only two other guests at the Brown's Beach resort hotel complex of several hundred rooms. Sadly, we bid our regular taxi driver, '*Vijaya*', good-bye, not knowing when we would see him again. Some months later, Sri Lankan police would shoot him to death in the course of an interrogation about his son's suspected JVP affiliation.

Our last dinner was taken in the hotel's spacious dining terrace overlooking a romantic tropical beach setting that was illuminated by moonlight and flickering kerosene torches. More than 70 tables were neatly set for the evening meal, but there was only one other diner. We slept fitfully that night. Rusting air conditioning units had not functioned for months and there were holes in the mosquito netting over our beds. Early the next morning, before driving to the airport, we shared remains of our breakfast with hungry crows that perched fearlessly on our balcony ledge. The sky was cloudless and gentle waves splashed along the shoreline of the pristine, empty beach.

Some hours later, our Singapore Airlines flight touched down safely in Hong Kong. Until we no longer experienced it, we did not recognise how draining the daily stressfulness of Colombo life those last few weeks had been. At the same time, we felt guilty about leaving our Sri Lankan friends to an uncertain fate. For a day or so, when we entered a hotel, restaurant, or store, we instinctively reached for our bags so that they could be checked for concealed weapons and explosive devices. There were no security guards standing by to inspect them.

2
Why Did Sri Lanka's Political Differences Escalate Into Protracted, Deadly Conflicts?

The debate about the causes of violent conflict escalation in Sri Lanka is really a debate about why successive Sri Lankan governments were, prior to the mid-1980s, unable to achieve effective, sustainable development.

Conjectures

Sri Lanka did not become the next Cambodia, as some feared, in 1988. The JVP was destroyed as a guerrilla organisation by 1990 and later re-emerged as a legal political party. The civil war with Tamil rebels has ebbed and flowed. Differences between the two sides remain intractable, though a fragile truce has temporarily ended the killing. Through years of deadly conflict, scholars (as they are wont to do) have struggled to answer the question that gives this chapter its title. These sometime contradictory conjectures comprise the current "state of knowledge" about causes of deadly civil conflict in Sri Lanka. Their relevance extends beyond the island. Here are the most important, briefly summarised.

1. Ethnicity: Cultural differences between ethnically distinct communities, deeply rooted in history, created a climate favouring the emergence of leaders who used ethnic appeals to gain political support. This pushed *all* political leaders who succeeded in gaining power to implement discriminatory policies, emphasising ethnic differences, which produced a radicalisation of political discourse and the emergence of militant movements on both sides of the ethnic divide.[1]

2. Un-remedied structural weaknesses in the post-colonial economy: Early successes in public health, mass education and provision of basic entitlements produced rapid population growth and a youthful population with high aspirations. But un-remedied structural weaknesses in the post-colonial economy meant that aspirations of young men and women for good jobs and a better way of life could not be fulfilled in many cases.[2] This created disillusionment

with the established order and a climate of hopelessness that attracted youth to militant movements, committed to violent means as the only way to effect needed radical change.[3]

3. Ruling class exploitation: The post-independence period simply continued a pattern of colonial-era exploitation, but with colonial rulers replaced by an indigenous ruling class. This ruling class, sometimes in league with former colonial masters, maintained a political-economic system that expropriated most of the benefits that the labour of the masses produced. Escalating violent conflict was the historically necessary consequence of such a system.[4]

4. Social disruptions caused by privatisation, deregulation and structural adjustment: Free market economic reforms and structural adjustment were implemented, beginning in 1977, to correct un-remedied structural weaknesses in the post-colonial economy and to eliminate disincentives and inefficiencies caused by years of failed social policies. But these reforms caused social disruptions, corruption and widening inequities that alienated Sri Lankan youth, many of whom remained unemployed or underemployed. This created disillusionment with the established order and a climate of hopelessness that attracted youth to militant movements, committed to violent means as the only way to effect needed radical change.[5]

5. Too much democracy: Sri Lanka's problems were caused by too much democracy. Early successes in public health, mass education and provision of basic entitlements conditioned citizens to view government, rather than the market as the principal source of both employment and benefits. Governments were replaced in successive democratic elections when they failed to deliver or opposition leaders promised more. The result was a succession of inconsistent, even contradictory, economic policies that produced economic stagnation and failed to implement necessary structural reforms.[6] Consequently, aspirations of young men and women for good jobs and a better way of life could not be fulfilled in many cases. This created disillusionment with the established order and a climate of hopelessness that attracted youth to militant movements, committed to violent means as the only way to effect needed radical change.

6. Democratic governance failures: Sri Lanka's problems were caused by declining even-handedness and transparency of its democratic processes and institutions. Beginning in 1970, Sri Lanka's security forces became increasingly politicised and its governments became increasingly repressive. This helped Sri

Lanka Freedom Party leaders and United National Party (UNP) leaders retain power longer than might otherwise have been possible, but did not facilitate long-term solutions to economic problems. Government electoral manipulations and repression created a climate in which growing numbers saw violence as the only form of political dissent likely to be effective.[7] This created disillusionment with the established order and a climate of hopelessness that attracted youth to militant movements, committed to violent means as the only way to effect needed radical change.

7. <u>Leadership failures</u>: Erosion of democratic processes and institutions was caused by leadership failures. This theory focuses on shortcomings of the nation's two most influential post-independence leaders, Sirimavo Bandaranaike and J.R. Jayewardene. Mrs. Bandaranaike's leadership weakened her own party so that it was in no position to resist the authoritarian tendencies of the UNP. J.R. Jayewardene used his considerable tactical skills to vitiate the credibility of his moderate opponents. The tactics he used to remain in power 'helped to undermine the moral basis upon which pluralist politics formerly rested.[8] This created disillusionment with the established order and a climate of hopelessness that attracted youth to militant movements, committed to violent means as the only way to effect needed radical change.

In the case of each conjecture, excepting the historically deterministic number 'three' (ruling class exploitation), proponents conclude that in the circumstances described, *violent militant actions, evoking violent government responses, escalating to full-scale civil war was then the almost inevitable scenario.*

Academic debates about which contending explanation "is best" often seem like the parable about six blind men who each felt part of an elephant and then disputed with his companions about the whole. One man said the elephant "is like a wall;" a second, that it was like a spear; a third that it was like a snake; a fourth that it was like a tree; a fifth that it was like a fan and the sixth than it was like a rope. Each argued that his partial information could be extrapolated to a complete image, rejecting the need to combine it with the information of his fellows, in order to describe a more complex whole. Nineteenth century poet John Godfrey Saxe's rendering of the parable in verse concludes:

> *And so these men of Indostan*
> *Disputed loud and long,*
> *Each in his own opinion*
> *Exceeding stiff and strong*
> *Though each was partly in the right*
> *And all were in the wrong!*

What might the 'elephant' partially described by these seven conjectures look like? A good way to begin is by grouping them according to the 'schools of thought' they exemplify.[9] In chapter 5, elements from these conjectures, along with others, will be linked in what I call *the development-deadly conflict system* to provide a more comprehensive view. Descriptions of four schools of thought follow. I have labelled them 'ethnicity, identity and culture;' 'political economy;' 'effective governance and democratic governance' and 'leadership.'

Ethnicity, Identity and Culture

The relevant time horizon of this school's proponents spans centuries, perhaps even millennia. Theories that viewed the world through this lens were influential in the late nineteenth and the early twentieth centuries but fell out of favour with the emphasis on modernisation that dominated international development thought in the immediate post-World War II decades. Following the end of the Cold War, the high visibility of 'ethnic' political movements and of violent conflicts between 'ethnic' protagonists has reawakened interest. Scholars debate whether ethnic identities are socially constructed and goal oriented (instrumental), or more fundamentally intrinsic (primordial), but agree that they must be included in explanations of many violent conflicts.[10] 'Ethnic conflict' has become popular shorthand label for conflicts such as the one in Sri Lanka, though clearly much more than ethnicity is at issue.

Political Economy

Conjectures two, three, and four on our list focus on interrelated economic, political and sociological variables over a shorter time horizon. Political economy is an umbrella label given to such views, though some scholars limit use of the label to theories owing deference to Karl Marx's influential writings. Theories emphasising exploitation by a 'ruling class' (number three) fit this more narrow definition best, but those emphasising inequalities created by policies of a power-maximising, greedy, exploitative political leadership (number four) also qualify. Radical contributors to this school argue that smashing the power structure via a violent revolution is the only way to effect meaningful change. Less revolutionary theories emphasising 'structural weaknesses' (number two), such as an over-reliance on plantation agriculture as a source of foreign exchange, would qualify broadly as political economy. However, proponents of these theories are more hopeful about implementing 'structural reforms' and less concerned about political-social structures that may block or vitiate them. Such theories provide the basis for 'structural adjustment' reforms that were pushed by the U.S., Great Britain and international lending agencies during the 1980s and 1990s as an economic growth strategy for developing nations. Marxist political economists argue that structural adjustment reformers are, wittingly or unwittingly, part of power structures that keep stagnation and inequality in place or make it worse.

Effective Governance and Democratic Governance

Five and six on our list, but also four, which overlaps two schools, focus on political institutions and emphasise shortcomings in *effective governance* and *democratic governance* as important considerations that help to explain violent conflict. Emphasis on effective governance (or state performance) is part of a venerable tradition in history and comparative politics exemplified by Crane Brinton's *Anatomy of a Revolution,* cited earlier, and the influential writings of Harvard University sociologist Theda Skocpol.[11] More recently the World Bank (mandated by its charter not to address political matters) began raising issues of corruption, transparency and state competence in a series of working papers on 'governance' that culminated in the landmark *World Development Report 1997: The State in a Changing World.* The report concluded that effective governance was, indeed, a pivotal contributor to economic development. It argued further that ambitious development strategies attempted by weak states would fail because their governments lacked the 'capabilities' to implement them successfully.[12]

Democratic governance was a major theme in the voluminous 'political development' literature of the late 1950s and 1960s[13] and received some emphasis in pre-Vietnam era policies of U.S. President John F. Kennedy's administration. Disillusion with modernisation theories, intensification of the Cold War, and a more realist foreign policy contributed to its loss of favour as a development goal in the 1970s. President Ronald Reagan resurrected democratisation as a tool of his Cold War strategy, but it did not really come into vogue until the end of the Cold War. In the 1990s, as democratic theorists began to give renewed attention to developing nations,[14] controversial Reagan-era pro-democracy institutions were given a new lease on life and democracy promotion became a major priority of the U.S. Agency for International Development (USAID).[15] There remains considerable ambiguity, however about the relationship between democratisation, development and conflict, illustrated here by contradictions between theories that too much democracy (number five) and the erosion of democracy (number six) explain Sri Lanka's escalating violent conflicts.

Leadership

Theories that focus on *leadership* (number seven), especially on qualities of specific leaders, are part of a tradition made famous by Thomas Carlysle's nineteenth century classic, *On Heroes, Hero Worship and The Heroic in History* but have always been controversial among historians and social scientists. The positive influence of towering figures such as Gandhi and Nelson Mandela as well as the pernicious influence of Iraq's Saddam Hussein, Serbia's Slobodan Milosevic and other 'rogue leaders' lend credence to the view that leaders do make a difference — for good and ill — at critical junctures. Interestingly, the authors of *Preventing Deadly Conflict* give particularly strong emphasis to the discretionary role of leaders in precipitating violent conflict and preventing it. There are many forces pushing groups toward conflict, they observe, but violence is not inevitable. 'The inescapable fact is that the decision to use violence is made by leaders to incite susceptible groups.' But they also have discretion 'to use peaceful measures of conflict resolution and structural approaches [that] can reduce the susceptibility of groups to arguments for violence.'[16]

Where Do 'Theories of Conflict' Fit In?

I have provided an identical conclusion for all but one[17] of the synopses to emphasise that while there are disagreements about root causes of violent conflict escalation in Sri Lanka, there is considerable agreement about proximate causes. Most important among these are unmet aspirations of youth (linked especially to poor employment prospects), hopelessness and disillusionment with the established political-economic order, the growing strength of militant movements committed to violence and the inability of government security forces to successfully contain them.[18] Explanations focusing on these proximate causes draw from proponents of three schools of thought in the 'conflict theory' literature, which can be labelled *relative deprivation, mobilisation* and *repression*.

Relative deprivation theories emphasise popular attitudes, *en masse*, as a cause of violent outbreaks. Outbreaks are more probable, proponents believe, when the social-political climate has become volatile, due to built-up collective anger, resentment and aggressions that unmet expectations produce. It is the *gap* between benefits and the experience of fulfilment that produces collective anger. Either heightened expectations (which political campaign rhetoric might produce) or declining benefits can widen the gap. Explanations of conflict escalation that emphasise disillusionment resulting from economic stagnation or governance failures reflect the influence of relative deprivation theories.[19]

Mobilisation theories emphasise the organised activities of groups as a cause of violent outbreaks. Outbreaks are more probable, proponents believe, when social movement leaders with a militant agenda have mobilised followers, organised them into a disciplined, cohesive group and secured sufficient resources to act on that agenda. Ethnic and class ties often provide a basis for group mobilisation, but are no substitute for resources, organisational ability and discipline. Understanding the group's dynamics may be critical to understanding how a particular conflict scenario unfolds. Explanations of conflict escalation that emphasise the pivotal role of militant movements and their leaders reflect the influence of mobilisation theories.[20]

Repression theories emphasise the role of state-sanctioned violence employed by the security forces and pro-government paramilitaries in catalysing violence. Outbreaks are more probable, proponents believe, when two elements are present. First, the security forces (possibly with paramilitary or 'thug' allies) are tasked to enforce an unpopular political-economic agenda or quell popular resistance to such an agenda. Second, these forces lack the resources, skill and/or motivation to carry out this task effectively. Their ineffective use of violence aids militant opposition in a variety of ways, from driving disgruntled neutrals and moderates into militant ranks, to actually enhancing militant firepower by failing to prevent thefts of weapons or having to surrender or abandon them. Explanations of conflict escalation that focus on politicisation and corruption of police and military forces along with the destabilising role of government-sanctioned thugs, paramilitaries and death squads, reflect the influence of repression theories.[21]

While I have grouped theories about the proximate causes of violent conflict into schools, it would be inaccurate to characterise them any more as 'contending' schools. Most conflict theorists now acknowledge that each school has something to contribute, though emphases and research foci may differ. Feelings of relative deprivation, whatever their cause, create a climate that facilitates mobilisation. Outbreaks of conflict may be spontaneous, but will not evolve into a protracted conflict in the absence of an effective social movement to sustain it. Similarly, repression alone, however inept, will not provide militant groups with the skill and wherewithal to challenge the repressors.[22]

From the perspective of this book's goals, the consensus regarding proximate causes among six of the seven conjectures summarised is of particular note. They reflect a growing consensus in the conflict theory literature.

Points of difference among at least five of the seven – those within the political economy and governance schools – focus on relationships between the effectiveness of country-level development and those proximate causes of conflict escalation. A deeper probing of ethnicity and identity literature would reveal that even with within this school of thought, most instrumentalists see ethnicity as a flexible construct that is at least partly manipulated by communities and their leaders in the service of development goals.[23] *Thus, the debate about causes of violent conflict escalation in Sri Lanka is really a debate about why successive Sri Lankan governments and other key actors were, prior to the mid 1980s, unable to achieve effective, sustainable development.*[24] Was this failure caused by irremediable ethnic divisions, a pernicious colonial legacy, ruling class exploitation, a flawed economic structure, counterproductive and destabilising reforms, bad leadership or what? My answer, to be elaborated in chapter 5, is that all these factors played a role, but it is the way they were (are) linked together in a system that is most important.

This is a good point to look back over the terrain that our exploration of linkages between development and the escalation of deadly conflict has covered so far.

Development-Conflict Linkages: What do we know and need to know?

What the current state of knowledge regarding development-conflict linkages communicates seems unambiguous, but incomplete. Here is what seems unambiguous.

- When development failures are widespread, large numbers of individuals will experience deprivation and are likely to see themselves as victims of injustice. When large numbers see themselves as victims of injustice, outbreaks of organised violent conflict that may well escalate into a protracted civil war are probable. The word 'organised' is used to emphasise that outbreaks and especially their persistence will not, primarily, be spontaneous, though elements of spontaneity may be present. If perceptions of injustice run along ethnic fault-lines, as they do in many poor, less-industrialised countries, the probability of violent outbreaks and escalation are greater.
- Incidents of organised violent conflict, even at relatively low levels of intensity, are early warning signals of development failure providing indications that the country is starting down a path that, in the absence of remedial action, may very well lead to violent civil war.
- Violent conflict leading to civil war may be perceived as 'the only way'

of remedying perceived injustices, but it is not a cost-effective strategy for doing so or for effecting fundamental social changes. Typically, civil wars are costly, brutal, protracted and leave most protagonists (especially numerous dead and physically maimed) worse off than when the war began.

- Both neighbouring countries and rich, industrialised countries far from the scene of battle ignore escalating patterns of conflict, leading to civil wars, at their peril. Once civil war breaks out, they are likely to be sucked into the process, incurring greater economic and political costs than early, timely, appropriate interventions would have required.

- The sooner corrective measures intended to move the country back on a path of effective, sustainable development are undertaken, the more productive and cost-effective they are likely to be.

This book focuses on two areas where filling gaps in the state of knowledge would contribute to preventing deadly conflicts. First, there are few accepted guidelines for identifying and implementing remedial measures in response to early-warning signals of development failure, in particular those measures that are most likely to move a country back on an effective, sustainable development path. Second, there is incomplete understanding of why – in the face of compelling evidence linking development failure and deadly civil conflict and of civil conflict's futility for most (not all) protagonists – such conflicts have become one of the most tragic social pathologies of the post-Cold War era. More specifically, we do not know why the irrefutable linkages between effective, sustainable development and conflict prevention have been taken into account so incompletely in implementing country-level and international-level development policies.

The questions this book seeks to answer, then, focus on knowledge gaps that, if filled, will help politicians/practitioners design and implement development policies effectively targeting deadly conflict prevention as a more specific objective. Among the most important questions are these:

- Viewed retrospectively, to what specific manifestations of development failure do the patterns in our violent political conflict fever charts (and the incidents that generate them) point? How were relationships between the circumstances generating these patterns and Sri Lanka's development scenario seen at the time? Why were early warning signals of development failure not heeded (or not heeded effectively?)

- What were the perceptions and what were the priorities of Sri Lanka's political leaders when they made the decisions that they made, especially decisions that affected economic policy, governance, democratic practice and employment of security forces? To what degree did they take conflict-development linkages into account when making their choices? When decisions produced unanticipated outcomes or side effects (especially violent ones) why did that happen?

- Under successive leaders and governments, what remedial measures, in the areas of economic policy, democratic practice and leadership, might have moved Sri Lanka back toward the path of sustainable development, on which it seemed to have made such a promising start? What guidelines might have facilitated the crafting of such remedial measures?

- What practical lessons can be drawn from Sri Lanka's experience with development-conflict linkages that will facilitate effective, sustainable development in other countries? How can these lessons be applied to Sri Lanka itself in order to move the country back towards a path of sustainable development?

Why View Conflict Development Linkages Through the Lens of Sri Lanka's Civil Wars?

This last set of questions shifted the focus back to Sri Lanka, even though augmenting the state of knowledge about development-conflict linkages more generally is the goal. This narrowing of focus needs to be justified. I propose to do so by answering the two most obvious questions that any case study with pretensions to generality must address: (a) Why ground the analysis so intensively (and almost exclusively) in a single case, and (b) having made that decision, why choose Sri Lanka's development experience and civil wars, specifically, as the lens through which to focus.

Why focus so intensively on a single case?

The project that produced this book began as a series of case studies. As already noted, my studies of Sri Lanka were preceded by development of a generic computer simulation model of development-conflict linkages, then refinement of the model through an application to Argentina, then further testing of the model's generality through an application to Mexico.[25] This model-based approach to international development problems used an applied systems analysis methodology called *system dynamics*, which has been part of my professional practice for many years. System dynamics has been widely applied to problems in business management, urban development, environmental policy and long-term global-scale problems involving relationships between population, political economy, resources and the environment.[26] A more detailed discussion of how development-conflict linkages are viewed as a complex system and why this is useful will be presented later. Here I only want to identify three precepts of system dynamics that point toward a case study approach.

First is the *importance of describing a problem as observable behaviour patterns of policy relevant variables that occur over relatively long time periods.* System dynamics practitioners call graphs of such behaviours, plotted against time, *reference modes.* The fever chart of violent conflict intensity pictured in chapter 1 is a good example. Reference mode patterns, for example exponential growth, goal seeking and oscillation, provide clues about the underlying structure of the complex system generating the behaviour.[27]

A belief that *reference mode behaviour patterns are generated by complex systems, where variables (elements) are linked together in feedback loops is a second precept of system dynamics.* A feedback loop is simply a circular connection of variables that impact one another. In the systems model of development-conflict linkages to be discussed later, examples of variables would be *violent conflict intensity* (our reference mode variable), *relative deprivation* and *economic performance.* Figure 2-1 illustrates a feedback loop that might be labelled a 'vicious cycle.' Relative deprivation increases the potential for conflict; conflict adversely impacts economic performance; declining economic performance further increases deprivation. System dynamics practitioners believe they only begin to understand a system fully when they have created a simulation that reproduces reference mode behaviour patterns.[28]

Belief that *a deep understanding of context is essential to creating fully accurate simula-*

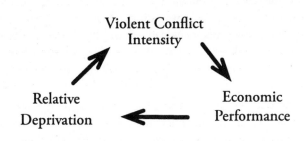

Figure 2.1 A 'Vicious Cycle' Feedback Loop

tions is a third precept of system dynamics. Apprentice modellers are told that they must *immerse themselves in the system* generating the problematic reference mode behaviour patterns. While they should use such quantitative data as is available, they should give equal attention to the mental models of individuals who know the system well and to the contextually rich writings that are produced by journalists, historians and anthropologists.[29]

Guided by these precepts, it is natural that systems dynamics practitioners interested in development and political economy are drawn to country level scenarios unfolding over relatively long time horizons. We tend to compare cases serially, rather than simultaneously.[30] It was this practice that led me to model Argentina first, then Mexico and then to seek the opportunity for a year-long immersion in Sri Lanka. In fact, I became so immersed that I have not yet created a computer simulation of Sri Lanka's development (though I have been guided by the model's underlying theory). Before doing so, I decided to share what I had learned, so far, by writing this book.

Why do Sri Lanka's experiences provide a useful lens?

I have already described what first led me to Sri Lanka. Before becoming an exemplar of 'ethnic conflict' it was widely cited as a leading development 'success story.' 'What happened to Sri Lanka?' had been a topic of discussion among development practitioners and was of a particular interest to someone who had been seeking to understand development-conflict linkages. As I deepened my understanding of the island and its people, it became apparent that Sri Lanka's multifaceted development scenario provided an opportunity to examine relationships between violent conflict patterns and an unusually diverse range of development policies and experiences.

First, Sri Lanka began life as an independent nation with what appeared to be extraordinarily good preconditions for a peaceful development scenario: a relatively robust economy, a relatively strong system of governance, and relatively strong traditions of democratic pluralism. Thus it was possible to reject the most common explanations of conflict that emphasised the heritage of colonialism, rather than development policies implemented after independence. To be more specific:

- Sri Lanka achieved independence without a revolution and with closer ties to its former colonial rulers than most developing nations.
- It seemed to have many socio-economic characteristics customarily

associated with political stability: a relatively strong middle class and civil society, high literacy, widely read newspapers representing diverse points of view, strong public health and entitlement programs, and a fairly equitable distribution of income.

• It also began independence with almost no military establishment and a very modest police establishment. Like their British counterparts, Sri Lanka's police were unarmed (many still do not carry firearms). The military did not become a really significant factor in national life until conflict with Tamil militants escalated in the 1980s.

• It had a relatively large cadre of talented political leaders, many of whom were British university graduates in law and economics.

• Most post-independence leaders were at least publicly committed to political pluralism; the nation had a relatively strong pluralist tradition to build upon, though there had been tensions between ethnic groups and, from time to time, severe outbreaks of violence.

• It was one of the few developing nations with a genuinely competitive multi-party system, dominated by two strong contenders and with strong democratic traditions dating back to the 1930s.

• It began life as an independent nation with substantial foreign exchange reserves and a balance of payments surplus, though the economy, like that of many developing nations, was dependent on exports from the plantation sector. Its systems of macroeconomic data collection and economic planning were unusually strong for a developing nation.

• Its cadre of higher level civil servants was professional, well educated and received a living wage. Public service was considered one of the most desirable career paths for top university graduates in Sri Lanka.

Second, Sri Lanka's leaders coped fairly successfully with the post-independence social and economic problems that produced political instability and economic setbacks in many developing nations and brought authoritarian, one-party regimes to power. They experimented with many of the economic development strategies whose merits and demerits were debated by international development practitioners. This provides an opportunity to compare divergent policies and assess which contributed more to circumstances that catalysed intensifying conflict. To be more specific:

- Sri Lanka began life as an independent nation with a mixed economy. This was followed by a period in which Marxists held key economic posts in successive governments and Sri Lanka's economy became one of the most centrally planned in the developing world. Following this, it was one of the first developing nations to implement 'structural adjustment' reforms that expanded the role of the free market, provided investment incentives, and linked Sri Lanka more closely with the global economy.

- It was a major recipient of development assistance, first from Western nations and multilateral donors, then from the USSR, its satellite nations and China and then again from the West.

- A 'populist revolution' that gave greater power to the Sinhalese majority and implemented polices making Sinhala the official language was achieved democratically and, despite some inflammatory rhetoric, peacefully.

- Two attempted military coups were easily foiled and, in 1971, the government successfully quashed a militant insurrection in less than a year. Though initial reprisals against militants by security forces were draconian, the government later implemented a wide ranging amnesty program that reintegrated many militant supporters back into society.

- The militant insurrection was not followed by a militarisation of the society (though the government did become more repressive). In fact, military budgets steadily declined in real terms, returning to almost pre-insurrection levels.

- The insurrection motivated government leaders to carry out (and many elite Sri Lankans to support) one of the few successful land reform and wealth redistribution programs implemented peacefully by any developing nation. Within less than a decade, the gap between average incomes of rich and poor Sri Lankans narrowed substantially.

- Between the time of independence and the general election of 1977, Sri Lanka's democratic institutions remained resilient. Seven general elections, all widely viewed as free and fair, produced six changes in the political party that controlled the government. Sri Lanka was one of a very few nations to supplant Marxist-oriented central planning with free-market-oriented policies via a general election.

- The victorious party in the 1977 general election tried to secure its free market economic reforms with constitutional reforms and a political strategy that attempted to emulate the 'Asian Tiger' model – a strong executive and a political system in which opposition was permitted, but a single party was clearly dominant.

Finally, as readers well know, beginning in 1983, violent political conflict became the dominant reality of Sri Lanka's political economic life and has remained so as this book is completed. Thus patterns and conditions that might theoretically have been expected to produce relative political stability failed to do so. More specifically:

- Militant Tamil groups, using violent confrontational tactics, came to supplant moderates as the dominant political forces in the Tamil majority regions of the North and East. Increasingly repressive measures undertaken by Sri Lanka's police and military forces failed to limit their activities and angered moderate Tamils.

- Anti-Tamil riots by Sinhalese mobs (that many believe were organised by government leaders) created thousands of Tamil refugees and motivated formerly moderate Tamil youths to become militant recruits.

- South Asia's dominant political power, India, which had once been a strong Sri Lankan ally, became a covert supporter of Tamil militants, providing them with resources, training facilities and sanctuaries. Eventually India intervened directly in the conflict, forcing Sri Lanka's government to accept a peace- keeping force of more than 50,000 troops. For several years, this force exercised de facto political authority over most of Sri Lanka's Northern and Eastern Provinces.

- Beginning in 1987, Sri Lanka's government also faced a second insurrection in Southern rural areas and major urban centres. This insurrection, organised by Sinhalese militant youth, was a 'class conflict' rather than an 'ethnic conflict.'

- The latter insurrection was defeated, over a four-year period by the most draconian, repressive measures ever seen in Sri Lanka. Subsequently, the party that had organised the insurrection was allowed to enter the political mainstream and won a number of seats in parliament.

- The conflict with Tamil militants more closely resembled other 'typical' civil wars. It was brutal, divisive, economically devastating, protracted, and apparently irresolvable.

Sri Lanka, then, provides a lens for viewing many challenges with which development practitioners and leaders of developing nations have grappled in the post-World War II era – and for learning from them. My intention is to provide answers to the question, 'how did we come to this' that will help craft more humane, peaceable, sustainable future development scenarios. Such scenarios could make it unnecessary for future generations to contemplate protracted deadly conflict's legacies – suffering, devastation and hopelessness – as Sri Lankans, Rwandans, Bosnians, Afghanis and many others have had to do. My vision is of a day when no citizens in today's developing nations will have to ask the question that chapter 1 posed: 'how did we come to this?' *Paradise Poisoned* will have achieved its purpose when that day comes.

3
What is 'Successful Development' and Why Does it Matter?

There is a wide gap between what most human beings are seeking out of life and what most country-level development scenarios of the last 50 years have provided. Within that gap lie the roots of protracted deadly conflict and terrorism. Crafting an early warning strategy for preventing deadly conflict and terrorism must begin by rethinking, fundamentally, what is meant by 'successful development.'

What has been said so far about links between conflict, terrorism and development, can be simply pictured in a feedback-loop diagram (Figure 3.1). Development failures cause social pathologies that contribute to intensifying violence. Intensifying violence makes development failures more probable. Frequent outcomes are deadly conflict and terrorism that, in turn, further exacerbate development failures and social pathologies. This is another example of a 'vicious cycle.'

Figure 3.1 - Development-Deadly Conflict Vicious Cycle

Supplanting 'development failures' with 'successful development' can break the cycle. But more than a half century of international development experience and scholarship has not produced consensus on how to achieve successful development or even what that means. Political leaders seeking guidance on such practical matters as how to alleviate poverty, stimulate economic growth, reduce youth unemployment and promote democracy, while maintaining political stability, are often frustrated by the responses that 'experts' provide. Sri Lanka's leaders experimented with both Marxist and 'free market' development models. They received 'development assistance,' consulted with experts, formulated detailed plans and measured their nation's progress. Both experiments were, for a time, touted as development success stories – before Sri Lanka became a poster case of deadly conflict and terrorism Failure to achieve targeted goals contributed to this tragic outcome. But what if the concept of 'successful development,' on which Sri Lanka's policies and programs were based, was fundamentally flawed?

What would an 'ideal' developed country look like?

Crafting a clear and specific picture of the 'end product'—an 'ideal' developed country—is where rethinking 'successful development' might begin. For many years, I have begun the formal education of prospective practitioner/scholars in American University's *Master of Arts in International Development Program* by challenging them to envision such an ideal.[1]

Like all development practitioners, our students come to realise that clearly envisioning an 'ideal' developed country is difficult. Should the model be an existing country—New Zealand? Singapore? Malaysia? The United States of America? Sweden? Israel? The Islamic Republic of Iran? Japan? Should it extrapolate from a smaller village-scale community such as an Ashram or Kibutz, or a larger intentional community such as Auroville[2] to an entire country? Should the model be a utopia than has not yet existed outside of a creator's imagination such as the Pure Land of the *Sukhavativyuha-sutra*,[3] the elitist polity of Plato's *Republic*, the agriculturally based traditional society of Austin Tappan Wright's *Islandia*[4], or the Marxist paradise of Edward Bellamy's *Looking Backward*[5] For many years, I have begun each semester's *International Development* core course, normally the first taken by our students, with the question: 'What would a country that was 'developed' *according to your ideal* look like?'

We seek answers in a guided visualisation exercise. Guided visualisation draws on scholarship and management practices that emphasise the power of *visioning* (creating visions) as a point of leverage for effecting change.[6] Proponents of this approach believe that 'visionary human intentions can bring forth not only new information, new behaviour, new technologies, but eventually new social institutions, new physical structures and new powers within human beings.'[7]

The exercise is a simple one. In a darkened room, with seats arranged in two long rows, three wide, and an aisle between, students are asked to close their eyes and imagine that they are journeying by passenger jet to a nation that is 'developed.' 'Developed,' I explain, means that individual and community life, the physical environment, the government and the economy are exactly as they would *choose* them to be. 'Voyagers' are urged to visualise what they really want, not what someone has told them to want or what they believe they must accept. They are encouraged to forget 'feasibility' and past disillusionments, allowing imagination to run free in the realm of their dreams and ideals.

They journey first to the seat of government, then to an agricultural area, then to an industrialised area, then to any area that particularly interests them. In each setting, they are asked, in their imagination, to answer these questions: 'What are you seeing? What are you hearing? What are the people around you doing and what to they look like? How do they relate to each other? How do they relate to you? What feelings are you experiencing?' The journey ends when they imagine themselves flying back to Washington, D.C. and, while the flight is in progress, imagine that the plane has turned back into a classroom.

Next, class members are asked to draw pictures of their visualisations—then to share them in small groups and with the entire class. Commonalties among them, across many sets of individuals with diverse cultural backgrounds and over many years, have been striking. Clearly this and similar exercises are touching something fundamental in the human spirit.

Three colleagues, who have facilitated similar visualisations in many parts of the world, synthesised them in their book, *Beyond the Limits: Confronting Global Collapse: Envisioning an Sustainable Future.*[8] Attributes of 'a sustainable world' they describe closely resemble what students, business executives, public servants, scientists and others report having experienced on imaginary journeys to the 'developed' country where they would most like to live.[9]

Here is a partial list:

- Sustainability, efficiency, sufficiency, justice, equity and community as high social values.
- Leaders who are honest, respectful, and more interested in doing their jobs than in keeping their jobs.
- Material sufficiency and security for all. Therefore, by spontaneous choice as well as by communal norms, low death rates, low birth rates and stable populations.
- Work that dignifies people instead of demeaning them. Some way of providing incentives for people to give of their best to society and be rewarded for doing so, while still ensuring that all people will be provided for sufficiently under any circumstances.
- An economy that is a means, not an end, one that serves the welfare of the human community and the environment, rather than demanding that the community and the environment serve it.
- Political structures that permit a balance between short-term and long-term considerations. Some way of exerting political pressure on behalf of the grandchildren.
- High skills on the part of citizens and governments in the arts of non-violent conflict resolution.
- Reasons for living and thinking well of oneself that do not require the accumulation of material things.

Models of society emerging from visioning exercises are almost uniformly peaceable. Indeed, police forces and natural security establishments rarely show up at all. This is hardly surprising. In a just and equitable society, led by honest politicians serving the public interest rather than their own, providing opportunities for meaningful work, with material sufficiency for all, where every individual was physically secure, where the perpetual accumulation of material things was not required to think well of oneself—few of the circumstances theorists identify as causing violent conflict would be present. 'Peace,' described by most of the world's great religions as a universal human want, would be the norm.

More that 30 years of studying, teaching and writing about 'international development' philosophies, strategies, plans, and programs lead me to conclude that most human beings are reaching towards ideals very similar to those pictured by my students and colleagues. The language may be less idealistic than evoked by visioning exercises, but is not inconsistent with them. '*Our dream* (emphasis added) is a world free of poverty,' states the World Bank's website.'[10] The mission statement of the United Nations Development Program (UNDP) speaks of 'helping countries to achieve sustainable human development by assisting them ...in poverty eradication, employment creation and sustainable livelihoods, the empowerment of women and the protection and regeneration of the environment, giving first priority to poverty eradication.' Further, it speaks of commitment 'to the principle that development is inseparable from the quest for peace and human security.'[11]   China's Ninth Five Year Plan (1996-2000) set as its goal: 'rais[ing] the people's living standard to that of a fairly comfortable life, with poverty practically eradicated.'[12]

When development visions are translated into operational plans, however, the ideal most human beings have in common – of a humane and peaceable society, characterised by material sufficiency, personal security and psychic fulfilment – is lost. There is a wide gap between what most human beings are seeking out of life and what most country-level development scenarios of the last 50 years have provided. Within that gap, I believe, lies the roots of protracted deadly conflict. Crafting an early warning strategy for preventing deadly conflict must begin by rethinking, fundamentally, what is meant by 'successful development'. Why do the visions embedded in current practices fall so far short of widely shared human aspirations?

Which 'development model' is best?

International development practice is about connecting ideals and results. The connections are policies and programs – five year plans, structural adjustment reforms, irrigation schemes, land reform laws, education schemes, governance structures and the like.   Collections of such policies and programs, linked by some theoretical/ideological perspective, are often termed 'development models.' Different models embody different development visions, though these visions may not be made explicit by proponents.

One popular text has identified five 'development models' as most influential. Three are 'capitalist or 'market-oriented' – laissez faire, import substitution industrialisation, growth with equity – and two are the 'socialist' 'Chinese' and 'Soviet' models.[13] Another volume identifies six models – monetarism, the open economy, industrialisation, green revolution, redistribution and socialism.[14] Post-World War II development practice can be viewed as a multiplicity of country-level trial and error experiments with such models. Particular models have won favour with development practitioners in different periods and then fallen from grace. Since the end of the Cold War, growth-oriented, capitalist, open economy models have been ascendant, but this is no guarantee that they will not be supplanted by an alternative in a few years. 'Which model is best' is always an important question for politicians and practitioners. Answering the question depends, in large degree, on the performance criteria chosen to measure 'successful development.'

Which performance criteria for measuring 'successful development' are best?

Performance criteria used to evaluate success or failure play important roles, not only in choosing from among contending development models, but in designing and refining them.[15] Common sense tells us that a model designed to maximise GNP per-capita will be quite different than a model designed to maximise income equality or to minimise infant mortality. For a systems analyst, performance criteria are key links in compensating feedback loops that determine a system's behaviour trajectory. Implicit in the performance criteria used by practitioners and politicians are definitions of 'successful development' and visions of an ideal developed country. All too rarely are these definitions and visions made explicit and then debated.

Surprisingly, the debates about which development model is best have not been matched by corresponding debates about which performance criteria are best. For decades, a single criterion, GNP per-capita, was the only performance index with institutional support and wide acceptance. An alternative that offered a contending world view, the Physical Quality of Life Index, gained some visibility in the 1970s, but lacked a solid institutional base and soon fell into disuse. Not until 1990, when Mahbub ul-Haq entrepreneured the first UNDP *Human Development Report*, featuring the *Human Development Index* (HDI), did a competitor to GNP per-capita become viable (though it remains far less influential).[16] While many readers may be familiar with these three indices and their associated worldviews, others may not. A brief synopsis seems appropriate.

Gross national product per-capita and economic growth

The World Bank defines Gross National Product (GNP) as 'the sum of value added by all resident producers, plus any taxes (less subsidies) not included in the valuation of output, plus net receipts of primary income from non resident sources.'[17] More simply, the concept is often defined as the total value of goods and services produced by a (country's) economy. Per-capita GNP, often used as a surrogate for per-capita income,[18] is simply a country's total GNP divided by its population. GNP became a popular performance measure as the centrepiece of a system of national income accounting first adopted by the U.S. and Great Britain in the 1940s.[19] In particular, the system was designed to provide fiscal planners and central bankers with theoretically grounded data that would help them to promote economic growth, damp the effects of business cycle downturns and prevent another great depression. Most governments now have national statistical offices, modelled after those of Britain and the U.S., that collect, compile and report national accounts data.

Simon Kuznets' seminal writings popularised and refined the use of economic growth as a development performance measure, though he also commented thoughtfully on its limitations.[20] It was the centrepiece of Walt Whitman Rostow's widely read volume, *The Stages of Economic Growth* (1960) and many other works that defined 'modernisation' as the goal of development. Most important, GNP-related measures have been the dominant performance criteria used by the World Bank and International Monetary Fund in their influential programs and publications and remain so to this day.

The implicit worldview emphasised by these criteria is straightforward. Maximising average personal income is the goal of development and the exemplars are nations that have done so, such as the United States, Switzerland, Scandinavian countries and, in the developing world, Singapore, Hong Kong and some Gulf States. Economists and other development scholars have developed a variety of models and policies intended to promote per-capita income growth. Most of the 'which model is best' debates focus on these growth-oriented models.

The Physical Quality of Life Index (PQLI)

Despite the early dominance of GNP-related performance measures, even proponents were well aware of their limitations as a measure of 'development' or welfare. Many productive activities (for example housewives' work) were excluded and some unproductive ones (expenditures on pollution clean up) were included. Important but subjective, non-monetised elements of human well-being – levels of happiness, justice, leisure, freedom and beauty – were not taken into account. Nor were important indicators of the physical quality of life – for example literacy, life expectancy and health – considered.

Imperfect relationships between GNP per-capita and human well-being raised a second set of problems. Focusing on average GNP per-capita took no account of how benefits were distributed in a country. Average incomes could be growing or high, but poor people could be losing out. A country's wealth could be directed to expenditures that had little impact on well-being – build-up of military forces, extravagant national monuments and deposits in foreign bank accounts of the politically powerful. Moreover, it was possible to improve well-being with targeted programs that required little increase in GNP per-capita or none at all.

The difficulty of making meaningful international comparisons raised a third set of problems. Though GNP-based performance measures were used widely to make comparisons, there were grave concerns about the meaningfulness of such analyses. Comparisons were most often made by adjusting exchange rates to a common currency and deflating currencies to a base year. But after abandonment of the Bretton Woods system introduced volatility into currency values, devising a consistent rationale for these adjustments became increasingly problematic. Adjusting for 'purchasing power parity' – the fact that a dollar equivalent could buy a great deal more of life's basic necessities in Dhaka than in Tokyo – added additional complexity to the problem of making meaningful comparisons.[21]

UN-sponsored committees, non-governmental organisations and individual scholars had periodically proposed alternatives to GNP per-capita that would address these problems but, until 1977, none gained much attention.[22] The breakthrough occurred when economic historian Morris W. Morris used a resident fellowship at the Overseas Development Council (ODC) to refine a deceptively simple composite index of human well-being that differed significantly from previous proposals.[23]

Morris sought an index that would satisfy six criteria:[24]

1. It should not assume that there is only one pattern of development.
2. It should avoid standards that reflect the values of specific societies.
3. It should measure results, not inputs.
4. It should be able to reflect the distribution of social results.
5. It should be simple to construct and easy to comprehend.
6. It should lend itself to international comparison.

He claimed that among more than 100 indicators identified by projects that had preceded his work, only three – *infant mortality, life expectancy* and *basic literacy* – met these criteria.[25] He combined these indicators into a composite index by setting a theoretically 'best' and 'worst' value for each and defining those values as equivalent to '0' and '100.' Indicator values were then scaled within this range.[26] The overall PQLI value for each country was simply the average (arithmetic mean) of the literacy, infant mortality and life expectancy indices weighted equally. This produced an easily understood result in which countries that did best scored near 100 and those that did badly scored near zero. Sweden, with a PQLI of 97 ranked highest, Guinea-Bissau, with a PQLI of 12 ranked lowest.

PQLI rankings presented a quite different worldview than GNP-per-capita rankings. Morris summarised these differences in two propositions: 'Money isn't everything.' And 'Low GNP countries don't all have low PQLIs.'[27] The first was illustrated by Saudi Arabia, the United Arab Emirates, Libya and some other Middle Eastern countries, which were distinguished by high per-capita GNPs and low PQLIs. Sri Lanka, Cuba, Grenada, Korea and the People's Republic of China provided examples of countries with very low per-capita GNPs that, nonetheless, did well in providing for the basic physical well-being of their people.

The implications of this new performance measure were significant for designing 'successful development' policies. Morris concluded that 'there is no automatic link between per-capita GNP and even the barest elements of well-being.' Moreover, 'it takes considerable time to build the institutional infrastructure that can generate and sustain a high PQLI even once the commitment to an improved quality of life is made.'[28] The research pointed to models through which poor countries could improve their residents' well-being with only modest increases in income. It concluded that relatively high PQLI scores were not associated with any particular type of political system.[29]

Professor Morris and James Grant hoped the PQLI would emerge as a competitor to GNP per-capita that would win favour with practitioners and politicians who were concerned with non-economic dimensions of development. In his major work, *Measuring the Condition of the World's Poor,* Morris argued for using the PQLI as 'a measure of performance,' 'criterion for international decision making' and 'tool for targeting and measuring progress.' So long as James Grant headed the Overseas Development Council, this seemed possible.

The index was featured in the Council's *Annual Reports* and energetically promoted. Research projects focusing on applying and refining the PQLI were initiated. But when Grant chose to become Secretary General of UNICEF in 1980, the PQLI lost the charismatic promoter and proponent who had been pivotal in its rise to prominence. It gradually faded into obscurity.[30]

The Human Development Index

The UN Charter called for 'promotion of the economic and social advancement of all peoples. Development-oriented UN agencies had long tried to position themselves as more sympathetic to 'human development' than the IMF, World Bank and major bilateral donors. Years before the PQLI was introduced, there had been efforts, under UN auspices, to devise an indicator that would win support as a people-centred alternative to GNP per-capita.[31] The limited success of these collaborative efforts highlighted the formidable challenges of coming up with a measure that was simultaneously rigorous enough to win support of academic communities (especially economists) and elegantly simple enough to be an effective communication device.[32] The PQLI, created by a single scholar, had met the second criteria, but Morris' decision to exclude economic variables entirely may have doomed it from the start.

In the end it was the UNDP that came up with a credible competitor to GNP per-capita, called the *Human Development Index* (HDI), providing the necessary institutional support to give it long-term viability.[33] In 1990, the UNDP showcased the HDI in its first *Human Development Report*. This included a technical description of the new index, a listing of 130 countries ranked according to their 'human development' performance, and a set of policy recommendations drawn from analysis of these new human development data in relation to other development indices. Interestingly, the project's leader, Mahbub ul-Haq, resembled James Grant in many ways. His effectiveness as an engaging, articulate spokesperson for this new way of evaluating development performance contributed greatly to its acceptance.[34]

The project's centrepiece was a broadly appealing concept of development that self-consciously differed from the more narrow frames of economic growth (GNP per-capita) and meeting basic needs (PQLI). 'The purpose of development is to offer people more options,' the 1990 UNDP report stated. 'One of their options is access to income - not as an end in itself but as a means to acquiring human well-being. But there are other options as well, including long life, knowledge, political freedom, personal security, and guaranteed human rights.[35] 'The use of statistical aggregates to measure national income and its growth have at times obscured the fact that the primary objective of human development is to benefit people.'[36]

Having defined 'human development' in the broadest possible terms, ul-Haq and his team crafted a composite index of modest scope, focusing on three indicators: *longevity* or life expectancy at birth; *knowledge*, measured as adult literacy; and *command over resources needed for a decent living*, measured as GNP per-capita, adjusted according to a complex scheme.[37] Choice of these three indicators reflected realities of data availability and 'the need to balance the virtues of broad scope with those of remaining sensitive to critical aspects of deprivation.'[38]

Translating numerical values for longevity, literacy and income into 'deprivation indices' was a distinctive feature of the HDI, part of the strategy necessary for aggregating these disparate numerical values into a single number. Here, the approach was similar to that used in calculating the PQLI. 'Best case' and 'worse case' values were chosen for each indicator. The deprivation index, then, was the ratio of numbers denoting each country's actual circumstances in comparison with the theoretical worst case.[39] By subtracting this index from one, country HDI values were obtained in the range of one to zero. Values near one denoted minimal deprivation and a corresponding high level of human development (top performer Japan = .996). Values close to zero denoted deprivation and low human development (bottom performer Niger = .116). In fact, HDI index values are rarely reported, perhaps because the index is too complicated for most people to grasp, intuitively. Relative HDI rankings and changes in HDI rankings have received considerable attention, however.

Though the worldviews embodied in the HDI and PQLI differed, country rankings were similar.[40] Top HDI performers in 1990 were Japan, Sweden, Switzerland, the Netherlands and Canada, all wealthy countries with relatively strong social welfare programs. Among developing countries with strong showings were free market success stories – Hong Kong (#22), Singapore (#34), and Chile (#23) – but also communist countries – German Democratic Republic (#20), Czechoslovakia (#24), and USSR (#25). After 12 years of free market reforms and six years of civil war, Sri Lanka (#47) still ranked well above the next best performing South Asian country, India (#96). Middle Eastern countries with high GNP's per-capita but low levels of literacy, for example Libya (#63), Saudi Arabia (#66) and Oman (#82), all ranked well below

Sri Lanka in the 'medium human development' category.[41] All but two of the countries ranked lowest in human development were located in Sub-Saharan Africa.[42]

The *Human Development Report's* policy lessons and recommendations were consistent with those presented in *Measuring the Conditions of the World's Poor,* but provided additional details. Like Professor Morris, the authors concluded that respectable levels of human development could be achieved with modest income levels, that the 'link between economic growth and human progress is not automatic'[43] and that country-level averages could conceal large within-country disparities between urban and rural areas, men and women, rich and poor. HDI statistics were used as justification for explicit, controversial recommendations to reduce population growth, increase funding for social programs and give greater attention to environmental issues related to sustainability. Such recommendations differed markedly from the conventional wisdom proffered by the UNDP's sister multilateral, the World Bank, in its country team and *World Development Reports.*

Some might quibble with technical details of the Human Development Index but few would dispute the importance of institutionalising it, through the *Human Development Reports,* as a counterweight to the strong economic growth emphasis that the World Bank's *World Development Reports* continued (and continue) to exemplify. Reports have been published focusing on relationships between 'human development' and issues such as globalisation (1992 and 1999), 'People's Participation' (1993), human security (1994), gender (1995), poverty (1997), human rights (2000) and technology (2001).

The annual *Human Development Reports* have also catalysed a growing number country level and even state level human development reports. Even the World Bank has moved away from its single minded emphasis on economic growth, though GNP per-capita remains its dominant performance measure and it has yet to include HDI values in its 'Selected Development Indicators' even where they might be relevant. Since 1991, five World Bank *World Development Reports* have addressed human development issues including environment (1992), health (1993), 'workers' (1995), governance (1997) and education (1998/1999). Among 'four crucial lessons' yielded by 'fifty years of development experience' enumerated in *World Development Report 1999/2000* is the following: 'growth does not trickle down: development must address human needs directly.'[44] The process of institutionalising an alternative development performance measure, which began with publication of Professor Morris' seminal work in 1977, has begun to have an impact, albeit modest.

Why do GNP-based performance indicators remain dominant?

Why do I use the word 'modest' to describe the progress made in strengthening alternative performance measures? Evidence that economic growth still dominates the design of development policies is so overwhelming that it hardly needs documentation. Economic growth is the central performance criterion shaping a cluster of neo-liberal, market-oriented economic policies, labelled the 'Washington Consensus' that were recommended (sometimes imposed) by the most influential and powerful donor agencies in the 1980s and 1990s.[45] Joseph Stiglitz, then Chief Economist of the World Bank, described this scheme with unusual clarity and candour in a 1998 lecture:

> The success of the Washington Consensus as an intellectual doctrine rests on its simplicity: its policy recommendations could be administered by economists using little more than simple accounting frameworks. A few economic indicators - inflation, money supply growth, interest rates, budget and trade deficits - could serve as the basis for a set of policy recommendations. Indeed, in some cases, economists would fly into a country, look at and attempt to verify these data, and make macroeconomic recommendations for policy reforms all in the space of a couple of weeks.[46]

Stiglitz is a particularly influential member of a scholarly cadre that has begun writing about a 'Post-Washington Consensus' that places greater emphasis on concerns beyond macroeconomic stability and 'getting prices right,' including sound financial regulation, competition, technology transfer and transparency. But mainstream critiques of the Washington Consensus continue to emphasise economic growth as the goal and GDP per-capita as the performance criterion to be maximised.

What explains the failure of the HDI to become more central in development planning, with all that implies for the relatively low priority given to 'human development' as a goal? Consider the qualities that widely used, popularly reported indices have in common:[47] GNP-based performance measures exhibit all of these qualities, while the HDI, arguably, meets none of them fully.

They include:

- A definition that is clear, operational, mathematically tractable and easy to understand.
- A well-established body of theory that predicts and explains index values and that can be used for policy design.
- One or more well-recognised, powerfully institutionalised academic disciplines whose members are committed to refining, elaborating and applying that body of theory.
- Credible, professional, well funded, officially sanctioned institutions that collect and maintain data relevant to the index and provide it to policy makers.

Once an index gains a degree of acceptance, these qualities become part of a self-reinforcing process that further enhances its stature. The process typically begins with theoretical, conceptual and technological breakthroughs that establish the index's credibility and relevance to a policy context that needs it, but uses of the index can then acquire their own momentum. The system of national accounts and corpus of economic theory it helped to spawn, in which GNP-based performance measures figure so centrally, illustrate this principle. If similar energies and resources had been devoted to developing and supporting a people-based system of indicators, beginning in the 1930s, human development measures would be far more influential.

Interestingly, problems and needs that produced the system of national accounts bear little relationship to the development problems and needs that less industrialised poor countries have faced in the post-World War II era. Rather, national accounts data and related economic theories were pressed into service because they were available and had a powerful constituency. The power of that constituency was further strengthened by one of the very few unalloyed development 'success stories,' the Marshall Plan.[48] Experience soon taught development practitioners that lessons drawn from the economic recovery of Western Europe and Japan were often worse than useless in designing policies to meet the development needs of poor countries in Asia, Africa and Latin America. But the worldview, performance measures and development models that shaped the Marshall Plan are still influential.

Which performance measure is best? This question remains unanswered. We have only been able to answer the question: 'Which performance measures currently dominate development policies and plans?' Dominance of GNP-based performance measures, however, has more to do with their intellectual and institutional history than the intrinsic merit of the worldview they promote. That worldview evokes few inquiries about the ideal society a country's residents might want or paths they might wish to follow in order to realise that goal, sustainably. Neither currently popular free market models nor discredited state-centric models are directly concerned with people's opinions and feelings.[49] More surprising, human development performance measures, too, are primarily based on expert judgements about what constitutes 'human development', not feedback from people about what they want.[50] That imposition, from above, of imperfect development models intended to maximise GNP per-capita or even 'human development' can evoke feelings hostility and alienation is hardly surprising.

Rethinking 'Successful Development?'

Can 'successful development' be defined in a way that takes human well-being and aspirations into account, while minimising the shortcomings of more widely used measures. I believe an approach that emphasises *subjective well-being* is most promising. My working definition is this: *'Successful development' is a scenario widely perceived by a country's residents*[51] *as constructively responding to their needs and aspirations. The measure of success is that residents feel good about their lives, the circumstances in which they live and future prospects for themselves and their children.*

How dies this definition relate to ongoing discourses about defining and measuring 'development'? As we have seen, contending definitions of 'development' and 'successful development' fill a voluminous literature.[52] Often the two terms are used, synonymously, as in the *U.S. Agency for International Development* (USAID), a foreign aid agency and the *Society for International Development* (SID), a leading non-governmental organisation for 'development' scholar practitioners. But this can be confusing. Drawing a clear distinction between 'development', 'successful development' and 'failed development' is more helpful.

'Development,' (successful or failed) can be seen most usefully as an unfolding or evolving process, rather than a snapshot. Two concepts used in the remainder of this book, *development trajectory*, and *development scenario* make this clear. A 'development trajectory' is the path that some distinct aspect of a country's political economy, political geography, natural environment or social order traces. Not all trajectories are easy to measure, but visualising them as numerical indices (such as GNP per-capita, infant mortality, or forest-cover depletion) graphed over time can be helpful. Such graphs are staples of international development policy analysis, as well as systems analysis practice. How a trajectory is viewed will depend on who does the viewing. Family planning was banned in Ceausescu's Romania after 1967,[53] but mandated in China after adoption of the one child policy.[54] Changes in birth rates and average family size were viewed very differently by the two regimes.

What about *development policies?* These are courses of action (decisions, programs, plans, strategies, etc.) that are intended to move one or more development trajectories in desired directions or maintain them within desired ranges. Structural adjustment, family planning, democratisation initiatives and drug interdiction programs are typical examples of such policies. Policies are normally termed successful if they produce the results intended and failed if they don't. Whether the results are widely viewed as beneficial by those impacted is taken into account much less frequently.

A country's *development scenario* is simply the unfolding sum-total effects of multiple development trajectories. That some trajectories will counteract or cancel others is part of the picture. For example a country's agricultural sector might be benefiting from foreign assistance but suffering from tariffs or restrictive quotas. This is a dilemma faced by sugar producers in some sub-Saharan countries. 'Sum total effect' cannot be rigorously objectified, but it is what shapes residents' overall perceptions about whether development policies are succeeding or failing. The subjective well-being of African sugar producers could be assessed, though little attempt has been made to do so.

We can now return to the definition given above: 'Successful development is a scenario widely perceived by a country's residents as constructively responding to their needs and aspirations...' Whether a scenario is 'successful' or a failure depends entirely on how it is viewed. Success and failure are neither intrinsic properties of the scenario nor objective measures that can be imposed by outside interveners.

The issue of an appropriate time horizon, which often challenges development practitioners, is addressed in the second part of the definition: 'The measure of success is that residents feel good about their lives, the circumstances in which they live and future prospects for themselves and their children.' As part of judging success or failure of development scenarios overall, assessing the trade offs between present and future – between benefits for the current generation and their grandchildren – is assumed to be within the purview of those impacted.

Until recently, use of this intrinsically appealing approach to assessing development effectiveness has hardly been debated, let alone seriously attempted.[55] In the last decade, however, a few scholars have begun to grapple seriously with the issue and even receive recognition for their work. Critics such as Robert Chambers, Arturo Escobar, John Friedman and David Korten have scored the shortcomings of 'top down' development, calling for more people-centred approaches.[56] They have warned political leaders and development practitioners that the objects of their ministrations are also human beings, that they have complex, fundamentally different world views and that ignoring these world views can be perilous. Amartya Sen's Nobel Prize-winning work emphasises that freedom, 'our individual ability to live as we would like', should not only be the primary end of development, but must be the principal means of development as well.[57] Attempts to measure subjective well-being lag far behind work on economic and human development indicators, but some progress is being made.[58]

Using subjective well-being to measure successful development seems appealing in principle, but is it feasible? Would it represent an improvement over what is being done now? Why do I believe the answer is 'yes?'

First, responding to self-defined needs and aspirations is a widely accepted norm in development practice that is affirmed by democratic theory. It simply has not been taken seriously as a frame for policy design and evaluation. Presently, democratic elections are the principal mechanisms used to judging subjective well-being, but they are very imperfect ones, at best.

Second, the link between subjective well-being and deadly conflict is unambiguous. People, especially young men of fighting age, are far more predisposed toward violence and the appeals of militant groups when they feel they are not getting what they deserve from life.[59]

Third, if changes in subjective well-being were be tracked effectively, the design of early warning systems that anticipated rising militancy and outbreaks of deadly conflict would be much easier. More important, better feedback about subjective well-being might lead to changes in obviously failed policies more quickly and highlight areas in which development practitioners and security practitioners should be collaborating.

Describing how subjective well-being could become an accepted, operational development goal is beyond the scope of this book. But this book adds to the evidence that failure to do so has been counterproductive and costly. Rethinking what successful development means and how it is measured should be an urgent priority.

4
Measuring Violent Political Conflict and State-sanctioned Violence In Sri Lanka

Measuring political conflict intensity and state-sanctioned violence intensity seem tasks that are far more complex than measuring temperature, but people once found measuring temperature confusing. Attempts to measure temperature produced false starts and scholarly debates. Eventually a consensus emerged. That consensus greatly enhanced our ability to understand physical and biological phenomena.

This chapter describes how *political conflict intensity* and *state-sanctioned violence* intensity are represented as numerical indices. Crane Brinton's 'fever chart' metaphor was used to introduce political conflict intensity in chapter 1, but state-sanctioned violence was not considered. It is the use of force by government officials and supporters to maintain public order and quell opposition. A cumbersome but neutral term is used to describe activities that might be simultaneously labelled, from different vantage points, 'maintaining law and order' and 'repression'. State-sanctioned violence is the therapy most commonly used to 'cure' the fever of escalating conflict, but often unsuccessfully.

Why measure social phenomena like violent conflict and state-sanctioned violence using numerical indices, an approach that many – including some reviewers of this manuscript – view sceptically? Let me answer first with an anecdote. Some years ago, I invited a senior Sri Lankan government official, making a brief Washington visit, to join a small group of students and me for lunch at American University's Faculty Club. Not surprisingly, Sri Lanka's 'ethnic conflict' was our principal topic of conversation. My students wanted answers to the same question that this book poses: 'How could Sri Lanka have come to this?' Our guest's response surprised me (it may have been an 'official' response he felt obligated to give). Current circumstances are not really abnormal, he suggested. Sri Lanka has periodically faced political unrest, some ethnically motivated, over the years. What is happening today is no different. He provided historical examples, dating back to Sinhalese-Muslim rioting in 1915 and the abortive JVP insurrection of 1971[1] to support his point of view.

The official was correct that Sri Lanka had periodically faced civil unrest, but wrong about similarities between 1985-92[2] and earlier eras. The fever chart in chapter 1 shows that after 1983, conflict become vastly more widespread, destructive and deadly. Any attempt to explain contemporary conflicts, beginning from the premise that they are essentially similar to conflicts occurring prior to 1984, would be seriously flawed. Yet focusing only on anecdotal information might mislead one to that conclusion. That is one important reason why it is important to find a way to measure relative conflict intensities.

Philosopher of Science John G. Kemeny provides additional reasons, using the numerical index we now call 'temperature' as an example.[3] A breakthrough came when scientists discovered that our perceptions of 'temperature – frigid, cold, tepid, warm, and hot – and a column of mercury's height corresponded. The hotter the temperature, the greater was the height. Measuring political conflict intensity and state-sanctioned violence intensity seem tasks that are far more complex than measuring temperature, but people once found measuring temperature confusing. Perceptions of 'hot' and 'cold' differed depending on circumstances.[4] It was not clear whether the 'hotness' of air, water and metal were the same or different. Attempts to measure temperature produced false starts and scholarly debates. Eventually a consensus emerged (though different measurement scales are still used). That consensus greatly enhanced our ability to understand physical and biological phenomena.[5]

When social scientists attempt to translate a concept like 'violent political conflict intensity' into numbers, they usually begin with an *operational definition*. Operational definitions are supposed to provide unambiguous guides to observation.[6] When one is collecting data, an operational definition serves a very practical purpose. It enables researchers to determine which incidents are 'violent political conflict' and which are not. It spells out clearly why a given incident should be scored as '7' and why another should be scored as '3'.

Most investigators who measure political conflict intensity – the exact concepts they use differ – have constructed indices from available numerical data such as number of deaths, number of injuries, number of participants in conflicts and/or value of property destroyed.[7] Such statistics, however, are impossible to obtain in Global South nations such as Sri Lanka. Accordingly, I opted for an approach that had proved useful in studies of Mexico and Argentina, recording and then scoring 'political conflict incidents'.[8] In Sri Lanka, competing daily newspapers were published in English, Sinhala and Tamil. While there were some restrictions on the press, instances of political conflict were extensively reported. Possible distortions in published materials could be crosschecked with knowledgeable individuals and with alternative sources such as police and army records. In all, my Sri Lankan team of researchers[9] recorded and scored more than 6,500 political conflict incidents.[10]

Two Illustrative Conflict Incidents

Becoming immersed in a large database makes it easy to lose touch with details. This is inevitable. Nevertheless, remembering that each 'conflict incident' was of surpassing importance to the individuals involved is important. Becoming familiar with the details of individual incidents makes it clear why development strategies should be sought that reduce violent conflict to an absolute minimum. It is appropriate to preface a description of the violent conflict database's technical details with two event descriptions that emphasise this.

The first, published in a 1988 edition of *Asia Week*, describes the action of a JVP hit squad against a minor official of the ruling United National Party (UNP). Hundreds of similar incidents, many unrecorded, took place in 1987-1991 during the height of the JVP insurrection.

> Gunasena Karunamunige lay moaning on a mat in the bedroom of his tiny home in Kolonne, a run down hamlet 130 kilometres southeast of Colombo. Hepatitis had ravaged his body, leaving him too weak to move. On that fateful night last October [1987], his wife, Wimalawathie, was bringing him a glass of water when three masked men suddenly burst in through the back door. Ignoring Wimalawathie's screams, they strode to the sick man. One intruder pulled out a pistol and stopped Gunasena's feeble attempt to escape with a bullet through his left eye. Another pummelled his wife to the ground and dragged her, kicking and screaming into an adjoining room. ...A few seconds later Gunasena was on the mat, dead, with a bullet in his brain and five stab wounds in his chest. ...The 26-year old victim was secretary of the Kolonne branch of the ruling United National Party (UNP). His assailants were members of the JVP (People's Liberation Front)...[11]

The second event, a 1985 massacre of worshipers by Tamil Tigers at one of Sri Lanka's most sacred Buddhist Shrines, received international attention and enraged the Sinhalese community. The matter of fact account quoted here is a report from the leader of the hit squad to Tamil Tiger leader Velupillai Prabakharan:

> My Dear Leader,
>
> On orders of VICTOR, we carried out the attack on the Sinhalese at Anuradhapura. ...We hijacked a vehicle and proceeded in the direction of Anuradhapura along Puttalam road. I drove the vehicle and having travelled for about 3 miles, we killed the driver and two others who were in the vehicle at the time of hijacking it. We came to the new bus stand at Anuradhapura and all of us got down from the vehicle. I went a little away from the bus stand to hijack a mini bus for our return journey and in the meantime some of our comrades had entered the Buddhist temple... and had killed more than 10 Buddhist Priests and 5 nuns. Then we got into the mini bus and proceeded back on the same route.[12]

How are political conflict incidents defined and scored?

The operational definition of political conflict used in the database can be understood best by quoting from instructions I wrote for my research team members.[13]

> A political conflict incident is a politically significant occurrence that falls outside the established legal procedures of political life and often involves violence. Usually political conflict incidents express some sort of protest against the government or the established order of things. For example:
> * Assassinations of government or party officials
> * Attacks or destruction of the symbols of government (attacks on police stations, post offices or Kacheries,[14] burning of trains or SLTB[15] busses, etc.)
> * Politically motivated strikes.
> * Riots or demonstrations with political overtones.
> Sometimes violent incidents may not be specifically anti-govern-

ment. For example, the Colombo ethnic riots in June of 1983 would be classified as a political conflict incident, even though not explicitly anti-government. Attacks on opposition party officials that frequently occur during election campaigns would be counted, although these attacks are, in some sense 'pro-government.'

Strikes are an example of an incident about which there may be ambiguity. A strike would not be included if it was directed against a private corporation and was only motivated by economic objectives (e.g. higher wages, better working conditions, etc.). However in Sri Lanka, most strikes do have political overtones because (a) the organisations struck are government agencies or affiliated with the government (Sri Lanka Transport Board, hospitals, universities, etc.) and/or (b) the labour unions have political affiliations and political objectives. If you are uncertain about whether or not to include a strike, fill out a coding sheet for it and explain the ambiguity in a 'comment' entry. I will make the decision as to whether to include or exclude it.[16]

Occasionally a political conflict incident may involve a protest or demonstration, but no violence. Our coding for intensity of violence provides a 'non violent' category. Examples would be non-violent work stoppages (with political overtones), boycotts and demonstrations, as long as they did not involve violence. A *satyagraha*[17] that did not deteriorate into violence would receive such a classification.

The composite index used to score of each incident's *intensity* was developed by Russian-born sociologist Pitrim Sorokin to measure what he called the 'fluctuation of internal disturbances' over very long time periods.[18] Sorokin's data problems were far more daunting than any I encountered. The breadth of his writings was similar to works of philosopher-historians such as Henry Buckle, Oswald Spengler and Arnold Toynbee.[19] Among the nations included in his analysis were Ancient Greece (600 to 126 B.C), Ancient Rome (525 B.C. to A.D. 500), Byzantium (526 to 1400) and France (526 to 1925). Sorokin's attitude toward his research also struck a sympathetic chord. He wrote:

Anyone who attempts to tackle these problems [of comparatively studying social and cultural dynamics over very long time periods] meets difficulties at every step, and realises the dangers possibly more fully and clearly than any critic. For this reason, the results are neither given as being perfectly accurate, nor are they claimed to be infallible. On the other hand, careful and laborious study has given the investigator an ever-increasing feeling of confidence that the most essential results are not misleading... Besides this study has an advantage possessed by neither the purely speculative studies nor the thorough historical studies based upon a limited number of cases: here all the data and the procedure are laid 'naked' before the reader; he can go through them, check each and all of them, and in this way test their accuracy or error. In the purely 'philosophising' studies, as well as those based upon a few cases, such a possibility is lacking. There is no evidence by which to verify whether or not the conclusions are accurate, or whether the generalisations derived from the few cases is or is not valid.

'Let these remarks be noted,' Sorokin concludes, 'and let them suffice here without further details concerning the lack of data, their uncertainty, [or] the difficulty of finding an adequate measuring stick.'[20]

An excerpt from the database, including event descriptions, codings and index values is presented in Table 4.1. Four dimensions of a political conflict event are measured: *duration, location, severity* and *size.*

The *duration* of an event is coded 1 if it lasts less than a week and 3 if its duration is longer than a week. Scores are reported for each month, so longer events are counted separately for each month in which they occurred.[21]

Scoring for *location* reflects Sorokin's view that the importance of an event is determined not only by size, duration and intensity, but also proximity to the political centre of the country. Events that occur in rural areas are scored 1. A similar event occurring in part of the capital city is scored 20. An event that inflamed the whole country would receive a score of 100. Adapting the location criterion to Sri Lanka required that each city, town and village for which events were reported be classified according to the size criterion. A hierarchy of locations was established that was appropriate to the Sri Lankan setting.

The *severity* of an event measures physical coercion, physical destruction, injury and deaths.[22] Non-violent events with no destruction of property, injury

| TIME PERIOD | | LOCATION | | EVENT DESCRIPTION | CODES | | | | |
START DATE	DURATION	PROVINCE	CITY/AREA		DURATION	LOCATION	VIOLENCE INTENSITY	SIZE	AVG.
4/21/86	Less than 1 day	Northern	Thondamanar in Jaffna District	Terrorists attacked army patrol killing 6 soldiers. They used a Hindu Kovil as cover	1	1	6	3	2
4/21/86	Less than 1 day	North Central	Palaththumanaichenai in Polonnaruwa Dist.	3 terrorists killed by the security forces in a raid on two houses	1	1	6	3	2
4/21/86	Less than 1 day	Eastern	Vandaramanai in Batticaloa District	Two terrorists were killed in a shoot out with the security forces.	1	1	6	3	2
4/22/86	Less than 1 day	Central	Matale	A former Chairman of the Matale Urban Council was killed by unknown gang	1	3	6	1	2
4/22/86	Less than 1 day	Northern	Thondamanar in Jaffna District	Forces attacked a group of terrorists. 6 soldiers and 15 terrorists died. Several more were injured	1	1	6	3	2
4/23/86	Less than 1 day	Northern	Wishwamadu in Kilinochchi area	A terrorist was killed when his group attacked the security forces	1	1	6	3	2
4/23/86	Less than 1 day	Eastern	Pullipanchigal in Batticaloa area	The security forces raided an LTTE hideout. They recovered explosives arms and other items	1	1	3	3	1
4/23/86	Less than 1 day	Western	Wellawatta (Colombo)	A bomb explosion rocked the police Station injuring 9 civilians and Police Constables	1	20	5	3	4
4/23/86	Less than 1 day	Eastern	Vakaneri in Batticaloa District	One EROS member was killed and 10 were captured by the security forces in an operation	1	1	6	3	2
4/23/86	Less than 1 day	Eastern	Batticaloa	A plan to attack the Special Task Force headquarters was foiled by the police. One terrorist arrested	1	5	3	1	1
4/23/86	Less than 1 day	North Central	Anuradhapura	A Petrol station was damaged and six people were killed in a bomb explosion	1	5	6	3	3
4/24/86	Less than 1 day	Northern	Mallakam in Jaffna District	Terrorists broke into Sri Lanka Transport Board workshop and robbed items valued at over Rs. 50,000.	1	1	5	1	1

Table 4.1 Political Conflict Data Base Excerpt

or death, such as peaceful demonstrations and work stoppages, are given a score of 1. An event described as a 'riot,' 'robbery,' 'hijacking' or another term suggesting coercion or confrontation is classified as having a 'slight' severity and given a score of 3 so long as there is no destruction of property and no shootings, injuries or deaths. A score of 5 is given to events where there is destruction of property, shooting or injury. Kidnapping and hostage taking are also included in this category. If deaths were reported, the event receives a score of 6.

The *size* of an event refers to the number of people participating. Events with less than 10 participants receive a score of 1. A 'small group' – 10 to 100 individuals – is scored 3. A score of 4 is given to events involving 'a large group but not a social class' – 101 to 5,000 people.[23] If 'a large social class' or 'an extensive occupational, economic, racial or religious group' (or any group of more than 5,001 individuals) are involved, the event receives a score of 5. If essentially 'all adults' participated, a score of 10 is assigned.

The composite index value for each event is the geometric mean (average) of the four dimensions.[24] In contrast to the arithmetic mean, which is more commonly used for averaging, the geometric mean gives considerably less weight to single extreme values. Thus, compared with the arithmetic mean, relatively high scores on all four dimensions would receive a higher total score than ones that receive a very high score on one dimension but low scores on all others.[25] Sorokin adopted this aggregation procedure after experimenting with a variety of alternatives. Numbers graphed on 'fever charts' such as Figure 1.1 (in Chapter 1) are the sum of all incident scores for each month. Figure 4.1 provides a second illustration, using a shorter time horizon. It compares the seven years of United Front rule with the early years of J.R. Jayewardene's administration, prior to the ethnic rioting of July 1983. The chart shows that after the JVP insurrection of 1970, conflict levels in the two administrations were roughly comparable, though Mrs. Bandaranaike's is widely regarded as the more turbulent.

As noted above, Sri Lanka's newspapers were used as the primary information source for incident descriptions. The fact that Sri Lanka has a tradition of press freedom and that the press was permitted to describe political conflict events even during periods of press censorship made this approach possible. However, newspapers are an imperfect source of information. Not every incident was reported, especially during the most turbulent periods. Knowledge-

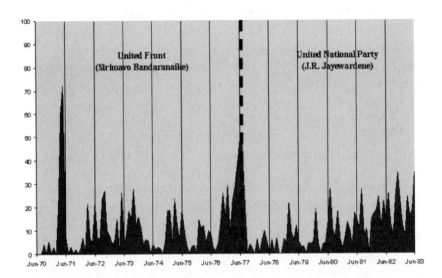

Figure 4.1 Violent Conflict Intensity: June 1970 – June 1983

able Sri Lankans – including security force officers with whom I consulted – felt that most major events would be reported, but that minor events might be under-reported by as much as 25 per cent in some rural areas. Since major events and events in urban areas have higher scores, this problem would produce roughly a 10 per cent margin of under-reporting in aggregate scale values. Another source of under-reporting was government suppression of incidents viewed as politically sensitive. Those I consulted felt that overall patterns would convey useful information, but caution should be exercised when reporting specific numbers. In addition to reviewing the concept of the database, my informants also sampled compilations of incidents and graphic output. The feedback I received was that the results seemed plausible, useful and far better than anything else available.

A different sort of problem was that some incidents interpreted as political might have robbery or the settling of personal scores as their motive. There was no consensus as to the magnitude of error this might create and no unambiguous way to differentiate these 'apolitical' events. My strategy was simply to review event descriptions carefully and to take this into account. I have assumed that coding created by this latter problem did not distort overall patterns significantly.

How is the intensity of state-sanctioned violence measured?

State-sanctioned violence is measured using a composite index developed by political scientists Ernest Duff and John McCamant for the study of *Violence and Repression in Latin America*.[26] The index measures four dimensions:

1. Suspension of constitutional guarantees.
2. Arrests, exiles and executions.
3. Restrictions on the organisation of political parties.
4. Censorship of media.

In contrast to the Sorokin scale, the *month* rather than the *conflict event* is used as the unit of analysis. Each month is scored for each type of state violence using a scale from zero to four. Index values are the sum of the scores on the four dimensions. Thus, the minimum intensity of state violence is zero and the maximum intensity is sixteen. Before considering details, it will be useful to take a broader view by looking at how the index and its components are graphed. Figure 4.2 shows this.

The figure reports state-sanctioned violence levels only for the Sinhalese majority provinces of Sri Lanka's western, central and southern regions. (During this period, government internal security policies in Tamil majority regions were sufficiently different to make separate graphs useful.) The topmost line reports the overall value of the index, which ranges from a low of 2, shortly after the Jayewardene Administration assumed office, to a high of 9, during campaigning prior to a controversial referendum that extended the life of parliament in December 1982. The width of each component shows the contribution of each to the overall index value. Thus between August 1979 and August 1980 the Jayewardene government's record on restricting opposition political parties and on 'arrests, exiles and executions' was relatively good (index values = 1), but its record on press censorship and suspension of constitutional guarantees was poorer. The arrows direct attention to points in time when changes in one or more values occurred and the text in the boxes provides a brief description of what happened. In October 1980, for example, a UNP-dominated parliament voted to strip the opposition party leader, former Prime Minister Bandaranaike of her civic rights. I interpreted this as meeting the criterion '...groups with large followings are harassed by restrictions and acts against leaders.' The index value for 'restrictions on political parties' was increased from one to two, where it remained for the duration of the period covered.

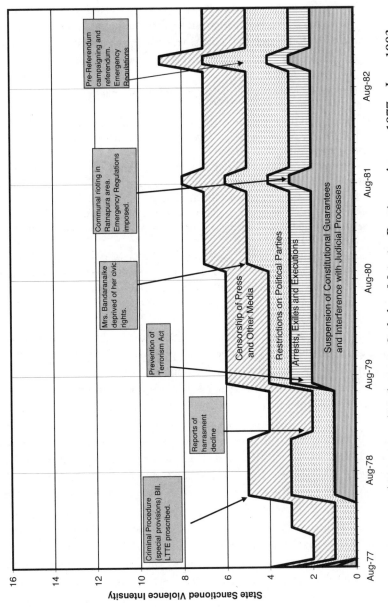

Figure 4.2 State-sanctioned Violence in Sinhalese Majority Provinces: August 1977 – June 1983

Operational definitions of the four component indices of state-sanctioned violence and how they were adapted to Sri Lanka are considered next.

Suspension of constitutional guarantees and other interferences with judicial process are one way in which Sri Lankan governments, like the Latin American governments studied by Duff and McCamant, have attempted to restrict opposition. The criteria for scoring this index are as follows:

0 - No report of any suspension of constitutional rights or intervention in the judiciary for internal purposes.

1 - Constitutional rights are suspended only temporarily (less than thirty days for entire country or less than sixty days for one part of the country) and no reported intervention with judiciary.

2 - Suspension of constitutional rights for more than thirty days but less than nine months for whole country or more than sixty days for one part of the country with no reported intervention with the judiciary.

3 - Suspension of constitutional rights for more than nine months for whole country, or intervention in the judiciary for the purpose of bypassing constitution, or both.

4 - Legal procedures dispensed with entirely as military, secret police or unofficial gangs replace judicial decisions for determining punishment. Such a situation may exist with or without the formal suspension of constitutional guarantees.[27]

As far as the formal suspension of constitutional rights is concerned, applying these criteria to Sri Lanka posed no problems. All of the nation's constitutions have included provisions for imposing 'emergency' regulations to deal with crisis situations. Emergency regulations were first imposed by Dudley Senanayake's government to deal with the general strike of August 1953. Later, S.W.R.D. Bandaranaike's government imposed emergency regulations to deal with labour unrest. In more recent times, the governments of Sirimavo Bandaranaike, J.R. Jayewardene and R. Premadasa have imposed emergency regulations in response to communal rioting and terrorist attacks.

A more complex issue was posed by the government's selective abrogation of Tamil minority rights. In 1948 and 1949 Parliament passed politically motivated laws that had the effect of disenfranchising and revoking the citizenship rights of the Indian Tamil plantation workers. I coded this legislation as a restriction on minority political parties rather than the suspension of a constitutional guarantee. This seems consistent with most interpretations of Prime Minister D.S. Senanayake's policies. In fact, many

Indian Tamils lost their citizenship because of a tactical decision by their leaders, later regretted, to boycott the procedures that had been established to give citizenship to long-standing residents.

The judgement to code the language policies of the S.W.R.D. and Sirimavo Bandaranaike governments as a 'suspension of constitutional rights for more than sixty days for one part of the country' will be more controversial. I made this judgement because the 'Sinhala only' language policy was so widely perceived by Tamils as an abrogation of an important fundamental right that had been constitutionally guaranteed at the time of independence. Since language policy was not an issue in the Latin American countries studied by Duff and McCamant, there was no specific provision in their coding for situations where a majority selectively revoked constitutional guarantees that had been established to protect the rights of a minority.

Arrests, exiles and executions are more active elements of state-sanctioned violence – the way in which the government enforces its rules and carries out its threats. Duff and McCamant 'consider any arrest, imprisonment, exile or assassination of a person known for his political opposition to the regime as fitting into this category'.[28] The criteria for scoring this index are as follows:

0 - No political arrests, exiles or assassinations.
1 - Only small-scale (less than ten per million) temporary arrests of one segment of the population for violation of public order when acting for political purposes.
2 - Large number of temporary arrests (ten to fifty per million), an occasional long-term arrest or exile of a political leader, or both.
3 - Mass arrests (more than fifty per million) with some held for more than few months or exiled, or simply numerous political leaders imprisoned or in exile, or any case of assassination by unofficial groups where not prosecuted by the government. Some opposition groups are not affected.
4 - Large number of political prisoners held or political leaders exiled. Leadership of all opposition political groups either dead, in prison or in exile.[29]

As noted above, Sri Lanka has had strong democratic traditions, however mass demonstrations, riots and violent attacks on the government have resulted in large numbers of temporary arrests. Beginning in the late 1980s and especially in 1989, there were numerous allegations of 'death squad activity,' both against terrorists and some opponents of the government who were not terrorists.

Because of the special problems created by terrorism and guerrilla attacks, I should emphasise that a rating of 2 or even 3 given to a period of pervasive violent anti-government activity does not necessary imply a negative value judgement against a government that is struggling to maintain or restore public order. In Sri Lanka, there has sometimes been widespread public support for vigorous action by the police and armed forces against dissident groups who used violence. The nation's political leaders have struggled to maintain a degree of normalcy in civil processes and to hold free, contested elections in the face of severe threats. Sri Lankans have been sensitive to criticism, sometimes ignorant and uninformed, of government 'repressiveness' and 'human rights violations.' Nonetheless, mass arrests of opposition group members and even some politically motivated assassinations have been a fact of political life in Sri Lanka and need to be taken into account in any serious attempt to understand the nation's multifaceted political conflicts.

Restrictions on political parties is the third dimension of state-sanctioned violence. The criteria for scoring this index are as follows:

0 - No restriction on the organisation of a political party, but there may be some minimum requirements for the running of candidates.
1 - Extremist groups with less than 10 per cent of adult population as a following are not allowed to run candidates and legally organise political parties.
2 - All but small extremist groups allowed to form political parties, but groups with large followings are harassed by restrictions on meetings and acts against leaders.
3 - Control prevents the organisation of a majority party. Major party or parties outlawed, many political leaders exiled or denied political rights, but tame opposition is permitted.
4 - No opposition is allowed to organise a political party[30].

Sri Lanka has had a more competitive party system than most Global South nations; however governments have not been reluctant to proscribe extremist parties, especially those engaging in violence. The JVP was proscribed after the 1971 insurrection and again after the ethnic rioting of 1983. Extremist Tamil groups such as the Liberation Tigers of Tamil Eelam (LTTE) have also been proscribed and after 1983, J.R. Jayewardene's government passed the Sixth Amendment to the Constitution, imposing a ban on political parties that advocated separatist policies. Individuals that advocated separatism faced criminal penalties[31]. This had the effect of proscribing virtually all Tamil political parties and expelling their representatives from Parliament. Tamil majority regions were assigned a score of three for this period. Even though some token political activity was permitted, the rating for restrictions on political parties was increased to 4 during the period when the Indian Peace Keeping Force occupied Sri Lanka's Northern and Eastern Provinces.

There have also been periods when 'groups with large followings [were] harassed by restrictions on meetings and acts against leaders.' For example, in 1958, the passport of former Prime Minister Kotelawala was impounded in England and he was not permitted to return to Sri Lanka. In the same year, the S.W.R.D. Bandaranaike government responded to demonstrations against 'Sinhala only' legislation by placing all Federal Party members of Parliament under house arrest and detaining more than 150 Federal Party members in the North and East. Emergency regulations were used to severely restrict political meetings. This period was given a score of two. A similar situation occurred during the period from April through September 1962 when Sirimavo Bandaranaike's government passed regulations establishing Sinhalese as the language of administration. The Federal Party responded with a civil disobedience campaign. The government, in turn, responded by implementing 'emergency regulations' and detaining Federal Party leaders.

Censorship of the press and other media is the fourth dimension of official violence. The criteria for scoring this index are as follows:

0 - No restrictions on newspapers or other media besides libel and slander laws.
1 - Minor restrictions, such as banning the publication of certain news for less than a week, use of import licences to restrict the supply of newsprint.
2 - Longer term restrictions on publication of some kinds of political information. Banning of Communist or other minority press.
3 - Censorship of all political news, but decision on news selection remains in private hands. Closure of major newspapers.
4 - Government directs what news shall be published. All other news excluded.[32]

During the period covered by this book, Sri Lanka's electronic media were under direct government control.[33] The government directed what news would be made available and dissenting voices were rarely heard, although limited time was given to opposition candidates during election campaigns. Newspapers, however, are another matter. Sri Lankans are avid newspaper readers.

In the years immediately following independence, Sri Lanka boasted ten daily newspapers selling over 350,000 copies a day and eight Sunday papers with a circulation of 450,000. Magazines and party newspapers, typically published weekly, served more specialised audiences. There was a strong tradition of investigative journalism; newspapers could be harshly critical of the government and of individual politicians.

Because newspapers are so widely read, successive Sri Lankan governments have been greatly concerned with what was published and press freedom has gradually eroded. The Bandaranaike governments were particularly known for harassing and censoring the press, perhaps because most newspapers and especially the powerful Lake House group favoured their principal opponent, the UNP. Press censorship scores of 2 were common, and scores of 3 were not infrequent during these regimes. When it returned to power in 1978, the UNP also imposed an informal press censorship. Control of the Lake House group of newspapers (which was seized by Mrs. Bandaranaike) remained in government hands. As far as political news is concerned, Lake House newspapers now function as a government house organ. The several independent newspapers were more likely to criticise government programs and report criticisms levelled by opposition members of parliament, but rarely criticised individual members of the government by name. I have assigned a score of two for press censorship during virtually the entire period of UNP rule after 1977.

Duff and McCamant's scale was intended to apply to nations as a whole. It seemed appropriate to apply it to Sri Lanka in this way prior to the period in which militant Tamil groups began to dominate the politics of the North, but not afterwards. I chose to use 1977 as a demarcation point for coding state-sanctioned violence in Tamil and Sinhalese majority regions separately. Before 1983, the differences in state-sanctioned violence levels between the two regions were relatively small, although the government did place increasing strictures on political activity in the North. However, after fall 1983, the majority political party in the North was outlawed and its leaders exiled. Beginning in fall 1987, civil administration in the North and East was under the overall control of the Indian army.

Assessments and scorings have been based on press reports, historical accounts, public documents, interviews, and reports by international groups that concern themselves with official violence, such as Amnesty International, Asia Watch, and World Priorities. Because Sri Lanka is a relatively open society and matters pertaining to official violence have often been debated in parliament, a substantial amount of information is available. However, assessing levels of official violence is a controversial business. I chose to do all the state-sanctioned violence scorings myself, with no direct assistance from anyone.

I have discussed my general impressions of state-sanctioned violence and, in some instances, specific scorings with a number of knowledgeable Sri Lankans across a broad spectrum of political persuasions. Because state-sanctioned violence is a sensitive area in which Sri Lankans were understandably reluctant to provide information for publication, the opinions I solicited were provided in confidence, with the guarantee of anonymity. I have done my best to be objective and to consider a broad range of information and opinion, however the judgements reflected in official violence scores are entirely my own.

Violent political conflict and state-sanctioned violence indices provide a clearer picture than anecdotes alone of the rising tide of deadly conflict in Sri Lanka. They confirm conventional wisdom, expressed by many Sri Lankans, that violent conflict and state violence escalated to a qualitatively different level in the 1980s. Protracted deadly conflict has now been the dominating fact of Sri Lanka's political and economic life for more than two decades. The remaining chapter of this section describes the development-deadly-conflict system that has provided, in Sri Lanka and other Global South nations, a context for violent conflict escalation.

5
The Development-Deadly-Conflict System

Insights from systems analysis can provide a deeper understanding of development-deadly conflict linkages. The approach is not a panacea, but does offer a relatively unexplored path that points toward policy recommendations we seek.

Introducing the Development–Deadly-Conflict System: A Personal Digression and Plea

Book publishers advise authors to keep diagrams, especially complex ones, to a minimum. Textbooks, which students must buy, are the only exception. I have included twelve diagrams, some complex, in this chapter. Some knowledgeable manuscript reviewers have advised me to keep theory to a minimum because readers will be 'put off.' I introduce in this chapter a body of theory that many readers will find new and some may regard as arcane.

An excerpt from Saxe's poetic rendering of the 'blind men describing the elephant' parable, quoted earlier, points to my rationale:

> *And so these men of Indostan disputed loud and long,*
> *each in his opinion, exceeding stiff and strong.*
> *Though each was partly in the right, and all were in the wrong.*

My goal, in this volume, is to redefine the 'loud and long' dispute about causes of deadly conflict, not to perpetuate it. This is done by combining theories that are 'partly in the right' into a more complete representation of the whole 'elephant,' the complex system that links development and deadly conflict.

Some grasp of systems analysis fundamentals is needed to understand this system. Understanding the system makes it clear why violent conflict escalation is difficult to reverse and deadly conflicts become intractable. Explanations of specific conflicts – such as that in Sri Lanka – and policy recommendations follow from this understanding. Systems analysis fundamentals, then, provide the foundation for both explanations and policy recommendations.

A Systems Analysis Fundamentals Briefing

My systems analysis fundamentals briefing begins with a discussion of elephants, still widely used as draft animals in Sri Lanka, and their *mahouts* (drivers)[1]. Consider first the mahout-elephant relationship pictured in Figure 5.1.

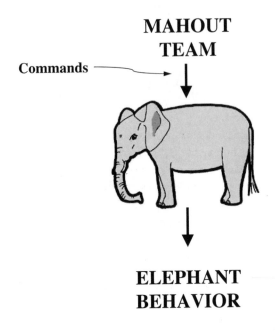

Figure 5.1 Casual Observer's View of an Elephant at Work

A casual observer may see a simple causal relationship between the mahout's commands, given by voice, feet, legs and prod, and the animal's behaviour, but the reality is quite different. Before beginning to train the animal in specific tasks, a mahout must first acquire a deep understanding of his elephant *as a system*.[2] Thus, when he views a working elephant or when a team[3] works their animal, perceptions are quite different. We could refer to Figure 5.2, which shows this as the 'Elephant-Mahout model.' The elephant is seen as a complex system, comprising many elements and subsystems. Elephant and mahout are linked by commands and information.

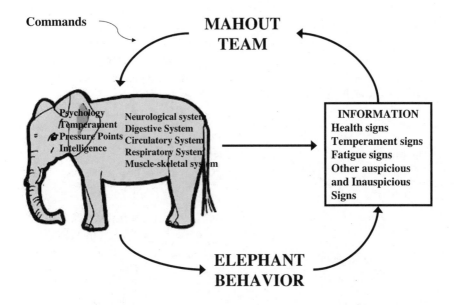

Figure 5.2　Mahout's View of an Elephant at Work

Years of training and experience are needed to understand elephants well enough to work with them, even though Asian elephants' behaviour is relatively predictable and controllable. This predictability and controllability has made it possible for the profession of mahout to evolve as a craft and for elephants to perform successfully as draft animals.

The mahout-elephant model provides a systems analysis lens for viewing development–deadly-conflict linkages. Figure 5.3 suggests how this might be done.

This diagram is labelled 'Politician/Practitioner's View' because I believe many politicians and development practitioners see their roles analogously to that of a Mahout. Decisions – I denote *choices, actions* and *policies* with this term – are effectuated through the 'country context.' This comprises structures of political economy, governance, citizen participation, ethnic identity discussed in chapter 3 – and more. Like the mahout, political leaders can use voice commands, push pressure points and if necessary, employ the steel hook at the end of the prod to try and get what they want.[4] Subsequent decisions will be responsive to information about changes in the country context and unfolding development scenarios, just as mahouts' commands are responsive to changing perceptions of the performance, well-being and temperament of their elephant.[5]

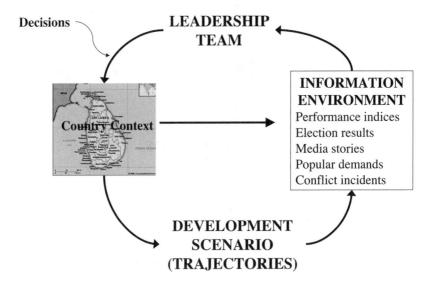

Figure 5.3   **Politician/Practitioner's View of How Decisions Shape Development Scenarios**

But the mahout-elephant model's worldview has its limitations. Those who internalise it uncritically as a guide to policy design and implementation are likely to be lead astray. Figure 5.4 shows why.

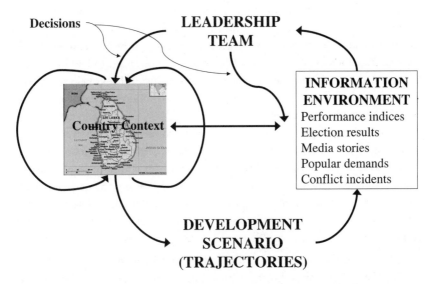

Figure 5.4 More Complete View of How Development Trajectories Unfold and Change

Comparing this 'more complete view' with the 'politician/practitioner's view' reveals three additional complexities. First, there are two feedback loops surrounding the country context. Second, there are arrows on both ends of the link between country context and information environment. Third, political team decisions are shown to impact the information environment as well as the country context. What do these changes denote?

The additional feedback loops remind us that structures and processes comprising the country context are themselves dynamically linked. Thus political team members' voice commands, applications of pressure to sensitive points and uses of the prod impact an ongoing stream of behaviours that may counteract, amplify or otherwise modify intended results. The double-headed arrow represents a feedback loop between country context and information environment. This is intended to show that representations of the context in the form of performance indices, media stories and other information elements can change the context directly, as well as impacting politician's decisions. Were it otherwise, governments would not accord such high priority to propaganda and 'spin.'

Finally, the causal link from decisions to the information environment shows that political team members' perceptions can be distorted by their own decisions. For example, the information environment of a highly repressive regime that responds to bad news by 'killing the messenger' is likely to be less complete and accurate than the environment of a regime that is more open to bad news and tolerant of dissent.[6] The collective impact of these additional links help to explain why many decisions have unanticipated side effects, produce different outcomes than those intended or seem to have no impact at all.

Development decisions, as we have seen, often provide prime examples of unanticipated outcomes. To understand why choices, actions and policies in this domain sometimes intensify deadly conflict, we need to probe more deeply into the country context. When probing, it is tempting to label development decisions as 'causes' and intensifying conflict incidents as 'effects', but we must resist this. Development – deadly-conflict linkages are strongly bi-directional. Over time, intensifying and protracted deadly conflicts significantly impact development policies.

Introducing the Development-Deadly-Conflict System Model

The 'model' that gives this chapter its name combines elements of Figure 5.4 with a more detailed representation of country context elements that have been described in earlier chapters – development visions, economic policies, satisfaction of human needs, political identities, ethnic identities, conflict trajectories and many others. They are linked in what systems analysts call a *causal loop diagram*. Such diagrams are an important tool of the System Dynamics methodology alluded to briefly in chapter 2 (and to be described more fully below).

The term 'causal *loop*' emphasises an important System Dynamics principle: understanding how system elements are linked in closed chains of cause-effect relationships, or feedback loops, is key to understanding behaviour trajectories that a system exhibits.[7] The behaviour of systems dominated by *reinforcing loops* is characterised by 'booms and busts,' like Asian financial markets, and cancerous growth, like deadly conflict in Sri Lanka during the 1980s. Such systems tend to be highly unstable. The behaviour of systems dominated by *counteracting loops* is characterised by goal seeking, like a well-designed policy implementation, and the maintenance of equilibria, like a smoothly functioning market. Such systems tend to be more stable. Not infrequently, loop dominance in a system will change, over time, producing changes in behaviour that seem contradictory and puzzling.[8] Figures 5.5 and 5.6 illustrate reinforcing and counteracting loops, which occupy an important place in the discussion that follows.

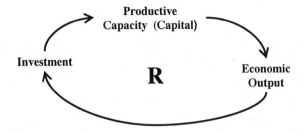

In this simplified reinforcing economic growth loop, productive capacity of the economy's capital stock determines the level of economic output, which provides resources for investment that increases productive capacity. The same loop structure that produces the 'boom' conditions of economic growth can also generate the "bust" conditions of recession where reduced investment leads to lowered productive capacity and reduced output, resulting in further investment reductions.

Figure 5.5 Reinforcing Feedback Loop

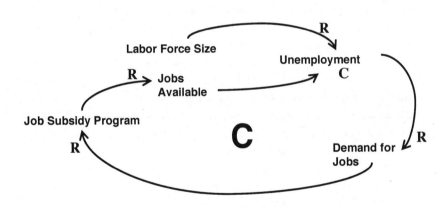

In this counteracting feedback loop, increases in labour force size that exceed job growth increase unemployment. The unemployed demand jobs and government responds with the expedient of a job subsidy program (for example by increasing public-sector jobs). In the short run this reduces unemployment, though the policy may not be sustainable. The "goal" of this loop is to keep unemployment within acceptable bounds. Note that there is only one counteracting relationship in the loop, between jobs and unemployment. A loop will be counteracting, whenever there are an odd number of counteracting relationships between its variables, even one!

Figure 5.6 Counteracting Feedback Loop

One additional feature of Figure 5.6 – the letters 'R' and 'C' at the end of each causal arrow – should also be noted. These tell us whether the causal linkages between variables are reinforcing or counteracting. When a relationship is *reinforcing* a change in the independent (cause) variable will produce a change in the dependent (effect) variable in the *same direction*. The relationship between 'productive capacity' and 'economic output' is a good example. An increase in productive capacity will cause economic output to increase. A decrease in productive capacity will cause economic output to decrease. In *counteracting* relationships, a change in the independent variable produces a dependent variable change in the *opposite direction*. The relationship between 'jobs available' and 'unemployment' illustrates a counteracting relationship. More jobs decrease unemployment. Fewer jobs increase unemployment. We will use the concepts of reinforcing and counteracting relationships between variables to help examine the dynamics of development–violent conflict relationships later in this chapter.

The System Dynamics perspective and what it has to offer

We have seen that leaders' decisions, development trajectories, and deadly conflicts are dynamically interwoven with the other elements that comprise a country's context. Development policy interventions (like other interventions) are attempts to leverage the behaviour of complex systems comprising multiple feedback loops and patterns of shifting loop dominance. More than a half century of systems research has provided a fairly well developed body of theory and numerous insights describing the behaviour of such systems. Five of the most important insights are these:

1. All systems, no matter how complex, comprise networks of reinforcing and balancing feedback loops. All dynamics arise from the interaction of these loops with one another.[9]

2. Complex multiple feedback loop systems far exceed the analytical capabilities of 'technologies' most widely used by leadership team members (politicians and practitioners) to guide their decisions, mental models.[10]

3. Complex system behaviour may not only be perplexing to the policy maker, but also misleading. In a classic paper on this subject, Jay Forrester writes '...a social system tends to draw our attention to the very points at which an attempt to intervene will fail.[11]

4. Complex systems resist or counteract most policy changes. When an

intervention is made, even a substantial one, the problematic behaviour often remains.[12] Many international development and conflict prevention programs provide evidence of this.

5. Complex systems mislead and resist us because we have been socialised to an event-oriented approach to problem solving. We are taught from an early age that every event has a cause, which in turn is an effect of some still earlier cause.[13] Widely used analytical methods, statistics in particular, reflect this linear causal world view.

Insights from systems analysis can provide a deeper understanding of Development – Deadly-Conflict linkages. The approach is not a panacea, but does offer a promising, relatively unexplored path that points toward policy recommendations we seek.

Why a 'relatively unexplored path?' Because international development scholar/practitioners and those concerned with 'national security' have primarily looked elsewhere – to the disciplines of economics, sociology, anthropology, political science and international relations – for theoretical insights. Systems analysts, on the other hand, look more to biology, information sciences and systems engineering.[14] Theories in these fields describe complex interrelationships between a large number of elements that comprise, for example, an organism like the human body, a complex piece of technology like a space station or a complex human organisation like a city.[15]

The type of systems analysis that has most influenced my own practice, called 'System Dynamics' was briefly introduced in chapter 2. There, I used it to justify a case study approach and close examination of 'reference mode' trajectories for clues to underlying system behaviour. MIT computer engineer Jay W. Forrester invented System Dynamics. His work brought together ideas from three fields that were then relatively new – control engineering (the concepts of feedback and system self-regulation), cybernetics (the nature of information and its role in control systems) and organisational theory (the structure of human organisations and mechanisms of decision-making). He supported software development, built path-breaking models, articulated guiding principles and trained students. Flight simulators (another technology in which he pioneered)[16] provided a metaphor for the project. Models, Forrester argued, could be used for experiments in the same way simulators are used to train pilots. Mistakes made on the model would not result in severe social costs or loss of life. Repeated experimentation would be helpful in solving difficult, complex problems.[17]

System Dynamics practice is grounded in four fundamental ideas.

1. The *structure* of a system, that is, the way its elements are inter-connected in cause-effect relationships is the key to explaining the system's behaviour patterns. Often included as model elements are the social goals, rewards and pressures that play such an important role in influencing human behaviour.

2. *Feedback loops* – closed chains of cause-effect relationships – are the most important components of a system's structure. (As discussed above.)

3. In social systems, *human decisions* play an important role in feedback processes. Decisions are based on goals and information, filtered through perceptions about those aspects of the systems that decision-makers believe to be relevant. 'We find that people perceive correctly their immediate environment,' Jay Forrester writes, adding that '[t]hey know what they are trying to accomplish. They know the crises that will force certain actions. They are sensitive to the power structure of the organisation, to traditions, and to their own personal goals and welfare.'[18] In System Dynamics, an accurate representation of how human beings perceive and act often plays a more important role in explaining behaviour patterns than 'hard data.'[19]

4. Feedback processes do not operate instantaneously; the timing of behaviour depends on the presence of system elements that create *inertia* or *delays*. These inertial elements are accumulations of material, information, attitudes or feelings, to name some examples. In System Dynamics jargon, they are referred to as 'stocks' or 'levels.' Typical levels are population, physical infrastructure, inventories and perceptions. Delays in feedback loops caused by stocks are often a source of oscillations or other unstable behaviour patterns.

Chapter 2 described how my own study of development-deadly conflict linkages began, first with a generic computer simulation model, incorporating contending conflict theories, then with applications of the model to Argentina and Mexico. The model's ability to qualitatively reproduce the two very different conflict trajectories that characterised these nations gave me confidence that I had captured at least some understanding of the complex system linking development and deadly conflict.

Often, insights gained from the model building process are more important than a model's technical details and generated computer runs. Model building deepened my understandings of how leaders' decisions, governance effectiveness, political attitudes, economic performance, the mobilisation of mainstream and militant political movements, the performance of the security forces and other elements in the development process were linked to violent conflict trajectories. These understandings shaped my study of the Sri Lankan case. One product of that study is the 'development-deadly-conflict system model.' It uses my computer model's structure as a point of departure, but has been enriched by more than a decade of immersion in international development studies and the Sri Lankan case. Additional details of the model are presented next.

The Development-Violent-Conflict System Model: sectors and linkages

Figure 5.8 shows the major sectors of the model and important variables within each sector. Like many such diagrams it seems complex, because the system it is describing is complex. This section will unravel the complexity by describing important variables and connections in each sector. Most have already been encountered in chapters 2 and 3. The two sections that follow will describe how important feedback loops produce common development scenarios in Global South countries.

<u>Leadership and governance</u>
- Development vision
- Leadership effectiveness
- Governance effectiveness
- Policy responsiveness
- Centralisation – devolution
- International political linkages

The leadership and governance sector is the source of decisions (choices, policies and actions) that impact other sectors of the model. It is most directly impacted by political feedback and by the availability of resources the economy provides for governance and policy implementation. If policy responsiveness is high, political feedback can produce changes in policies and, via the electoral process, changes in governments. Violent conflict, too, can have an impact, altering priorities and, in extreme circumstances, producing leadership changes.

International linkages include the political influence of hegemonic powers and international lending agencies such as the World Bank, as well as refugee

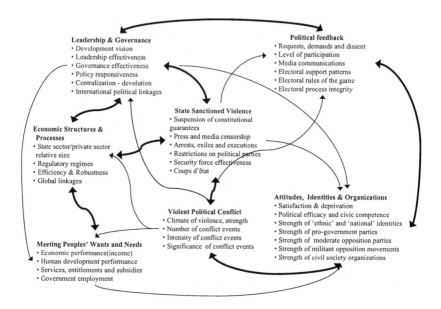

Figure 5.7 Development – Deadly-Conflict System Model

Heavy, double-ended arrows denote feedback loops.

flows and migrations. Other spillover effects from international conflicts also fall within this category. For example U.S.-led wars in Afghanistan and Iraq have affected all of the bordering nations and many others.

In addition to impacts noted above, decisions are also impacted by the 'information environment,' discussed earlier. To keep the diagram relatively simple, most information flows have been omitted. An important influence on the information environment's fidelity is the 'openness' of the country's society, including the robustness of the media and civil society institutions. Governance and leadership effectiveness affect the skill with which information is processed and interpreted.

Economic structures and processes
- Relative size of the private sector/state sector
- Regulatory regimes
- Robustness and efficiency
- Global economic linkages

This is simply called the 'economic sector,' or the economy, in most development models and literature. It provides the wherewithal for activities of government – something politicians can sometimes forget – for its own growth via investment, and for meeting peoples' wants and needs. Efficiency and robustness[20] are impacted by policies that shape the country's 'development model,' discussed in chapter 3 including, most importantly, regulatory regimes and the degree of state sector economic involvement.

Global economic linkages, via commodity markets, capital markets and currency markets, play important, complex roles in country economies that are being hotly debated by proponents and opponents of 'globalisation.' Such linkages provide investments, markets and competitive pressures that promote efficiencies. But they also can be the source of severe structural and labour market dislocations that contribute to human suffering and political instability. Country leadership teams may have very limited control over the impacts of global linkages, but bear the consequences when impacts are adverse.

The relative emphasis given to different performance criteria often has an impact on economic structures, regulatory regimes and entitlement programs, as noted in Chapter 3. The arrow from '…wants and needs' to the economic sector shows this. High state-sanctioned violence levels can adversely impact the functioning of free markets, but also lower the robustness and efficiency of state controlled systems, as the breakdown of Communist economic systems made clear. Violent conflict can scare off investors, diverting capital to national security concerns, motivate capital flight, both financial and human, and destroy physical capital, i.e. productive facilities and infrastructure.

Meeting people's wants and needs
- Economic performance (income)
- Human development performance
- Direct services, entitlements and subsidies
- Government employment

Meeting peoples' wants and needs is the ostensible – through rarely measured – purpose of development. It is a major focus of development visions and governance. The economy provides the resources for meeting wants and needs. Policy decisions and governance influence how resources are allocated and how productively they are used. Of course, violent political conflict, the other direct input to this sector, impacts people's lives directly as well as through its indirect effects on governance and the economy.

Government also directly involves itself in meeting people's needs through services such as health and education, or entitlements and subsidies, though these are overlapping categories. Government employment is identified separately because it is so often viewed more as an entitlement, provided in return for political support, than as a vehicle for providing services. Not only meeting wants and needs but meeting them sustainably is a perpetual challenge for leaders and governments.

Attitudes, Identities and Organisations

- Feelings of satisfaction and deprivation
- Feelings that one can make a difference
- Strength of 'ethnic' and 'national' identities
- Strength of pro-government parties
- Strength of moderate opposition parties
- Strength of civil society groups
- Strength of militant opposition movements

When wants and needs go unmet, when expectations are unfulfilled, when gaps between 'haves' and 'have nots' widen, these circumstances are manifest as changed feelings, attitudes and identities. But performance trajectories relating to wants and needs represent only one input to this complex, pivotal sector, comprising processes and structures with the greatest direct impact on violent conflict. Other impacts are from the electoral process in democratic countries; from state-sanctioned violence and security force effectiveness; and from violent conflict itself.

Within-sector dynamics are more important in this sector than most. Parties, movements and organisations partly derive 'strength' from levels of popular support, which, in turn, are a product of attitudes. But the effectiveness of parties as organisations, as well as popular support, contributes to 'strength.' In fact support levels partly depend on organisational effectiveness in mobilising support and retaining support.[21] Feelings of satisfaction and deprivation too, have an institutional component. Their source is a gap between expectations and fulfilment. Arguably, whether wants and needs are met has the major impact on fulfilment, though even this could be debated. Nevertheless, parties, organisations, and movements play a major role in creating expectations. Democratic political campaigning is particularly known for its inflationary effect on expectations, denoted here by the feedback arrow from the '...elections' sector. Chapter 3 argued that even 'ethnic' identities are at least partly constructions that are significantly shaped, if not entirely created, by organisations.

This sector has another distinctive trait: the number of connections to other sectors via double-headed arrows, denoting reciprocal cause-effect relationships. Here we will focus on 'effects,' reserving consideration of how this sector impacts others until we examine the impacted sectors.

The impact of state-sanctioned violence is complex since it depends not only on the form of repressive policies – the several dimensions of the state-sanctioned violence index – but the effectiveness of security forces in carrying them out. Beginning with James C. Davies' pioneering work and expressed most recently in research on 'weak states,' there is strong evidence that adequately resourced draconian measures intended to weaken or crush opposition movements can be quite effective. Repressive measures that are ineffective, however, are more likely to strengthen opposition forces, especially militant movements, though they may effectively weaken moderate opposition parties and civil society. Intensification of violent conflict contributes to this polarising effect. It elevates those with authoritarian, militaristic predispositions to opposition, and government, leadership positions, providing a rationale for stifling dissent on both sides, and over time, socialising a widening cadre of young men and women to violent conflict as a way of life.

State-sanctioned violence
- Suspension of constitutional guarantees
- Press and media censorship
- Arrests, exiles and executions
- Restrictions on political parties
- Security force size and effectiveness

Inputs to the state-sanctioned violence sector are from leadership/governance, from the economy, and from political feedback. Leaders' decisions determine how the security forces are constituted, how they are being employed, the degree to which they are politicised and how well they are funded. Senior military officers and, less frequently, police officers, may be members of political leadership teams or initiate transfers of power, via military *coups d'etat*. Funding levels depend on leader's decisions, but also on revenues that the economy provides for this and other government functions. Police and soldiers in Global South nations are often underfunded, and poorly trained and equipped. Thus, governance effectiveness impacts security force effectiveness. Leaders may fail to take this into account when defining their missions and ordering them to take action. Other inputs to this sector are from 'political feedback' – for example, security forces may respond aggressively to peaceful protests – and 'violent conflict.' These linkages emphasise that decisions to use state-sanctioned violence are often reactive.

Outputs from this sector are the two faces of state-sanctioned violence, maintenance of 'law and order' and repression. When members of the security forces, such as the army and police, are well-funded, well-paid, well-trained, non-political and professional they are more likely to be effective in preventing political conflict from escalating out of control. In Global South nations, however, this level of effectiveness is rare. More typically security forces are not only underfunded but also politicised. Often governments use them to stifle dissent and harass political opponents. Some economic activities may also be repressed. Sometimes the police and military forces are visibly or covertly involved in repressive acts. Alternatively, they may simply stand aside while pro-government thugs, unions, death squads and the like carry out repressive acts. Typically, politicised security forces lack widespread popular support. They are more likely to be resented and feared than respected. This hampers their effectiveness both in normal circumstances and times of crisis.

The first four variables listed, components of the state-sanctioned violence index discussed in chapter 4, focus on repression. In addition to stifling dissent, repression can play an important role in catalysing conflict escalation. Our discussion of how repressive measures, ineffectively implemented by the security forces, can strengthen militant movements emphasised this. As they become stronger, militant movements are better able to sustain protracted conflict and more predisposed to do so. The foot soldiers in government military forces are often poorly paid conscripts. Political reliability may be a more important criterion for promoting officers than professional competence. As escalating conflict weakens the government, prospects of military victory become increasingly slim, but leaders may find it difficult to face the alternatives.

Political feedback
- Requests, demands and dissent
- Media communications
- Level of participation
- Electoral support patterns
- Electoral rules of the game
- Electoral process integrity

The political feedback sector is a principal information source and the principal non-violent error correction mechanism in the Development-Deadly-Conflict system. It provides information about political attitudes and the relative strengths of political organisations. Indirectly the sector is the best source of information about whether development policies and programs are proving to be 'successful' or not. It can also be the sector where political change is initiated.

Elements of political feedback, apart from free elections,[22] are present in both democratic and non-democratic systems, though in highly authoritarian regimes, they communicate little that is useful. Free elections, along with rules and norms that sustain them are unique to democratic systems.[23] Election results (electoral support patterns) determine whether a government remains in power or gives way to another. Indirectly such patterns constitute a referendum, albeit imperfect, on the government's leadership and policies. Electoral rules of the game and the integrity of electoral processes are like filters or refractors intervening between voter attitudes and the outcomes of elections. How legislative boundaries are drawn and whether members of legislative bodies are chosen in single member districts or through proportional representation can make a real difference in how attitude changes manifest themselves in leadership and governance changes. Since elections confer power as well as communicating information, those in power routinely strive to manipulate the rules of the game in ways that will perpetuate them in office.[24]

In addition to changes in attitudes, identity configurations and the relative strengths of contending political organisations, both state-sanctioned violence and violent political conflict can impact political feedback. Governments may use state violence to muzzle opposition media, restrict opposition party campaigning and keep opposition voters away from the polls. Violent conflict can impact feedback directly by creating a climate in which the powers of security forces are strengthened and opposition to the government is equated with disloyalty or even treason.[25]

A common effect of political feedback distortions is that governments are perpetuated in power, but leaders are less and less well informed about the degree to which their policies are succeeding. As the quality of leaders' information declines, the probability of development failures increases. As development failures increase, popular dissatisfaction rises, but this dissatisfaction is given diminishing opportunities to express itself. As popular dissatisfaction rises, so too does the likelihood that violent conflict will intensify.

Violent political conflict
- Number of conflict incidents
- Duration of conflict incidents
- Intensity of conflict incidents
- Significance of conflict incidents
- Climate of violence, intensity

The elements listed for this sector, excepting the last, correspond to the elements of Sorokin's violent conflict index, discussed extensively in chapter 4. Increases in intensity of a 'climate of violence' are not measured specifically, but I assume this is highly correlated with violent conflict intensity. The phenomenon has been noted by many commentators and most eloquently in Edward Azar's characterisations of 'protracted social conflict.'[26] As a climate of violence becomes more pervasive, country residents are more and more predisposed to use violence as a 'normal' mode of policy implementation, political behaviour and conflict resolution. Those not directly involved come to accept elevated violence levels as a 'normal' part of daily life.

Inputs that cause violent conflict to escalate and become deadly come from the state-sanctioned violence sector and the attitudes, identities and organisations sector. As we have seen, high levels of deprivation and how those feelings are mobilised by organisations, especially militant movements, are major sources of conflict escalation. Depending on the effectiveness with which it is applied, state-sanctioned violence can either dampen violent conflict or by raising deprivation levels and increasing support for militants, escalate it still further.

Only violent conflict impacts every other sector in the development-deadly-conflict system. Escalating conflict changes the character and focus of leadership and governance. It weakens the economy and has direct, adverse impacts on human development. It alters the political culture, making it more confrontational, reducing the influence of moderate groups, weakening civil society and strengthening the hand of militant movements. It redirects resources to the security forces and strengthens leaders' predispositions to use state-sanctioned violence, both to try and quell violent conflict and for other political purposes. It distorts electoral processes and other political feedback. The impact of violent conflict is pervasive and pernicious.

Development-Deadly-Conflict System Dynamics

Why does violent conflict escalate and become deadly? Our discussion of the violent conflict sector provided a simple answer, focusing on proximate causes and simple cause-effect relationships. But System Dynamics practice warns that focusing on proximate causes can be misleading and dangerous. It also provides better answers. In brief, violent conflict escalates and becomes deadly because of the way elements of the system are linked together in feedback loops.

Not all loops will influence system behaviour at all times. When a particular loop is influencing a trajectory's behaviour, we say that the loop is *dominant*. If violent conflict levels are low for a period of time, we know the system is being dominated by one or more counteracting feedback loops. To understand stable democracies (and stable authoritarian regimes, as well), we need to identify those counteracting loops. If a key trajectory exhibits rapid growth or decline, on the other hand, we know that the system is dominated by one or more reinforcing loops. Thus to understand conflict escalation, we need to identify the dominant reinforcing loops in the Development-Deadly-Conflict that are producing that escalation.

Our examination of Development-Deadly-Conflict dynamics will describe three patterns of counteracting loop dominance that can limit conflict escalation. I label these patterns *stable democracy*, *one party/ ethnic group dominant state*, and *dictatorship*. For each of these patterns, potential destabilising linkages that can shift the system to reinforcing loop dominance, producing an escalation of violent conflict, will be considered.

Stable democracy and its discontents

Figure 5.8 pictures dominant linkages and loops in a stable democracy. It shows how effective error correction mechanisms, via political feedback, contribute to maintaining stability. Leadership and governance are effective. The economy is relatively robust and efficient, though not without normal business cycle fluctuations. Satisfaction of economic and human development needs of most country residents comes reasonably close to expecta-

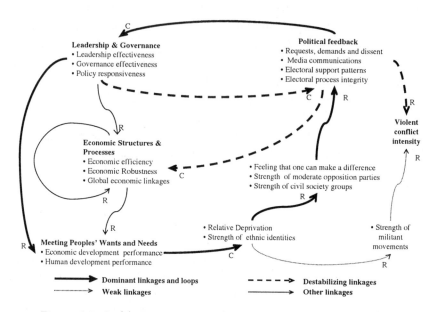

Figure 5.8 Stable Democracy and its Discontents

tions. People feel more satisfied than deprived and moderate parties dominate political discourse. Political leaders and governance structures are open to feedback. When dissatisfaction and deprivation increase, they are manifested first as support for legitimate opposition parties, demands for policy change and non-violent expressions of dissent. Either the government responds with policy changes that improve performance or, eventually, elections are held that shift power to a new group of leaders. Because corrective mechanisms are working properly, feelings of deprivation produce few violent incidents, political discourse is mostly in the 'moderate' range, and militant movements remain on the fringes.

Three potentially destabilising linkages, typically faced by Global South democracies, may weaken corrective mechanisms. Dashed and dotted lines in the diagram show these. First, demands may be expressed in forms that adversely impact the economy. For example, politically motivated strikes may slow production, perpetuate inefficiencies and scare off investors. Second, leaders' policy goals may be frustrated by erratic or unfavourable behaviour of world markets for a few commodities on which a country's economy depends. Third, development policies may be ineffective. Free market economic policies may worsen the lot of the poor. Initiators of a nationalised economy may promise more growth and greater wealth for all, but produce unemployment, inefficiency and stagnation instead. A succession of democratic governments that fail to deliver may produce disillusionment with democracy itself.

Failure to meet expectations, leading to rising, persistent escalation and deprivation, will cause opposition parties to become stronger and demands more strident. Government leaders may perceive a threat to public order, feel that expression of dissent is disrupting the economy or simply fear the loss of power. To right matters they may invoke state-sanctioned violence to clamp down on opposition and dissent. Attempts may be made to rig elections or postpone them. A military coup to 're-establish order, for the good of the country' is another possibility. Sri Lanka demonstrates that a degree of democracy can coexist with chronic political instability, but transition to a second pattern of loop dominance, the one party state is more common. This is pictured in Figure 5.9.

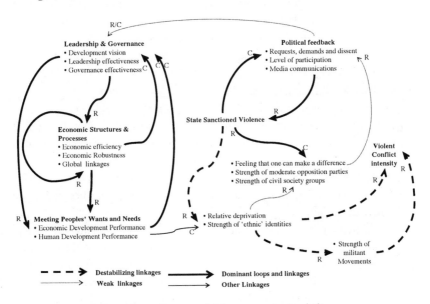

Figure 5.9 One Party State and Threats to its Stability

The one party state and threats to its stability

The ideal of the one party state is the 'Asian Tigers' during their rapid growth stage, especially Singapore, South Korea and Taiwan.[27] South Korea and Taiwan have now moved toward more democratic competition, but Singapore remains as a relatively pure and highly successful example of this type.

The rationale of the one party state is that economic development and human development goals can best be served if democratic competition and popular expressions of dissent are kept within strict bounds. The dominant loops and linkages in this system sustain a robust economy and satisfy wants and needs through bureaucratic planning and regulatory regimes. These regimes are the leadership team's principal sources of feedback. Print and electronic media are strictly controlled and popular disruptions of economic activity are forbidden. A professional, efficient civil service provides leaders with timely, accurate information about the economy and human development performance. Leaders have a good understanding of people's wants and needs. An effective governance system supports them in choosing and implementing good policies. The left hand side of Figure 5.9 shows these traits. Opportunities for country residents to directly express feelings of deprivation are limited. The country may be ethnically diverse, but expressions of ethnic identity are permitted only so long as they do not assume political overtones.

A professional, well-funded security establishment limits dissent and maintains public order. Counteracting links from 'state-sanctioned violence' to 'political feedback,' 'opposition parties and civil society groups' and 'violent conflict intensity' show this. Parties and groups are permitted to organise and engage in clearly circumscribed political activities, but their role in mobilising dissent and communicating it to leadership team members is marginal. In such systems, capable individuals who are motivated toward political careers typically seek leadership positions within the government party. Violent conflict incidents are rare. When they break out, security force intervention to restore order is swift and effective.

The dominant loops that support successful development and political stability reinforce one another and make the system work. Political stability creates a 'favourable climate for investment' which in turn contributes to economic growth. Economic growth, combined with good governance, sustains high levels of economic and human development. High levels of development keep deprivation levels low, which contributes to political stability. Most country residents regard the trade-off between material well-being and political freedom to be acceptable. Those opposed to the regime are lacking in power and relatively small in number. They are viewed as fringe elements that are not acting in the public or national interest.

Though the Asian Tigers have been exhibited as 'successful' development models (especially before the Asian financial crisis), there are far more failed one party states than successful ones. Sub Saharan Africa's post-colonial history, in particular, is replete with such failures. A tendency to respond to adversity with repression rather than reform is the major threat to stability of one party states.

A cycle of adversity is most likely to begin with economic development and human development performance that fail to meet expectations. Fluctuations in global markets, declines in economic efficiency or governance effectiveness, unrealistic promises or bad leadership decisions could all contribute to this. Unmet expectations contribute to rising deprivation levels, increased support for moderate opposition forces and a rising volume of dissent. In one party states, the normal response to these trends is heightened levels of security force intervention. Often dissent will be viewed primarily as a 'law and order' or 'internal security' issue. This can have three destabilising impacts. First, information to leadership team members about rising dissent and its causes is likely to be delayed and distorted. Policy changes, if they do occur, may be wrong and too late. Second, country residents may become disillusioned with the limited channels available for mobilising and expressing dissenting views. If circumstances continue to worsen, and the only response is heightened security force interventions, some residents may come to see violent dissent as their only option. Increasingly, younger residents may turn to militant movements. In ethnically diverse countries, ethnic identity is likely to play an important role in mobilising support for such movements. As one or more militant movements gain strength, violent conflict intensity will grow stronger. Increasingly draconian levels of state violence, if ineffectively applied, will drive additional recruits to militant movements and increase their credibility with country residents at large.

The real danger of this scenario is that increasing government preoccupation with order and increasing levels of violence will have further adverse impacts on development performance. This in turn will contribute to rising levels of militancy and conflict. If this cycle continues, the pattern of loop dominance I have labelled 'dictatorship' may well emerge. Figure 5.10 shows this.

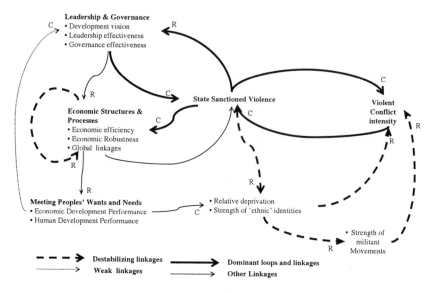

Figure 5.10 Dictatorship and the Abyss of State Failure

From dictatorship to failed state

Contemporary dictatorships in their purest form (I hesitate to use the word 'ideal') include North Korea, Myanmar and, until recently, Iraq.   Among recently failed versions of this species one might include Mobuto Sese Seko's Zaire, Sani Abacha's Nigeria, Mengistus Haile Mariam's Ethiopia, Samuel Doe's Liberia and among former Communist states, Nicolae Ceauçescu's Romania. These dictatorships' early years looked more like one-party states, however they succumbed to the pathology of the one party state model, becoming increasingly repressive and increasingly impoverished.

Dictatorships may masquerade under the guise of the one party state (Ethiopia), religious fundamentalism (Taliban-led Afghanistan) or messianic nationalism (Iraq, Yugoslavia under Milosevic) but perpetuating the regime in power, using state-sanctioned violence, is the rationale that all such regimes have in common. Enrichment of the 'supreme leader' and a few intimates is also a common feature, but in long-surviving dictatorships, remaining in power takes precedence.

The loops linking leadership/governance and violent conflict intensity with state-sanctioned violence dominate this system. The state security forces are the principal instrument of governance and the leadership team's principal source of information.[28] They also dominate economic policy, ensuring that government policies take precedence over market-responsive or entrepreneurial activity. No organised political activity or expressions of dissent are permitted. Outbreaks of violence evoke a draconian response. Feedback regarding economic and human development performance, apart from that provided by the security apparatus, is weak or non-existent.[29]

North Korea and Myanmar – especially North Korea – provide examples of regimes that have been able to perpetuate themselves for extended periods, by making political survival the overriding policy goal. Superpower intervention was needed to topple Iraq's Saddam Hussein. However, most regimes succumb to one of three pathologies. The first is economic. In a competitive global environment, repressive regimes are not able to compete effectively. As the tenure of such regimes lengthens, economic stagnation and negative growth rates are more probable. Flawed economic ideologies and lack of accurate information complicate the task of responding effectively to these problems. North Korea's problems of stagnation and starvation may provide the most revealing examples, but there are many others. Apart from contributing to high levels of deprivation, economic shortfalls may become severe enough, over time, to weaken the readiness and morale of the security forces.

Rising deprivation levels is a second pathology. Interestingly, deprivation levels in very repressive regimes may be less than one would expect, not because economic and human development performance levels are high, but because expectations are so low. By controlling all information that a country's residents receive, repressive regimes may try to convince them that they do, indeed, live in a 'worker's paradise' or to substitute nationalist rhetoric for decent living conditions and opportunities. However, it is increasingly difficult to cut off all information at the border, especially when a regime needs advanced technology to modernise its economy and maintain the readiness of its security forces. Information about the world outside makes privations less endurable and tarnishes an omnipotent dictator's reputation.

A third pathology, inability to maintain security force readiness and morale, in the face of development failures that repression creates, is the Achilles heel of dictatorships. As adversity mounts, the supreme leader's position is analogous to 'riding a tiger.' Relaxation of draconian measures is certain to catalyse the formation of militant opposition movements, especially in ethnically diverse dictatorships where repression is seen as ethnically based. Repressive measures, ineffectively applied, strengthen the hand of militants and weaken the regime's credibility. Ethnic separatist movements in remote regions, far from the centre of power, as in Myanmar and Indonesia, pose particularly difficult challenges as the effectiveness and credibility of the security forces erode. The next stage can be for the contagion to spread to economic and political power centres, including the capital city. Protracted conflict, collapse of the regime or collapse of governance structures entirely are all possible scenarios for ending the fragile 'stability' that characterises dictatorships. While a more benign successor regime may emerge, this is by no means guaranteed. Afghanistan, Somalia, the Democratic Republic of the Congo, Liberia and several Balkan states illustrate worst case scenarios of post-dictatorship regimes.[30] The post-dictatorship scenarios in Afghanistan and Iraq are still uncertain.

The syndrome of escalating deadly conflict

A syndrome is defined as the 'concurrence of several symptoms in a disease.'[31] Contending theories of violent conflict escalation, along with our consideration of instability dynamics in democracies, one party states and dictatorships have all pointed to common symptoms. There are five:

1. Deteriorating economic performance.
2. An increasing number of development failures.
3. Rising levels of relative deprivation; in ethnically diverse societies manifested as strengthening ethnic identities and groups mobilised around those identities.
4. Declining effectiveness in the application of state-sanctioned violence.
5. Growing strength of militant movements.

Returning to the overall structure of the Development-Deadly-Conflict system, we find these symptoms are linked in two reinforcing feedback loops, both characterised by significant delays between causes and effects. The first is *conflict escalation from development failures*. The second is *conflict escalation from state-sanctioned violence ineffectiveness*. Reinforcing loops, it will be recalled, are sources of growth and instability in systems. Delays make it more difficult to understand a system's behaviour. They are also sources of momentum that postpone or frustrate the impacts of corrective actions intended to reverse unfavourable trends. The fact that escalating conflict is being driven by two reinforcing loops – both with significant delays – helps explain why escalating conflict trajectories are so difficult to reverse and why deadly conflicts become protracted. We need to examine each of these loops in more detail.

Conflict escalation from development failures

A cycle of deadly conflict is likely to be catalysed first by development failures, typically caused by some mix of bad policies, ineffective governance and deteriorating economic circumstances. Development failures evoke heightened feelings of relative deprivation which, in ethnically diverse countries, are typically accompanied by heightened levels of ethnic consciousness. These attitudes and feelings create a climate in which militant movements grow stronger. Stronger militant groups are better able to sustain and escalate violent conflict.

Policies that reduce development failures are the high leverage interventions that can reverse trends produced by this loop, but implementing such policies becomes increasingly difficult because of the adverse economic impacts that violent conflict produces.

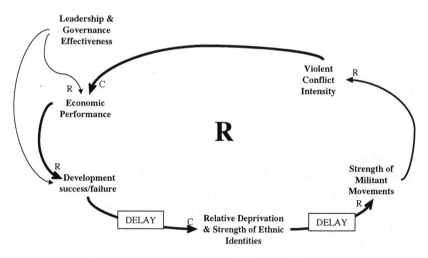

Figure 5.11 Conflict Escalation from Development Failures

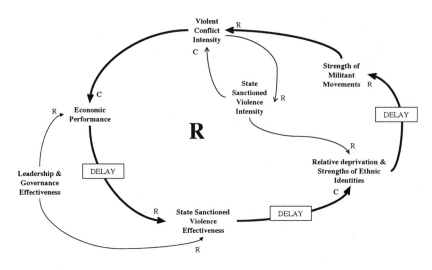

Figure 5.12 Conflict Escalation from State-sanctioned violence Ineffectiveness

Conflict Escalation from state-sanctioned violence ineffectiveness

The second reinforcing loop is catalysed by ineffectiveness in implementing state-sanctioned violence. The agents of state-sanctioned violence – principally police forces and army – will be ineffective to the degree that they are
underresourced, corrupt, undermanned, poorly trained, poorly lead and politicised. Bad policies and adverse economic conditions contribute to ineffectiveness. Corrupt and repressive security forces can provoke insurgency even in
peaceful times. But violent conflict escalation due to development failures,
evoking state-sanctioned violence, is the more common scenario.

When violence does break out, security forces will be called upon to quell
it, irrespective of their effectiveness.[32] To the degree that effectiveness is defi-
cient, this activates the loop pictured in Figure 5.12. Attempts by an ineffective
security force to clamp down on violence, may appear to succeed in the short
term, but are almost always counterproductive in the longer term. Typically
manifestations of ineffectiveness are an inability to subdue militant forces and
the imposition of harsh measures and reprisals on broader populations. The
problem is compounded, as in Sri Lanka, when the security forces are members

of one ethic group and the forces they are attempting to subdue, along with a larger civilian population in a region, belong to another.

Policies that increase security force effectiveness, while maintaining high levels of state-sanctioned violence until violent conflict subsides, are the high leverage interventions in this loop. Implementing these policies while a conflict is ongoing is difficult, however. Deteriorating economic performance complicates matters still further, especially since security force and development budget priorities will be competing. This is why outside intervention, both to restore order and restart the development process, is so often necessary.

How delays impact feedback loops and decision making

Delays make it more difficult for leaders to identify problems in a timely manner. By the time they do respond, the loop has generated so much momentum that the intervention comes too late. The delay between relative deprivation and strength of militant movements is common to both loops that reinforce conflict and may be the most important delay in the entire system. The two attributes that this delay represents are interrelated. First, militant movements do not arise instantaneously in response to worsening conditions. Initially most country residents will be reluctant to turn to movements with a militant agenda. The requisites of a strong militant movement are the requisites of any strong organisation: effective leaders, and motivated, loyal employees; also a vision, resources, a resilient organisational structure and plans appropriate to the mission. Because violent engagements are part of the mission, militant movements also have special requirements – training facilities, command and control technologies, weapons and ammunition. Creating such resources takes time. There may little visible evidence of the movement's existence during the organising phase.

From the standpoint of conflict management, the delay between changed circumstances (for example reforms) and the de-escalation of militant violence is even more important. Once a militant movement grows strong, a growing number of adherents, especially those in top leadership positions, have a vested interest in its perpetuation. Military discipline enables them to maintain control over those whose loyalty to the cause may be flagging and to stamp out dissent. Redressing the 'grievances' that helped mobilise the movement in the first place will rarely be enough. 'Total victory' may be the only satisfactory resolution. Reaching some negotiated 'political solution' may be an extraordinarily difficult, time consuming process.

Feelings of relative deprivation and, especially, strong ethnic identities also take time to form and are difficult to change. It may take 10 years or more for a development project to succeed or fail. When failure does occur and people react, the project may have fallen off the political radar screen. The impact and memories of development failures can last for a generation or more. This is especially true where heightened identities are part of the syndrome. 'Playing the ethnic card' as a way of mobilising support and distracting attention from development failures is an all too common political tactic. In can be analogous to opening 'Pandora's Box' from which 'all manner of misery and evil...flew out over the earth.'[33] The ethnic identities thus heightened may become, for all intents and purposes, a permanent feature of the political landscape.

The final delay, between economic performance and state-sanctioned violence effectiveness, remains to be considered. The effect of budget cutting on security forces, especially cuts in real expenditures that are masked by inflation, may produce no visible effect in the short run. Senior officers closest to the leadership team may be the least impacted by the cuts and have the most to gain politically by going along. Effects on the lower ranks may be masked, especially in police forces, as officers take graft to narrow the widening gap between income and needs. Soldiers in lower ranks are often conscripts, from the poorest classes, who are in no position to express grievances. They may have little will – or skill – to fight when the need arises. The 'feedbacks' leaders are most likely to receive are rising levels of crime and civil unrest on the domestic front. If an effective, highly motivated militant movement threatens the government, a succession of military defeats may provide warning signals of deteriorating effectiveness. But by then, it may be too late.

The role of leaders and effective governance

Skilled leaders, supported by good governance, can often counteract the reinforcing feedback loops that escalate violent conflict intensity. They can strengthen the efficiency, resiliency and productivity of the economy. They can direct resources toward programs that meet country residents' wants and needs. They can ensure programs are managed efficiently and sensitively. They can maintain security forces that are professional, highly motivated and adequately funded. Discretion to do these things is much greater, as we have seen, when violent conflict intensity is low.

As violet conflict intensity rises, the two reinforcing feedback loops that reinforce violence become dominant, leaders' zone of discretion shrinks and they are swept along with the tide. Soon they are justifying deteriorating economic conditions, development failures, and repression and escalating conflict with the plaintive cry 'we had no choice.' Once, these leaders did have choices, but they failed to heed early warning signals of development failure and implement timely corrective measures. Often leaders' desire to remain in power motivates them to ignore or suppress feedbacks that could have helped them turn the tide of escalating violence, instead of being swept along.

This describes Sri Lanka's tragic development scenario. In Parts II-IV of this book we will see how it unfolded.

Part II

Homeostasis – Reality or Illusion :
Was Sri Lanka a Development
'Success Story'?

6

The 'Uncle-Nephew Party' Years: Elitist Pluralism

Our overall goal is to explain changes in political conflict intensity, but for this period, it is consistently low levels of conflict that must be explained.

Sri Lanka became an independent nation, within the British Commonwealth of Nations, on 4 February 1948. In contrast to its neighbours, India and Pakistan, relatively amicable relations between Sri Lankan and British leaders had marked the pre-independence years.[1] The colonial Board of Ministers, elected by universal suffrage (including women), strongly supported the British war effort. Sri Lanka served as the headquarters for Lord Louis Mountbatten's Asia Theatre Command and is fondly remembered as a rest and recreation stopover by many British and American sailors and airmen.

During more than eight years of United National Party (UNP) rule, Britain's 'model colony' appeared to have become a model developing nation. When D.S. Senanayake, the father of Sri Lankan independence, died, there was a smooth transition to a government headed by his son, Dudley. Contending factions within the UNP quickly united behind the new leader, a decision that was ratified by an overwhelming general election victory. When Dudley Senanayake resigned, soon thereafter, transition to new leadership was again peaceful. In 1956, a vigorously contested general election with broad popular participation conferred power on the major opposition leader, S.W.R.D. Bandaranaike and his coalition.

Our overall goal is to explain changes in political conflict intensity, but for this period, it is consistently low levels of conflict that must be explained. Was this because post-independence Sri Lanka conformed to the 'stable democracy model'? Was its government effective? Were its development policies successful? Were its leaders responsive to political feedback? Chapter 6 will explore this conjecture, but also an alternative. The alternative is that Sri Lanka's government was more elitist than democratic and experienced development failures similar to those of many Global South nations. The absence of conflict was due more to delays in the *conflict escalation from development failures feedback loop* – first between development failures, deprivation and identity formation; second between these phenomena and the strength of militant movements. The development – deadly-conflict system model also points to a third question: to what degree did Sri Lanka's development scenario under the UNP strengthen destabilising linkages that could create instability under future governments?

Violent political conflict: a period of 'good health'

The UNP's first term in office was the most tranquil in Sri Lanka's years of independence; however violent political conflict events did occur. Discussing these in some detail provides a useful point of comparison for more turbulent periods that followed.

Conflict intensity per month, readers will recall, is measured by summing the intensities of conflict events that occurred during that month. For example, in the month of September 1948, the following three events were recorded and scored for intensity:[2]

Date	Location	Event Description	Score
Sept.19	Trincomalee, Eastern Province	Speakers at a mass rally organised by the Communist Party were pelted with stones. Protestors pulled down the Communist Party Flag. Order was restored by the police. One person was taken to the hospital with injuries.	2
Sept. 26	Kurunegala, Northwestern Province	Protesters hurled stones at the platform during a Communist Party meeting. There is some evidence that the protest was instigated by the UNP. No injuries were reported.	2
Sept. 27	Kurunegala, Northwestern Province	A Communist Party supporter was killed. A subsequent court proceeding convicted a man affiliated with the UNP and found that the motivation for the killing had been political.	2

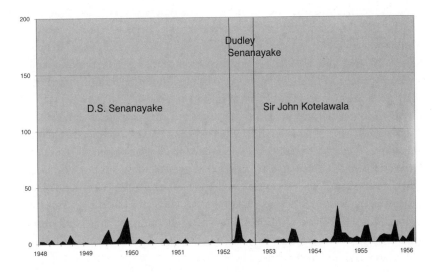

Figure 6.1 Violent Conflict Intensity: January 1948 – March 1956

Chapter 4 also discussed how the score for each event takes into account *duration, location, severity of violence* and *size* (number of participants). The event on 19 September scored highest because a relatively large number of individuals participated and injuries were reported. The event on 27 September received a higher score for severity because it resulted in a death, but a lower overall score because only two individuals were involved.[3] The total conflict intensity for the month of September was 7.8. Of course, specific numerical values of individual events or months are of little significance. The numbers are useful because they permit comparisons of political conflict from month to month, year to year and period to period.

A magnified 'fever chart' of the 87 months from January 1948 through March 1956 (Figure 6-1) will be a good place to begin looking at this period more closely.[4]

The most obvious topographical feature appearing on the chart is eight 'peaks' of relatively intense conflict. The three most intense have maximum values greater than 25. The remaining five have intensities greater than 10 but less than 20. A second topographical feature might be called 'changing ambient conflict intensity' (during periods when there were no distinguishable peaks). Prior to June 1954, the typical pattern was a mix of months with no conflict reported and months with intensity levels of less than four. Between June 1954 and March 1956 the ambient level of conflict increased. There were only three months with no reported events. Reported monthly intensities, apart from peaks, tended to be five or more.

Both municipal and parliamentary elections were apparently major catalysts for violence. The three most intense peaks all included election-related incidents. There was factional fighting between parties, political rallies that turned violent and attempts by one party to intimidate supporters of another. Some candidates were roughed up after results were announced and on one occasion, a victorious candidate was shot and killed by supporters of an opposing faction.[5] Although there was labour unrest in tea and rubber growing estates, the majority of violent events during these peak periods occurred in Colombo and nearby towns.

Labour unrest was a major contributor to the five less intense peaks. Sri Lanka's left wing parties, who controlled most urban labour unions during this period, used strikes to discredit officials in power, mobilise supporters and intimidate opponents. Issues provoking strikes were primarily procedural and jurisdictional, rather than economic. Prime Minister Kotelawala's strong anti-Communist governmental stance contributed to a confrontational atmosphere. Pro-UNP goon squads were sometimes used to disrupt both strikes and opposition party meetings. Confrontations between these squads and leftist party supporters often led to violence.

Two factors contributed to rising ambient conflict intensities after mid-1954. First, incidents of labour unrest – strikes, demonstrations and confrontations – became much more frequent. Second, there were a growing number of incidents related to the revival of Buddhism and confrontations over a "Sinhala only" official language proposal. These were the first issues to evoke significant communal conflict, involving Sinhalese and Tamils, since independence.

In addition to graphing fever charts, I have grouped conflict incidents into six categories, and tabulated the frequency of each. This too, provides useful baseline data for comparisons with later period. Results are shown in Figure 6.2.[6]

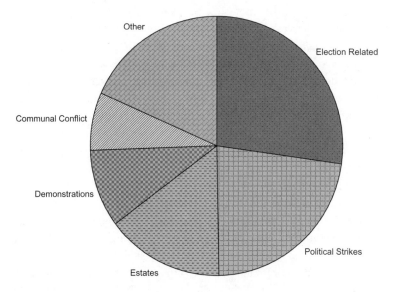

Figure 6.2 Conflict Incident Frequencies

Election related events were the most prevalent form of conflict reported. Although the number of events were relatively small, the use of intimidation and violence in campaigning on election day and, occasionally, to exact retribution after a victory or defeat was clearly part of Sri Lankan political life, especially in urban areas. Next in frequency were *strikes* that occurred throughout the period. Only strikes that appear to be linked to some political agenda are included, however that includes many strikes in Sri Lanka.

Strikes and demonstrations involving estate workers came next in frequency, comprising nearly 20 per cent of all events reported. These are treated as a separate category because the Indian Tamil population that provided most protagonists for these events. They were concerned with regionally specific issues and thus fell outside of the political mainstream. During this period there were lengthy strikes at several estates over a combination of political and economic issues and strikes of shorter duration in which hundreds of thousands of workers participated. The government's decision to disenfranchise most Indian Tamils contributed to this unrest. Paradoxically, estate sector revenues, which depended on Indian Tamil labour, were a major foreign exchange source. Without estate income, social welfare and economic development programs that provided few benefits to estate workers could not be sustained.

Political demonstrations and incidents at political meetings is the next category. Demonstrations, like political strikes, were held to protest unpopular policies such as reduction of the rice subsidy or government involvement in the Buddha Jayanthi 2,500 year anniversary commemorative celebrations. University students demonstrated in support of various political causes, and when police intervened, violence could result. Supporters of a rival faction could disrupt a political meeting by yelling slogans, setting firecrackers or, in rare cases, firing shots. This could lead to stone throwing and fights, especially between members of rival goon squads.

Communal violence ranked low among categories of violence during this period. Two early events, reported in 1948 and 1952, were Sinhalese–Muslim and Tamil–Muslim communal clashes. Beginning in 1953, incidents of communal violence began to be associated with rising Buddhist Sinhalese political movements and with Tamil community concerns that these movements generated. For example, two incidents involved clashes between Buddhist processions and the police. Another was the looting and burning of Tamil and Muslim shops by a crowd that had gathered to protest the beating of several Buddhist priests. The priests had tried to disrupt a Communist Party political meeting. The major Tamil response to growing Sinhalese militancy was one-day general strikes in Tamil majority areas, organised by the pro-Tamil Federal Party. Although *hartals* were supposed to be non-violent they could degenerate into stone throwing and more violent confrontations. Communal conflict incidents scored highest in intensity because they often produced injuries, sometimes severe. In three of the nine reported incidents, there were deaths.

The geographical distribution of conflict events is also worth noting as a baseline. Nearly 40 per cent of recorded events occurred in Colombo or immediately surrounding communities. Less that 15 per cent occurred in Tamil majority areas of the north and east.

Political conflict during the post-colonial period provided relatively few harbingers of what was in store for Sri Lanka. It was primarily secular, urban, and non-communal. Outbreaks of conflict were primarily linked to the activities of more-or-less mainstream organisations – political parties, labour unions and resurgent Buddhist groups. Despite the revolutionary rhetoric of some Marxist factions, there were no organisations that were committed to force and violence as the principal means of attaining their goals. The goon squads used by many political parties – including the major parties – were not part of the political mainstream. Mainstream political leaders were quick to disavow and deny responsibility for goon squad activity (even when they initiated it). Finally, Sri Lanka's institutions appeared to be resilient in the face of conflict. Most incidents were of short duration. Where necessary, the police were relatively effective in restoring order. It would be an exaggeration to describe Sri Lanka's political life as tranquil, but violent conflict was rare, rather than the norm.

Leadership and governance

The new nation's Westminster style constitution was a collaborative effort. When the Soulbury Commission was appointed, in July 1944, to consider the terms for Sri Lankan independence, a constitution had already been drafted and approved by the elected ministers.[7] In deference to minority fears that the majority Sinhalese would control the constitution writing process, the Commission maintained the pretence of beginning its deliberations, *de novo*, but its final report strongly reflected the views of Sri Lankan political leader, Don Sebastian (D.S.) Senanayake and his constitutional advisor, Sir Ivor Jennings.[8] The 'Soulbury Constitution' provided for a bicameral legislature, with a directly elected House of Representatives.[9]

Colleagues have described D.S. Senanayake, who became independent Sri Lanka's first Prime Minister, as a skilful politician and consensus builder. He saw Sri Lanka as a democratic, secular state that would be dominated by the majority Sinhalese but sensitive to minority concerns. He respected British institutions and opposed radical change. In his view, political, economic and social development should proceed gradually in a climate of moderation, civility and stability.[10]

Senanayake knew Sri Lanka Tamils feared independence would lead to discrimination and oppression by Sinhalese. He also knew that Sinhalese chafed under what many viewed as a privileged status given to Tamils under colonial rule. In pre-independence governments, British minority representation schemes had given Tamils a disproportionate voice. Superior education, especially in English, had contributed to high proportions of Tamils in many professions and prestigious civil service posts. English was the language of government, professional life and higher education, though only a small proportion of Sinhalese spoke it.

In pre-independence negotiations, Sri Lanka Tamil leaders G.G. Ponnambalam and S.L.V. Chelvanayakam had campaigned aggressively, though unsuccessfully, for a representation scheme based on the '50-50' principle – 50 per cent representation for the majority Sinhalese, 50 per cent representation for the minorities. Senanayake was steadfastly insistent on a territorial franchise, but favoured drawing electoral districts so that roughly proportional minority representation would be probable.[11] He favoured a provision in the Soulbury Constitution that prohibited Parliament from enacting discriminatory laws against ethnic or religious groups, restricting the free exercise of religion or giving special privileges to any community or religion.[12]

Only with regard to the Indian Tamil workers did Senanayake align himself with the views of more chauvinistic Sinhalese politicians. The Ceylon Workers Congress, which represented the majority of Indian Tamils, had opposed the Prime Minister's UNP in the 1947 election. Further, the plantation workers were viewed as a potential rural base of support for Sri Lanka's vociferous, but numerically weak, left-wing parties. Following independence, parliament quickly passed a series of laws that disenfranchised most Indian Tamils.[13] This created a divisive issue between Sri Lanka and India that would not be resolved for several decades.

Senanayake's cabinet included four men who would subsequently serve as Prime Minister, three of whom were relatives. His son, Dudley, became Prime Minister when D.S. Senanayake died suddenly. Sir John Kotelawala, who succeeded Dudley, was D.S. Senanayake's nephew (hence the nickname given to the UNP by wags, 'Uncle-Nephew Party'). J.R. Jayewardene, a more distant relative, became Prime Minister in 1977 and later Sri Lanka's first Executive President. The fourth, Solomon West Ridgeway Dias (S.W.R.D.) Bandaranaike, would successfully challenge Senanayake's vision of a secular state on the English model, when his newly created SLFP defeated the UNP in the 1956 general election.

There will be more to say of Bandaranaike later in this chapter and chapter 8. This flamboyant and mercurial man of aristocratic origins[14] had established the *Sinhala Maha Sabha* (Great Sinhalese League) in 1936, which mobilised support for the view that Sinhalese communal interests should be weighted more heavily in Sri Lankan politics. Although Bandaranaike differed from Senanayake on communalism, he nonetheless viewed himself as the number two man in the government and as 'heir presumptive'.[15] He had served as a member of the State Council (the representative body that preceded Parliament) since 1931 and held a ministerial portfolio since 1936. His work as Minister of Local Government and extensive speaking provided him a base of mass support in rural areas, especially among village leaders and Buddhist priests (*Bhikkhus*). As Health Minister, he had directed a successful malaria eradication campaign. But his flamboyant style and opposition to Senanayake's conservative philosophy cost him influence in the cabinet and party, relative to potential rivals.[16] It became clear that he would never head a UNP government as Prime Minister. On 11 July 1951, Bandaranaike accepted the reality of his position, resigned from the government and crossed to the opposition benches in Parliament. On 3 August, he chaired the inaugural meeting of the Sri Lanka Freedom Party, which he hoped would serve as a focal point for those who opposed the UNP but were uncomfortable with Marxist alternatives.[17]

D.S. Senanayake's premature death on 26 March 1952 led to a test of strength that neither Bandaranaike, nor the UNP leadership, anticipated.[18] Senanayake had made it clear that he wished his son, Dudley, to succeed him.[19] After some hesitation, Dudley agreed.[20] The UNP leadership moved quickly to capitalise on public sentiment for the father of Sri Lankan independence and disorganisation of the newly-founded SLFP. Parliament was dissolved and a general election called for May. The results produced an overwhelming victory for the UNP and a clear majority of 54 in the 95-member House.[21]

Dudley Senanayake's tenure was short lived. In July, budget deficits and dwindling foreign exchange reserves forced Finance Minister Jayewardene to propose reducing the popular rice subsidy, which directly benefited more than half the island's citizens. The cost of importing rice to sustain the subsidy appeared to threaten the government with insolvency. Political opponents were quick to capitalise on popular discontent by staging demonstrations[22] and a *hartal* (general strike).[23] Police overreaction, resulting in deaths, injuries and arrests, was followed by angry speeches in Parliament. Senanayake's gentle temperament, personal indecisiveness and frail health were unable to withstand the crisis and he resigned 12 October. Sir John Kotelawala was named as his successor.

Sri Lankans remember Sir John for decisiveness, a sharp tongue and an uninhibited style. Some also recall crudity, insensitivity and politically costly flamboyance.[24] His administration continued Senanayake's conservative economic and social policies without significant initiatives. He stage managed a successful visit of the Queen of England to Sri Lanka, adopted a strong anti-Communist foreign policy and viewed the Marxist parties rather than Bandaranaike's SLFP as his primary opponents. J.R. Jayewardene, whose subtlety and political skills to some degree compensated for the Prime Minister's stylistic shortcomings, managed parliamentary strategy.

Only in the areas of language and religious policy did Kotelawala blunder seriously. These blunders epitomised an insensitive, parochial outlook in the face of growing mass political consciousness that spelled the end of Sir John's political career and reversed the electoral fortunes of the UNP.

His attempt to reinforce D.S. Senanayake's even-handed policy on language played into the hands Sinhalese-Buddhist nationalists, led by S.W.R.D. Bandaranaike. Plans for celebrating the 2,500-year death anniversary of the Buddha (*the Buddha Jayanthi*) had catalyzed "a formidable array of forces which had hitherto been unable if not unwilling to unite in a common program."[25] Supporters greeted Kotelawala's 1954 announcement, given on an official visit to the North, that he would propose constitutional changes for parity of status between Tamil and Sinhala, with a firestorm of protest.[26] In February 1956, with a general election on the horizon, the Prime Minister reversed himself and endorsed Bandaranaike's proposal that Sinhala become the only official language. It was too late. The move alienated Tamils and was viewed as politically expedient by the Sinhalese. The latter continued to shift their allegiance to the SLFP and other parties in Bandaranaike's anti-UNP coalition.[27]

While waffling on language, Kotelawala tried unsuccessfully to cast his government in a leadership role of the pro-Buddhist movement and the Buddha Jayanthi preparations. But the Prime Minister who, though a Buddhist, had been described as "Asia's playboy politician," was an improbable choice as leader of a Buddhist resurgence. He compounded his problems by calling an early general election during the Jayanthi year in the hope of capitalising on public enthusiasm for his government's pro-Buddhist policies and his own official appearances at Jayanthi functions. This further infuriated Buddhist leaders who had strongly urged the Prime Minister to keep the year of celebration free of political activity.[28]

The 1956 General Election has been described as an election more lost by the UNP than won by Bandaranaike's coalition.[29] Bad leadership, organisational weaknesses and mismanagement of rising Buddhist Sinhalese consciousness contributed most visibly to the demise of D.S. Senanayake's centrist coalition and his vision of a secular, pluralistic Sri Lankan polity. As we shall see, UNP economic and social policies also played a role in vitiating Senanayake's political settlement and moving the Sri Lankan society in the direction of a more volatile polarised state.

Development goals and the economy

Sri Lanka's development goals under the UNP were similar to those of many new nations: expansion of agricultural production and exports, food self-sufficiency, strengthened social programs, full employment, and economic diversification. But how were these goals to be attained? Chapter 3 emphasized that 50 years after Sri Lanka became independent, development specialists still argue about which policies will promote economic growth, diversification and social well-being.

Like contemporaries in other nations, Sri Lanka's new leaders faced the difficulties of managing an export-oriented economy, subject to the fluctuations of international markets, in the face of rising popular aspirations created by independence and the competition for political power. Reconciling ambitious economic development and social welfare goals with the realities of limited export income became and remains to this day a major problem. In 1948, Marxist economics provided the principal body of theory to guide development. Leaders of Sri Lanka's small but vocal Marxist parties advocated central planning and broad-based government intervention to achieve a diversified, industrialised economy.[30] The economic policies of D.S. Senanayake's men, experienced in politics and often trained in the law, were more incremental and pragmatic.

Increasing rice (paddy) production, a long-standing personal interest of D.S. Senanayake and his son, was a centrepiece of the government's program. Their views drew sustenance from and reinforced the myth of the independent rice-growing smallholder, which was deeply rooted in Sinhalese culture.[31] This may have helped Sri Lanka avoid the errors of many new nations, which emphasised industrial development and food subsidies for urban dwellers at the expense of the agricultural sector. The government initiated a multifaceted campaign that included guaranteed prices for rice, equal to or above world market prices, and subsidies for fertiliser. A major river development scheme was initiated to provide dry zone irrigation and funds were provided to restore the "tanks" and irrigation works that had been a hallmark of Sinhalese civilisation at its height.[32] With passage of the Paddy Lands Act of 1953, the government began to grapple with the problem of reducing large land holdings and share-cropping. While the act produced few concrete results, it paved the way for more stringent and effective legislation passed in later years.[33] The agricultural programs had shortcomings, but succeeded in establishing a set of ongoing development priorities, with strong political support.

In delivery of social services, the government moved well beyond colonial era programs. Interestingly, the expansion of social services in health care, public health and education was more the result of individual ministers' initiatives than an overall plan. In 1947, C.W.W. Kannangara, Sri Lanka's dynamic education minister, was successful in implementing a system of free education at all levels.[34] A system of free medical care for all was also introduced[35] and Health Minister S.W.R.D. Bandaranaike's mosquito eradication program began to show significant results in the form of reduced death rates from malaria.[36]

More than 50 per cent of investments came from government. Investment priorities emphasised traditional rice paddy agriculture and promoted its extension to a broader area through land development and irrigation schemes. Construction of expanded facilities in education, power, health and transportation was also given some attention. In contrast to the Marxists, expansion and diversification of the nation's industrial base were viewed as responsibilities of the private sector.

Sri Lanka's post-colonial economic structure made expansion and diversification difficult. Export production was dominated by the plantation sector, especially the tea plantations. Plantations were largely foreign owned. Rice production for domestic consumption was insufficient to meet local needs, especially with the government's commitment to food subsidies. Industrial development tended to be undercapitalised and unfocused. The nation lacked the physical infrastructure, technical expertise and entrepreneurial skills needed to support industrial development.[37] Credit markets, dominated by foreign bankers, did not generally support local business initiatives. Progress in developing alternative export markets or domestic industries that could provide alternatives to expensive imported goods was slow. Because both demand and prices for Sri Lanka's export products were high in the first years after independence, weaknesses in the economy were at first not fully exposed.[38]

But the government's economic policies had far less impact on economic conditions than the prices of locally produced commodities that the nation exported and the prices of foreign products, both commodities and finished goods, that it needed to import. At the time of independence, export income, almost exclusively from tea, rubber and coconuts, contributed more than 30 per cent to Sri Lanka's GNP and even more to government revenues. In most years, 50 per cent or more of export income came from the tea plantations alone. Despite plans to encourage local industry and diversify the economy, this pattern changed little during the first eight years of independence. Moreover, the government was heavily committed to food imports, especially rice for the politically sacrosanct food subsidy program. Thus, changes in Sri Lanka's terms of trade (the relative prices of exported versus imported goods) as well as fluctuations in demand for its products could have disastrous consequences.

During the post-colonial years, Sri Lanka's leaders faced the consequences of deteriorating terms of trade only briefly. The Korean War had produced a boom in the export markets for Sri Lanka's products, especially rubber. However, with the end of the war, these markets collapsed. Sri Lanka's terms of trade index plummeted 24 points in 1952 and remained low in 1953 as well. At the same time, both the price and volume of Sri Lanka's imports rose substantially. As a result, Sri Lanka's balance of trade (the difference between import costs and export revenues) dropped from a surplus of 13 per cent of exports to a deficit of 21 per cent. Steps taken to cover the deficit reduced the value of Sri Lanka's foreign assets by more than 30 per cent (of their 1948 value) in 1952 and by an additional 22 per cent in the following year. As noted above, the government's attempt to deal with the situation pushed Dudley Senanayake to resign.[39] Fortunately for the UNP leadership, commodity prices boomed again in 1954, the balance of trade recovered and the crisis was averted. However, this was an object lesson in the sensitivity of political support to economic conditions and of economic conditions to the vagaries of international trade.

The importance of foreign asset management in an import-dependent economy forced the adoption of the unpopular austerity programs. Imports, of course, could only be purchased with foreign currency. Sri Lanka began its life as an independent nation with a relatively large stock of foreign assets. However, generous social programs, coupled with a downward turn in prices for Sri Lanka's primary commodities, began, by 1952, to drain foreign assets at an alarming rate and create major budget deficits. Anticipating possible problems, Finance Minister Jayewardene had established a system of exchange controls and import licences as early as 1948. Thus, quick implementation of the politically disastrous austerity program, discussed above, was possible. By 1954, fiscally conservative policies and improved commodity prices had resulted in a 50 per cent increase in assets.

Like democratic politicians everywhere Sri Lanka's leaders tended to give greater priority to immediate, rather than long-term, concerns. But emphasis on short-term benefits in an undeveloped economy limited its capacity to meet the needs of a rapidly growing population and the nation's vulnerability to fluctuations in commodity prices.

Emphasis on short-term benefits was reflected in government budgets. More than half of expenditures (more than 60 per cent in two years) were allocated to programs intended to provide immediate benefits for Sri Lanka's people or support for the nation's growing number of public corporations. The bulk of funds went to health, education and other social services. There were also substantial "transfer payments" to subsidise food, transportation and local government. Because these services represented an ongoing commitment, it was difficult or impossible to make cuts during bad economic times. Cuts prior to general elections were viewed as politically suicidal. To support expanded programs the government began to rely on deficit financing. Deficits were recorded in all of the first five post-independence years. Government spending and the size of the deficit rose most in 1952, when real GNP declined. In three years (1950, 1952 and 1953), deficits exceeded 20 per cent of expenditures. During this period, Sri Lanka's public debt more than doubled.

By the end of 1953, rising debt, coupled with a precipitous drop in Sri Lanka's external assets had pushed Prime Minister Kotelawala toward more conservative policies. These policies, coupled with rising demand for Sri Lanka's exports (export taxes and plantation industry taxes were major sources of government revenue) actually produced small surpluses in 1954 and 1955. However, as noted above, the government's austerity measures were viewed by many as among the pre-election errors that contributed to Kotelawala's repudiation in the 1956 general elections. This error, if error it was, would not be repeated by his successors.

The post-colonial UNP governments have been criticised as elitist and committed to maintaining the status quo. Many UNP leaders, especially the flamboyant Kotelawala, were out of touch with the rising political consciousness of rural Sinhalese. D.S. Senanayake and to a lesser degree, his successors moved slowly because they were concerned about the destabilising effects of radical change and of ideological appeals that would raise the level of tension in Sri Lanka's multi- communal society.[40] However these "conservative" leaders undertook radical – and costly – initiatives intended to improve the well-being of Sri Lanka's people. In its agricultural development and food subsidy programs, Sri Lanka was unique among Third World nations of its era. Moreover, the government's economic and social programs, by and large, produced good results. These results are examined next.

Meeting people's wants and needs

National-level measures of economic performance and social well-being are available for Sri Lanka.[41] However, as for many Global South nations, the accuracy and interpretation of such measures can be problem. Statistical data may not be of much use in determining absolute levels of well-being, either economic or social, and I am dubious about comparisons between nations. Moreover, as chapter 3 emphasised, index values often do not measure country residents' perceptions of well-being. I do believe, however, that data on trends within a single nation, over time, can communicate useful information. My approach to making qualitative judgements about the satisfaction of wants and needs reflects this.

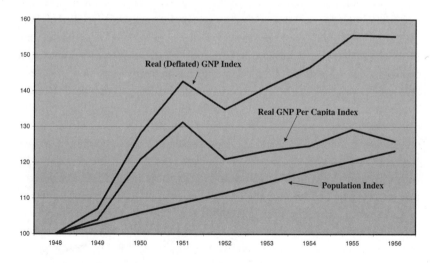

Figure 6.3 GNP and Population Trends

The budget crisis of 1952 notwithstanding, economic trends were generally favourable (see Figure 6.3).[42] Real GNP growth averaged nearly six per cent annually and GNP per-capita averaged nearly three per cent. The population growth rate of 2.6 per cent per year was already lower than most Global South nations. Sri Lanka's prospects for escaping from the demographic trap of population growth rates that outran economic growth rates seemed promising.

Improvements in education and public health contributed to declining population growth rates. In these areas, the success of government programs intended to meet basic educational, health and nutritional needs can be documented. School enrolments increased by a remarkable 42 per cent under the UNP government. By 1956, more than half a million more students were attending schools than at independence. School construction and teacher training programs, which emphasised rural as well as urban areas, had more than kept pace with a school age population that was, thanks to parallel improvements in health, exploding at a rate of nearly four per cent per year. Adult literacy had increased from about 63 per cent at the time of independence to nearly 70 per cent. The literacy rate for males was nearly 80 per cent. These were extraordinarily high numbers for a Global South nation in the 1950s.

Progress was slower in meeting a growing demand for higher education. Sri Lanka's university system was highly regarded internationally and, during this period, was able to admit about 30 per cent of those who applied.[43] Further, sons (and more rarely daughters) of the nation's English speaking elite often completed their education in England. However, lack of emphasis on technical education essential for a developing economy was a serious problem. Sri Lanka's university system did not produce its first engineering graduate until 1953. Arts and oriental studies were by far the most popular fields of study. This reflected the emphasis of the nation's elite secondary schools, modelled on English public schools, and the high prestige accorded to careers in law, medicine and government service. Sri Lanka's educational system was not, by and large, producing the men and women who could expand and diversify the nation's economic base. Instead, the men and women it was producing would face increasing difficulties finding employment. Thus the country's 'success' in education was a double-edged sword. Government policies began to create a literate, upwardly mobile population with high expectations, but these expectations were growing faster than Sri Lanka's economy and political institutions were capable of meeting them.

Statistics also documented significant achievements in health care. Mortality rates fell by 24 per cent, infant mortality rates by 27 per cent and maternal mortality rates by an astonishing 54 per cent. Sri Lanka was well on the way to establishing the reputation for which it later became recognised internationally. Its policies seemed to demonstrate that despite limited economic resources, a nation could achieve very high levels in meeting the basic needs of its people.

Thus, after eight years of independence, Sri Lankans, on average seemed better off in many ways and few seemed worse off. Although rural life remained unchanged in most respects, the government was providing visible, tangible services and subsidies to many citizens. A relatively benign international environment supported the expansion of the nation's export economy. Favourable terms of trade and high export prices provided needed revenues to support expanded services and entitlements. Investment programs targeted small agricultural producers, a numerous and politically powerful segment of the population. The nation's rapidly expanding cadre of young people, the beneficiaries of malaria eradication and public health programs had, by and large, not yet entered the labour force and so unemployment levels remained relatively low. As far as meeting residents' basic economic and human needs, few factors seemed to intensify relative deprivation; rather, they seemed to promote a climate of well-being. Indeed, one might have predicted that voters would have rewarded the UNP government with a parliamentary majority in the May 1956 general election. An examination of changing attitudes, deepening identities and newly powerful organisations that capitalised on them, will help explain why this did not happen.

Political attitudes, identities and organisations

Sri Lanka's political parties were the principal organisations through which political attitudes were mobilised and expressed during this period. From the vantage point of some non-Sri Lankan observers, this fledging democracy seemed to have quickly evolved into a western-style, competitive multiparty system. Politically, as well as economically, this pro-western anti-Communist island nation seemed to point the way towards democratic development for Global South nations.[44] Within a decade, it would become apparent that the reality was somewhat different.

Political mobilisation at the centre: the UNP

The UNP not only controlled the government, but also dominated the island's political life, for most of its term. Leaders saw its philosophy as centrist, inclusive and secular. Economic programs emphasised agricultural development and social programs. Party manifestoes described the UNP as the sensible alternative to Sri Lanka's Marxist parties which, at the time of independence, constituted the principal organised opposition leadership.

D.S. Senanayake viewed the UNP as a broadly inclusive ruling coalition rather than a tightly organised structure. Supporters could be members of the UNP while retaining their affiliation with other political groups such as Bandaranaike's *Sinhala Maha Sabha* or the Ceylon Muslim League.[45] Real power, however, was concentrated and centralised. Though a 10-15 man "working committee ostensibly governed the party," important policy decisions were made by a small coterie of officials, members of the *Goyagama* (landowning) caste,[46] with close family and personal ties to D.S. Senanayake.[47]

Party organisation and party loyalty were weak. Political relationships were based more on personality and position than party. Members of parliament gained support through close personal ties to constituents and benefits they distributed. Often, they resisted proposals to form local party branches because they did not wish to be subject to party discipline.[48] The party organisation's major role was to distribute modest funding to candidates, staging campaign rallies featuring party notables and mobilising transportation to bring voters to the polls on election day.

UNP supporters spanned the island's ethnic and caste divisions, with landowners, shopkeepers (*mudilalis*) and upper level civil servants playing the most influential roles. Virtually all of the nationally distributed newspapers supported it. But links to lower economic classes were weak. UNP's success with the agricultural and urban working classes in the 1947 and 1952 elections had been largely due to the influence of landowners and employers and to respect for D.S. Senanayake, personally, as a man of the people. Workers and peasants were often ill informed about candidates, issues and programs. They tended to vote the way their employers wished unless labour unions or other similar groups exerted a countervailing influence.[49] However, this relatively passive 'employee vote' was ripe for mobilisation by a party program that could frame the issues of a general election in terms that touched the lives of ordinary Sri Lankans more closely. Under Sir John Kotelawala's leadership, the UNP became increasingly out of touch with the masses.

Political mobilisation on the left: the Marxist parties

Sri Lanka's left-wing or Marxist parties claimed to represent 'the masses' but they were not very effective in organising a united, credible opposition to the UNP. All traced their origins to the *Lanka Sama Samaja Party* (LSSP) founded in 1935 by a group of upper class intellectuals who had been imbued with Marxist and Fabian socialist ideals while students at the London School of Economics.[50] The combined vote for left-wing parties was second only to the UNP in both the 1947 and the 1952 general elections.

Initially, UNP leaders viewed the Marxists as their most serious political opposition, however Marxist leaders often seemed more interested in doctrinal purity than political power. Issues such as membership in the Third International, shifts in Soviet foreign policy and interpretations of Marxist-Leninist dogma were of little concern to most Sri Lankans, but caused Sri Lanka's left-wing movement to fragment into a cast of bewildering and ever-changing factions.[51] This seriously limited effective political campaigning on a party basis, although a number of individual party leaders were effective and personally popular with the voters.[52] Further, the left-wing parties were never able to frame a credible appeal to rural Sinhalese who held the balance of power in parliamentary elections.[53] The parties' major source of strength in rural areas, the Indian Tamil plantation workers, was lost when their citizenship and voting rights were revoked in 1949.

Domestic programs advocated by left-wing parties emphasised nationalisation and collectivisation. Speeches and manifestoes spoke of "working class revolution" and "overthrow of the capitalist system," but leaders generally accepted democratic practices.[54] When more radical Marxist parties committed to violent tactics emerged in later years, they were generally condemned by the older leaders. Most Marxist parties made common cause with S.W.R.D. Bandaranaike in the 1956 election, but their purpose was only to establish a united front against the UNP. Such expedient alliances were common practice in Sri Lanka. Generally, Marxists opposed the two policies of government support for Buddhism and preferential treatment for the Sinhalese that were centrepieces of Bandaranaike's program.[55]

Party organisations were modelled after their counterparts in the international Communist movement. A Central Committee, dominated by the leadership, was responsible for determining policy that was then communicated to rank and file members. As with other Sri Lankan parties, personal loyalties to individual leaders were a more important basis of support than organisation. Relatively small membership, shifting loyalties and limited financial resources made it difficult for any of the Marxist parties to develop an effective grass roots organisation, although individual workers were quite successful in some villages. In fact, the largest of the parties, the LSSP, never contested more than 39 of the 95 parliamentary constituencies during this period.[56] Labour unions, to be discussed below, constituted the parties' greatest source of organisational strength but were not particularly effective in mass mobilisation or election campaigning.

Marxist party supporters were found largely in Sri Lanka's more urbanised South and West and among lower level wage earners in both the public and private sectors. These workers tended to have higher levels of literacy and greater exposure to "Western" ideas. University students and recent secondary school graduates, as in most Third World nations, were also receptive to Marxist appeals. Buddhism and other traditions were less strong among these segments of society. Further, class differences emphasised by Marxists were more apparent in urbanised areas and to those with access to radios and newspapers. In urban areas, moreover, Marxist parties were quite effective in organising discussion groups and social activities that would appeal to young people. Some Marxist leaders would later play a major role in shaping Sri Lanka's domestic policies, but emergence of the communally oriented SLFP forever ended the hope of the Marxist parties to become a dominant political force.

Emergent communalism: the 'Sinhala Only movement' and the SLFP

The SLFP's rise from a modest faction within the UNP coalition in 1947 to the dominant party in the 1956 general election testifies to the power of communal issues, the charisma of S.W.R.D. Bandaranaike's leadership and the ineptitude of its opponents. It also lends weight to instrumentalist views, discussed in chapter 3, about the 'construction' of communal identities.

Bandaranaike first discovered the power of communal appeals when he toured the island as a member of the State Council between 1934 and 1936. He discovered that appeals on behalf of Sinhalese language, religion, culture and interests caught the imagination of people who had been previously apathetic. This was particularly true of some influential rural leaders, for example Sinhala medium school teachers and ayurvedic (traditional medicine) physicians.[57] This motivated Bandaranaike to hold preparatory meetings which, in 1936, led to the formation of the *Sinhala Maha Sabha* (Great Sinhalese Union). This new political association came to be dominated by Sinhalese cultural revivalists. Its stated goals envisioned a Sri Lankan nation dominated by Sinhalese culture and language and by Buddhism (with which Sinhalese culture was inextricably linked).[58] Although Bandaranaike viewed himself as a moderate, he was soon speaking on behalf of a 'genuine nationalism [that] could only emerge from common language, culture, customs, history and Race'.[59] Even while Bandaranaike served as D.S. Senanayake's Minister of Local Government, he continued to speak out independently on communal issues and to take positions that differed strongly from the Prime Minister's view of a secular, multi-ethnic Sri Lankan nation.[60]

Bandaranaike's resignation from the UNP in the summer of 1951 reflected both ideological and personal differences with the UNP inner circle. He had been a supporter of reform within the cabinet, advocating strengthened social programs, greater use of vernacular languages, decentralised administration and special status for Buddhism. But personal rivalries and an abrasive personal style made it difficult for him to make common cause with other reformist cabinet members such as Dudley Senanayake and J.R. Jayewardene. By resigning from the government and founding the SLFP, Bandaranaike acknowledged that his goal of becoming Sri Lanka's Prime Minister could never be achieved under UNP auspices.

D.S. Senanyake's death and the 1952 general election occurred before Bandaranaike had the opportunity to fully crystallise either his party organisation or program. It was not until 1956 that the issues of "Sinhala only" and special status for Buddhism assumed centre stage. In 1952, the party's platform emphasised a broad range of programs and issues designed to appeal to Sinhalese national sentiment. Bandaranaike advocated economic programs that would improve the well-being of Sinhalese peasants, including the repatriation of estate workers so that their jobs could be made available to the Sinhalese. He promised "socialist" reforms that would tax the rich, nationalise basic industries and solve the problem of unemployment. He proposed a new constitution, arguing that the Soulbury constitution reflected colonial influences rather than Sinhalese national character. Indigenous languages, *both Tamil and Sinhalese,* were to be promoted to official status.[61]

According to some observers, the Sinhala Buddhist revival of the mid-1950s occurred largely independently of the SLFP.[62] It was motivated by a combination of economic issues, the growing strength of the *swabasha* (indige-nous language) movement, rising religious consciousness related to the *Buddha Jayanthi* and Prime Minister Kotelawala's shortcomings. Leaders of this move-ment were 'political Buddhist priests (*bhikkhus*), Buddhist intellectuals, Sinhala language schoolteachers, *ayurvedic* (traditional medicine) physicians and leaders of local village organisations.[63] By 1955, however, Bandaranaike had formed an alliance with the advocates of cultural revival. His policy of elevating both indigenous languages to official status had been replaced by advocacy of Sin-hala as the *only* official language. His advocacy of government support for Bud-dhism had become explicit and his attacks upon Sri Lanka's Tamil minorities had become increasingly strident. The SLFP's electoral victory provided strong evidence that language, religion and ethnicity could be powerful tools for politi-cal mobilisation in Sri Lanka.

The SLFP's rudimentary organisational structure reinforces this conclu-sion. It was perhaps the most personalised of Sri Lanka's political parties in a political culture where personalised parties were the norm. In the months following his resignation and the SLFP's founding, Bandaranaike campaigned tirelessly, especially in rural areas where he believed the UNP to be weak. In contrast to UNP politicians, he drove a battered Austin, often travelled alone and mixed freely with local villagers. But his attempts to build a grassroots party organisation were largely unsuccessful. Bandaranaike did begin to build a personal following of able young leaders for whom neither the UNP nor the leftist parties seemed to offer any real opportunity.[64] The SLFP was only able to field 48 candidates for 95 parliamentary seats in 1952, but its popular vote total of more than 350,000, second only to the UNP, testifies to both Bandara-naike's effectiveness and the timeliness of his issues he was raising.

Although Sri Lanka's political and economic life has always had a strong Colombo-centric bias, most Sri Lankans lived in rural areas. The SLFP was strongest in rural areas inhabited by Sinhalese. It was in these areas that Bandaranaike had campaigned most diligently, where the issues of language and Buddhist revivalism carried greatest weight and where indigenous groups supporting his candidacy were most influential.

The 35,000 plus teachers in Sinhalese day schools (comprising 70 per cent of all teachers on the island)[65] provided a strong support network They be-lieved that establishing Sinhala as the sole official language would reverse their second class status in wages and facilities and open up new economic opportunities for their students. Sinhala medium (language) students, who were filling the ranks of the unemployed in growing numbers, were barred from most of the high paying high prestige positions in the government service, where business was done in English. Unemployed or underemployed recent graduates made good campaigners. They had motivation, energy and time for political activities. Resentment at second-class status for Sinhalese was reinforced when villagers had to deal with government bureaucrats and a justice system in a language they did not fully understand or understand at all in many cases.

Ayurvedic physicians, a second cadre of Bandaranaike supporters, numbered between 7, 000 to 10,000. Like the teachers, they worked primarily in Sinhala and were personally close to people in rural areas. Ayurvedic medicine and Sinhalese culture were closely intertwined.[66] The physicians felt threatened by a government health system that had downplayed ayurvedic traditions and was drawing away their patients to Western-style medicine by providing free services at subsidised clinics.[67] As early as 1954, organisations representing these groups, along with Buddhist priests and peasant leaders, had banded together in a loose federation, to promote 'Sinhala only.'

In urban areas, the issues of language and Sinhala-Buddhist cultural revival drew not only Buddhist intellectuals, but also some small businessmen into the ranks of SLFP supporters. The latter group were men whose commercial success, because of language or caste prejudices, had not been matched by social acceptance. Under Bandaranaike, they believed, there would be a new social order that was more egalitarian, but non-Marxist. They contributed funds and organisational skills to the SLFP in areas that had been strongholds of the left-wing parties or the UNP.

Many leading Buddhist priests opposed political action[68], but a new breed of politically active *Bhikkhus* became active SLFP supporters.[69] Justification for their activities came from a report of the All Ceylon Buddhist Congress entitled (in its English version) *The Betrayal of Buddhism*. The report claimed that Sri Lanka's post-independence governments had been complicit in a process that had reduced the status and strength of Buddhism on the island to a perilous state.[70] Groups of younger *Bhikkhus*, clad in their distinctive saffron robes, canvassed for SLFP candidates in the weeks prior to election day.[71] This type of canvassing was particularly effective in rural areas where traditional values were strong.

Sinhalese political mobilisation under the banners of "Sinhala only" and the Sinhala-Buddhist cultural revitalisation inevitably evoked a counter-mobilisation in Sri Lanka's North and East. The moderate Tamil Congress and Tamil politicians who had favoured accommodation with the UNP were discredited as "Sinhala only" became the pledge of both major parties and Tamil bashing became a campaign staple of many Sinhalese politicians.

The Tamil response: from accommodation to 'federalism'

With less than 13 per cent of Sri Lanka's population, Sri Lanka Tamils had no chance to command a parliamentary majority. Geographic separation plus caste and cultural differences made co-operation with the Tamil plantation workers difficult. At the time of independence, Tamils did have the advantage of a highly literate population and a disproportionate number of positions in government service, law and medicine.

Basically, two political options seemed open: coalition building with a Sinhalese party in hopes of sharing the benefits of political power, or a communally-oriented strategy that would protect Tamil interests by achieving a degree of regional autonomy. G.G. Ponnambalam, leader of the Tamil Congress, advocated coalition building with the dominant UNP. S.L.V. Chelvanayakam, founder of the Federal Party, favoured the communal strategy.[72] The decision of Sinhalese politicians in both the SLFP and UNP to pursue communal politics secured the Federal Party's dominant position among Sri Lanka Tamils in the North and, to a lesser degree, in the East.

Ponnambalam and Chelvanayakam had both contested the 1947 elections under the Tamil Congress banner, gaining eight out of nine seats in the Northern Province and one out of seven in the East. In 1948, Ponnambalam joined D.S. Senanayake's cabinet as Minster of Commerce and Industry, but was unable to obtain a post for his lieutenant, Chelvanayakam.[73] When Ponnambalam did not oppose the government's legislation stripping Indian Tamils of their citizenship rights, Chelvanayakam resigned from Tamil Congress and, in 1949, formed the Federal Party.[74] A resolution passed at the party's inaugural convention rejected Ponnambalam's accommodationist strategy. Federal Party leaders were not specific about their concept of federalism, but broad political, economic and linguistic autonomy for 'the traditional Tamil homelands,' comprising the Island's Northern and Eastern provinces, was the centrepiece of their program.[75]

Initially, the Federal Party did not win wide support among Tamils in the North and East. Although Ponnambalam was denounced by some as a "traitor to the Tamil cause,"[76] his spirited, though unsuccessful, defence of Tamil rights during the pre-independence period was still widely respected. Moreover, as minister, he had been able to deliver some tangible benefits to the North. In the 1952 general election, the Tamil Congress-UNP coalition defeated the Federal Party soundly.

By the 1956 election, the position of the two parties was reversed. Sir John dropped Ponnambalam from the cabinet when he succeeded Dudley Senanayake as Prime Minister. By 1955, both major parties were attempting to outdo each other in advocating communal policies and denouncing the Tamils. This lent credence to Chelvanayakam's warnings, discredited Ponnambalam, intensified the separatist rhetoric of Tamil politicians and drove moderate Tamils into the ranks of Federal Party supporters. The 'ethnic' polarisation of Sri Lankan politics had begun. The Federal Party polled 142,036 votes in the 1956 general election, made strong gains in the volatile Eastern province and sent 10 representatives to Parliament. The Tamil Congress nominated only one candidate, Ponnambalam himself, (who was re-elected by his loyal Jaffna constituents) and polled only 8,914 votes. From 1956 until the early 1980s, when leadership of Tamil politics would be seized by far more militant forces, the Federal Party and its successor, the Tamil United Liberation Front, would be the dominant political voice of the Sri Lanka Tamils.

Labour unions as political actors

Labour unions also played a political role in Sri Lanka, although they became more influential after the 1956 general election.[77] At the time of independence, perhaps a third of Sri Lanka's 2.7 million labour force could be classified as wage earners and thus potentially receptive to the appeals of trade union organisers. Sri Lanka was unusual in that the majority of its wage earners, about 75 per cent, were estate workers, mostly Indian immigrants. The remaining wage-earners were found largely in urban areas, employed in manufacturing, transport, services and the public sector.[78] Trade union membership grew from about 160,000 in 1948 to more than 300,000 in 1956.[79]

The largest trade union by far was the Ceylon Workers Congress (CWC), representing the Indian Tamil estate workers. Membership may have approached 200,000 before it split into two factions in 1956.[80] Initially, the CWC was affiliated with the estate workers' political party, the Ceylon Indian Congress. The party contested eight seats in the 1947 general election and won seven, but political campaigning became irrelevant after 1949. Now proscribed from direct political influence, the CWC concentrated more on traditional labour issues, wages and working conditions, and on strengthening its internal organisation. A number of strikes were held, but demands were strongly resisted by the estate owners who were then well-organised and supported by a sympathetic government. In 1952 the CWC orchestrated a 140-day *satyagraha* to protest the new citizenship regulations, but with no tangible results.

Most urban labour unions had either formal or informal ties with Marxist political parties. (Later, the SLFP and even the UNP would also form their own labour unions.)[81] Examples were the Government and Clerical Service Unions, affiliated with the LSSP and the Public Service Workers Trade Union Federation, affiliated with the Communist Party (Moscow-wing). Like the Marxist parties, Sri Lankan trade unions tended to be small, shaped by strong personalities and prone to fragmentation. Workers might join unions for economic reasons, but union leaders with party affiliations were often able to involve some of them in political action. During election campaigns, unions provided campaign workers with offices for meeting places and ready-made audiences to whom candidates could appeal.[82] Sometimes union members could be mobilised for demonstrations or to disrupt the functions of rival unions and candidates.[83]

Was polarisation inevitable?

Like Gandhi in India, D.S. Senanayake may have recognised, better than most, what might be the dangers of injecting communalism into Sri Lanka's political discourse. The grievances of the Sinhalese were real. Apart from an elite class who often seemed more British than the British themselves, Sinhalese had lived as second-class citizens in their own country throughout the colonial period. UNP economic policies improved their well-being but the opportunities that independence and democracy seemed to offer raised their expectations more. In S.W.R.D. Bandaranaike, the Sinhalese had a leader who heightened consciousness, articulated a vision of a Sinhalese dominated Sri Lanka, and provided an organisation through which that vision could be manifest, politically. Sir John Kotelawala was no match for him. Bandaranaike's movement offered the possibility of meaningful change, a democratic error-correction that would bring Sinhalese into the political mainstream. But the movement was also destabilising. It heightened political differences and pushed Tamil politicians to take the first steps down the road toward militancy.

I noted earlier that politicians do make a difference. When he belatedly realised the threat Bandaranaike's movement posed, Sir John Kotelawala chose to play Bandaranaike's game, embracing strident communalism and rejecting the

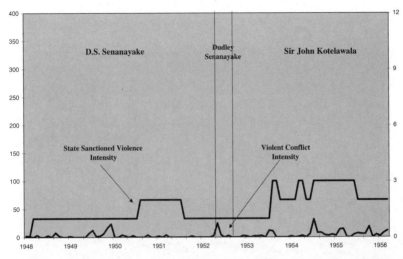

Figure 6.4 State-Sanctioned Violence and Violent Conflict Intensity

centrist, secular philosophy of the party's founder. His decision, represented in our model by destabilising feedbacks from leadership and political feedback, reinforced the communalist political discourse that Bandaranaike had initiated. Under D.S. Senanayake's leadership, or even that of Dudley Senanayake, the UNP would almost certainly have responded to Buddhist-Sinhalese concerns and those of Tamils as well with more deftness and sensitivity. The momentum of polarisation might have been slowed, if not stalled. Bandaranaike's movement made the heightening of identities, both Sinhalese and Tamil, inevitable, but it might have been channelled more constructively.

State-sanctioned violence

State-sanctioned violence, we saw in chapter 5, can have either a stabilising or destabilising impact. During this period, its impact was preponderantly stabilising, but modest. State violence intensity remained low (Figure 6.4). This reflected both low levels of violent conflict and a government that was basically committed to civil liberties, an uncensored press and open political competition. Police and military force effectiveness was sufficient for the tasks they were called upon to perform.

The political use of state-sanctioned violence was not entirely absent. Like other parties, the UNP occasionally used goon squads to intimidate opponents and settle political scores, but reports of such activity were sporadic.[84]

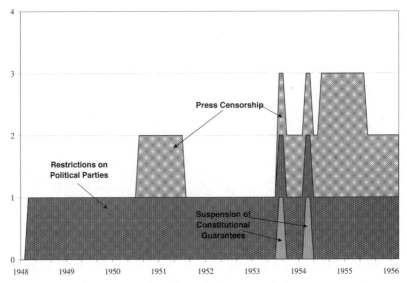

Figure 6.5 State-Sanctioned Violence Components

Emergency regulations were briefly imposed in 1953 and 1954 to deal with specific problems, but quickly relaxed. There were no reports of arrests, exiles or assassinations. Figure 6.5 shows how each of the four state-sanctioned violence indices contributed to the overall scoring. I should emphasise again that these scorings and plots are important for the long-term qualitative patterns they show, not specific numerical values.

Disenfranchisement of Indian Tamil Estate workers, described above, was an exception to an otherwise tolerant policy toward dissent and opposition. Stretching Duff and McCamant's definition (see chapter 4, above) I have scored this as a 'level 1' restriction on political parties.[85] Later, Prime Minister Kotelawala's government closed down two Marxist party printing operations. Subsequently police raided the offices of two radical newspapers and seized 'communist' literature. The anti-Communist Prime minister labelled the offending organisations 'agents of a foreign power.' Emergency regulations were imposed on two occasions, but quickly lifted. Later governments would keep states of emergency in force long after circumstances motivating the suspension of constitutional guarantees had passed. By no stretch of the imagination could Sri Lanka's government be labelled 'repressive' during this period.

The security forces

Even had political leaders been inclined towards repressiveness, the institutions available for this purpose were modest in size and limited in capabilities. The British trained police force numbered less than 6,000 at the time of independence and did not increase greatly.[86] They had adequate training for performing normal duties in a relatively tranquil society. They were generally free from corruption and respected by the public. However, they were ill prepared to manage large-scale demonstrations. Burghers, Tamils and Sinhalese Christians[87] dominated the officer corps. Most were committed to the non-political character of the force, but generally sympathetic to the UNP.

The military forces were similarly modest in size and capability. At the time of independence, Sri Lanka had no army, navy or air force, relying instead upon Great Britain for protection. The first army units were formed in 1949. In 1950, Navy and Air Force units were organised. Officers and non-commissioned officers were largely drawn from Sri Lankans who had previously served in the British armed forces. Sri Lanka's leaders had no pretensions that these token forces would allow it to play a significant international role. While other Third World nations were allocating 30 per cent or more of government budgets to the military, Sri Lanka's allocation was less than five per cent. Apart from ceremonial duties, internal security, control of illegal immigration and attempting (mostly unsuccessfully) to catch smugglers were the armed forces' principal missions. In 1956, total manpower numbered less than 6,000.[88]

Neither the police nor the military forces could be counted upon as instruments of repression; they could only be counted upon to maintain public order in a relatively peaceful society. One major challenge to public order, the *hartal* of 1953, stretched the forces beyond the limits of their capabilities. Excessive violence in responding to the strike contributed to the resignation of the Prime Minister. Nonetheless, most still viewed the security forces as free of political taint and relatively impartial protectors of public order when the UNP concluded its term in office.

Political feedback – electoral support patterns

Political feedback was taken seriously by citizens and political leaders in Sri Lanka. In this respect, the island nation conformed to the 'stable democracy' model. Politically aware Sri Lankans saw elections as an effective way of securing benefits from government, expressing opposition and affecting political change. Members of Parliament and government officials were held accountable on polling day for their effectiveness in dispensing government services and political favours. A degree of "thuggery" was accepted as normal, especially during political campaigns[89], but elections were widely viewed as fair and free.

Examining elections returns points to four observations about patterns of support for and opposition to major parties during this period:

1. Neither the UNP, nor the SLFP, which succeeded it as the *dominant* party in Parliament, were *majority* parties. More Sri Lankans voted for candidates opposing the winning party in the first three general elections than for winning party candidates.

2. Though the SLFP did not gain an absolute majority of votes in the 1956 election, the movement away from the UNP was substantial. However, despite its shortcomings, the UNP retained the allegiance of many Sri Lankans.

3. Sri Lanka's single member district system tended to inflate the number of seats held by the dominant party. Minority views in the electorate were underrepresented in Parliament.

4. Patterns of electoral support and opposition were very different in the Northern and Eastern provinces from those in the rest of Sri Lanka. Moreover, Northern and Eastern Province voting patterns were very different from one another.

Figure 6.6 pictures per cent vote totals for the 1947, 1952 and 1956 general elections. In 1947 there was no single, credible alternative to the UNP. Yet despite this and D.S. Senanayake's personal popularity, the UNP received less than 40 per cent of the vote overall and gained an absolute majority in only three of Sri Lanka's nine provinces. The large vote total for communally oriented Tamil parties included more than 70,000 votes from Tamil plantation workers who, soon after the election, were disenfranchised. In 1952, the UNP increased its percentage but by less than five per cent. This was despite sentimental support for D.S. Senanayake's son in the months following his death and removal of Indian Tamil voters (most of whom had voted against the UNP) from the rolls. SLFP candidates gained at the expense of the Marxist parties and independents.

In 1956, the SLFP-led coalition gained votes from the UNP and some Marxist parties (others were allied with the SLFP in no contest pacts), but did less well than had the UNP in 1952. Despite Buddhist revivalism, the 'Sinhala only' issue, Kotelawala's unpopularity and Bandaranaike's charisma, the UNP received more than 27 per cent of the votes, even though it did not contest

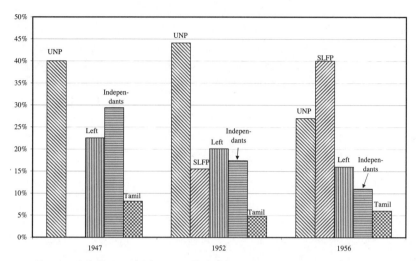

Figure 6.6 General Election Results: Percent Vote Totals

in either the Northern or Eastern provinces. All of these results point to a relatively stable body of public opinion that may have been less susceptible to extremist appeals than many Sri Lankan politicians supposed. The SLFP made remarkable strides filling the vacuum created by the Marxist parties' lack of credibility as an opposition, but the UNP retained a solid and substantial base of support.

'Electoral rules of the game' dictated that this base of support would not be well represented in Parliament after 1956, for two reasons. First, the SLFP made its most substantial gains in rural areas where each MP represented a relatively smaller number of voters. In the Western Province (where Colombo is located), for example, each MP represented 52,000 registered voters in 1956. Parliamentarians from rural Uva Province, located on the Southeastern part of the island, represented only 19,000 voters. Even more important, Sri Lanka's system of single member districts overweighed parliamentary representation in favour of the majority party. The UNP had been the beneficiary of this system in 1947 and 1952, but its delegation of 8 MPs was smaller than the 10 member delegation of Chelvanayakam's Federal Party after the 1956 debacle. This meant that a parliamentary majority could enact policies that might be opposed by a substantial minority or even a majority of Sri Lankans.

The fact that the Federal Party, which received less that 150,000 votes, was represented by 10 members of Parliament, while the UNP which received more than 700,000 had only eight parliamentarians highlights political differences between the Tamil majority regions and the rest of the island. Results also reflected the differing communal composition of the two Tamil majority provinces. In the Northern Province more than 82 per cent of population were Sri Lanka Tamils. In the East, Tamils were the largest communal group, but there were also substantial Sinhalese and Muslim populations. As communal issues came to dominate political debate in the 1956 election, this was reflected in sharpened communal voting patterns.

In the Northern province Tamil parties dominated, although both the UNP and independent Tamil candidates contested some seats. Making Sinhalese Sri Lanka's only official language was a policy that not only provoked hostility but was, as a practical matter, impossible to implement. But these matters were of little concern to the rural Sinhalese living in the island's centre and south to whom the policy was intended to appeal. Had those Sri Lankans visited the Jaffna Peninsula, it would have seemed an alien land, but they were not likely to do so.

Sri Lanka's multi-communal Eastern Province posed complex problems for political leaders and continues to do so. It commands much of the island's eastern coastline, including the incomparable natural port of Trincomalee.[90] It has been the focus of major irrigation projects. "Colonisation" of Sinhalese from the densely populated wet zone has been encouraged by the government and resisted by Tamil political leaders. The entire province is claimed by Tamil nationalists as part of the "traditional homelands of the Tamil people," a claim hotly disputed by Sinhalese politicians and historians as well as by Muslim and Sinhalese residents.[91] Prior to independence, the province's different communal groups lived in relative harmony, although there were sporadic outbreaks of violence. D.S. Senanayake's model of a multi-ethnic secular state was supported by many. But by 1956, the success of Bandaranaike's mobilisation strategy for the Sinhalese was beginning to polarise Eastern Province politics and poison relations between its ethnic groups.

Electoral results from the Eastern Province's seven electoral districts illustrate this transformation clearly. In 1947 three of seven seats, including one constituency with a Tamil majority, were won by the UNP. The Tamil Congress, which would shortly join the government, won one seat. In 1952, the

UNP actually increased its vote total[92] in the province but won only two parliamentary seats. The Federal Party replaced the Tamil Congress in Trincomalee district. In 1956, as noted above, neither the UNP nor the SLFP chose to run candidates in the East. Four seats, including two from districts with Muslim majorities, were won by the Federal Party and a fifth by a communally oriented splinter party. In the space of three years, advocacy of Buddhist-Sinhalese nationalism by Sri Lanka's major parties had communalised and radicalised the politics of the Eastern province.

Sinhalese politicians had realised by 1955 that Sinhalese-Buddhist nationalism could be a powerful mobilising force. Tamils viewed promises of 'Sinhala only' as excluding them from effective participation in the political process and reneging on promises made at the time of independence. They responded by giving their support to communal parties and groping for a new political strategy that would protect their political rights and economic position. The failure of the Sinhalese parties to contest the Northern and Eastern Provinces in 1956 was symbolic.[93] From the standpoint of Sinhalese politicians, Tamil Sri Lankans were increasingly viewed as politically irrelevant. This tactically expedient decision would ultimately prove to be a strategic disaster.

For many Sinhalese, however, 1956 was a turning point that reinforced their belief in the efficacy of democratic political institutions. Bandaranaike's supporters believed that the newly elected government could provide economic opportunity and increase government benefits to the Sinhalese, restore Buddhism to its rightful place and narrow class differences. Opposition to policies that had guided the nation since independence could be expressed with ballots, not bullets. Bandaranaike entered office with high expectations. High expectations benefit those campaigning for office, but not necessarily those entrusted with the responsibility of governance. The new government's challenge was to fulfil the expectations they had created and to prevent those who would be losers in the new political economic order from disrupting it.

Conclusion

Two conjectures began this discussion of independent Sri Lanka's first eight years. First was that effective democratic feedback and error correction explained low levels of conflict. The alternative attributed low conflict levels more to delays than successful development and democratic institutions. The reality seems somewhere in between.

Having gained power through a peaceful transition and with solid finances, the UNP government made strides in increasing economic output, meeting the basic needs of its people and creating stable, responsive political institutions. Opposition to the government and desires for fundamental change could be expressed in an uncensored press, open campaigning and free elections. Yet many Sinhalese felt post-independence reforms had not gone far enough in redressing inequities of the colonial era and effecting fundamental changes. S. W.R.D. Bandaranaike's reformist platform catered to their aspirations and their resentments.

The 1956 general election tested democratic institutions and they performed effectively. New leaders gained power promising revolutionary change, but the transition to new leadership was non-violent. It was a revolution of the ballot, not the bullet. Sri Lanka's new leaders now faced the challenge of maintaining gains already achieved and delivering on their promises.

The revolution of 1956 was not, however, a revolution that was intended to benefit all Sri Lankans. Its most important feature, the promise of 'Sinhala only,' was a promise to re-distribute economic and political benefits to Sri Lanka's majority community by withdrawing them from the nation's most populous minority community, the Sri Lankan Tamils. Thus, Sri Lanka's leaders faced two contradictory challenges. First, they would have to meet heightened Sinhalese expectations that had partly been created by political mobilisation and general election campaigning. Failure to do so would raise deprivation levels in the majority community. On the other hand, meeting Sinhalese expectations was certain to raise feelings of deprivation and intensify communally oriented mobilisation of Sri Lankan Tamils. Since both major party leaders had promised to curtail Sri Lankan Tamil rights and reduce their political power, resentments in this community were likely to be expressed in support for more radical movements and a heightened potential for violence. Dealing with these divisive consequences of 'Sinhala only' was the second challenge that Sri Lanka's new leaders would face.

7
Opening Pandora's Box – The Bandaranaike Era Begins

S.W.R.D. Bandaranaike's term marked the beginning of a 'poisonous' cycle in Sri Lankan politics that has worked to polarise society along communal lines. When in power, leaders of both parties have seen the need for reasonable concessions to Sri Lanka Tamils in order to maintain national unity. But when in opposition, these same leaders have become uncompromising advocates of Sinhalese nationalism in order to gain political support.

Popular expectations soared as S.W.R.D. Bandaranaike's government took office in April 1956. Members of the new cabinet were sworn in wearing national dress.[1] Traditional dishes and fruit juice replaced the liquor and Western fare that had been served at official functions. It was announced that the first 'Speech from the Throne' would be given in Sinhala rather than English.[2]

> On the day the new Parliament opened, people from distant villages crowded into the galleries and when the proceedings ended, they pushed their good-humoured way onto the floor of the House. With cries of 'Now we are the government,' they took turns sitting in the Speaker's chair. 'From the well of the Chamber they gazed upwards into the galleries and from the galleries the remaining MPs and guests looked back at them.' For this moment of mild bewilderment at least it seemed (in a much used phrase) that *ape anduwa* 'our government'—had arrived.[3]

S.W.R.D. Bandaranaike, the self styled 'people's prime minister' is remembered by admirers as a visionary leader, champion of the less privileged, and also a tragic figure, cut down in his prime by an assassin's bullets. Critics describe him as a demagogue, lacking in principle, whose policies opened the Pandora's Box of communal strife in Sri Lanka.[4] Bandaranaike's electoral triumph, pro-Sinhalese policies and tragic death made his 40 month regime pivotal in Sri

Lankan history. Bandaranaike's successor, his aristocratic, strong willed-widow, Sirimavo, gave her husband's brief tenure as Prime Minister legendary proportions and made his policies a permanent part of Sri Lanka's national life.

Conflict patterns during this period exhibit some intensification, but appear to be counteracted by an effective 'homeostatic response.' Despite the assassination of a popular Prime Minister and an attempted security force (army and police) coup, conflict did not escalate out of control. Both the intensification and apparent stabilisation need to be explained. Was conflict intensification more a product of divisive populist and ethno-nationalist appeals or a delayed response to failed development policies of the UNP? Did conflict remain within tolerable bounds because of government responsiveness and security force effectiveness or because of delays in mobilising more militant sentiments among government opponents? Did the policies of successive Bandaranaike governments promote 'successful development' or fail to do so? Did they sustain Sri Lanka's democratic institutions or catalyze destabilising linkages that could weaken them?

Violent political conflict within bounds

By any measure, the 1956-1965 period witnessed a several-fold intensification of political conflict. Comparing this period's 'fever chart' (Figure 7.1) with its predecessor (Figure 6.1) shows the transformation from a relatively tranquil to a more turbulent society that all chroniclers of the Bandaranaike years have described. As in Chapter 6, I will focus on conflict 'peaks' as a way of presenting some details of this turbulence. 'Peaks,' readers will recall, appear in the topology of our charts during periods of a month or more when an unusually large number of conflict incidents and/or incidents of high intensity occur. Events in a peak need not be related, but do highlight types of incidents that were more prevalent in a particular time period.

Five 'peaks' stand out during S.W.R.D. Bandaranaike's administration. In 1956 and 1957, communal conflict was sparked by Tamil demonstrations against the government's language policy. In 1958, Sinhalese demonstrated against the Prime Minister's compromise on Tamil-minority rights (the Bandaranaike-Chelvanayakam pact)[5] and then Sri Lanka Tamils demonstrated against his decision to back away from his compromise. Most communal conflict episodes began with peaceful demonstrations organised by the Federal Party, by Sinhalese dominated political parties or by Sinhalese militant groups, however there was an increasing tendency for some participants, especially Tamil and

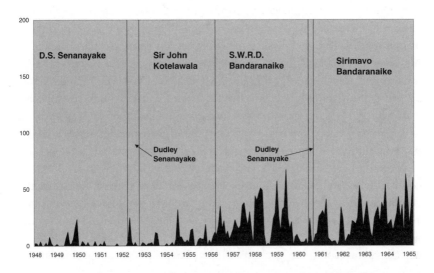

Figure 7.1 Violent Conflict Intensity: April 1956 – March 1965

Sinhalese youth, to become violent. In Tamil majority areas, particularly in the multi-ethnic Eastern Province, mobs and gangs would attack Sinhalese homes and shops, as well as government installations. In Colombo and other Sinhalese majority areas, there were similar attacks against Tamils. Attacks by members of one community in areas where they were dominant evoked retaliatory attacks by members of the other community in areas where *they* were dominant. Often, the victims of attacks were innocent shop owners and householders, who had lived in harmony with neighbours belonging to other ethnic groups for years and had no particular desire to become politically involved.

Strikes in the commercial, public and estate sectors contributed to the overall climate of conflict in 1956-1958 and became the principal components of conflict 'peaks' during final year of S.W.R.D. Bandaranaike's administration. The strongest public sector and industrial-commercial unions in urban areas were Marxist oriented with either indirect or direct links to Marxist political parties. Bandaranaike's government supported union membership and legislation favouring 'worker rights.'

Where UNP governments had used the security forces to control (sometimes even break) strikes and pro-labour demonstrations, 'people's government' ministers instructed the police and army to adopt a more tolerant attitude. Paradoxically, the resulting growth in union strength and pre-disposition to strike encouraged Marxist party leaders to use strikes as a weapon against the Prime Minister. The rash of public sector strikes in April-July 1959, which at times brought the island's economy to a halt, were largely motivated by the Marxist parties' desire to punish Bandaranaike for making concessions to conservative members of his government. By reducing the credibility of the government, strike leaders hoped both to extract concessions from a leader perceived to be pliable and to gain support among voters for upcoming general elections.[6]

A pattern of public sector political strikes is repeated in seven peaks of conflict during Sirimavo Bandaranaike's administration. A small fraction of the conflict incidents that took place during the turbulent years from 1960 through 1965 involved communal or religious issues, but the overwhelming majority were motivated by political-economic agendas of Marxist leaders. Indivisibility of politics and economics is, of course, central to the Marxist worldview, and Sri Lanka's government became, increasingly, the principal actor in the economy. Thus it is not surprising that the strike became an often-used tool of political action, directed at areas of high leverage and vulnerability such as transportation, telecommunications, petroleum distribution and especially the Colombo Port. In the last three years of Mrs. Bandaranaike's administration, not a single month passed without disruption from a political strike.

The preponderance of strikes as well as the increase in all forms of conflict during this period shows up in Figure 7.2, which compares numbers of conflict incidents in major categories during the two Bandaranaike governments and their UNP predecessors.[7] (As with fever charts, what is important about charts like this is qualitative order-of-magnitude distinctions, rather than specific numerical values.)[8] While there was nearly an eight-fold increase in the total number of conflict events, the number of strikes increased by nearly double that amount. Moreover the preponderance of strikes occurred in the capital city, where political leaders could not miss their impact on political stability and economic performance.

Only about six per cent of reported conflict events were 'communal' in nature. Sri Lankan Tamils experienced significant political deprivation during the Bandaranaike years, but far reaching changes in government policy regarding language and religion may have had little impact on Tamils daily lives, especially in the overwhelmingly Tamil North. With the exception of a small

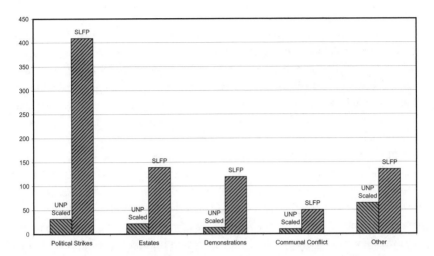

Figure 7.2 Conflict Incident Frequencies: SLFP (scaled) and UNP Governments Compared

number of youth, Tamils did not adopt violence as a strategy. They continued to look, by and large, to relatively conservative Federal Party leaders to organise peaceful demonstrations and remedy their grievances within the framework of the nation's established political processes.[9] Where communal conflicts did lead to violence, it was as likely to be produced by Sinhalese counter-demonstrations as by the Tamils.

Thus, while conflict intensity increased under successive Bandaranaike governments, the overall character of conflict events, described in Chapter Six as 'predominantly secular, urban and non-communal' changed much less. There appeared to be a continued commitment to democratic political processes. Indeed the increased intensity of violent conflict - apart from communal conflict - may have been due in part to the fact that political violence was tolerated and at times even encouraged by the government. During this period the security forces became less professional, more subject to political interference and, after a 1962 coup attempt, more Sinhalese-nationalist in outlook. The government's more tolerant attitude to strikes and violent tactics of its supporters replaced a generalised commitment to maintaining public order under the UNP. Our examination of state-sanctioned violence patterns, later in the chapter, will return to this theme.

Leadership and governance

Few politicians in any nation take campaign rhetoric seriously. In Sri Lanka, inflammatory political speechmaking is a tradition. There was a wide gap between S.W.R.D. Bandaranaike's campaign strategy and his conception of the Prime Minister's role as national leader. As candidate, he had used the issue of 'Sinhala only' to appeal to extremist groups, mobilise popular support and catalyze opposition to the UNP. Tamils were a convenient scapegoat for failures to quickly deliver on unrealised - and unrealistic - expectations of poor Sinhalese for a better life following independence. Making Sinhala the sole official language and recognising the special status of Buddhism represented easily understood, if simplistic remedies for complex social and economic problems.[10]

Once elected, Bandaranaikes sensitivity regarding communal issues more closely resembled the moderate Senanayakes than that of the Sinhalese nationalist factions whose support had been pivotal in bringing him to power.[11] He wanted to make government more responsive and egalitarian, but within the context of British liberal traditions, including protection for minority rights. He saw the Prime Minister's role as 'arbiter' between contending interests and factions in Sri Lanka's complex plural society and did not expect the promise to make Sinhala the sole national language 'within twenty-four hours' to be taken seriously.[12] As head of government, he expected to be given discretion and flexibility to implement promised language, religious and economic reforms in a spirit of 'fair play to all.' James Manor points to excessive generosity and an absence of political toughness as Bandaranaike's greatest shortcomings. By trying to please everyone, vacillating in the face of pressure and intervening personally in relatively minor matters, he squandered his authority.[13]

Making Sinhala Sri Lanka's 'official language'

Bandaranaike's shortcomings as leader were most tragically visible in the divisive area of language policy. The original draft of the Official Language Act, which the Prime Minister steered through his majority parliamentary group, combined establishment of Sinhala as the sole official language with provision for the 'reasonable use of Tamil.' But he backed down on the use of Tamil when Sinhalese extremists protested and one engaged in a brief hunger strike. Instead, the act provided only for a transition period, until December 31, 1960, during which Tamil could continue to be used for official purposes.

Introduction of the Act in Parliament provided a catalyst for the Federal Party to mobilise strident opposition by a Sri Lanka Tamil community already demoralised by pro-Sinhalese platforms of both major political parties. A general strike was declared in Tamil majority areas and Tamil demonstrators marched on Galle Face Green, opposite the Parliament Building. Pro-Sinhalese groups organised counter demonstrations that became violent; roving gangs of thugs stoned restaurants and looted shops in Colombo's commercial districts.[14] Sporadic communal violence also broke out in other cities: Efforts to maintain order stretched the resources of Sri Lanka's unarmed police force and largely ceremonial army to the limit. Already, the observation of one Tamil Parliamentarian seemed prophetic: 'One language, two countries,' he said, 'two languages, one country.'[15]

The drift toward 'two countries' quickened when the Federal Party convention, held later in the year, agreed on four demands as major platform planks. They included autonomy for Tamil majority provinces under a federal constitution, parity for Tamil as an official language, full citizenship for Indian Tamil estate workers and cessation of 'colonisation' programs that were moving Sinhalese migrants into Tamil majority areas. The party promised to initiate a program of 'direct action' should their demands be unmet within a year's time, on 1 August 1957.

The Prime Minister responded with negotiations that sought common ground between Sinhalese and Tamil demands. In consultation with leading Buddhist priests, he framed a proposal that included devolution of some central government power to newly created regional councils, constitutional amendments to safeguard minority rights and provisions for 'reasonable use of Tamil' within the scope of the Official Language Act.[16] Negotiations culminated with direct talks between Federal Party leader Chelvanayakam and the Prime Minister that produced an agreement, the ill-fated 'Bandaranaike-Chelvanayakam Pact,' on 25 July. Bandaranaike promised the pact would be submitted quickly to Parliament and Chelvanayakam called off direct action.

The pact's provisions, which included major concessions from Tamil leaders, represented a victory for the Prime Minister. In return for regional autonomy, far short of federalism, and an agreement to submit legislation providing for 'reasonable use' of Tamil, Chelvanayakam agreed to defer other demands. Bandaranaike also promised to give Tamil demands not covered by the pact his early attention.[17] With the immediate crisis averted, however, he turned his attention to other matters, allowing opposition to the pact from the UNP and from extremists within his own coalition to mobilise.

Faced with mounting opposition Bandaranaike first defended the pact. He travelled around the country making supportive speeches to large, friendly crowds and obtained a favourable, though divided vote from his cabinet. But at a critical juncture, he succumbed to the importuning of Buddhist priests who had engaged in a *satyagraha* near his private residence and refused to move until the act was rescinded. After negotiations, Bandaranaike agreed to announce dissolution of the pact to the nation on radio. The betrayed Tamil leader, Chelvanayakam, gathered his allies and laid plans for mass civil disobedience.

Standing aside from the Bandaranaike-Chelvanayakam pact weakened the Prime Minister, heightened communal tensions and strengthened the hands of extremist factions on both sides. It marked the beginning of what James Manor has called a 'poisonous' cycle in Sri Lanka politics[18] that polarised the society on communal lines. When in power, leaders of both parties have seen the need for reasonable concessions to Sri Lanka Tamils in order to maintain national unity. But when in opposition, these same leaders have become uncompromising advocates of Sinhalese nationalism in order to gain political support. Opposition to proposed compromises, often taking the form of disruptive violent demonstrations, has pushed successive Sri Lankan governments toward more extreme positions on communal issues, with tragic consequences. Moderate Tamil leaders have felt betrayed, and either radicalised their own positions or have been supplanted by proponents of more aggressive, violent responses.

At the end of May, incidents in the Tamil-majority Batticaloa district, and in the adjoining Sinhalese-majority Polonnaruwa district sparked communal violence that threatened to become island wide.[19] By 26 May, rumours of 'Tamil atrocities' had motivated harassment of Tamils by angry crowds throughout the Sinhalese majority areas and especially in the capital city, where numerous Tamil-owned shops were looted and burned.[20] Senior police officers, fearful that firm action would bring them before commissions of inquiry, were reluctant to intervene. Shortly after noon, a reluctant Bandaranaike finally acquiesced to a State of Emergency declaration. The declaration imposed a dusk to dawn curfew and press censorship. Public meetings, processions and strikes against essential services were banned. The Federal party and a Sinhalese extremist group were proscribed. More than 150 Federal Party members, including the entire parliamentary group, were arrested and detained. The armed forces were mobilised and both army and police were given extraordinary powers. Order was not restored until 3 June, 13 days after the first incidents had been reported.

Despite the relatively prompt restoration of order, emergency regulations were to remain in force until March of 1959, setting a precedent that would be emulated by subsequent governments.

The final acts of language policy under S.W.R.D Bandaranaike's administration continued the slow process of giving Sinhala official status while attempting to reach a widely acceptable compromise with the Tamils. In July 1958, the first Sinhala telephone directory was introduced. In August, with Federal Party MPs still in detention, Parliament agreed to the *Tamil Language (Special Provisions) Act*, which provided for use of Tamil in education, public service examinations and administration in the Northern and Eastern Provinces. In December, more than 10 years after independence, Parliament passed the first legislation to facilitate the use of Sinhala in the courts.

Giving Buddhism its 'rightful place'

'According to Buddhism its rightful place in the country' had been a second major campaign promise and like 'Sinhala only,' a major concern of groups that helped Bandaranaike gain power. To address this concern, while postponing action until the debate over language policy subsided, the *Buddha Sasana Commission*[21] comprising both priests and laymen, was appointed. Commissioners were given a broad mandate to investigate the vitality of Buddhist institutions, the reform of the priesthood and the relationship of Buddhism to the state. A contentious political issue was a constitutional provision that no law shall 'confer on persons of any community or religion any privilege or advantage which is not conferred on persons of other communities or religions.'[22]

The Commission took two years to prepare its report, which gave priority to establishing a government sponsored corporate governing body that would reform the priesthood and adjudicate disputes between contending factions. However the political environment in November 1959, when the report was released, had changed radically. A leading political faction of priests had been discredited as conspirators in the Bandaranaike assassination and the unity of the Buddhist revivalists had been fractured. Sirimavo Bandaranaike's government, preoccupied with other matters, did not follow up on the Commission's recommendations.

Political and social reforms

A third major concern of Bandaranaike's government was political and social reforms. Steps were undertaken to make the political system more accessible by reducing the cost of political campaigning and lowering the voting age to 18. The number of polling stations was increased, especially in rural areas, and by nationalising private bus companies, the government eliminated a major UNP advantage in getting its supporters to the polls.[23] A constitutional amendment was passed that redrew the boundaries of Parliamentary constituencies, increasing their number from 95 to 151.[24] A process was initiated to replace traditional village headmen with government officials (*grama seva niladharis*) recruited by examination.[25] A number of economic and agricultural reforms intended to move Sri Lanka in the direction of a more egalitarian and government-controlled economy, were also proposed and, in some cases, implemented.

Proposals for economic and social reform revealed a deep fissure in Bandaranaike's cabinet, which threatened the stability of the government in 1959. The ruling coalition was an improbable alliance of conservative, rural aristocrats who dominated the SLFP[26] and more cosmopolitan, left-wing social reformers who dominated Sri Lanka's oldest Marxist party, the LSSP. Cabinet members agreed on language reform, but were sharply divided on social and economic reforms, especially those intended to benefit rural smallholders. The superior abilities of the minority Marxist ministers, sometimes publicly acknowledged by the Prime Minster, made consensus-building more difficult.[27] The divisions came to a head over the Paddy Lands Bill, which proposed a major land re-distribution, and the Co-operative Bank Bill, which proposed establishing multi-purpose co-operatives for poor rural villagers. Both bills were introduced by the Minister of Agriculture and Food, LSSP leader Philip R. Gunawardena. Faced with conservative opposition from within his own party, the Prime Minister abandoned Goonewardene. The LSSP parliamentarians moved to the opposition benches, talking six left-leaning SLFP MPs with them. This left Bandaranaike with a bare majority and precipitated a cabinet crisis that was unresolved at the time of the Prime Minister's assassination.

Foreign Policy: Moving Sri Lanka toward 'non-alignment' and India

Maintaining foreign policy independence is a continual problem for small states that are located in geo-strategically sensitive regions. Meddling by 'great powers' can significantly impact domestic politics and political stability. The UNP governments' policies emphasised close ties to the West. Bandaranaike chose to become a leader of the emerging 'non-aligned movement,' gaining heightened international visibility both for himself and Sri Lanka.[28] Reversing Prime Minister Kotelawala's anti-Communist stance, Sri Lanka granted diplomatic recognition to the USSR, China and the Communist nations of Eastern Europe. Bandaranaike spoke eloquently on behalf of non-alignment and neutralism at meetings of Commonwealth ministers and at the UN General Assembly, distancing Sri Lanka from British foreign policy.[29] He established close personal ties with India's Nehru, drawing his views on non-alignment from Nehru's philosophy, but also maintained friendly relations with the other major powers in the region, China and Pakistan. No doubt the opportunity to function as a leader in the world diplomatic arena provided a welcome relief from the turbulence of Sri Lankan domestic politics.

On 25 September 1959 the forces that Bandaranaike helped unleash wrote a premature and tragic *finis* to his political career. At about 9:30 in the morning, the Prime Minister completed a meeting with the new American Ambassador and walked with him out to the veranda of his home, where the usual crowd of petitioners and well wishers waited. Among the crowd was the Venerable Talduwe Sonarama, a disgruntled Buddhist priest and ayurvedic physician who had been angered by the government's lack of support for traditional medicine and the slow pace of promised reforms.[30] As Bandaranaike bent towards the saffron robed assassin, hands clasped in the traditional gesture of greeting and respect, Sonarama drew a pistol and fired. Four shots entered the Prime Minister's body, causing mortal wounds.

For nearly 24 hours, it appeared that Bandaranaike might survive the assassin's bullets, as he had survived so many political challenges. Fully conscious, he was driven to the hospital in his official vehicle. He insisted on dictating a lengthy statement, urging Sri Lankans to show patience and restraint, before being taken into the surgery. The next morning, he met with the Governor General and was joking with his doctors when he had difficulty breathing and became unconscious. Within a few minutes, 'the people's Prime Minister' was dead.[31]

'Ape Mathiniyata Jayawewa' ('Hail and Praise to Our Mother')

Following Bandaranaike's death, the already fractured SLFP cabinet group, now dominated by conservatives, soon dissolved into squabbling factions. One faction was able to enlist the support of Bandaranaike's widow, who made tearful campaign appearances in her white mourning garments and urged voters to support those former cabinet colleagues who had remained loyal to her late husband's party and program. The election results provided no clear mandate. The UNP gained a plurality of the votes, with the SLFP a close second and Dudley Senanayake was asked to form a minority government. Within a month, Senanayake had lost a vote of confidence in the divided Parliament and asked the Governor General to schedule a new general election for July.

Sirimavo Bandaranaike's emergence as a formidable campaigner was the most important development of this interregnum period. It soon became apparent to SLFP leaders that only she, despite scant political experience, had the charisma to mobilise voter support in behalf of her husband's legacy and the stature to unite warring factions of his party. She agreed to become the SLFP President and led an SLFP- dominated coalition to a decisive general election victory. As cheering supporters shouted *'Ape Mathiniyata Jayawewa'* ('Hail and Praise to Our Mother'), Mrs. Bandaranaike was driven to Government House to be sworn in as Sri Lanka's – and the world's – first woman Prime Minister.[32] Over the next 40 years, she would be one of the two or three most influential figures in the island's politics. She would serve as Sri Lanka's Prime Minister for more than a third of that period.

Her background, prior to 1960, provided few clues to her subsequent political skill and stature. Sirimavo Ratwatte was raised in the conservative, traditional environment of the upland Kandyan aristocracy in rural Sabaragamuwa province.[33] Her father and maternal grandfather carried out the patriarchal, semi-feudal role of *Ratemahatamaya* (Headman) of Balangoda village, near the provincial capital of Ratnapura district. From the age of 8 until 19, she received her education at St. Bridget's Roman Catholic Convent in Colombo, afterwards returning home to live for six years with her parents until a suitable marriage could be arranged. Not surprisingly, her friends at St. Bridget's did not anticipate that the tall, reserved young woman would become Prime Minister, but they recalled qualities that would subsequently characterise her political style – steadfastness of purpose (which some described as stubbornness) – and attention to detail.[34] During the six years between school and marriage, she apparently became quite close to her father, Barnes Ratwatte, spending long hours with him as he walked on foot along jungle and mountain paths to visit the remote villages of his territory. Mrs. Bandaranaike reports that her upbringing and especially the circuits with her father bred empathy with the problems and aspirations of the rural poor.[35]

Sirimavo Ratwatte's marriage to S.W.R.D. Bandaranaike, was not only an alliance between two of Sri Lanka's best known *Goyigama* (landowning caste) families, but also between the conservative, traditional Kandyan aristocracy and the more sophisticated, cosmopolitan low country Sinhalese. That his alliance with the Ratwattes would enormously strengthen his political base in a vote-rich area that had been a Senanayake stronghold cannot have escaped the politically astute Bandaranaike.[36] Apart from political advantage, the aspiring politician had gained a helpmate with experience in managing a large household who had been trained from birth in the Buddhist marital ideals of *Pativata*.[87]

During their nineteen years of marriage, there is no evidence that Sirimavo Bandaranaike did more than provide 'matrimonial purity, faithfulness and devotion' to a husband whose unpredictable, frenetic lifestyle was often taxing and who showed scant respect for her intellectual abilities.[38] But when the time came for her to assume a leadership role, in a time of great personal and political crisis, she did so skilfully and effectively. She recognised and vowed not to emulate her husband's shortcomings of excessive idealism and generosity.[39] In fact her own shortcomings, inflexibility and a toughness that sometimes crossed the boundary to vindictiveness, were the opposite of her husband's.[40] She became custodian of the Bandaranaike legend and by skilfully nurturing that legend, probably far exceeded what S.W.R.D. Bandaranaike would have accomplished had he lived.

Mrs. Bandaranaike's policies

Language policy continued to be a major and socially divisive priority of Sri Lanka's government. Reneging on a pre-election pledge to the Federal Party, Mrs. Bandaranaike moved decisively to implement the Official Language Act, requiring that Sinhala become the language of administration throughout the island on 1 January 1961. Despite her pledge, her husband's oft-stated commitment to 'reasonable use of Tamil' and legislation already on the books, the new Prime Minister refused to make any concessions to Tamil demands.[41] Predictably, the Federal Party declared a civil disobedience campaign in Tamil majority provinces, to which Mrs. Bandaranaike responded by declaring a state of emergency and sending the army north to restore order. When the troops were dispatched on emergency duty, communalism was raised as a contentious issue in the Army's officer corps, for which apolitical British traditions had been a model. Two Tamil officers commanding the Third Artillery Regiment were relieved of their commands and replaced by an infantry officer, Mrs. Bandaranaike's relative and Sinhalese nationalist, Col. A.R. Udagama.[42]

On this occasion, Sri Lanka's traditions of civility and security force professionalism, still relatively strong, prevailed. Order was restored and the civil disobedience campaign subsided. Federal Party leaders, still dominant in Tamil politics, opted to continue with a political strategy, first by joining an abortive coalition government in 1964 and then by endorsing the UNP in the 1965 election. In a 1964 Parliamentary debate, however, the Federal Party Secretary spoke prophetically of the nation's growing communal divisions. 'If the leaders of the Sinhalese people persist in this attitude,' he said,

> '...when you will be advocating federalism, we will rather choose to have a division of this country even at the cost of several lifes (*sic.*)... We will rather have a division of this country than surrender as a nation without self-respect and be eternal slaves in this country.'[43]

Mrs. Bandaranaike's government also pressed forward with educational reform, a cause supported by the Buddhists on religious grounds and the Marxists on ideological grounds. Legislation was passed to secularise and bring under full government control the nation's publicly funded, but privately administered, denominational secondary schools. Nationalisation affected the schools of all religions, but the principal target was the prestigious Christian mission schools (including Mrs. Bandaranaike's alma mater, St. Bridget's). Education in one of these English-language schools, which hired few non-Christian teachers, was considered essential for students who aspired to top positions in government and business. Their elitism, proselytising and discrimination against non-Christians were regarded as intolerable by members of the parliamentary majority and their supporters. Sri Lanka's powerful Roman Catholic community, who were the biggest losers, bitterly opposed nationalisation, but to no avail.[44]

Under the leadership of the SLFP's Marxist coalition allies, the government's commercial and financial enterprises were also nationalised. The Bank of Ceylon was brought under government control and directed by the Finance Minister, 30-year-old Felix Dias Bandaranaike, 'to assist local enterprise in a more liberal way than it had done in the past.'[45] A newly created 'People's Bank' established branches in a number of smaller towns that had hitherto had no banking services. A 'Co-operative Wholesale Establishment' began taking over responsibility for the import and distribution of food and other essential commodities. Later, the petroleum and insurance industries were nationalised.

Mrs. Bandaranaike's policies and decisiveness in implementing them threatened entrenched interests in the business community, senior civil service and military. Increasingly, the Prime Minister was seen as a political figure in her own right rather than the legatee of her slain husband. In 1961, opposition leaders began to mobilise. Their increasing strength, reinforced by poor economic conditions and doubts about the competence of key ministers, might have threatened the government's viability were it not for a failed military coup, initiated by senior (and largely Christian) military officers and civil servants in January 1962.[46] Although the plotters appear to have been more concerned with preserving a secular national state in the model of D.S. Senanayake than with communal issues,[47] it was portrayed by the government as a pro-Christian, anti-Buddhist-Sinhalese movement. The coup reinvigorated both Buddhist-Sinhalese-nationalist and Marxist support for the government and, for a time, precluded any effective challenge from the right.[48] This enabled Mrs. Bandaranaike and her supporters to move forward more aggressively with programs of language reform, preferential treatment for Buddhism[49] and nationalisation initiated after the 1960 victory.

Regularising the Indian Tamils' status

In one area of communal relations, bridging domestic and foreign policy, the Prime Minister did achieve a notable success. This was the vexing status of the Indian Tamil estate workers, who had been disenfranchised and rendered stateless by the D.S. Senanayake government's citizenship legislation. By the time Mrs. Bandaranaike came to power, there had been more than 12 years of fruitless negotiations between Prime Minister Nehru and successive Sri Lankan governments. Nehru's death, and the more flexible stance of his successor, La Bahadur Shastri led, in 1964, to signing of the 'Sirima-Shastri' agreement providing for the repatriation of about 525,000 Tamil estate workers over a 15-year period, granting of Sri Lankan citizenship to 300,000 others and subsequent negotiations to resolve the fate of the remaining 150,000.[50] The pact, and its gradual implementation by successive Sri Lankan governments, helped pave the way for the Indian Tamils, skilfully lead by H.R. Thondaman, to join the mainstream of Sri Lankan party politics.

In broader areas of foreign policy, Mrs. Bandaranaike soon emerged as a non-aligned movement leader in her own right. With Presidents Tito and Nasser and Prime Minister Nehru, she hosted the first conference of non-aligned nations in Belgrade (held in June 1961) and participated in drafting the 'five criteria of nonalignment' adopted by the conference.[51] In 1964, she hosted the preparatory conference of foreign ministers for the Second Conference of Non-Aligned nations and co-hosted the conference in Cairo. Under Mrs. Bandaranaike, non-alignment did not mean strict neutrality. Like many other non-aligned nations, Sri Lanka's policies tended to be 'anti-colonialist,' which meant anti-Western in tone.[52] This bias was reinforced by domestic political considerations—the need for parliamentary support from Sri Lanka's Marxist parties. Relations with the United States became particularly strained when the two nations could not agree on compensation for the nationalised assets of U.S. oil companies and the U.S. government retaliated by terminating its foreign aid program.[53] However the simplistic perception, widely held in the United States, that Mrs. Bandaranaike's government was 'pro-communist' was far from accurate. Like most small nations, Sri Lanka's foreign policy reflected more continuity than change between regimes and could best be explained by the need to respond to geopolitical and economic forces over which the government had little control.[54]

The first Bandaranaike era ends

Accumulating economic and political discontents helped end the first Bandaranaike era, however it was Mrs. Bandaranaike's penchant for tackling one controversial issue too many that precipitated her government's defeat. The issue was government control of Sri Lanka's vibrant free press, then dominated by government opponents. A proposal to nationalise newspapers had first surfaced in the 1962 'Speech from the Throne,' however the government had retreated in the face of domestic opposition and widespread criticism from the foreign press.[55] In 1964, the issue resurfaced: the government proposed legislation to nationalise the nation's major private newspaper group, Lake House, and institute a 'Press Council' to oversee all newspapers. Opposition to the proposal united factions that could agree on little else and the government fell to a vote of no confidence in December. For the ensuing general election, Dudley Senanayake and J.R. Jayewardene pulled together a disparate coalition including both the Tamil Federal Party and several Sinhalese extremist groups in the name of 'democratic forces' united to fight 'the totalitarianism of the left.'[56] The coalition triumphed in a relatively close vote, with 18- year-old Sri Lankans participating for the first time. In defeat, Mrs. Bandaranaike still characterised herself as the bearer of S.W.R.D. Bandaranaike's legacy, and renewed her commitment to the political career she had chosen at the time of his death. 'It was frustrating to think that a 'road block' was placed in the path to democratic socialism in Sri Lanka; that the future my husband envisioned for his country was now a little further away on the horizon; the full implementation of his policies would take a little longer time than we had anticipated,'[57] she later recalled. When the new Parliament convened, Sirimavo Bandaranaike occupied her husband's old seat as Leader of The Opposition, the first woman in the world to hold that position.

Development goals and economic policies

Like its predecessor, S.W.R.D. Bandaranaike's government was committed to improving the well-being of Sri Lanka's masses by creating opportunities for the rural poor, strengthening the domestic industrial sector, broadening social welfare programs and making basic education available to all. Unemployment and underemployment in a rapidly expanding labour force were recognised as the nation's most serious problem. Indeed, the government's language policies were justified, in part, as a way of broadening economic opportunities for poor Sinhalese. Sri Lanka's economic planners recognised that improving social welfare and economic opportunity would require long-term economic growth. Long-term growth would require, in turn, long-term equilibrium in balance of payments, limits on deficit financing and a diversified domestic economy that was less vulnerable to fluctuations in export prices.[58]

In strategy, the new government differed radically from the pragmatic, incremental approach to economic management of the UNP regime. Bandaranaike and his Marxist-oriented ministers favoured a more activist role, including nationalisation of major productive sectors.[59] Their views – that government management of the economy was the quickest route to diversification, economic growth and full employment[60] – sound fanciful today, but were widely shared by leaders in the emerging nations of Africa and Asia.[61]

Not all members of Bandaranaike's unstable coalition shared these views. Traditional, rural elite leaders who dominated the SLFP cared little about industrial diversification, but strongly opposed policies that proposed to raise investment capital by taxing wealthy landholders. Proposals to re-distribute land, provide greater security of tenure and politically empower rural smallholders were even more repugnant. However, despite opposition, some agricultural sector reforms were initiated. As already noted, the Paddy Lands Act, designed to improve the lot of tenant smallholders, was the most contentious.[62] It provided for secure land tenure, along with government regulation of rents and wages. There were also rarely enforced provisions intended to improve the quality of production by giving the Department of Agrarian Services oversight over cultivation practices and power to requisition the land of inefficient producers. In fact 'rarely enforced' could be applied to most provisions of this act on which so much political capital had been expended. The debate over paddy lands may have raised the aspirations of Sri Lanka's tenant smallholders, but did little to improve their well-being.[63]

There were fewer political obstacles to implementing Marxist-oriented industrial reform policies and little serious debate of the proposition that nationalisation would re-distribute wealth, while simultaneously improving efficiency. Nationalisation schemes were not only consistent with Marxist dogma; it was also correctly assumed by Sri Lanka's politicised labour unions that government appointed managers would be more receptive to demands for wage increases.[64] Buddhist Sinhalese factions viewed nationalisation as a way of reducing the economic power of foreigners and more cosmopolitan local (often Christian) elites.[65] Thus, during the time that the nation was preoccupied with matters of language, religion and education, expansion of the government's role in the economy proceeded rapidly. By the time of the assassination, the government was engaged in producing diverse products including cement, cotton cloth, kaolin, iron and steel, tires, ceramics and plywood.[66]

As discussed above, nationalisations under Mrs. Bandaranaike's government included the Bank of Ceylon (1961) and foreign oil companies (1961). The government assumed control over distribution of all petroleum products throughout the island.[67] A 'People's Bank' was created to make credit more readily available in rural areas.[68] Establishment of the State Engineering Corporation (1962) moved the government into the field of heavy construction. By the time Mrs. Bandaranaike lost the election of 1965, she had succeeded in transforming Sri Lanka's economy into one of the most state dominated in Asia.[69] Surprisingly, Sri Lanka's tea plantations, a major producer of foreign exchange, were an exception to this trend.[70] However, high taxes and export duties, plus the fear of expropriation made foreign owners reluctant to invest new funds. Failure to modernise reduced the international competitiveness of Sri Lanka's most important industry. The plantations were nationalised during Mrs. Bandaranaike's second administration.

For Marxist and Sinhalese-Buddhist ideologues in the Bandaranaike government, nationalisation and the re-distribution of wealth were the desired end results of economic policies. However the widely held belief that central planning, implemented by politically appointed administrators was the most effective way promote economic growth and distribute its benefits equitably in a developing nation was based on optimism and untested theories, rather than proven results. Sri Lanka's new leaders faced the same problems of uncertainty about the best development strategy as their UNP predecessors, but with a commitment to radical activism and, in the wake of successive nationalisations and strengthened regulatory controls, vastly more power to influence the structure and performance of the economy.

The problem of defining economic priorities faced by the new government is highlighted by the recommendations of seven 'visiting economists' who visited Sri Lanka for short periods in 1958-1959 for the purpose of examining the nation's economic problems and preparing recommendations for the Planning Secretariat.[71] While there was a degree of consensus regarding the need for economic growth, diversification, maintaining export competitiveness and more effective planning, conflicting recommendations for setting priorities covered the entire spectrum of possibilities.

Since even experts could not agree, it is hardly surprising that capital investment allocations during the Bandaranaike years were the result of a shifting, often conflicting mix of pressures including inertia, economic planning goals, economic analysis and ideological preconceptions, personal interest and political power of responsible decision makers.[72] Under the government's ten-year plan, the bulk of public-sector investment was earmarked for agriculture, as in the Senanayake regime, with a strong emphasis on 'traditional' agriculture.[73] However, government funds were required for capitalisation of the expanding state industrial sector and there was a limited program of subsidies to some selected private industries as well. Increasingly, government became the primary source of investment capital. High taxes, government hostility toward foreign-owned business and fear of expropriation had not only closed off foreign sources of investment but also motivated foreigners to disinvest where that was possible. The government's Marxist rhetoric and nationalisation programs also discouraged domestic investors, many of whom had close ties to the UNP.

Unfortunately, the new government's optimism about the growth potential of a command economy and about its own capacity to implement ambitious economic development plans proved to be unfounded. While changes in the international economy contributed to the nation's problems, ill-conceived domestic economic policies also played a major role. In keeping with its 'import substitution industrialisation' approach to economic development, the government created a number of new industries, and then quickly erected high tariff barriers to protect them. As intended, this reduced or eliminated international competitive pressures. As government-owned monopolies, they were also freed from domestic competition and from the normal free-market pressures to show profitability and provide a return on investment.

A shortage of technical competence and managerial experience was also a problem. Sri Lanka's system of free education was among the best in the developing world, but it mostly produced liberal arts graduates who aspired to positions in the government civil service. Increasing emphasis on the use of Sinhala meant that managers used a language that was unknown outside of Sri Lanka and in which there was virtually no published technical literature. In this environment it is hardly surprising that technical sophistication, efficiency of production and profitability was given little emphasis in the management of Sri Lanka's new industries.[74] Indeed many public officials and managers, who had been given responsibility for major economic decisions and enterprises for the first time, viewed the opportunity to benefit personally or politically from their positions as legitimate fruits of power.[75]

Over the long run, government policies decoupled Sri Lanka's economy from an expanding world market at a time when competitor nations in Southeast Asia were positioning themselves to benefit from that expansion. Moreover, despite expert advice and ambitious industrialisation plans, the basic structure of an export-oriented economy that the People's United Front government had inherited from the UNP (and that the UNP government, in turn, had inherited from the British) remained unchanged. When Mrs. Bandaranaike lost the 1965 general election, nearly a quarter of Sri Lanka's GNP was still provided by exports (down from 32 per cent in 1956, but still substantial). Virtually all (92 per cent) of that export income was provided by the plantation sector, including 60 per cent from the tea plantations alone. While the nation did make some progress in producing - often inferior - goods for domestic markets, the overall contribution of plantation crops to total exports actually increased by three percentage points (from 89 to 92 per cent) during the nine years of *dirigiste* economic management.

This meant that domestic economic performance continued to be highly vulnerable to declining demand and market prices for three commodities—tea, rubber and coconut products. Declining export income was not matched by declining import expenditures. In fact, the demand for imported food and consumption goods remained robust, contributing to trade deficits. When trade deficits occurred, the government had to draw down its dwindling stock of foreign assets to cover the import bill. To stem the haemorrhaging, politically unpopular import and exchange controls were necessary. The controls were successful to some degree, but had the undesirable side effect of further discouraging investment and slowing economic growth.

Sri Lanka's critically important stock of foreign assets, which had remained relatively stable during the period of UNP rule, also seriously eroded, and with more drastic consequences than its terms of trade. The problem was precipitated by significant trade deficits in the politically turbulent years of 1957, 1959 and 1960. The deficits were caused by a combination of factors not under the government's control - rising import prices, remittances from plantation workers to relatives abroad, poor weather conditions, and repatriation of profits from foreign-owned businesses. Simultaneously there was growing demand for imported food and consumption goods generated by an increasingly educated population that had high expectations and was expanding by more than two per cent per year.[76]

The remedies available for dealing with trade deficits were expanding exports, drawing down foreign assets and reducing imports. By the time Mrs. Bandaranaike's second government had taken office, it was apparent that no dramatic reversal of the nation's fortunes on export markets would occur. Selling off foreign assets was becoming a less and less viable option; in less than five years, the value of Sri Lanka's foreign holdings had diminished by nearly 60 per cent. But the obvious need to pursue the third option – reducing imports – created both political and economic dilemmas for the government.

The responsibility for dealing with these dilemmas fell to Mrs. Bandaranaike's nephew and finance minister, Felix Dias Bandaranaike.[77] Under his direction the government introduced a moderately successful program of economic austerity that included increased tariffs, tariff surcharges, quotas and the issuance of import licences to reduce imports and favour domestic production. Some rationing was also introduced. From 1961 through 1965 there was only one trade deficit year, 1964,[78] and Sri Lanka's stock of foreign assets was stabilised at about 30 per cent of its 1965 level. However, the deterioration of Sri Lanka's trade position meant that a government that had come to power with a commitment to long-term planning that would foster economic expansion became preoccupied with short-term damage control.[79]

Preoccupation with the short term was also reflected in government finance. The UNP government's policy of providing a broad range of entitlements including free education, free medical care and a weekly rice ration was continued.[80] Since these entitlements were made available on a per-capita basis, their costs increased as the population expanded. Generous subsidies helped to make transportation, communication services and electricity more widely available; it was accepted that the nationalised concerns that provided these services would run at a loss.[81] There were increased subsidies to rural agriculture, as noted above, however the expectation that these would reduce food imports, especially the costly imports of rice, were largely unfulfilled. Finally, government subsidies were regularly required for a broad range of nationalised industries that were intended to produce a profit, but did not do so. Overall, annual government expenditures on short-term benefits grew by nearly 15 per cent per year during the 1956-65 period, from a total of 917 million to more than two billion rupees, annually.

Earlier in this chapter, I described a philosophy and set of policies which ensured that public officials – the cabinet ministers and planners in successive Bandaranaike governments – would be the major actors in raising and allocating investment capital. This economic philosophy was similar to that of Marxist governments in the Soviet Union, Eastern Europe and other Global South regimes, where it was possible to nationalise the economy and divert substantial resources from present consumption to investment, with the objective of achieving long-term economic growth.[82] However, the circumstances faced by Sri Lanka's political leaders were vastly different from those of Communist and non-democratic 'non-aligned' nations.

Sri Lanka's political environment included an uncensored and critical press, hostile scrutiny of government policies in Parliament and the prospect that leaders would be called to account by Sri Lanka's people in regularly scheduled genuinely democratic elections. The degree to which Sri Lanka's democratic system created nearly irresistible pressures on politicians, both government and opposition, to endorse extremist nationalist sentiments has already been described. In a time of budgetary stringency, democracy created analogous pressures in favour of maintaining short-term benefits rather than reallocating scarce resources to provide for long-term economic growth. It is hardly surprising that over a nine year period when spending on short-term benefits increased by 132 per cent and spending on administration and defence by 65 per cent, annual capital investments by the government increased by only 10 per cent. In fact, expenditures on capital investment were actually decreased in five of the nine government budgets enacted during the 1956-65 period.

Finding sufficient funds to provide social services to a growing population, to support a burgeoning government bureaucracy and meet ambitious investment targets was further complicated by revenue shortfalls. During a period when government expenditures grew by more than 100 per cent in real terms, revenues increased by less than 50 per cent, just slightly more than the rate of increase in GNP. Sri Lanka's program of nationalisation and centralised economic planning did little to alter the relatively static sources of revenue that the Bandaranaike government had inherited from the UNP and the British.

Practical problems of determining tax liabilities and actually collecting the money faced by all developing nations made the imposition of new taxing schemes more difficult. In 1956, almost 90 per cent of the nation's revenue came from four sources[83], import levies (23 per cent), export levies (26 per cent), income taxes (24 per cent) and gross receipts from trading enterprises (14 per cent). Of these, only the first three could be counted as discretionary income sources, since government enterprises, with rare exceptions, required government subsidies to keep them afloat. The government's strategy for raising revenues involved steep increases in import and export levies, higher taxes on incomes, new taxes on accumulated wealth and a variety of new taxes on corporate profits and commercial transactions.[84] Of course it was also hoped, unrealistically as it turned out, that existing, newly nationalised, and newly established government enterprises would be revenue producers rather than additional drains on government resources. The major outcome of these revenue enhancement programs can be seen by comparing the listing above with the following listing of the government's most productive revenue sources in 1965:[85] sales and turnover taxes (11 per cent), import levies (30 per cent), export levies (12 per cent), income taxes (16 per cent) and gross receipts from government trading enterprises (14 per cent). By 1965, the new sales and commercial taxes had become significant revenue producers and revenues from import levies had nearly doubled. However, these new revenues had to make up for significant declines in the contribution of export levies and income taxes to the total.

Overall, the problem was that government revenues were dependent on the performance of the economy as a whole and were not likely to grow at a rate much faster than overall economic growth. This important reality was not fully taken into account in the theories of Sri Lanka's economic planners. Thus some of the taxes that produced increases in the short run could be counterproductive in the long run by reducing the revenue base. Attempts to milk the maximum revenues from the plantation sector had already begun to produce this effect as plantations became less efficient and less competitive on world markets. The myriad of business taxes, imposed on a still fragile domestic economic sector, had the effect of discouraging private investment and the growth of private sector enterprise. As we have seen, government investment and government enterprises proved to be poor substitutes as revenue sources and as engines of economic growth.

Faced with the political liabilities of curbing welfare and subsidy programs, plus the failure of its revenue policies, successive Bandaranaike governments succumbed to the temptations of a 'solution' that many other nations, including most notably the United States, have also found expedient – chronic deficit financing. Beginning in 1956, government expenditures began to grow at more than twice the rate of GNP. Budget deficits averaging more than 25 per cent of expenditures were incurred in every year after 1956 (which completed the last budget of the Kotelawala government.) Moreover, after 1956, methods of financing the deficit were increasingly inflationary, 'amounting to little more than use of the printing press.'[86] During the 1956-65 period, Sri Lanka experienced nearly a fourfold increase in public indebtedness and its level of indebtedness rose from 17 to 47 per cent of GNP. Domestic indebtedness was a less immediate problem than the decline in foreign assets – interest payments were less than 6 per cent of expenditures in 1966[87]– however the pattern of chronic deficit spending established by the Bandaranaike governments was clearly not sustainable in the long run.

Lack of viability over the long run is, in fact, the distinguishing characteristic of development policy during the 1956-65 period. As the next section will show, the governments of S.W.R.D. and Sirimavo Bandaranaike were generally successful in delivering a high level of benefits to their constituents, if not fully meeting their expectations. Nationalisation, together with an expansion of government and agricultural development policies, produced some re-distribution of wealth. However, the government's economic policies, in conjunction with changes in the international economy, resulted in erosion of the nation's foreign assets, decline in international competitiveness of the plantation sector, failures of import substitution industrialisation, chronic revenue shortfalls and growing domestic indebtedness. This meant that politically unpalatable reductions in social benefits and availability of consumer goods were the inevitable legacy of the People's United Front governments to their successors. It is paradoxical that a regime that came to power with a commitment to rationalising economic management and promoting the long-term growth of a more diverse, industrialised economy would have implemented policies with far more detrimental long-term consequences than the ad hoc and incremental policies of its predecessor.

Meeting people's wants and needs

How well did Bandaranaike era governments deliver on promises to improve the lot of ordinary Sri Lankans? The record is mixed, but generally positive. Greatest success was achieved in providing benefits *directly*, through subsidised programs of health, transportation and food distribution. Opportunities for government employment, the highest career goal of many Sri Lankans, increased (although these were mostly restricted to the Sinhalese majority community). There were also expanded educational opportunities. On the other hand, programs to provide good jobs and economic opportunities *indirectly* through industrial diversification, improved competitiveness and growth-producing investments were less successful.

As in chapter 6, it is useful to begin discussing performance by examining overall trends in population, Gross National Product (GNP) and per-capita GNP (Figure 7.3). Sri Lanka's population continued to grow at a rate about 2.5 per cent per year and surpassed 11 million in 1965.[88] This was a net addition of nearly 2.5 million people. Nearly half of this rapidly growing population was under 20; youths who had completed basic education and, with high aspirations, were seeking entry into the labour force. While population growth created increased population densities and increased pressures on the government to provide jobs, Sri Lanka was spared the problems of rapid urbanisation that many developing nations faced. During this period, less than 20 per cent of the population lived in towns and cities with a population of 10,000 or more.[89]

Sri Lanka's GNP grew steadily but at a pace just sufficient to stay ahead of population growth. GNP per-capita grew by only 14 per cent, an average rate of little more than one per cent per year. In four years during the 1956-65 period, real GNP per capita either remained stagnant or declined. Given the government's deficit financing policies, inflation remained surprisingly low.[90]

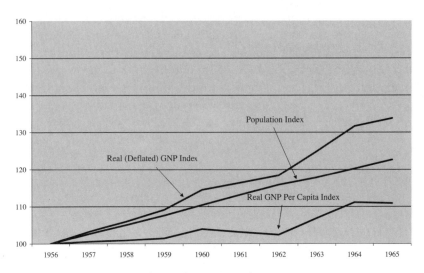

Figure 7.3 GNP and Population Trends

Sri Lanka's poor, especially the rural poor, benefited the least, economically. Wages in the agricultural sector increased little, if at all, so that by 1965 urban workers (the beneficiaries of aggressive union activity) earned, on the average, three times as much as their rural counterparts.[91] In fact the most striking effect of the Bandaranaike economic policies on income was to strengthen the economic position of the middle class, largely at the expense of the poor. During the period between the 1953 and 1963 censuses (which correspond closely, but not precisely to the Bandaranaike years) the income share of Sri Lanka's poorest 20 per cent declined by 24 per cent.[92] Among the nation's wealthiest, only the top 10 per cent saw their income share decline.[93]

Unemployment and underemployment among the poor also increased significantly, although the precise magnitude is difficult to quantify.[94] Government studies report that about 200,000 jobs were created during the 1953-63 intercensual period, a growth rate of less than one per cent per year and far less than the increase in the size of the labour force.[95] Some of these jobs were in the paddy cultivation and fisheries sectors, viewed by many newly educated Sri Lankan youth as worse than no jobs at all. Another indicator of an increasingly severe unemployment problem was the number of registrants at government employment exchanges, which doubled from about 150,000 to nearly 300,000.[96] Despite these problems, however, the government programs succeeded in providing subsidies and entitlements that made Sri Lanka unique among Global South nations.

Among these, the most important by far were subsidies on basic food-stuffs, particularly the rice subsidy. Four pounds per week of this essential staple were made available to low-income Sri Lankans at far below market prices. Rice distribution was island wide, unlike some other benefits which were more readily available in urban areas. Not only did the availability of rice meet basic nutritional needs – starvation was virtually unknown in Sri Lanka – it also served as an income supplement for the poor. Many who drew their subsidised ration then sold some of it at higher market values, using the difference to purchase other foodstuffs and goods.[97]

Sri Lanka's system of free health care, backed up by strong public health, continued to be one of the best in the developing world. Between 1955 and 1965, the number of doctors and nurses employed increased by more than twice the rate of population growth.[98] Moreover, traditional Ayurvedic physicians were SLFP supporters and government funding for this parallel health care system, which was strong in rural areas but used by all economic groups, increased.[99] Government policy endorsed the view, shared by most Sri Lankans, that Ayurvedic and Western medicine were complementary. The popularity of Ayurvedic health care relieved pressure on the government-supported Western health facilities and provided a level of quality health care not fully reflected in official statistics.[100]

The combined impact of food subsidies, strong public health and expansion of quality health care services, produced continued improvement in indicators measuring the overall health of the nation's population. Maternal mortality per 1,000 births declined by 37 per cent and infant mortality by 21 per cent. These improvements were in rates that were already low for global south nations and compared favourably with many industrialised nations of the north.

Subsidised fares combined with the widespread availability of transport throughout the island also benefited the poor.[101] It meant that large numbers of people could commute daily to Colombo and other commercial centres, while continuing to live in more rural areas. At the same time it facilitated the location of some industries away from major centres. Because people could travel with relative ease from rural areas to government offices in the towns, government officials were better informed about what was going on and could provide better services. This did not ensure that the rural poor received equitable treatment but it compelled the government officials to look more carefully at circumstances where delivery of services was not consistent with political leaders' promises.[102]

Finally, this period witnessed a massive expansion and transformation of educational opportunities at the primary and secondary level. The number of schools and teachers increased by more than 80 per cent.[103] The transition to education in vernacular languages (*swabasha*) had been initiated by UNP governments and completing this process was high priority goal. By 1960, virtually all secondary education was conducted in Sinhala or Tamil.[104] Because of these changes, many rural Sri Lankan families, especially rural Sinhalese families, were able to send their children to school for the first time. By 1965, school enrolment had increased to 2.5 million and most eligible children, excepting children of the Indian Tamil estate workers,[105] were attending at least some school.[106]

Rapid expansion of educational opportunities did not, however, solve the problems of offering a diverse curriculum that would train Sri Lanka's young men and women to meet the needs of an expanding, industrialising, export-oriented economy. Teachers of commerce and science, Sinhala instructional materials,[107] and the necessary laboratory facilities to support science education were in short supply, which meant that most students were compelled to choose a field of concentration in 'arts.'[108] Thus, in 1964, the 'arts' field of concentration was designated by 85 per cent of the candidates sitting for the nation wide basic (GCE Ordinary) level examination. Changes in the language of instruction and expansion of rudimentary basic education had proved to be easier than curricular reform and expansion of facilities to meet development needs.

The problem of expanding facilities to provide more advanced, technically sophisticated curricula was even more evident at the university level. Historically, the quality of education offered by Sri Lanka's university campuses at Peradeniya and Colombo had been high, but spaces were very limited (only 658 were accepted in 1955) and competition for admission was fierce. Only students enrolled the nation's elite 'colleges' (high schools) even considered applying, and less than an a third of the applicants were accepted.[109] This was clearly unacceptable to leaders of 'the people's government' in a society where a university degree was viewed as the ticket to social status, political power and economic security. Accordingly, expanding opportunities for university education was a high government priority that was pursued vigorously, if somewhat haphazardly, throughout the 1956-65 period.

With encouragement from the Education Ministry, applications for university admission expanded by an astonishing fifteen-fold, from 2,061 in 1955 to more than 31,350 in 1965. The number of admitted students grew by almost ten-fold, from 658 in 1955 to 6,359 in 1965. To cope with this influx, the education ministry converted two traditional Buddhist schools (*Pirivenas*), to universities[110] and attempted to expand facilities at the Colombo and Peradeniya campuses. The newly matriculating students found, however, that it was easier to make the politically popular decision to expand admissions than to provide quality education to a student body that increased by more than 400 per cent in four years. Few books were available, and books that were available were written in English, which the new cadre of *swabasha* students (and even some instructors) could not read. Thus the educational experience in many classes became little more than the verbatim transcription of lecture notes which young and ill-prepared instructors had, themselves, recently transcribed.

What the universities provided most effectively was a venue for raising student consciousness, especially the consciousness of rural students, about shortcomings in Sri Lankan political, social and economic institutions. They could engage in endless political discussions with equally idealistic and disillusioned compatriots about ways in which 'the system' could be changed. Many young instructors and some older ones too shared their views. As this new group of students completed their education – about half were awarded degrees – and discovered that a university degree, especially an arts degree, no longer guaranteed employment, their disillusionment toward 'the system' and desire to change it increased.

Thus, in contrast to other benefits the government had been so successful in providing, the expansion of educational opportunities in a relatively stagnant economy did not contribute to a view that the government was keeping its promises to improve the well-being of ordinary Sri Lankans. Rather it contributed to a growing sense of dissatisfaction and disillusionment in the segment of society most likely to express that dissatisfaction, if mobilised, in aggressive – even violent – political action intended to effect radical change.

8
Political Responses and Feedback in a New Era

During a decade marked by the assassination of a Prime Minister, temporary disintegration of the ruling party, an attempted military coup, periodic suspension of constitutional guarantees, press censorship and harassment of opposition parties, plus the emergence of sharp communal divisions, Sri Lanka's democratic institutions continued to function, with broad public support.

Political attitudes, identities and organisations

Prior to the 1956 election, the island's 'masses', that is ordinary Sri Lankans, were not really conscious of their power to shape political events. Marshall Singer, one of the most insightful observers of this period, asserts that 'deference' was the prevalent attitude toward authority. 'If a caste or class or man was in a position of power, that was the way things should be. Society had always been a hierarchy and no individual or group of individuals was going to alter this structure.'[1]

The structure of Sri Lanka's political parties and labour unions reflected this traditionalist view. Top leaders from both the 'right' and the 'left' were drawn from the same strata of society, the English speaking, and often English educated, elite.[2] Unless they chose to retire, they could expect to hold office for long period of time and be given broad scope, with little accountability for the exercise of power.[3] Parties lacked a grass-roots structure and the leadership often communicated with voters through intermediaries. The structure of labour unions has been described as 'oligarchic,' with few – or no – democratic procedures for choosing leaders, setting policy or even deciding on strike actions.[4]

If Sri Lanka's people resembled inhabitants of other traditional societies in their deferential attitudes toward authority, high literacy and wide exposure to mass communications set them apart and provided a receptive environment for the mass appeals of charismatic populist figures such as S.W.R.D. and Sirimavo Bandaranaike. A 1964 survey reported that more than half of Sri Lanka's men and about 25 per cent of its women were regular newspaper readers and radio listeners, with significantly higher proportions in urban areas. Only the Tamil estate workers reported relatively low media exposure.[5] In 1964, Sri Lanka possessed four daily newspapers with an average circulation of more than 50,000 and three weekly newspapers with a circulation of more than 100,000. Additionally, there were six more widely circulated dailies and four other major weekly newspapers.[6] Political coverage, often highly partisan, was featured in these publications as well as many smaller ones.[7]

In the hands of S.W.R.D. Bandaranaike and his followers, traditional Sinhalese nationalism became a force that empowered the majority Sinhalese population. Using the institutions of parliamentary democracy, they rejected D.S. Senanayake's model of a secular, multi-ethnic state in favour of a more populist ethnic-oriented model that they believed would better serve their interests. Bandaranaike's electoral reforms ensured that rural voters and members of disadvantaged castes, to whom the SLFP's platform was most appealing, could not, as under United National Party (UNP) governments, be kept from the polls. By 1965, when Dudley Senanayake became Prime Minister again, the need to appeal to Sinhalese-Buddhist nationalism was accepted by all major political factions, excepting the Tamils.

Incorporation of Sinhalese-Buddhist nationalism into the rhetoric and platforms of all major political parties diminished its influence as a pivotal factor in determining electoral outcomes. This gave renewed importance to the factors of personality, family affiliation, economic opportunity, delivery of benefits and party organisation in shaping voting behaviour. Faith in competitive elections and parliamentary democracy remained strong in Sri Lanka, despite the 1962 military coup. For the most part, major parties did not challenge the electoral 'rules of the game' and there were peaceful transfers of power following the April 1960, July 1960 and March 1965 general elections.

If empowerment of Sri Lanka's Sinhalese majority altered traditional patterns of deference and created new feelings of identity with 'our government', the 1956-65 period was, nonetheless, as much a return to values perceived as 'traditional' as a movement from them. There was little change in the personalised and hierarchical leadership structure of major political parties and groups. Personalities, as much as policies, continued to provide the focal point for political organisation and the mobilisation of political support. S.W.R.D. and Sirimavo Bandaranaike's Sri Lanka Freedom Party (SLFP) was the most personalised political party of all, and remains so to this day.

The Sri Lanka Freedom Party

The SLFP was a paradox. S.W.R.D. Bandaranaike had described its philosophy as 'the middle way,' capitalising on both Buddhist sensibilities and the idea that economic programs of democratic socialism would seek a middle ground between the pro-business philosophy of the UNP and the Marxist radicalism of the left-wing parties. The paradox was that the SLFP-led People's United Front coalition did not include any real 'middle ground.' Rather, it was an uneasy alliance between some of Sri Lanka's most conservative land-owning families,[8] rural peasants, Sinhalese- Buddhist traditionalists and Marxist radicals, the latter being willing to accommodate Sinhalese nationalism in order to win political power and influence economic policy. Earlier, I described S.W.R.D. Bandaranaike's failed attempts to mediate between these contending factions. Few believe that the SLFP could have successfully contested a general election in 1960 or 1961 under his leadership.[9]

Mrs. Bandaranaike's revitalisation of the SLFP's fortunes in the April 1960 election campaign and her decisive victory in July were uniquely personal triumphs, which made it clear to other SLFP leaders that their political fortunes were inextricably tied to hers. Recognition that her popularity was more personal than linked to any specific policies made it difficult even for experienced SLFP parliamentarians, let alone the rank and file, to question the Prime Minister's authoritarian leadership style and the influence of trusted family members who were close to her. To retain power, even the more conservative SLFP members were willing to co-operate with Marxist parties. They muted their opposition to socialist economic policies impacting areas of Sri Lankan life in which they had relatively little interest.

Despite Mrs. Bandaranaike's personal popularity and control of Parliament, the SLFP was never organisationally strong, nor a true majority party.[10] Family dominance of the party precluded the recruitment of talented young men who subsequently became mainstays of a revitalised UNP. Mrs. Bandaranaike's ability win elections and to govern always depended on her personal popularity, plus alliances and no contest pacts that even included, to their subsequent discomfiture, the Tamil parties. Sustaining a coalition whose members had little in common, proved to be difficult. In 1964, the combined effects of failed economic policies, opposition toward proposals for press censorship and personal antagonism toward what was seen as a Bandaranaike family cabal had produced a 'no confidence' vote in Parliament and precipitated a general election.

A coalition of Buddhist priests and lay Buddhist organisations had been key allies of S.W.R.D. Bandaranaike in 1956. The influence of priests soon declined but lay Buddhists played a decisive role in elevating Buddhism's political role under Mrs. Bandaranaike's government. Largely Colombo-based and occupying senior positions in industry and the government bureaucracy, the most influential among them banded together in a shadowy but powerful pressure group, the *Bauddha Jatika Balavegaya* (Buddhist Nationalist Force). Their goal was to shape language and education policy to redress 'historical grievances' against the Sinhalese and Buddhism.[11] The abortive military coup of 1962 strengthened their position by mobilising political support for the government's education reforms and greatly reducing the political influence of Colombo's English-speaking Roman Catholic elite. They were less politically active by 1965 because many of their objectives had been achieved[12] and were basically supported by the UNP, as well as the SLFP.

The Marxist parties

We have seen that S.W.R.D. Bandaranaike's SLFP became the UNP's principal opponent, largely because Sri Lanka's bewildering mosaic of left-wing parties lacked credibility. Their Colombo-based, English-educated leaders were never able to connect with an electorate that was largely poor, rural, Buddhist and Sinhalese. Utopian visions of a secular, classless society that would be governed by a 'workers and peasants government', formed through academic study and ideological debate at elite British Universities, were out of touch with Sri Lankan reality. Factional strife further weakened the Marxist parties by dividing, confusing and alienating their core supporters who must often have thought that their principal political opponents were not the UNP or SLFP, but other Marxists.

Some argue that Marxist parties became marginalised under the Bandaranaikes, but this ignores the pivotal influence of Marxist leaders and their Marxist doctrines over Sri Lanka's economy. To gain this influence, it was necessary for them to mute or abandon positions on minority rights, language policy and religion that they had staked out in the 1940s and early 1950s. An opportunity to defeat the UNP and implement the Bandaranaikes' vaguely defined ideal of democratic socialism proved sufficient inducement to do so. As the UNP narrowed its differences with the SLFP on communal issues and the Tamils became increasingly alienated, more moderate Marxist factions often found they held the balance of power. This enabled them to leverage strategic voting blocs plus control over powerful labour unions into cabinet positions responsible for shaping economic policy. As we have seen, conservative SLFP notables had little interest in these posts.

The United National Party

In many developing nations, the triumph of charismatic, populist leaders such as S.W.R.D. Bandaranaike was followed by the demise of opposition parties as viable competitors for political power. In Sri Lanka, on the other hand, the UNP recouped electoral losses with modest victories in the April 1960 and 1965 general elections and with a resounding victory in 1977. UNP resiliency played a key role in sustaining Sri Lanka's democratic institutions. It remained viable because top leaders were able to learn from defeat, be ideologically flexible, back up personal appeals with solid organisation and recruit new blood. Most important among the leaders who revitalised the party was the politically astute J.R. Jayewardene. Jayewardene, his biographers note, 'would have endorsed R.A. Butler's dictum that 'power is the first goal of party politics, the *sine qua non* of political effectiveness.'[13]

Following the 1956 election, party leaders formed a special committee to identify reasons for the UNP defeat and recommend reforms. Committee members concluded that the party's manifesto (platform) had lost touch with popular aspirations, due in part to a party organisation that provided no real linkages between top leaders and the Sri Lankan people, or even the party's rank and file members. Recommendations provided a blueprint that would transform the UNP from a loose confederation of notables that D.S. Senanayake had created to a more structured organisation that could appeal to ordinary people and win elections.[14]

The UNP's defeat by a resurgent SLFP in July 1960 provided new impetus for the reorganisation schemes that J.R. Jayewardene had been urging on a reluctant Dudley Senanayake. Again, a committee of senior party leaders conducted a post-election assessment, this time with Jayewardene himself as chair. Their report echoed many of the concerns and proposals that had been presented in 1956, but this time, with much greater prospect of prompt implementation. It urged party leaders to shed the UNP's elitist image and be more welcoming to those who had been educated in Sinhalese and wore national dress. It advocated strengthening branches in all parts of the country, a more aggressive propaganda campaign and a program to strengthen the party's finances. Many of the recommendations were implemented in a new constitution, adopted at the party's Twelfth Congress, held in 1961.[15]

A notable success was the recruitment of strong new leaders, some of whom had previous affiliations with the SLFP. One was I.M.R.A. Iriyagolle, a man with strong ties to the powerful lay Buddhist community and an effective orator in Sinhala. Another was Ranasinghe Premadasa, a spellbinding Sinhala orator who had begun his political career with the Labour party in 1949, and began to rise rapidly in the UNP leadership.[16] Because he was of low caste, in contrast to *goyigama* (landowning) caste members who had occupied most top positions in Sri Lankan politics, Premadasa's visibility tangibly demonstrated the party's openness to new blood.[17]

The Federal Party (Tamil)

S.W.R.D. Bandaranaike's triumph and passage of the Official Language Act discredited the accommodationist policies of G.G. Ponnambalam's Tamil Congress and virtually ensured that S.J.V. Chelvanayakam's Federal Party would become the focal point for Tamil opposition to government policies.[18]

Sinhalese politicians portrayed the Federal Party as a militant group and it was perceived as militant by many Sinhalese. However, political scientist A.J. Wilson describes the party as 'basically middle class' and committed to achieving its goals by peaceful and constitutional methods.[19] Nor did it have a strong organisation, even in the Northern and Eastern Provinces. The absence of a serious competitor for the Sri Lankan Tamil vote made this unnecessary. For the most part, the Federal Party drew its candidates from locally prominent men who attracted voters through their own personal influence structures.[20] Apart from Chelvanayakam, these men were typically conservative Hindu members of the *Vellala* (land-owning) caste, who supported Jaffna's rigid class structure. The Federal Party had no counterpart to the UNP's youth league and no effective mechanism for recruiting talented young men – especially lower caste young men, such as the UNP's Ranasinghe Premadasa or LTTE leader Velupillai Prabhakaran, into its leadership ranks.

Increasingly strident demands for autonomy over the 'Traditional Homelands of the Tamils,' coupled with parallel developments in the South Indian province of Tamil Nadu, magnified Sinhalese fears of Tamil irredentism more than the Federal Party's loose organisation and relatively peaceful tactics. According to party politicians, 'Traditional Homelands' included not only the Northern Province, which had indisputably been the home of an independent Tamil kingdom for several hundred years, but also the Eastern Province, with its substantial Muslim and Sinhalese populations, over which Tamil rule had been extended only for brief periods of time. Moreover it was during this period that in South India's Tamil Nadu State, the *Dravida Munetra Kazhagam* (Dravidian Progressive Front) supplanted the Indian National Congress as the dominant party. Leaders of this overtly communal party preached the politics of ethnicity and made 'Tamil rights,' including the citizenship rights of the Indian Tamil plantation workers, a major theme of inflammatory speeches in political campaigns and the Tamil Nadu legislative assembly. The 'Tamil Nadu factor' opened even modest proposals for regional autonomy and decentralisation to sinister interpretations in Sinhalese eyes.[21]

In fact, Federal Party pronouncements and its mobilisation of an increasingly aroused Tamil community reflected a belief that some variant of 'business as usual' politics was likely to prevail in Sri Lanka over the long run. Party leaders believed that a combination of political action in parliament, non-violent demonstrations and negotiations with Sinhalese leaders could achieve their goals of protecting Tamil minority rights throughout the island and attaining a degree of regional autonomy in the North and East.[22] The party won some tactical successes, but failed to win sufficient concessions to justify its approach. Sinhalese leaders proved to be more concerned about the power of Sinhalese nationalists than the Federal Party. In time, Tamil party leaders came to be seen by an increasingly militant Tamil youth movement as not only ineffective, but more concerned with preserving their own privileged status than responding to the aspirations and needs of Sri Lankan Tamil society as a whole.

Labour unions' political roles

In contrast to UNP leaders of the post-colonial era, S.W.R.D. Bandaranaike, along with left-wing members of his cabinet, strongly supported the expansion of trade unionism. Helped by pro-labour legislation and regulations, union membership expanded fourfold.[23] The government encouraged the formation of unions in state-managed enterprises and supported unions that were seeking recognition from private employers as bargaining agents. Labour tribunals were established to hear workers' complaints and legal assistance was given to unions engaged in disputes with employers.[24] Unions quickly learned that the authorities would not interfere with strike actions and that laws proscribing political strikes or those threatening to the public interest were rarely enforced.[25]

Bandaranaike's government soon found that a philosophical commitment to empowering the working classes through trade union membership did not necessarily translate into political benefits, especially during a period when government become one of the nation's principal employers. For the non-estate sectors of the economy, the average number of man-days lost to strikes grew more than five-fold, from 42,611 in 1951-55 to 244,919 in 1956-60 and 370,257 in 1961-65. The average duration of strikes tripled, reflecting a labour movement that was not only much larger, but also better organised.[26]

Prior to 1956, as noted in chapter 7, nearly 75 per cent of Sri Lanka's trade union membership was found in the estate sector, mostly in S. Thondamann's Ceylon Workers' Congress (CWC). The Tamil estate workers did have a degree of political power, because of the nation's economic dependence on tea-export revenues, but the leverage of the CWC over mainstream Sinhalese politics was limited.[27] After 1956, there was a significant increase in the political strength of organised labour because state-managed industries – where strikes could bring the nation's economy to a standstill – became unionised. Simultaneously, union members became more widely visible and dispersed, because they were to be found in the numerous offices, outlets and branches of State Corporations throughout the island.

Despite the explosion of union membership and marked growth of union influence during this period, there was no fundamental change in the organisa-

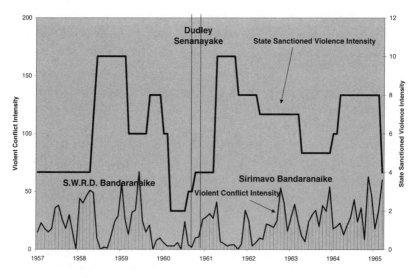

Figure 8.1 State-Sanctioned Violence and Violent Conflict

tion or leadership of Sri Lanka's trade union movement. Top union leadership remained elitist and oligarchic, although competition for members between two or more unions in the same industry created some accountability. Apart from the CWC, the largest and most powerful labour organisations were four trade union federations, enrolling more than 300,000 members, all affiliated with Marxist parties,[28] and four strategically placed independent unions. There were also numerous unions with very small memberships of 50 or even fewer which had little influence.

Even more than the electoral success of the SLFP, the quadrupling of labour union membership provided evidence that growing numbers of Sri Lankans were becoming actively involved in holding economic managers and political leaders accountable. Strong trade unions, like Buddhist pressure groups, were part of an emerging civil society in the island nation. As Robert Kearney notes:

> The much criticised partisanship of the labour movement...may have assisted in the development of the competitive political process based on mass participation in meaningful elections that [was] one of the most impressive achievements of contemporary Ceylon.[29]

But political feedback to economic management, as noted in chapter 5, can be destabilising. What was not clear was whether the pressures exerted by strong, politically influential trade unions on political leaders and on the managers of Sri Lanka's government-controlled economy would facilitate or impede economic performance that could meet the aspirations of their members in the long run.

State-sanctioned violence

Rising values of the state-sanctioned violence index after 1956 show clearly that in this area, as in many others, S.W.R.D. Bandaranaike's election victory marked a turning point. The government's language policy was viewed by Sri Lankan Tamils as an abridgement of a fundamental right and had to be forced upon culturally distinct Tamil majority areas. Likewise, Tamils did not passively accept government decisions to adopt Sinhalese symbols as national symbols.

Government permissiveness also contributed indirectly to more frequent and vigorous use of state violence. 'The People's Prime Minister' was much less inclined by temperament to coerce opponents than his predecessor, Sir John Kotelawala, and he recalled the adverse political fallout from Dudley Senanayake's decision to call out the police against rioters in 1952. On several occasions, as we have seen, Bandaranaike caved in to demonstrators rather than standing firm. This created a climate in which opposition forces, or groups opposing a policy, viewed confrontation as a tactic that would make the government back down and would weaken it in the eyes of the public. Mrs. Bandaranaike was far less tolerant toward those who demonstrated against her government, but the trend of disruptive – sometimes violent – confrontations escalating out of control and provoking a forceful government response continued. In fact, her willingness to press forward with divisive policies on several fronts made confrontations more likely. Provisions of emergency regulations, especially censorship, were also used to deal with opponents who had not necessarily resorted to confrontational tactics.

Figure 8.2 shows changes in the four factors comprising the state-sanctioned violence index – suspension of constitutional guarantees; arrests, exiles and executions; restrictions on political parties; and censorship of the press. It will be useful to refer to this diagram as a more detailed description of events underlying the numerical coding is presented.

Passage of the Official Language Act marked the first increase in state-sanctioned violence. Though some Sinhalese might disagree, I classified it as 'suspension of constitutional guarantees for part of the country' because it was widely perceived by Sri Lanka Tamils as a cancellation of a constitutionally guaranteed right. Initially, the act's significance was only symbolic. Through the period of the Bandaranaike-Chelvanayakam negotiations in 1957 there were few government attempts to coerce the Sri Lanka Tamils and the Tamils generally avoided provocative action. Mainstream Tamil leaders, parliamentary rhetoric aside, recognised the need for some concessions to majority sentiment and had faith in the Prime Minister's ability to deliver on his promise of a workable compromise. Even during the turbulent early months of 1958, when violent conflict intensified, security force responses were limited by a government policy of 'maximum restraint.'

Things changed when, at the Prime Minister's request, Governor General Goonetileke belatedly declared a state of emergency to quell communal rioting in May 1958.[30] Protected by emergency regulations, Bandaranaike's government pushed use of state-sanctioned violence to new levels for post-indepen-

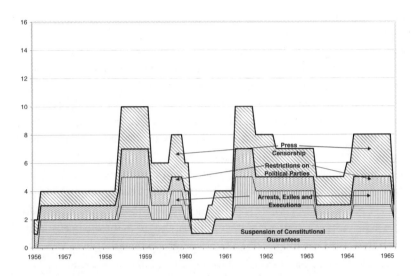

Figure 8-2 State Sanctioned Violence Components

dence Sri Lanka. Freed from the 'maximum restraint' directive, the army and police were able to restore order in both Sinhalese and Tamil areas.[31] The Federal Party was proscribed and its leaders placed in detention.

Restoration of order was not immediately followed by a restoration of constitutional guarantees, as government leaders found that emergency regulations made it easier to deal with opponents and critics. Between May when the emergency was declared and the following March, when emergency regulations were lifted, there was police harassment of opposition party activities and some further arrests of opposition politicians. Former Prime Minister Kotelawala's passport was impounded, preventing him from leaving the country. Press criticism from both right and left, which had been a thorn in the side of Bandaranaike's government since it came to power, was stifled by government censors. When emergency regulations were lifted, official harassment of the opposition and press censorship lessened, but did not disappear entirely.[32]

Emergency regulations were imposed for a second time following Prime Minister Bandaranaike's assassination and remained in force until January 1960. There was less harassment of the opposition or censorship, despite upcoming general elections. The caretaker government that succeeded the slain leader seemed less inclined and perhaps was less able to use the state of emergency for political purposes. Once the state of emergency was lifted, state-sanctioned violence returned to pre-1956 levels, where it remained through the March 1960 general election, the brief tenure of Dudley Senanayake's minority government and the election campaigning of June - July, 1960.

Under Sirimavo Bandaranaike's administration, the use of state-sanctioned violence soon rose once again. Less than two weeks after the new government took office, 1,000 copies of the U.S. magazine, *Time*, containing an unflattering article about the new Prime Minister were seized. Following the incident, Finance Minister Felix Dias Bandaranaike informed customs officials that hereafter, all American periodicals were to be approved by him personally before being offered for sale.[33] Domestic publications could not be censored without Parliamentary approval, but government officials began to threaten censorship – especially against the pro-UNP Lake House group – and to define the limits of acceptable criticism through both official and unofficial channels.[34] In December, Radio Ceylon stopped its long-standing practice of relaying BBC news broadcasts, replacing them with government-generated broadcasts featuring local news.[35]

Government pressure on the Tamil speaking population[36] also began to increase. Disillusioned Federal Party leaders quickly learned that the new Prime Minister had no intention of honouring a pre-election agreement, promising to implement major provisions of the Bandaranaike-Chelvanayakam accord, which had contributed to her victory. In October 1960, the government announced plans to require that all government officials speak Sinhala and made it clear that implementation of the Official Language Act would proceed as scheduled on 1 January 1961.[37] State power also backed up government initiated legislation taking control over the nation's denominational – largely Christian – schools and seizing their property.[38]

It became clear to Sri Lankans that their government was now more willing to censor the media, limit individual freedoms and harass political opponents. Among numerous acts of censorship were legislation controlling publications on horse racing,[39] establishment of a 'Special Conference Unit' to review and approve all international participants in conferences,[40] the banning of a textbook because of objectionable material dealing with the 1956-60 period,[41] censorship of all news pertaining to the Ceylon Transport Board strike of January-February 1963, removal of one page containing objectionable material from the 3 August 1962 edition of *Time* magazine[42] and withholding of an entire December 1964 edition.[43] There was a new requirement that any proposed imports of books and literature be reviewed by the Attorney General.[44] All foreign news bulletins broadcast by Radio Ceylon were subject to censorship.[45] Political films 'which refer disparagingly to political principles or ideology of other countries' could be banned.[46] The proposed 'Press Bill' of 1964, which contributed to Mrs. Bandaranaike's defeat in Parliament and then in the general election, was an attempt to further restrict freedom of expression by government leaders who viewed most of the nation's newspapers as hostile to their interests.

The free expression of ideas was not the only area in which freedoms previously taken for granted were curtailed. New regulations prohibited the departure from Sri Lanka of any medically or technically trained person to accept positions abroad[47] and required that all foreign travel by government and corporate officials be approved by the Prime Minister.[48] Later, Sri Lankan students were prohibited from sending applications to foreign educational institutions. In three contested bi-elections the use of flags, distribution of handbills and holding of public meetings by opposition parties was restricted;[49] three Tamil parties with at least philosophical links to the Tamil nationalist *Dravida Munetra Kazhagam* (DMK) party of India were banned.[50]

Federal Party resistance, civil disobedience campaigns and continued unrest in the North and East did not deter the implementation of additional regulations that favoured Sinhalese and discriminated against Tamils. Reversing historical patterns of discrimination against Sinhalese was the stated rationale for these regulations. The Education Department barred admission of all Tamil candidates to teacher training colleges, except for teachers already in service.[51] Public servants recruited after November 1948 who could not document claims to Ceylonese citizenship were discontinued with three months notice.[52] Some promotions in the public service were predicated on the ability of the applicant to pass a Sinhala proficiency test [53] (a later amendment softened this requirement somewhat.)[54] The government's concern also extended to English users who were informed by the Commissioner of Official Language that a record would be maintained listing the names of all public officials who addressed letters, correspondence or official papers to any other public officials (including officials of public corporations) in English.[55]

After an 11-month period, during which normal constitutional guarantees were in force, the government responded to an island-wide strike of electrical engineers and technicians by again declaring a state of emergency on 6 March 1964. This was the government's first use of emergency regulations to deal with the numerous strikes and demonstrations that had plagued the country since Mrs. Bandaranaike became Prime Minister. Strikes were forbidden, with some initial success, in 11 'essential services' including electricity, public transport, water supply, postal services, hospitals and banks. (Later there were strikes in most of these areas despite the prohibition.) The state of emergency enabled the government to impose censorship again, including censorship of news about cabinet deliberations.[56] Emergency regulations remained in force until Dudley Senanayake, following the general election of March 1965, succeeded Mrs. Bandaranaike as Prime Minister.

The security forces

The discussion above has made it clear that both S.W.R.D. Bandaranaike and especially Sirimavo Bandaranaike were prepared to use state-sanctioned violence to impose a distasteful language policy and Sinhalese national symbols upon a resistant Sri Lankan Tamil population. Under the umbrella of emergency regulations, which were in force for more than half of her term in office, Mrs. Bandaranaike was prepared to go further in attempting to consolidate and exercise power as Prime Minister. The threat or use of force was required to suspend constitutional guarantees, take over the Christian schools and expropriate their property, seize foreign publications, censor and seize Sri Lanka's newspapers, harass her political opponents and place Tamil majority areas in the North and East under military rule. When her protégé, Felix Dias Bandaranaike returned from a trip to Russia in 1961, he is reported to have observed that Sri Lanka could use 'a little bit of totalitarianism.'[57]

The small size and limited capabilities of the police and military forces, as well as their non-political British traditions, made it highly unlikely that Sri Lanka would move very far in the direction of the Soviet and Eastern European authoritarian regimes that the young finance minister admired. During a period marked by policies that provoked increased communal conflict and fostered a more organised and militant labour movement, there was surprisingly little attempt to strengthen the forces responsible for maintaining public order and enforcing the government's will on recalcitrant segments of the population.

The potential for conflict escalation from state-sanctioned violence ineffectiveness was significant.

In the 1956-1965 decade, Sri Lanka's police force increased less in size than the population as a whole, from about 9,000 to about 10,000 men of whom about 7,800 were 'constables and police drivers,' mostly unarmed.[58] Rank and file police suffered from low pay and poor training, although corruption was less common than in later years. They were reasonably effective at maintaining public order under normal conditions in a basically non-violent society with a tradition of respect for authority. However, controlling massive civil disorders, such as in 1958, was beyond their capabilities.[59] Under S.W.R.D. Bandaranaike's administration, both respect for authority and respect for the police diminished. SLFP politicians criticised the police and ordered them to 'stand aside' at some demonstrations, even where mobs were destroying property. The policy of exercising 'maximum restraint' in dealing with disorders made constables fear that they might be hauled before a Commission of Inquiry if they took strong action.[60]

Senior officers who had political leanings toward the UNP, but supported the idea of a professional and non-political police force, resented S.W.R.D. Bandaranaike's push to Sinhalise the police, especially when he appointed a civilian with little police experience, but close political ties and a Sinhalese-nationalist, agenda to the rank of Inspector General, the top position in the force. They also complained that the Prime Minister, through his policies and actions, created problems requiring police intervention and then failed to back the police up when they did intervene. Mrs. Bandaranaike's appointment as Prime Minister and her delegation of broad powers to Felix Dias Bandaranaike lowered the morale of senior police officers still further. Like S.W.R.D. Bandaranaike, Sirimavo and Felix Dias Bandaranaike were viewed as initiating policies that created problems for the police. Unlike the slain Prime Minister, they were regarded as inexperienced and arrogant.[61] A number of senior police officers were implicated 1962 attempted military coup against Mrs. Bandaranaike's regime.

Policing problems were compounded in Tamil majority areas, where a thinly stretched and increasingly Sinhalese police force was expected to exercise normal police functions and quell civil disturbances against unpopular government policies and symbols. Good police work always requires the support of the local community. In Jaffna and Tamil-majority areas of the East, more and more police were Sinhalese, often from rural areas, who did not speak the language, understand the culture or want to be there. Sri Lanka Tamils, who had a tradition of respect for authority would, over this and subsequent periods, come to view police as agents of a hostile occupying power. In this climate, the potential for imagined and real 'police brutality' grew. To some degree the presence of a few Tamil police constables and senior officers mitigated this problem. However, over time this too would change. It is difficult to imagine a more volatile situation than that which was building in Tamil majority regions, especially Jaffna: an ethnically alien police force of modest size, with weakened morale and limited capabilities, asked to enforce policies that were viewed by an overwhelming majority of the population as illegitimate and repressive.[62]

Many generalisations I have made about Sri Lanka's police force also apply to the 6,000 man army, but there were significant differences. British traditions were stronger, especially in the artillery. Many senior officers were Sandhurst trained and had World War II experience. The army was more respected by the public than the police and regarded as more free from corruption. Standards of training were higher and, of course, army officers and men were not involved in day-to-day police functions. Thus, when it was called upon, the army was in a stronger position to deal with civil disturbances, and more effective in doing so, as in the communal riots of 1958.[63]

The army also remained ethnically diverse for longer, despite government pressures to give preferential treatment to Sinhalese. Resistance against communalisation and politicisation was strong among senior officers, and the accommodating S.W.R.D. Bandaranaike did not give priority to transforming the army into a predominantly Sinhalese force. Of the 25 army commissions awarded from 1956 through 1960, more than half went to minority groups, including eight to Tamils. Among the Sinhalese officers, most were high caste, all spoke English and Christians outnumbered Buddhists. It is hardly surprising that many senior army officers were even less sympathetic to the Bandaranaike program of populism and Sinhalese-Buddhist nationalism than their counterparts in the police. Some junior officers and most notably among senior officers, Mrs. Bandaranaike's relative, Colonel Richard A. Udagama, were exceptions.[64]

Paradoxically, preserving the professional and non-political character of the army was one of the stated goals of the 1962 coup plotters. Failure of the coup did reinforce the tradition of a civilian controlled military at a time when military forces in many developing nations were becoming increasingly influential political actors. But in other respects, the result was precisely opposite from what the rebellious officers intended. The attempted coup convinced Sirimavo Bandaranaike that she could only count upon an army that was dominated by politically reliable Sinhalese Buddhists and she moved with characteristic decisiveness to transform the army along those lines. Col. Udagama was named army Chief of Staff and officers judged to be unreliable were retired.[65] During the period from 1963 through 1969, nine out of every ten newly commissioned officers in the army were Buddhist and Sinhalese. After 1960, every Sri Lankan cadet selected to be trained at Sandhurst was Sinhalese. Sri Lanka's army was on the way to becoming a cadre of ethnic soldiers.[66]

When the army moved North and East to establish a military government and quell Federal Party initiated demonstrations, it was still respected by many Tamils as a relatively non-communal, professional force that could be counted on to carry out its duties in a relatively even-handed manner. Despite demands on the part of Sinhalese politicians that Tamils be 'taught a lesson,' the conduct of the army in general justified this respect. However, this was the last time there would be mutual respect between the Tamils and the army. In the future, when preponderantly Sinhalese military units were called upon to maintain order in Tamil majority areas of the North and East, they would face a non-cooperative, even hostile population, with whom communication was difficult. They would only be able to carry out their mission through the fear of force and the use of force.

Political feedback – electoral support patterns

The 1956 general election had presented Sri Lanka's voters with an unambiguous choice between personalities and policies. Popular support for the SLFP-led coalition gave S.W.R.D. Bandaranaike a clear mandate to effect fundamental changes in language and economic policies. Had Bandaranaike lived, a general election in 1960 or 1961 would have given voters the opportunity to choose five more years of Bandaranaike's leadership and policies or to moderate the pace of change by turning to Dudley Senanayake and the UNP. Since the UNP had, by 1958, become a strong advocate of Sinhalese-Buddhist nationalism, the communal issue would have diminished in importance as a factor distinguishing the two major parties. The principal choices posed to Sinhalese voters in 1960 or 1961 would have been between personalities – Bandaranaike versus Senanayake – and economic policies – nationalisation and import sub-

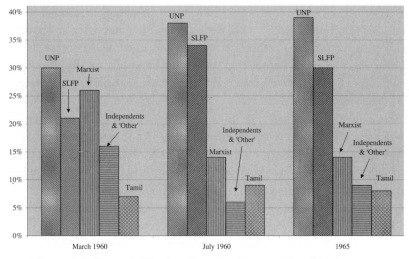

Figure 8.3 General Election Results: Percent Vote Totals

stitution industrialisation versus a mixed economy. Since 1960 and 1961 were years of poor economic performance – real GNP per-capita declined in both years – and would have been years of political turbulence as well, there is reason to believe that Bandaranaike would have been hard pressed to repeat his 1956 triumph at the polls.

Bandaranaike's assassination and the surprising emergence of his widow as a successful campaigner fundamentally changed the choice that Sinhalese voters faced in the March and especially in the pivotal July 1960 general elections. Rather than facing a choice between well-known political personalities and contrasting economic philosophies, they were asked to render a verdict on the Bandaranaike legacy, as embodied in the emotionally appealing, but politically unknown persona of Sirimavo Bandaranaike. By 1965 the immediate political impact of the assassination had receded and the choice was once again between philosophies and personalities. Voters now had ten years of experience with nationalisation and import substitution. Mrs. Bandaranaike was a well-known political personality in her own right, although she still missed few opportunities to evoke the image of her slain husband when campaigning.

Figure 8.3 pictures the per cent vote totals for Sri Lanka's major political parties in the March 1960, July 1960 and March 1965 general elections. As during the preceding period of UNP dominance, there was no clear relationship between number of votes received and parliamentary strength. Pre-election "no contest agreements" and post-election parliamentary negotiations played a crucial role in determining which of the two contending personalities, Mrs. Bandaranaike or Dudley Senanayake, would be called upon to exercise political power.

In March 1960, the UNP increased its vote total only slightly, but benefited from a weak and divided opposition. The SLFP lacked strong leadership. Its caretaker Prime Minister, W. Dahanayake,[68] had resigned and formed a rival faction shortly before the election. Leaders of the rival Marxist parties fielded large slates of candidates and received more than 25 per cent of the votes cast, but divided the support of pro-Marxist and pro-SLFP voters in the more populous urban working-class areas. Both the UNP and SLFP received a larger percentage of parliamentary seats than votes. The Marxist parties, on the other hand, fared poorly in parliamentary races.

Dudley Senanayake's appointment as Prime Minister and the prospect of losing power for a minimum of five years to a 'capitalist' UNP government reminded SLFP and Marxist leaders that allowing ideological and personal differences to supersede the practical arrangements necessary to gain political power could be costly. Opposition forces in Parliament coalesced quickly to deny Senanayake's minority government a vote of confidence, precipitating the nation's second general election in a year. Strategically, the subsequent campaign was similar to 1956, with the UNP forced to campaign against a relatively united opposition that picked candidates and negotiated 'no contest' agreements so as to maximise parliamentary strength. The outcome gave the SLFP and its allies a clear parliamentary majority and placed the reins of political power in Mrs. Bandaranaike's strong if inexperienced hands.

Arguably, the most significant consequence of Mrs. Bandaranaike's victory was aggressive nationalisation of Sri Lanka's economy and the imposition of high tariff barriers, both to spur domestic production and protect dwindling foreign assets. The negative impact of these policies on Sri Lanka's economic performance has already been described. Nevertheless, it is unlikely that economic policy was a central concern of the new Prime Minister. There was nothing in her experience or training to prepare Mrs. Bandaranaike for dealing with the complexities of managing Sri Lanka's economy. She was quite willing, however, to support ministers whose policies would strengthen the political power of her government. These ministers interpreted Mrs. Bandaranaike's' electoral mandate as a licence for sweeping changes that would move Sri Lanka's economy decisively to the left.

Close scrutiny of both the March and June 1960 election returns, however, raises serious doubts about this view. Support for free enterprise and opposition to a command economy had been centrepieces of UNP election manifestos since the time of independence and remain so to this day. The UNP's move toward – and even beyond – the SLFP on the communal issues of language and religion was not accompanied, despite occasional populist rhetoric, by a move to the left on economic issues. The election returns, even though the UNP did not win a large number of parliamentary seats, showed a solid and growing base of support for its more moderate economic philosophy. In March 1960, the UNP had reasserted itself as the party receiving the largest plurality of votes, nearly 10 per cent more than the SLFP. In the June 1960 election victory of Mrs. Bandaranaike, the UNP increased its popular vote total by nearly 10 per cent and was once again the party receiving the largest number of votes. In 1965, the UNP once again increased its popular vote total, albeit modestly, but Dudley Senanayake's return to power was due more to the UNP's success in the two areas of Sri Lanka where popular support for government policies was less critical, negotiation of strategic pre-election alliances and formation of a workable, though hardly robust parliamentary coalition.

The leading Marxist parties[69] also moved toward the SLFP on communal issues but clearly differentiated themselves as a 'non-capitalist alternative' on economic policy. Their election manifestos favoured nationalisation of most private sector enterprises, in particular the plantations, banks and insurance companies, as well as direct government management of all imports and exports.[70] Unlike the UNP, and despite considerable power in the labour movement, they were never able to mobilise broadly based popular support for their program. Marxist leaders made a serious bid to capitalise on SLFP weaknesses and reestablish their coalition as a credible alternative to the UNP in the March 1960 general election. The result, in the words of one observer, 'provided evidence that the electorate was not prepared to vote the left-wing parties into power.'[71] Subsequent elections continued a trend of declining popular support. Despite this Marxist leaders and their allies were skilful in gaining ministries that shaped economic policy. Economic policies of Mrs. Bandaranaike's government were hardly distinguishable from the Marxist parties' election manifestos. Thus, paradoxically, nationalisation and strict government control over all aspects of economic life was becoming more entrenched during a period when many Sri Lankans seemed less and less inclined to favour this approach.

Despite an apparent disparity between what the public wanted and what Mrs. Bandaranaike's government provided in the area of economic policy, members of Sri Lanka's newly mobilised and empowered majority community had much reason to be satisfied with the responsiveness of their democratic political institutions. The overwhelming victory of S.W.R.D. Bandaranaike and the SLFP in 1956 had not only transformed government policy regarding language and religion, it had also transformed the platforms of the major opposition parties regarding communal issues. Support for Buddhist and Sinhalese nationalist agendas were now accepted as a prerequisite for political success in Sinhalese majority areas. Popular social programs that had been initiated under UNP leadership were continued and even enhanced by the new regime. Broadened indigenous-language public education, coupled with the policy of 'Sinhala only', offered Sinhalese youth (especially rural Sinhalese youth) expectations of a life very different from that of their parents and the generations that had preceded them. Realisation that Sri Lanka's economy might not provide the jobs and productivity to meet these expectations would not come until later. Bandaranaike's political shortcomings or his assassination might have made this peaceful revolution temporary, resulting in widespread disillusionment among the Sinhalese. But just as the revolution appeared to be faltering, the Prime Minister's martyrdom, plus the charisma and political skills of his widow, reunified the SLFP and provided Sinhalese voters, in the election of July 1960, with the opportunity to reaffirm their commitment to Bandaranaike's vision. In Sirimavo Bandaranaike, they gained an appealing new political leader who would, for an additional five year term, ensure that the work of her slain husband was carried on with tenacity and decisiveness.

This did not mean there was no possibility of reversing the course set by Mrs. Bandaranaike's government. For Sinhalese who opposed a centrally planned economy, were dissatisfied with economic stagnation and growing unemployment or simply believed in Dudley Senanayake's leadership, the UNP remained a viable alternative. By the early 1960s, its advocacy of a Sinhalese nationalist agenda had become convincing and it had managed to shed its elitist image, at least to some degree. UNP leaders challenged government policies skilfully in parliamentary debates. A strengthened organisation and recruitment of some charismatic young party leaders made the UNP a visible and increasingly credible political force throughout the nation's Sinhalese-majority areas.

The 1965 general election showed that even a personally popular leader like Sirimavo Bandaranaike could be called to account. Factors contributing to her defeat have already been catalogued. They included poor economic performance, an unpopular press-censorship proposal, labour unrest, organisational weaknesses in the SLFP, effective campaigning by the opposition and, perhaps, a simple desire for change on the part of many Sinhalese after 10 years of SLFP rule. But from the perspective of Sri Lanka's Sinhalese majority what may have been most important was the message the election communicated about the responsiveness of Sri Lanka's democratic institutions. As in 1956 and 1960, voters had been given the opportunity to freely express approval or disapproval of their government's policies and leadership. When Mrs. Bandaranaike's hand-picked Governor General (and uncle), William Gopallawa, named Dudley Senanayake Prime Minister, this was evidence that once again voters' choices had made a difference.

Non-responsiveness of democratic institutions to Tamil concerns

Ten years of SLFP rule gave Sri Lanka Tamils a very different message about responsiveness of democratic institutions. As Sinhalese-Buddhist nationalism became the prerequisite for electoral success in Sinhalese majority areas, Parliament lost its value as an institution where 'normal' political processes could be used to further Tamil interests. The result was hardening of support for an increasingly militant Federal Party. In Sri Lanka's Northern and Eastern Provinces, communal identity became the principal guide to voting behavior for many Tamils.

By 1960, neither the SLFP nor the UNP was seriously contesting for any Northern Province seats: they had ceded them to Tamil communal parties. The Federal Party won 10 of the 13 seats in each of the three elections. The remaining seats were won by independents and by G.G. Ponnambalam's Tamil Congress. Voting was also along communal lines in the Eastern Province. Tamil majority districts gave overwhelming support to the Federal Party. Amparai district, populated mostly by rural Sinhalese, supported the SLFP while Muslim majority districts tended to support Muslim candidates with varied party affiliations.

Thus, most Tamils looked to the Federal Party for political leadership in redressing their grievances, both within Parliament and via extra-parliamentary means during this period. Federal Party leaders represented the status quo in the North and understood the customs and rules of Sri Lankan politics as it had been practiced since before the time of independence. But the Federal Party's record under the Bandaranaikes was a record of failure. Unless things changed for the Tamils, it was clear that there would be an opportunity for new political leadership proposing fundamentally new approaches to making the Sri Lankan state more responsive, or for freeing the Sri Lankan Tamils of the north and east from majority control entirely.

Conclusion

The general election of 1965 ended a decade of political, social and economic transformation during which Sri Lanka was dominated by two of the most influential personalities in its history, S.W.R.D. and Sirimavo Bandaranaike. Using Sinhalese-Buddhist nationalism, S.W.R.D. Bandaranaike mobilised political forces that gave him the power to transform an elitist political and economic system, long dominated by his opponents. A populist campaign based on the slogan 'Sinhala only within twenty-four hours' became his vehicle for gaining Sri Lanka's highest political office.

Having been named Prime Minister, evidence suggests that Bandaranaike recognised the need for compromise in language policy and hoped to meet the expectations of his supporters without alienating the Sri Lankan Tamils. His inability to find a middle path between these conflicting interests helped catalyse the successful assassination plot by leaders of extremist forces with whom he had been allied. In economic policy, Bandaranaike's 'democratic socialism' also sought a middle path between the doctrinaire socialism of the Marxist parties and the pro-business philosophy of the UNP. However his plans for economic reform were even less complete than his plans for language and religious reform when he was assassinated in September 1959.

Sirimavo Bandaranaike's commitment to her husband's legacy provided the *raison d'être* for her successful July 1960 election campaign and subsequent administration. Her tenacity and courage became legendary in Sri Lankan politics. She compensated for lack of experience with qualities essential for success in high office – focus and decisiveness in dealing with matters that might enhance or threaten her political power.[72] S.W.R.D. Bandaranaike had defined a broad agenda for transforming Sri Lanka. Under Sirimavo Bandaranaike, fundamental changes that her husband had initiated, or in some cases only hoped for, were accomplished and began to take root, though perhaps in a form different than he had envisioned.

Most important, certainly, were the cluster of new language, religious, economic and administrative policies that placed Sri Lanka's government in the position of aggressively supporting Sinhalese-Buddhist nationalism and giving preferential treatment to members of the majority community. Electoral districts that gave preponderant influence to rural Sinhalese and reforms that supported more active rural voter participation in elections ensured that no party favouring D.S. Senanayake's model of a secular multi-ethnic state would ever again win power in Sri Lanka. As we have seen, by the end of Mrs. Bandaranaike's administration, Sinhalese dominance had been established over the civil service, government-managed enterprises, the military forces, the police and the symbols of the state.

Of nearly equal importance was the transformation of Sri Lanka's economy from free market to state controlled along with the adoption of import substitution-industrialisation policies. Nationalisation and strong import controls produced short-term economic and political benefits. However, longer-term negative impacts on economic efficiency, economic growth, balance of trade and foreign reserves meant that the high aspirations of Sri Lanka's youth for better jobs and economic opportunities, created by Bandaranaike's populist revolution, could not be fulfilled. Even worse, poor economic performance intensified ethnic conflict by providing a smaller pool of economic benefits to be shared by the Sinhalese and minority ethnic communities. Disappointment with stagnant per-capita income and high unemployment created almost irresistible temptations for politicians to redirect the anger of their still-disadvantaged Sinhalese constituents against minority groups. This intensified ethnic divisions created by the government's preferential language, education, religious and public employment policies. Had the economy been more productive, political pressure to discriminate against the Tamils as well as the consequences of this discrimination might well have been less. Though negative economic and social consequences of nationalisation and import substitution industrialisation programs have been characterised as 'long-term,' they had begun to appear well before Mrs. Bandaranaike's 1965 defeat and almost certainly contributed to it.

Alienation of the Sri Lankan Tamil community from the Sri Lankan state was a third major transformation during this era. Tamils felt that the national government in Colombo, now controlled by Sinhalese politicians pursuing an avowedly pro-Sinhalese agenda, had lost its legitimacy. These feelings intensified when that government tried to enforce its will in Tamil majority areas with a predominantly Sinhalese army and police force. The army and police were also seen as having failed to protect Tamils, or even as collaborators with Sinhalese rioters who attacked Tamils in the South.

By 1965, M. Sivasthamparam's prediction in the Parliamentary debate on the Official Language Act: 'two languages... one country; one language ...two countries' was becoming a reality. Sri Lanka had not become 'two countries' – that would not be countenanced by the Sinhalese community, so long as it had the force to resist – nor was separatism yet a demand of any but the most militant Sri Lankan Tamils. But the growing polarisation of the island along communal lines, resulting from a decade of inflammatory rhetoric and discriminatory policies, had produced two distinct political systems. In the South, a political system dominated by the Sinhalese functioned as a representative democracy but with Sri Lankan Tamils, especially those living in the North and East, excluded from meaningful participation. This political system controlled the institutions of the Sri Lankan state. In the North, and in Tamil majority districts of the East, mechanisms of representative democracy also continued to function, but with little power to influence the national government. The politics of Sri Lanka Tamils focused almost exclusively on problems of discrimination and strategies for reaching a new constitutional settlement that would protect minority rights.

A fourth transformation, less sharply defined, but easily seen from the data on political conflict and state-sanctioned violence, was the decline in public civility and respect for the forces charged with responsibility for maintaining public order. Why did this happen? S.W.R.D. Bandaranaike must bear major responsibility. As a campaigner and as Prime Minister, he seemed to view public demonstrations, at least by Sinhalese, as an acceptable, even desirable way for individuals and groups to express themselves politically. 'Maximum restraint' directives given to police and concessions given to demonstrators sent a message that under the people's government, disruptions of public order were, within vaguely defined limits, permissible and potentially productive forms of political action. Mrs. Bandaranaike, as we have seen, made few concessions and attempted to deal sternly even with legitimate democratic opposition. But she was unable to reverse the rising level of strikes and demonstrations that had gained momentum during her husband's administration, fostered by rapid political mobilisation in a permissive environment.

In Tamil majority areas the pattern of declining civility was the same, but the causes were different. Strikes and demonstrations were a predictable result of Tamil alienation from mainstream political institutions. Sri Lanka Tamil protests were not viewed tolerantly by the authorities and did not win concessions. But as Sinhalese control over the nation's democratic institutions tightened and discriminatory laws multiplied, Tamils came to see strikes and demonstrations as the only meaningful option for political self-expression. For members of both communities, the politicisation, communalisation and diminished effectiveness of the police also contributed to a climate in which protests, demonstrations and disruptions of the economy, not infrequently accompanied by violence became a more 'normal' part of Sri Lankan political life.

The introduction to this chapter posed two questions regarding conflict patterns during this period: why did conflict intensify and what 'homeostatic mechanisms' constrained it within reasonable bounds. The answer to the first question is easy. Communally divisive policies and an inconsistent mix of permissive and authoritarian interventions made violent outbreaks more probable and more difficult to contain. In the light of more recent developments, it is tempting to emphasise communal conflict incidents, but labour unrest precipitated by Marxist unions was far more prevalent. This occurred mostly in Sinhalese majority areas with high urban concentrations, not in the North and East. During this period, it was the Marxist unions that were most capable of *organising* violence. Permissive government policies and declining security force effectiveness encouraged unions to engage in strikes and demonstrations, but also kept them from escalating out of control. Leaders knew that the government was more likely to back down in the face of pressure than to take a firm stand which might not be enforceable. In Tamil majority regions, anger and disillusionment was growing, but government polices had not yet impacted young Tamil men sufficiently to push them across the threshold of militancy. The conjecture that delays in mobilising militant sentiments helped to keep violent conflict within bounds seems reasonable.

A widespread belief that democratic institutions would, in the end, produce needed political changes may have been the strongest homeostatic mechanism of all. In contrast to many developing nations, Sri Lanka did not become a one party state and Sirimavo Bandaranaike did not become an authoritarian ruler, governing without democratic accountability. During a decade marked by the assassination of a Prime Minister, temporary disintegration of the ruling party, an attempted military coup, periodic suspension of constitutional guarantees, press censorship and harassment of opposition parties, plus the emergence of sharp communal divisions, Sri Lanka's democratic institutions continued to function, with broad public support. Ordinary Sri Lankans, even in Tamil majority areas, participated vigorously in hotly contested elections. The outcomes of elections produced significant changes in leadership and public policy. The leading opposition party emerged from two election defeats better organised, less elitist and more responsive to the concerns of the Sinhalese majority. Because Sri Lanka remained a democracy, with an opposition that offered a real alternative to Sirimavo Bandaranaike and her policies, citizens had the option in the 1965 general election of moderating or even reversing the preceding decade's changes. As we have seen, Mrs. Bandaranaike's SLFP coalition was defeated, ushering in five years of 'middle path' policies under Dudley Senanayake's leadership. Moreover, Sri Lanka's voters opted for another change in 1970. They turned again to Sirimavo Bandaranaike, who led a government committed even more strongly to vigorous implementation of the communal and economic policies of the 1956-1965 period. How that scenario unfolded, and with what consequences, will be told in later chapters.

9
'Middle Path' – Dudley Senanayake's Imperfect Governance Strategy

At a time when experts were divided regarding the efficacy of free market versus centrally planned economies, political considerations weighted more heavily than economic ones in shaping economic policy. Senanayake attempted to steer a middle path between the advocates of structural adjustment and Marxists in his own cabinet. This approach slowed the deterioration of Sri Lanka's economic and fiscal health, but failed to deal with fundamental issues.

A 'National Government'

Sri Lanka's third closely contested general election in a row gave the United National Party (UNP) a plurality of parliamentary seats but not a majority. Dudley Senanayake became Prime Minister by patching together a euphemistically labelled 'National Government' coalition. Despite a slim majority, he was able hold office for a full five-year term.

The UNP Manifesto included the now-obligatory advocacy of Sinhalese-Buddhist nationalism, but promised a more conciliatory approach to Tamil concerns. To deal with unemployment, a stagnant economy and chronic trade deficits, Senanayake proposed a 'middle path' strategy that would preserve social benefits and maintain state control over key industries, but also encourage investment and strengthen the private sector. During his term, Senanayake tried to keep these promises by striking a series of compromises between the increasingly confrontational class and communal factions into which Sri Lanka was becoming divided. Despite some setbacks, he enjoyed a fair measure of success. Sri Lankan Tamils came to feel that some accommodation with the majority Sinhalese community might be possible. The economy began to grow, though benefits trickled down to wage earners more slowly than government planners had hoped.

Violent political conflict returned to the relatively low levels that preceded S.W.R.D. Bandaranaike's election to office. Use of state-sanctioned violence diminished, although lightly administered emergency regulations were in force for three years. The security forces become somewhat less politicised and somewhat more effective.

What explains the relative tranquillity of Senanayake's five year term? Security force reforms point to one possible explanation. Was the influence of the *escalation from state-sanctioned violence ineffectiveness* feedback loop reversed? Did security force reforms slow or reverse the trend towards organised militancy as well as damping down outbreaks of violent conflict – spontaneous and organised? Impact of National Government development policies must also be examined. How did improved economic performance and more conciliatory policies toward Tamils impact feelings of deprivation and alienation in the society? Were Sinhalese and Tamil youths, in particular, more or less content with their lot in life and future prospects? Were they more or less receptive to preachings of radical leaders that militant direct action was the only strategy for realising their aspirations? Answering these questions will help us judge whether the apparent homeostasis this period's conflict fever chart reveals was real or illusory.

National Government leaders *believed* they had turned Sri Lanka away from communally divisive politics and economic stagnation of the previous decade. They were confident voters would affirm these accomplishments. Instead, the 1970 general election results repudiated Dudley Senanayake's government more decisively than any since the island had gained independence. Mrs. Bandaranaike became Prime Minister once again. She interpreted her overwhelming parliamentary majority as a mandate to move forward aggressively with communal, economic, religious and foreign policies that had been implemented only partially during her first term. Many observers believe these polices set the stage for civil war, beginning in the 1980s. Were these policies, in fact, what Sri Lankans voted for in 1970?

Violent political conflict – a return to 'normalcy' ?

Dudley Senanayake's 1965 campaign promised a government that would work to reconcile class and communal differences and reduce violent conflict in Sri Lankan political life. He expressed support for the rule of law and promised to maintain public order. Our political conflict 'fever chart' shows he mostly succeeded (Figure 9.1). By any measure, Senanayake's five years in office were less turbulent than the preceding decade.

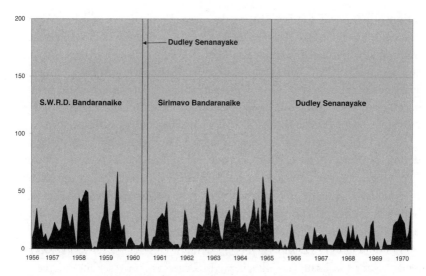

Figure 9.1 Violent Conflict Intensity

Most discernible peaks in this period's conflict topology reflect tensions and confrontations between the government and Marxist allied labour unions, but the first, in late 1965 is an exception. This maps a series of violent student demonstrations beginning at Kelaniya's Vidylankara campus near Colombo which escalated quickly and spread to other institutions.[1] Dudley Senanayake took a firm stand against politically motivated strikes early in his term and was more successful than his predecessor in keeping labour unrest under control. Peaks (or hillocks) of conflict intensity that do show up after 1965 all map politically motivated strikes. After 1967, strikes by Marxist and SLFP labour union allies that included violent confrontations began to play an increasing role in a revitalised opposition's strategy to discredit and defeat the Prime Minister.

A general strike of public sector employees that disrupted postal deliveries, communications, transportation and some administrative functions in late 1968 was a typical example. Officials declared that 'essential services' were threatened and ordered strikers back to work, however 23 days elapsed before normal conditions were restored. Student strikes, mob violence against police sentries and some acts of sabotage added to the state of unrest.

In the following year, a series of strikes called by the powerful Ceylon Mercantile Union (CMU) were even more disruptive. They produced the most turbulent period of Dudley Senanayake's term, five months of labour unrest that while less intense, resembled the last two years of Mrs. Bandaranaike's administration. Because economic issues provided the initial rationale for striking and because the CMU had at least passively supported the government, Senanayake was reluctant to intervene. University students contributed to the general unrest with demonstrations at four university campuses that required police intrusions and, in two instances, closure of the institutions to restore order.

Conflict subsided to some degree in March and April, but escalated again during the May general election campaign, which was the second most violent since independence.[2] Among the events reported were kidnapping and assaults of candidates, stoning and bombing of busses en route to political meetings and bombing of the Colombo Batticaloa train. Campaigning was violent, but it was not yet lethal. No deaths resulting from pre-election violence were reported.[3]

Figure 9.2, which compares the frequency of conflict events during Dudley Senanayake's administration with its two predecessors, provides another picture of how violent conflict intensity lessened. Under the National Government, the frequency of strike events and demonstrations fell by more than half.[4] The incidence of communal conflict and conflict in the estate sectors fell by more than two-thirds. Less than three per cent of reported events included deaths. As in earlier years, violent conflict primarily remained an urban and secular phenomenon resulting from the activities of organised groups, particularly labour unions and student organisations.

A noteworthy characteristic of violent conflict during this period was the near absence of clashes between Sinhalese and Tamils or Tamil demonstrations against the government over communal issues. There was 'communal conflict' in the North, which became violent during a five month period beginning in September 1967, however it was between Tamil upper and lower castes in Jaffna's rigidly stratified society. Lower caste Tamils demonstrated for the right to enter Hindu Temples and gain other privileges that were guaranteed to them by Sri Lankan law but denied to them by custom. In these conflicts, Sri Lankan police, many of them Sinhalese, but skilfully directed by a Tamil Deputy Inspector General,[5] were viewed by many as protectors of lower caste Tamils rather than oppressors of an occupying government. In the Eastern Province, the only reported incidents of communal conflict were between members of the Tamil and Muslim communities. In this respect at least, Senanayake's conciliatory 'middle path' strategy succeeded.

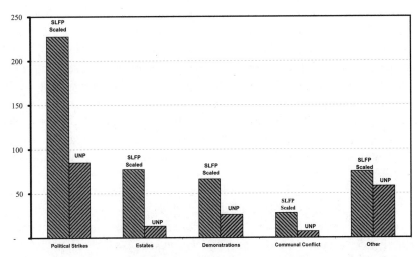

Figure 9.2   Conflict Incident Frequencies: First SLFP Government (scaled) and Second UNP Governments Compared

Leadership and governance

There was no triumphal post-election march to Queen's house for UNP leader, Dudley Senanayake, on 23 March 1965. Because neither contender commanded a parliamentary majority, it was uncertain whether Governor General William Gopallawa[6] would call upon Senanayake or Prime Minister Sirimavo Bandaranaike to form a new government. For two days, both Queen's House and the Prime Minister's residence, Temple Trees, were surrounded by noisy demonstrators who urged Mrs. Bandaranaike to remain in office and threatened to attack Senanayake if he attempted to meet with Gopallawa.[7] Paradoxically, Tamil leader S.L.V. Chelvanayakam emerged as kingmaker following an election campaign where both the Sri Lanka Freedom Party (SFLP) and the UNP had extolled Buddhist-Sinhalese nationalism. Because Parliament was almost evenly divided between UNP and SLFP coalitions, the 14 Tamil seats were pivotal in determining which party leader could command a majority. Despite last minute personal appeals from Mrs. Bandaranaike's allies, Chelvanayakam found Senanayake's promises more credible and stood firm on his pre-election pledge of support for the UNP.[8]

Senanayake's National Government was 'national' in name only. Principal coalition members were the UNP (66 seats), the (Tamil) Federal Party (14 seats), and the Tamil Congress (3 seats). Remaining participants were 'a motley collection of parties with little in common except a desire for office and an anxiety to keep Mrs. Bandaranaike out of power.'[9] Nearly one-third of National Government MPs had, at one time or another, been supporters of the People's United Front Government and remained strongly committed to a pro-Sinhalese-Buddhist stance.[10] Since, in contrast to the British Parliament, pro-government MPs who disagreed with the Prime Minister's policies could vote with the opposition and even change parties with relative ease, the task of accommodating the Tamils, while avoiding defections leading to fatal votes of confidence, was an enormously difficult balancing act.

Dudley Senanayake was a reserved and diffident man who might have chosen private life as a barrister had he not been pressed into politics by his father. He never married and had few close friends, his principal confidants being older women who were relatives. Throughout his later life, particularly in stressful times, he was plagued by a painful, debilitating digestive ailment and by bouts of depression. In contrast to his UNP senior colleagues, J.R. Jayewardene and Sir John Kotelawala, he had little interest in party organisation or in the rough-and-tumble side of Sri Lankan political life. When in good health and spirits, however, he could be both an effective campaigner and skilful parliamentary debater. Apparently he was one of those rare political leaders who served his nation out of a genuine sense of commitment, and in response to entreaties from political allies, but did not relish the exercise of political power. Senanayake's leadership was needed by his UNP colleagues because, whether in or out of office, he was always held in high affection by Sri Lanka's people. Perhaps they sensed that unlike most politicians, he sought their support more because he felt obligated to serve, than for personal motives.[11]

With a very slim majority and a cabinet that was divided on communal issues, Senanayake's lack of interest in party organisation might have posed more serious problems for the new administration but for his long-standing alliance with J.R. Jayewardene, whose organisational talents and zest for politics compensated for the Prime Minister's shortcomings. Despite the unprepossessing title, 'Minister of State,'[12] Jayewardene was the second most powerful man in the cabinet, with day-to-day responsibility for the details of government operations. When Senanayake travelled abroad, Jayewardene became acting Prime Minister.

By the end of its first year in office, Senanayake's government had already faced two major political crises and dealt with them skilfully. The first was Sri Lanka's second military coup plot in four years, which was uncovered while the Prime Minister was out of the country mending fences and seeking foreign aid in the United States. This time, the intention of the plotters was the opposite of their colleagues who had schemed to overthrow Mrs. Bandaranaike's government in 1962. All were Sinhalese, Buddhist and SLFP supporters who had either been recruited or promoted during the previous administration.[13] Failure of the Burmese rice harvest in the fall of 1966 precipitated the second crisis. International shortages made the cost of rice imports to support Sri Lanka's politically sacrosanct two kilogram per person per week ration prohibitively expensive. J.R. Jayewardene advised abolition of the ration and redirection of rice subsidy funds to economic development, but Dudley Senanayake well remembered the last time – in 1953 – when he had heeded his deputy's counsel on the subject of rice. Public outcry, fanned by the opposition, had precipitated a breakdown in his fragile health and ultimately his resignation as Prime Minister in favour of Sir John Kotelawala. This time Senanayake, with the advice of other cabinet members, engineered a classic political compromise that provided a short-term solution and disarmed political opponents. The government cut the ration by half, reducing imports to a manageable level, but agreed to provide the ration for free.[14]

Backing down on language rights and devolution of power

Minority rights – as manifested in conflicts about language, devolution of power, religion and education – remained the most difficult political issue. On language, Senanayake kept a pre-election pact with Federal Party leaders by introducing legislation to liberalise the use of Tamil.[15] The new law provided that Tamil could be used to conduct government business and maintain public records in the Northern and Eastern Provinces, including the official correspondence of local government bodies. All legislation, subordinate rules and orders and official publications would be issued in Tamil as well as Sinhala. On the more sensitive issue of using Tamil *outside* the North and East, however, the new rules were silent.[16] Senanayake also relaxed regulations requiring government civil servants to demonstrate proficiency in Sinhala, saving the jobs of a number of Tamil officials.[17]

The Prime Minister and Jayewardene may not have been surprised that the opposition used these conciliatory moves to mobilise Sinhalese public opinion against the government. They had employed similar tactics when S.W.R.D. Bandaranaike negotiated concessions with Chelvanayakam regarding language and regional autonomy in 1957.[18] Mrs. Bandaranaike personally led demonstrations against implementing the language provisions that her late husband had pushed through Parliament. When the demonstrations became violent and police responded, those who opposed any official recognition of Tamil language rights gained a martyr. A young Buddhist priest, whom organisers had placed in the front ranks of the mob to forestall police baton charges, was killed by a stray bullet. Despite this unrest, the government stood firm and the legislation passed. This provided opposition parties with an opportunity to make Tamil language rights and Tamil participation in the National Government coalition a campaign issue in three by-election campaigns. The by-elections were all in Sinhalese areas, and all were eventually lost by UNP candidates.[19] In the face of opposition militancy and election losses, Senanayake's government backed off on enforcing the new regulations. Tamil critics later characterised implementation of the Tamil Language (Special Provisions) Act as 'a dead letter.'[20]

Opposition pressure forced the Prime Minister to back down even more abjectly on the second part of his pre-election pact with the Federal Party, establishing District Councils that, while remaining under central government control, would exercise a degree of local autonomy.[21] A draft bill was finally approved by the cabinet in 1968,[22] but the proposed legislation aroused a storm of protest, spearheaded by an interest group alliance that could agree on little else. The SLFP and Sinhalese-Buddhist traditionalists, who opposed any concessions to Tamils, welcomed another opportunity to embarrass the Prime Minister. Allied with them were Sinhalese local government officials afraid of losing power, Marxist factions who opposed decentralisation in principle, and Muslims who feared they would lose power to Tamils in the multi-ethnic Eastern Province. Even some cabinet members opposed the bill.[23]

As the debate raged on, it became clear to the Prime Minister that passing District Councils legislation would be politically impossible. He explained his difficulties to the Federal Party leaders and offered to resign. The Tamils asked him to remain in office, fearing that a government lead by Sirimavo Bandaranaike would treat them even more badly.[24] They withdrew from the coalition, but continued to provide the votes needed for Senanayake to hold on. The government survived, but not without cost; failure to pass the District Councils Bill contributed to growing Tamil disillusionment, especially among youth, with their own leaders and with Sri Lanka's Colombo-based and Sinhalese dominated democratic institutions.[25]

Sri Lanka's 'Indian Tamil' plantation workers fared better. Dudley Senanayake's pledge to this minority, in return for their support, had been abolition of the separate electoral register established by Mrs. Bandaranaike for the 300,000 Indian Tamils who were granted Sri Lankan citizenship under the Bandaranaike-Shastri pact.[26] By this scheme, she had hoped to protect the disproportionate influence of rural Sinhalese voters living in the old Kandyan Kingdom, who were among her strongest supporters.[27] The legislation abolishing the register was passed by Parliament in 1967,[28] a move that produced a double political benefit for the United National Party. Support for the SLFP was weakened in key rural constituencies that had provided safe parliamentary seats since the 1956 general election. Even more important, the pragmatic Savumiamoorthy Thondamann, head of the Ceylon Workers Congress, led his organised, disciplined cadres into a mutually beneficial alliance with the UNP that remained strong into the 1990s.[29]

Affirming Buddhism's pre-eminence

While Senanayake's cabinet sought compromise on Tamil language rights and decentralisation of power, it took the lead in making Buddhism pre-eminent in Sri Lanka. This stand was consistent with the Prime Minister's religious beliefs and those of several cabinet members.[30] For a government whose Sinhalese-nationalist bona fides were suspect, it also seemed to make political sense. Early in its term, the government passed broadly supported legislation mandating that weekend holidays based on the Buddhist full-moon *Poya* day would replace Saturday and Sunday. The Prime Minister regularly worshipped in public, included Buddhist priests in political functions and acknowledged the integral role of Buddhism in the affairs of the Sri Lankan state.[31] A program to establish a number of Buddhist shrines as 'protected areas' with government support was also initiated.

Politically, however, the government lost rather than gained from its pro-Buddhist stance, which angered traditional United National Party constituencies, but moved few of Mrs. Bandaranaike's supporters.[32]

Lowering Sri Lanka's international profile

Dudley Senanayake was more successful in international affairs where, unlike the Bandaranaikes, he did not seek to become a major actor. Upon assuming power, he pledged foreign policy continuity but soon made it clear that Sri Lanka would lower its profile and try to apply the principle of 'nonalignment' even-handedly.[33] 'My conception of nonalignment,' he emphasised in a 1965 address to Parliament, 'does not vary with the nature of the power bloc that does a wrong act...'[34]

Restoring the flow of foreign aid to Sri Lanka and repairing strained relations with the United States were the Prime Minister's first priorities. In response to overtures from his government, aid donors quickly established an 'Aid Group for Sri Lanka' under World Bank auspices.[35] While granting of aid was made conditional on changes in economic policy, arousing some domestic criticism, the conditions were generally compatible with the National Government's free market philosophy.[36] In June 1965, negotiations to compensate U.S. oil companies for property that had been expropriated by Mrs. Bandaranaike's government were completed.[37] Early in 1966, Senanayake visited the U.S. and signed an agreement to resume foreign aid.[38]

In regional foreign relations, Sri Lanka's government faced the continuing challenge of balancing pressures created by conflicts between its two powerful neighbours, India and China. Cordial relations with India were symbolised by an exchange of state visits with Mrs. Gandhi and a similar exchange between India's President and Governor General Gopallawa.[39] Sri Lanka spoke on behalf of India in its conflict with China's Communist government and also condemned the Chinese invasion of Tibet.[40] On the other hand Sri Lanka supported China's admission to the UN and, in 1967, successfully negotiated a third five-year renewal of the advantageous rice-rubber agreement.[41] Senanayake also bowed at the last minute to pressures from China, supported by left-wing opposition parties at home, by choosing not to have Sri Lanka become a founding member of the Association of South East Asian Nations (ASEAN). ASEAN later negotiated a free trade agreement with the Common Market and became a major regional economic force. When Sri Lanka did ask to become a member in 1981, its application was rejected.[42]

The decision not to join ASEAN seems to have been one of Senanayake's few foreign policy failures. Even this assessment benefits from the wisdom of hindsight: in 1967, few anticipated the phenomenon of 'newly industrialising countries' which gave ASEAN its strength a decade later. Overall, his low-key 'middle path' approach to foreign policy deserves higher marks than it has received from most scholars. During the 1965-1970 period, Sri Lanka was a small, strategically located nation, with virtually no military power, in a region plagued by great power rivalries, political instability and armed conflict. Two of Sri Lanka's opposition parties avowedly supported, respectively, the USSR and China, two nations pre-disposed toward intervening in small nations. Faced with this environment, Dudley Senanayake followed his personal inclination not to seek visibility on the world stage and to adopt a cautious, non-doctrinaire, even-handed and at times even 'indecisive' approach to his nation's foreign relations. His strategy achieved results which could arguably comprise the pre-eminent goals for any small, militarily weak, and strategically placed nation. Sri Lanka remained independent. Its domestic politics were largely free of international meddling. Relations with all of its powerful neighbours remained civil, if not always cordial.[43]

Middle path options diminish and lose their appeal

Civility and cordiality were, regrettably, becoming less and less characteristic of Sri Lankan domestic politics as Senanayake's five-year term drew to a close. A large number of newly enfranchised and newly educated unemployed youth added a volatile mix of frustration and high aspirations to the political process. As the general election drew nearer, Mrs. Bandaranaike's United Front Coalition stepped up its efforts to discredit the government. It capitalised on indiscretions of Senanayake allies while highlighting communal and class differences to mobilise its followers. By this time almost every issue touching on communal relations (which meant *most* issues) had became a no-win situation for the government.

Senanayake was also weakened by the strains within his own government. The Federal Party had withdrawn from the coalition and, while supporting the government passively, was trying to negotiate a better deal with Mrs. Bandaranaike. The United National Party was tainted by a highly publicised foreign currency fraud; one of the accused was both head of Lake House publications (whose newspapers supported the UNP) and husband of the Prime Minister's niece.[44] Estrangement of Senanayake from J.R. Jayewardene deprived the UNP of organisational and political skills that had contributed to its 1965 election victory.[45] For an increasingly beleaguered Prime Minister, practical challenges of devising policies that would embody his 'middle path' ideal were proving to be insurmountable.

Development goals and economic policies

Dudley Senanayake and his advisors knew that breaking the pattern of economic stagnation, which had contributed to Mrs. Bandaranaike's defeat, must be given high priority. Economic revitalisation, with a strong emphasis on the agricultural sector, became the National Government's overriding development goal.[46] Achieving an annual five per cent growth rate in national income – the minimum judged necessary to provide employment to Sri Lanka's burgeoning labour force – was established by economic planners as a target that was both essential and attainable. A targeted nine per cent annual growth rate was established for the struggling industrial sector.

Dudley Senanayake and J.R. Jayewardene had their own experience as well as Mrs. Bandaranaike's to remind them that promising economic benefits to Sri Lanka's electorate could be a risky business.[47] Even assuming that sufficient foreign exchange and investment capital were available, experts continued to disagree about how best to diversify, improve efficiency, and promote economic growth in developing economies. Success in correcting Sri Lanka's chronic balance of payments deficit so that foreign exchange would be available was more likely to be determined by fluctuations in the international markets for rice, tea, rubber and coconuts than by decisions of political leaders.

The National Government's multifaceted development strategy reflected Dudley Senanayake's lifelong interest in strengthening Sri Lanka's traditional agriculture. First priority was given to programs designed to achieve self-sufficiency in rice and subsidiary food crops – primarily chillies, potatoes and onions. Reducing costly imports of these essential foods was seen as the quickest way to gain a foreign-exchange surplus that could be allocated to industrial development.[48] Private and public sector industrial development, supported by a combination of private investment, foreign aid and government resources were to be targeted toward areas that used domestic raw materials and either stimulated agricultural development or produced saleable goods for export.[49] The nation's tea, rubber and coconut plantations were not targeted for growth but were expected to continue as major producers of foreign exchange and government revenues.[50]

As in other areas of policy, the National Government's development strategy emphasised compromise, in this case between agriculture and industry and between central planning and free markets. The Prime Minister hoped this 'middle path' approach would accommodate contending factions in his own fragile coalition and in the electorate, while giving priority to politically appealing programs that responded to the needs of Sri Lanka's rural poor. Agriculture would be emphasised, but as a means to spur industrialisation. Private investment would be encouraged, but to complement rather than supplant Mrs. Bandaranaike's popular nationalisations. State sector corporations would not be returned to private ownership, but would be made more efficient and productive. The tea plantations would remain under foreign ownership, but were expected to be major contributors to the public good.

Agricultural development

Short-term programs to increase and diversify food production were first on the government's priority list. A *productivity improvement program*, intended to increase yields on land already under cultivation, targeted institutions that had already been put in place by the previous government, but had not functioned effectively.[51] A *land development program* leased tracts of state-owned forest land to private individuals for clearing and cultivation of food crops. A 'land army' of young men was formed to clear and cultivate newly opened land. They were given some training in scientific agriculture and promised that they could eventually become owners of their own plots.[52]

The most notable result from these programs was an increase in rice production. By 1970 about 100,000 additional acres were under cultivation; the total rice harvest for 1969/70 was more than 70 per cent greater than the 1964/65 harvest.[53] This did not fully resolve the nation's balance of payments problems as we shall see, but reduced needs for imported rice did reduce trade deficits. Other programs appear to have contributed more to the well-being of UNP politicians than agricultural output.[54]

In addition to these short-term programs, Senanayake's government embarked on a long-term initiative intended to provide agricultural land for Sri Lanka's growing population, make the nation self-sufficient in food and produce enough hydroelectric power to meet the needs of a modern industrial society.[55] These goals were to be attained by building dams, reservoirs, and irrigation canals that would fully exploit the waters of Sri Lanka's longest river system, the Mahaweli.[56] Dudley Senanayake took a strong personal interest in what came to be known as the *Mahaweli Development Program*, an ambitious undertaking that proposed to realise his father's vision in what would be the world's largest integrated river development project.

Politically, this massive scheme was presented as another way of revitalising Sinhalese culture. The maxim of King Parakramabahu I (1153-1186 AD), 'Let not a single drop of rain that falls on this island flow into the ocean without first serving humanity'[57] was known to all Sinhalese school children. Parakramabahu had presided over the birth of the world's greatest hydraulic civilisation, the remnants of which were still tourist attractions in modern Sri Lanka.[58] In the UNP plan, many of the remaining reservoirs ('tanks') and channels that had been constructed in the twelfth and thirteenth centuries were incorporated into the modern system.

As news of the project, especially the terms of World Bank financing for construction, became available, United Front Coalition leaders seized upon it as another way to attack Dudley Senanayake's already weakened government.[59] A storm of criticism from both within and outside of Parliament delayed the implementing legislation establishing a Mahaweli Development Board until March of 1970, just two months before Mrs. Bandaranaike resumed office. An irrigation project south of the ancient capital of Anuradhapura and a hydroelectric power project near Kandy were begun, but other work was placed by hold by the new government.[60] Limited work was resumed after a two-year delay, however Mahaweli Development would not again become a priority until the United National Party was returned to power, under J.R. Jayewardene's leadership, in 1977.

Economic restructuring and industrial development

Agriculture would have been given high priority in any government headed by Dudley Senanayake, but the foreign exchange crisis of fall 1966, caused by a jump in rice prices, revealed starkly the vulnerability of Sri Lanka's economic position.[61] Government leaders recognised that the reduced free rice ration was only a temporary expedient; new industrial, investment and trade policies were urgently needed. As in the late 1950s they responded by seeking economic expertise from outside Sri Lanka and strengthening the government's planning and analysis capabilities. These steps provided the basis for new industrial development policies in both the private and public sector.

Recommendations for economic restructuring were provided in a government-commissioned study by Indian Professor B.R. Shenoy, an early proponent of free market economics who had been chosen to provide a counterweight to the *dirigiste* policies advocated by virtually all Sri Lankan economists.[62] Like previous analyses, Shenoy's study pointed to slow economic growth, high inflation and chronic balance of payments deficits as the nation's major problems. Shenoy advocated shifting primary responsibility for industrialisation to the private sector, which would be encouraged to invest by reduced taxes and other incentives. A balanced budget would be achieved by curtailing subsidies, selling off many government-run industries and managing the remaining ones profitably. These proposals received an enthusiastic response from J.R. Jayewardene, who would implement many of them when he gained power seven years later, but were opposed by most cabinet members, including the ever-cautious Prime Minister.[63]

Typically Dudley Senanayake responded to Shenoy's radical proposals with a more incremental approach to the nation's economic ills. His government strengthened its planning and analysis capabilities, while giving greater emphasis to foreign investment and private sector development through a series of organisational changes. A new Ministry of Planning and Economic Affairs was established, under the Prime Minister's direct authority, with responsibility for setting priorities, collecting data and monitoring plan implementation.[64] On the other hand, much of the day-to-day responsibility for approving new industries, providing incentives, channelling investment and promoting exports fell to the Ministry of Industry, headed by left-leaning Philip Gunawardena,[65] formerly S.W.R.D. Bandaranaike's Minister of Agriculture. Gunawardena reorganised and strengthened the capabilities of his ministry, but resisted proposals to reduce the size of the state controlled sector.[66]

Despite problems, progress in promoting new and efficient industries in the private sector was made. There was little growth in 1965 and 1966, despite extensive planning efforts, due to foreign exchange shortages. However, opportunities for new ventures improved somewhat in 1967. By 1970, annual registrations of new private companies had more than doubled, in comparison with 1965. The capitalisation of these new companies was nearly seven times as great as during the previous administration.

Unfortunately, the impact of this expansion on overall employment and economic growth was limited by the small size and geographic concentration of Sri Lanka's industrial base. Most privately-owned industries employed 150 workers or less in a single location and were managed as small proprietorships or partnerships. More than 80 per cent of production facilities, both public and private, were located in the Western Province, close to Colombo, where they could take advantage of a more developed infrastructure, availability of raw materials and access to markets. Lack of foreign investment capital remained a problem. Senanayake's government had hoped to make Sri Lanka more attractive to foreign investors who had been scared off by the nationalisations and Marxist rhetoric of its predecessor. The government had no intention of nationalising any private undertakings, would-be investors were assured; adequate compensation for losses would be made in the unlikely event that nationalisations were required 'in the public interest.' A new Foreign Investment Committee was established to implement an incentive program and expedite approvals for new projects.[67] Despite a variety of initiatives and policy statements, government efforts to promote investor confidence failed. Foreign investment continued to show a net outflow with little improvement over the previous decade.[68]

The modest size of Sri Lanka's private industries meant that the major impetus for industrial growth and job creation had to come from the state controlled sector which by this time dominated heavy industry, transportation, communications and public utilities. The problems facing this sector were detailed in a report commissioned by the Ministry of Economic Affairs. Deficiencies in organisation, location, quality of staff, planning, project evaluation, marketing, pricing and labour management relations were identified.[69] Prime Minister Senanayake's goal was to eliminate subsidies in most industries and generate public revenues by utilising production facilities at full capacity, improving management efficiency and, with the exception of a few politically sensitive areas such as transportation,[70] pricing goods more realistically.[71]

Fuelled by more than a doubling of state investment,[72] the public sector did expand, though at a slower rate than the private sector.[73] However, conflicting political pressures, disagreements within the cabinet, resistance from beneficiaries of the old system and the Prime Minister's penchant for compromise limited the overall impact of a reform program that was more successful in generating elegant action plans than in actually implementing the actions described. When Dudley Senanayake left office most state-run enterprises were still plagued by over capitalisation, excess capacity, bloated labour forces and low profitability.[74]

Overall, the government's industrialisation initiatives had a generally constructive but marginal impact. Measured in constant rupees, overall investment in private and public corporations increased by nearly 70 per cent, investment in government and public enterprises by about 24 per cent and investment in the industrial sector by more than 50 per cent in comparison with Mrs. Bandaranaike's administration.[75] Overall manufacturing output increased by one-third, an average of seven per cent per year, however this was primarily due to a 24 per cent spurt of growth in 1968, resulting from increased availability of foreign exchange. The problem was that this growth, however encouraging, did not represent a significant change in the structure of Sri Lanka's agriculturally-based economy. In fact, manufacturing output contributed slightly *less* to Sri Lanka's gross national product in 1970 than in the last year of Mrs. Bandaranaike's administration.[76] Thus, success in generating the export income necessary for domestic industries to grow still depended on international prices for tea, rubber and coconut products. These three commodities were still producing 88 per cent of Sri Lanka's export income when Dudley Senanayake left office.[77]

Because imported raw materials accounted for 75 per cent of the materials used in industrial production, expansion of the industrial sector had at least the short-term effect of increasing the import bill. Under Dudley Senanayake's government Sri Lanka experienced trade deficits in every year but 1965, with particularly severe deficits in 1966 and 1969. Predictably, high trade deficits had to be covered, in part, by depleting foreign assets, which experienced a 23 per cent drop in value between 1965 and 1969.

As chronic trade deficits depleted foreign assets, the government was increasingly forced to resort to foreign borrowing. Foreign debt nearly doubled during the five years of National Government rule with more than 60 per cent of the loans being financed by banks at commercial rates.[78] Loan repayments and interest become a significant factor in the budget and a burden for subsequent governments. Because growth in overall economic output was slow, and the all-important income from exports was stagnant, the rise in debt was not accompanied by a commensurate increase in Sri Lanka's ability to repay. Under Senanayake's government the size of foreign debt increased from 34 to 47 per cent of GNP. In 1965, Sri Lanka's total foreign debt was only 35 per cent larger than its income from a year of exports. Five years later the ratio of foreign debt to exports had increased by nearly 100 per cent. Two full years of export income (even assuming the funds were put to no other use) was no longer sufficient to retire the nation's foreign debt.

Trade deficit and debt problems would have been even worse were it not for Dudley Senanayake's success in restoring good relations with Western aid

Paradise Poisoned

donors, especially the United States, International Monetary Fund and World Bank. Total foreign aid receipts nearly doubled, from $US 20.8 million in 1965 to $US 38.1 million in 1970. The increased flow of aid, however, was a mixed blessing for Sri Lanka. On the average, more than 80 per cent was in the form of loans, which had to be repaid eventually, although on more favourable terms than those charged by commercial banks. Total grant assistance received by Senanayake's more pro-Western government during its term in office ($US 28 million) was only marginally higher than that received by Mrs. Bandaranaike's administration ($US 25 million).[79] Much of the aid was for commodity purchases, which provided short-term economic damage control, but contributed nothing to long-term development or the capacity to repay. Some of the aid, particularly aid from the United States, came with conditions attached, such as the requirement that goods be purchased from the nation providing the aid. These conditions meant that Sri Lanka could not negotiate for the best price or most suitable range of products. When foreign donors provided substandard goods at inflated prices, the government had little recourse.[80] Shortcomings in aid programs, when revealed, provided further ammunition for Dudley Senanayake's opponents.

British scholar James Jupp, who authored one of the best books on the politics of this period, provides a scathing indictment of British and U.S. aid policies which, he asserts, 'destroyed their credibility as patrons of democracy in underdeveloped nations.' British aid, he notes, 'rose from negligible proportions to a sum of five millions per annum, or rather less than had been paid for many years to support autocratic regimes in Jordan and Muscat.' Jupp contrasts U.S. policy toward Sri Lanka with its policy toward Viet Nam, noting that U.S. military expenditures could have financed Sri Lanka's external debt many times over. 'Enormous resources were spent for the military defence of a democracy that did not exist,' he writes, 'while small sums were grudgingly made available, accompanied by suitable sermons on thrift to a democracy which not only survived, but enjoyed the active support of most of its people.'[81]

Foreign and domestic critics not withstanding, Senanayake's government was able to slow, if not reverse some of the disturbing trends in government finances that had appeared during the previous two administrations. Most important, government managers made modest progress in shifting budgetary priorities from short-term benefits toward investment. Thanks to the reforms initiated in 1967, total expenditures on the troublesome food subsidy increased by only 31 per cent. In 1970, annual spending on subsidised food was only 10 per cent greater than it had been in 1965, compared with an increase of more than 100 per cent during Mrs. Bandaranaike's administration.[82] By keeping short-term expenses down, the government was able to increase investment, while ensuring the cost of government did not grow more rapidly than the economy as a whole.[83]

Success in curbing costs did not, however, solve a chronic deficit problem. The government ran a deficit in every year between 1965 and 1970, averaging nearly 25 per cent of expenditures. The size of Sri Lanka's public debt grew by 61 per cent, an annual increase of more than 10 per cent per year and nearly twice the growth rate for the economy as a whole.[84] While this compared favourably with a 90 per cent increase during Mrs. Bandaranaike's administration, this level of deficit spending was clearly unsustainable and potentially inflationary over the long run. Revenues rose slightly more than expenditures, but the increase was not remotely sufficient to reverse the pattern of high deficit spending institutionalised by the Bandaranaikes.[85]

If Dudley Senanayake had been in power during the early 1990s, his economic program might have been viewed differently. Now we know more about the adverse long-term consequences of unsustainable economic policies emphasising central planning, currency controls, restriction of imports, state-managed industrialisation and chronic deficit spending. Policies similar to those initiated by S.W.R.D. and Sirimavo Bandaranaike produced crises in the finances of many developing nations, but it has often taken several decades for the crises to be come severe enough to provoke a political response. The most widely adopted remedial strategy, though it has had its critics, is called *structural adjustment*.[86] A program of structural adjustment mandates selling off state run industries (privatisation) to improve efficiency, slashing subsidies to restore fiscal discipline, reducing import duties to promote exports and eliminating currency restrictions to encourage trade and foreign investment.[87]

As noted in chapter 7, economic trends during Mrs. Bandaranaike's administration already pointed to serious shortcomings in the Marxist approach to economic management and contributed to the UNP victory in 1965. However, the longer term consequences of these policies were not readily apparent to Sri Lanka's voters, which had benefited from new government programs and jobs provided by the expanding state sector. The alternative offered by Dudley Senanayake's government was a very mild version of structural adjustment, which slowed (but did not stop) the growth of the state sector, encouraged private enterprise, maintained government supplied benefits and subsidies and featured political compromise rather than shock therapy as the implementation strategy. At a time when experts were divided regarding the efficacy of free market versus centrally planned economies, political considerations weighed more heavily than economic ones in shaping economic policy. Senanayake attempted to steer a middle path between the advocates of structural adjustment and Marxists in his own cabinet. This approach slowed the deterioration in Sri Lanka's economic and fiscal health, but failed to deal with fundamental issues. At the time of the 1970 general election, which turned on political as much as economic issues, a return to the economic policies of the Bandaranaike years still appeared to be a promising, viable alternative to many Sri Lankans. It would take seven more years of Marxist economics to demonstrate unequivocally this was not the case.

Meeting people's wants and needs

We have seen that National Government economic policies increased domestic food production, reduced troublesome food subsidy costs, gave priority to investment and encouraged private enterprise. Stimulating economic growth was the primary goal of these policies. Government planners believed that economic growth, in turn, would provide jobs for a burgeoning population and improve the well-being of the poor. Achieving these latter goals, within its five-year term in office, was viewed as key to the government's political success.

Economic growth was stimulated and, had the mass of voters directly benefited, Dudley Senanayake would probably have returned to power triumphantly in 1970. Gross national product grew at an average rate of nearly seven per cent annually (contrasted with a 4.5 per cent annual growth rate under Sirimavo Bandaranaike). Per-capita GNP also surpassed the near-stagnant performance of the previous administration (Figure 9.3).

The downside of growth was inflation. Prices were stable during Dudley Senanayake's first three years in office, but soared by more than 13 per cent in 1968, the year that expansionary policies and currency reforms had their first major impact. This record level of inflation for Sri Lanka cost the government politically, even though prices stabilised in 1969.

Wage earners and the poor benefited less than anticipated from economic growth. Predictions that income generated by an expanding economy would soon 'trickle down' as hopes for higher wages went unrealised, for the most

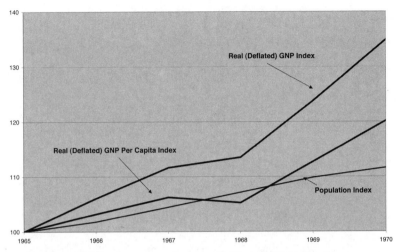

Figure 9.3 Trends in Population, GNP and GNP Per Capita

part.[88] Minimum average wages rose less than 1 per cent per year from 1965 through 1970, a rate actually *lower* than under Mrs. Bandaranaike. The average annual rise in non-agricultural minimum wages was about 1.2 per cent, a marginal improvement over the previous five years but far slower than per-capita economic growth.[89] An exception to the overall pattern was wages set by the government directly. There were several increases for public sector employees, including augmentations to compensate for inflation and the customary pre-election raises.[90]

Labour force and unemployment statistics complete the picture of a growing economy that failed to improve the well-being of many Sri Lankans.[91] In the 1960s, one consequence of Sri Lanka's public health successes was a large increase in the number of young men and women seeking employment. Between 1953 and 1963, Sri Lanka's labour force had grown at a modest annual rate of about 1.6 per cent, more slowly than the rate of population growth.[92] During the five years following 1963, however, labour force growth spurted to about four per cent per year, adding more job seekers to the economy in five years that had been added during the entire *10 year period* between 1953 and 1963. A more detailed labour force survey, completed in 1970 confirmed the growth in the labour force and, despite economic growth rates of nine per cent in both 1969 and 1970, reported even higher levels of unemployment.[93] Paradoxically, during a period when the number of unemployed reached record levels, Sri Lanka's economy also generated record numbers of new jobs.[94] But this was of little comfort to half a million Sri Lankans who had no jobs.

Even unemployed Sri Lankans could take comfort from the social services provided to them. Dudley Senanayake's government did not innovate in this area, but affirmed the programs established by its predecessors. Overall spending on education and other direct benefits grew at about the same rate as per-capita gross national product, a somewhat lower rate than under Mrs. Bandaranaike. The modified food subsidy was available to all and total spending on free food increased by 27 per cent. Few people starved to death in Sri Lanka, which made it unique among Global South nations. Train and bus service remained widely available and heavily subsidised. Public transport services continued to function as employers of last resort, especially for the government's political supporters.

Sri Lanka's health care services continued to be among the best in the developing world. During the 1965-70 period, increases in the numbers of doctors and nurses providing health services and in the number of hospital beds more than kept pace with population growth.[95] Maintaining health professionals in rural areas to supplement widely used services of *ayurvedic* practitioners continued to be a priority. Widely available free health care, plus the near absence of serious malnutrition, produced further improvement in public health indicators that had already compared favourably with some European nations. Maternal mortality rates fell by 50 per cent and the bellwether infant mortality rate fell below the threshold of 50, regarded by many as distinguishing between success and failure in meeting basic human needs.[96]

Thanks to Sirimavo Bandaranaike's reforms, Sri Lankans were also eligible for free education. This free education was readily accessible at the primary level. By 1965, the process of transforming the language of instruction from English to Sinhala and Tamil was nearly complete.[97] Dudley Senanayake's Education Minister, I.M.R.A. Iriyagolle,[98] made no attempt to reverse the major restructuring and expansion of educational institutions initiated by the Bandaranaikes. State control over the Roman Catholic schools that had been nationalised in 1960-61 was affirmed, despite UNP opposition to this reform at the time. As we have seen, the Prime Minister retreated from his campaign pledge to once again allow these schools to levy fees.[99] Only in the plantation sector, where privately run schools were still permitted to charge modest fees, was education not widely available. Only 10 per cent of Tamil plantation workers' children were enrolled in school.[100]

Now that primary education was widely available, Education Minister Iriyagolle could focus on improving teacher training. His program increased the number of teachers with university degrees and reduced the number who had failed to pass government qualifying examinations ('uncertificated teachers') offering instruction in Sri Lanka's schools.[101] While the overall quality of instruction improved, wide regional disparities remained. Teachers were assigned to their positions by the Education Ministry, but elite schools in Colombo and Kandy, nonetheless, received the most highly qualified. Less qualified teachers were assigned to schools in low income and rural areas.[102]

Iriyagolle also turned his attention to problems in the nation's universities created by rapid expansion under Mrs. Bandaranaike's government – overcrowded classes, teacher shortages, dissatisfaction with admissions procedures and a preponderance of graduates in 'arts' subjects that did not meet the nation's employment needs. Reform legislation passed in 1966 established a National Council on Higher Education with responsibility for long-range planning, admissions and university funding levels.[103] Over protests from faculties about 'loss of autonomy,' the National Council was also given responsibility for nominating candidates to serve as vice chancellor[104] of Sri Lanka's four universities.

The Council attempted to deal with the twin problems of severe overcrowding and a preponderance of arts graduates by simultaneously expanding facilities and tightening admissions standards. Sri Lanka's educational planners learned, however, that it was easier to draft new university charters than to provide adequate faculty and facilities for the reorganised institutions. New hires helped to reduce student/faculty ratios in arts curricula to 14:1 at Peradeniya and 20:1 at Colombo,[105] but the quality of instruction continued to suffer as large numbers of were assigned to marginally qualified junior assistant lecturers. In science, engineering and medicine, the problem of finding qualified new faculty was compounded by academic salary levels that were considerably lower than those offered in the private sector.

The government was more successful in curtailing admissions. During Mrs. Bandaranaike's term in office, the number of students taking university entrance examinations had increased six-fold from about 5,200 to more than 31,000. In 1965, more than 6,300 students (about 20 per cent of those applying) were granted admission. Political considerations, rather than the availability of qualified faculty and adequate facilities weighed more heavily in determining the number of new students who would be allowed to matriculate, each year. By 1970, admissions procedures administered by the National Council had reduced the number of acceptances by nearly 50 per cent, to about 11 per cent of the more than 30,000 students who applied.[106]

Perhaps because of the high prestige accorded traditional university degrees, UNP leaders moved slowly in an area that could have both provided employable skills and stimulated the economy: commercial and technical training. Institutes providing this training were established, but given far lower priority than the universities. The government also established a small number of 'practical farms' where young men and women (mostly men) could complete a one-year course in agricultural management.[107] Agriculture, however, was not a high prestige occupation and this program was viewed as a very poor second best alternative to university admission. In a nation where 90 per cent of gross national product and the preponderance of foreign exchange were generated by the agricultural sector, enrolments in agricultural training were far smaller than in arts and oriental studies.

What can be said, overall, about the success of National Government policies in delivering benefits to Sri Lanka's people? In his own assessment, James Jupp points to a difficult problem faced by Sri Lanka's governments and, indeed, by most democratic regimes in developing nations: 'vulnerability created by the need to cater to the strong distributive pressures generated by their electoral clientele.' Dudley Senanayake's middle path policies responded to these pressures by maintaining the high levels of social benefits and subsidised services established by previous administrations. His government tried to provide for long-term needs with a gradualist approach to deep-seeded problems in Sri Lanka's economy and educational institutions.

The policies partially succeeded. Economic growth improved, revitalisation of the private sector was begun and the pattern of government resource allocation was shifted, albeit marginally, from short-term benefits toward long-term investment. But Senanayake's gradualist approach failed to deal with the long-term problem of dependence on agricultural commodities for foreign exchange and was unable to cope with further declines in the prices of Sri Lanka's principal exports. Chronic trade deficits continued, with the resultant adverse economic and political consequences that had plagued previous governments.

Economic successes and failures during Dudley Senanayake's administration illustrate both the possibilities and limits of development policy in developing nations with export oriented commodity-based economies.

More important from a political standpoint, the performance of Dudley Senanayake's government fell short in four areas where it was most vulnerable to attacks from the radical populist left and to repudiation at the polls: wages, income distribution, employment and education. As we have seen, during a period when there were significant price increases for the first time in Sri Lanka's post-independence history, real wages lagged behind economic growth, income distribution skewed more toward the rich and unemployment rose. Relaxed university admissions during the previous administration added large numbers of young men and women with high aspirations but few employment prospects to the labour force. When Sri Lanka went to the polls in 1970, more than 10,000 of the unemployed were recent university graduates. These disaffected graduates mostly lived in urban areas, had ample free time and were predisposed toward political action. Added to the ranks of the disaffected were large numbers of young men and women who had failed university entrance examinations. Although only one out of five candidates had been admitted even under Sirimavo Bandaranaike's administration, it was easy for those who failed to blame the new admissions policies of Senanayake's National Council of Higher Education for their failure. As campaign rhetoric became more heated, they would have another 'injustice' on which to blame their failure as well – allegedly preferential treatment given to Tamil candidates for admission. Disaffected secondary school and especially university graduates, along with many of their teachers, played a key role in the Dudley Senanayake's 1970 General Election defeat.

10
Political Responses to the 'Middle Path'

Dudley Senanayake's greatest achievement was to provide Sri Lankans with their last full governmental term that was relatively free from violent political conflict. …His unequivocal commitment to maintaining civil order discouraged violent disruptions. He used the security forces to keep the peace, but rarely called upon them for overtly political tasks or to impose unpopular policies on a resisting minority.

Political attitudes, identities and organisations

Dudley Senanayake's overwhelming 1970 general election defeat would mark a turning point in Sri Lanka's post-independence history and culminate the peaceful revolution initiated by S.W.R.D. Bandaranaike in 1956. For the first time, a party coalition won more than a two-thirds majority in Parliament. This gave Sirimavo Bandaranaike's government unfettered power to legislate a radical program and to amend Sri Lanka's constitution. The way in which this power was used will be described in the next chapter. Here, we examine the changing balance of political and popular forces that so fundamentally altered Sri Lanka's electoral landscape.

Since 1960, there had been a near balance of power between UNP and SLFP-led coalitions, with Tamil and Marxist parties in pivotal positions to influence policy and even bring down a government if they chose to do so. After June 1970, the SLFP's control of 91 seats (a 60 per cent majority) gave Mrs. Bandaranaike the option of governing alone, although she chose to keep pre-election pledges to her 'United Front' coalition partners, the Trotskyite *Sri Lanka Equal Society Party* (*Lanka Sama Samaja*, LSSP) and the Communist Party (Moscow wing). She and her allies interpreted the general election outcome as reflecting a major shift in mass political attitudes. According to this view, 'the masses' had rejected the UNP's elitist-capitalist-imperialist program and mandated a fundamental restructuring of Sri Lanka's economy and society along Marxist lines, with preferential treatment for Sinhalese Buddhists. How accurate is this view of the 1970 general election results?

James Jupp provides a revealing picture of the complexity and intensity of Sri Lankan political life during the late 1960s, which he depicts as a blend of traditional and 'modern' elements.[1] At the highest levels, parliamentary and party politics continued to be a game that was dominated by a British-educated, English-speaking, Colombo-based elite drawn mostly from the land-owning (*goyigama*) caste. More than half the MPs maintained residences in or near Colombo. Many of the most influential belonged to one of Sri Lanka's four politically dominant family groups.[2] Most Marxist party leaders were also wealthy and English-educated, but from lower castes or lacking family ties and thus de facto disqualified for top leadership posts in the two major parties.[3] Even the marginalised Tamil parliamentary leaders were part of this system. Jupp notes that top politicians had faced each other in the legislature for 30 years or more, contributing to a 'conspiratorial and paranoid style of local politics.'[4]

Because hotly contested elections conveyed real political power, politicians tried to be aware of popular attitudes and constituent demands,[5] but they were often out of touch with the lives and concerns of ordinary Sri Lankan peasants, industrial workers, shopkeepers and especially the younger generation. Day-to-day 'political feedback' was weak and distorted. Many politicians, including Prime Minister Senanayake, may not have realised that Sri Lanka's voters, even rural voters, had become more politically discerning.

A variety of newspapers, which circulated widely in a population more than 80 per cent literate, now played an important role in raising political con-sciousness and voicing opposition concerns. The conservative Lake House and Times newspapers, which supported the UNP, still had the largest cir-culations,[6] however pro-UNP organs no longer dominated print journalism as in the past. Two pro-SLFP dailies, the *Sun* (English) and *Dawasa* (Sinhala) supported the Sinhalese nationalist cause and mounted strong attacks on the government for 'excessive' concern with Tamil rights.[7] The Communist Party daily, *Aththa* (Truth), and the LSSP daily, *Janadina* (People's Daily), wrote sen-sational stories about high-level corruption and splashed eye-catching head-lines on their front pages that ridiculed government leaders.[8] Modest reported circulations did not fully reflect the influence of these papers, because they were shared among many readers and became the basis for political gossip that reached remote areas via bus and truck drivers, travelling salesmen and returning relatives.[9]

Access to radio and newspapers, 40 years of reasonably fair elections, exposure to propaganda from competing parties, the reforms of the Bandaranaike years and periodic changes in government had made it clear even to rural Sri Lankans that political participation could produce tangible benefits. Moreover, participation was encouraged by political rallies, meetings and elections that were among the few forms of mass entertainment in rural areas. Events were held throughout the years as well as during political campaigns to provide opportunities for party organisers, members of Parliament and potential candidates to meet with the people and mobilise support.[10] According to Jupp, competition between political parties produced 'the sort of enthusiastic interest attached to sporting teams' in other nations.[11]

By 1970, Sri Lanka's historical pattern of voter loyalty to individual candidates was being supplanted by loyalty to political parties, which had become the principal intermediary between the people and the government. At least 600,000 people, over 10 per cent of the electorate, were enrolled in major parties, youth leagues and partisan union groups.[12] In 1956, following Indian practice, each party was assigned a distinctive symbol, which designated its candidates on the ballot.[13] Parties also had adopted their own colours – green for the UNP, blue for the SLFP, red for Marxist parties – which were featured at rallies and on election posters. Candidates for both local and national offices counted on a small number of party professionals and a larger number of volunteers to organise rallies, distribute posters and banners, serve as drivers and bodyguards and make up the core of uniformed marchers that led parades. In some constituencies, party organisations also included gangs of thugs who were responsible for the darker side of Sri Lankan political activity: disrupting and breaking-up meetings, instigating riots, intimidating opponents' supporters on election day and, occasionally, even bombings and murder. Strong party organisations, with some capability to maintain order and discipline, reduced the prevalence of party switching that had been a common practice following independence.[14] By 1970, parties had come to play a central role mobilising support and developing strategies necessary to win elections.

The UNP

At a time when strong organisation and strategic planning were becoming more important, it was the UNP's misfortune to be torn by the personality conflict between its most effective vote getter, Dudley Senanayake, and its most skilful political manager, J.R. Jayewardene. Causes of the rift between the top

UNP leaders have already been described.[15] Differences regarding economic policy and political style were magnified by the intrigues of close associates, especially confidants of the Prime Minister with grudges against Jayewardene. Dudley Senanayake's own leadership style had changed little from the 1950s when Sri Lanka's politics were dominated by notables who relied on their personal reputations to win votes. Preoccupied with governing and confident of his popularity with voters, the Prime Minister neglected grass-roots organisation, underestimated the strength of a resurgent opposition and overestimated the force of his personal charisma in tipping the balance toward UNP candidates in a closely contested election.[16]

The UNP's program of recruiting talented, energetic young men to leadership roles faltered with Jayewardene's decline in influence and Senanayake's neglect of grassroots organisation. The Prime Minister could be personally engaging with younger party members, but preferred to govern with a small group of associates whom he had known for years. During the 1965-70 period, young men with political ambitions saw little opportunity for advancement in the UNP and many gravitated toward the revitalised opposition.[17] Not only was there a shortage of new blood, but key leaders of the 1965 campaign either dropped out of politics or joined Mrs. Bandaranaike.[18] Senanayake's elitist governance style reinforced a popular image of the UNP as representing the upper classes and catering primarily to conservative commercial interests that had been its mainstays during the governments of D.S. Senanayake and Sir John Kotelawala.[19]

The UNP's difficulties were compounded by losing the unqualified support of two minority groups that the party had always counted as reliable allies, Roman Catholics and Muslims. Roman Catholics were disaffected by the Prime Minister's broken promise to rescind the ban on fee-paying private schools, by his failure to appoint one of their number to the cabinet and by replacement of the traditional Sunday Sabbath with Buddhist *poya* holidays based on phases of the moon.[20] After 1967, Muslims seeking an alternative to the UNP could look to a new organisation, the Islamic Socialist Front, which was founded by a Vice President of the SLFP, Al-Haj Badiuddin Mahmud. The Front quickly developed a grass-roots organisation of more than 100 branches and in 1970, won four parliamentary seats as a member of the victorious United Front coalition.[21]

The United Front coalition

Formation of the United Front coalition in May 1967 culminated a move toward more pragmatic politics by its three leading members, the SLFP, the LSSP and the Communist Party 'Moscow wing'. In the SLFP, many conservative feudal landowners had been supplanted by men who were more sympathetic toward Marxist economics, less strident advocates of a Sinhalese-Buddhist nationalist agenda and loyal supporters of Mrs. Bandaranaike.[22] Leaders of the two Marxist parties agreed to put aside ideological differences in the interest of gaining political power. Electoral power bases of the three parties were complementary. Rural constituencies in the Kandyan highlands had been dominated by the SLFP since the time of S.W.R.D. Bandaranaike. LSSP control over labour unions made it a strong contender in Colombo and Southern Province constituencies with high concentrations of wage labourers and government civil servants. The Communist Party also controlled several labour unions, held a 'safe' parliamentary seat in Colombo[23] and was influential in the island's southernmost district, Matara.[24]

While the three coalition members maintained their own identities, the United Front manifesto made it clear that a fully integrated 'people's government' would be formed following a general election victory.[25] This consensus, unusual in Sri Lankan politics, created a formidable parliamentary opposition at a time when the UNP was struggling with its own internal divisions.[26] Even more important, consensus made it possible to negotiate no-contest agreements, ensuring that voters who opposed the government in a given constituency would be able to support a single candidate rather than having to choose from among candidates representing the SLFP and one or more Marxist parties.

Fear of losing power for another five years helped to solidify the United Front but leaders of the three member parties each saw advantages to be gained by maintaining the coalition after an election victory. With the Marxists now in her camp, Mrs. Bandaranaike hoped to avoid the labour unrest that had plagued her previous administration. She also expected at least passive support from Marxist legislators for constitutional changes and legislation that would further institutionalise the Sinhalese-Buddhist agenda in Sri Lanka.[27] For their part, Marxist leaders were guaranteed cabinet positions that would allow them to reassert government control over the economy.[28] The United Front's 25 point 'Common Program'[29] promised the nationalisation of banks, heavy industry, the foreign-owned tea plantations and imports of 'essential commodities'.

On communal and religious issues, the United Front moved away from the militant pro-Sinhalese position favoured by conservative elements in the SLFP, while still making it clear that the Sinhalese people and the Buddhist religion would be given favoured treatment. Coalition members sought a middle ground that would appeal to disaffected minorities (even Tamils) by attacking the UNP for its pro-Tamil stands, but simultaneously offering vague promises of 'fundamental rights for all citizens.'[30] Few Tamils were converted, however this strategy, coupled with UNP blunders described above, did contribute to splitting members of the Catholic and Muslim communities from their traditional support for the UNP.

Sinhalese militancy: The People's Liberation Front (Janata Vimukti Peramuna)

The pragmatic decision of SLFP and Marxist leaders to mute ideological differences and join forces reflected a time-honoured strategy for winning power in a democracy by moving toward the political centre where electoral majorities are found. Formation of the United Front was made easier by two distinctive characteristics of Sri Lanka's party systems that have already been described. First, leaders of the UNP, SLFP and Marxist parties were all drawn from the nation's English-educated elite. Second, party leaders were given broad authority to negotiate alliances and reshape programs.

A shortcoming of this cosy arrangement was that by the late 1960s, many young voters had become alienated from political leaders who seemed distant, unresponsive and self-serving. For Sinhalese youth, especially those living in the densely populated south, the promises of S.W.R.D. Bandaranaike's 1956 revolution remained unfulfilled. They faced high unemployment and limited opportunities. Those who did work were employed as poorly paid labourers in agriculture, services and small manufacturing concerns.[31] Colombo-based party leaders saw 'the class struggle' as subject matter for political debate and the rhetoric of party manifestos; they were out of touch with the frustrations of Sinhalese youth who were struggling to overcome low wages and limited opportunities every day. These youth were alienated from Sri Lanka's established parties, but ripe for the appeals of a leader who would address their concerns and provide political opportunities that could make a difference in their lives.[32]

Patabandi Don Nandasira Wijeweera, was a leader who responded to their needs. He took the name 'Rohana Wijeweera' ('The Victorious Hero from Ruhuna') when he founded the People's Liberation Front (*Janatha Vimukti Pera-*

muna – JVP) in 1967.[33] This militant guerrilla movement, espousing an ideology that improbably combined Sinhalese-Buddhist nationalism with radical Marxism, seriously threatened Sri Lanka's government on two separate occasions, in 1971 and 1987-90.

Wijeweera's chosen name recalled the warrior traditions of Sri Lanka's independent southern kingdom which had stood as a bulwark of Sinhalese-Buddhist nationalism against the 'foreign' encroachments of Sri Lankan and South Indian Tamils prior to the colonial era.[34] The future militant leader grew up in Kottegoda, a small coastal town near Sri Lanka's southernmost city, Matara, and was the son of an ardent but relatively minor Communist Party functionary.[35] In 1960 he received a scholarship to study medicine at Moscow's Patrice Lumumba University, but was forced to return home because of illness in 1964. Wijeweera's application for a visa to return to the Soviet Union was denied, apparently because he had engaged in pro-Chinese political activities while in Moscow, and he became for a brief period, a full-time paid functionary of the Communist Party (Peking Wing).[36] A chicken farm near the small inland town of Kirinda, northeast of Matara, was purchased by Wijeweera and some followers in 1967 and became the Front's permanent base of operations. Here, Wijeweera codified the ideology of his movement in 'The Five Lectures,' which became the basis for an aggressive recruitment and indoctrination program for Sinhalese youth, beginning in 1968.

Major themes emphasised in the five lectures included the dangers from Indian expansionism, vulnerability of Sri Lanka's neo-colonialist economy, failure of post-independence governments to improve the lot of most Sri Lankans, shortcomings of the old-line Marxist leaders and strategies for seizing political power in 24 hours.[37] The Front's goal was fundamental social revolution which, Wijeweera argued, must be led by the Sinhalese and organised for their benefit. He was vague about how the new Sri Lanka would be organised, but the Maoist states of China, Cuba, and Albania were suggested as models.[38]

The JVP was an authentic grass-roots movement of the southern Sinhalese. In contrast to every other left-wing group, it had no historical links with the Sri Lanka Equal Society Party (LSSP) and no ties with British Marxism of the 1920s and 1930s. Core leaders were graduates of former Buddhist seminaries that had been reorganised by the previous government as universities. Others were high school graduates and teachers from smaller rural towns. Many were lower caste and appealed to caste-based resentments against the dominant landowning (*goyigama*) caste.[39] The Front built support *de novo* by organising a series of 'educational camps' where Wijeweera and other leaders gave lengthy discourses on the five lectures. In 1969, when the Front was publicly supporting Mrs. Bandaranaike, military training was added to the curriculum. Most recruits trained with model replicas, pictures and black-board drawings since few actual weapons were available. However a small elite cadre of highly trained armed militants also became part of the party organisation at this time. A dual structure, comprising both a 'democratic' po-litical party and a clandestine network of militants, would be a feature of the JVP throughout Rohana Wijeweera's lifetime. By 1970, thousands of youths had participated in one or more programs and accepted Wijeweera's leader-ship.[40] Interestingly, a number were former members of Dudley Senanayake's agricultural 'land army.'[41]

The Sri Lanka Tamil parties

Chapter 6 described how the two Sri Lanka Tamil parties failed to protect Tamil language and religious rights against the rising tide of Sinhalese-Buddhist nationalism that S.W.R.D. Bandaranaike's leadership catalyzed. Dudley Senan-ayake's return to power, supported by Tamil Members of Parliament, offered hope that the Tamils' traditional strategy of high-level negotiation and balance of power parliamentary politics might once again prove successful. Both the Federal Party and Tamil Congress were included in the National Government coalition. Nevertheless, despite the transformation in Sri Lankan politics be-tween 1956 and 1965 and the Tamils growing alienation from the political mainstream, the structure and leadership of the two Tamil parties remained basically similar to the early 1950s–authoritarian and elitist.

Unlike the Sinhalese parties, the Federal Party had failed to develop a grass-roots organisation and broaden its popular base. It was dominated by a loose confederation of wealthy landowning (*vellala*) caste members. They still relied heavily on the political ingenuity of their infirm and aging leader, C.L.V. Chelvanayakam. When Sinhalese pressure forced Dudley Senanayake to aban-don the Regional Councils bill, this provided further evidence that Chelvanay-akam's strategy had outlived its usefulness, but the Federal Party leadership had no real alternative to offer. The party's position was further weakened by its strong opposition to reforms that would grant greater freedoms to lower caste Tamils and untouchables, which party leaders saw as threatening Jaffna's rigid caste-based society.

Ponnambalam's Tamil Congress, supported largely by Colombo-based civil servants with roots in Jaffna, continued to advocate the type of multi-ethnic Sri Lankan society, deemphasising regional differences, that had been favoured by the nation's first post-independence leader, D.S. Senanayake. Tamil Congress leaders opposed viewing ethnic differences as a problem of north versus south and favoured parity of status for the Tamil and Sinhalese languages throughout the island. While many Tamils viewed the Tamil Congress as an anachronism, Ponnambalam had been regularly returned to Parliament by his loyal Jaffna constituents. His strategy was to promote the Tamil cause by exploiting long-standing personal ties with top UNP leaders. This approach, too, was increasingly ineffective against the overwhelming pressures that Sinhalese nationalists, within the UNP as well as the opposition, could now muster.

Why did Tamil youth remain passive?

Earlier we saw how high unemployment in the south, coupled with the unresponsiveness of Sinhalese political leaders, created conditions that made Sinhalese youth responsive to the appeals of the militant JVP. What of *Tamil* youth in the north, where political leaders were even less aware and responsive? During this period, there is little evidence of the militancy among Tamil youth that would, in later years, come to dominate the politics of the north and even threaten the existence of Sri Lanka as an independent state.[42] While no detailed study has been done to explain why this was so, it would appear both economic and educational opportunities were somewhat better for Tamil than for Sinhalese youth. Tamil youth benefited from superior schools that gave them some knowledge of English and better preparation than their Sinhalese counterparts for university entrance examinations in law, medicine, engineering and science. Admission to Indian universities in India's Tamil Nadu State was also common. Under Dudley Senanayake, Tamil youth could expect reasonably fair treatment in applying for positions in the civil service and state corporations (though the police and armed services were now largely off limits). Youth from north-western coastal villages in Mannar and Jaffna could combine income from fishing with a highly profitable smuggling trade.[43] Thus, despite Sinhalese dominance of the central government, Tamil youth could still see paths for advancement within Sri Lankan society, where intelligence, superior education and hard work would be rewarded. When Sirimavo Bandaranaike returned to power, she moved quickly, if unintentionally, to close off these paths. These steps were taken in the name of providing greater opportunities for Sinhalese youth. The resultant rise in militancy among Tamil youth during her administration was a predictable result.

The Diminished influence of labour unions under Dudley Senanayake

The government's decisive response to labour unrest contrasted with its vacillation on communal issues. First targeted were members of the Ceylon Teacher's Union (*Sri Lanka Jathika Guru Sangamaya*) who had campaigned aggressively for Mrs. Bandaranaike in the 1965 campaign. While political activity by government employees was against the law, the teachers felt protected by the tacit encouragement of the government in power and pre-election UNP pledge not to retaliate against political opponents. They learned this pledge did not apply to them when, shortly after the election, 239 teachers were suspended and ultimately, 140 were dismissed for illegal political activity. Within a year, according to union records, nearly 3,000 teachers were either transferred or suffered some other form of 'political persecution.'[44]

The government also responded resolutely to a demonstration and general strike called by opposition parties on 8 January 1966 to derail the passage of legislation providing for some use of Tamil in the Northern and Eastern provinces.[45] When order had been restored, the government suspended many union leaders, fined public servants who had stayed away from their jobs and fired large numbers of public corporation and Ceylon Transport workers (some were later reinstated with loss of seniority). Not only did this send a message to the pro-opposition unions, it provided the UNP with the opportunity to fill vacant positions with their own political supporters.[46] Nearly three years elapsed before another politically motivated general strike was organised. This, too, failed to achieve its objectives.[47]

Reining in the unions did have a down side for the government. Union leaders who had lost power were strongly motivated to campaign for a United Front victory in 1970 as well as encouraging their members to do so. This added to the long list of problems that Dudley Senanayake's beleaguered and divided government faced as it set the general election date, 27 May, and appealed to Sri Lanka's voters to renew its mandate for another five-year term.

State-sanctioned violence

Even Dudley Senanayake's political opponents do not describe his government as repressive. In personal recollections, contemporaries almost always emphasise his support for British liberal traditions and basic democratic freedoms. Senanayake believed that freedom should be exercised with restraint,

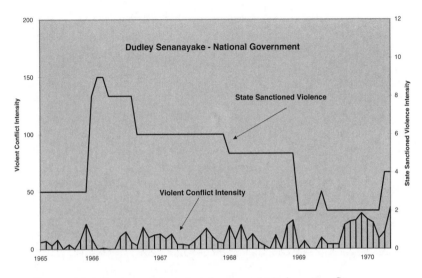

Figure 10.1 State-sanctioned violence and Violent Conflict

however, and that maintaining public order was an important function of government. He rejected populist rhetoric, which gave precedence to 'popular will' over the rule of law. Although a liberal, Dudley Senanayake was also a realist who accepted at least some of the unwritten 'rules of the game' that most believed were necessary for political success in Sri Lanka. Like other parties, the UNP had its enforcers and squads of thugs whose actions were countenanced, although not publicly acknowledged, by top leaders.

Overall patterns of state-sanctioned violence and political conflict during the National Government's years in power are shown in Figure 10.1. Political liberalisation characterised Dudley Senanayake's early months in office and this is reflected in an initially low value of the State-sanctioned violence Index. His government did not aggressively promote a pro-Sinhalese agenda or try to restrict publication of critical material.[48] Tamil parties, now members of the governing coalition, discouraged acts of civil disobedience.

In January 1966, the index rises sharply, reflecting the government's response to protest demonstrations against Senanayake's compromise with the Tamils on official language policy. This response included imposition of emergency regulations. Discovery of the military coup plot, allegedly organised by the army Chief of Staff and a Buddhist priest with SLFP ties, provided a rationale to

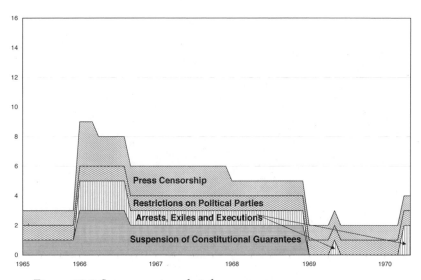

Figure 10.2 State-sanctioned violence components

keep emergency regulations in force after the protest demonstrations subsided. Government actions after declaring a state of emergency included suspension of constitutional guarantees, detentions without trial, and heavy censorship of opposition publications judged 'inflammatory.' As we have seen, this strong response, along with a firm stand against politically motivated strikes and Senanayake's more conciliatory approach to communal issues all contributed to a relatively low level of violent political conflict for the remainder of the 1965-70 period. With political conflict apparently under control, the government gradually relaxed enforcement of emergency regulations and lifted them entirely in January 1969. For the last 15 months of National Government rule, use of state-sanctioned violence was at a low level, comparable to the pre-1956 period and the early months of Mrs. Bandaranaike's administration.[49]

Figure 10.2 provides more detail on the use of state-sanctioned violence during the National Government's term in office. During the early months, there was some harassment of extremist parties and censorship of their publications, but no restriction of the mainstream SLFP and Marxist opposition. The government's attitude toward implementing Sinhala-only language policies was conciliatory although more restrictive policies, viewed by Tamils as an abridgement of their constitutional rights, remained on the books.[50]

Dudley Senanayake's State of Emergency declaration provided a legal umbrella under which more repressive measures were taken against the opposition.[51] When the LSSP newspaper, *Janadina,* printed a harsh attack on the Prime Minister, government censors judged the article to be 'defamatory' and suspended publication for five months.[52] Other left-wing papers were denied access to state managed transport facilities. Commercial advertisements from state run corporations and government departments were withdrawn from opposition papers allegedly publishing 'defamatory' or 'inflammatory' materials. Emergency regulations also simplified the arrest and extended detention of Chief of Staff Major General Richard Udagama, along with 27 other alleged coup ringleaders. Some of these men were imprisoned for more than three years, but none were convicted.[53]

Although emergency regulations remained in force for three years, there were few reported uses of state-sanctioned violence after 1966. Knowledgeable individuals from across the political spectrum agree that censorship was soon relaxed. There were few arbitrary arrests or harassments of opposition political parties. In January of 1968, the government issued identity cards to all Sri Lankan citizens over 18 years of age.[54] This is rated as a minor instance of state-sanctioned violence; however it did not appear to arouse much concern in Sri Lanka.

Two incidents involving arrests of Marxist party members occurred as Dudley Senanayake's term drew to a close, but these appear to have been isolated, rather than part of a pattern of repression.[55] More significantly, in the spring of 1970, Sri Lanka's Inspector General of Police became increasingly concerned about reports describing clandestine military training activities of Rohana Wijeweera's JVP, which was also functioning as a legal political party. (As noted above, military training of JVP cadres had been in progress nearly a year, despite the party's public denials.)[56] A special police unit was formed which found evidence of preparations for an insurgency and a number of party leaders, including Rohana Wijeweera himself, were arrested. The special unit was disbanded and Wijeweera released shortly after the United Front Government assumed power.[57] In chapters that follow, we will see that Mrs. Bandaranaike lived to regret this decision.

The Security Forces

Under a regime that was committed to civil order, but that also sought conciliation on divisive communal issues, the police and armed forces were able to play a role more commensurate with their modest size and capabilities. Indeed, what is most noteworthy about the published literature on Dudley Senanayake's government is how rarely matters pertaining to security force policies, organisation and activities are discussed.[58] Even the abortive coup plot by Buddhist officers is dismissed as a relatively minor event, though symbolising the degree to which the previously non-political armed services had become entangled in communal issues.[59] The Prime Minister made some attempts to reform and reassert professionalism in the security forces, but these were not, apparently, major priorities. 'Inadequately armed,'[60] 'neglected'[61] and 'minuscule'[62] are phrases used to describe the institutions of state-sanctioned violence available to Sri Lanka's government during this period.

As under previous administrations, the police were called upon to control political demonstrations, quell civil disturbances, and intervene in labour disputes judged to threaten public order. When emergency regulations were in force, they were given the additional power to arrest and detain individuals without charge as well as to prevent offending publications from reaching the public. Police intervention in the Tamil-language and rice-ration demonstrations of 1966, in a number of student demonstrations on university campuses, in two general strikes, and in strikes at the Colombo and Trincomalee ports have already been described. What distinguishes these interventions from similar actions under S.W.R.D. and Sirimavo Bandaranaike's administrations was their relative infrequency, relatively short duration and relative success in restoring order.

We have seen that more consistent political support for the police (in contrast to S.W.R.D. Bandaranaike's orders to 'stand aside' from demonstrators) no doubt contributed to making commanders more confident and effective in their roles as guarantors of public order. Dudley Senanayake's strong defence of police action in the Colombo Tamil Language Riots of January 1966, despite the accidental killing of a Buddhist Priest, made it clear to both the police and the public that the new government would be much less accepting when violent civil disturbances were used as a political tactic. Although the composition of the police remained overwhelmingly Sinhalese, Senanayake's policies reduced communal tensions so that Sinhalese officers no longer had to play the role of a foreign occupying force. The Prime Minister appointed a Tamil to the senior police post in the Northern Province. This officer, a highly respected professional, developed strong ties with the community, sensitised his officers to cultural differences and emphasised traditional police functions.

The Prime Minister announced his attention to strengthen the organisation and management of the police by appointing, shortly after assuming office, the nation's first independent police commission to be named since independence. Commission members were mandated to review department activities and to recommend measures that would keep the service up to date, strengthen performance and improve effectiveness.[63] Some changes were made in recruitment, training and administrative procedures following the Commission's appointment;[64] however the relationship between these changes and the Commission's work is not clear.

Despite these changes, funding the police department was, apparently, not a top budget priority. Not only was equipment primitive, but staffing was below authorised levels. A 1967 report from the nation's top officer complained that staffing of the Colombo division was inadequate to control the numerous festivals and political events that drew huge crowds to the capital city. He was frequently faced with the need to draw men from neighbouring towns to meet urgent needs, thus weakening law enforcement in the region surrounding Colombo.[65] In 1968, a leading Sinhalese daily newspaper reported that the government's ability to control smuggling in the north had been limited by the fact that the single patrol boat assigned to Northern Province police had been brought to Colombo for repairs in 1965 but the repairs had not yet been completed.[66]

There were few changes in Sri Lanka's armed forces during Dudley Senanayake's term in office. Expenditures on defence rose by about 15 per cent, but dropped as a percentage of total government expenditures. The size of the forces remained about the same as under Mrs. Bandaranaike–a 6,000 man army, 2,000 man navy and 1,500 man air force.[67] Establishment of new training academies for the three services reflected an increased emphasis on professionalism, but despite fears that had motivated the 1966 coup plot, there was no attempt to restore Christian and minority dominance over the officer corps.

During this period military service, like other forms of government service, was considered a desirable and prestigious career. Numbers of applicants far exceeded the number of positions that could be filled. Reduced levels of communal conflict meant that calls for the army to support the police in civil disturbances were fewer;[68] training and ceremonial functions were its principal activities. The Navy's 30 patrol boats and the Air Force's 24 aircraft[69] were called upon to assist police and customs officers in controlling the smuggling trade from India, but with limited effectiveness. In contrast with other Asian states, indeed most developing nations, Dudley Senanayake's Sri Lanka was described by one observer as 'virtually demilitarised.'[70]

Political feedback – a 'landslide' election

As supporters telephoned election results to Dudley Senanayake's Colombo home on 27 May 1970, UNP leaders gathered there realised they had suffered the worst general election reversal in Sri Lanka's history. Among 129 UNP candidates who campaigned for Parliament, only 17 won victories. Eleven of Senanayake's 17 cabinet ministers were defeated. In his rural home district, Dedigama, the Prime Minister won against a political unknown by only 1,067 votes. Only in Colombo, where J.R. Jayewardene and three other UNP leaders were re-elected by comfortable margins, did the party retain something of its traditional base.[71]

Voters turned against the UNP most strongly in constituencies with large Sinhalese-Buddhist majorities, especially rural districts dominated by Kandyan Sinhalese. Among Sri Lanka's 114 Sinhalese dominated constituencies, the UNP was able to win only three (one of which was Senanayake's Dedigama). Four UNP candidates won in Muslim majority constituencies, three in those with a large Roman Catholic population, two where Sri Lanka Tamils were in the majority. In five other constituencies, support from large minority populations contributed to the UNP victories. In thirteen of the Island's 21 administrative districts and three entire provinces no UNP candidates won seats.

The United Front victory mirrored the UNP's defeat. The coalition won a plurality of votes in all 16 Sinhalese dominated administrative districts, carrying 14 of these by absolute majorities. It won 84 of the Sinhalese majority constituencies by more than 3,000 votes and 54 by more than 5,000 votes. This gave Sirimavo Bandaranaike's new government substantially more than the two-thirds majority needed to amend the constitution, without depending upon a single vote from the Tamil parties.

What explains this overwhelming repudiation of a popular Prime Minister and a government that had begin to reinvigorate economic growth? As in many democratic nations, elections were used by Sri Lankans to express dissatisfaction with the economic circumstances of their daily lives. Factors contributing to this dissatisfaction in 1970 were described earlier in this chapter. Economic growth had not yet trickled down to wage earners, especially in rural areas. Unemployment was at an all time high, especially among youth who had swelled the voting rolls by nearly 20 per cent since 1965.

Popular discontent was focused on the UNP and then translated into votes by a campaign strategy that worked to discredit the government in Parliament, appealed to class and communal differences and promised an extensive package of social benefits that would be financed by redistributing wealth from the rich to the poor.[72] Implementation of this strategy began in earnest with the formation of the United Front coalition in March 1968 and was based on the '25 point program' that has already been described. Unlike previous coalitions in Sri Lanka, the United Front maintained cohesion and unity of purpose throughout the two-year period preceding the general election. According to one observer, 'it spoke with such unanimity and confidence on every issue that it was sometimes almost a parallel government.'[73]

Mrs. Bandaranaike's pre-election manifesto introduced themes that United Front candidates, publications and supporting organisations would effectively emphasise throughout the campaign. Dudley Senanayake's government was characterised as an 'odd collection' of opportunists that depended on defectors and Tamil federalists for support. Its economic policies were derided for creating inflation, indebtedness and unemployment, while making Sri Lanka dependent on 'international finance capital, imperialist economic agencies and international trade cartels.' While communal issues received less emphasis than in 1956, United Front candidates reminded Sinhalese audiences that Tamils had held the balance of power in the 1965 Parliament; Tamil support had tipped the balance in favour of Dudley Senanayake and kept his government in office for its full term. Only by giving the Front an overwhelming majority, they argued, could the Tamil parties be barred from holding the balance of power. As election day approached, a number of leading Buddhist priests issued a warning to both leading candidates that 'the Sinhala race is now facing a severe national calamity' and urged them to exclude Tamils from power by forming a national unity government in the event of a close election.[74]

In their own campaign, UNP candidates and their allies attempted to defend the government's record, while arousing fears that an administration allied with Marxist parties would end democracy in Sri Lanka.[75] They pointed to improved economic growth, higher wages, and the free rice ration. Economic revitalisation was attributed in part to the restoration of foreign aid. The Mahaweli irrigation project was defended as an embodiment of centuries-old Sinhalese traditions that would help achieve food self-sufficiency and lay a solid foundation for long-term economic growth.

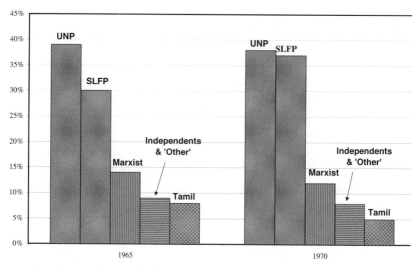

Figure 10.3 General Election Results: Percent Vote Totals

Although the UNP emerged from the election with only 17 of the nation's 151 parliamentary seats (13 per cent), it retained a solid core of support in the electorate (Figure 10.3). Nearly 300,000 *more* voters cast their ballots for the UNP in 1970 than in 1965 and it was once again the party receiving the largest number of votes. It received virtually the same per cent of the popular vote that had provided a narrow margin of victory in 1965. UNP candidates won the largest number of votes in four of Sri Lanka's nine provinces comprising 61 per cent of the nation's total registered voters. Interestingly, the two Marxist members of the United Front coalition saw their share of the popular vote drop from 14 to 12 per cent. This was due in part, however, to tactical decisions by party leaders not to contest seats where the SLFP candidate had the best chance of winning.

These 'no-contest pacts,' which capitalised on Sri Lanka's single member electoral system and the disproportionate parliamentary representation given to Kandyan Sinhalese, were pivotal in giving the United Front the overwhelming parliamentary majority necessary to ignore both UNP and Tamil objections to fundamental social and economic changes. These pacts were designed so skilfully that, apart from symbolic candidacies in the Tamil dominated Northern Province, *neither the LSSP nor the Communist Party lost in a single constituency that it contested.* The SLFP lost in only 15 of the 106 constituencies that it contested seriously. It was no-contest pacts that enabled the United Front to translate a 49 per cent popular majority into an 83 per cent parliamentary majority.

Despite this wide gap between popular and parliamentary majorities, Sirimavo Bandaranaike clearly came to power with a broad mandate for change from Sinhalese voters. Dudley Senanayake's five-year term in office had failed to sway those Sri Lankans whose votes made a real difference in elections, Sinhalese Buddhists, from their commitment to S.W.R.D. Bandaranaike's unfinished social and economic revolution. A substantial majority of the Sinhalese favoured the more egalitarian and overtly Sinhalese-Buddhist, language, educational, government employment and religious policies advocated by the SLFP. Mrs. Bandaranaike's view that any exercise of political power by Tamils should be regarded by Sinhalese as a 'severe national calamity'[76] was shared, no doubt, by many of her supporters. Talk of minority rights—especially rights for Sri Lanka Tamils – was viewed as affronting a democratically mandated reformist agenda, intended to restore the Sinhalese race to its rightful place in Sri Lanka.

The electorate's verdict on economic policy must be regarded as more equivocal. It would be hard to argue that there was overwhelming support for Marxist approaches to economic and social policies. Indeed, Marxist leaders joined the United Front in part because they recognised, after 1960, that their parties would never win a parliamentary majority. Their share of the popular vote had continued to shrink in almost every election and shrunk again in 1970. On the other hand, the United Front's overall economic goals had broad appeal. A majority of Sri Lanka's voters were still poor, and in 1965, a substantial fraction was either unemployed or underemployed. Workers in the agricultural sector had seen prices rise faster than wages. Teachers and government workers, who benefited from public-sector wage increases, feared that a UNP-dominated government would further limit labour union power. Voters knew that nationalisation and new social programs would increase employment and educational opportunities for Sinhalese. They hoped that promises of continued economic growth and of economic management that was not only more equitable, but more efficient, would also be fulfilled.

What of the Tamils in this pivotal election? Tamil voters in the north and east were also dissatisfied with the status quo, but had less reason to hope that casting their votes would improve matters. They faced the same economic problems as the Sinhalese plus the growing threat to their political and economic rights posed by Sinhalese-Buddhist nationalism. Support from Tamil members of Parliament had kept Dudley Senanayake in power, but the Prime Minister had broken his promise to support regional autonomy and vacillated on Tamil language rights. Sri Lanka's major political parties had little to offer the Tamils; they no longer seriously contested most Tamil majority constituencies. Federal Party and Tamil Congress campaign propaganda continued the acrimonious 20-year debate over whether confrontational or accommodationist strategies would most effectively protect Tamil rights; in fact, both strategies had repeatedly failed.

Voting patterns in Tamil majority constituencies revealed no clear pattern, but less stability than in previous elections. In the Northern Province, voters replaced all three Tamil Congress members of Parliament, including party leader G.G. Ponnambalam, with Federal Party candidates. However they also replaced three sitting Federal Party MPs with Tamil Congress candidates.[77] Thus, while six seats changed hands, the number of seats held by the two parties remained the same.

The Federal Party was a big loser in the more ethnically mixed Eastern Province . It retained control of two out of three Tamil majority districts, but lost the third to the UNP. In the Muslim majority Muttur district, it lost a seat to the SLFP.[78] In the past, Federal Party advocacy of Tamil language rights had gained it support from Tamil speaking Muslims, but in the face of SLFP and UNP appeals, community leaders felt there was more to be gained by co-operating with the increasingly dominant Sinhalese than with the Tamils.[79]

If Tamils needed further evidence that their traditional parties' business-as-usual approach to Sri Lankan politics would not work, the 1970 general election provided it. The overwhelming United Front majority in Parliament erased any possibility that Tamil Members could exercise influence by holding the balance of power. Advocates of Sinhalese-Buddhist nationalism could now legislate as they pleased, using their two-thirds parliamentary majority to pass a new constitution that would mandate preferential treatment for the Sinhalese race and for Buddhism.

Conclusion

The UNP's narrow general election victory in March of 1965 was no mandate to change Sri Lanka's development trajectory. Dudley Senanayake came to power because S.W.R.D. Bandaranaike's populist revolution had lost momentum, not because the Sinhalese majority that now dominated Sri Lankan politics wished to repudiate it. Senanayake's pledge to seek a 'middle path' (echoing S.W.R.D. Bandaranaike's similar pledge in 1956) affirmed that there would be no turning back, but offered an alternative to the Bandaranaikes' left-leaning populism. Senanayake argued that compromise and gradual change, in the British liberal tradition, rather than confrontation and revolutionary change, in the Marxist tradition, would be a better approach to economic development and social reform in Sri Lanka.

Senanayake remained committed to compromise and gradual change throughout his five years in office, despite criticism from political opponents and allies alike that his policies were vacillating and inconsistent. He included Tamils in the political process and partially accommodated their demands for language rights but gave in to Sinhalese pressure on the issue of regional autonomy. His unpopular *poya* holiday scheme acknowledged the special place of Buddhism in Sri Lanka, but he tried to deal sensitively with the desires of Hindus, Christians and Muslims to practice their religion freely. He compromised by halving the politically sensitive rice ration, saving critically needed foreign exchange, but partially assuaged critics by making rice available for free. His economic polices were less hostile to the private sector and included half-hearted structural changes to address long-term economic problems that had become more visible during 10 years of central planning: stagnant growth, negative trade balances, declining foreign reserves and chronic government deficits. Nevertheless, industrial policy (directed by a Marxist Minister of Industries, Phillip Gunawardene) remained firmly committed to strong government controls. Finally, Dudley Senanayake orchestrated a non-ideological foreign policy that improved relations with Western nations, but maintained more or less amicable ties with both India and China. Overall, he approached democratic governance in the manner described by political economist Charles Lindblom as 'the science of muddling through.'

A 'muddling through' strategy is most appealing to those who have a stake in the status quo and are sceptical of millennial ideologies. Those disadvantaged by the status quo are often opposed to compromise and receptive to millennial appeals. Sri Lanka's Sinhalese majority, and especially Sinhalese youth, fell disproportionately into this latter category. Both their expectations and political awareness had been raised by S.W.R.D. Bandaranaike. In 1970, they still remained deeply committed to the goals of his social revolution: economic opportunity, social equity, Sinhalese pre-eminence and government support for Buddhism.

In 1970, many of these goals were, as yet, unrealised. The nation that named Dudley Senanayake Prime Minister in 1965 was very different from the nation his father, D.S. Senanayake, had been named to govern in 1948. However, 10 years of rule by S.W.R.D. and Sirimavo Bandaranaike had done more to legitimise the principles of a Sinhalese-dominated social revolution than to actually transform Sri Lankan society according to those principles. When Dudley Senanayake assumed power, a small number of wealthy high caste families still controlled large tracts of land as virtual feudal overlords, lived ostentatiously in Colombo mansions and, through complex kinship networks, dominated the nation's economic, political and social life. The Official Language Act had been passed in 1960, but English still remained the most important prerequisite for political and economic power. Sri Lanka's legal system, in fact, continued to function almost entirely in English, even at the lowest-level magistrate's courts. The nation's tea plantations, which provided critically needed foreign exchange, were still owned by foreigners. Exclusive British clubs in both Colombo and the tea growing areas still refused to admit Sri Lankan citizens as members.

Yet, as noted in the introduction to this chapter, violent conflict returned almost to 1946-56 levels under the National Government. The drop in communal conflict incidents was especially marked. Which policies of Dudley Senanayake's government, and the trajectories those policies helped shape, contributed most to this change?

The Prime Minister's principled yet conciliatory leadership style may have been the most important factor. He sympathised with Sinhalese-Buddhist aspirations but was not prepared to give up democracy and civil order to fulfil them. In a society that still respected authority (and respected Dudley Senanayake personally) the Prime Minister's public statements stressed the importance of public order. He avoided both the communally divisive rhetoric favoured by SLFP leaders and the revolutionary rhetoric of the Marxists. His political strategy stressed reconciliation between Sinhalese and Tamils rather than trying to gain Sinhalese support by pitting the two communities against one another. Even where Senanayake failed to keep his promises, Tamil leaders viewed him as a sympathetic figure and felt there was little to be gained by confronting his government. Buddhists, too, acknowledged the Prime Minister's devout Buddhism though many preferred the more overtly pro-Buddhist stance of Sirimavo Bandaranaike. Extremist Buddhist groups did not receive the tacit support for confrontational tactics that S.W.R.D. and Sirimavo Bandaranaike's administrations had given.

A stance of respect for authority was coupled with more even-handed management of the security forces. *Conflict escalation from state-sanctioned violence ineffectiveness* was not a problem under the National Government, as it had been under the Bandanaraikes. Through its strong response to illegal campaigning by the teacher's unions and to an abortive January 1966 general strike, the government sent a message to union leaders that would it use the power of the state to oppose political strikes. Dudley Senanayake's unequivocal defence of the security forces role in quelling the strike, despite a Buddhist priest's 'martyrdom', demonstrated to police and army leaders that stern measures to maintain order would be supported. Student leaders received a similar message when the Prime Minister took the politically risky step of ordering police onto university campuses in order to quell demonstrations that had gotten out of hand. These interventions angered student leaders and in that way may have contributed to the UNP's general election defeat, but they also deterred violent student demonstrations and, to some degree, controlled those that did occur. Despite their limited capabilities, Sri Lanka's police and army became, once again, relatively effective instruments that the government could call upon to control disorder, rather than instruments of uncertain value that were as likely, in a given situation, to fuel the flames of violent conflict as to put out the fire.

Improved economic growth may also have reduced the potential for violent conflict, despite the problems of stagnant wages and unemployment. An expanding economy gave employers (including Sri Lanka's largest employer, the government) greater ability to avoid long strikes by raising wages. This offered workers the hope of further gains through measures short of violence. The growing strength of the United Front during the final two years of Senanayake's term may have fostered similar attitudes on the part of factions opposed to the government.

Dudley Senanayake's greatest achievement was to provide Sri Lankans with their last full governmental term that was relatively free from violent political conflict. Viewed retrospectively, the ability to keep peace in Sri Lanka's divided society seems a greater achievement than it may have appeared to be in 1970. He succeeded in reducing the level of confrontation and revolutionary rhetoric that had pervaded Sri Lankan politics during the previous decade. His unequivocal commitment to maintaining civil order discouraged violent disruptions. He used the security forces to the keep the peace, but rarely called upon them for overtly political tasks or to impose unpopular policies on a resisting minority. Even Senanayake's political opponents respected his commitment to democracy and knew they would be given a relatively unfettered opportunity to compete for political power in 1970. This made political violence seem less attractive as a political tactic and less easy to justify.

Part III

Symptoms of Infection and Immune
System Responses:
How Sri Lanka's United Front
Government Coped with a Violent
Insurrection and Shortcomings of its
Marxist Development Model

11
Populism and Sinhalese Nationalism Resurgent

In international settings, Mrs. Bandaranaike could speak movingly of oppression and its costs and of the feelings of oppressed people. Her words were not so different from those of Tamil leaders expressing their aspirations for political freedom. Had Sirimavo Bandaranaike brought the brilliance and energy to domestic communal problems that she brought to international affairs, relations between Sri Lanka's Sinhalese and Tamil communities might have followed a different path.

Sirimavo Bandaranaike's government assumed power, as we have seen, with an unprecedented mandate to effect the political, social and economic reforms described in the United Front's 'Common Program.' To symbolise a new political order, Parliament's ceremonial opening was held for the first time in Colombo's Independence Hall, modelled after the grand audience chamber of Sinhalese Kandyan kings. Independence Hall, located in the centre of a large plaza, has no walls; its massive roof is supported by columns that leave the precincts open. Ordinary Sri Lankans, who gathered in large numbers to cheer United Front leaders and jeer the tiny cohort of opposition parliamentarians, could witness the entire proceedings.

The new government moved quickly to implement its programs, but within the framework of Sri Lanka's laws and democratic institutions. United Front ministers were reform-minded members of the established political order, not revolutionaries. New legislation sailed quickly through a compliant parliament, but implementation moved more slowly. Drafting a new constitution, a top government priority, took nearly two years to complete. In the economic arena, ministers worked to strengthen central planning institutions and prepare a detailed five-year plan. As with constitutional reform, the first results from months of work were complex documents, not tangible benefits for the poor.

Early in its term, Sirimavo Bandaranaike's new regime faced two crises that made achieving its ambitious goals more difficult. In April 1971, youthful People's Liberation Front (JVP)[1] cadres, impatient with the slow pace of reforms, mounted a full-scale armed insurrection that nearly toppled the government. The insurrection diverted resources to the security forces and delayed reforms still further. Peace had scarcely been restored when a combination of skyrocketing oil prices and declining rice production produced the worst trade deficits Sri Lanka had faced since independence. Foreign exchange reserves dwindled, imports were curtailed and the economy stagnated. A government that had promised poor Sri Lankans a cornucopia of benefits was instead forced to reduce the weekly measure of rice by half and impose bread rationing.

Economic deterioration was paralleled by deterioration in relations between the Tamil and Sinhalese communities. Pro-Sinhalese provisions of the new 'Republican Constitution' were rammed through by an overwhelming Sinhalese majority, over Tamil protests. The document eliminated minority protections, prohibited federalism explicitly, and mandated privileged status for Buddhism. 'Ceylon' became 'Sri Lanka,' a name that evoked ancient Sinhalese traditions. The changes convinced many Tamils that no Sinhalese government would treat them fairly. Pro-Sinhalese university admissions procedures angered Tamil youth, who began to throw their support to militant separatist movements. Tamil United Liberation Front was the new name chosen for a coalition of leading Tamil parties in 1976. The choice was intended to symbolise Tamils' growing belief that fair treatment, political rights and economic opportunity were now only attainable in a separate state, which they called Tamil Eelam.

In a seven-year period characterised by development failures, heightening ethnic identities, communal polarisation and some decline in security force professionalism, one might expect to see a fever chart showing heightened levels of conflict throughout the period. This is not the case. After an initial paroxysm, denoting the JVP rebellion, conflict patterns seem more like the relatively tranquil United Front years than the more turbulent period of S.W.R.D. and Sirimavo Bandaranaike's first years in office. Deeper probing shows differences as well as similarities. Militant-inspired conflict, communal conflict and political killings were more frequent, though the overall level of conflict intensity remained low.

What are we to conclude from this: that development failures and polarisation do necessarily increase the likelihood of violent incidents, but may change their complexion? Another possible explanation for low conflict levels is that despite the limited capabilities of its security forces, Mrs. Bandaranaike's government used state-sanctioned violence effectively to clamp down on dissenters. In contrast to later eras, Sri Lanka's political institutions and security apparatus were capable of responding to violent outbreaks with an effective homeostatic response. A third possibility is that virtually inevitable preconditions for civil war were created during the United Front years, but did not manifest themselves until after Sri Lanka's voters had removed Mrs. Bandaranaike's coalition from office. In the development conflict system model's language, Mrs. Bandaranaike benefited and her successor was victimised by delays in the *conflict escalation from development failures* and *state-sanctioned violence ineffectiveness* feedback loops. Sri Lanka's premier historian, K. M. de Silva, argues this position powerfully in his book, *Reaping the Whirlwind*, and other publications.

As the scheduled date for general elections drew near, it appeared that Sri Lanka's democratic institutions still offered an alternative to violence, providing a feedback mechanism to peacefully effect leadership changes when a government lost favour. A revitalised UNP under J.R. Jayewardene's leadership was aggressively exploiting government misfortunes in its political campaigning. United Front leaders responded with tightened press censorship and banned UNP public meetings, but holding together an increasingly fractious coalition proved more difficult. In 1975, The Sri Lanka Equal Society Party (LSSP) left the government and precipitated strikes by its labour union allies that further damaged an already stagnant economy. Early in 1977, the Communists joined them in opposition. When voters went to the polls in July 1977, Sirimavo Bandaranaike's rump Sri Lankan Freedom Party government was defeated by an even greater landslide than its 1970 triumph.

Violent conflict: Sri Lanka's first militant insurgency

If you ask Sri Lankans for recollections of Sirimavo Bandaranaike's second term 'the JVP Rebellion' almost always looms large[3]. The failed attempt of youthful revolutionaries to install a radical Marxist regime by force, followed by an aftermath of repression, were common occurrences in developing nations, but shocking new experiences for Sri Lankans. Despite sporadic outbreaks of ethnic conflict, most still viewed their society as 'peaceful' and 'civil'. The rebellion shows up as the first and highest peak on our 'fever chart' for this period (Figure 11.1).

There were also more political killings and more conflict attributable to communal differences during Mrs. Bandaranaike's seven years in power. Between 1972 and mid-1976, communal strife between Sinhalese and Tamils replaced strikes and demonstrations as a principal contributor to conflict 'peaks'. After the United Front Coalition fractured in late 1975, Marxist unions began

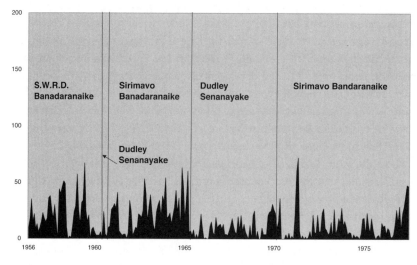

Figure 11.1 Violent Conflict Intensity, May 1956 – July 1977

harassing the government again with strikes and demonstrations. When the 1977 General Election date was set and campaigning intensified, thuggery, bombings, arson and politically motivated killings became more intense than during any previous pre-election period. Violence was now a more widely used political tactic in Sri Lanka.

The People's Liberation Front (JVP) Insurrection

The JVP guerrillas who threatened Sirimavo Bandaranaike's government early in its term typified this acceptance of violence. Chapter 10 described how thousands of Sinhalese youths, predominantly from the rural South, participated in JVP indoctrination classes and how a smaller number received at least rudimentary military training. During the general election campaign and following the United Front's overwhelming victory, JVP leaders continued to pursue a dual strategy of overt political organising and clandestine military preparations. In an August 1970 newspaper interview entitled 'Not guns, but criticism', student leader Mahinda Wijesekera characterised the JVP's public stance: 'Our movement consists of true lovers of this country and poor masses,' he said. 'We have emerged to liberate our country from all imperialists and capitalist strangulation, even at the cost of our lives, to establish pure socialism and bring prosperity to the poverty stricken masses of our beautiful motherland.'[4]

Senior police officers in Dudley Senanayake's government viewed the JVP's threats seriously. They increased surveillance of the organisation early in 1970 and arrested its leader, Rohana Wijeweera, in March. However, Mrs. Bandaranaike at first viewed Wijeweera as sympathetic to her government. In pre-election publications and public speeches, he had called upon 'democratic and peace loving people' to support the United Front and warned that the UNP's goal was to establish a dictatorship. Releasing Wijeweera from prison was one of the new Prime Minister's first decisions.[5]

Once freed, Wijeweera began holding a series of public rallies that drew large, supportive audiences and solidified his leadership position within the JVP. As it became clear that the government's 'revolution' would be entrusted to old line Colombo politicians, for whom elaborate plans and constitutional legalisms took precedence over action, his speeches became more strident and the JVP one again began to attract police attention. In a 27 February address at Colombo's Hyde Park, Wijeweera, perhaps carried away by audience enthusiasm, referred specifically to 'the day of revolution.'[6]

Sri Lanka's Marxist politicians had spoken of 'revolution' and 'class warfare' on political platforms for years, but Wijeweera was serious. Plans for an armed insurrection were in advanced stages and had been largely ignored by a government that was more concerned about threats from the right. By early 1971, the JVP's stock of arms had grown to more than 3,000 home-made bombs, plus shotguns, revolvers and ammunition. These were cached in a network of hideouts, many in Buddhist temples and on university campuses, throughout Sinhalese areas of the country.[7] The revolutionaries' plan was to begin the insurrection with simultaneous attacks on more remote police stations and jails that would drive security forces from rural areas. As those attacks gained momentum, a team of men was to seize the Colombo Main Power Station, blacking out the city. Following this, the Prime Minister would be abducted (possibly killed), key government installations in the capital captured, and the new revolutionary government proclaimed.[8] JVP leaders compiled long lists of counter revolutionaries to be killed after state power was seized. Dead bodies were to be dumped and buried in roadside ditches prepared in advance for this purpose.[9]

Fortunately for the government, stepped up JVP bomb production in the first two weeks of March 1971, produced a rash of accidents that aroused police suspicions.[10] On two successive days small villages in rural Sabaragamuwa

Province were rocked by explosions that left several youths dead and revealed bomb-building workshops.[11] Two weeks later, an accidental detonation blew the entire roof from a Peradeniya University residence hall. Investigators who rushed to the scene discovered the hall was a hideout for a large cache of explosives and weapons. By this time, the police had already moved against the JVP leadership. Wijeweera was arrested on 12 March, apparently while he was on a final mission to 'brief the leaders of the revolution'.[12] By 16 March, acting under newly imposed emergency regulations; police had taken more than 100 JVP activists into custody, transported them by military convoy to the north and incarcerated them under Spartan conditions in an old Dutch Fort near Jaffna city.[13]

The arrests pushed JVP leaders not in custody to implement their plans prematurely.[14] Early on the morning of 5 April, armed youths began a series of attacks on rural police stations that surprised the security forces and alarmed the government, but failed to capture any major centres of power. According to official sources, as many as 94 police stations were captured in nearly simultaneous attacks directed by a centralised leadership. More recent accounts describe the JVP as faction riven and the attacks as disorganised. They say initial JVP gains were due as much to decisions to withdraw police from rural areas by a government that had lost its nerve, as to rebel effectiveness.[15] However there is no debate that at the high watermark of the rebellion, only a few days after the first attacks, Sri Lanka's security forces had ceased to function effectively in many rural areas of the South.[16]

Despite early successes, it soon became clear that youthful enthusiasm, a simplistic ideology and wishful thinking had been major ingredients in planning and initiating the insurrection. When the plan to seize power in a lightning stroke failed and there was no spontaneous popular uprising, JVP cadres were ill prepared to repel an offensive mounted by the Sri Lankan Army. Top JVP leaders, many now incarcerated in Jaffna or Colombo, had made no plans for a hit-and-run guerrilla campaign against superior forces that might have sustained the movement.[17] Young men and women who had chosen to follow Rohana Wijeweera – as well as many who had not – would pay dearly for these miscalculations.

After a brief period of uncertainty, Sirimavo Bandaranaike's government sought international assistance and soon counterattacked decisively and harshly. Prime Minister Indira Gandhi of India sent small arms and ammunition, a squadron of four frigates to patrol the island's coastline, 150 Gurkha soldiers to guard the international airport, and six helicopters that flew combat missions under the direction of the Sri Lankan army. Army firepower was soon augmented by fighter aircraft from the Soviet Union, helicopters from the Soviet Union and the United States, armoured cars from the Soviet Union and Britain and police communications equipment from East Germany.[18] Strengthened by these additional resources, the army moved quickly to re-establish control over settled areas and round up dissidents. Often, their sorties were preceded by strafing aircraft or helicopters that killed local peasants and villagers indiscriminately.[19] By June, most organised resistance had ended and more than 14,000 'young men and women gone astray' (the words of Prime Minister Bandaranaike's amnesty declaration) had given themselves up. Government detention camps, including two university campuses, held more than 16,000 prisoners. Small groups of JVP followers that had retreated to the jungle continued the fight until early 1972.

As they re-established control over disputed areas, government forces often dealt severely with rebels and suspected rebels; reserve units in particular became known for cruelty and indiscipline. Anonymous tips were solicited by security teams to identify JVP members and sympathisers. Those identified, as well as their relatives, were tortured to extract confessions and additional names. As in later conflicts, individuals were sometimes fingered as JVP supporters by personal enemies who wished to settle scores or gain a business advantage.[20]

One of the most vivid stories told by Sri Lankans to illustrate the cruelty of army retribution during this period concerns the death of Premawathi Manamperi, a beautiful young woman who, in 1970, had been named New Year's festival Queen for Kataragama District, home of one of the nation's most sacred Buddhist shrines. An informant identified Premawathi as a JVP leader and an army unit that had entered Kataragama took her into custody. After questioning by the lieutenant commanding the unit (many allege that she was repeatedly raped as well as questioned) Premawathi was stripped of her clothing and forced to march naked through the city where she had reigned as festival queen. Bursts from the lieutenant's sub machine gun ended her march and she was buried in a pit with her clothing.[21]

There is no accurate count of the death toll from the rebellion. Official records list 53 security force personnel dead and 323 injured. Estimates of the number of non-security force personnel killed vary from about 1,000 (in official reports) to more than 10,000 (in some popular accounts). Officials spent more than two years interrogating the detainees. About 10,000 were released without charge. 2,492 pleaded guilty and were given suspended sentences. Three hundred and ninety, including 31 top leaders, were convicted and jailed. Twelve years imprisonment at hard labour (rigorous imprisonment) was the most severe sentence imposed.[22]

Rising Tamil militancy

Between the end of the JVP insurrection and the rash of strikes that began in 1976, Tamil militancy was a major contributor to violent conflict 'peaks.' Beginning in May 1972 and continuing through the end of the year, there were a series of violent incidents in the Northern Province involving attacks on moderate Tamil politicians, sabotage of power lines, bombings and burnings of public buildings. Underlying many of these incidents was an issue that divided the Tamil community: government supported attempts to break down Jaffna's rigid caste barriers.[23] Youthful militants, often from lower castes, were as much concerned with fighting discriminatory practices in Jaffna society as with reversing government imposed discrimination against Tamils.

In early October, a more traditional form of Tamil resistance reappeared when the Federal Party, Tamil Congress and Ceylon Workers Congress, now allied as the Tamil United Front (TUF),[24] staged a widely supported one day general strike in the Northern and Eastern Provinces to protest ratification of Sri Lanka's new constitution. This was followed by a six week civil disobedience campaign, organised by the TUF, to express opposition to the new constitution and postponement of a by-election to fill a vacancy in a Tamil majority constituency. Adding to an unstable climate was labour unrest in many tea estates culminating in a massive ten-day strike involving more than 500,000 workers in December. These work stoppages were a particularly severe problem because of a foreign exchange crisis that made Sri Lanka more dependent than ever on revenues from tea exports.

An event that has become part of the mythology of Tamil-Sinhalese conflict in the north grew out of The Fourth International Conference on Tamil Research held in Jaffna during 3-10 January 1974. The Conference was one of a series of meetings where international and regional scholars presented papers on Tamil (Dravidian) culture. During a period of rising Tamil political consciousness in both South India and Sri Lanka, the conferences also provided a venue for political statements, which, in 1974, were not likely to be friendly toward Prime Minister Bandaranaike's government. Officials could have used Emergency Regulations to ban the Conference entirely, however they allowed it to go forward, subject to the condition, accepted by conference organisers, that no 'political or controversial' speeches would be made. Events proceeded smoothly until the concluding plenary session, which was open to the public and drew an overflow crowd, perhaps as many as 50,000. Whether or not the Sri Lankan police (probably all Sinhalese) who had been assigned crowd control duties were 'provoked' is disputed. Indisputably, they interrupted the proceedings in mid session and attempted to break up the crowd using tear gas. In the resultant stampede, seven or more persons died, and a number were injured. For Tamils, this became yet another often-cited example of government 'persecution.'[25]

Tamil militant activity continued in 1975 and included the shooting deaths of two police constables escorting a Jaffna to Trincomalee bus. In March a UNP rally in Jaffa was halted by a jeering crowd that refused to allow party leader J.R. Jayewardene to speak. In July, Jaffna Mayor Alfred Durayappah, a SLFP member and ally of Prime Minister Bandaranaike, was shot to death by a hitherto unknown militant youth named Velupillai Prabakharan. Prabakharan was a *Kariarar* (fisherfolk) caste member and former boy scout, who enjoyed reading about Napoleon's exploits and, at age 21, could hit a cigarette with a pistol at 100 paces.[26] In the next decade he would become undisputed leader of one of the twentieth century's most feared and effective guerrilla movements, the Liberation Tigers of Tamil Eelam.

A government under siege in 1976 and 1977: labour unrest and pre-election violence

Strikes and student demonstrations broke out shortly after Sri Lanka Equal Society Party (LSSP) members were dismissed from the government in September 1975. Now, the government had become a target for harassment from its erstwhile political ally. Disruptions reached a peak between October 1976 and January 1977, before subsiding briefly. Health workers, transit workers and government clerical workers all participated. Officials were forced to invoke the politically unpopular Essential Services Act to get trains running again. Student disruptions at universities were increasingly widespread.

As the 21 July general election date approached, pre-election political violence escalated to its worst level since independence. Among the reported incidents were bomb throwings, burning of election offices and platforms erected for political rallies, fights between rival party members, clashes between police and party members, and attacks on political candidates. On the day before the election, 'armed thugs' hijacked a truck carrying an issue of the pro government ment *Sun* newspapers and burned all 12,000 copies. Overall, six deaths and 22 serious injuries, plus substantial property damage were attributed to pre-election violence. Political campaigning had now become lethal as well as violent in Sri Lanka.

Changing conflict patterns

The degree to which violent political conflict patterns changed during the United Front era is pictured in Figure 11.2. As with versions of this figure in previous chapters, National Government data has been scaled for comparability, taking into account Mrs. Bandaranaike's longer term in office.[27]

Features that stand out from these data are significant increases in militant activity and communal conflict. During Sirimavo Bandaranaike's administration, types of violent conflict that would come to dominate Sri Lankan political life in the 1980s begin to show up in significant numbers. The many-fold increase in 'militant' events is most striking. Such events were rarely reported prior to 1970, but were the most frequently reported between June of 1970 and July of 1977. Many of these (about two-thirds) were attributable to the JVP insurrection, but, as we have seen, Tamil militancy was on the rise as well. At least half of the communal conflict events involving Tamils were attributable to militant activities.

A change that I have not attempted to graph, because graphing would convey more precision than widely divergent estimates justify, is a very significant increase in the number of deaths, resulting from political conflict. At a minimum, probably 3,000 to 5,000 JVP supporters, civilians and security force members died as a result of the JVP insurrection. One hundred or more almost certainly perished as a result of Tamil militancy or in election related violence. During the entire five years of Dudley Senanayake's government, there were probably no more than 50 politically related deaths and the number might have been considerably smaller.[28]

In the light of subsequent events, the differing order of magnitude of conflicts linked to Sinhalese agendas and Sinhalese militancy as contrasted with those linked to Tamil agendas and Tamil militancy merits additional comment. Political leaders give priority attention to political conflicts that are perceived

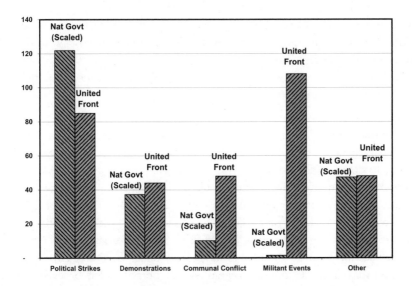

Figure 11.2 Conflict Incident Frequencies: National Government (scaled) and United Front Government Compared

to threaten their power and the stability of their governments. For Sri Lanka's leaders, Sinhalese militancy, labour unrest, demonstrations in Colombo city and perhaps even unrest in the economically critical estate sector must all have seemed more threatening than political unrest among Tamils. After seven years of rhetorical bashing and discriminatory policies, Tamil political protests were still relatively peaceful and mostly concentrated on the Jaffna peninsula, an economically unimportant region, remote from Sri Lanka's centres of power. While Tamil militancy was on the increase, it must have seemed fragmented and insignificant, in comparison with the threat posed by the JVP in 1971 and 1972. Indeed, during the early days of the JVP rebellion, when the loyalty of young Sinhalese officers and enlisted men was called into question, government leaders counted on the loyalty of Tamils in the armed forces to help stabilise the situation.[29] Just prior to the 1977 general elections, leaders of the traditional Tamil parties even seemed willing to overlook past betrayals and to consider negotiating a political accommodation with Mrs. Bandaranaike (although the negotiations eventually fell through).

Five years after he assumed power, one of Sri Lanka's most shrewd and experienced political leaders, J.R. Jayewardene, faced with a crisis situation, would
seriously miscalculate the potential threat posed by Tamil militancy, with disastrous consequences. The data on political conflict during his predecessor's
term in office provides one indication of why his miscalculation may have
seemed reasonable at the time.

Leadership and governance

Sirimavo Bandaranaike's 1970 campaign addresses, like those in 1960,
spoke of fulfilling S.W.R.D. Bandaranaike's 'revolution.' Now she had the
power to do so. With supporters holding 120 seats in a 151 member Parliament, her United Front Government could provide Sri Lanka with a new constitution as well as passing reform legislation, virtually unopposed. For more
than two years, United Front study groups, including some of the nation's
brightest left-leaning intellectuals, had been preparing working papers on Sri
Lanka's economy and institutions. Broad goals resulting from these efforts had
been set forth in the 'Common Program.' United Front leaders believed they
could leave as their legacy a document that would permanently establish socialism while legally sanctioning Sinhalese preeminence and a 'special place' for the
Buddhist religion in Sri Lanka.

The stately woman who became Prime Minister in 1970 differed greatly
from the young widow who had reluctantly entered political life a decade earlier.[30] Sirimavo Bandaranaike brought to her new responsibilities nearly five
years of previous experience as Prime Minister and five years experience as
leader of the opposition. She was the undisputed leader of the SLFP and
of the United Front coalition, which she had played a decisive role in forming. She was acknowledged worldwide as the post-war era's first woman Prime
Minister.[31] As an early leader of the non-aligned movement, she had established close personal relationships with other non-aligned leaders, especially
Yugoslavia's Marshall Tito, which continued during her years out of power.
Close personal ties with Indira Gandhi, now Prime Minister of India, were
based on years of friendship between the Gandhi and Bandaranaike families.

As Prime Minister, Mrs. Bandaranaike exhibited the sharp differences between personal and political styles characteristic of many successful politicians.
Among close associates, she was known for warmth, consideration and sensitivity even during times of severe political pressure. Her genuine concern for
the well-being of Sinhalese rural poor, dating back to the days when she had ac-

companied her father on the rounds of his semi-feudal estate, was reciprocated with loyal political support and warm responses to her public appearances. Her relationship by birth and marriage to two of the nation's most aristocratic families added to her stature in a society that respected authority. To the courage and decisiveness she had exhibited in her first term was added a new self-confidence in dealing with both parliamentary opponents and members of her own cabinet. While she fully trusted only a small group of close advisors, mostly from her own family, she was now more accepting of counsel from a wider circle, including not only cabinet members, but members of the United Front's parliamentary group and some academics.

The Prime Minister's growing stature and self confidence did not, however, make her more tolerant of dissenting views. She could deal ruthlessly with opponents, using the full weight of state power, when it served her purposes. In part, this ruthlessness may have stemmed from disillusioning and painful experiences to which she had been subjected in the past. After becoming Prime Minister in 1960 she had been ridiculed by political opponents during a period when her inexperience and vulnerability made an effective response difficult. Close allies of her slain husband, after promising support, tried to advance themselves politically by exploiting her naiveté and in some cases even defected to the opposition. She viewed this as a personal betrayal. Perhaps most disillusioning was evidence that Dudley Senanayake, reputedly a man of high integrity, had been complicit in the unsuccessful 1962 coup attempt by senior police and army officers.[32] After the UNP's 1965 election victory, Dudley Senanayake's government also initiated well publicised – and subsequently discredited – charges of corruption against Mrs. Bandaranaike and her brother.[33] In Parliament, during her years as opposition leader, she was often heckled from the government benches by members who capitalised on her limited debating skills. Having been restored to power, Sirimavo Bandaranaike may have felt more than justified in treating her opponents harshly.

Mrs. Bandaranaikes' two daughters, Sunethra and Chandrika had completed their education in Europe and returned home during this period to play an increasingly influential political role.[34] Sunethra, the eldest, was appointed Co-ordinating Secretary to the Prime Minister and placed in charge of the government-directed food production campaign. Along with her husband she had been strongly influenced by Marxist development philosophies that were current in Europe and placed herself in the vanguard of those pressing for more encompassing socialist measures in Sri Lanka. Chandrika, the younger daughter, was named a Director of the Land Reform Commission and, reflecting her exposure to left-wing student movements in Paris, was also active in Marxist causes.[35] Anura, the youngest Bandaranaike child, was only twenty when his mother became Prime Minister and remained mostly in England until he completed his education at The University of London in 1974. When he returned to Sri Lanka, he became head of the SLFP Youth League and of the party's official journal, *Sinhale* (The Sinhala Land). Using these positions as platforms, he proclaimed himself a liberal democrat, allied himself with more centrist party members and became a political rival to his left-leaning sisters. This personal and ideological rift between the Bandaranaike children posed serious problems for a political party whose leadership was so strongly tied to one family. Later, it added to the Prime Minister's burdens as she struggled to hold her weakened government together and mount an effective campaign against the resurgent UNP in 1977.

United Front policy initiatives

The possibility that voters might once again turn to the UNP for leadership seemed a remote possibility to Sri Lanka's confident new leaders in June of 1970, as they began to capitalise on the opportunities for radical change their overwhelming parliamentary majority offered. Once in office, Sirimavo Bandaranaike's government moved quickly to reverse the pro-Western tilt of Dudley Senanayake's foreign policy and implement domestic legislation that would narrow the gap between rich and poor, while strengthening government control over the economy. Simultaneously, longer-term processes of economic planning and constitutional reform were initiated.

Foreign policy initiatives, requiring no legislative approval and under the direct control of the Prime Minister,[36] came first. Sri Lanka granted full diplomatic recognition to North Korea, East Germany and the Provisional Government of the National Liberation Front of South Viet Nam. Diplomatic relations were severed with Israel, a decision popular with Sri Lanka's Muslims and with Middle East Arab nations (who were major purchasers of Ceylon tea). The United States was asked to send its Peace Corps volunteers home and the Asia Foundation, a non-governmental organisation headquartered in the United States, was asked to discontinue its operations in Sri Lanka. To further emphasise Sri Lanka's independence from the United States, then deeply enmeshed in Viet Nam, Mrs. Bandaranaike chose to welcome Madam Nguyen

Tai Binh, 'Foreign Minister of the Revolutionary Government of Viet Nam' to Colombo as the first official state guest of her administration. Another visitor to the Capital in 1970 was Pope Paul IV, whose reception by Mrs. Bandaranaike reflected improved relations between the United Front and Sri Lanka's Roman Catholic minority.[37] The new government also made an important symbolic concession to Roman Catholics by replacing the Buddhist weekly calendar based on phases of the moon with the more widely used seven day Sunday based week. This reform was welcomed by business leaders with international ties and evoked little protest from Buddhists.[38]

Successful domestic reforms, United Front leaders believed, required a sympathetic press, a supportive civil service and politically reliable security forces. A sympathiser was named Editor in Chief of the Lake House Newspapers. This was the first step on the road to making Sri Lanka's most influential media outlet a virtual 'house organ' for the government. The tradition of a politically independent professional civil service, which had begun to erode under the two previous Bandaranaike administrations, was now virtually abandoned, as party loyalists replaced senior career officers. Members of the lower bureaucracy already tended to be government supporters because of their membership in SLFP and Equal Society Party (LSSP) affiliated trade unions.[39] Reflecting its populist philosophy, the government also established internal Workers Councils and external People's Committees to serve as watchdogs over the civil service.[40] Commissions of senior police and military officers, judged to be politically unreliable, were withdrawn so that the positions held by these men could be given to government loyalists. By this time, most police constables, military enlisted men and junior officers were Sinhalese Buddhists and thus assumed to be pro-government.[41]

To reshape Sri Lanka's economy, analysts in the Planning and Finance Ministries, following the practice of other socialist states, began drafting a five year plan to spell out how newly created mechanisms of a state controlled economy would marshal the nation's resources to attain long-term development goals. Parliament passed legislation to legalise government take-overs of privately owned enterprises. A State Trading Corporation was established and given control over both external and internal trade in 'essential commodities.' It was hoped that these steps would make commodity distribution more equitable, direct imports toward the most essential economic development needs, rationalise foreign exchange expenditures and reduce the nation's chronic balance of payments deficit.

To reshape Sri Lanka's political institutions, Parliament was reconstituted as a 'Constituent Assembly', with responsibility for drafting the promised constitution. In July, Prime Minister Bandaranaike convened the Assembly's inaugural session, which began with Buddhist ceremonies, at Colombo's Navarangahala stadium, about three miles from the Parliament building. Choice of this venue emphasised a break with institutions established by the British-mandated Soulbury Constitution, which were labelled 'alien' by government leaders.[42] In her opening address, Mrs. Bandaranaike emphasised that 'our constitution must be such as helps to strengthen the 'one-ness' of our nation.' She made it clear that one alien institution slated for elimination was the concept of democratic pluralism embodied in the Soulbury Constitution's clause 29(2), which safeguarded minorities against discriminatory legislation.[43] An institution that was retained however, was the single member district electoral system that had given the United Front its overwhelming majority. UNP and Tamil objections to new constitutional provisions were, for the most part, steamrollered by the overwhelming United Front majority. There was little attempt to achieve consensus or take minority concerns into account.[44]

Responding to the JVP insurrection: Authoritarianism and centralisation of power

The short-lived JVP insurrection, as we have seen, was partly caused by youthful disillusionment over the slow pace of reform. However, its initial impact slowed reforms still further. Restoring order became top priority for government officials. Scarce foreign exchange earmarked for economic development was diverted to arms purchases. Military and police budgets were increased. Repairing physical destruction caused by the fighting deferred construction of new infrastructure and productive capacity. Incarcerating, and interrogating more than 15,000 young men and women over a period of two years was also costly and removed potentially productive workers from the labour force (though many youths might have been unemployed).

Government leaders, especially those affiliated with Marxist parties, were stunned that lower class Sinhalese youth from rural areas, which they regarded as strong supporters had risen in rebellion against a United Front government. Their first response was disbelief – they erroneously described the JVP as a right wing movement, covertly supported by UNP reactionaries. Later, in a typical response of true believers to schismatics, Marxist leaders were among those pressing for the most severe punishments to be meted out to the rebels.

A tilt toward greater centralisation and authoritarianism, by a government already predisposed toward authoritarian rule, was one political consequence of the rebellion. Emergency regulations were imposed after the first attacks, but then remained in force until Prime Minister Bandaranaike dissolved Parliament in May of 1977, more than six years later. A Criminal Justice Commission was established which limited the rights of defendants in state security cases.[45] The need to deal expeditiously with youthful detainees was used to justify establishment of the Commission, but later, its writ was expanded to other matters.[46] Local government elections were suspended and subsequent local government reforms, while described as enhancing 'popular participation' contained strong elements of central government control.[47] Parliamentary by-elections were delayed, despite vacancies, for more than a year.

Anthropologist Gananath Obeyesekere observes that one paradoxical fallout from the rebellion was a further increase in the elitism and Colombo-centrism against which the United Front had campaigned. 'Immediately after the insurrection,' he noted in a 1974 publication, members of the elite located in the outstations pulled into Colombo and this trend has continued. In the city, social and political life goes on in isolation from rest of the country. 'Confronted with massive economic and social problems,' he wrote, 'elite bureaucrats, planners and politicians seek bizarre solutions. Planners, for example, are preoccupied with paper plans impossible of implementation.' Obeyesekere's description provides one explanation of why results from the United Fronts' complex programs of social and political reform often failed to meet expectations.[48]

Though the insurrection slowed reforms initially, it may have speeded them and broadened their scope over the longer term. 'Responding to the concerns of our youth' was an often-heard rationale in debates over reform proposals. The spectre of a Pol Pot type regime made upper class Sri Lankans more willing to accept reforms than might otherwise have been the case.[49]

Soon after restoring order, the government began implementing reforms by abolishing the appointive Senate, which had functioned as a brake on the more populist House of Representatives.[50] Over the next two years, the now autonomous House passed laws intended to narrow the gap between rich and poor by targeting assets and property of Sri Lanka's wealthiest citizens. [51] There were substantial increases in income tax rates at upper levels in April 1972, the government required that all income over 2,000 rupees per month be invested in government approved industries.[52] These measures were followed by a land reform law that set a 25-acre limit on private ownership of paddy (rice growing) land and a 50-acre limit on other agricultural land.[53] After a short grace period, holdings greater than this limit were expropriated. In January 1973, passage of the Ceiling on Housing and Property Act imposed a limit on the number of residential homes that a single family could own.[54] Implementation of these redistributive laws had a visible impact on many wealthy families, providing concrete evidence of government seriousness about redistributing wealth from the rich to the poor.

Coping with economic adversity: austerity measures

The United Front government needed to assuage poor Sri Lankans by exacting visible sacrifices from the rich because harsh economic realities had forced a precipitous retreat from 1970 campaign promises.[55] Government leaders had the power to make reforms, but discovered, like their predecessors, that they could not legislate economic productivity or world market prices. Austerity was the theme of speeches by a sombre Prime Minister and Finance Minister in early November 1971, which introduced their government's Five-Year Plan and annual budget to Parliament.[56] The Plan set ambitious targets for economic growth, industrialisation and agricultural production, but the budget proposed curtailing benefits that Sri Lankans had long taken for granted. These were necessitated, the Finance Minister stated, by chronic budget and balance of payments shortfalls.[57]

Austerity measures eventually accepted by a reluctant Parliament[58] were particularly hard on the poor. Lives were made more difficult by bottlenecks and shortages, resulting partly from inexperience in managing the new state controlled distribution system and partly from peasant suspicion of the new government purchasing monopoly. These resulted in long waits in line at distribution centres, especially prior to the Sinhalese New Year holidays when demand was high.[59] Since the government was now both the purchaser and supplier of essential commodities it became the focus of public frustration when things went wrong.

Political problems related to food in 1972 were dwarfed by those encountered in the following year.[60] Most serious were high prices and unreliable supplies of rice, Sri Lankans most essential staple food. Compounding the problem was a steep rise in oil prices, resulting from formation of the OPEC cartel. This not only raised Sri Lanka's petroleum import bill, but also pushed up the prices of imported wheat, wheat flour, and sugar and further increased costs of imported rice.

Government leaders knew that tampering with the rice ration and failing to maintain an adequate supply of rice at affordable prices would be politically costly. But draconian measures introduced to maintain stocks at distribution centres and fight a burgeoning black market also had political costs and may actually have compounded the supply problem.[61] Selling rice was declared a government monopoly. Hoarding and the transport of rice by private individuals was prohibited. Highway checkpoints, manned by police constables and soldiers were set up to search vehicles for hidden stocks of rice. In response, Sri Lankans figured out ingenious ways of evading the regulations. One family told me how they would hide rice under sleeping children and appeal to police at checkpoints not to wake them. Sri Lankan security forces had neither the resources nor the will to enforce regulations effectively in the face of widespread resistance. Sometimes, police searches seized legitimate stocks of rice, angering the public further. Poor people who could not afford black market prices suffered most, sometimes spending hours waiting in line or doing without rice entirely. In 1974 and subsequent years, food was more plentiful, but the political damage had been done. Food distribution problems were still a live issue with voters when Mrs. Bandaranaike campaigned unsuccessfully for President in 1988, more than 14 years later.

While economic conditions in Sri Lanka did not reach their nadir until the end of 1973, it was clear much earlier that economic policy would be a political liability rather than an asset. This placed added pressure on working groups who were drafting the new constitution to incorporate popular political reforms that might compensate for economic policy shortcomings. The constituency to which government leaders felt reforms most needed to appeal was the Sinhalese majority.

A new constitution

Sri Lanka's 'Republican Constitution,' adopted on 22 May 1972, incorporated new provisions in three areas to which Sinhalese Community leaders had given high priority: establishment of Sri Lanka as a unitary state, strengthening Sinhala's pre-eminence as the nation's official language, and obligating the government to 'protect and foster Buddhism.' Other provisions legitimised socialist economic reforms and strengthened government control over the administrative service and judiciary.

The new document's *Preamble* emphasised that 'power and authority' to establish a new constitution and effect changes in Sri Lanka's fundamental law derived from the 'sovereignty of the people.'[62] Practically, the 120 recently elected United Front MPs wielded this power, with the Prime Minister and close associates playing key roles. That there would be few concessions to minority rights had become clear by early summer 1971, when the Constituent Assembly overwhelmingly rejected Federal Party proposals for constitutional protection of minority rights and UNP proposals for constitutional protection of property rights.[63] In June 1971, Federal Party delegates walked out of the Assembly and did not return. UNP delegates remained, but had little influence over the proceedings.

Descriptions of Sri Lanka's Republican Constitution can be found in a number of sources;[64] most details of this landmark document need not concern us. However some provisions, especially those that strengthened Sinhalese and Buddhist dominance, thus contributing to increased communal tension, do need to be discussed. Perhaps most important, because it was both integral to Sinhalese national identity and strongly opposed by Tamils, was characterisation of Sri Lanka as a 'Unitary State.'

'Unitary State,' was the legal form used to express Sinhalese attachment to 'our land' (*ape rata*), which one Sinhalese scholar has summarised thus:

> *Ours is a Sinhalese country.*
> *Ours is a land of Buddhists.*
> *This is the only place where the Sinhalese race exists.*
> *Foreigners have come and exploited our country*
> * and we Sinhalese have become poorer and poorer.*
> *We will not allow anyone to divide our country.*
> *Why can't these Tamils go back where they came from?*[65]

'The National State Assembly may not,' the Constitution stated, 'abdicate, delegate or in any manner alienate its legislative power, nor may it set up an authority with any legislative power other than the power to make subordinate laws.'[66] This language had the effect of precluding power sharing between regions and the central government, which the Federal Party had long demanded.[67] It gave credibility to more extremist Tamil leaders who regarded an independent nation, *Tamil Eelam,* as the sole remaining option for protecting Tamil political and economic rights.

'Official Language' provisions of the new Constitution gave Tamil extremists additional ammunition. Legislation that established Sinhala as the Official Language and provided for some use of Tamil in the north and east was reaffirmed.[68] The constitution mandated that new laws would be written originally in Sinhala and then translated into Tamil. No formal provision was made for English, which most educated Tamils spoke fluently and was still widely used both in government and as a communication medium between the two communities. Thus the Republican Constitution ratified the inferior status of the Tamil language and made it clear that Tamil public servants and lawyers who wished to work outside Tamil majority areas would need to be fluent in Sinhala.[69]

Religion alone had rarely been a major cause of communal conflict in Sri Lanka, so a constitutional provision that elevated Buddhism above other religions in the eyes of the state concerned Federal Party leaders less than those relating to power sharing and language.[70] Reforms fell far short of demands to establish Buddhism as the state religion, name Sri Lanka 'the Buddhist Socialist Republic of Sri Lanka' and require the President to be a Buddhist.[71] Nonetheless, giving Buddhism privileged political status was one more example of the extent to which Sinhalese-Buddhist cultural traditions and aspirations had become those of the state.[72]

Apart from giving Sri Lanka's government a more explicitly Sinhalese identity, strengthening central government authority was probably the greatest change in the Republican Constitution.[73] Both the civil service and judiciary were placed firmly under cabinet control [74] and courts were precluded from ruling on the constitutional validity of legislation.[75] Moreover, the JVP insurrection motivated constitution writers to retain the Soulbury Constitution's *Public Security Ordinance* though Marxist parties had originally opposed this.[76] Under emergency conditions, the National Assembly was authorised to delegate broad powers to the President and Prime Minister, including the power to issue regulations with the force of law. As we have seen, Sirimavo Bandaranaike exercised emergency powers under this provision from the time of the insurrection until she dissolved Parliament in May 1977.

The *Principles of State Policy* article, which affirmed socialist doctrine, was borrowed from India. It mandated national goals of full employment, equitable distribution of the social product, development of collective forms of property, elimination of economic and social privilege, social welfare and maximum participation of the people in government. The *Principles* lacked legal force – officials could not be taken to court for failing to maintain full employment – but emphasised the United Front's commitment to a managed economy and re-distributive social policies. Including these commitments in a constitution presented to the people with great fanfare may have increased poor Sri Lankans' sense of deprivation when many of these goals were not fulfilled.

The government's attempted use of the constitution writing process to extend its term in office from five to eight years was particularly controversial. A simple expedient was used to legitimise this extension. First the term in office for the new National Assembly was increased from five to six years.[77] Second, former members of the House of Representatives, elected in 1970, were designated as the members of the new body. Finally, the Constitution stated that the six-year term of the National Assembly would not begin until the Constituent Assembly (also the same group of parliamentarians) ratified the new document.

Opposition leaders were outraged by this manipulation of the legal fiction that the 'House of Representatives', 'Constituent Assembly' and 'National Assembly' were different entities, rather than the same compliant and self-interested body of United Front parliamentarians, choosing to legislate themselves three additional years in power.[78] After a storm of protest, the government backed down to the extent of shortening the first National Assembly's term to only five years. This gave them seven years in power, rather than eight. Opposition parties and the Sri Lankan people, reflecting continued respect for legal processes (however convoluted), and despite growing unpopularity of the government, accepted the new dispensation.

Facing political adversity: Break-up of the United Front Coalition

United Front leaders knew they faced serious political problems as early as April 1973. Commemorative events following the sudden death of Dudley Senanayake provided an opportunity for Sri Lanka's volatile electorate to combine massive demonstrations honouring the former Prime Minister with expressions of opposition to Sirimavo Bandaranaike's government. The outpouring of public grief that followed the announcement of his death amazed even his close supporters and was deeply disturbing to government leaders, who had already been unsettled by recent by- election losses.[79]

A period of political sparring between the new UNP leader, J.R. Jayewardene, and an increasingly defensive government followed Senanayake's death. Jayewardene's strategy was to mobilise public opinion by holding non-violent demonstrations (*satyagraha's*) intended to focus attention on the government's economic failures. Government leaders responded with counter demonstrations and increasingly repressive measures. Daily newspapers were censored and placed under direct government control. Police were directed to prevent would-be demonstrators from assembling. Finally, on the one-year anniversary of Dudley Senanayake's death, Prime Minister Bandaranaike invoked emergency regulations to ban all public meetings of the UNP.[80]

Ideological conflicts within her own coalition posed even more serious political problems for Sirimavo Bandaranaike. There was a widening gap between Marxist and more conservative coalition members over economic policy. The Prime Minister, supported by Felix Dias Bandaranaike and her son, Anura, had come to believe that a moratorium on further nationalisations, plus incentives for both foreign and domestic investment, were needed to stimulate economic growth.[81] Finance Minister N.M. Perera and other Marxist leaders, supported by the Prime Minister's daughters, favoured completing the program to transform Sri Lanka into a socialist society that had been initiated in 1970.

The differences became public when N.M. Perera proposed increasing taxes on the rich and reducing investment tax incentives at the same time Prime Minister Bandaranaike was appealing for additional foreign investment.[82] Despite widening differences, along with intensifying public acrimony between Marxist and conservative factions, the LSSP remained a coalition member until the fall of 1975. Finally, on 2 September, Mrs. Bandaranaike sacked the three LSSP cabinet members, including the Republican Constitution's principal architect, Dr. Colvin R. de Silva. All but two of their LSSP parliamentary colleagues joined them in opposition, opening the government to attacks from left as well as the right and reducing its majority below the pivotal two-thirds threshold. Although Communist Party MPs continued to support the government until February of 1977, firing the LSSP Ministers marked the end of major social and economic reforms.[83] Foreign policy initiatives and attempts to postpone almost certain repudiation at the polls preoccupied the Prime Minister and her close associates during their remaining months in power. Their lives were further complicated by deteriorating relations between Sri Lanka's Sinhalese-dominated government and its Tamil citizens.

A widening gap between Sinhalese and Tamil communities

The amicability and civility of Sinhalese-Tamil relations progressively worsened during the United Front years. By 1977 many Tamils living in the north and east felt so marginalised and alienated, they no longer considered themselves part of Sri Lanka. These feelings were unmistakable in the pre-election *Manifesto* of the Tamil political party coalition, now called the Tamil United *Liberation* Front.[84]

> ...What is the alternative now left to the nation that has lost its rights to its language, rights to its citizenship, rights to its religions and continues day by day to lose its traditional homeland to Sinhalese Colonisation. What is the alternative now left to a nation that lies helpless as it is being assaulted, looted and killed by hooligans instigated by the ruling race and by the security forces of the State?...There is only one alternative and that is to proclaim with the stamp of finality and fortitude that we alone shall rule over our land our forefathers ruled. Sinhalese imperialism shall quit our homeland.

Even discounting typical rhetorical excesses, this manifesto marked a sea change in Tamil political organisations and attitudes in the short space of seven years – from Federal Party to Tamil United Liberation Front, from demands for language rights and devolution of power to demands for political independence. Moreover as we have seen, the escalation of political demands was accompanied by an escalation of violence. By 1977, two of Mrs. Bandaranaike's leading Tamil supporters had been felled by assassins bullets, bank robbery had become a principal source of funds for militant groups and a Tamil organisation had staged pro-independence demonstrations in London. In attempting to maintain order, an increasingly embattled police force routinely detained and sometimes tortured demonstrators and suspected militants. In June 1974, 17-year-old Ponnundari Sivakumaren, facing arrest for bank robbery, became the first Tamil youth to take his own life by swallowing a cyanide capsule. How had things come to this in a nation once regarded as a model of civility and democratic pluralism?

When two ethnic communities, like two lovers, become estranged, invariably both parties have contributed to the estrangement and each tends to blame the other. This certainly applies to Sri Lanka in 1977. However many observers, Sinhalese as well as Tamil, view divisive policies, indifference, and miscalculations by Sirimavo Bandaranaike's government as the major causes of Tamil alienation. These followed logically from the political philosophy of the Prime Minister, close associates and many supporters. At its core, this philosophy viewed Sinhalese-Buddhist cultural-religious values as indistinguishable from the core values of the Sri Lankan State. Even the name *Sri Lanka*, which replaced *Ceylon* under the Republican Constitution, harked back to Sinhalese traditions.[85]

What were these 'Sinhalese cultural values'? Sirimavo Bandaranaike's heritage and political power base were *Kandyan Sinhalese*. Among Sinhalese, those who owed allegiance to the Kandyan kingdom had been least impacted by Colombo's commercialism and cosmopolitanism.[86] They took pride in their racial distinctiveness and, in contrast to many Sri Lankans, had little use for cultural and institutional legacies from British colonial rule. Kandyans often expressed resentment toward those living in more westernised (and wealthier) parts of the island. Poverty and the decline of traditional values in Kandyan areas were blamed on intrusions of commerce and of outsiders.[87]

Prime Minister Bandaranaike and her mainstream supporters were prepared to accept minority members as citizens, to accommodate their culture and language, even to include them in the governing coalition.[88] However two principles, the indivisibility of the Sri Lankan nation and political supremacy of Sinhalese-Buddhist culture throughout that nation, were not open to accommodation. Acknowledging these two principles was unacceptable to many Tamils. So long as each side held to their positions, the gap between them was unbridgeable. Failure of United Front leaders to recognise this, when they also lacked the military resources to impose their will on the north and east by force, proved to be a serious miscalculation. Throughout the 1970s, they pressed onward with their program mandating Sinhalese-Buddhist political hegemony, with little regard for the growing intensity and militancy of Tamil opposition.

To understand how this miscalculation could occur, one must remember that in the years following independence, leaders of Sri Lanka's other influential minorities, Sinhalese Christians[89] and Muslims had come to accept the reality of Sinhalese-Buddhist political hegemony. Their political strategies emphasised accommodation and defined goals compatible with a political culture acknowledged to be predominantly Sinhalese-Buddhist. Sri Lankan Tamils who lived outside of Tamil majority areas, particularly the large number of

Colombo residents, also largely accepted this reality. It was members of these accommodationist minorities with whom government leaders most frequently came in contact. Even the Tamil United Front leader, S.J.V. Chelvanayakam, was an accepted member of the Colombo political scene, with a reputation for negotiating compromises and a commitment to Gandhian principles. To most Sinhalese leaders, the Northern Province was a place they had visited rarely and only in carefully managed circumstances. It existed more as an abstraction, on the periphery of their concerns than as a real place where real people lived. Sirimavo Bandaranaike could not empathise with Northern Tamils as she emphasised with Kandyan Sinhalese peasants, living lives similar to families she had visited a teen-age girl. Nor was there any political incentive for her to do so. The 1970 general election proved that Tamils no longer held a balance of power between the major Sinhalese parties.

Knowledge of top United Front leaders' perspectives makes it easier to understand why they used their two-thirds plus majority to adopt policies that Tamils viewed as discriminatory. The Republican Constitution, which stripped Tamils of rights they had previously enjoyed and legitimised principles of Sinhalese-Buddhist hegemony, institutionalised discriminatory policies in Sri Lanka's fundamental document. When the new constitution was adopted, all government employees, including all lawyers, were compelled to give a formal oath to uphold it. Apparently most Tamils took the oath, however a young Tamil public servant that refused was not only fired, but imprisoned for nearly three years.[90]

Changes in university admissions policies contributed most to alienating Tamil youth.[91] The changes were intended to remedy perceived discrimination against disadvantaged Sinhalese and Muslim youth resulting from the competitive merit-based examination system that had been used in Sri Lanka since colonial days. Under the merit system, Tamil youth, who benefited from a superior school system, strong English language instruction and a greater cultural emphasis on education, had secured a disproportionate number of university places, especially the most coveted places in science, engineering and medicine.[92] By 1970, expanded primary and secondary education had produced a many-fold increase in applications but no comparable increase in the number of available places. Less than 10 percent of those taking entrance examinations were now admitted; the success ratio for coveted places in scientific and professional fields of study was even smaller. University admissions had become a ferociously competitive zero-sum game in Sri Lanka.

Indigenous language (*swabasha*) education introduced by S.W.R.D. Bandaranaike made changes in merit-based admissions easier to justify. Beginning in the 1960s students had been educated in one of three language 'streams': Sinhala, Tamil or English. This meant three sets of entrance examinations, one in each language, evaluated by three sets of examiners. Now, the higher scores received by Tamil applicants could be blamed on biased Tamil language examiners.[93] 'Media [language] wise standardisation' was introduced as a remedy for this alleged bias. Numerical scores of applicants in each language were adjusted to a common scale, based on the number of applicants in that language. Invariably, this meant that scores of Sinhala language applicants were raised, relative to their Tamil and English counterparts. Because proportionately more Tamils than Sinhalese applied to science fields, media wise standardisation had only a modest impact.[94] But the change, introduced shortly after the United Front took power, was seen by young Tamils as a message that ethnicity would increasingly be replacing merit in determining who was given the opportunity to pursue higher education.

'District quotas' for university admission, introduced in 1974, made the message of ethnic discrimination unambiguous. Under this system, residents of 'backward' districts were given preferential admissions treatment. Under criteria devised by the Education Ministry, these were mostly districts with heavy Kandyan and Muslim populations. Kandyan Sinhalese gained additional preference from the large number of Indian Tamil plantation workers living in their districts who increased the size of quotas, but rarely sought university admission. Implementation of district quotas reduced the number of Tamils admitted to university science programs by a third in a single year, causing great concern among Tamil youth.[95]

While the new educational policies closed off opportunities for Tamil youth in Sri Lanka, new foreign exchange restrictions made it virtually impossible for them to attend Tamil Nadu universities, which had been a financially viable option for even middle class Tamils in the past. While their own educational opportunities were eroding, young Tamil men and women could observe that Prime Minister Bandaranaike's children were completing their university educations in Paris and London.[96]

The government's principal gesture toward improving Tamil educational opportunities was opening a Jaffna Campus of the University of Ceylon to its first class of 103 students in October 1974. However this produced few political dividends. Instead of building a new facility, the Education Ministry chose to close one of Jaffna's most popular secondary schools, so that university classes could begin quickly. Subsequent tinkering with district quotas, which improved opportunities for Tamils somewhat, came too late to dampen the anger and growing militancy of young Tamil men and women who longer believed that the 'Sinhalese government' in Colombo would treat them fairly.[97]

Even those Tamil youths who were admitted to a university and successfully completed courses, faced discrimination when seeking employment in an economy dominated increasingly by state managed concerns, with top positions given to political supporters of the government. This was a third divisive area, though it receives less emphasis than the constitution and University admissions in accounts of the period. By the 1970s, there was little Tamil employment in public sector corporations – for example 98 per cent of those working for Sri Lanka's largest employer, the Ceylon Transport Board – were Sinhalese. Of 100 persons selected for the government's Higher Administrative Service in 1973, 92 were Sinhalese, four were Muslims and only four were Tamils.[98]

To complete the picture of deteriorating government-Tamil relations during Prime Minister Bandaranaike's term, it is useful to list a brief chronology of escalating Tamil protests. The list begins with unsuccessful attempts to change the draft Republican Constitution and ends with an election manifesto pledging to establish a separate state of Tamil Eelam.

June 1971. Federal Party delegates walked out of the Constituent Assembly when the Government's official language proposals, which they viewed as weakening agreements made in 1966, were accepted.

May 1972. At a meeting held in the Eastern Province seaport of Trincomalee, leaders of the Federal Party, Tamil Congress and Ceylon Workers Congress voted to form the Tamil United Front. The new organisation voted to reject the Republican Constitution because it had '...completely failed to meet the legitimate aspirations of the Tamil speaking people...'[99] and to boycott the ceremonial opening of the National State Assembly on May 22. TULF leader S.J.V. Chelvanayakam resigned his National Assembly seat, with the intention that the by-election to fill the empty seat would serve as a referendum for the Tamil people on the Republican Constitution and the alternative proposed by the TUF. The government postponed holding the by-election for three years.

January 1973. Tamil cabinet minister Chelliah Kumararsuriar made an official visit to Jaffna at Sirimavo Bandaranaike's request. 'Black flag demonstrations', organised by students adversely affected by the new university admissions policies, greeted him. In March, Jaffna visits by ministers N.M. Perera and Pieter Keuneman also evoked 'black flag demonstrations.'

January 1974. The Fourth International Conference of the International Association for Tamil Research was held in Jaffna. Police intervention in the final plenary session resulted in several deaths (see above).

October 1974. Prime Minister Bandaranaike attended opening ceremonies of the University of Ceylon's new Jaffna Campus. Her visit went off without incident, but was preceded by several acts of violence, including an attempted assassination of the Jaffna Mayor.

January 1975. The Eelam Revolutionary Organisers (later, the Eelam Revolutionary Organisation of Students – EROS) was formed in London and demonstrated publicly for an independent Tamil state in Sri Lanka.

February 1975. The long delayed by-election for Chelvanayakam's constituency was held and he won an overwhelming victory. In his victory address, he interpreted the election verdict as a 'mandate' for a separate Tamil state and gave his 'solemn assurance that we will carry out this mandate.'

July 1975. Alfred Duraiappah, the SLFP affiliated Mayor of Jaffna, was shot and killed by Velupillai Prabakharan, future leader of the Liberation Tigers of Tamil Eelam.

March 1976. Under Prabakharan's leadership, a gang of Liberation Tigers robbed the state-run People's Bank Office at Puttur near Jaffna, escaping with about 500,000 rupees in cash and jewellery valued at 200,000 rupees.[100] The notoriety enabled Prabakharan to recruit a small band of followers, who initially called themselves the Tamil New Tigers (TNT).

May 1976. At a convention of the TUF, held in the Northern Province Constituency of Vaddukodai, the party coalition reconstituted itself as the *Tamil United Liberation Front* and resolved to restore and reconstitute the 'Free, Sovereign, Secular, Socialist State of Tamil Eelam.'[101]

Also, the Liberation Tigers of Tamil Eelam was founded, as successor to the Tamil New Tigers.

April 1977. With the death S.J.V. Chelvanayakam, negotiations between the government and Tamil United Front leaders broke off, having failed to reach an agreement that would use Tamil votes to postpone scheduling of a general election. He was succeeded as TULF leader by Appapillai Amirthalingam.

Despite separatist rhetoric, Amirthalingam, like his predecessor, was more Colombo politician that revolutionary. His critics note that he spoke of independence in Jaffna, but continued to talk about federalism when in Colombo. In contrast to Chelvanayakam, however, he was prepared to use violence as a tactic and initially established close ties with the Tamil Tigers. His strategy was to use Sinhalese fear of militants as a lever for winning concessions from the government that would grant a measure of independence to the north and east. When the TULF won an overwhelming victory in 1977 and Amirthalingam became leader of the opposition, it appeared this strategy, which was basically the same as followed by his predecessor, might finally succeed.[102] However, the policies of Sirimavo Bandaranaike's government had set a process in motion that would ultimately shift power to militant leaders. We will return to this topic in chapter 12.

Problems faced by the Indian Tamil and Muslim minorities

United Front policies also made things worse for the 'Indian Tamil' plantation workers. We have seen that in 1972, their leaders found it useful, for the first time since the 1940s, to form a united front with the Sri Lanka Tamil parties against the Republican Constitution. However, as in the past, problems faced by Indian Tamils were fundamentally different than those of their compatriots in the north and east. These problems were rooted in racist attitudes of many Kandyan Sinhalese, a tradition of exploitation by plantation managers dating back to colonial times, and the uncertainty of their status as citizens in Sri Lanka. For these largely uneducated men, women and children, whose ancestors had been transported by the British to the Kandyan hill country, an independent Tamil Eelam in Sri Lanka's north and east had little to offer. Agitation for this goal was more likely to worsen their situation by fuelling the resentment of their immediate Sinhalese neighbours, who already felt that traditional lands had been 'stolen' for foreign-owned plantations. Indian Tamils were not responsible for creating the plantations. They were mostly brought to Sri Lanka to do low paid work that local Sinhalese were unwilling to do. But they made convenient scapegoats.

Indian Tamils, whether Sri Lankan citizens or not, were viewed by many political leaders and government officials as second or third class human beings. Even Sri Lanka Tamils viewed estate workers through a prism of caste and anti-immigrant prejudice. Estate workers had always been an exception to Sri Lanka's development 'success story'. Their infant and maternal mortality rates were significantly higher than national averages. Their literacy and life expectancy were considerably lower. Food shortages and subsidy cuts of the early 1970s impacted them with greater severity than most. Government welfare services were less available, and when available, were grudgingly dispensed by Sinhalese officials. During the worst of the food crisis, some officials refused Indian Tamils permission to stand in line for government issued bread rations, whether they were Sri Lankan citizens or not.[103]

Economic problems many plantations faced made their workers' living conditions even worse. With nationalisation, experienced plantation managers had been replaced with inexperienced political appointees, almost all Sinhalese. Often, the new men were not only corrupt, but inefficient. Plantations had traditionally been expected to provide welfare services, medical care, and education to their workers but reduced plantation income and indifference of Sinhalese managers further curtailed services that had already been the worst in the nation. Workers on some plantations experienced severe malnutrition. Some even died from starvation-related causes.

Work stoppages were the principal weapon that Indian Tamils could use to fight discrimination and economic hardship. Both the government and plantation owners wanted to avoid strikes. Tea growing is a labour intensive enterprise. The thousands of bushes that cover every steep hillside in the tea country must be regularly tended and the deep green leaves selectively picked by hand at precisely the right time to ensure good flavour.[104] Overripe leaves make bad tea that won't fetch top prices in a competitive world market. Sri Lanka depended on foreign exchange from tea sales to cover urgently needed imports of food and industrial raw materials. On the other hand, estate workers' slim margin of existence made any work stoppage difficult and long strikes out of the question. Workers were paid on an hourly or piecework basis, with no guarantees. They could not stockpile food or money to provide for a long strike and plantation managers knew it.[105] Strike breaking activities of pro-government unions also made strikes more difficult.[106] Short strikes and demonstrations held during the 1970s did get the government's attention, and improved working conditions in a few instances.[107] However they could not fundamentally change the biases of government officials who depended on estate workers' labour but were at best willing to grant them second class citizenship.[108]

Sirimavo Bandaranaike did make further progress in resolving the problem of 150,000 'stateless' estate workers remaining in Sri Lanka. Statelessness had complicated Indian-Sri Lankan foreign relations and in January 1974, Prime Ministers Bandaranaike and Gandhi met in New Delhi to resolve the matter. The agreed to divide the remaining Indian Tamils between them, with 75,000 being given Sri Lankan citizenship and 75,000 repatriated to India. Administration of the agreement was plagued by problems that continued into the next decade, however eventually more than 400,000 gained Sri Lankan citizenship, including full voting rights.[109] Sirimavo Bandaranaike's role in granting citizenship to some Indian Tamils was not sufficient to compensate for the hardships inflicted by her government on this community. In the 1977 general election, Indian Tamils turned out in large numbers to vote for candidates opposed to the SLFP and contributed to the UNP's overwhelming victory.[110]

Sinhalese-Muslim relations also worsened, especially toward the end of Sirimavo Bandaranaike's term. As with Tamil-Sinhalese relations, problems were caused by different views regarding communal entitlements and by government support for the Sinhalese side when conflicts occurred. Sinhalese were angered by policies of Education Minister Al-Haj Badiuddin Mahmud, perceived as favouring Muslims unduly.[111] We have seen that his 'district quota system' favoured Kandyan Sinhalese and Muslims, but discriminated against low country Sinhalese as well as Tamils. Sinhalese youth could be as volatile as Tamil youth when they saw their educational opportunities limited by discriminatory ethnic quotas. Also, special government-supported primary and secondary schools had been established for Muslims, with calendars governed by Muslim religious law and Arabic offered as a language of instruction along with Tamil, Sinhala and English. This deviation from the principle of secular education was resented by both Buddhist and Roman Catholic Sinhalese. Under Mahmud's administration, some of these 'Muslim Schools' were funded more generously than neighbouring schools and the disparities were evident to all.

Sporadic clashes had broken out between Sinhalese and Muslims over these issues and there were serious outbreaks in December and February 1975. In February, Sri Lankan police, virtually all Sinhalese, fired into a crowd gathered in a mosque, killing several Muslims. When Muslim community leaders levelled charges of ethnic partiality and excessive use of force, Prime Minister Bandaranaike endorsed the police version of events and personally defended the officers in Parliament. These events led Muslims to believe that a future Bandaranaike government would be biased against them and contributed, along with economic problems that impacted all Sri Lankans, to a shift in Muslim support away from the United Front. When Mrs. Bandaranaike's Education Minister Badiuddin Mahmud stood for Parliament in 1977, he ran fourth in a field of five.[112]

Prime Minister Bandaranaike's 'non-aligned' foreign policy

If economic policy and communal relations are viewed as problematic areas for the United Front Government, most observers give it high marks in international affairs, due mostly to the Prime Minister's personal diplomacy. As in her first term, Sirimavo Bandaranaike was a visible actor on the world stage, travelling extensively and cultivating personal relationships with leaders of the Non-Aligned Movement as well as the two regional powers most important to Sri Lanka, China and India. Like Dudley Senanayake, she recognised that international neutrality and even-handedness toward the major powers must be pillars of Sri Lankan foreign policy; however the climate of international affairs had changed in ways that fit well with her predispositions.

In the 1970s, leaders of newly independent nations had additional manoeuvring room and were able to play a more assertive role. Both the Cold War and the competition between socialist and capitalist economic philosophies were unresolved. China's presence as an alternative development model, foreign aid source and ally provided smaller powers with additional leverage. Many Global South nations were experiencing rapid economic growth. Those with petroleum resources benefited greatly from the OPEC cartel's new strength. Those without oil could often negotiate generous loans from an international banking system that was awash with funds. Formerly dominant colonial powers, France, Britain and the United States were struggling with weak governments, domestic economic problems and foreign policy reverses, of which the United States' Viet Nam debacle was the worst. In this new environment, three global organisations the Non-Aligned Movement, the Group of 77 and the United

Nations' General Assembly became vehicles for Global South leaders to express points of view that differed from those of the superpowers and former colonial nations. Sirimavo Bandaranaike was active in all of these organisations and played a particularly influential role in the Non-Aligned Movement.

Like Dudley Senanayake, however, Sirimavo Bandaranaike was sensitive to Sri Lanka's vulnerabilities as a small, geo-strategically significant state attempting to survive in an international system dominated by contending superpowers and in a region where the world's two most populous nations confronted one another suspiciously across a lengthy international border. Thus when JVP insurgents seemed about to topple her government, she sought help from both Western and Communist nations. The People's Republic of China provided Sri Lanka with the largest total of foreign aid grants; however the United States remained the largest provider of foreign aid loans. In the United Nations General Assembly, Sri Lanka's representative voted more often with socialist and newly independent nations than under Dudley Senanayake, but also supported the United States more frequently. On controversial issues where India and China were on opposite sides, Sri Lanka typically abstained or was recorded as 'not present.'[113]

An initiative that reveals both the strengths and shortcomings of Sirimavo Bandaranaike's foreign policy was her proposal, first introduced in 1970, for an international agreement that would establish the Indian Ocean as a 'Zone of Peace.'[114] Over the next seven years, the Prime Minister and Sri Lanka's diplomats pushed this proposal at Non-Aligned Movement meetings, Commonwealth Prime Minister's meetings and the annual sessions of the United Nation's General Assembly. A measure of diplomatic success was rising levels of support for successive General Assembly Zone of Peace Resolutions, from 60 nations in 1970 to 106 nations in 1976.[115] But seven years of intensive diplomacy appear to have had no impact on actual military force levels.[116] The Indian Ocean did not, in fact, become a zone of peace, which leads one to speculate whether the time top Sri Lankan officials, especially the Prime Minister, expended on this enterprise could have more usefully been given to other priorities.

Sri Lanka was more successful in its bilateral relations with China and India. Sirimavo Bandaranaike's skilful personal diplomacy maintained an officially neutral stance vis-a-vis these two regional rivals, while cultivating friendly ties and obtaining assistance from both. A June 1972 state visit where Mrs. Bandaranaike met personally with Chairman Mao and received the warm Chinese welcome reserved for favoured foreign dignitaries, cemented cordial relations between Sri Lanka and China. During her term in office, Sri Lanka received more than 400 million rupees ($U.S. 66.5 million) in long-term loans and nearly 150 million rupees in grants from China. The spacious Bandaranaike International Memorial Conference Hall, venue for the Fifth Summit Conference of Non-Aligned Nations, was entirely constructed and funded by the Chinese at a cost of 35 million rupees (nearly $U.S. 6 million). It remains today as a visible symbol of Sirimavo Bandaranaike's success in managing Sino-Sri Lankan relations.

Unlike China, India had been quick to respond to Prime Minister Bandaranaike's request for assistance to quell the JVP insurrection and had, as we saw earlier, even sent troops to help guard Sri Lanka's international airport. However, Sri Lankan neutrality during Pakistan's civil war, which broke out in March 1971, temporarily strained relations. Close ties between India and Sri Lanka that developed after the Pakistan war concluded were cemented by close personal ties that developed between the two prime ministers.

Events during their last two years in power further strengthened these ties. In 1975, Sri Lanka's government was one of the few to support Prime Minister Gandhi's use of emergency regulations to assume near authoritarian powers. Prime Minister Bandaranaike had, of course, been governing under emergency regulations, albeit sporadically used, since the first days of the JVP insurrection in 1971. Both leaders attempted to postpone the dates of general elections they feared they would lose. Both attempts failed and both were turned out of office, Prime Minister Gandhi on 20-21 March and Prime Minister Bandaranaike on 21 July 1977. Following Indira Gandhi's defeat, UNP orators, including party leader J.R. Jayewardene, used typical Sri Lankan campaign hyperbole to call attention to parallels between the two Prime Ministers and urged Sri Lankan voters to emulate their Indian counterparts.[117]   Mrs. Bandaranaike would not be returned to office as Prime Minister for 18 years and then only when her daughter, Chandrika, named her to the post after winning election as the Sri Lanka's third Executive President.[118] However, only three years elapsed before Indira Gandhi once again took the oath as India's Prime Minister. She had a long political memory and neither Jayewardene's political exploitation of her 1977 defeat, nor his subsequent move to deprive Sirimavo Bandaranaike of her civic rights were helpful to Sri Lanka's relations with its most important neighbour during his years in power.[119]

When Non-Aligned Movement leaders chose Colombo for their Fifth Summit Conference, this set the stage for a culminating event of Sirimavo Bandaranaike's term in office.[120] For a brief period Sri Lanka was highly visible on the international stage. This happened at a time when the world's developing nations achieved what may have been their greatest degree of collective unity and influence. Preparations for the Summit were a major priority of Sri Lanka's government for most of 1975 and 1976. There were logistical arrangements to be made for more than 2,000 international visitors, including 85 heads of state. The task of drafting numerous conference 'working documents' was given to a small team of Sri Lankan Foreign Service officers headed by Felix Dias Bandaranaike, who served as the nation's *de facto* foreign minister.[121]

The Fifth Summit, which opened on 16 August 1976, was a personal triumph for Prime Minister Bandaranaike, at a time that her weakened government was struggling with serious domestic political problems. As leader of the host country, she became President of the Non-Aligned Movement, a position Sri Lanka's head of government would hold until the Sixth Non-Aligned Movement Summit in 1979. It was her privilege to give the conference's inaugural address, following the pageantry of opening ceremonies, to an audience that included Indira Gandhi, Yugoslavia's Marshall Tito, Egypt's Anwar al Sadat and the Secretary General of the United Nations. By all accounts, the organiser's hard work resulted in an event that was both a diplomatic and logistical success. At its concluding session, conference delegates ratified a set of 'resolutions and declarations' emphasising some of Sirimavo Bandaranaike's favourite foreign policy themes.[122]

As August drew to a close, the Bandaranaike Memorial Centre's vast plenary hall had quieted and the last official delegates had departed. Life in Colombo was returning to normal. Exhausted exhilarated government officials could begin catching up on their day-to-day responsibilities. We can pose the question they and other Sri Lankans were no doubt posing to themselves: what tangible benefits had this commitment to high visibility in international diplomacy produced for Sri Lanka?[123] UNP leaders, already preparing for the general election, were clear on their verdict. They disparaged the Summit as a *'Kaberi Mangula'* (a festival of niggers). It had been a colossal waste of public resources, they said, at a time Sri Lanka's economy was stagnating and many of its citizens wanting for basic needs.[124] Government leaders who had promised constituents that international visibility and contacts resulting from the conference would bring additional foreign aid, especially from oil rich Middle Eastern countries were disappointed.[125] Nor did Sri Lanka's role as summit host boost the government's flagging popularity at home, as some had hoped.[126] Those who later wrote positively of the conference results placed more emphasis on its symbolic significance, as did Prime Minister Bandaranaike herself.

On 30 September Sirimavo Bandaranaike stood before the United Nations General Assembly, as President of the 85 nation Non-Aligned Movement, to present the results of the Colombo deliberations. On the dais behind the speaker's rostrum sat Sri Lanka's Permanent Representative, Shirley Amerasinghe, who had recently been elected President of the General Assembly. For the Prime Minister, this symbolised international recognition of the principle that had guided her foreign policy since she first assumed office in 1960: emergence of newly independent nations as a political counter-force to the great powers through political non-alignment and collective economic self reliance. Her view was that developing nations must stand on their own because they had learned that co-operation between unequal partners meant dependency and exploitation.[127] She spelled out her position even more clearly in an address, given on the following day, to representatives of the non-aligned countries:

> Our self-respect demands that when we speak of self-reliance we should not have to address appeals to other nations for succour and sustenance. The world is indeed interdependent, but interdependence was never intended to mean almost total dependence for some and grudging concessions by others.

Had the key Colombo Summit recommendations – solidarity among developing nations and a new international economic order – been realised in the years that followed, Sirimavo Bandaranaike's UN address might be remembered as a landmark, rather than a footnote. However the economic theories which the non-aligned leaders applied to their own nations and advocated for others failed them. The combined impacts, beginning in 1978, of soaring petroleum prices, rising interest rates and a global recession, made shortcomings of the Marxist economic model clear to all but the most ideologically blinded. As their centrally planned economies stagnated and they were forced to appeal for help to international lending agencies, any hope that left-leaning non-aligned nations would become a powerful third force evaporated. It was the 'Asian Tigers', nations that wholeheartedly embraced the free market, both globally and domestically, that provided 'success stories' for other nations to emulate.[128] After 1977, Sri Lanka, too, under J.R. Jayewardene's leadership, attempted to embrace the free market model. In retrospect, Sirimavo Bandaranaike's address to the United Nations was more epitaph that prophesy.

Viewed with the wisdom of hindsight, it would appear that Prime Minister Bandaranaike's management of bilateral relations with India and China, rather than her high profile international activities, contributed most to the well-being of her nation. The words I used to measure the success of Dudley Senanayake's foreign policy also seem applicable here. During the period from 1970 through 1977, Sri Lanka remained independent. Its domestic politics were largely free of international meddling. Relations with all of its powerful neighbours remained civil, if not always cordial.

Sirimavo Bandaranaike's leadership: achievements and opportunity costs

Having said this, it would be grossly unfair not to acknowledge the brilliance of Sirimavo Bandaranaike's personal achievements in international diplomacy. She began her political career with little knowledge of international affairs. She was a women who, in order to succeed, had to function effectively in the male dominated culture of world leaders. Her country was small, militarily insignificant and on the periphery of world affairs. The resources of Sri Lanka's Foreign Service were modest. Her domestic political base, in one of the few real democracies among developing nations, was far more precarious than most of her contemporaries. Despite these handicaps, she rose to the Presidency of the Non-Aligned Movement, orchestrated a successful Non-Aligned Summit and was widely recognised as a pre-eminent spokesperson for the Global South. This says much about Sirimavo Bandaranaike's intelligence, capacity to learn, sensitivity, political skills and toughness.

While acknowledging her achievements, one must question her priorities. Economists define 'opportunity costs' as benefits that were foregone because of decisions made and resources allocated. Opportunity costs are the 'what might have beens.' For most of her years in office, both Sirimavo Bandaranaike and the most able, powerful and trusted member of her cabinet, Felix Dias Bandaranaike, were preoccupied with international affairs. Of necessity, less important matters were delegated to officials who were lower in rank and often, in ability. It would appear that managing communal relations – perhaps managing the economy as well – fell into this category of 'less important matters.' While the Colombo summit was being planned, Jaffna Major Duraiappah was assassinated, the LSSP Ministers were fired from the government, Velupillai Prabakharan emerged as a top Tamil militant leader and the Tamil United Liberation Front issued the Vaddukkodai resolution calling for an independent Eelam. In international settings, Mrs. Bandaranaike could speak movingly of oppression and its costs and of the feelings of oppressed people. 'Our self-respect demands that when we speak of self reliance, we should not have to address appeals to other nations for succour and sustenance,' she told assembled UN delegates. These words were not so different from those of Tamil leaders expressing *their* aspirations for political freedom. Had Sirimavo Bandaranaike brought the brilliance and energy to domestic communal problems that she brought to international affairs, relations between Sri Lanka's Sinhalese and Tamil communities might have followed a very different path.[129]

12
Sri Lanka's Marxist Experiment - Promises and Performance

An overall appraisal of Sri Lanka's Marxist experiment needs to do little more than reiterate this oft-repeated theme: benefits derived fell short of promises and plans. Ideology had played some role in the United Front's 1970 election victory, but it was dissatisfaction with high unemployment, stagnant wages and access to higher education that brought Sirimavo Bandaranaike and her Marxist allies to power. Populist and ethnic nationalist rhetoric could not obscure the fact that in all of these areas, most Sri Lankans were worse off in 1977 than they had been in 1970.

United Front economic policy makers believed that Marxist theories they had advocated for decades provided the strategy needed to accelerate Sri Lanka's economic development. Key elements of this strategy were central planning, state ownership of major industries, services and financial institutions, import substitution and redistribution of wealth.[1] This approach contrasted sharply with Dudley Senanayake's incremental approach, which had attempted to find a middle path between free market and Marxist development models.

Commitment to a single development model simplified the task of formulating consistent economic policies, but there was a potential problem. In Marxist economics, recommended policies are not viewed as options to be discarded if they fail to achieve intended goals – such as economic growth, full employment and benefits to the poor. Instead, policies and goals are linked ideologically. That state planning best promotes economic growth is an article of faith, not a proposition to be tested against evidence. Economic policies backed by strong ideological commitments are difficult to abandon, even in the face of mounting evidence that they are not working.[2] This became a serious problem for Sirimavo Bandaranaike's government during the latter part of her term.

Promises: The five-year plan
United Front leaders spelled out an ambitious development agenda. Macroeconomic targets and broad strategic guidelines were described in the

government's Five-Year Plan, presented to Parliament in October 1971. The Plan targeted a six per cent average annual rate of growth, which was projected to raise per-capita annual income and create 810,000 new jobs. Accelerated growth was to be attained through substantial increases in savings and investment, plus surpluses that would be generated by public corporations. Planners acknowledged that public sector corporations had often generated losses in the past, but projected that an expanded public sector, with monopoly control over key industries and services, would now become profitable through efficient management, use of labour intensive technologies and the adoption of appropriate pricing policies. Emphasis on labour intensive technologies would aid in job creation and conserve foreign exchange by reducing the need for imported capital goods. Success of the plan also depended on the public's willingness to accept reduced consumption in the short run in order to achieve economic growth over a longer term.[3]

Shortly after the Five-Year Plan was introduced, economist Janice Jiggins, who had lived in Sri Lanka for more than two years, completed an independent analysis of Sri Lanka's macro economy focusing on prospects and strategies for promoting growth. Her report called attention to problems noted in earlier studies, particularly the problem of urban-rural imbalance, as well as problems caused by the new government's policies.[4] She warned of declining productivity in the rural sector, where farmers appeared to be producing primarily for subsistence and black market sales. Jiggins attributed this to disincentives resulting from the government monopoly of food purchases at controlled prices. Her examination of rapidly expanding state corporations raised questions about the government's plans for simultaneously expanding employment, improving efficiency and generating investment from this sector. Government officials appeared to view public sector concerns as providers of jobs and patronage rather than levers for economic growth.

As control of commercial activity was increasingly centralised in Colombo government offices, management efficiency appeared to be deteriorating, rather than improving. 'Bureaucratic and Government centralisation in Colombo,' Jiggins noted, 'provides an ever-expanding number of white-collar jobs and increasingly adds to the paralyzing administrative bottleneck.'[5] She also raised questions about the 'foreign exchange crisis' that had been so strongly emphasised by the government leaders as justification for austerity measures. In Colombo, she observed that Wilkinson razor blades, Nescafe, Indian saris,

Kenwood mixers, stereo equipment and expensive cars were readily available, despite being banned. Although no foreign exchange was officially available for foreign travel or education, between 1,000 and 2,000 young Sri Lankans were studying in American and European universities, while 'anyone who is somebody' seemed able to travel abroad without impediment. She urged the government to take seriously its commitment to efficiency in the public sector by eliminating political patronage as a primary basis for employment[6] and cutting 'hidden subsidies' to senior public officials.[7]

Agricultural sector policies and programs

In 1970, agricultural outputs comprised more than 25 per cent of GNP and provided more than 90 per cent of export income.[8] More than half of the nation's work force was employed in agriculture.[9] This politically sensitive sector was a primary target of United Front economic policy initiatives.

The policy with greatest impact on agriculture, land reform, has already been mentioned. Beginning in 1972, a series of legislative enactments reduced large holdings of paddy land to a 25-acre maximum, and other large holdings to a 50-acre maximum.[10] Larger holdings than this were still possible because family members could pool and jointly manage their individual allocations, but there was a significant increase in smallholdings and shifts in ownership from large private proprietors to state corporations. Nationalisation of foreign-owned tea plantations in 1975 largely completed this process.[11] Of course land reform was not really an economic policy. Rather, it was motivated by multiple political concerns: a felt need to respond to the JVP insurrection, the rural populism of SLFP supporters, the class consciousness of their Marxist allies and the hope that land reform would diminish the political power of UNP supporters who were large landowners. Land reform became a frame of reference within which government planners pursued multiple and sometimes conflicting agricultural policy goals.

Nowhere were these conflicts more perplexing than in the rice-producing sector.[12] Improving living standards and increasing the productivity of Sri Lanka's numerous small rice growers had been a top priority of Dudley Senanayake's government. United Front land reforms increased the number of smallholders who were in need of fair prices, accessible markets, agricultural credit and technical assistance. But Sri Lankan politicians, whatever their party, needed to be sure that all Sri Lankans had an adequate supply of their most important staple and that the sacrosanct rice ration was maintained. As we have seen, a combination of international shortages, rising prices and declining domestic production created devastating political problems for the United Front in 1972 and 1973.

Policies of the newly created Paddy Marketing Board, which in 1971 had been given monopoly control over all facets of rice, were major contributors to this decline. The Board was given sole responsibility for operating the Guaranteed Price Scheme, which had been established in the 1950s to provide a government subsidised minimum price for rice. However, monopoly control placed Paddy Board officials in a very different position than their predecessors.[13] Responding to budgetary pressures, they allowed the government's guaranteed price to fall below market levels and remain stagnant almost until the end of 1973.[14] Officials' inexperience – they were mostly political appointees – resulted in inefficiencies that created further disincentives for producers. Predictably, producers responded by reducing output and, when opportunities presented, sold to black market traders. In its first year, the Paddy Board had been able to purchase 32.3 million bushels of rice from Sri Lankan producers. In 1976, total purchases amounted to only 12.8 million bushels.[15] Other government initiatives intended to help small-scale paddy farmers produced mixed results. In response to attempts to promote the 'Green Revolution,' farmers modestly increased their use of high yielding rice strains, only to see their productivity plummet when the government was forced to temporarily cut fertiliser subsidies. Political pressure restored the subsidies, but fertiliser use remained far below optimal levels. The new Comprehensive Rural Credit Scheme increased loans by 25 per cent, but defaults also increased due to low income levels and crop failures. To protect against crop failures, the government established an Agricultural Insurance Board to administer a Comprehensive Insurance Scheme for all loan recipients. In fiscal year 1976-77, however, only 22 per cent of eligible acreage was covered and premiums were 80 per cent in arrears.[16]

In contrast to rice, officials decided that Sri Lankans could get along without imported vegetables or produce them at home. Importation of potatoes and Bombay Onions was prohibited in 1972 and the ban was extended to chillies, maize (corn), beans and peas in 1973. In contrast to the relatively modest increases in rice harvests, there were very significant increases in the production of all of these vegetables. Onion production more than doubled with an increase in yield per acre of more than 60 per cent. Domestic production of chillies, a staple almost as important to the Sri Lankan diet as rice, increased five-fold, with a doubling of per-acre productivity. Interestingly, the greatest beneficiaries of the domestic vegetable boom were Tamils in Sri Lanka's volatile Northern Province where the production of these crops had traditionally been concentrated.

Exports of coconuts, rubber and especially tea continued as Sri Lanka's major source of foreign exchange and a principal source of capital for other sectors.[17] Heavy dependence on these sectors placed government planners at the mercy of problems that vagaries in international markets and weather could create for a commodity-based export-dependent economy. To these normal problems were added the uncertainties created by fears of nationalisation, and inefficiencies created by complex government management schemes. Uncertainty was a greater problem for these three crops because judicious harvesting, careful tending and disciplined replanting of rubber trees, coconut trees and tea bushes was necessary to ensure good harvests of high quality products over the long-term. Plantation maintenance required skill and a willingness to plough back some short-term profits. Even during Dudley Senanayake's term in office, plantation owners had cut back on maintenance in anticipation that a socialist government would come to power eventually. After the 1970 general election, plantation owners tried to recoup their investments as quickly as possible. Rubber trees were 'slaughter tapped' to produce unusually high short-term yields. Between 1970 and 1977, rubber replantings dropped by 35 per cent and tea replantings by more than 55 per cent. Fertilisation of coconut palms, the principal means of ensuring long-term productivity, dropped by 55 per cent.

In contrast to the coconut industry, where most production remained in the hands of smallholders, tea continued to be produced on large plantations, which, after nationalisation, were managed directly by government officials. Nationalisation of privately owned plantations had mostly been completed by 1973 and control of plantations owned by public corporations passed to the government in 1975.[18] Anticipating nationalisation, private owners had already cut back on maintenance and replanting. This pattern continued, after nationalisation, despite government subsidies that grew to more than 100,000,000 rupees (about $US 11.8 million). By 1977, the government was in charge of 804 plantations, covering more than 230,000 acres and employing nearly 340,000 workers.[19] Managing these enterprises, plus 481 factories producing tea was a challenging task for the newly designated political appointees, although former plantation owners and supervisors were sometimes placed in charge of day-to-day operations.[20] Under government management, the plantations were less well maintained and less profitable, however the volume of production and volume of export sales remained relatively stable.[21]

Chapter 9 devoted considerable attention to the Mahaweli Development project, which Dudley Senanayake had made a high priority. The project's cost became a campaign issue, which may be one reason that a government strongly committed to interventionist policies in other areas chose to put it on hold for two years. Phase one of the project, which irrigated about 132,000 acres, brought nearly 29,000 acres of new land under cultivation and resettled nearly 1,700 families, was completed in 1976. Virtually all were Sinhalese. The region in which they were resettled was part of the 'Traditional Tamil Homelands' in the Eastern Province.

Investment Promotion and Industrial Development

Non-agricultural sectors of the economy were also targeted for policies emphasising central planning, nationalisation and re-distribution. A new industrial policy, announced soon after the government assumed power, outlined plans to place all 'heavy, basic and essential' industries under government management. Other industries were permitted to remain in the private or co-operative sectors, but they too could be nationalised if they employed more than 100 persons or were judged by government officials to be managed inefficiently or dishonestly.[22] The Five-Year Plan outlined priorities for resource allocation, especially the allocation of scarce foreign exchange, with emphasis given to export promotion, development of underdeveloped areas and job creation. Sectoral Development Committees were established with the responsibility for coordinating production to fulfill plan targets and meet overall national needs.

Planners recognised that growth required investment, including private and foreign investment, but promoting investment from non-government sources conflicted with the United Front's Marxist-populist ideology. Foreign investors expected a reasonable return on their funds, a predictable business climate, freedom to take profits out of the country and security against expropriation. Domestic investors needed surplus funds to invest, plus security and the expectation of a reasonable return.

Economic policies during Sirimavo Bandaranaike's early years in power have been described as creating 'a formidable climate of hostility to private enterprise and initiative.'[23] The one-time tax on assets exceeding 200,000 rupees has already been described. Beginning on 1 April 1972, a ceiling of 2,000 rupees ($US 325) per month was placed on disposable incomes. Those earning incomes in excess of this amount were required to invest the surplus in government approved enterprises. High denomination currency notes were demonetised. Using authority granted by the Business Acquisitions Act, government officials reorganised virtually all heavy and capital goods industries as public corporations. Businesses that remained in the private sector were subjected to a compulsory capital levy and a graduated tax on profits that was virtually confiscatory at high levels.[24] The State Trading Corporation monopolised marketing and distribution of 'essential commodities' and many consumer goods.

It is hardly surprising that voluntary private investments plummeted and private businesses failed to flourish in an environment characterised by ever more stringent government interventions, plus ever more strident political rhetoric intended to divert public attention from economic policy failures. Gross domestic capital formation in the private sector dropped by 50 per cent in 1971 and did not reach 1970 levels again until 1975.[25] Seizing assets of a small wealthy class and providing the treasury with a one shot infusion of funds contributed to higher than normal public sector capital investments in 1971, but re-distributing assets and imposing high taxes in a stagnant economy could not provide the revenues needed to sustain long-term growth.[26]

When the Five-Year Plan was released, it was already clear that combined effects of deteriorating terms of trade, foreign exchange shortages and declining domestic production would cause economic performance to fall short of plan targets. In the face of mounting evidence that massive government intervention would not turn Sri Lanka's economy around,[27] the economic recommendations of moderate cabinet members carried additional weight with the Prime Minister and the climate for private business began to improve. The debate over whether to solve Sri Lanka's economic problems with more vigorous government intervention, or by giving private sector investors and businesses greater scope, was a major contributor to tensions that eventually resulted in expulsion of LSSP cabinet members from the government.[28] Felix Dias Bandaranaike's appointment as finance minister represented a triumph for the moderates, although international activities and political concerns took priority over economic policy initiatives during Sirimavo Bandaranaike's final years in power. In a more favourable business climate, local entrepreneurs were able to take advantage of Sri Lanka's protected domestic markets along with special tax breaks and foreign currency allocations intended to stimulate exports.[29] Measured in real terms, private sector investment did not surpass 1970 levels until after the more business friendly UNP government assumed power in 1977. However, despite severe setbacks in the early 1970s, it represented almost half (49 per cent) of total investment for the 1971-77 period. Sri Lanka's heavily subsidised government enterprises and public corporations did much worse, with capital formation in the latter falling to less than half of the peak 1971 level by 1977.[30]

Government attempts to seek foreign investment also brought ideology and economic realities into conflict. Areas where foreign investment would be welcomed were included in the Five-Year Plan. These included tourism, some areas of manufacturing (including some public sector corporations) and areas requiring specialised skills.[31] However, government planners had little appreciation of the incentives needed to attract foreign investment in a competitive market. Anti-capitalist rhetoric, replacement of foreign import-export agencies with government monopolies and the virtual certainty that plantations would soon be nationalised contributed to a climate that international investors viewed as unwelcoming. The lengthy approval process for foreign investments, often administered by left-leaning officials, reinforced this view.[32] At a time when future 'Asian Tigers' were beginning to aggressively seek foreign capital, Sri Lanka's stagnant, bureaucratically encumbered socialist economy had little to offer. In 1972 and again in 1974, the government announced policies that were intended to reassure foreign investors, but, like proposals intended to encourage domestic investment, these were opposed by Marxist ministers and had little impact.[33] An idea floated by the Prime Minister, establishing two duty-free export processing zones, was rejected after cabinet debate.[34] Foreign investment would not become a major contributor to Sri Lanka's economic growth until J.R. Jayewardene's 'open economy' policies made it clear that entrepreneurial activity in the private sector was once again welcome.

State sector management problems

While private investment and a private sector did have a place in their plans, United Front leaders' primary commitment was to a state managed economy. Armed with legislative authority to nationalise existing concerns and with government funds to create new ones, they implemented policies that expanded Sri Lanka's state sector and contracted its private sector. Between 1970 and 1977, 45 new state enterprises were created and the capitalisation of public sector industries increased fourfold. By 1976, state controlled enterprises were contributing 30 per cent of GNP and employing 40 per cent of the Sri Lanka's labour force. Among the largest 20 per cent of economic concerns on the island, all were state owned. State owned concerns were responsible for 62 per cent of Sri Lanka's industrial output and 70 per cent of its industrial exports.[35]

By 1976, cabinet ministers and political appointees were managing the production of such diverse products as milk, distilled liquors, tobacco, textiles, plywood, chemicals, tires, ayurvedic drugs, steel, hardware and processed fish. They controlled organisations that monopolised purchases of most staple foodstuffs and all imports. As under previous administrations, appointees managed electricity production along with the refining and distribution of petroleum products. They ran the state railroad, bus lines, telephone system and banking system.[36]

Private enterprise was discouraged because of a strong belief that national rather than personal priorities should be served by economic activity; that social goals should be at least equally weighted with profitability. Most important among these goals were re-distributing income, providing employment, correcting regional development imbalances, training Sri Lankans in industrial skills and making 'essential goods' available at affordable prices.[37] While it was the 'duty' of public enterprises to conduct their operations so as to break even over five years and to generate a rate of return specified by the government minister in charge,[38] this 'profitability' was rarely attained.

With rare exceptions, Sri Lanka's state managed establishments did not play their planned role as engines of economic and employment growth.[39] They did not attract private investment, produce goods that could compete on international markets or generate surpluses that could be reinvested or redirected to other public purposes. Many required substantial subsidies to remain viable. Shortcomings in public sector enterprises were not the only cause of economic stagnation and continued high employment during the early 1970s – deteriorating terms of trade and several years of adverse weather conditions also contributed. But shortcomings in state sector management must bear substantial blame for the United Front's inability to deliver on its campaign promises. What were these shortcomings, why did they occur and why were their economic consequences so adverse?

Many critics point to political patronage at the principal villain. While political considerations had played a role in appointments before Sirimavo

Bandaranaike became Prime Minister, the practice reached a new level after 1970.[40] Political considerations seem to have weighed more heavily than professional qualifications in filling most positions. Expansion of the state sector meant nearly half a million jobs were subject to some sort of government oversight. 'The [state] corporations have become providers of jobs, not levers of economic growth,' wrote Janice Jiggins. 'They are areas of political patronage and intervention, not creators of a new managerial class.'[41]

Ethnicity, too, became a criterion for employment in most state sector corporations as new managers with Sinhalese nationalist leanings implemented hiring practices that discriminated against Tamils. Thus, politicisation of state employment contributed to ethnic tensions as well as reducing efficiency and productivity. Sri Lanka began to experience a 'brain drain' as talented managers, engineers and technicians who failed to secure domestic employment sought jobs abroad.[42] Many of these were Tamils and this period marked the beginning of a Tamil diaspora that would flood Western and Southeast Asian nations with talented migrants during the 1980s.

The strategy chosen to expand productive capacity also contributed to inefficiency and was a factor in Sri Lanka's inability to expand employment opportunities.[43] Government planners responsible for industrial development faced a conflict between using capital intensive technologies and providing full employment. Since Sri Lanka lacked its own capital goods sector, creating new industrial enterprises required imports of machinery and technical assistance from abroad. Communist countries were the most willing to supply needed capital goods on affordable terms. The USSR provided machinery for manufacturing steel, fertiliser, tires and tubes and for flour milling. Textile looms came from China, the German Democratic Republic and Poland. Machinery for manufacturing hardboard and refining sugar came, respectively, from Romania and Czechoslovakia.[44] Unfortunately, the production scale of these imported technologies was not well suited either to Sri Lanka's need for labour intensive facilities or modest level of domestic demand.

Further problems were created by government regulations that proscribed importation of consumer goods and encouraged development of industries that produced for the domestic consumer goods market, but placed fewer constraints on importation of intermediate factors of production.[45] This meant, for example, that Sri Lankans were forbidden to import finished textile products from China, but the State Textile Corporation could import machinery and raw materials to produce such products, even though the total foreign exchange cost of the domestically produced goods exceeded that of purchasing finished goods from China. A principal consequence of United Front industrial policies was to create oversized and capital intensive industries that contributed little to solving the nation's employment problems. Finished products produced by these industries might use as much as 100 per cent of imported raw materials. Moreover, because of oversized production facilities, low demand and foreign exchange shortages, average capacity utilisation during the 1970 -1977 period was only 53 per cent.[46]

Pricing policies that reflected 'social goals' further contributed to the unprofitability of state enterprises. Often prices charged for goods were lower than costs of production.[47] This could be due to decisions by inexperienced managers or poor cost accounting, but political considerations also entered in. Pricing decisions for many goods were made at the ministerial level. For items designated as 'essential commodities' or deemed to significantly impact the cost of living, price changes required cabinet approval. Since most goods priced in this way were produced by government monopolies, there was no domestic competition to provide efficiency checks or quality checks. High tariffs protected inefficient domestic producers from external competitors. Five-Year Plan growth projections assumed that state enterprises would soon return profits to 'the people' (i.e. to the government), but instead the government had to provide operating subsidies to keep them afloat and investment subsidies to help them expand. Subsidies added to government deficits and, when deficits had to be covered by Central Bank 'loans', to high levels of inflation.[48]

International trade and finance

Whatever their economic philosophy, policy makers knew they must better insulate Sri Lanka's agriculture-based export-dependent economy against fluctuations in international commodity prices and adverse weather conditions. How successful were United Front leaders in achieving this goal?[49]

From 1970 through 1975, Sri Lanka experienced progressive deterioration in its terms of trade caused by rising energy and imported food prices, along with stagnant or declining prices for tea, rubber and coconuts. Price increases in imported goods needed to keep Sri Lanka's industries functioning further added to import costs. Attempts to expand sales of the major export crops failed.[50] This combination of factors, plus limited foreign assets, declining foreign investment and declining foreign aid created severe pressures to reduce imports.

Government control over an increasingly centralised economy, plus the Prime Minister's support for draconian measures, produced success on this front. In 1971, 1972, and 1973, sharp cuts in imports, especially of consumer goods, kept Sri Lanka's trade deficit below five per cent and enabled Central Bank managers to substantially increase the nation's external financial assets.[51] Even food imports were kept below 1970 levels except in 1972, when the government responded to bad harvests with emergency imports of grain. In 1974 and 1975, when the deterioration in terms of trade was most severe, Sri Lanka ran trade deficits of more than 30 per cent and was forced to draw down its foreign assets, but strict import controls kept the reductions within manageable proportions. In 1974, when controls were most stringent, the Central Bank's volume index of imports had fallen to 55 per cent of 1970 levels and the value of Sri Lanka's external financial assets was still more than 25 per cent higher than in 1970.

Conservative trade policies produced a relatively strong financial balance sheet that made the nation less vulnerable to economic intervention from foreign powers or international lending agencies. However, it failed in two important respects, one political, one economic. The adverse political consequences of restrictive import policies have already been described. Import restrictions and rationing were a precipitous retreat from glowing promises made during the 1970 campaign. High prices and limited availability of wheat and rice impacted all but the wealthiest Sri Lankans, leaving the SLFP and its allies with a legacy of public mistrust that would take more than a decade to overcome. Economic stagnation produced a broad range of negative impacts, to which conservative trade policies contributed. Given state sector management problems, starving Sri Lanka's industries of raw materials and investment capital may have been a rational, albeit unintended policy. However these shortages imposed further strictures on an already stagnant economy, making it even less probable that economic expansion would occur.[52]

Sri Lanka's foreign debt was both positively and negatively impacted by trade policies. The increase in debt denominated in U.S. dollars was modest; however, effects of economic stagnation plus a 60 per cent loss in the rupee's value on international currency markets[53] weakened the ability of the government to repay. Foreign debt increased from 14 per cent of gross national product in 1970 to 41 per cent in 1977. As a percentage of exports, it increased from 87 to 160 per cent. As in other developing nations, increased debt relative to exports and productivity, contributed to a vicious cycle causing further losses in the rupee's value.

Foreign aid: an unheralded success story

Prime Minister Bandaranaike's success in maintaining flows of foreign aid from capitalist nations, while increasing foreign aid from the Communist world is one of the unheralded success stories of this period. Foreign aid provided desperately needed jobs in the domestic economy and helped to maintain Sri Lanka's international financial position. Among major donors were China, Canada, Australia, and the World Bank. The United States, which terminated grant assistance with great political fanfare in 1973, nonetheless continued to be Sri Lanka's largest provider of foreign loans. Deterioration in terms of trade during the mid-1970s led the government to give particular priority to commodity assistance, which in total dollar value exceeded the amount of project assistance. China continued to be a major supplier of rice. Denmark shipped critically needed supplies of wheat flour and fertiliser.[54] Canada provided asbestos fibre, newsprint, wood pulp and telecommunications. Both Denmark and Hungary provided capital equipment for the government's industrialisation program. As noted in chapter 11, the spacious Bandaranaike Memorial International Conference hall, serves as both a memorial to S.W.R.D. Bandaranaike and a reminder of Sirimavo Bandaranaike's success in soliciting foreign aid.[55]

Describing Sri Lanka's relations with foreign donors as a success story contradicts 'conventional wisdom' perpetuated by some scholars that Marxist participation in the government, along with socialist economic policies caused major reductions in aid.[56] In fact, receipts of both foreign loans and grants during Sirimavo Bandaranaike's regime were greater than under Dudley Senanayake, who has always received high marks for his management of relations with foreign donors. Annual receipts of foreign aid grants (which did not require repayment) under Sirimavo Bandaranaike were more than three times the amount received by Dudley Senanayake's government.[57] Without foreign aid, the United Front government's economic and political problems might have been far worse, especially during the early 1970s.

Government finance: not a success story

Despite reduced trade deficits and increased foreign aid, Sri Lanka's overall financial position worsened during Sirimavo Bandaranaike's term. Interventionist economic policies resulted in rising government spending levels that exceeded the economic growth rate. Growth in revenues was less than the overall growth in the economy.[58] One result of government economic policies was a dwindling stock of privately held funds that could be loaned to cover deficits. Increasingly, Central Bank 'loans' were called upon to bridge the revenue-expenditure gap. Use of the Central Bank to monetise government deficits was, as already noted, highly inflationary. Between 1970 and 1975, the Sri Lankan rupee lost 40 per cent of its value. By 1977, the rupee's purchasing power had dropped by more than 50 per cent. Measured in current rupee values, Sri Lanka's public debt grew by more than 200 per cent between 1970 and 1977.[59]

Both direct declines in government income sources and indirect consequences of economic stagnation contributed to revenue shortfalls. Deterioration in Sri Lanka's terms of trade and management problems in the export sector resulted in declining revenues from export taxes, one major government funding source. Declining import volumes, a product of foreign exchange shortages plus preferential treatment given to many state sector concerns, produced a drop in revenues from import taxes. Increases in sales and income taxes, along with the foreign exchange entitlement scheme, produced revenue increases, but also slowed economic growth. When adjusted for inflation, even the gross receipts of state owned trading enterprises, recipients of generous subsidies and investments, contributed less to government revenues in 1977 than in 1970.

Tax increases and spending cuts intended to shrink deficits contributed to a vicious cycle that slowed economic growth, resulting in greater deficits, generating additional pressures for tax increases and cost-cutting that slowed economic growth still further. Growth in revenues that did occur was produced by increased income from sales taxes, value added taxes, income taxes and the Foreign Exchange Entitlement Scheme. New taxes and tax increases extracted additional wealth from an already stagnant domestic economy and fuelled inflation by raising prices. Incentives offered by the Entitlement Scheme improved economic performance in some sectors, as in the case of the gem industry, but used dubious criteria to allocate scarce foreign exchange, often to unproductive enterprises. Attempts to cut spending, often implemented with political fanfare, were sporadic and inconsistent. The result was volatile government expenditure patterns, in an economy increasingly dominated by the government. This further contributed to an uncertain economic climate, adding to the concerns of investors already frightened by re-distributive tax schemes, nationalisations and Marxist rhetoric. Declining foreign and private investment, as already noted, also slowed economic growth.

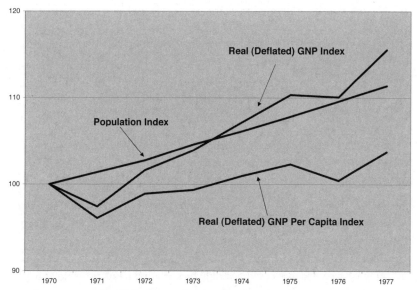

Figrue 12.1 GNP and Population Trends

Performance: meeting people's wants and needs

How effectively did Sirimavo Bandaranaike's government meet constituents' expectations for good wages, employment opportunities, health care and education? Adjusted for inflation, Sri Lanka's gross national product grew only by an average of 2.2 per cent per year, compared with 7.5 per cent under Dudley Senanayake.[60] Sri Lanka's annual population growth rate of 1.6 per cent was the lowest of any Global South nation; however population growth reduced average increases in per-capita gross national product to less than one per cent (Figure 12.1). The comparable figure for Dudley Senanayake's government was 4.5 per cent. Slower economic growth meant there were fewer resources and jobs to go around.

Rates of inflation averaging more than 11 per cent per year eroded the value of savings and wages. For 1973 and 1974, inflation averaged more than 20 per cent, by far the highest in modern Sri Lankan history. Under Dudley Senanayake, the average inflation rate was 3.5 per cent and a single year of double-digit inflation – in 1968 – had been a political crisis. Declines in the rupee's international value caused especially steep price increases for imported goods and for manufactured goods that depended on imports.

Rampant inflation in 1973 and 1974 discouraged private saving and added to the uncertain economic climate created by nationalisations and re-distributive taxes.

High inflation nullified improvements in well-being that wage increases would have provided in a more stable economy. Official indices of real wages showed little growth between 1971 and 1977.[61] The minimum day rate in agriculture declined in four of Sirimavo Bandaranaike's seven years in office, and showed a positive annual increase over the term only because of large rise in 1977.[62] The minimum day rate in non-agricultural occupations decreased in five of the seven United Front years and declined by 12 per cent, overall. Government employees fared worse than those in the private sector. Purchasing power of wages declined in every employment category with teachers experiencing the most severe decline; more than 10 per cent.[63] Reductions in food subsidies and rationing of essential commodities described earlier in this chapter eroded living standards still further. On the other hand, continued distribution of free rice that could not only be consumed, but also sold at market prices, provided at least some 'income' to poor Sri Lankans.[64]

As economic conditions worsened, government leaders hoped to mute popular dissatisfaction by imposing sacrifices disproportionately on the rich. Re-distributive legislation – the one time levy on assets, a steeply graduated income tax, ceilings on housing and land reform – has already been described. How successful was this legislation in shifting wealth from upper to lower income groups? Because periodic *Consumer Finances and Socio Economic Surveys* were only completed in 1963 and 1973, overlapping three administrations, this question can not be precisely answered.[65] However, since re-distributive measures were not implemented prior to 1970, it is probable that levelling of incomes taking place between the 1963 and 1973 surveys was due more to United Front policies than other factors. All but the top 20 per cent of income earners improved their position between 1963 and 1973, with the greatest improvement occurring among members of the 'middle class.' On the other hand, Sri Lanka's wealthiest decile experienced a precipitous income share decline of nearly 25 per cent. This re-distribution of income in favour of middle and poorer classes proved to be transient, however. The 1978/79 surveys show that top income earners had regained their position, while the poor and middle classes had lost most of their gains.[66]

Unemployment and job creation

Despite the Five-Year Plan's ambitious job creation targets, unemployment continued to worsen during the United Front's years in power. [67] Sri Lanka's population age structure was still skewed toward the young, which meant that the labour force continued to grow more rapidly than the population as a whole. Between 1963 and 1971, it grew by more than 40 per cent, adding about 1,300,000 job seekers to the population. Between 1971 and 1978 1,300,000 more men and women joined the labour force. This 30 per cent increment was nearly three times the rate of population growth and nearly twice the growth rate of Sri Lanka's stagnant economy. [68]

While job creation plans predicated on industrialisation and economic growth fell short of the mark, United Front leaders were able to create new government and state sector jobs directly. This increased the cost of government but did provide employment, especially for political supporters (virtually all Sinhalese). More than 100,000 new government jobs were added during Sirimavo Bandaranaike's first year in office (a 50 per cent increase) and by 1977 the size of the government work force had almost doubled. [69] Employment in 'semi-government institutions' (public corporations, universities, boards [70] and banks) grew from 170,000 in 1970 to 617,000 in 1977. However, much of this growth resulted from nationalisation of existing jobs rather than the creation of new ones. [71] Many newly created jobs were make-work positions that added little to productivity. [72]

Moreover, new government and state sector jobs could make only a small dent in the unemployment problem. For reasons already discussed, determining the exact level of 'unemployment' in Sri Lanka is impossible. However, there appears to be some consensus that the number of 'unemployed' grew from around 12 per cent to around 20 per cent between 1970 and 1977. [73] By 1977, more than one million men and women were seeking jobs and unable to find them. [74] Unemployment was higher among men than among women; higher in urban than in rural areas and highest of all among young people. [75] Unemployment was lowest for those with university degrees. Many who did have jobs were classified as 'underemployed,' adding another one million or more to the ranks of those who may have been dissatisfied with their work situation. [76] The presence of more than two million unemployed or underemployed, out of a five million member work force, was a matter of great concern to leaders who had nearly been overthrown by a rebellion of dissatisfied youth at the beginning of their term in office. [77]

Ethnic disparities in income and employment

To what degree do significant income and employment disparities show up between Sri Lanka's two largest ethnic groups, the Sinhalese and Tamils, during this period? This is an important question because Sirimavo Bandaranaike's government used the claim that Sinhalese were systematically disadvantaged to justify policies that gave them preferential treatment in employment and education. Tamil leaders, on the other hand, used economic discrimination as one justification for their secessionist platform and later, for armed rebellion. In an unpublished study, 'Ethnic Conflict and Economic Development in Sri Lanka' (1988), economist S.W.R.D. Samarasinghe has tried to sort out these contending claims. With regard to income, he concludes that Tamils were neither systematically advantaged prior to the 1970s nor systematically disadvantaged during the United Front's years in power.[78] The picture was more complex than strident advocates on either side of the ethnic divide would have us believe. The greatest disparity was between low country and Kandyan Sinhalese, with Tamils doing somewhat worse than the low country Sinhalese but better than the Kandyans. However, given the strong Kandyan influence in Sirimavo Bandaranaike's government, one can see how the disadvantaged position of Kandyans contributed to a perception, reinforced by SLFP politicians, that all Sinhalese were worse off than Tamils.

How was the Jaffna community's well-being affected by United Front economic policies and with what consequences for the Tamil secessionist movement? Political scientist Amita Shastri concludes that economic development and employment policies contributed to secessionist sentiment, but import controls provided a countervailing pressure.[79] Historically, Jaffna had never provided sufficient employment for its youth, forcing them to seek employment elsewhere on the island. Because of out-migration, population growth in Jaffna had been less than in other districts. In the 1970s, this changed and Jaffna District experienced greater population growth rates than the rest of the island.[80] Shastri attributes this to discriminatory government and state sector employment policies that kept many Jaffna youth at home. In-migration by Tamils who feared discrimination and violence in the south also contributed. The combination of new migrants and shutting down the out-migration safety valve escalated demand for nonagricultural jobs in Jaffna.

Jobs were not plentiful anywhere on the island, as we have seen, and less available in Jaffna than in the more developed Western province where Tamils had previously found employment. Job shortages reminded Tamils of the long-standing economic development pattern that had concentrated industry close to Colombo.[81] This pattern became more pronounced as Sinhalese dominated governments became the principal source of capital investment. When the government did fund an oil prospecting project in the North and a new flour mill near Trincomalee, Tamils were angered by 'island wide' employment quotas that favoured Sinhalese.[82] The Mahaveli irrigation project, which began to come on line in the early 1970s, also impacted Tamil-majority areas, but was viewed by Tamils as a 'colonisation' scheme intended to attract Sinhalese migrants.

Probably the only Tamil community members improving their lot under the United Front were Jaffna vegetable farmers, who became unintended beneficiaries of stringent import controls. Earlier, we saw that one government response to dwindling foreign exchange reserves was outright bans on 'minor vegetable' imports. These bans, especially bans on onion and chilli imports, were a bonanza for entrepreneurial Tamil smallholders who saw demand for their products skyrocket. Taking full advantage of rural credit schemes, hiring additional labour, and intensifying land use, they spearheaded a five-fold increase in domestic chilli production and nearly a doubling of onion production.[83] The United Front gained little political support from Jaffna farmers, but the windfall prosperity may have kept Tamil alienation from becoming even more severe. [84] When vegetable imports from India resumed, under J.R. Jayewardene's 'open economy' policy, agricultural income quickly dropped back to near 1970 levels.

Heath care services

Health care was an arena where the connection between government programs and results was demonstrable. The high priority given to public health and nutrition since before independence had been reflected in steadily improving public health indicators and this improving trend continued under Sirimavo Bandaranaike's government [85] Both maternal and infant mortality continued to decline. Mortality rates rose throughout much of the United Front's term, but had fallen to below 1970 levels by 1977.[86]

The priority given to health care, however, was less than under most previous governments. During a period when overall government spending increased by more than 20 per cent and spending on administration and defence by more than 50 per cent, health care spending in 1977, adjusted for inflation, had dropped nearly three per cent below the 1971 level.[87] While the total government workforce grew by nearly 100 per cent, the number of non-physician personnel employed by the government health service dropped by more than 10 per cent.[88] To reduce health care costs, modest fees were levied for visits to medical facilities and for drugs.[89] The only major health care initiative appears to have been construction and staffing of a number of small hospitals in rural areas.[90]

Why did health care spending decline? It seems unlikely that budget and personnel cuts were a high-level government policy.[91] More probably, they emerged from budget negotiations where the views of the Health Minister, an old SLFP stalwart representing a rural constituency in distant Uva Province, carried little weight.[92] At a time when Sri Lanka was being lauded by international development specialists as a model of the 'basic human needs' approach, the heavily burdened Prime Minister and her close advisors may simply have been unaware that heath care had dropped to near the bottom of the government's priority list. Or they may have felt that successful programs for which Sri Lanka had been internationally recognised in the past could withstand cuts that would be more burdensome and politically costly if made elsewhere.

Primary and secondary education

Education, too, ranked relatively low among spending priorities. Average annual funding was 12 per cent higher than during 1966-70 but, as in the case of health care, failed to keep up with inflation. Taking inflation into account, the education budget for 1977 was seven per cent less than in 1977. After years of growth, primary and secondary enrolments declined by about five per cent. This drop resulted from reforms that raised the age of eligibility from five to six years. Though Sri Lanka's pre-university education system was now superior to most developing nations and vernacular (*swabasha*) education was widely available, this transition by no means meant that every eligible child was in school. Educational opportunities for children in rural areas and especially for children of estate workers were still limited. Drop out rates among poorer families were high. Some urban schools were overcrowded and access to elite secondary schools, especially Colombo's Royal College, Mt. Lavinia's St. Thomas College and Kandy's Trinity College, was mostly restricted to upper class children. Apart from the poor schooling available on the tea plantations, there appears have been little discrimination by ethnic group at the primary and secondary level. Neither is there evidence to support assertions that Sri

Lanka Tamils, as a group, had better schools available to them. Educational opportunities in Jaffna, Sri Lanka's second largest urban area, were superior to those in the Kandyan region, but inferior to those in Colombo. Of course many Tamil families lived in Colombo and their children attended Colombo schools, including the elite schools.

Higher education

The pattern of reduced funding and ambitious but unfulfilled plans was repeated in higher education, but in this always volatile arena, challenges facing the government were far greater. University faculty and students had been one of the new government's important constituencies. They had been promised a relaxation of centralised controls imposed by Dudley Senanayake's Education Minister, expansion of the university system and greater faculty and student involvement in university administration. Proposed legislation that would have kept these promises was introduced in Parliament but passage was delayed by the People's Liberation Front (JVP) insurrection. When order was restored, the belief (subsequently proved wrong) that the rebel vanguard was dominated by university students, led Education Minister Badiuddin Mahmud to supplant initial government proposals with a reorganisation plan making university administration even more centralised than under Dudley Senanayake.[93] Considerable amounts of time and resources were devoted to imposing administrative 'rationalisations' and new experimental curricula on increasingly hostile constituencies.[94]

Bertram Bastiampillai's description of attempts to implement 'job-oriented' curricula in Sri Lanka's universities shows why well intentioned programs mandated by Colombo officials so often angered faculty, and disillusioned students.[95] These curricula were proposed in the Five-Year Plan as multidisciplinary courses, integrating academic study with practical training that would 'combine disciplines relevant to the needs of a developing country.'[96] With jobs almost impossible to find, students welcomed the new courses of study, which appeared to promise almost certain employment after graduation, with considerable enthusiasm. When few graduates found jobs, and most employers seemed to prefer graduates of more traditional programs, enthusiasm turned to disillusionment. Bastiampillai's study concluded that planners had based the program on a false premise, that unemployment among graduates was based upon lack of training, when in fact the problem was simply lack of jobs. Setting up the new programs had not been preceded by manpower studies to determine what skills were needed or plans to hire or retrain faculty qualified to teach the new courses. Faculty were highly resistant to 'practical training' as a component of academic study, a concept almost entirely foreign to Sri Lanka's British-influenced university traditions. Moreover, too many students were admitted to the programs for practical training to have been effective, even if supervised by enthusiastic faculty. Following complaints by students, some voiced in meetings with Education Ministry officials, the government attempted to interest employers in the program's graduates and to make some modifications in the curricula, but to little avail. Though vocationally-oriented practical training was widely acknowledged as a need in Sri Lanka, the shortcomings of the job-oriented curricula caused them to be added to the long list of United Front educational innovations that were scrapped in 1977.

The process of reforming Sri Lanka's universities was not helped by declining staff morale, produced by the 1972 budget crisis. Austerity measures required Ministry officials to impose spending cuts that curtailed library acquisitions and purchases of laboratory equipment, shrunk research funds (funds for foreign research were virtually eliminated), and cancelled subscriptions for scores of foreign academic journals. During intermittent periods, faculty and students even faced writing paper shortages. At a time of overwhelming pressure to expand university education, the combination of administrative turbulence and scarcity motivated an exodus of many talented faculty to foreign universities. This exodus, to which civil strife in the 1980s gave additional impetus, would seriously erode the quality of Sri Lanka's strongest academic programs, which had been among the finest in the Global South.

Reviewing plans devised by Sirimavo Bandaranaike's Ministries of Education and Plan Implementation, one cannot fail to be impressed by the awareness of issues facing Sri Lankan higher education and the seeming promise of proposed reforms. However, attempts at reform made little headway in solving fundamental problems – pressure on admissions, faculty resistance to change, an excess of unemployable 'arts' graduates and a shortage of graduates in science and engineering. Between 1970 and 1977, the number of students receiving marks high enough to be eligible for university admission nearly doubled, while the number admitted grew by only 20 per cent.[97]

The corrosive effects of discriminatory admissions policies based on ethnic quotas, which were one government response to the growing demand for scarce university places, have already been described.[98] What the government did not do – perhaps could not do – was provide the funds needed to expand higher education. Between 1970 and 1977, the total number of university graduates dropped by more than 20 per cent. While the output of science graduates nearly doubled, there was a drop of one-third in the number of engineering graduates. Overall, higher education was yet another area where benefits delivered fell short of ambitious promises and plans.

Sri Lanka's Marxist experiment: an appraisal

An overall appraisal of Sri Lanka's Marxist experiment needs to do little more that reiterate this oft-repeated theme: benefits delivered fell short of promises and plans. Ideology had played some role in the United Front's 1970 general election victory, but it was dissatisfaction with high unemployment, stagnant wages and access to higher education that brought Sirimavo Bandaranaike and her Marxist allies to power. Populist and ethnic nationalist rhetoric could not obscure the fact that in all of these areas, most Sri Lankans were worse off in 1977 than they had been in 1970. Some improvement in the international trade picture, beginning in 1975, could not reverse the impact of unfavourable economic trends on Sri Lanka's standard of living. As we have seen, even the equalising effect of redistributive policies had mostly worn off by 1977.

It would be wrong to lay all of the blame for Sri Lanka's economic decline on the United Front government. As early as the mid-1960s, Donald Snodgrass' meticulous dissection of Sri Lanka's export-dependent economy had made it clear that problems were looming on the horizon.[99] Given Sri Lanka's democratic institutions and an electorate habituated to generous benefits, every Prime Minister from D.S. Senanayake on faced the challenge of effecting structural reforms while retaining sufficient political support to avoid defeat in the next general election. The United Front government, which assumed power with such high hopes, also faced an incredible run of bad luck during its first years in office – the JVP rebellion, deteriorating terms of trade and unusually low yields of staple food crops.

Any economic program would have faced problems in the early 1970s, but the United Front's interventionist strategy made things worse.[100] Moreover, when it must have been apparent to all but the most ideologically blinded that *dirigiste* industrial, agricultural and trade policies were not working, the Prime Minister acceded to additional doses of the same medicine, prescribed by her Marxist political allies. This made an already ailing patient sicker. Finally, she became convinced that a change in direction was needed, but it was too late to recoup political losses from five years of failed policies and broken promises. Preoccupied with other matters, Sirimavo Bandaranaike's rump government had nothing to offer to a skeptical electorate that could counter J.R. Jayewardene's 'open economy' proposals. Postponing the July 1977 electoral reckoning or forming an improbable coalition with the Tamil United Liberation Front offered the only hopes of retaining power. When these stratagems failed, Sri Lanka's voters responded to seven years of United Front economic leadership with an unequivocal 'no confidence' vote.

The campaign strategy of Sirimavo Bandaranaike's erstwhile coalition partners provided voters with an even clearer opportunity to pass judgement on Marxist economics. Prior to the general election, The LSSP and Communist Party (Moscow Wing), along with some left-leaning SLFP defectors, joined together as the United Left Front. The Front nominated nearly a full slate of candidates to contest against nominees of the UNP and SLFP. Their platform promised that if elected, they would further strengthen economic policies of the 1970s. United Left Front candidates failed to win a single seat in the new Parliament.

13
Political Climate, Institutions and Feedback in the United Front Era

Had the United Front remained united, it is hard to say how much further down the path towards a Titoist regime Sri Lanka's government might have travelled. Disputes among coalition members, coupled with UNP resilience and Sri Lanka's strong democratic traditions. produced a different scenario.

How did Sri Lankans participate politically during the 1970s? What changes occurred from previous decades? What role did political movements and intensifying identities play in rising levels of political conflict? How did growing incivility and violence impact political identities and movements? How did the United Front government attempt to sustain its power and maintain public order using state-sanctioned violence? These are key questions about Sri Lanka's political climate, institutions and feedback examined in this chapter.

Political attitudes, identities and organisations

Landslide opposition victories in 1970 and again in 1977, in contrast to the closely contested elections of earlier decades, reflected qualitative changes in Sri Lanka's political life. In most electorates, support for national leaders rather than local candidates determined winners and losers. Overwhelming parliamentary majorities, first of the United Front coalition and then of the UNP, diminished the importance of Parliament. Government leaders had the power to steamroll their proposals into law and write new constitutions that reflected their political philosophies. In this 'winner take all' climate, opposition parties were more willing to use extra-constitutional means to press their views, and government leaders were more willing to use state power to prevent those views from being heard. Political competition became more confrontational and less civil. Mainstream opponents were demonised as 'enemies of the people' rather than acknowledged as 'loyal opposition.' There was greater willingness to achieve political ends and hold on to power by changing previously accepted 'rules of the game.'[1] On the political fringes, frustration of both Sinhalese and Tamil youth spawned militant movements pledged to transform 'business as usual' politics by violent means. These new patterns first emerged clearly during Sirimavo Bandaranaike's years in power. They would continue as the norm under J.R. Jayewardene.

How ordinary Sri Lankans viewed their government

Despite these new patterns, Sri Lankans' view of government changed little. People were less interested in ideology than improving the circumstances of their daily lives. They expected public officials to help with mundane matters, such as jobs, subsidies and community services. Often, members of Parliament served as intermediaries, especially between rural people and Colombo officialdom. Tumultuous political campaigns notwithstanding, elections were basically referenda on which political parties and personalities could deliver economic and social benefits most effectively.

Political scientist Robert Oberst provides a revealing picture of day-to-day concerns that led Sri Lankans to seek government assistance, based on interviews with members of the Seventh (1970-77) and Eighth (1977-88) Parliaments.[2] He writes that even government ministers set aside several days each month for meetings with district constituents.[3] Ministers told Oberst that national issues were rarely the subject of these conversations. Those seeking assistance could be very persistent in pressing their demands.

> The wife of one MP stated: 'My husband and I have been woken up in the morning by a constituent walking into our bedroom and seeking a favour.' One MP complained, 'One day, while meeting with my constituents, I had to answer a call of nature. While squatting there, I heard 'sir, sir, I think now is an excellent time to bring up a problem that has been bothering me.'[4]

Legislators might meet personally with 500 or more constituents each week and with almost every voter in their district during a term in office. While this was an important function, and by providing a channel for expressing basic demands may have contributed to political stability, it left little time for dealing with larger issues or educating constituents about them. Many requests asked for help in areas where MPs had little control. As we have seen, most policy decisions, even relatively low-level decisions, were made by the Prime Minister and a very small number of key ministers. Despite talk of 'popular participation' there was little input from backbenchers, except on politically volatile issues such as the rice subsidy and on some local development projects.

New roles for political organisations

The major national parties' influence continued to grow, supplanting the influence of notables and local level politicians. They employed full time staffs, supported local organisers, published newspapers, ran youth groups and either directly controlled or collaborated closely with labour unions. Most important, they nominated candidates, drafted manifestos and orchestrated the election campaigns featuring national party leaders that were key to securing parliamentary majorities. By 1977, the SLFP, Marxist parties, UNP, and Tamil parties were principal vehicles through which most individuals formed political identities and participated politically.

Militant groups, as we have seen, were also playing a larger, more visible role. These included the People's Liberation Front (JVP) and a number of Tamil Militant organisations, most with only a few members. Such groups sometimes represented themselves as political parties, but an acknowledged willingness to use violent force as a principal strategy set them apart. No mainstream party ever organised an armed insurrection as the JVP did or carried out high profile assassinations and bombings as some Tamil groups did.[5]

Interest groups were a third vehicle of political identity and participation, but were less influential than in the early 1950s when they had played such an instrumental role in pushing the Sinhala-only language policy.[6] Among the more influential were labour unions and religious organisations such as the All Ceylon Buddhist Congress and the Buddhist Nationalist Force (*Bauddha Jatika Balavegaya*). Political parties tried to control labour union and other interest group activity by organising their own. Party-based interest groups contributed to political polarisation along party lines rather than providing cross-cutting pressures, as in societies such as the United States, where they had more independent status.

The United Front coalition

A respected leader, coherent message and effective electoral strategy enabled the United Front to win broad support from an electorate that believed change was needed. However, the coalition's three member parties never achieved unity as an organisation. Each appealed to somewhat different constituencies. Each had its own structure and network of affiliated organisations. Significant doctrinal differences, particularly on economic management and foreign policy issues, divided party leaders. Adverse circumstances early in the government's administration intensified differences among member parties, which had been easier to ignore when campaigning for office. Eventually, as we have seen, conflicts over economic policy and political strategy splintered the United Front.

Factionalism within the SLFP paralleled divisions within the coalition. By 1970, pro-socialist SLFP leaders had become prominent while the influence of conservative rural and communalist leaders had waned. Rural Kandyan Sinhalese still comprised the party's most reliable electoral base, although large landowners had less power than in S.W.R.D. Bandaranaike's era. For these supporters, bread and butter economic issues, along with Sinhalese and Buddhist communal agendas, ranked higher in priority than any doctrinaire commitment to socialism. Personal identification with the Bandaranaike family was also an important consideration for many supporters.

As early as 1973, Sirimavo Bandaranaike and her close advisors could see signs of eroding public support. Harbingers were by-election losses, the mass turnout for Dudley Senanayake's funeral and widespread support for J.R. Jayewardene's civil disobedience campaign. Despite opposition from Marxist ministers, her daughters and left-leaning members of her own party, she became convinced a rightward tilt in economic policy was needed. This precipitated the conflict with LSSP Ministers described earlier.

Dealing firmly with opponents posed no problems for the Prime Minister. When LSSP Ministers published criticisms of government policies and then refused to resign, she sacked them from the cabinet. However, now the Prime Minister faced divided councils among her remaining supporters, not to mention her own family, which made major policy changes difficult. The rash of strikes precipitated by the sackings made prospects of a significant economic turnaround, regardless of what policy changes were implemented, even less probable.

Despite the problems it created, Sirimavo's Bandaranaike's dismissal of her LSSP colleagues is not difficult to understand, but their decision to break with her is harder to grasp. With public support for the coalition eroding, why did these men pick a fight that made a UNP victory in the upcoming general election all the more certain? Ideology, personal rivalries, caste and the views of core LSSP supporters all appeared to have played a role. As we have seen, the top Marxist leaders were among the nation's most respected British-trained intellectuals. Economic policies they wrote into the United Front's 'Common Program' reflected beliefs to which they had been committed for more than 30 years. They were willing to compromise on the rate of progress toward socialism,[7] but not on the ultimate goal. In an interview given a few months after the United Front's victory, cabinet member Colvin R. de Silva described his party as 'the soul of the United Front,' adding that 'the dominant issue in contemporary Ceylon is the overthrow of capitalism.'[8] Another party theorist described the Common Program as 'not so much a stage in a journey, but as a spring board from which the journey itself will really commence.'[9]

Party leaders also had to take constituent views into account, even in Sri Lanka's hierarchical and relatively disciplined political parties.[10] Youth and labour union members were core Marxist supporters. LSSP and Communist youth league members were far more militant than Sri Lanka's political mainstream. The JVP insurrection sharply reminded 'old left' leaders that they needed to be more attentive to this segment of the community. Labour union members were mostly government employees and employees of state corporations who had been direct beneficiaries of government programs and were mostly likely to lose by any move away from socialism. When the LSSP and Communist parties formed their ill fated United Left Front to contest the general election, their leaders were able to return to the more comfortable ideological terrain of class struggle and uncompromising socialism that they had occupied even before independence. Since politicians listen more to supporters than opponents and ideology is a powerful filter, they may have genuinely believed, despite overwhelming contrary evidence, that Sri Lanka's 'masses' would support their program at the polls.[11]

The United National Party

How did the UNP, within seven years, recover from its most devastating defeat to achieve its most decisive victory? United Front misfortunes, policy failures and factional disputes, described above, are part of the story. The remaining part – how UNP leader J.R. Jayewardene reorganised his party and capitalised on his political opportunities – will be told here.[12] In 1970, it seemed highly improbable that Jayewardene, then 66 years old, would rise above the number two leadership position he had occupied since the early 1950s. Following the United Front election landslide, a despondent Dudley Senanayake had asked him to lead the UNP's Parliamentary Group,[13] but as the government's political fortunes soured, Senanayake recovered his enthusiasm and appetite for leadership.

Senanayake advocated restoring the UNP's credibility by strongly attacking the government's Marxist ties, authoritarian tendencies and economic policies.

Jayewardene, who had supported Prime Minister Bandaranaike unequivocally during the insurrection, argued for a more conciliatory stance. Their differences escalated to public feuding that threatened to split the party, but eventually the two leaders reached an accommodation. Jayewardene acknowledged his old ally's authority as party president, while Senanayake agreed that Jayewardene should stay on as parliamentary leader, with the additional responsibility of rebuilding the party organisation.[14]

Dudley Senanayake's untimely death, at a time when he had regained much of his personal popularity with the electorate, was viewed as a UNP setback. However, it gave Jayewardene the opportunity to revitalise the party leadership and broaden its base of support in ways that would not have been possible had Senanayake lived. Skilful management of the politically sensitive funeral arrangements helped win him unanimous support as the next party leader from a UNP Working Committee heavily stacked with old-line Senanayake supporters. With this vote of confidence, Jayewardene moved quickly to tighten party discipline and place his own allies in key positions.[15]

These moves presaged fundamental changes that were intended to broaden the party's appeal and strengthen its campaign organisation. Membership rolls were swelled and party revenues increased by reducing the minimum membership fee. Increased revenues helped to staff an expanded party headquarters which, at Jayewardene's insistence, was now managed by a full time professional party secretary.[16] A program was initiated to form permanent branches in every polling district and give branches limited representation on the UNP Executive Committee. Branches were given equal representation at the party's National Convention, replacing a system that allowed cronies of the party leader to appoint large numbers of delegates

With these and other moves, Jayewardene began to transform the UNP's image from an elitist organisation dominated by the Senanayake family to a party in which young men and women from all castes and regions could aspire to leadership roles. Many of the new Working Committee members and more than a third of the party's candidates for Parliament in the 1977 campaign were younger than 40 years of age. A revitalised UNP leadership made the SLFP's practice of selecting top leaders almost exclusively from among Sirimavo Bandaranaike's relations an important campaign issue.

Opposing the government during this period was not an easy task. Emergency regulations gave the government broad powers to repress criticism and intimidate opponents. Each time the UNP tried to mobilise public opposition, government leaders strengthened repressive measures. Even parliamentary debates were not fully reported in the censored media. Maintaining the UNP's credibility as a party that could legitimately aspire to lead the nation was a constant struggle.[17]

Had the United Front remained united, it is hard to say how much further down the path towards a Titoist regime Sri Lanka's government might have travelled. Disputes among coalition members, coupled with UNP resilience and Sri Lanka's strong democratic traditions, produced a different scenario. In addition to coping with economically crippling strikes, the government had to fight off two votes of confidence in which former coalition members played leading roles. J.R. Jayewardene and his new UNP leadership team realised that attempts to further postpone general elections would probably fail and they would have the opportunity to present their case to Sri Lanka's voters by mid-1977 at the latest.[18]

As in 1970, proposals for solving the nation's economic ills dominated the campaign. The UNP election manifesto, *A Program of Action to Create a Just and Free Society*, promised reforms that would end Sri Lanka's experiment with Marxist economics, provide full employment, eliminate scarcities and broaden economic opportunities.[19] Among the proposals were establishment of export processing zones, reduction of the government's role in industry, investment incentives and competition between public and private sectors. This 'open economy' philosophy drew upon ideas that J.R. Jayewardene had pushed unsuccessfully under previous UNP governments and was strongly influenced by Singapore's successful economic development programs. In 1975 Jayewardene had acknowledged the popularity of socialist ideals by announcing that his party now embraced 'democratic socialism.'[20] Nevertheless, virtually every reform proposed in 1977 moved away from socialism toward a free-market economy.

On communal divisions between Sinhalese and Tamils, the UNP proposed a more conciliatory approach without committing to any specific reforms. Party leaders promised they would take 'all possible steps' to remedy grievances in such areas as education, colonisation, language and public employment. 'We will summon an All Party Conference...,' the manifesto stated, 'and implement its decision.'[21] Surprisingly, in view of the Tamil parties' call for a mandate 'to establish an independent sovereign state,' communal issues do not seem to have played a major role the election, outside of the Tamil majority areas. This reflected the degree to which politicians of both major parties viewed Sinhalese voters as their primary constituency and the concerns of Tamil voters as peripheral.

J.R. Jayewardene also tried to cloak himself in the Buddhist tradition of the 'righteous' (*dharmista*) ruler and promised that under his leadership, Sri Lanka would move toward the ideal of a '*dharmista society.*[22] This was intended to provide a powerful, easily understood moral appeal to the Sinhalese-Buddhist community. Later critics targeted this pledge as hypocrisy,[23] yet it reflected ideas that the UNP leader, himself a devout Buddhist, had thought about for years. An idealistic young J.R. Jayewardene had first described his vision of the *dharmista* ruler and the *dharmista* society in an essay on *Buddhism and Politics*, written before Sri Lanka became independent.[24] 'The ideal man,' Jayewardene wrote, '...is the unattached man, the man who is not attached to wealth or possessions, to power and to the object of his desires. He serves others, rather than himself.' 'The ideal state,' he continued, 'must be composed of ideal men; men without greed, hatred or ignorance.'[25] For a decade after the 1977 general election, the man who had 35 years earlier described the 'ideal state' and political leaders would exercise greater power than any Sri Lankan before him. Jayewardene would have his chance to put those ideas into practice.

Sinhalese militancy: the People's Liberation Front (Janatha Vimukti Peramuna - JVP)

Much has already been said about the origins, organisation, and ill-fated insurrection of youthful JVP miilitants. However, some of the questions that most troubled Colombo's ruling elite in the aftermath of rebellion remain to be answered: From what segments of Sinhalese society were the rebels recruited? What motivated them to take up arms against a socialist/Marxist government in the Global South's most democratic and welfarist society? If they had successfully seized power, how might they have restructured that society?

Answers to the first question have been provided by Sri Lankan anthropologist Gananath Obeyesekere who analyzed statistical data collected by government officials on 10,192 'suspected insurgents' in police custody. Not surprisingly, the rebels were overwhelmingly male, youthful and Buddhist. Although many JVP leaders came from Rohana Wijeweera's *karava* (fishing) caste, more than half of the suspected insurgents were from the landowning *goyigama* caste and Obeyesekere discounted caste as a factor in the rebellion. Data on education and economic status pointed to factors that were more significant. More than 85 per cent of those incarcerated reported they attended rural secondary schools where Sinhala was the language of instruction. These beneficiaries of language and education reforms were often the first in their families to have attended secondary school. When educational background was combined with data on occupation and income, a clear picture of frustrated economic aspirations emerged. More than 90 per cent of the youths in Obeyesekere's sample held poorly paid, low status positions or were unemployed. In an earlier era, secondary education would have qualified these men for a reasonably paid secure job at least and possibly for entry into lower rungs of Sri Lanka's middle class. Population growth, coupled with economic stagnation, ruled this out for most. Contradicting the views of many Colombo officials, Obeyesekere found that few suspected insurgents had university educations or high status jobs. 'Casual labourer', 'cultivator', 'student' and 'unemployed' were the occupations most frequently reported.

Trends and social structures that contributed to youthful frustrations have been described earlier. Population growth was pushing down the size of rural landholdings, particularly in the South. Children could no longer expect to be fully supported by produce from their father's land. Many joined a growing agricultural 'lumpenproletariat' whose members were under constant pressure to produce additional income.[33] When they sought a job or tried to start a small business, they were often blocked by interlocking systems of political patronage and elite dominance. Anthropologist Paul Alexander points to the pervasive influence of rural elites who maintained their power through networks of patron-client relationships based on trading jobs, credit and gifts for political support. Their approval was necessary to open a market stall, theater or bar, to run a truck or bus route, or to produce the fermented coconut liquor (toddy) popular with poor Sri Lankans. They served as intermediaries for government programs that supplied loans and basic supplies. They became involved in the government-managed systems for purchasing and distributing basic consumer items such as rice, textiles and kerosene. They collaborated with members of parliament to allocate government and state sector jobs. The substantial incomes they received from gifts, fees and bribes helped them to maintain their privileged position.[34]

When rural youth spoke of reform, it was this elite dominated rural patronage system they were most interested in reforming. We have already seen how the slow pace and legalistic orientation of reform measures initiated after Sirimavo Bandaranaike's government came to power frustrated them. But even more frustrating was a growing belief that the 1970 election landslide had changed nothing as far as the rural patronage system was concerned. ' Rightly or wrongly,' Obeyesekere concludes, 'the youths I interviewed felt their local MP had been bribed by persons of wealth in the area.' The use of job quotas by newly elected MPs to build alliances with former opponents was, apparently, a common and disillusioning pattern.[35] This contributed to a widespread sense of injustice that strongly motivated young men to join the JVP.[36]

What social and political order did JVP cadres envision as a replacement for Sri Lanka's social and political institutions? Rohana Wijeweera was somewhat vague on this point, but expressed admiration for the Maoist states of China, Cuba and Albania.[37] His model was a self-sufficient, egalitarian society, based on agriculture, with peasants as the backbone (as in Mao's China) and with land fully collectivised to ensure equality. Buddhist nationalist ideals harked back to heroic myths of the Southern Sinhalese kingdom of Ruhuna.[38] There was hardly a pretence that the movement would govern democratically once in power. Strong leadership and one party rule were needed, Wijeweera argued, to implement a consistent development strategy that would transform Sri Lanka.

Despite this commitment to centralised, authoritarian leadership, the degree to which the JVP itself had a centralised controlled organisational structure is debated, with early reports accepting the government's view of a centralised command directing a network of cells and later revisionist scholars expressing scepticism.[39] Two recent studies, which claim to be based on 'insider' information, fail to resolve the debate.[40] The 1987-1989 JVP rebellion's devastating impact provides evidence that Wijeweera, despite idiosyncrasies,[41] was a ruthless and inventive guerrilla leader who could command a significant following. Without such leadership, and with many members in detention, the JVP fragmented into small factions and ceased to exist as an effective force after 1971.[42] This did not mean, however, that the social and economic problems which motivated JVP supporters to take up arms had been solved. When J.R. Jayewardene repeated Sirimavo Bandaranaike's error by releasing Rohana Wijeweera from prison, the movement was resurrected and nearly achieved its goal of toppling Sri Lanka's government.

Tamil militant groups begin to take shape

While Sirimavo Bandaranaike's government was preoccupied with promoting Sinhalese-Buddhist agendas and with foreign policy, militant groups began to reshape the Tamil community's political agendas. Earlier, we saw how militant-initiated violence began to erode government authority in Tamil majority regions and push traditional Tamil parties toward more extreme positions on communal issues. How and why did Tamil militant groups emerge and become viable during the United Front's years in power? Who were their members and leaders; what was their relationship to the larger Tamil community? What potential did these groups have to marshal resources and mobilise support that would enable them to achieve their goal of an independent Tamil Eelam? Few Sinhalese political leaders were concerned with finding answers to such questions at a time when answers might have made a difference to the future of their nation.

Before addressing these questions a brief review of where Sri Lanka's Tamil population was concentrated at the time of the 1981 census will throw useful light on Sri Lanka's widening ethnic divisions and on proposals for an independent Tamil Eelam, to be discussed below.[43] Figure 13.1 shows this concentration, with heaviest shading showing regions where the concentration of Tamils is 80 per cent or more, the lighter shading showing regions where the Tamil concentration is from 50 to 80 per cent and other marked areas showing predominantly Sinhalese, predominantly Muslim and ethnically diverse regions.[44]

The highest concentration of Tamils, more than 95 per cent, was found in Jaffna district, located on the northernmost part of the island and the location of the island's second largest city. Not surprisingly it was in Jaffna district that government attempts to forcibly impose Sinhalese culture on a homogenous Tamil population of more than 800,000 met greatest resistance. Batticaloa district, located far to the south of Jaffna on the east coast, numbered more that 70 per cent Tamils among its population of 328,000, with a concentration of more than 90 per cent in Batticaloa city.

Batticaloa Tamils were separated from their counterparts in Jaffna district and Trincomalee coast by a band of predominantly Sinhalese and Muslim areas of settlement. In contrast to Jaffna, Batticaloa was one of Sri Lanka's poorest regions and accessible from the nation's economic and political heartland only by circuitous highway and train routes through mountainous terrain.   A significant number of Tamils were also concentrated on the coast of Trincomalee district, just south of Jaffna district. Tamils shared multiethnic Trincomalee city, surrounding one of the world's most spectacular natural harbours, with

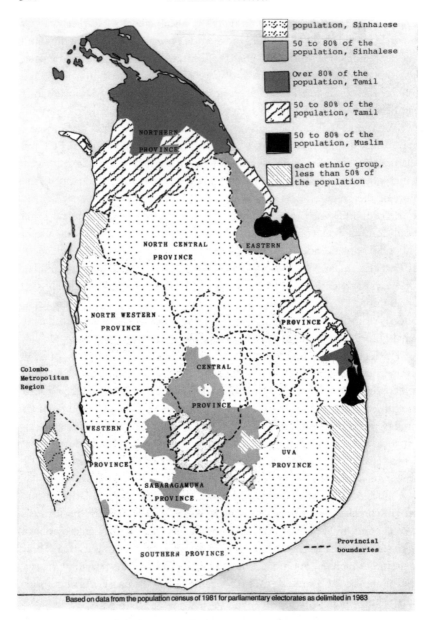

Based on data from the population census of 1981 for parliamentary electorates as delimited in 1983

Figure 13.1 Population Concentrations of Major Ethnic Groups

a large Tamil-speaking Muslim population, but few Sinhalese. The predominantly Sinhalese population surrounding Trincomalee city and the coastal strip to the north included a number of recent migrants who had been relocated by government 'colonisation schemes.' These schemes were, as we have seen, highly unpopular with Tamils.

Tamils also comprised the majority of the sparsely settled Vavuniya district's population of only 83,000. About 180,000 Tamils lived in Colombo, representing approximately 10 per cent of the capital city's 1.75 million population. Interestingly, Tamils living in Colombo were the third largest Tamil grouping in Sri Lanka and, on a per-capita basis, the wealthiest and most highly educated. Many were successful lawyers, physicians, businessmen and, despite 20 years of preferential treatment for Sinhalese, senior officials in Sri Lanka's government.

Political activism among the Jaffna Peninsula's educated youth was not new, but had never been viewed as a major threat.[45] After independence, Jaffna youth had actively participated in the intensifying confrontations between Tamils and government officials over communal issues including the anti-*Sri* campaign, 'black flag' demonstrations, civil disobedience campaigns (*satyagrahas*) and general strikes (*hartals*). In 1961, a young group of Federal Party activists who rejected Chelvanayakam's Gandhian philosophy formed The Army of Tigers appropriating for their symbol the standard of the ancient and powerful Tamil Chera Kingdom. Members met secretly in the precincts of Koneswaren Hindu temple, overlooking Trincomalee Harbour, and swore a solemn oath to fight for an independent Tamil Eelam.[46]

The 'army' did not survive Federal Party participation in Dudley Senanayake's government, but even during the relatively tranquil 1965-70 period, young Tamil activists distributed pamphlets advocating militant action against the government that included a poetry collection allegorising a 'Tiger Army.' Tamil youth were also influenced by the domestic politics of Tamil Nadu state where, in 1967, the Tamil nationalist Dravidian Progressive Front (*Dravida Munnethra Kazhagam*) ousted Indira Gandhi's Congress Party from control of the state government for the first time. There was little overt militant activity, however, perhaps because Tamil youth with ability could still anticipate that a superior education plus hard work would provide opportunities for a good job and reasonable economic security.

The 1970 election landslide, followed by United Front policies that Tamil youth viewed as overtly racist, changed this optimistic outlook, making young Tamils more receptive to militant appeals. As we have seen, successively more discriminatory university admissions standards, beginning in 1970, contributed most to youthful alienation.[47] Pro-Sinhalese hiring practices by government departments and by the increasingly dominant state economic sector motivated youths who might previously have migrated south to remain in Jaffna, even with no prospects of a good job. Youths who might have travelled to Europe, the United States or India for university degrees, but were kept home by foreign exchange controls, also remained in Jaffna, where they nursed grievances against the Colombo government.

Many of the problems faced by Tamil youth – university admissions pressures, scarcity of jobs and restrictions on foreign travel – impacted Sinhalese youth as well. Tamil politicians, like their Sinhalese counterparts, encouraged racial scapegoating. Simultaneously, Tamil pride was strengthened by a Tamil Nadu cultural revolution that produced a flowering of literature, poetry and especially films. Many of these contributions were available in Sri Lanka, as well.[48] The fact that Sinhalese politicians, including Prime Minister Bandaranaike herself, often blamed 'Tamils' for the nation's problems further strengthened the feeling of ethnic identity and alienation among this most volatile sector of the Tamil population.

The early 1970s were also a time when two violent uprisings in South Asia – the JVP rebellion and the secession of Bangladesh from Pakistan – captured the imagination of Tamil youth. For secondary school and university students, the uprising of their Sinhalese counterparts against an unpopular government made the possibility of revolutionary violence more concrete.[49] There were also direct contacts. Some JVP detainees in Jaffna shared prison facilities with young Tamils, including young men who had been incarcerated for political protests.[50] Tamil youths were able to learn about tactics that had been successful in the South and discuss reasons why the rebellion failed.

Events leading to the creation of an independent Bangladesh provided a more useful model for young Tamils. Democratic elections held in December 1970, had given Mujibur Rahman's Awami League an overwhelming victory in West Pakistan. Responding to delays in recognising the election by Pakistan's military regime, the Bengali leader mobilised Gandhian style demonstrations to back political autonomy demands. When Pakistan's government responded with armed intervention, Mujibur proclaimed the independent Republic of Bangladesh. He was immediately arrested and condemned to death. The insurgents would almost certainly have been defeated by Pakistan's well-equipped army but for India's intervention. First, India provided sanctuaries and arms for the Awami League's 'Freedom Force'. When this proved insufficient, India's army intervened directly and quickly overwhelmed the Pakistani forces. Mujibur was freed and by the spring of 1972 an independent Bangladesh had gained international recognition. For Tamil youth, contrasts between the JVP's defeat and the Awami League's victory illustrated the value of a sanctuary and of Indian support. They further concluded that Indian military forces might support an armed struggle for independence under some circumstances. 'Yuri Desh' and 'Eela Desh' became part of the political graffiti that young Tamils scribbled on Jaffna walls.

In contrast to the JVP leadership's limited political-economic vision, Tamil youth and academics had thought seriously about the economic viability of an independent Eelam. Initial plans developed by a group of Peradeniya undergraduates were refined by faculty and students at the newly founded Jaffna Campus.[54] Their proposals looked much more like Singapore or Taiwan than the self-sufficient agrarian society envisioned by the JVP. In broad outline, their analysis and plan was as follows: Tamil regions already produced rice, fish and vegetables that could be consumed or used for trade but lacked industrial capacity. This obstacle would be overcome by establishing an export processing zone, capitalising on Trincomalee's natural harbour. A wealth of entrepreneurial talent and capital to initiate development would be available from successful Tamil businessmen. Educated Tamil youth would provide a high quality labour force for new enterprises. Once a critical mass had been established, it would be easy to attract additional capital and technology from the Tamil diaspora and other investors. The Tamil Eelam government's role would be to raise revenue and co-ordinate development plans for the benefit of the local population. Freed from Sinhalese oppression and exploitative policies administered from Colombo, this would not be difficult to accomplish. The Eelam proposals made it clear that linking Jaffna's and Batticaloa's Tamil populations by incorporating the multi-ethnic Trincomalee region was essential to the new nation's viability. However, no serious attention was given to issues of self determination or minority rights for the region's large Sinhalese and Muslim populations.[55]

Given the circumstances I have described – economic hardships, cultural revitalisation, government policies viewed as oppressive, dissatisfaction with mainstream Tamil parties and the vision of an economically viable Eelam – formation of youthful militant groups was not surprising. Initially, the form these groups assumed was very different than the JVP's relatively centralised structure. Their lineal ancestor was the Tamil Students' League (*Tamil Manavar Peravai*), founded in 1970, which became the Tamil Youth League (*Tamil Elaingyar Peravai*) in 1973. The League had no formal links with the Tamil United Front (TUF), but under the direction of the Front's second in command, Appapillai Amirthalingam, its youthful members sometimes served as TUF footsoldiers.[56] If the TUF announced a general strike, those who did not comply were often beaten and their businesses vandalised by gangs of young men operating with Amirthalingam's tacit approval.[57] A small number of Tamil youths, however, were becoming dissatisfied with Chelvanayakam's pacifist principles and attempts to compromise with Sinhalese leaders that seemed to produce defeat after defeat. Some Tamil politicians, too, had begun using the rhetoric of 'armed struggle.' For example, at a 1972 public meeting, a speaker described government supporters as 'enemies of the Tamil nation.' 'They do not deserve to die a natural death,' he told his audience. 'Nor do they deserve to die in an accident. The Tamil people, especially the youth, must decide how they will die.'[58] Some Tamil youths were taking such statements seriously.

Militant sentiment was particularly strong among young men of the *Karayar* (fishing) caste who lived on the Jaffna Peninsula's northernmost 'smugglers coast'. Resistance to authority was nothing new among these coastal dwellers whose families had combined smuggling with seafaring for generations. As in the South, fishing caste members were known for their independence and entrepreneurial ability.[59] Not only did *Karayar* youth oppose Sri Lanka's government, they had little use for the *Vellala* (landowner caste) dominated mainstream political parties or for the caste conscious rigidities of Jaffna society. It is not surprising, then, that two of the early militant groups trace their origins to Velvettiturai town, a conservative fishing community of about 10,000, nicknamed 'smuggler's paradise'. The first of these, which became the Tamil Eelam Liberation Organisation (TELO), was conceived by two Velvettiturai youths, Nadaraja Thangavelu and his friend Selvaraja Yogachandran[60] who were then living in Jaffna. By 1971 they were holding secret meetings, collecting weapons and experimenting with bomb manufacture. Ponnandi Sivakumaran, whom we encountered earlier as the first Tamil youth to die by biting a cyanide capsule, was also an early TELO member. While ineffective at first, TELO would later establish close ties with Tamil Nadu's movie-actor-turned-Chief Minister, Mulhuvel Karunanidhi, and receive support from India's clandestine services organisation, RAW.[61]

Vellupillai Prabakharan and the Liberation Tigers of Tamil Eelam

The second militant group with Velvettiturai roots was founded by another early TELO member, Velupillai Prabakharan. First called the 'Tamil New Tigers,' the group became known as the Liberation Tigers of Tamil Eelam (LTTE) after 1976. Since Prabakharan later become a major protagonist in Sri Lanka's protracted Tamil-Sinhalese civil war, a brief recounting of his early life – primarily as told by Indian Journalist Narayan Swamy – is in order.[62]

His father, Tiruventkatam Velupillai, was employed by Sri Lanka's government as a district land officer. His upbringing has been described as 'typical middle class.' Tiruventkatam was no militant, but his home and homes of his friends were venues for endless political discussions of the Tamil community's worsening position under the United Front. Young Prabakharan is described as listening quietly by his father's side at these gatherings.

Even in his mid-teen years, Prabakharan is remembered as having set his sights on becoming a militant leader who would free the Tamil people from Sinhalese domination. Subash Chandra Bose, the Bengali nationalist who rejected Gandhi's pacifism and formed an 'Indian National Army' to fight the British, became a role model. Bose's slogan, 'I shall fight for the freedom of my land until I shed the last drop of blood' inspired young Prabakharan. America's 'tough guy' movie actor Clint Eastwood, and Veerapandia Kattabomman, a legendary warrior featured in a popular Tamil movie, were also personal heroes. Prabakharan studied Napoleon's campaigns and, for lighter reading, 'devoured' *Phantom* comic books. While other boys played sports, the future guerrilla leader practiced shooting squirrels, birds and chameleons with his home made slingshot and learned the rudiments of martial arts. Later, an air gun replaced the slingshot and he recruited friends to practice making bombs, using ingredients stolen from their high school chemistry laboratory. Teasing family members nicknamed him *veeravan*, the brave one.[63]

Personal bravery was important to Prabakharan. His commitment to a protracted armed struggle was more serious than many of his TELO compatriots and he had begun to discipline himself for what lay ahead. To practice withstanding torture, he would lie on bags in which hot chillies had been stored or remain tied in a bag under the hot sun in Jaffna's 100 plus degree heat for a full day. He stuck pins under his nails to increase his endurance for pain and pricked insects to death with needles so that he would be mentally prepared to torture 'the enemy.'[64] Before leaving Velvettiturai in the early 1970s to become a full time militant, Prabakharan went through his home and destroyed every family picture in which he appeared. From that time on, he lived constantly under cover and rarely slept in the same place twice. On two occasions he fled across the Palk straits and hid out in Madras to escape police capture.

Despite these exploits, Prabakharan did not emerge as a leading guerrilla figure until his successful assassination of Mayor Durayappah on 27 July 1975. The Liberation Tigers of Tamil Eelam was not formally established until March of the following year. Prabakharan personally chose the new organisation's symbol which featured the head of a roaring tiger and crossed rifles.[65] Robbery proceeds provided funds for establishing self sustaining training farms in remote jungle hideouts south of Jaffna, where carefully selected recruits were indoctrinated and drilled in marksmanship.[66] Even with these resources, total LTTE membership was less than 100 at the time of the 1977 general election.

The most visible Tamil militant group formed during Sirimavo Bandaranaike's term was founded not in Sri Lanka, but at the London home of long-time Tamil student activist, Eliyathambi Ratnasabapathy. The Eelam Revolutionary Organisation of Students (EROS), as the group named itself, began in 1975.[67] They organised demonstrations in London and at the World Cup Cricket matches in Manchester that gave Tamil separatism its first international visibility.[68] EROS established ties between Tamil separatism and Yasser Arafat's Palestine Liberation Organisation when the PLO Ambassador, after attending a Tamil student meeting where he met Ratnasabapathy, offered to train Tamil guerrillas at Fatah camps in Lebanon. Three EROS members completed a six-month training course in 1976 and an additional seven took the course a year later. Ratnasabapathy also agreed to include Tamil Tigers in the training program, but these plans became a casualty of factional disagreements between the two groups.[69] EROS did not gain significant support in Sri Lanka until after 1977 when it began building strength among Tamil youths living primarily in Batticaloa District.

Tamil militant groups would not become a serious threat to Sri Lanka's government until the 1983 ethnic riots drove thousands of youths into their ranks. However, the parallel growth of TELO, LTTE, EROS and PLOTE, along with less well-known groups, established a pattern that continued into the 1980s. Published lists of militant groups typically included a dozen entries or more. This differed greatly from JVP domination of Sinhalese militancy both at the time of the 1970 insurrection and in the 1980s. Anthropologist Michael Roberts argues that multiple competing groups made Tamil militancy more resilient. Different groups tapped different regions, castes and social strata for recruits. The police's task of controlling militancy was more complex than if actions had been orchestrated by a central command.[70]

Competition between groups for support also tended to push all of them toward more extreme positions.[71] Groups proposing compromise or opposing violence risked being branded as 'traitors to the Tamil nation.'[72] Militant groups became increasingly militaristic and, coupled with police repression, this gave Tamil political life a more authoritarian caste.[73] Loyalty to 'the leader' was paramount and dissenting views were not tolerated. Open discussion of political issues necessary for a democracy to function became less and less possible.[74] With the death of S.J.V. Chelvanayakam in 1977, the last influential Tamil leader committed to non-violence passed from the scene.

The Mainstream Tamil political parties

Chelvanayakam's deputy and successor, A. Amirthalingam, was a less principled man. His professed commitment to non-violence included tacit acceptance of bombings and assassinations. Occasionally he used militant cadres as enforcers. Later, when Amirthalingam was named leader of the opposition in Sri Lanka's Parliament, it appeared that he was at the height of his power, but this was an illusion. The era when mainstream Tamil politicians could speak of independence in Jaffna, while negotiating deals with Sinhalese politicians in Colombo was ending. Power to direct political life in the North was passing to the militant leaders.

In 1970, it was not inevitable that extremists would come to dominate a society that, despite political reverses, was still politically conservative and relatively peaceful. When Sirimavo Bandaranaike became Prime Minister, Chelvanayakam still believed that accommodation between Tamil and Sinhalese communities in a united Sri Lanka was possible. Switzerland was the Federal Party's model for power sharing, hardly a radical stance.[75] Its 1970 election manifesto urged Tamils 'not to lend their support to any political movement that advocates the bifurcation of the country.'[76] In 1971, Sri Lankan government leaders viewed Jaffna as a safe location for incarcerating People's Liberation Front (JVP) leader Rohana Wijeweera and his top lieutenants.

In Chapters 11 and 12, we saw how Sirimavo Bandaranaike's government enacted policies viewed as humiliating by many Tamils. These policies unintentionally targeted Tamil community members most likely to respond militantly. Policies discriminating against Tamil youth were intended to appease Sinhalese youth, a volatile population that government leaders feared more, but this evoked no sympathy from idealistic young men such as Eliyathambi Ratnasabapathy, Ponnundari Sivakumaren and Velupillai Prabakharan. For them, every new enactment and humiliation was viewed not only as Sinhalese oppression, but political failure of mainstream Tamil politicians.

This combination of government intransigence and rising youth militancy placed Chelvanayakam and his moderate colleagues in an impossible position. Beginning with the 1971 Constituent Assembly boycott, their actions and declarations sent increasingly strong messages to the Prime Minister about opposition to government policies in the Tamil community. By staking out more and more militant positions themselves, Tamil politicians were responding to pressures from their own community to move beyond 'business as usual' politics. Public demonstrations, *hartals* and Chelvanayakam's overwhelming victory in the long-delayed Kankesanthurai by-election provided solid evidence of Tamil community opposition to policies equating 'national values' and 'Sinhalese values' in a region than was more than 90 per cent Tamil. Bombings and assassinations showed the direction Tamil resistance might take if non-violent expressions of opposition continued to be ignored. We have seen, however, that by 1975, Sirimavo Bandaranaike's government was both weakened politically and preoccupied with other matters. Like Chelvanayakam, the Prime Minister faced conflicting pressures. Demands from Tamil leaders, coupled with threats to government authority, evoked counter-pressures from more militant elements among her own supporters who felt that 'teaching those Tamils a lesson' was the appropriate response to demands for greater autonomy.[77]

Although voters did not realise it, the 21 July 1977 elections were the last time Tamils living in Sri Lanka's Northern and Eastern provinces would have an opportunity to express the political goals of their community in a relatively free election. In their election *Manifesto*, Tamil United Liberation Front leaders presented the election as a referendum on whether or not the Tamil people endorsed an independent Eelam. Winning TULF candidates, the *Manifesto* stated, will 'form themselves into the National Assembly of Tamil Eelam which will draft a constitution for the state of Tamil Eelam and establish the independence of Tamil Eelam by bringing that constitution into operation, either by peaceful means or by direct action or struggle.'

Whether or not Tamil United Liberation Front leaders received their 'mandate' is open to interpretation. In the Northern Province, TULF candidates won every seat and a large majority of the popular vote. In the Eastern Province, viewed by Tamils as an integral part of their 'traditional homeland,' the UNP was the clear victor, by a margin of eight seats to four and a popular vote plurality. This highlighted a problem rarely addressed by TULF orators in Jaffna audiences, but with serious practical implications for Sri Lanka's new leader of the opposition, Appapillai Amirthalingam. Whether or not the Eastern Province belonged to the 'traditional Tamil homelands' could be debated by historians, but its inclusion in an independent Tamil state was an economic and political necessity. This meant Tamil Eelam would have its own minority problem. A majority of the Eastern Province's population were either Sinhalese or Muslim, had voted for UNP candidates and wanted to remain in Sri Lanka.

Amirthalingam also faced a second problem. Northern Province voters at least had given him a clear mandate to lead them to an independent Tamil Eelam, but it soon became apparent that he had no strategy for attaining this goal.[79] By speaking of a 'secret plan' for independence, he raised Tamil expectations and Sinhalese fears, but his real objective seems to have been no different than Chelvanayakam – some kind of compromise settlement with the newly installed UNP government.[80] As leader of the opposition, Amirthalingam was unable to deliver either an independent Eelam or a compromise that would grant Tamils limited autonomy. This failure disillusioned many Tamils who had been strong TULF supporters. It eroded their already fragile faith in democracy and made them more receptive to militant appeals. As Amirthalingam showed his true colours, many young Tamils who had welcomed the TULF victory came to view him as a traitor to their cause.[81]

The Indian Tamils

Both in economic position and political power, Indian Tamil plantation workers remained at the bottom of Sri Lankan society throughout Sirimavo Bandaranaike's years in office. They experienced severe discrimination at the hands of Agriculture Minister Hector Kobbekaduwa and some other Sinhalese officials. Nevertheless, successive agreements resolving the statelessness problem were adding Indian Tamils to Sri Lanka's voting rolls. By the next general election it was possible that in some districts they might be represented in Parliament by members of their own community rather than by Sinhalese nationalists who opposed their interests.[82] Thus, Indian Tamil leaders hoped voting power could be added to the very limited arsenal of weapons at their disposal to bring pressure on plantation owners and Sinhalese politicians. Since even a fully enfranchised Indian Tamil community would always be a small minority, gaining political power meant choosing political allies. Choosing how to relate to the increasingly militant Tamil parties of the north posed a severe challenge.

Economic deprivation and exploitation rather than lack of political freedom were Indian Tamils' most pressing problems. They had the highest infant mortality, highest illiteracy and lowest life expectancy in Sri Lanka. Working conditions were poor and wages were low.[83] Conditions faced by women were particularly harsh. Often they had to walk long distances to work and then spend 12 hours picking tea. They had to pick a certain volume of tea to earn their wages, but if they met their quota early, they were required to continue picking. Latrine facilities and drinking water were limited. Supervisors could discipline workers, without recourse, for minor infractions.

With more than 300,000 members Savumiamoorthy Thondaman's Ceylon Worker's Congress (CWC) continued to be the most powerful Indian Tamil labour organisation. His power, however, was lessened by Sri Lanka's custom of having multiple competing unions, many affiliated with political parties, in the same industry. Twelve unions competed for plantation workers' allegiances and four of those were government allies.[84] Thondaman pursued a dual strategy of negotiating with more sympathetic government ministers and attempting to build independent political strength. The first track, which involved a combination of demands, threats, short work stoppages and compromises, achieved only limited concessions from a government in increasingly straitened circumstances and with a strong anti-Tamil bias. The political track was to prove more successful in the long run.

Initially, as we have seen, Thondaman responded to anti-Tamil provisions of the Republican Constitution by joining with the Federal Party and Tamil Congress to form the Tamil United Front.[85] For a period of time, the collaboration was close. As Northern leaders responded to militant pressure by moving toward separatism, however, Thondaman began to develop an alliance with the UNP.[86] CWC cadres supported the UNP civil disobedience campaigns against government economic policies, turning out in large numbers for a *satyagraha* in the heart of the tea country. Thondaman also campaigned for J.R. Jayewardene in Colombo when he resigned and then ran for reelection to protest the government's extension of its term in office.

Formation of the Tamil United Liberation Front (TULF) and passage of the resolution advocating an independent Tamil Eelam widened the gap between Thondaman and northern leaders. He formally dissociated the CWC from the resolution. Indian Tamils were all comparatively recent migrants to Sri Lanka. They had no historical links, real or imagined, to the 'traditional Tamil homelands.' It was clear to the politically astute Thondaman that his followers had nothing to gain and much to lose from calls for an independent Tamil Eelam in Sri Lanka's northern and eastern regions.[87]

J.R. Jayewardene's alliance with the CWC was long lasting. In 1977, Savumiamoorthy Thondaman was elected to Parliament, representing Nuwara Eliya-Maskeila constituency. This was part of the old constituency that he had represented in 1947, before the Indian Tamils lost their citizenship. In 1978, J.R. Jayewardene, now Sri Lanka's Executive President under a newly ratified constitution, asked Thondaman to become a member of his cabinet. He remained an influential cabinet minister throughout Jayewardene's term in office and during the terms of the two UNP Presidents that succeeded him.

How labour unions lost power under the United Front

Thondaman's CWC was a rarity in the Sri Lankan labour movement – a union that dominated its industry, using both strikes and political influence to improve the well-being of its members. In many sectors, a number of small unions competed, but none represented enough workers to be a significant force. In others, one or two unions did represent large numbers of workers, but their leaders often cared more about politics than members' well-being. The largest and most powerful unions, especially those enrolling public sector employees, were directly or indirectly affiliated with the LSSP or the Communist Party.[88]

Unions had been closely linked with the government during much of the 1956-1965 period but the problems this created were not so evident as they became after 1970. During Mrs. Bandaranaike's second term, Marxist parties were more influential in policy-making, a larger number of workers were unionised, more workers were employed by the government and, most significantly, the government was committed to austerity programs that affected many union members adversely. This created conflicts of interest for those Marxist Ministers closely affiliated with labour unions, including N.M. Perera and Colvin R. de Silva of the LSSP and Pieter Keunemann of the Communist Party (Moscow Wing). For the most part, these conflicts were resolved in favour of the government.[89] Despite adverse conditions, unionised workers mostly supported their leaders in government by staying on the job. During the first five years of United Front rule, days lost to strikes in the private sector dropped by a factor of ten[90] and the public sector was virtually free of debilitating politically motivated strikes.[91]

The unwillingness of Marxist trade unions to strike against deteriorating wage and economic conditions created an opportunity for the UNP affiliated National Workers Organisation (*Jatika Sevaka Sangamaya*). When the JSS was first organised in 1958, J.R. Jayewardene had been one of the few party leaders to see the advantages of a labour union linked to the pro-business UNP.[92] He had little interest in labour relations, but saw the effective political role played by unions affiliated with Marxist parties. Dudley Senanayake was deeply opposed to the JSS and it made little headway while he lived. When Jayewardene became UNP leader, however, he made the JSS a key element in his revitalised party organisation. A darker side of the JSS was its emulation of Marxist unions' role in providing thugs to catalyze violent demonstrations and intimidate political opponents.[93] Factional fighting among Marxist unions and their support of unpopular economic policies swelled JSS membership rolls especially as the prospects of a UNP general election victory grew. After the UNP's landslide victory, this once insignificant union grew to be Sri Lanka's largest and most powerful labour organisation.

Though Marxist unions had lost members and influence, they were still strong enough to make trouble for Sirimavo Bandaranaike's weakened government after the LSSP assumed its more traditional opposition role in the fall of 1975. An escalating series of strikes targeted essential health and transportation services, plus key government agencies and state sector businesses. During the pre-election months of 1977, use of labour unrest to cripple essential services, slow the economy and discredit the government reached a crescendo. Sirimavo Bandaranaike paid dearly for past policies that had encouraged labour union membership and political activism by union members. At least one major labour action took place on 138 of the 202 days between 1 January and the 21 July general election. Many were island wide, affecting multiple locations.

Labour unrest contributed to the image of a government that not only failed to keep its promises, but also could not cope with challenges to its authority.

Despite these successes, Sri Lanka's labour unions, excepting the CWC, emerged from the United Front years weaker than they had been in 1970.[94] Membership had increased, but less so than the number of unions. Unions affiliated with Marxist parties were first discredited by their leaders' support for policies that failed to benefit workers and then by the United Left Front's shattering election defeat. These events highlighted problems in a system of close ties between unions and political parties but failed to stimulate reform of that system. Improbably, J.R. Jayewardene's National Workers' Organisation was the principal beneficiary of labour movement failures during the 1970s. This self-consciously political union lacked even an ideology that placed people's interests first.[95] Its primary goal was to serve the interests of the UNP and, when the party was in power, of a UNP government.

State-sanctioned violence

Apart from moves against the Lake House Newspapers, United Front leaders respected democratic practices during their first months in office. With an overwhelming election mandate, there was little reason not to do so. The JVP rebellion changed this. Sri Lankans became more willing to grant broad emergency powers to a popularly elected and widely respected leader. As the JVP threat receded, Sirimavo Bandaranaike used her parliamentary majority to keep emergency regulations in force and to write some emergency powers permanently into law. This made it easier to legally clamp down on dissent as economic hardships strengthened support for government opponents and Tamils in the north became restive. We saw in chapter 11 that authoritarian trends were only reversed when internal divisions splintered the United Front coalition.

Graphs of the state-sanctioned violence in Figures 13.2 and 13.3 show these patterns. The index value remained low until March 1971 and then rose to 9, reflecting suspension of constitutional guarantees, arrests, detentions, legally sanctioned killings, proscription of 'extremist' parties and press censorship. Toward the end of 1972, it appeared there might be some relaxation of authoritarian measures, however new measures were imposed in 1973 and 1974. Sirimavo Bandaranaike's government found that emergency powers were a useful tool for responding to both Tamil militancy and initiatives of the revitalised UNP opposition. 1974 and 1975 witnessed the highest levels of state-sanctioned violence, impacting both Sinhalese and Tamils, that Sri Lankans had yet

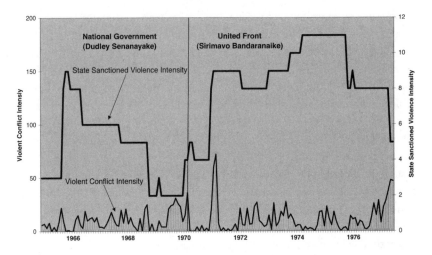

Figure 13.2. State-sanctioned violence and Violent Conflict 1965-1977

experienced. Gradual relaxation of repressive measures, following the United Front coalition's breakup is shown by index values of 7 throughout most of 1976, dropping to 5 beginning in May of 1977.

From the first days emergency powers were granted, Prime Minister Bandaranaike made it clear her government would interpret its mandate to restore and maintain public order broadly. Her initial speech to Parliament on the emergency targeted not only People's Liberation Front (JVP) supporters, but also 'hoarders and such other people responsible for creating shortages' for arrest and detention.[96] Later the net was widened to include exchange control violators and evaders of the government's rice distribution monopoly.

Emergency regulations facilitated quick anti-terrorist action by the security forces but offered few safeguards against abuse of power by inexperienced, frightened, vengeful or sadistic officers. Detainees were routinely assaulted by guards and interrogators. Use of torture to extract confessions and information was commonplace. Confessions made to police while in custody were admissible before the specially created Criminal Justice Commission that had been established to expedite trial procedures. Since police were not required to report arrests and could bury or cremate dead bodies without an inquest, they literally had power of life and death over detainees. It was easy to cover tracks when errors were made or torture went too far.

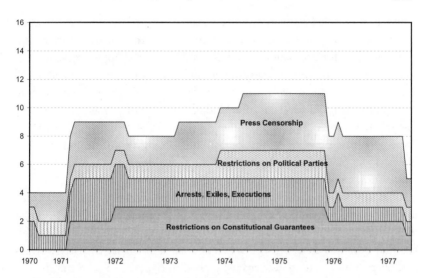

Figure 13.3 State-sanctioned violence Components

Official resistance to public scrutiny further increased the potential for abuse. Critical comments about the security forces and especially reports of atrocities or human rights violations were certain to be excised by censors. Foreign correspondents who evaded censorship by filing stories in India risked expulsion.[97] For example, Britain's Lord Avebury, representing Amnesty International, visited Sri Lanka in September 1971 and prepared a detailed report documenting abuses and offering recommendations for protecting detainees' human rights. Officials responded with an expulsion order and forbade distribution of the report in Sri Lanka.[98]

Sirimavo Bandaranaike had always viewed most newspapers as enemies and could react strongly to critical coverage. Parliament had blocked attempts to curtail press freedom during her first term. Now, she was quick to capitalise on opportunities for suppressing critical coverage that emergency regulations provided. Once censorship authority had been granted, it was broadly applied to matters unrelated to the JVP insurrection. In fact, all news reports, feature stories and editorial comments were subject to review by a 'competent authority.' No 'posters, handbills or leaflets' could be distributed or 'posted in a public place' without prior police permission.[99]

After some informal relaxation of controls in 1972, passage of the Press Council Bill in February 1973, made censorship a permanent government function.[100] Detailed rules governing criticism of officials, economic reporting and reporting of policy discussions within the government were spelled out. The Minister of Information[101] had broad discretion in applying these rules. In May, the nation's largest newspaper group, Lake House, was nationalised.[102] Prime Minister Bandaranaike and her family apparently pressed for this final step against their old adversary after reading coverage of Dudley Senanayake's funeral they viewed as critical to the government.[103] Nationalisation of the *Times* group of newspapers (in August) and closing down the Independent Newspapers of Ceylon (in April 1974) completed the task of placing a once vibrant newspaper industry under direct government control.[104]

Those concerned about democracy's health in Sri Lanka pointed not only to censorship, but to the first-ever attempt to suppress activities of a major opposition party (as opposed to extremist parties) using state power. Authorities first began to cross the line between 'normal' thuggery by party workers and overt use of state power against a political opponent in the summer of 1973, following Dudley Senanayake's death. The by-election campaign to represent Senanayake's Dedigama constituency, viewed as a major test of strength between newly named UNP leader J.R. Jayewardene and the Prime Minister, provided the occasion.[105] During pre-election campaigning, senior government ministers directed police to arrest a number of UNP campaign workers on 'trumped up charges.' Some UNP booths near polling places were burned. On election day, government ministers used Dedigama's main police station as their command-central to direct picketing and blockades by SLFP cadres intended to keep UNP voters from the polls. When complaints were lodged with police, the ministers' presence discouraged a strong response.[106] These tactics did not prevent a high voter turnout and UNP victory,[107] but further eroded public confidence in police impartiality.

Any doubts about Prime Minister Bandaranaike's willingness to use the security forces against political opponents was erased by her spirited defence of government intervention to block a UNP civil disobedience demonstration (*satyagraha*) in her home constituency of Attanagalla.[108] As recounted earlier in this chapter, there was widespread use not only of police but of regular army troops to block roads leading into Attanagalla and intimidate demonstrators. When demonstrators were stoned and vehicles carrying them had widows smashed and tires slashed, security force personnel did little or nothing to interfere. All of this was characterised by an unrepentant Prime Minister as 'Attanagalla's people' exercising their right to forcefully prevent outsiders from disturbing their community.[109]

Sirimavo Bandaranaike's most crippling move against the UNP came on 21 April 1974 and was provoked by Jayewardene's plans to simultaneously hold 145 meetings throughout the island in commemoration of Dudley Senanayake's first year death anniversary. Not only did the Prime Minister declare an island wide curfew to prevent the meetings from being held, she published new emergency regulations that effectively banned all public meetings of Sri Lanka's principal opposition political party.

In addition to moves against the UNP, and later against LSSP allied labour unions, the government stepped up attempts to bring militant action in the North under control. Emergency regulations were used to arrest and detain a number of Tamil youths, especially following Mayor Durayappah's assassination. Reportedly, physical assaults and torture by police were almost routine.[110]

An amendment to the Emergency Regulations in December 1974, which reduced police discretion to arrest and detain, marked the end of Sri Lanka's most repressive period since independence, but abuses continued. For the most part, officers were still protected from public scrutiny by government information controls and defended by government ministers when accusations did become public. After communal rioting that broke out in the multiethnic community of Puttalam, police were accused of killing seven Muslims unnecessarily and standing by while a gang of Sinhalese youths burned two Muslim youths alive. When the matter was raised in Parliament, Prime Minister Bandaranaike personally endorsed the police version of events.[111]

The security forces

Sri Lanka's security forces were often accused of abusing their power and the rights of individual citizens during the United Front's years in office. Opportunities for abuse grew because of unprecedented demands imposed by terrorist threats and enforcement of emergency regulations. To support the army and police in meeting these demands, Sirimavo Bandaranaike's government gave them broader *authority* and insulated them from public scrutiny. There was less willingness, however, to match broadened authority with strengthened *capabilities* – training, adequate pay, modern equipment, and good working conditions – needed to effectively carry out new missions and meet new demands. Life was made more difficult for security force personnel by pressures to treat United Front political allies preferentially and, sometimes to ignore violence and intimidation directed at government opponents. Because of their responsibilities for day to day interaction with citizens, the problems faced by Sri Lanka's police officers were particularly stressful and made abuses almost inevitable. Many shortcomings of Sri Lanka's police became apparent during the JVP insurrection and its aftermath, but only half-hearted reforms were undertaken. When police were ordered to repress militant Tamil youth and enforce the writ of a Sinhalese dominated government in Jaffna, communal animosities made their task even more difficult than dealing with JVP militants. By 1977, the risks of giving police a challenging, complex mission, without the skills or resources to carry it out effectively, were becoming apparent.

We have seen that as Dudley Senanayake's term drew to a close, Sri Lanka's security establishment was among the weakest in the world. Its lightly armed military forces had occasionally been called upon to quell civil disturbances, but were otherwise untested. Police were mostly unarmed, a legacy of British traditions, but nonetheless widely unpopular. According to James Jupp, 'their relationship with the public had been destroyed by years of bribery, intimidation and arrogance, especially in rural areas.'[112] Rural police stations were a natural target for JVP rebels, because they symbolised Sri Lanka's government at its worst. After assuming power, Prime Minister Bandaranaike withdrew the commissions of some senior police and military officers, however political reliability rather than efficiency appears to have been her primary motivation.[113] New appointees, including one active politician, were predominantly Sinhalese, Buddhist and SLFP loyalists.[114]

Ineffectiveness in dealing with the JVP and suspected complicity in numerous missing persons cases further eroded public confidence in the police.[115] Credit for defeating the militants went primarily to members of the armed forces who had, in fact, assumed police functions in many areas. Once order was restored, rural police sometimes collaborated with local politicians to reestablish authoritarian and exploitative mini-regimes. The protective umbrella of emergency regulations and government censorship gave them nearly unlimited power to take action against those who opposed them. Writing of this period, anthropologist Paul Alexander observed that 'it would be difficult to overstate the hatred many peasants feel for the police.'[116] In 1972, Sri Lanka's senior police officer, hardly an anti-government source, told a Ceylon Daily Mirror reporter that he had received 'numerous complaints of assault and the public attitude towards the police is one of fear.'[117]

A security force buildup had been one early government response to the JVP rebellion. Spending for the Army, Navy and Air Force grew by 85 per cent in 1971 and an additional 10 per cent in 1972.[118] Military manpower grew by about 3,000 during this period, with the lion's share going to the Army. Much of the increased spending was allocated to new weapons that were mostly purchased from Sri Lanka's Communist bloc allies – China, Yugoslavia, and the Soviet Union. For the first time, some army units were equipped with automatic weapons and relatively modern light artillery, replacing World War II-era Lee-Enfield Rifles and 4.2 inch heavy mortars.[119] The army was reorganised into three area commands. Training exercises emphasised counterinsurgency and jungle warfare.

For the remainder of the United Front's term in office however, the military forces reverted to their more or less passive role, apart from occasional policing responsibilities and continued efforts to control the island's northern borders. A decline in the inflation-adjusted value of military budgets reflected this diminished role. By 1977, the real value of defence expenditures by Sirimavo Bandaranaike's financially strapped government was only six per cent above 1970 levels. This meant reduced funds for training, new equipment and maintenance, plus military pay scales that failed to keep up with inflation.[120] Sri Lanka's elite Squadron Number Four, whose helicopters had played a vital role in against the JVP in 1970, was reconstituted as 'Helitours.' In order to earn foreign exchange for fuel and maintenance, squadron pilots provided wealthy foreign tourists with aerial views of Sri Lanka's ancient shrines.

Sri Lanka's police force, too, experienced manpower increases and was faced with budgets that failed to keep up with inflation. Between 1970 and 1977, manpower increased by more than 50 per cent. But in contrast to the military forces, police responsibilities increased significantly. New emergency regulations, which permitted forceful government intervention in many areas of Sri Lankan society, usually involved additional police missions. Civil disobedience was a traditional form of dissent in Sri Lanka, which meant that unpopular government interventions often provoked confrontations.

Consider the burdens imposed on this small,[121] lightly equipped, modestly trained force by events described earlier in this chapter. Following the JVP insurrection, supervision of detention camps and interrogation of detainees were primarily police responsibilities. When the government banned hoarding and internal transport of rice to enforce its distribution monopoly, police constables were required to man roadblocks and conduct searches. Prime Minister Bandaranaike's strict orders to suppress the UNP civil disobedience campaign, meant that each *satyagraha* announced by J.R. Jayewardene called forth a massive police presence. Sometimes officers were also ordered to play an overtly political role as during the Dedigama by-election campaign and the Attanagalla *satyagraha*, further complicating their mission. Police were responsible for enforcing the ban on UNP public meetings and later on strikes and demonstrations by LSSP affiliated unions. When orders were issued to prevent distribution or close down the presses of offending publications, police constables were responsible for carrying out the orders. In addition to these new 'political' functions, there were also significant increases in the normal police responsibilities for community policing and crime control. Annual numbers of 'total crimes' and annual numbers of 'prison receptions' increased respectively by 67 and 89 per cent compared with the previous administration.[122]

Problems posed for police by a combination of new responsibilities and limited resources were nowhere more evident than on the Jaffna peninsula.[123] The widening political gap between Tamils and Sinhalese meant that police were increasingly viewed as agents of an oppressive 'foreign' security establishment. Civil disobedience demonstrations often became confrontations between police and demonstrators that assumed ethnic overtones. Normal crowd control at public events could quickly escalate into violence, as during the Fourth International Conference on Tamil Research. Militant youth targeted police facilities and patrols for terror attacks. In an environment of escalating ethnic hostility, Tamil officers were viewed by Colombo officials as having a conflict of interest and the ethnic composition of the police became overwhelmingly Sinhalese. For the most part, Sinhalese police constables assigned to Jaffna spoke neither Tamil nor English which made even elementary communication with residents difficult. Many constables were newly appointed probationary recruits on their first assignment and resentful at being detailed to a 'hardship post.' Sometimes officers with disciplinary problems were posed to Jaffna as punishment.

As militant youth turned to bank robbery and extortion to support their activities, boundaries between 'patriotism' and criminal activity began to blur. Tamils who co-operated with police were labelled 'traitors.' Thus even those few police who could speak Tamil or English often encountered a wall of silence when seeking information from the community. Performance of normal functions became impossible as Tamils' faith in the ability of police to maintain law and order eroded. The frustrations of an impossible situation, coupled with the immunity emergency regulations provided, made violent and abusive police behavior more probable.[124] By the late 1970s, police-community relations in the Jaffna peninsula had deteriorated to a state of mutual alienation, suspicion and paranoia that was ripe for exploitation by militants on both sides. Political leaders and politicised senior police officers in Colombo had little grasp of how grave the situation had become. Sri Lanka was ripe for *conflict escalation from state-sanctioned violence ineffectiveness.*

Political feedback – a landslide reversal of fortunes

Long before voters queued at the polls on 21 July 1977, Sirimavo Bandaranaike knew there would be no repeat of her 1970 triumph. Public protests, well attended UNP rallies and by-election losses provided evidence of declining public support. SLFP and Marxist candidates now competed for votes in districts where 'no contest pacts' had contributed to 1970 victories. Some left-leaning SLFP parliamentarians had defected to the United Left Front. Despite these harbingers, few anticipated the overwhelming vote of 'no confidence' registered by Sri Lanka's voters on election day (Figure 13.4). SLFP candidates won only eight of the 127 seats the party contested. Among those eight seats, three were in multi-member districts where one SLFP nominee was virtually guaranteed a seat.[125] Only one cabinet member, apart from the Prime Minister herself, won reelection.[126] Voters in formerly safe Dompe constituency defeated Felix Dias Bandaranaike, the government's second most powerful leader, by more than 2,000 votes.[127]

Results for Mrs. Bandaranaike's erstwhile partners were even more disastrous. United Left Front parties contested 177 seats in Sinhalese majority areas but failed to carry a single one. Party stalwarts lost in electorates they had represented since independence.[128] Rendering an unequivocal verdict on Marxist economic policies, only six per cent of Sri Lanka's voters cast ballots for United Left Front candidates.

On election night, UNP leader J.R. Jayewardene drove to his *alma mater,* Royal College,[129] to follow the returns. Royal's elegant colonial-era precincts, training ground for most of Sri Lanka's top leaders, were just a short walk from Colombo's Independence Square, where triumphant United Front supporters had jeered Jayewardene at the ceremonial opening of Parliament, seven years earlier. By midnight, he knew this year's ceremonial opening would be different. Reports of UNP poll watchers throughout the island conveyed news of

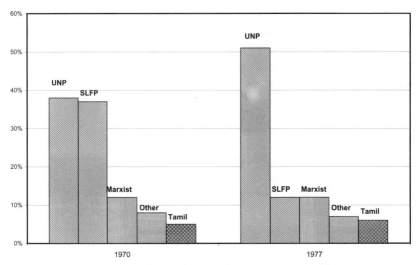

Figure 13.4 Per-Cent Vote Totals for the Major Parties

an overwhelming victory.[130] 'I'm going home,' the 70-year-old leader told an increasingly jubilant group of supporters and counting agents. 'It's time for some sleep. I'll need it tomorrow.'[131]

Many factors contributing to the UNP triumph have already been discussed. Even a lackluster campaign would probably have defeated Prime Minister Bandaranaike's unpopular and weakened government. In fact, J.R. Jayewardene and his principal lieutenants mounted an aggressive campaign that targeted government shortcomings and proposed an alternative economic development strategy emphasising free market principles. As we have seen, the UNP also promised righteous (*dharmista*) leadership, based on Buddhist moral precepts. The reorganised party held 140 well attended rallies where its three principal leaders – Jayewardene, Ranasinghe Premadasa and Gamini Dissanayake spoke. Party officials in every Sinhalese majority polling district ensured that supporters turned out to vote.[132]

The UNP manifesto promised radical economic and constitutional reforms. These reflected ideas Jayewardene had been advancing for years; as undisputed leader he now had the power to make them centrepieces of his party's platform. To eliminate scarcities, promote economic growth and generate employment, the UNP proposed to replace central planning with an 'open economy' program. Key elements were relaxation of currency and import controls, establishment of duty-free export processing zones and foreign invest-ment promotion. In agriculture, the UNP promised to replace cumbersome state monopolies with programs that recalled Dudley Senanayake's agricultural development philosophy. Artificial price controls for farm products would be removed, the guaranteed price scheme for farmers extended, agricultural credit made more widely available and the Mahaveli development irrigation scheme revitalised. The UNP education proposals promised to reverse unpopular re-forms based on Marxist doctrine, implementing a philosophy 'to ensure that Sri Lanka's people are not isolated from the Western countries.'

Jayewardene believed the United Front's Republican Constitution must be scuttled to attract foreign investment and ensure the success of economic re-forms. The UNP manifesto promised a new constitution that would strengthen democracy by reestablishing an independent judiciary, guaranteeing individual rights and protecting press freedoms. Concentration of executive authority was the centrepiece of Jayewardene's proposals for restructuring Sri Lanka's government. If elected, he promised to replace Sri Lanka's Westminster Model Parliament and largely ceremonial President, with an 'Executive Presidency' modelled roughly after Charles de Galle's Fifth French Republic. Only a Presi-dent with executive powers, he had concluded, would have sufficient authority to implement reforms, some initially unpopular, that were necessary to start Sri Lanka's economy on a path of sustained economic growth.

If Sri Lankans may not have understood the full implications of these proposals, they at least knew they were being offered something fundamentally different from the past seven years. The contrast was unintentionally reinforced by a dispirited SLFP campaign[133] that emphasised negative messages about the opposition rather than concrete plans for the future. Prime Minister Bandara-naike characterised the UNP as a 'reactionary capitalist party', and accused J.R. Jayewardene of being personally unfit to serve as Prime Minister. In response, Jayewardene castigated SLFP nepotism and abuse of power. Sinhalese populist Ranasinghe Premadasa, who exemplified the revitalised UNP, delivered slash-ing, sarcastic attacks on United Front economic policy failures to enthusiastic audiences.

Either SLFP leaders did not link the nation's economic problems with their policies or simply had nothing new to offer, because their manifesto prom-ised few fundamental changes. Central planning was offered as the best route to 'economic emancipation' for working people. Voters were reminded that

600,000 new government and state sector jobs had been created and promised that additional jobs would be created in the future. SLFP leaders conveniently omitted mention of a significant increase in unemployment. A program of economic self sufficiency that extended state control over basic industries, controlled consumer goods imports and discouraged foreign investment[134] was proposed to bring inflation under control. In agriculture, the problem of basic goods scarcities was to be solved by extending government involvement still further, through production boards and transport units that would manage the purchase, distribution and marketing of all essential agricultural products. To provide evidence that it could keep its promises, the government relaxed import controls shortly before the election and flooded markets with consumer goods that had long been unavailable. Interestingly, Sirimavo Bandaranaike used 'consistency' as a major talking point in her campaign. In contrast to the UNP, she pointed out, her party had made few changes in its image or policies since S.W.R.D. Bandaranaike was first named Prime Minister in 1956. By 1977, however, young Sri Lankan voters had no memories of the assassinated Prime Minister; many had not even been born when he assumed office. They wanted change, rather than consistency, from their political leaders.

The United Left Front's losing campaign, like its decision to withdraw from the government coalition, gave priority to doctrinal purity over political realities. A United Left Front government, voters were promised, would build a 'truly socialist state', by extending state control to all sectors of the economy. This would include a state monopoly on banking and credit, plus nationalisation of industrial and commercial enterprises, wholesale trade, import-export trade and foreign-owned businesses. Community-level development councils were proposed to more fully involve 'the masses' in economic planning. Little attention was given to how state management failures of the past seven years would be remedied. Despite repeated electoral evidence that a 'truly socialist state' appealed to relatively few Sri Lankans, Marxist political leaders clung tenaciously to this vision.

We have seen in past elections how parliamentary representation based on single member districts favoured the majority party disproportionately. The UNP, too, was a beneficiary of this system, winning over 80 per cent of the seats in Parliament with only about half of the popular votes. Despite its shortcomings, Sirimavo Bandaranaike's SLFP held on to its core supporters, comprising between 25 and 30 per cent of the electorate. J.R. Jayewardene, like Mrs.

Bandaranaike before him, had the legislative power to push the constitutional changes through a compliant Parliament. But pushing changes that were too radical risked alienating Bandaranaike supporters and more extreme Sinhalese nationalists whose views were no longer fully represented in the political process.

Results in the Tamil majority regions

Seven years of policies that equated Sri Lankan nationalism with Sinhalese-Buddhist nationalism had already alienated many Northern Tamils. Earlier in this chapter, we saw that militant youth were playing an increasingly influential role in Tamil politics. More conservative mainstream Tamil parties had adopted the rhetoric of 'liberation' and described the 1977 election as a referendum on establishing an 'independent, secular, socialist state of Tamil Eelam.'[135] Election results in the Northern Province showed that the process of marginalising those who favoured some accommodation with Sinhalese in a united Sri Lanka was nearly complete. The avowedly secessionist Tamil United Liberation Front won an overwhelming 70 per cent of the popular vote and carried every parliamentary seat. Having won the victory they sought, TULF leaders now faced the prospect of having to deliver on their promises.

Results in the pivotal Eastern province, viewed as part of the 'Traditional Tamil Homelands' and critical to the economic viability of an independent Tamil Eelam, were more equivocal. Tamil United Front candidates won in three of the four Tamil majority districts, but lost narrowly to UNP in the fourth despite a 64 per cent Tamil population majority. Of the remaining six seats, all but one went for the UNP.

The results indicated only lukewarm support for a secessionist agenda among Eastern Province Tamils and almost no support among Muslims – most of whom spoke Tamil – or among Sinhalese. In the province's two predominantly Sinhalese districts, Amparai and Seruvila, the TULF did not even nominate candidates. Thus, results in most Eastern Province electorates were more reflective of island-wide trends than the special concerns of Jaffna Tamils. That an independent Tamil Eelam, incorporating the Eastern Province, would have to forcibly assimilate large Sinhalese and Muslim populations who opposed secession was a subject not often addressed by either TULF orators or militant Jaffna youth.

Assessing the United Front years

In 1970, Sri Lankans chose a strong leader who was protective of her power and unflinchingly committed to her goals. Prime Minister Bandaranaike's method of governing differed greatly from Dudley Senanayake's conciliatory middle-path approach and muddling-through political strategy. She was willing to act decisively and had little patience for her opposition. 'Consistency,' a theme of the SLFP's unsuccessful reelection campaign, was another of her virtues.

These attributes served Mrs. Bandaranaike well in responding to the JVP rebellion, by far the most serious threat Sri Lanka's government had faced since independence. Skilfully managed appeals to Western, Non-aligned and Communist nations brought immediate military aid that strengthened the anemic security forces. Emergency regulations, coupled with strong government support, gave police and army officers power to move decisively against the rebels. Abuses of power and human rights inevitably occurred, but were accepted by most Sri Lankans as permissible costs to prevent the installation of a draconian regime, controlled by youthful Marxist-Sinhalese radicals.

Emergency regulations also strengthened the government's hand in implementing constitutional reforms. By structuring a 'constituent assembly' based on parliamentary representation, Sirimavo Bandaranaike guaranteed herself a pliant forum that would rubber stamp her government's proposals. Press censorship ensured that information on assembly debates made available to the public would primarily reflect the government's point of view. Those opposed to institutionalising Sinhalese-Buddhist values and socialism in a new constitution were able to make little headway with their objections. Bodies of minority opinion represented by the UNP and mainstream Tamil Parties received little more than lip service in the drafting process.

As we have seen, the new constitution was only one facet of a comprehensive reform agenda that was swiftly implemented, following the JVP's defeat. By the end of 1972, Sirimavo Bandaranaike's government had stripped Sri Lanka's wealthiest citizens of multiple residences and large landholdings. Re-distributive taxes on wealth and large incomes gave the poor tangible evidence that their government was powerful enough to mandate a more egalitarian society. Large private concerns and most foreign owned businesses were nationalised. Members of the upper classes, for the most part, accepted the reforms passively or expressed their opposition ineffectively. Political coalitions of wealthy landowners of the kind that had successfully resisted re-distributive measures in the Philippines and most Latin American countries failed to gain headway in Sri Lanka.

Unfortunately, decisiveness, maintaining a consistent policy line and immobilising opposition parties proved less beneficial in the areas of economic management and communal relations. Here too, the United Front government used political power to steamroll opposition and attain its policy goals. As we have seen, major economic sectors were placed under direct government control, with cabinet ministers responsible for important pricing and resource allocation decisions. Tariffs and quotas were established to conserve foreign exchange and nurture domestic industries. Preferential treatment for Sinhalese in matters of religion, education, employment and cultural symbolism became the law of the land. Tamils were warned that resistance would be dealt with sternly, using force when necessary. Unfortunately, these policies contributed to economic stagnation and heightened communal strife.

The government's economic management failures were fully detailed in chapter 12. Political skills necessary to legislate a Marxist political-economic agenda provided no guarantees that farmers would grow sufficient rice; that tea, rubber and coconut plantations would produce efficiently; that state-managed industries would produce quality goods, generate surpluses and create jobs; that Sri Lanka would be insulated from adverse fluctuations in terms of trade and the value of its currency. When inefficient management of the newly centralised agricultural sector and soaring international prices caused stocks of essential foodstuffs to dwindle, the government's 'decisive' response – rationing and tighter controls on distribution – made things worse. When centralised planning and nationalisations produced inefficiency, economic stagnation and rising unemployment, the government stuck with policies shaped more by ideology than a candid assessment of what was working and not working in the economy. Economic stagnation also reduced government revenues, with resultant cuts in social services to poor Sri Lankans who had been among the government's strongest supporters. Budget cuts reduced police and military capabilities at a time when the government was placing increasing demands on the security forces to enforce unpopular policies, control public opposition and play an overt political role. Prime Minister Bandaranaike's strong legislative and rhetorical support for the forces was not backed up – perhaps could not be backed up – by needed financial resources.

In communal relations, the government's commitment to imposing a Sinhalese and Buddhist political agenda on an increasingly resistant Tamil community was unwavering. In part this can be explained by the need to appease the United Front's primary constituency with preferential treatment and symbolim as compensation for mounting economic adversity. However, there was little appreciation of how this agenda was radicalising more volatile elements among the Jaffna Peninsula's overwhelmingly Tamil population of more than 700,000. Few Sinhalese politicians, including opposition UNP politicians, appear to have questioned Tamil willingness to more or less passively – and loyally – accept whatever indignities a Sinhalese dominated government chose to impose. Prime Minister Bandaranaike's uncompromising response to demands of mainstream Tamil politicians – typical of her dealings with *most* opponents – ensured that demands would become more strident and that reputations of Tamil leaders who took a moderate stance would suffer. Assuming that Sri Lanka's lightly trained and lightly equipped Sinhalese police officers could enforce unpopular decrees, maintain public order and contain militant activity in an increasingly hostile community where few even spoke the language, was an ill-informed and potentially dangerous miscalculation.

Beginning with the JVP insurrection, authoritarian measures, legally facilitated by emergency regulations, played an increasingly important role in the United Front's governing strategy. Suspension of constitutional guarantees, restriction of opposition political activity, use of the security forces for political purposes and press censorship are reflected in higher values of the State-Sanctioned Violence index than for any previous period. This could be viewed as another manifestation of the Prime Minister's 'toughness' in pushing forward with her agenda, even in the face of strong opposition.

Willingness to use authoritarian measures helps to explain the United Front's success in effecting radical reforms, but may also explain its miscalculations in the economic and communal spheres. A weakness of authoritarian measures, especially censorship and strictures on opposition parties, is that they restrict the flow of information about what is not working in a society. Apart from its inability to postpone or manipulate elections, Sri Lanka's government under the United Front functioned more like an authoritarian one party state than a democracy. Authoritarian systems tend to reward purveyors of 'good news' and penalise the bearers of 'bad news.' Officials are pre-disposed to tell the leader only what they think she wants to hear. When censorship is imposed, it not only restricts the flow of information to the public, which is the goal of censorship, but also to leaders. Most information channels are likely to be controlled by sycophants, making it more and more difficult for leaders to hear 'bad news.' While bad news may be disquieting to leaders, it is the news they most need to know. An effective early warning system that alerts leaders to problems in sufficient time for remedial action is essential for effective governance. In the area of communal relations and perhaps in the area of economic management as well, Sirimavo Bandaranaike's early warning systems appear to have been flawed. Thus many decisions, especially during the latter years of her term, may have been based more on her own preconceptions and those of close confidants than on accurate information about what was actually taking place in Sri Lanka.

Despite these shortcomings, Sirimavo Bandaranaike's leadership deserves high marks for success in social reform and foreign policy. Sri Lanka completed a genuine social revolution between 1970 and 1977, something few developing nations achieved without violence – and many have yet to achieve. Moreover, even though Marxist economics failed to produce economic growth, Mrs. Bandaranaike should not bear all the blame. In 1970, the question of which economic polices contribute most to broad-based growth and also helped poor people was still hotly debated. Leaders and scholars who were far more knowledgeable about economics than Sri Lanka's Prime Minister still advocated some variant of state managed development.

Did Prime Minister Bandaranaike 'sow the wind of ethnic conflict' so that her successor was forced to reap the whirlwind, as Professor K.M. de Silva asserts? In many respects, this talented and tough-minded woman did leave Sri Lanka worse than she found it. Its economy was less vibrant and its ethnic communities more divided in 1977 than they had been in 1970. Implementation of reform programs in education and local government was slowed by over-centralisation, political squabbling and limited funding. The politicised and underfunded security forces were no better prepared to deal with Tamil militancy than they had been to quell the JVP insurrection in 1970.

But assessments that Sri Lanka's ethnic civil war was caused by Sirimavo Bandaranaike's policies need to be weighed carefully. To be sure, assuming that in the 1970s, Jaffna's Tamil community of more than 700,000 would still accept business as usual politics, Sinhalese style, was a serious miscalculation. That politicians of both major parties shared this view, including even some Tamil leaders, partially explains the miscalculation. However, this makes it only slightly less excusable for leaders with Sirimavo's and Felix Dias Bandaranaike's abilities. A point made earlier bears repeating here: If Prime Minister Bandaranaike had given communal relations the same attention and talent she brought to foreign policy, Sri Lanka's history might have followed a different path.

In 1977, however, that other path was still open. Despite secessionist rhetoric, Amirthalingam's TULF was Jaffna's dominant political force and it was open to conciliatory government moves on sensitive issues. Most Jaffna Tamils – even young Jaffna Tamils – had not yet become revolutionaries. They were social and cultural conservatives who respected education, hard work and authority. Though militants had grown in stature on the Jaffna peninsula and gained some modest international visibility, the total number of hard core supporters was still minuscule, certainly less than 200. Militant groups lacked the popular support, the recruits, the international funding and the foreign sanctuaries that were critical ingredients of their strength in the 1980s. In particular, Sri Lanka's warm relations with India, buttressed by Sirimavo Bandaranaike's close personal ties with Indira Gandhi, made it unlikely that the region's dominant power would support a secessionist guerrilla movement in its small neighbor. The small size of militant groups and their lack of foreign support help to explain the failure of violent outbreaks to escalate into a protracted civil war.

When Sri Lanka's most sophisticated and experienced political leader, J.R. Jayewardene, was sworn in as Prime Minister in 1977, Sri Lankans had every reason to hope for a better economic future and more tranquil communal relations. For several years, that scenario seemed probable. In fact, more than seven years would elapse before Tamil militants marshalled the resources to mount a serious threat against Sri Lanka's government. When a serious threat was mounted in 1985, militants were still divided into sometimes hostile factions. However, they had gained the necessary ingredients to sustain a viable guerrilla movement, including widespread popular support, large numbers of motivated recruits, and international funding. Most importantly, they had gained protected sanctuaries and covert military assistance from India. Only then did Sri Lanka's ethnic conflict assume its present character. Part IV, which follows, describes how this transformation occurred. Sirimavo Bandaranaike's policies contributed, but policies and decisions of her successor, during the ensuing seven years, were far more pivotal.

Part IV

Failure of Radical Therapies:
How Sri Lanka's 'Open Economy'
Development Model and
Strengthened Presidential Authority
Failed to Prevent Conflict and
Terrorism from Escalating Out of
Control

14
Symptoms of Development Failure

Comparative data reinforces the message of our fever charts and narrative of political conflict events: even before the July 1983 explosion of ethnic strife, President Jayewardene's attempt to find some middle path between Tamil separatism and Sinhalese nationalism was not succeeding.

Electoral triumphs enclose J.R. Jayewardene's first term like bookends, but their circumstances differed greatly, providing a measure of government successes and shortcomings. The 1977 electoral landslide reflected widespread popular support for new leadership and an appealing reform agenda. United National Party leaders gained virtually unfettered authority to implement radical therapies, intended to return Sri Lanka's ailing economy and political institutions to good health. In 1982 President Jayewardene won re-election and then secured his overwhelming parliamentary majority for six more years in a controversial referendum. These victories did not represent an unambiguous vote of confidence, however. Promises of sustained economic growth and widely shared benefits had been only partially fulfilled. Two other campaign promises, communal reconciliation and a righteous (*dharmista*) society remained unfulfilled. Sinhalese-Tamil relations had worsened. Many Sri Lankans viewed President Jayewardene's government as more corrupt than its predecessor. Fear of an electoral rebuke motivated the decision to replace scheduled parliamentary elections with a referendum to extend the life of the existing parliament. The UNP leaders' no holds barred tactics in pre-referendum campaigning and on polling day made this clear.

We saw in Chapter 13 that J.R. Jayewardene began his term with a coherent development model and program of political restructuring. Economic development, he believed, would create a climate in which proposals leading to communal reconciliation would be viewed more favourably. Political restructuring was the simpler task. Sri Lanka soon had its second new constitution in a decade, featuring an 'Executive President.' This new office amalgamated 'head of government' and 'head of state' powers in a single office that was less beholden to parliamentary votes of confidence. But strong executive powers did not guarantee that sweeping free market economic reforms could be implemented quickly or that they would produce envisioned results. By now, government's role in Sri Lanka's economy was deeply entrenched. Some UNP leaders resisted ceding control over large budgets and cadres of political appointees that privatisation proposals entailed. Though some open economy reforms were enacted, it was easier for President Jayewardene to move forward with massive government-funded development programs than to reform the public sector.

The new government's term began propitiously with relaxed import controls and infusions of foreign aid, catalyzing a spurt of economic growth. Sustaining growth and distributing its benefits equitably proved to be more difficult. Sri Lanka's export oriented and import dependent economy remained vulnerable to global market shocks. By 1980 prices of three critical imports – petroleum, wheat and rice – had risen precipitously, causing deterioration in terms of trade and outflow of foreign reserves. These trends contributed to high inflation, reduced purchasing power, and cutbacks in government entitlement programs. The psychic impact of this reversal in economic fortunes was worsened by the fact that government promises and three years of visible prosperity had led Sri Lankans to believe hard times might be behind them. President Jayewardene's hope that a favourable economic climate would facilitate communal reconciliation proved to be illusory.

Thus, it is not surprising that our fever chart covering the June 1970 – June 1983 period (Figure 14.1) shows rising conflict intensity levels, beginning in 1980, though the peaks are lower than those mapping the 1971 JVP insurrection and the paroxysm of violence coincident with the 1977 general election and its aftermath. Two probable causes – reversals in favourable development trends and the president's inability to damp down communal tensions have already been described. We need to examine two other probable causes suggested by the development – deadly-conflict system model: a growth in support for militant movements and security force ineffectiveness. Obviously Sri Lankan political leaders, like leaders of other small nations, have little control over global market fluctuations. But policies that weaken or strengthen militant movements and policies that use security forces effectively or ineffectively are within their discretion. In these discretionary areas, to what degree did President Jayewardene and his colleagues make choices that diminished and to what degree did they make choices that amplified the potential for violent conflict

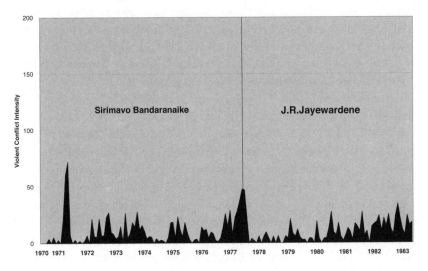

Figure 14.1 Violent Conflict Intensity: June 1970–July 1983

Figure 14.1 Monthly Intensities of Political Conflict: June 1970-June 1983

escalation? Answering these questions will be a primary concern in this chapter and the two that follow.

Violent conflict: becoming more frequent and more communal

When J.R. Jayewardene assumed office, Sri Lankans had every reason to hope that the turbulence marking Prime Minister Bandaranaike's final months would be supplanted by more peaceful times. Until mid-1980, this optimism seemed justified. In 1981, however, conflict events became more frequent and more intense. Beginning in 1982, there were no longer any months of respite. Violent political conflict was becoming endemic.

Rising conflict levels in Tamil majority regions, especially the Jaffna Peninsula, were especially pronounced. Figure 14.2, which distinguishes conflict events by region, shows this clearly. Between 1970 and 1980, there were few months where incidents in Tamil majority regions contributed significantly to nationwide monthly totals. After 1981, conflict in Tamil regions was more frequent and more intense than elsewhere. Only 10 per cent of Sri Lanka's population was found in the Northern and Eastern Provinces, now claimed by Tamil leaders as 'traditional homelands', making the preponderance of violent conflict in those provinces even more striking. Militant actions, coupled with inflammatory rhetoric from some Tamil politicians, enraged growing numbers of Sinhalese. Militancy and its spill-over effects increasingly distracted top government leaders from their ambitious reform agendas.

Jaffna was geographically remote from Colombo, Sri Lanka's political and economic power centre, but events in mid-August 1977 sharply reminded new government leaders that events in the north could generate island-wide reverberations. Confrontations between Tamil youths and police, resulting in the destruction of a police vehicle, were followed by clashes in which Jaffna's central market was set on fire and more than 140 shops burned. Reports of these events in the Sinhalese press, amplified by Sri Lanka's always active rumour mill, reached the South at a time when pro-secessionist statements by Tamil parliamentarians had already fanned Sinhalese resentments. This volatile mix produced six days of communal rioting, directed primarily against Tamils living in Sinhalese majority areas. Houses and shops were looted and burned. Several hundred men, women and children – mostly Tamil – were killed. After some initial hesitancy, Sri Lanka's security forces (now virtually all Sinhalese) intervened effectively, enforcing an island-wide curfew and making numerous arrests. But according to some Sinhalese community leaders, the riots were 'a lesson' Tamils needed to be 'taught' for demanding a separate state.[1] This view was not endorsed by President Jayewardene. He moved quickly to appoint a neutral commission of inquiry[2] and invited an influential Indian businessman to meet with him personally so that India's Prime Minister Morarji Desai could be fully briefed.

Restoration of order ushered in a relatively peaceful period that lasted until the spring of 1981, however sporadic, highly visible militant actions continued to capture Sinhalese attention and dispel illusions that communal violence could be easily controlled. In January of 1978, a TULF parliamentarian who had switched allegiance to the UNP was gunned down in Colombo.[3] In April of 1978, a feared Tamil police inspector and his squad of men were trapped in a Tamil Tiger ambush and shot to death. Later in the summer, militants added a police district supervisor and a retired police inspector to their list of killings. In September, a bomb destroyed the regularly scheduled Air Ceylon Flight from

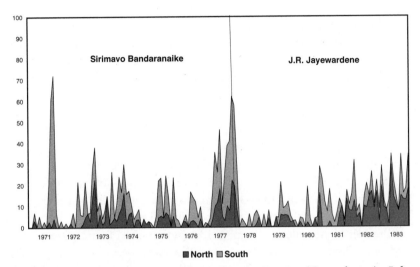

Figure 14.2 Violent Political Conflict, by Region (Cumulative): July 1970 – June 1983

Jaffna to Colombo on the runway of Colombo's Ratmalana airport. Only an early arrival forestalled the bomber's intention to blow up the plane over the capital, in the midst of festivities celebrating Sri Lanka's new constitution. None of these militant actions represented serious military threats, but they created a climate of resentment among police detailed to Tamil areas, inflamed Sinhalese public opinion, eroded the government's credibility and poisoned the climate for negotiations with Tamil moderates.

Jayewardene's government responded to the attacks with a series of increasingly severe retaliatory measures intended to restore its credibility, appease Sinhalese public opinion and reassure anxious foreign investors.[4] Despite campaign criticism of Sirimavo Bandaranaike for similar emergency measures, legislation was passed in May 1978, outlawing the Liberation Tigers of Tamil Eelam 'and other similar organisations.' The government followed this a year later with the Prevention of Terrorism Act, modelled after similar legislation in Britain, which gave security forces widespread authority to arrest, detain and interrogate 'suspected terrorists' without judicial oversight. Armed with this legislation, Jayewardene imposed a state of emergency on the North and dispatched Brigadier Tissa I. Weeratunga to Jaffna with orders to 'eliminate... the menace of terrorism in all its forms' and to complete the task by 31 December

1979.[5] Weeratunga's mission was the first of many failed military initiatives to quell Tamil militancy.

That Weeratunga's mission had failed was by no means obvious during 1980. Reduced levels of violence seemed to suggest a trend toward normalcy, though occasional armed robberies and killings of police officers continued. During seven months of that year, there were no reported conflict events in the Tamil regions.[6] In fact, a Sinhalese air force detachment, assigned security duty in the mixed community of Vavuniya, was responsible for the worst outbreak. Thus, as 1980 drew to a close, it appeared that government policies blending conciliation and firmness, coupled with robust economic growth, were contributing to increased political stability in both Sinhalese and Tamil areas. J.R. Jayewardene, it seemed, had every reason to contemplate the remaining two and a half years of his first term in office with optimism.

President Jayewardene's optimism rose further when Prime Minister Premadasa received a warm welcome from Jaffna residents, in late January, while on an official visit to open new housing and development projects. UNP leaders interpreted this reception as evidence that the government's new scheme for decentralising power through District Development Councils, coupled with some high profile investments in the North, were drawing popular support from militants and the Tamil United Liberation Front. They decided to capitalise on their improved prospects and deal a blow to the TULF by vigorously contesting elections for the new District Development Councils in Jaffna District. The President appeared to have good reasons to anticipate success at the polls.[7] First, UNP campaigns were known to be the most efficiently organised in Sri Lanka. Jayewardene and Premadasa were among the nation's most skilful political tacticians. In 1981, they could support their candidates with state resources and draw upon increasingly numerous National Workers' Organisation (JSS) cadres when aggressive action to disrupt opposition meetings and intimidate opposition supporters seemed called for. Additionally, government economic reforms had generated a flood of foreign investment and produced tangible benefits for many Sri Lankans.

Militancy –Tamil and Sinhalese – returns to centre stage (May 1981 - August 1981)

In deciding to run a business-as-usual Sri Lankan political campaign for District Development Council seats representing the Jaffna peninsula, President Jayewardene and his advisors miscalculated seriously. Campaign events gave militants new opportunities to attack UNP candidates and the security forces. News reports describing these gave Sinhalese politicians new ammunition for inflammatory speeches. To restore order and maintain credibility, the government was forced to implement retaliatory measures using the modest resources at its disposal – poorly trained police and army detachments that were almost 100 per cent Sinhalese. Security force indiscipline, in the face of militant provocations, led to violent attacks against Tamil property and civilians that further polarised two communities. Heightened polarisation created a climate in which minor incidents in one area sparked organised attacks by Sinhalese against Tamil minorities elsewhere in the island. In short, Jayewardene's decision precipitated prototypical circumstances of *conflict escalation from state-sanctioned violence ineffectiveness.*

This vicious cycle of deteriorating communal relations between Tamils and Sinhalese had been played out before and would be played out again as Sri Lanka slipped toward the abyss of protracted, violent civil war. Events during the months of May through August of 1981 proved to be a milestone. As the summer of 1981 drew to a close, mistrust between Tamil leaders and President Jayewardene's government escalated. Tamil hopes for a political solution to their problems within a unified Sri Lanka faded. In the South, proposals of Sinhalese factions supporting draconian solutions to 'the Tamil problem' became more strident and widely supported.

No event that occurred during this turbulent four month period is recalled more vividly than the torching of Jaffna's public library housing a collection of more than 90,000 volumes including many irreplaceable Tamil manuscripts. President Jayewardene's ill-conceived decision to contest Jaffna's District Development Council elections set the stage for this incident, which played into the hands of Tamil militants.

Here is how events leading up to this tragedy unfolded. The police presence in the North had been strengthened following the execution-style shootings of two alleged police informants and subsequent killings of two police constables during a bank robbery.[8] Militants responded with an intimidation campaign directed against UNP District Development Council Candidates. The assassination of the UNP's chief political organiser in Jaffna on May 24 sent a strong message that militant threats should be taken seriously.[9] Many UNP candidates withdrew from the race or maintained a low profile.

Three-hundred additional police officers, including a number of hastily mobilised reservists, were dispatched quickly to Jaffna for emergency election duty. President Jayewardene also dispatched an additional 150 'poll watchers', all UNP loyalists and virtually all Sinhalese. To provide on site leadership for these reinforcements, the President sent a number of senior party officials to Jaffna. Inexplicably, the UNP team was lead by Industries Minister Cyril Mathew, arguably the government's most outspoken anti-Tamil cabinet member.

When two police constables assigned to election duty were shot to death, the Jaffna tinderbox ignited. Senior police officers lost control of their men, who retaliated with three days of arson attacks. The Jaffna Public Library, the Tamil United Liberation Front's Jaffna headquarters and a TULF Member of Parliament's Jaffna home were targeted by the arsonists, who also destroyed a number of commercial establishments. Cyril Matthew's presence in Jaffna helped convince many Tamils that the library burning was part of a Sinhalese plot to obliterate Tamil cultural identity in Sri Lanka.[10] Jayewardene's plan to build Tamil support for the UNP had ended in disaster. When the Jaffna District Development Council Elections were held later, TULF candidates captured nearly 85 per cent of the total votes polled and every Council seat.[11]

Violence directed against Tamils living in the South broke out in mid August, when a fracas between rival students at a sports meet escalated into arson and looting by gangs of Sinhalese in a number of areas. Victims were mostly poor peasants and agricultural wage labourers living in Sinhalese majority areas rather than militant Northern separatists. International press reports speculated that some government officials might have been complicit in the attacks, which appeared to be more organised than previously. President Jayewardene criticised members of his own party for escalating communal tensions and even threatened to resign if inflammatory speechmaking was not curtailed. In a pattern similar to August 1977 the security forces responded passively in many areas and only took firm action after a state of emergency had been declared, seven days after disturbances first broke out.[12]

Endemic communal violence (December 1981 - June 1983)

In 1982, politics increasingly preoccupied Sri Lankans, due to J.R. Jayewardene's decision to advance the date of Sri Lanka's Presidential election by nearly a year. As already noted, this political stratagem was rewarded by an overwhelming election victory. Victory in the subsequent referendum to extend the life of Parliament, with its overwhelming UNP majority, for six more years further strengthened Jayewardene's position.[13] The UNP landslide did not extend to Jaffna or Batticaloa districts, however, where President Jayewardene lost badly. Referendum results provided further evidence of Tamil alienation. The government won only 14 per cent of the votes in the Northern Jaffna and Vanni districts and failed to carry any Tamil majority area.

While President Jayewardene focused on maximising UNP vote totals and demoralising Sirimavo Bandaranaike's factionalised Sri Lankan Freedom Party[14] the influence of youthful militants in Tamil majority areas grew, while the capacity of Sri Lanka's beleaguered security forces to maintain order diminished. Elevated conflict levels after 1981 shown on our 'fever chart' reflect this. Events in Tamil majority regions were almost entirely responsible for the turbulence that sets this period apart. In fact, with one notable exception,[15] conflict intensity in Sinhalese areas was somewhat *lower* than in many previous months. Stories of armed robberies, violent demonstrations, arson, sabotage and execution style killings in Tamil areas became increasingly regular fare in Sri Lanka's newspapers. Moreover the militants, although still small in number, were now beginning to launch attacks on security force convoys, patrols and installations.

Local government elections held on 22 May 1983, provided circumstances for a further escalation of violent conflict. Growing militant influence (and possibly fear of defeat at the polls) lead Jayewardene to postpone parliamentary by-elections in the North, but he decided to hold local government elections as scheduled. Despite the problems encountered in the District Development Council elections, UNP candidates were nominated to run against Tamil United Liberation Front and Tamil Congress nominees. Liberation Tiger spokesmen responded by calling for an election boycott and reinforced their message by gunning down three UNP candidates in quick succession. Other UNP candidates withdrew their names or hid out during the remaining days of campaigning. Shortly after he received a 'request' from Tamil Tiger representatives who visited his Jaffna office, Kumar Ponnambalam officially withdrew his Tamil Congress party from the local government contests.[16]

On election day militants killed a soldier and wounded two police constables who were standing guard duty at a Jaffna polling station. The government responded by declaring a state of emergency in the North, a move officially supported by the TULF, but militant robberies, bombings and attacks on government property continued throughout the month of June. One knowledgeable observer described conditions in Jaffna as 'out of control.'[17]

As tensions escalated, the security forces often responded to violent incidents by arresting and harassing Tamil civilians. Most solders and police officers spoke no Tamil, had few contacts with the local population and were unfamiliar with the areas they were patrolling. This made it almost impossible to separate 'Tigers' from innocent bystanders. Moreover, provoking security force excesses was an important part of the militants' strategy. When civilians demonstrated against harassment or sought help from higher government authorities, security forces often responded with even harsher retaliations. Sometimes these incidents were severe enough to find their way into local and international newspapers, or into reports of local and international human rights organisations.[18] Nevertheless, security force excesses against civilians are surely underreported in our data base, which relies heavily on published materials. Even when official censorship was not in force, officials could influence news content informally and newspaper editors, themselves, often deleted sensitive material.

Though political conflict in Sinhalese majority areas was not a serious problem, killings of Sinhalese soldiers and police officers, now occurring on an almost weekly basis, not only aroused Sinhalese anger against 'Tamils' but weakened government credibility. Maintaining order in areas where slain Sinhalese police constables were returned home for burial, especially in multi-ethnic neighbourhoods, required special precautions.[19] There was no repeat of the August 1981 anti-Tamil rioting, but senior officers were concerned about the reliability of their poorly educated cadres who had been exposed to a steady diet of nationalist rhetoric and seemed likely to sympathise more with families of their slain 'brothers' than with Tamil Sri Lankan citizens whom they might be ordered to protect.[20]

J.R. Jayewardene's early years and Sirimavo Bandaranaike's second term compared

Comparing the number and types of conflict events during J.R. Jayewardene's early years and Sirimavo Bandaranaike's second term, it seems surprising that August 1977 - June 1983 appears to be the more turbulent period and that communal strife was far more frequent under J.R. Jayewardene than Sirimavo Bandaranaike. I say surprising only because many observers, particularly those writing before July 1983, picture Jayewardene's first term not only as an era of economic prosperity, but also of political stability, relatively speaking. Comparative data in Figure 14.3 reinforce the message of our fever charts and narrative of political conflict events: even before the July 1983 explosion of ethnic strife, Jayewardene's attempt to find some middle path between Tamil separatism and Sinhalese nationalism was not succeeding.

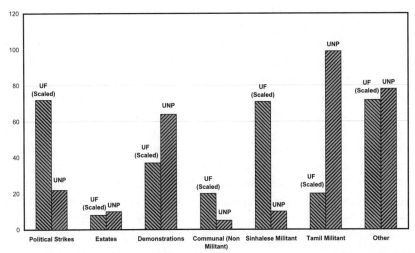

Figure 14.3 Conflict Incident Frequencies: United Front (Scaled) and UNP Governments Compared

Both militancy and communal strife were on the rise in Sri Lanka. Labour-management relations were the only area where President Jayewardene was more successful than his predecessor in keeping violent political conflict at bay.[21] A combination of economic prosperity, firm anti-strike measures and growing power of the government's National Workers' Organisation (JSS) all contributed to labour peace. In this area at least, UNP leaders largely succeeded in creating a climate that was receptive to the foreign aid and investment needed to sustain their open economy program. Leading Sri Lanka to a position among the 'Asian Tigers' had, as we have seen, been one of J.R. Jayewardene's top priority political objectives for a decade or more.

What he did not grasp was that events in Jaffna, the seat of Tamil militancy, could be more than a troublesome and frustrating political side show. President Jayewardene was a quintessential political realist. Sri Lanka's demographic realities seemed to make it obvious that concessions made to Jaffna politicians would cost him support in Sinhalese majority regions. Only three per cent of Sri Lanka's voters lived in Jaffna district, where calls for secession originated. An additional two per cent lived in Batticaloa district, where opposition to the government was also becoming strong. As late as spring 1983, the highly visible militants numbered in the hundreds at most. UNP leaders viewed most

Tamils living in the North as law abiding men and women who opposed violence and were ambivalent about separatism.

For President Jayewardene, the political main event continued to be in the South. His principal political adversaries continued to be Sirimavo Bandaranaike, along with her allies in the Sri Lanka Freedom and Marxist parties. His goal was to keep these adversaries demoralised, maintain his hard-won base of Sinhalese political support and use the six year window of opportunity provided by his 1982 electoral victories to complete the transformation of Sri Lanka's economy. By so doing he believed he could reverse the pattern of conflict escalation from development failures and security force ineffectiveness that had become symptomatic in his first term. The two chapters which follow look more closely at the radical therapies his government initiated during its first term, and how they contributed to this pattern of violent conflict escalation.

15
Strengthening Executive Power to Sustain Open Economy Reforms

Following the UNP's Referendum victory, it was easy for demoralised government opponents to conclude that Sri Lanka was moving irrevocably towards a one party state, which was the model in several Southeast Asian nations that J.R. Jayewardene admired.

As we have seen, J.R. Jayewardene's development vision for Sri Lanka differed fundamentally from that of his predecessor and her Marxist allies. 'Asian Tigers,' such as Singapore, which emphasised export-led growth, open financial markets and incentives for foreign investment, provided his model for transforming Sri Lanka's economy. The government's direct role would be to build up infrastructure, while ensuring continuity and political stability.

With 138 seats in the 168-member Parliament and firm control over a unified party, Jayewardene was in a position to give Sri Lanka its second new Constitution in less than a decade. He planned to combine the Head of State and Head of Government roles in an 'Executive Presidency,' with tenure independent of Parliament and centralised authority far greater than any Sri Lankan leader had exercised in modern times. Using this authority and his parliamentary majority, Jayewardene believed he could create a robust free-market economy and resilient political institutions that would chart Sri Lanka's development path for decades. I believe he hoped to create a *de facto* one party state, reducing the opposition SLFP to permanent minority status.

Prime Minister Jayewardene and his cabinet

We have already encountered J.R. Jayewardene as an important political leader. First elected to the pre-independence State Council in 1943, he served in Parliament almost continuously until he became Executive President in February 1978.[1] Thanks to a fortunate marriage[2], he was independently wealthy. He could devote his full energies to politics and had little temptation to use political office for personal financial gain.[3] He held ministerial portfolios in every UNP cabinet, and played the role of 'second in command' during Sir

John Kotelawala's administration and much of Dudley Senanayake's third term in office.[4] His skills as a political organiser were instrumental in returning the UNP to power after general election defeats in 1956 and 1970. He served as leader of the opposition during the United Front years and easily took over the UNP's top leadership post, following Dudley Senanayake's untimely death. At age 71, he was the oldest person ever to have been named Prime Minister of Sri Lanka.

No Sri Lankan leader has been written about as widely as this multifaceted, enigmatic man, nicknamed 'the old fox' by some contemporaries. A largely positive view is found in the pages of K.M. de Silva and J. Howard Wriggins' massive two-volume biography. These authors emphasise his elitist heritage, his experience, his intelligence, his foresightedness, his mastery of Parliamentary debate and the nuances of legislative procedure, his skills as a political organiser and strategist.

Placing political expediency ahead of principle is a theme Jayewardene's numerous critics emphasise. One argues that he had no long term strategy other than remaining in power and destroying his political opponents. This created a climate in which opponents despaired of regaining power democratically and some turned to armed opposition.[5] Another describes him as a 'loner' in a calling where gregariousness is valued, who became increasingly reliant on his wife and a few trusted advisors as his term progressed.[6] A third claims that Jayewardene's reputation as a politically dominant figure was exaggerated. On communal issues, especially, he was unable to follow through on promises made to Tamil leaders and seemed to cave in to more extremist factions in his party.[7]

One Jayewardene trait that may help us to better understand his style of governance as Executive President has received surprisingly little emphasis. I refer to a rootedness in Sinhalese and Asian cultural traditions, including traditions of kingship.[8] Like other young men of his class, he was well-trained in English history and literature. During his years out of power, he studied the career of Benjamin Disraeli; he is said to have regarded the great nineteenth century British leader as a model.[9] But Jayewardene seems less 'English' and more 'Asian' than many of his contemporaries, including S.W.R.D. Bandaranaike. His formal academic training and professional experience was entirely in Sri Lanka. He was an early proponent of indigenous language (*swabasha*) education. He converted from the Anglican Church to Buddhism and adopted 'national dress' long before it became fashionable to do so. His thoughtful collection of essays on the relevance of Buddhism to contemporary ethics, science, society and governance was first published in 1942.[10] In a memorable address to the 1951 San Francisco Peace Conference, Jayewardene not only asked that Japan be forgiven, but also emphasised its pre-eminence as an independent Asian and Buddhist nation.[11]

J.R. Jayewardene often reflected on the inherent tension between using power to achieve good ends and the obligations of 'the righteous ruler.'[12] As Executive President, he became the most monarchical head of state since independence, using ancient traditions to help legitimise his authority.[13] He asked Sinhala speakers to address him as 'your Excellency,' with a Sinhalese phrase connoting kingly, even divine, status. He chose Kotte, the capital of a fifteenth and sixteenth century Sinhalese kingdom, as the site for a new parliamentary complex and resurrected the capital's traditional name. Fortuitously, that name, *Sri Jayewardenepura*, was the same as his own.[14]

A picture of the cabinet, taken shortly after newly named ministers were sworn in, shows a somber, formally attired group of 24 men and one woman seated beside and standing behind the Prime Minister. They were a diverse group in terms of class and caste, reflecting successful efforts to broaden the UNP's base of support. Only six members had previous ministerial experience and only two were of the same generation as their leader. The cabinet's large size reflected a trend of granting ministerial perquisites to a relatively large number of individuals, in order to cement ties with religious, geographic, caste and occupational groups.[15] Only a few exercised real influence, however.

Jayewardene seemed comfortable surrounding himself with strong personalities holding divergent views. For the most part, he was skilful in preventing any single subordinate from becoming too powerful. Whether he could have imposed greater discipline on his ministers had he chosen to do so is a matter on which observers of the President differ widely.[16]

The new government's policy initiatives

UNP leaders moved quickly to effect changes and reforms emphasised in their campaign manifesto: constitutional restructuring, political liberalisation, economic liberalisation and economic development. Severe ethnic rioting in mid-August 1977 slowed the pace of change temporarily, but momentum was quickly regained. By the end of the year, a Constitutional amendment and a mass of new legislation had been ratified by the UNP's overwhelming, compliant parliamentary majority.

Establishing an 'Executive Presidency' to replace Sri Lanka's Westminster Model executive topped the new government's priority list. Jayewardene had favoured a strong chief executive along the lines of Charles de Galle's Fifth French Republic ever since Dudley Senanayake bowed to political pressure and compromised on strong economic reforms during the 1966 budget crisis. Chief executives in developing nations must be insulated from short-term political pressures that arise both within and outside parliament, Jayewardene reasoned, in order to implement economic policies that would be beneficial in the long-term, but have adverse short-term consequences.[17] His proposal was introduced in September 1977 and quickly approved.[18] J.R. Jayewardene was sworn in as Sri Lanka's first Executive President on 4 February 1978.

The government also moved quickly to abolish the Criminal Justice Commission and Foreign Exchange Control Act which, in the view of UNP leaders, leaders in the previous government had used for political harassment and repression. Abolishing the Criminal Justice Commission raised questions about the status of 147 prisoners, including Peoples Liberation Front (JVP) leader Rohana Wijeweera who had been imprisoned by the Commission. Jayewardene chose to release them. Later, the President explained that he set Wijeweera free so that imprisonment would not enhance his popularity 'like Nelson Mandela.' Shortly after regaining his freedom, Wijeweera visited his benefactor for an extended political discussion. 'He did not impress me,' J.R. Jayewardene later recalled.[19]

Centrepieces of the UNP's economic development program were the creation of an 'export-processing zone' and what came to be known as the Accelerated Mahaweli Development Project, discussed in greater detail below. Readers will recall that the latter project was initiated by Dudley Senanayake, but stalled under the United Front. J.R. Jayewardene inherited a plan that envisioned completing the project's three remaining dams, associated irrigation works and land development projects over a 30-year period. However, he quickly obtained cabinet approval for a greatly accelerated timetable that would complete the project during his government's six-year term.[20]

Sri Lanka's Housing Program, which targeted completion of 100,000 houses during the government's first term, was not initially envisioned by J.R. Jayewardene as a government priority on par with the Export Processing Zone or the Mahaweli Program. It assumed this status because of Prime Minister Premadasa's desire to have a major project of his own, coupled with his political skills, managerial ability, and exceptional energy. Despite protests that the target was unrealistic – Sirimavo Bandaranaike's government had completed only 3,000 houses – not to mention international donor concerns that other construction projects would compete for resources with Mahaweli, Premadasa won cabinet support for his 100,000-house target.[21] He pledged that new houses and supporting community services – schools, electricity, roads, and running water – would be constructed in each of Sri Lanka's 195 electoral districts.[22]

Sri Lanka's new constitution

The United Front's Constituent Assembly had spent nearly two years drafting its 'Republican Constitution' but made only modest changes in governance and electoral structures. The UNP's 1978 Constitution, drafted and ratified in less than nine months, changed fundamentally the balance of power between executive and legislative branches of government as well as how Sri Lanka's top leaders and legislative representatives would be chosen.[23]

The office of Executive President freed its occupant from cabinet and legislative oversight and provided greatly expanded powers. He spelled out how ministries were structured, selected ministers and presided over cabinet meetings. New provisions for filling vacant seats also strengthened the President's position. New members could be appointed to these seats by political parties rather than having to face by-elections. Thus, shifts in public opinion against the government could not reduce its parliamentary majority. The President could also dissolve Parliament and call an early general election. If the President's party did lose a general election before his term expired, he would be required to appoint the Prime Minister from the majority party, however this requirement did not extend to other cabinet members.[24] The President also had broad authority over the judiciary. Though the Supreme Court held limited powers to review the constitutionality of legislation and adjudicate human-rights cases, no real separation of powers existed.[25]

The authority to declare a state of emergency and then enact emergency regulations with overriding effect was another major area over which the President had sole discretion. The Constitution required, however, that a majority in Parliament ratify both the state of emergency and emergency regulations within 30 days or they would lapse automatically. If Parliament was not in session, the President would have to reconvene it within 10 days. After 90 days, only support by two-thirds of Parliament could keep emergency regulations in force.[26]

Provisions for referenda offered a mechanism by which a President could overcome parliamentary opposition, reflecting some preservation of the populist philosophy that had so dominated the 1970 Constitution. If the President judged the matter to be 'of national importance' he was empowered to submit any bill rejected by Parliament to the people for approval by a popular vote. Referenda were also required for some constitutional changes, as well as prior approval by a two-thirds parliamentary majority. Among these were the 'unitary' nature of the Sri Lankan state, provisions governing the franchise and matters relating to the nation's sovereignty. A two-thirds majority, plus approval by popular referendum were also required to extend the terms of either Parliament or the President. For other constitutional changes, judged to be less fundamental, only a two-thirds majority was required.

Thus, provisions for amending the Constitution by Parliament alone were retained. However, President Jayewardene and his colleagues on the Parliamentary Select Committee shared a widely held view that the huge swings in Parliamentary representation produced by the 1970 and 1977 general elections were potentially destabilising in a plural society such as Sri Lanka's. To correct this problem Sri Lanka's single member districts were replaced by with a complex proportional representation scheme designed to provide minority views with a significant voice, while avoiding the fragmentation that had paralyzed some legislatures elected under a proportional franchise.

The designers of this new scheme argued that in the future, Constitutional changes would only be made if supported by a broad national consensus. This meant, further, that the governance mechanisms put in place by the 1977 Constitution were likely to be more permanent that those established by its predecessors. Thus, the Parliament elected in 1977, with its overwhelming UNP majority, would probably be the last in which a president could impose Constitutional changes and take other actions requiring two-thirds majority support, virtually at his discretion. After the next general election, which could be held no later than 21 July 1983, this window of opportunity would close.

Even with the increased authority given to Sri Lanka's chief executive, there was much in the new Constitution that appeared to place democracy and protections for human rights on a firmer foundation. However, Constitutional scholar M.P. Jain, writing shortly after the document had been ratified, emphasised that '[m]uch would ....depend on the spirit with which the Constitution is implemented in practice.' Jain observed that '[e]ven the best of paper Constitutions may break down if not worked in the right spirit,' adding that 'even a bad Constitution may result in good government if worked in the right spirit. Human failure and not inherent defects in the Constitution pose the greatest danger.'[29]

Depriving Sirimavo Bandaranaike of her civic rights

Stable democracy requires clear channels for political feedback. A vibrant opposition is the best mechanism for keeping those channels open. But strong political leaders, especially in new democracies, are reluctant to acknowledge this. When in power, Sirimavo Bandaranaike had used an overwhelming parliamentary majority and emergency regulations to mute dissenting media voices and harass the UNP. Some UNP leaders had been incarcerated for lengthy periods on what they viewed as 'trumped up charges.'[30] President Jayewardene 'could see no reason why he should be more generous to her [Mrs. Bandaranaike] than she had been to him or his party colleagues ... [31]

The United Front government's two most powerful figures, Sirimavo and Felix Dias Bandaranaike, were accused of corruption and abuse of power, stemming from lucrative land sales that were consummated two days before passage of the law mandating confiscation of all land holdings in excess of 50 acres. To investigate the charges, UNP leaders crafted legislation empowering the President to name Special Presidential Commissions of Inquiry. Commissions, to be composed of Supreme Court Justices, were charged with investigating alleged political victimisation, misuse or abuse of power and other 'fraudulent acts.' The law applied retroactively: Alleged offences that occurred before the law's passage were not to be immune from investigation. Nor were Commission proceedings bound by legal rules of evidence; Commissioners could consider evidence that was not admissible in court. In the event of an adverse finding, determination of an appropriate punishment was left to Parliament. A two-thirds majority was required to impose the penalties provided for in the legislation: expulsion from Parliament and imposition of civic disability for a period not to exceed seven years.[32]

Commissions of inquiry were an accepted mechanism in the British legal tradition,[33] but it was no secret that the UNP legislation was specifically targeted against the former Prime Minister and her deputy. Initially, Mrs. Bandaranaike stated that she wished to present her case and expected vindication. Later, she challenged the legislation in court and refused to participate in the proceedings, which nonetheless moved forward to their inevitable conclusion. In late August, the Commission submitted to the President a finding that Sirimavo and Felix Dias Bandaranaike had abused their power, and the cabinet affirmed this ruling a few weeks later. As the 16 October date for debating the Commission's findings drew closer, Mrs. Bandaranaike and her allies tried unsuccessfully to mobilise mass demonstrations to show public support for her cause and perhaps even halt the proceedings in Parliament. The failure of this effort provided further evidence of J.R. Jayewardene's political skills and Sirimavo Bandaranaike's diminished stature. She vigorously defended herself in the final Parliamentary debate, reminding members of her services to the nation and accusing the government of attempting to subvert the two party system, but to no avail. The motions of expulsion and imposition of civic disabilities passed by a vote of 139 to 19.[34]

Parliament's verdict further weakened an already demoralised opposition. While Mrs. Bandaranaike retained her position as President of the SLFP, inability to campaign or make political speeches seriously limited her effectiveness. In particular, it meant she could not lead her party in the next general election, scheduled for 1983, or the next Presidential election, to be held in 1984. The prospects that Sri Lanka's voters would return the UNP and J.R. Jayewardene to power for another six years, thus giving them the opportunity to solidify their reform program, seemed excellent. Only one dark cloud loomed on an otherwise clear political horizon – relations between the Sinhalese and Tamil communities.

In this area, too, President Jayewardene believed that strong leadership, backed up by strong executive powers, would be needed to set Sri Lanka on a new path.

Relations between the Tamil and Sinhalese communities

Promoting greater communal harmony proved a more difficult task than demoralising the SLFP had been. Despite a promising start, J.R. Jayewardene's attempts to find common ground with moderate Tamil leaders fell short. As reported in chapter 14, sporadic but well publicised outbreaks of violence in the north had compelled some Sinhalese leaders to criticise the government, and even provoked retaliatory violent outbreaks. The President thought that broad powers would enable him to balance Sinhalese and Tamil interests more effectively, but he struggled to find an acceptable formula that would do this.

When speaking of relations between 'Sinhalese' and 'Tamils,' we need to periodically remind ourselves that neither 'community' is monolithic. The existence of differing views within ethnic communities always complicates conflict management and resolution. Among the Sinhalese, those living in rural areas of the south and the Kandyan highlands tended to be most militant on communal issues, though personal contacts with Sri Lanka Tamils were rare. These areas were traditional bastions of the SLFP. In urban areas, poorly educated men at the bottom of the economic ladder, often of lower caste, comprised a discontented *lumpenproletariat* whose hostility could erupt spontaneously into violence or be mobilised by politicians for attacks on opponents. Many Sinhalese were tolerant of Tamils or indifferent about communal issues, though political campaigns and publications describing communal strife could arouse latent sensitivities. Some members of the Buddhist priesthood provided spiritual and even political leadership for militant nationalist groups, but others preached toleration and steered clear of militancy. Attitudes concerning communal issues among Sinhalese political and economic elites ran across a wide spectrum. Nevertheless, even sophisticated, cosmopolitan political leaders like J.R. Jayewardene and Felix Dias Bandaranaike, often characterised as moderates, sometimes found it politically advantageous to 'play the ethnic card.'

By 1977, the political agenda of the Tamil community had become increasingly dominated by the concerns of those living in Jaffna district, where fewer than half of Sri Lanka's Tamils lived. Even in Jaffna, an independent Tamil Eelam enjoyed far less than unanimous support. Many viewed the Eelamist rhetoric of TULF politicians as political posturing or as staking out an extreme position that could provide a basis for compromise. Some leaders of Batticaloa's Tamil community also spoke of Eelam, but there was little support for a settlement in which the east which be dominated by Jaffna. Indian Tamil plantation workers had many grievances against the Sri Lankan government, but nothing to gain from an independent Eelam. Their best hope lay in the political alliance that Ceylon Workers Congress leader Thondaman had negotiated with J.R. Jayewardene. Colombo's large Tamil community of professionals, civil servants, businessmen and traders had, for the most part, made their peace with a Sinhalese-dominated political order and stood to lose the most from an independent Tamil state. Eelam's strongest supporters, as we have seen were the increasingly influential youthful militants. For them, the war for Tamil independence had already begun and *all* Tamils, whether residents of the northeast or not; whether supporters of Eelam or not, were potential soldiers.

Recognising diverse communities and diverse points of view is important, but only one facet of Sri Lanka's communal setting in the late 1970s. For all this diversity, Sri Lanka is a small island, with one of the highest population densities in the world. Newspapers and other political tracts circulated widely among a citizenry that was both highly literate and politically aware. This meant that news of events in one part of the island spread quickly to all parts. The death of a Sinhalese police constable at militant hands in Jaffna could become a news story in the southern town of Matara the following day. An inflammatory, anti-Tamil speech in Parliament could be discussed on Jaffna street corners and in tea houses soon afterward.

While news spread quickly, the 'news' reported to Sinhala and Tamil readers could be quite different. Newspapers, especially Sinhala and Tamil language newspapers, often sensationalised accounts to appeal to their respective audiences. Stories about security forces' indiscipline, ethnic rioting or a new Mahaweli settlement would have very different communal slants, depending on where they appeared. Since Tamils and Sinhalese read different newspapers, their perception of events touching on communal relations could be quite different. This increased mutual distrust between the two communities.

While communal reconciliation numbered among J.R. Jayewardene priorities, it did not dominate the others. Awareness of Tamil concerns was reflected in new constitutional protections for minority rights and in recognition of Tamil as a 'national language.' He saw the need to reform discriminatory university admissions policies and initiated controversial 'District Development Councils' legislation, which few Sinhalese supported. At times, he took a strong stand against chauvinist elements in his own party.[35] But he believed that over the long run, free-market economic reforms would contribute most to communal harmony by expanding economic opportunities for all Sri Lankans and reducing dependence on state sector programs.[36]

His positions on communal issues were tempered by political realism. He knew that a national leader must have a broad base of Sinhalese support; the Tamil United Front's core constituency represented no more than six or seven per cent of the electorate. From time to time, he felt the need to prove his *bona fides* to supporters who viewed him as too cosmopolitan and lukewarm in his support for Sinhalese stances on key issues. He seemed to adjust his positions to maintain political advantage, leading both supporters and opponents to observe that they never could entirely determine where he stood.

Jayewardene's principal Tamil protagonist, TULF leader Appillai Amirthalingam, found himself in a fundamentally new position in 1977. Because the TULF held the second largest number of seats in Parliament, Jayewardene had named Amirthalingam Leader of the Opposition, even though he had campaigned on a separatist platform.[37] This gave the TULF leader national stature, the perquisites of a senior government official and a seat in the cabinet. But close ties with militant groups, especially Prabakharan's LTTE, limited his flexibility. Militants viewed Amirthalingam's new role in Colombo with suspicion and were averse to compromise. Successful actions against the security forces gave militant leaders a sense of greater power and they began to assume an increasingly dominant role in their partnership with the TULF.

A.J. Wilson described relations between President Jayewardene and TULF leaders as characterised by 'mutual contempt.' The three Tamil leaders whom Jayewardene knew best – G.G. Ponnambalam, Murugesan Tiruchelvam, and S.J.V. Chelvanayakam – had all died during 1976-77. Amirthalingam and his principal deputy came from a new generation. Neither had served in Parliament during the 1970-1977 term. Jayewardene referred to these leaders privately as 'small minds, small people.' The Tamil leaders, on the other hand, remembered Jayewardene as the man who successfully opposed the 1958 Bandaranaike-Chelvanayakam pact and for virulently anti-Tamil speeches that he had given from time to time.[38] As a result, they distrusted him deeply.

Misgivings between the two communities and their principal leaders, coupled with pressures from extremist elements on both sides, combined to complicate government efforts to resolve long-standing divisive issues, though some progress did occur. The open economy program contributed relatively little to communal harmony. Rather, unanticipated consequences of the program created new frictions. The massive Mahaweli development project caused divisions because the availability of newly irrigated land raised the issue of 'colonisation,' i.e. settlement of Sinhalese migrants in Tamil majority areas, to new levels of salience. To understand why communal relations deteriorated rather than improved during J.R. Jayewardene's first five years in office, we need to examine more closely the issues of economic reform, language policy, religion, the Mahaweli development program and devolution of power to the regions.

The new communal frictions that resulted from open-economy policies may have surprised President Jayewardene, because he believed so strongly that free markets and economic growth would contribute to a more harmonious social climate. However, economic reforms produced losers as well as winners. In the north, protectionist trade policies hurt Jaffna vegetable farmers, one of the few Tamil groups that had improved their lot during Sirimavo Bandaranaike's years in power. These entrepreneurs now found prices undercut by Indian competition. Many suffered severe losses and had to lay off casual labourers. Both farmers and unemployed workers had reason to be angry at the government.

In the south, deregulation meant there were fewer ways that Sinhalese businessmen could use political patronage to gain advantages in the market place over Tamil rivals. Competing on more equal terms, some lost out. An expanding economy, coupled with skyrocketing inflation, widened the gap between rich and poor. Poor Sri Lankans in urban and semi urban settings – mostly Sinhalese – experienced declines in real income and continued risks of unemployment at the same time the government slashed food and other consumer subsidies.[39] Those who fared badly – even as others apparently fared well – sought somebody to blame. Minorities, including Indian Tamils, Muslims and foreigners, as well as Sri Lankan Tamils, became prime targets for feelings of deprivation, resentment and aggression. Inflammatory speeches and tracts by extremist leaders fuelled this scapegoating. Conservative Sinhalese were distressed by adverse cultural impacts of open economy policies due to the influx of foreign films, music and consumer goods, along with tourists whom they viewed as insensitive and immoral. Those who had been swayed by J.R. Jayewardene's promise to create a *dharmista* (righteous) society were particularly outraged.[40]

Some Tamils acknowledged the 1978 Constitution's recognition of their mother tongue as an important symbolic change,[41] but it had little practical impact. By this time, language had receded in importance, as different segments of the society accommodated to the appropriate use of Sinhala, Tamil and English in dealings with the government and in their own lives. As Sri Lanka's economy became more internationalised, the tourist trade grew and opportunities for foreign education expanded. Those who could afford to do so educated their children in English. Increasingly, English became the language of modern-sector businesses, and of local graduate education in many fields. English enjoyed wide use in government as a preferred, though unofficial means of communication, and as a 'link' language between Tamil and Sinhalese officials. Tamils often communicated with the central government in English or Sinhala for practical reasons: they felt that communications in Tamil were less likely to receive attention or produce favourable results.[42]

Pressures from contending factions on another divisive issue, religion, challenged the President to seek out a middle path that would lessen communal friction while not swelling the ranks of his opponents. The 1978 Constitution reaffirmed Buddhism's 'foremost place' and went a bit further than the 1972 document by stating that 'it shall be the duty of the state to protect and foster the Buddha *Sasana*,' i.e. Buddhist doctrine and institutions.[43] To provide other religions a voice, the government created a Department of Hindu Affairs in 1978 and a Department of Muslim Religious Affairs in 1980: Nevertheless, many complained that these departments provided little more than window dressing.[44] President Jayewardene did resist pressures to establish a Buddhist state, however.[45] The government's policy was to provide symbolic support for Buddhism as a religion, while limiting organised Buddhism's political influence. Anthropologist Stephen Kemper writes that in choosing monks to receive patronage, the government 'signalled its support ...for a certain kind of Buddhism – the kind that is lived out in monasteries, not on political platforms or behind police barricades.'[46]

Government overtures to Tamils in the touchy area of university admissions also sought a middle path. 'Standardisation', the practice of adjusting scores to equalise performance within language groups, was abandoned shortly after the new government assumed power. This increased the number of Tamils gaining admission and, if the size of entering classes had remained the same, would have reduced the number of Sinhalese. To minimise this, universities received directions to increase acceptance rates and establish some special quotas favouring Sinhalese. This seemed to satisfy many, though critics remained. To create some insulation between university administration and politics, a multi-ethnic University Grants Commission was created with overall management responsibilities, including responsibility for admissions policy. President Jayewardene also split off higher education from the Ministry of Education, naming himself as Higher Education Minister. These changes succeeded in reducing the amount of time devoted to university matters in Parliament and cabinet meetings. However, total political insulation was impossible in a climate where factions scrutinised data for ethnic winners and losers at the end of each admissions cycle.[47]

The widening gap between Sinhalese and Tamil communities made the issue of settler 'colonisation,' with its implications for control over territory, more politically consequential and contentious than either language, religion or university admissions. Compromise was difficult because the interests of the two communities seemed so diametrically opposed. Proposals for decentralisation of authority to regions, discussed subsequently, raised the political stakes associated with control over territory higher still.

Readers will recall that Sri Lanka divides topographically into a 'wet zone,' located in the central and southwestern part of the island and a 'dry zone' in the north and east.[48] Population densities are highest in the wet zone, where conditions allow for intensive agriculture.[49] Sinhalese predominate among wet-zone residents. Sri Lanka's more sparsely populated Northern and Eastern Provinces, identified by Tamils as their 'traditional homelands,' lie in the dry zone. One goal of the Mahaweli Development Project involved irrigating dry-zone lands so that they would support higher levels of agricultural production and thus, of settlement. The major point at issue in the 'colonisation' debate was the ethnic identity of settlers who would populate these newly opened lands.

Even before implementation of the Mahaweli scheme, policies implemented by Sri Lanka's Sinhalese-dominated government tended to favour Sinhalese settlers. These policies angered Tamils, but probably stemmed more from political than overtly ethic considerations. Elected public officials, mainly Sinhalese, had a great interest in assisting their constituents and supporters, also predominantly Sinhalese.[50] Political commitments to preserving the nearly mythical values of Sinhalese peasant culture[51] and restoring the greatness of Sri Lanka's ancient hydraulic civilisation[52] also gave settlement policy a markedly Sinhalese bias, especially when viewed through Tamil eyes. Redrawing political boundaries to give Tamil and Sinhalese populations more distinct political identities facilitated a pro-Sinhalese bias.[53] A pattern developed of disproportionate assistance to Sinhalese living in the interior, along with neglect of coastal areas in all three Eastern Province districts. Population shifted markedly as a result of this preferential treatment. In Trincomalee District, Tamils outnumbered Sinhalese by nearly two to one in 1971. By 1981, the proportions had become approximately equal. In Amparai, the margin of Sinhalese over Tamils over the same period increased from 8 per cent to 18 per cent.[54]

When the government decided to 'accelerate' completion of the Mahaweli Project from 30 to six years, they also eliminated or indefinitely postponed some irrigation projects that had appeared in the original plan. President Jaye-wardene's choice of areas where projects would go forward opened him up to charges of pro-Sinhalese bias on two fronts: First, Sinhalese predominated in the inland areas of Trincomalee and Ampara district that he chose; by con-trast, the government cancelled or postponed projected work in areas closer to the coast, populated largely by Tamils and Muslims. Second, the fact that Sinhalese majorities already lived in the areas chosen for irrigation provided a rationale for settling additional Sinhalese there.[55] While the criteria for choos-ing prospective settlers emphasised geography rather than ethnicity, Tamils and Muslims received a minuscule proportion of new lands. Data compiled by the government in 1985 showed that of 39,622 settlers who had received new land, 38,208 or 96.4 per cent were Sinhalese; 1,050 or 2.7 per cent were Muslims; and only 364 were Tamils.[56] In 1985 – when communal conflict had escalated into civil war and government representatives met with militant leaders in Thimpu – the inequitable settlement or 'colonisation' patterns promoted by the Mahaweli Project figured high on the agenda.

A related and even more contentious issue was devolution of power, name-ly the transfer of authority and resources from central-government ministries to elected regional governments. While the 1977 Tamil United Front election manifesto had demanded an independent Eelam, moderate Tamil leaders were willing to accept meaningful devolution. J.R. Jayewardene, too, had recognised that devolving power to Tamil majority regions could be an important step toward restoring communal harmony.

Decentralisation and local government reform had become matters of concern throughout Sri Lanka, not only in the north and east.[57] Historically, central government authorities had demonstrated somewhat greater willing-ness to cede power to Sinhalese regional authorities than to those headed by Tamils. However, neither devolution proposals nor establishment of District Development Councils evoked much interest in Sinhalese areas, except to the extent that they aroused the ire of Sinhalese-Buddhist nationalists who op-posed any move toward federalism.

District Development Councils may have provided Sri Lankans their last opportunity to defuse communal tensions before violent conflict erupted. Pos-sibly, these institutions could have legitimised the eroding position of moderate Tamil leaders before militant forces on both sides gained control of the politi-cal agenda. The failure of this initiative, which left each side more distrustful and resistant to compromise, provides yet another illustration of how short-comings in political leadership intensified communal differences in Sri Lanka and strengthened the hand of militant factions. Two contrasting accounts of the District Development Councils initiative, by highly regarded Sinhalese and Tamil scholars, K.M. de Silva and A.J. Wilson, show how greatly the perceptions of 'moderate,' knowledgeable members of the two communities could differ regarding the same events.[58]

The goal of establishing Councils had appeared in the government's post-election 'policy statement,'[59] but it was clear that economic restructuring, Constitutional reform and the Mahaweli Development Project had a higher priority. The first specific proposals for devolving power did not appear until June 1978, in the form of a 'white paper' rather than as a specific legislative proposal. This document represented President Jayewardene's attempt to find a middle path between Tamil demands for federalism and Sinhalese insistence on a unitary state by creating regional authorities, but then greatly limiting their autonomy.

In informal discussions, TULF leaders expressed a reluctant willingness to experiment with this mechanism, but negotiations over the ethnicity of district ministers highlighted deep differences between the TULF and the government over the multi-ethnic Eastern region. Discussions of 'self determination' have often foundered over disagreement about the geographic unit within which different groups would exercise 'self determination'. From the TULF perspective, both the Northern and Eastern Provinces, each with three administrative districts comprised single Tamil-speaking territorial units, with a Tamil majority, in 'the traditional homelands of the Tamils.' At a minimum, they wanted Tamil district ministers appointed to the five districts where Tamil speakers predominated, including both Trincomalee and Batticaloa in the east. Jaye-wardene agreed that Tamil district ministers should be appointed in the north, but proposed a more complex scheme of joint ministers for the two Eastern Province districts. Negotiations bogged down for more than a year, with mistrust between the major protagonists rising and northern militants becoming more aggressive. Declaration of a state of emergency in the north and appointment of an Army brigadier as commander of all security forces in Jaffna further heightened tensions between the protagonists.[60]

In August 1979, President Jayewardene attempted to break the stalemate by appointing a 10-member multiethnic Presidential Commission on Development Councils charged with finding a workable compromise. After six months of deliberations, the Commission put forward a set of overdue recommendations, which TULF Commissioners nevertheless found unacceptable. As with the earlier government white paper, District Ministers still lacked real autonomy and the Development Councils had only an advisory role. However, the proposal that councils be elected did represent a step forward from the Tamil perspective. President Jayewardene decided to use the Commission report as a basis for legislation. Further delays ensued, and Parliament did not finally approve the Development Councils Act until 21 August 1980.[61] On 4 June 1981, the government held elections to fill District Development Council positions. Polling proceeded peacefully in most parts of the island, but had to be postponed in Jaffna after killings, rioting and the Public-Library fire, all described earlier. The first stage of this fragile devolution experiment finally ended in October, with the election for Jaffna's District Development Councillors.

The lengthy process of creating councils and holding elections highlighted deep divisions within Sri Lanka over devolving power which had contributed to previous failed attempts by S.W.R.D Bandaranaike and Dudley Senanayake. Viewed from this perspective, passage of the Development Councils Act 'constituted a major political achievement,' as K.M. de Silva emphasises.[62] President Jayewardene saw the need for communal reconciliation, pressed forward with politically risky legislation and maintained party discipline to achieve passage. But A.J. Wilson's reflections on the lengthy negotiations, in which he was personally involved, emphasise his growing distrust of the President's motives. He came to believe that Jayewardene, despite periodic good intentions, could not control extremist factions in his own party and the larger Sinhalese community. Shortcomings in the negotiation process and final legislation reflected this. At best, President Jayewardene is portrayed as a weak leader who was unable to keep his promises. At worst, Wilson concludes, the President may have been a disingenuous man who never intended to carry out his promise to devolve power.[63]

Passing District Development Councils legislation required Jayewardene to overcome visceral Sinhalese opposition to any regional power sharing with Tamils. Actually making the councils work ran into a second challenge, countervailing powerful cabinet ministers' and senior civil servants' opposition to sharing power. The task of persuading officials to give up power was also complicated by limited funding. Massive government expenditures on development had contributed to soaring government deficits and inflation levels that aroused the concerns of World Bank and International Monetary Fund economists. Donor agencies cut back on aid and pressured Sri Lanka's government to reduce expenditures. Finance Minister Ronnie de Mel was forced to impose budget cuts of as much as 25 per cent on some ministries, just at the time that the budgets and programmatic authority of District Development Councils were being worked out.[64] Among additional complications, President Jayewardene decided to advance the Presidential election to 20 October 1982, and subsequently to hold a referendum on extending the life of Parliament. Budget cuts and campaigning provided already resistant ministers with further excuses to push District Development Council matters to the bottom of the priority list.

Election results in October provided the President with little motivation to make politically risky concessions to the TULF. In Northern Province Presidential polling, J.R. Jayewardene came in third behind the SLFP and Tamil Congress candidates.[65] Tamil opposition to the government was expressed even more strongly in the referendum to extend the life of Parliament, which went down to defeat in most Tamil majority districts. The Northern Tamils had responded to President Jayewardene's devolution initiatives by making common cause with Sirimavo Bandaranaike's SLFP.

The process of devolution did continue to move forward, but only at glacial speed. The government formally delegated certain powers to newly-appointed District Ministers in September 1982. By December 1982, more than 16 months after most Council members' election, District Ministers received a formal description of their roles and responsibilities. Delays in funding Council activities continued.

Analysts dispute the effectiveness of this tentative step toward regional autonomy before the July 1983 riots made it a dead letter: K.M. de Silva notes that the multi-ethnic Trincomalee Council was 'a pronounced success,' and that some councils with strong leadership in Sinhalese areas had also made headway. Even the Jaffna Council, from which citizens expected a greater measure of success than that of any other regional council, 'appeared to have blunted the edges of separatist agitation' for a period of time.[66] Most Tamil leaders, however, saw District Development Councils as 'an empty shell' because of delays in appointing ministers, their limited authority, and lagging delivery on funding commitments.[67] The report of a Presidential committee, chaired by respected civil servant Bradman Weerakoon, largely confirmed this view.[68]

As a mechanism for restoring communal harmony, District Development Councils must be judged a failure. By the spring of 1983, Tamils and Sinhalese had become far more divided than in 1977. Jaffna's militant leaders had stepped up their use of violence and began to take control of Tamil communities' political agendas. Amirthalingam no longer stood as the pre-eminent leader. In fact, when the government imposed a state of emergency in May 1983, the TULF leader supported the decision.[69] After receiving Weerakoon's report, President Jayewardene began holding meetings with District Ministers to take steps toward increasing the effectiveness of Development Councils. These discussions, however, took on a surreal quality, divorced from the pressing reality of conflict in the north. In cabinet meetings, ministers argued with increasing effectiveness that that Tamils had been given 'too much' and that the government should use military force to restore order.[70]

Resolving communal differences in Sri Lanka had proven difficult enough in peaceful times. The escalating violence described earlier in this chapter made the task more urgent, but simultaneously made it more difficult. Violent actions by the most militant Tamils and Sinhalese complemented one another in eroding any middle ground for compromise. In a political climate characterised by real political differences and escalating violence, speechmaking by political leaders on both sides made things worse. A Tamil or Sinhalese politician, facing a sympathetic audience or, perhaps, addressing Parliament would deliver a speech that combined intransigent stands on sensitive issues, appeals to chauvinist values and demeaning ethnic stereotypes of the rival group. The speeches most inflammatory phrases would be quickly reported in the indigenous-language press of the rival group, along with critical editorial comments and, possibly a cartoon caricature of the offending speaker. Such accounts were regular fare in Sinhalese and Tamil language newspapers.

Amirthalingam, who was new to national level politics and to his role as official leader of the opposition, quickly aroused Sinhalese ire. During the election campaign he had spoken of a 'secret plan' for establishing an independent Eelam. It was easy for average Sinhalese to conclude that this 'plan' involved violence or even worse, colaboration with India.[71] The TULF leader chose 18 August 1977, during the height of island-wide ethnic rioting to introduce an amendment to the government's policy statement that reiterated pre-election calls for independence. He was well aware that Tamil 'self determination' was unacceptable to even moderate Sinhalese. Retired Chief Justice Sansoni's report on causes of the 1977 rioting strongly criticised Amirthalingam for statements that showed disrespect for the law, condoned militant killings and incited violence.[72] As time passed and conflict intensified, TULF rhetoric became less and less tolerant of opposition. Platform oratory portrayed party loyalists as embodying the 'Tamil Nation.' All others were branded as 'traitors.'[73]

Among Sinhalese political leaders, Minister of Industries Cyril Mathew is most often identified as one who used strong, confrontational rhetoric when discussing communal matters. Two books, published during President Jayewardene's first term made his views clear. *Diabolical Conspiracy* (1979) characterised Tamil officials and military officers as 'Sri Lankans who did not regard this blessed island as their motherland and who did not consider the pristine religion of this country as their own religion.' According to Mathew, these men had colluded with British colonial rulers to gain special privileges. After independence, they used their privileged positions to deprive deserving Sinhalese of opportunities that were rightfully theirs.[74] *Sinhala People - Awake, Arise and Safeguard Buddhism* (1981) urged decisive action by Sinhalese to regain what was rightfully theirs. Among other strategies, Mathew proposed aggressive Sinhalese colonisation of Tamil majority areas, including the Jaffna peninsula and even a Buddhist *Jihad* if there was resistance.[75] Mathew's positions as head of a powerful government Ministry and of the UNP's labour union signalled Tamils that his extremist views carried weight with the Cabinet and with President Jayewardene.

Propaganda activities of the international Tamil community, were a final irritant to Sinhalese, as well as a serious foreign policy problem for Sri Lanka's government. Tamil students had begun organising, demonstrating and propagandising prior to 1977, but these activities intensified during J.R. Jayewardene's first term. Paradoxically, the government's relaxation of currency restrictions made foreign travel easier, swelling the ranks of Tamils living abroad. Journalist Sinha Ratnatunga reports that by the mid-1980s there were more than 40,000 Tamils resident in Britain and France and nearly 10,000 in Germany. Australia, Canada and the United States were also home to large Tamil communities.[76]

Quotas for permanent migrants were small in the West, but governments and citizens were more receptive to political refugees.[77] Thus there was motivation for 'economic refugees', political refugees and Eelamists to join forces in publicity campaigns that would picture life for Sri Lanka's Tamils in the bleakest possible terms. Lobbying groups were formed in most major Western nations to mobilise support for Tamil militants and pressure Sri Lanka's government.[78] Tamil students and youths living abroad on temporary visas (or no visas at all) were the foot soldiers of these organisations. Wealthy Tamil businessmen and professionals, who had often migrated some years earlier, provided funds. Tamil groups held public demonstrations, gave newspaper interviews, and lobbied government organisations and human rights organisations. In Germany, they campaigned to reduce the lucrative tourist trade to Sri Lanka. In England demonstrations were held urging the British not to drink Ceylon Tea.[79] Representatives visited the World Bank and other donor organisations, lobbying for cutbacks in foreign aid to Sri Lanka. The U.S. Eelam Tamil Association obtained a pro-Tamil resolution from the Massachusetts legislature's lower house, which was sent to the U.S. Congress. When the Governor declared that 22 May 1979 was 'Eelam Tamils Day' in Massachusetts, TULF President M. Sivasthamparam was on hand to personally receive a copy of the declaration.[80] Not all activities were non violent. In August of 1981, there were Arson attacks against Sri Lanka's high Commission Offices in both Bonn and London.

Tamil groups developed a network that ensured wide publicity for anti-Tamil rioting, security force excesses and legislation such as the Prevention of Terrorism Act. When such excesses occurred, support for Tamil refugees and pressure on Sri Lanka's government grew. For the most part, Tamils were far more effective in presenting their point of view than Sri Lanka's official missions. Reports by the UN human rights division, the International Commission of Jurists, the World Council of Churches and Amnesty International highlighted repressive acts against Tamils, but gave little attention to militant attacks against Sinhalese or other Tamils.[81] An increasingly beleaguered government began to view international human rights organisations as adversaries, a view that continues to this day.

Whether international propaganda activities helped or hurt Tamils living in Sri Lanka is difficult to judge. Successive reports by human rights organisations and communications from donor governments made J.R. Jayewardene's government more sensitive to the international implications of domestic communal policies, but to the Presidents inner circle, the options for changing policies seemed limited. Many cabinet members resented the international attention and considered it unfair. Moreover international criticism of Sri Lanka, widely publicised in Sri Lankan newspapers, was yet another factor poisoning communal relations. It strengthened the voices of Sinhalese nationalists, angered ordinary Sinhalese who were proud of their country and made the task of those who favoured conciliation more difficult.

How J.R. Jayewardene's foreign policies won support from the west, but alienated India.

Internationalisation of Sri Lanka's ethnic conflict was a source of frustration to President Jayewardene. He felt that Sirimavo Bandaranaike's high profile leadership of the Non-Aligned Movement had impeded Sri Lanka's development. Left-leaning non-alignment, he believed, discouraged both private investors and aid giving agencies from providing the funds necessary to build the economy. A major foreign policy goal was to lower Sri Lanka's international profile so that top priority could be given to domestic economic programs and export promotion. Jayewardene hoped to deal with Tamil militancy as an 'internal' domestic problem, but India's increasing support for Tamil aspirations and militant movements greatly complicated the President's agenda.

The new UNP government got off to a promising start in foreign affairs, thanks largely to effective personal diplomacy by the President and members of his inner circle.[82] President Jayewardene named A.C.S. Hameed, a Muslim, to be Sri Lanka's first independent Minister of Foreign Affairs.[83] Replacing Sirimavo Bandaranaike as the official head of the Non-Aligned Movement, Jayewardene eloquently endorsed the movement's goals, while distancing Sri Lanka from activist stances. In international forums, he appealed for creation of a World Disarmament Authority, a proposal that was later adopted by the UN General Assembly. On a 1979 visit to Japan, he was enthusiastically received by a government and people still grateful for his support at the San Francisco Peace Conference, nearly 30 years earlier.[84]

Though Sri Lanka remained officially non-aligned and socialist, its new economic policies and political leanings were viewed favourably in the West. Sirimavo Bandaranaike's close personal ties had been with leaders such as Marshal Tito, Gamal Abdul Nasser, Anwar Sadat and Indira Gandhi. In contrast, J.R. Jayewardene cultivated Malaysia's Prime Minister Mahathir Mohammed and Singapore's Lee Kwan Yew, as well as the new conservative leaders of Britain and the United States, Margaret Thatcher and Ronald Reagan. Sri Lanka joined with Pakistan in speaking out strongly against the Soviet invasion of Afghanistan and later stood with Great Britain when it sent a carrier task force to recapture the Falklands/Malvinas Islands.[85] The U.S. Peace Corps was invited back to Sri Lanka to organise rural education programs and the U.S. Information Agency was given a 1,000 acre tract to install high powered Voice of America transmitters. Trincomalee's superb deep water harbour was opened to naval vessels from all nations, so long as they did not carry nuclear weapons. Relations were strengthened with the World Bank, the International Monetary Fund and western bilateral donor agencies. Substantial funds and large contingents of Western advisors began to flow into Sri Lanka.

Sri Lanka's pro-western tilt changed policies that had aligned it closely with India during Sirimavo Bandaranaike's and Indira Gandhi's terms in office, however President Jayewardene quickly established close ties with India's new Janatha government and Prime Minister Moraraji Desai. The Janatha government, too, was taking tentative steps toward a more open economy policy and more centrist foreign policy. An exchange of official visits in 1978 and 1979 strengthened personal ties between the two leaders and their close advisors.[86]

Unfortunately for Sri Lanka's government, strengthening ties with India's leaders, who were also Indira Gandhi's political opponents, proved to be counterproductive. Opposition to Mrs. Gandhi had brought the Janatha coalition members together, but factional squabbling broke out once they gained power. In July, Prime Minister Desai was forced to resign and his replacement, Charan Singh, was unable to secure a majority in Parliament. The ensuing general election returned Indira Gandhi to power with a large majority.[87]

This did not bode well for Sri Lanka. Mrs. Gandhi had been personally insulted by J.R. Jayewardene's criticisms of her in the UNP's 1977 election campaign and in speeches he subsequently made during a visit to India. At the September 1980 meeting of Asia-Pacific Commonwealth leaders, Jayewardene made things worse with a speech fulsomely praising Mahatma Gandhi and Prime Minister Nehru (Mrs. Gandhi's father) that seemed to imply India's present leadership had fallen considerably below their standards. Finally, there was Mrs. Gandhi's political and personal friendship with Sirimavo Bandaranaike and her family. When the UNP dominated Parliament voted to deprive Mrs. Bandaranaike and Felix Dias Bandaranaike of their civic rights, India's Prime Minister publicly accused Sri Lanka's government of 'harassing' the Bandaranaike family.[88]

In contrast to Desai, Mrs. Gandhi was concerned with asserting India's role as south Asia's dominant power. Mrs. Gandhi's hegemonic pretensions were reinforced by a bureaucratic military elite that, in the early 1980s, exercised increasing influence over India's domestic and foreign policy. Making India a world power was the goal of this elite, Journalist Anuradha Gupta argues.[89] India's central intelligence agency, the Research and Analysis Wing of the Department of Defence (RAW), was responsible for the clandestine aspects of this agenda. As with other intelligence establishments throughout the world, RAW's leaders would sometimes act independently when they felt it was in their interest or their nation's interest to do so.[90]

J.R. Jayewardene's overtures toward the West, undertaken without consulting India, were viewed with concern by Mrs. Gandhi and India's defence establishment. Especially worrisome were moves that seemed to enhance the United States' strategic influence in the Indian Ocean – the Trincomalee tank farm deal, the possibility of U.S. Naval visits to Trincomalee and the expanded Voice of America listening post. Following the invasion of Afghanistan, the U.S. had strengthened ties with Pakistan which was enlisted as a conduit for U.S. supplied arms to Afghan guerrillas. India's government, on the other hand, continued to maintain close ties with the USSR. U.S. strategic interests in the south Asia region were viewed as at least potentially hostile to those of India.[91] An assertively independent Sri Lanka, pursuing strong ties not only with the United States but also with Pakistan, was not perceived to be in India's national interest. Weakening J.R. Jayewardene's government and asserting more control over its foreign relations became a goal of India's intelligence establishment.

This goal was symbiotic with the pressing domestic concern of the Congress (Indira) political party of cultivating political support in Tamil Nadu state. Tamil Nadu returned 39 seats to the *Lok Sabha*, the seventh largest state delegation in India. Mrs. Gandhi believed she would need those seats in the 1985 general election to remain in power, but knew her party could never carry them directly. Alliance with one of Tamil Nadu's two dominant political parties, the All India Dravidian Progressive Front (AIDMK) or the Dravidian Progressive Front (DMK) were the only options.[92]

Muthuvel Karunanidhi's DMK had spearheaded the creation of Tamil Nadu as a linguistically distinct state in the late 1960s. While passage of the sixteenth amendment to India's Constitution had forced Karunanidhi to disavow separatism, the party remained strongly nationalistic and did not hesitate to endorse separatism in Sri Lanka. In the late 1970s, the DMK divided into two factions. The schismatic AIDMK, lead by movie star M.G. Ramachandran, won control of the state government but was dismissed by Mrs. Gandhi.[93] When the AIDMK triumphed over the DMK in the 1980 general election, however, Mrs. Gandhi negotiated an alliance with Ramachandran, who was considered the more 'moderate' of the two Tamil leaders.

No matter which party was in power, Sri Lankan separatism remained a volatile issue in Tamil politics, with politicians on both sides competing for stature as the true champions of Sri Lanka's Tamils. Anti-Tamil rioting, security force excesses and government repression in Sri Lanka invariably unleashed a flood of nationalist oratory along with demands that India's central government intervene on behalf of the Tamils. Such demands provided yet another rationale for Mrs. Ghandi to intervene in Sri Lanka. By this time, too, both party leaders had established links with Tamil militant groups and were providing some covert support to them.

How international, national and Tamil Nadu politics intermingled was illustrated graphically by Sri Lanka's futile attempts to extradite militant leaders Velupillai Prabakharan and Uma Maheswaren who had fled to India in early 1982. On 19 May Prabakharan spotted Uma coming out of a restaurant in Madras' Pondi Bazaar and both men opened fire with revolvers. They were soon apprehended by Tamil Nadu police and Sri Lanka's government sought extradition to prosecute them for multiple crimes, including 27 murders between them.

It was not to be. Collaborating with the militants' Tamil Nadu-based political surrogates, DMK leader Karunanidhi organised street demonstrations and sent emissaries to Prime Minister Gandhi. Gandhi promised she would not press for extradition. Tamil Nadu Chief Minister Ramachandran instructed his police to take no precipitous action. On August 6, both men were released on bail. To prevent renewal of their feud, they were directed to live in different cities, where sympathisers welcomed them. Sri Lanka's Inspector General of Police, himself a Tamil, who had travelled to Madras to take the two men into custody, had to return to Colombo empty handed.[94]

Sri Lanka's failure to obtain custody of Prabakharan and Maheswaren from India was one of a number of signals that J.R. Jayewardene was failing to give sufficient priority to his nation's most important bilateral relation. Overtures to the west had produced financing that was strengthening Sri Lanka's economy, but support in a political conflict with India was another matter. The Soviet Union was India's ally. The United States, still wounded by its experience in Viet Nam, was already mounting a covert action against Soviet dominated Afghanistan in colaboration with Pakistan. U.S. leaders were unlikely to engage India on another front over matters that had little relation to their strategic priorities. In Prime Minister Gandhi, moreover, J.R. Jayewardene faced an adversary far more formidable than Sirimavo Bandaranaike. Her mastery of realpolitic easily matched 'the old fox' and the resources at her command were vastly greater. Cordial personal relations between Jayewardene and Indira Gandhi would not have altered geopolitical realities nor the realities of Tamil Nadu politics. But one has to wonder why a leader of Jayewardene's intelligence and experience chose to administer gratuitous slights, rather than reaching out to India's leader.[95]

Renewing the government's mandate: the presidential election and referendum of 1982

The deterioration in relations with India and the setback in Tamil Nadu occurred at a time when J.R. Jayewardene was contemplating the prospects of another six years in power with growing optimism. The economy seemed relatively strong, despite nagging inflation problems. Unemployment had fallen, though job opportunities for young men and women were still below expectations. Mahaweli construction projects were gaining momentum with the prospect that increased hydro power would spur industrialisation and expanded irrigation would reduce the need for costly rice imports. Replacing the rice ration with food stamps had been accepted with a minimum of protest. Depriving Mrs. Bandaranaike of her civic rights had left the SLFP in disarray with factions headed by her son and younger daughter fighting to control party machinery. Only in the area of communal relations did the UNP face serious problems, but it appeared that the impact of these problems on the upcoming general and Presidential elections would be modest.

Though omens seemed propitious, nearly 50 years in politics had taught President Jayewardene that no election is a sure thing. The UNP been defeated by SLFP-led coalitions in 1956, 1960 and 1970 when many of its top leaders were confident of victory. Transformation of Sri Lanka's economy, which Jayewardene viewed as a major legacy, was far from complete. World Bank economists and an outside consultant had recommended tough, potentially unpopular measures to reduce government deficits and curb inflation. If implemented, these measures were likely to have an impact that coincided with the scheduled dates of upcoming elections. There was a strong case for advancing the election date to capitalise on the favourable economic climate and Sri Lankan Freedom Party disarray.[96]

Choosing a general election date that coincided with strong government popularity was a time honored tradition in Great Britain and other Westminster Model systems. However the recently revised Constitution created problems. While the date of parliamentary elections could be moved up, the Executive President's term of office had been fixed at six years. Thus, Jayewardene could campaign for his party in a general election, but without any guarantee that he would remain head of state after the subsequent Presidential election. Moreover, the new proportional representation system increased the chances that his party might lose the general election, or only win with a small majority. UNP strategists and the President himself were convinced that maximum political advantage would be gained by holding the Presidential election first. Assuming that J.R. Jayewardene won convincingly, he would then be strongly positioned to campaign for UNP parliamentary candidates.[97]

Altering the length of the President's term required a Constitutional amendment, still an easy matter with the UNP's overwhelming majority. A potential obstacle was that the Supreme Court might judge the amendment to be a 'fundamental change,' requiring that a referendum be held. The justices' ruling (by a 4 to 3 vote) that no referendum was necessary cleared the way for phase one of the UNP's plan. J.R. Jayewardene's 76th birthday, 17 September 1982, was chosen as the auspicious date for nominations.[98] October 20 was set as the Presidential election date.

The Presidential campaigning and election results will be examined more fully in chapter 17. At this point, suffice it to say that the UNP strategy, combined with a vigorous campaign that left as little as possible to chance, was effective. Running against a relatively weak SLFP candidate, former Agriculture Minister Hector Kobbekaduwa, and several splinter candidates, Jayewardene triumphed with nearly 53 per cent of the vote. Only in Jaffna district were the results disappointing. There, as already noted, Jayewardene placed third behind Tamil Congress candidate Kumar Ponnambalam and Kobbekaduwa, with only 20 per cent of the vote. An uncharacteristically low voter turnout, only 44 per cent, was an additional signal of Tamil alienation.

With an additional six years in office assured, President Jayewardene now faced the prospect of imminent Parliamentary elections under the proportional representation system that the UNP had written into the 1978 Constitution. The goal of this system, readers will recall, was to make attaining the overwhelming majorities of the 1970 and 1977 Parliaments difficult or impossible. Arguing for proportional representation, UNP leaders had taken the principled stand that a parliamentary majority large enough to amend the Constitution should reflect broad national consensus, not the partisan goals of a single party.

Once in power, however, UNP leaders found the temptation to use Constitutional amendments for partisan purposes irresistible. Now it appeared that proportional representation would achieve its intended purpose in the upcoming general election, by returning 60 or more SLFP members and coalition partners to opposition benches. The UNP government would no longer be able to unilaterally amend the Constitution and its power to impose emergency regulations for an extended period of time would also be limited.

Faced with this prospect, President Jayewardene maneuvered to guarantee himself six more years of essentially one party government. He called for a popular referendum to extend the life of the current Parliament for an additional six years, rather than holding a general election. If a simple majority of the electorate approved the referendum, he could retain a five-sixth majority in Parliament, along with the power to amend Sri Lanka's Constitution. His generally sympathetic biographers termed this 'an adroit legal and Constitutional move, but one which paid little heed to the niceties of democratic politics.'[99] This was not the first time the life of a parliamentary majority had been extended. Readers will recall that Sirimavo Bandaranaike's government used a different constitutional stratagem to extend its term in office for two years (and was roundly denounced by the UNP for doing so). But the referendum violated Sri Lanka's well established tradition of regular, competitive elections It was viewed as a cynical self-serving move, even by some traditional UNP supporters.[100]

J.R. Jayewardene always used national security as the principal justification for calling a referendum rather than general election. He referred to intelligence information that a radical SLFP faction was plotting to assassinate the President, along with Anura Bandaranaike and senior government officials, to imprison Mrs. Bandaranaike, seize power and establish a military government. An SLFP victory, he argued, would fill the opposition benches with Naxalites (anarchists) whose goal would be to disrupt the work of his government.[101] Critics and supporters offered a variety of additional rationales including belief that a two-thirds majority would be necessary to complete a settlement with the Tamils, the need to impose a state of emergency to control militant violence,[102] concern that a less supportive parliament would derail the nation's growth strategy[103] and fear that a robust opposition might expose government misdeeds.[104]

Having committed themselves to the referendum, the President and other UNP strategists embarked on a no-holds-barred campaign strategy intended to guarantee a victory. Use of government power and resources placed the opposition, led by Mrs. Bandaranaike, at a severe disadvantage. Using its two-thirds majority, J.R. Jayewardene's government extended the State of Emergency that had been declared following the presidential election to cover not only the period prior to the referendum, but the 23 December polling date itself. Emergency regulations required government approval for public meetings; often partisanship intervened in the approval process. Displays of the 'lamp', symbolising a 'yes' vote, on public facilities were widespread, a blatant violation of the election laws. Orders from the Inspector General of Police to remove illegal displays were ignored. Some citizens who complained to the police were harassed by thugs and even detained under emergency regulations. Sri Lanka's police had long been vulnerable to political pressure. During the run up to the referendum, they appeared to tolerate widespread violations of the law, so long as the perpetrators were government supporters.

The campaign to ensure a majority 'yes' vote reached a crescendo on election day, with systematic intimidation of voters, opposition poll watchers and election officials that far exceeded the sporadic outbreaks of thuggery in previous elections. Widespread impersonation of voters and violations of the secret ballot were reported to Sri Lanka's Commissioner of Elections. The most blatant *prima facie* evidence of possible vote fraud occurred in the electorates of Attanagala and Dompe, which had long been Bandaranaike Family strongholds. In the UNP's 1977 landslide, Mrs. Bandaranaike had still carried Attanagala by more than 10,000 votes, though Felix Dias Bandaranaike had lost in Dompe. Hector Kobbekaduwa had carried both electorates in the Presidential election. In the referendum, however, 'yes' won in Dompe by nearly 11,000 votes and in Attanagala by an improbable margin of more than 18,000 votes. Overall, the government won by a margin of 45 to 54 per cent, which was large for Sri Lankan national elections. The referendum lost in four Tamil majority districts, with a 90 per cent 'no' margin in Jaffna and in three of the four districts on the southwest coast. In his *Report on the First Referendum in Sri Lanka*, Sri Lanka's Commissioner of Elections concluded that '...some participants in the referendum are alleged to have thrown away every inhibition to the winds and behaved as if the law was not there...' and, further, that 'Some of the salutary features at elections, which had come be taken for granted, were conspicuous by their absence.'[105]

Democratic elections provide political feedback, intended to hold government leaders accountable for their performance. J.R. Jayewardene chose to deny Sri Lanka's voters an authentic opportunity to express their views. In totalitarian regimes and one party states this is taken for granted, but not in Sri Lanka. Whether the government's proposal would have won in a fair vote preceded by a fair campaign is difficult to say. But observers of Sri Lankan politics and government are virtually unanimous in concluding that the referendum not only eroded J.R. Jayewardene's reputation but the faith of ordinary Sri Lankans in their political institutions and the rule of law. Political scientist C.R. de Silva concluded the Constitution was now seen not as fundamental law, but an instrumental device, to be manipulated by politicians for their advantage.[106] A Sri Lanka Civil Rights Movement publication later concluded that disrespect for the law, engendered by the referendum, contributed to the widespread anti-Tamil rioting in July 1983.[107] This view is widely shared.[108]

Political patronage, corruption and loss of legitimacy

After a half year of intensive political activity and two national elections, UNP leaders had achieved their goal: six more years of power with a five-sixth parliamentary majority. Now they hoped to return to a 'business as usual' mode. At the top of President Jayewardene's priority list were the Mahaweli project, cabinet reorganisation and improving Sinhalese-Tamil relations by tinkering with the District Development Councils. Electoral politics too, remained on the agenda, with nationwide local government elections and 18 parliamentary by-elections scheduled for May. The President's new term began officially on 4 February. A large crowd assembled in Colombo for a tradition-breaking public swearing in, but there was none of the spontaneous, enthusiastic outpouring that had welcomed J.R. Jayewardene in 1977.[109]

Observers of Sri Lanka's public mood following the referendum speak of widespread 'disillusionment and demoralisation,'[110] of bitter feelings and a sense of injustice.[111] Even UNP supporters acknowledged that government performance, despite successes, had fallen far short of promises to rule righteously and transform Sri Lanka into a righteous society. Many benefited from open economy reforms, but some were worse off and the gap between rich and poor had widened. 'Business as usual' politics, including thuggery and use of state power for partisan purposes, had characterised the first six years of UNP rule.

Following the catastrophic breakdown of law and order that occurred in July of 1983, scholars would point to a climate of government-sanctioned corruption and lawlessness as major contributing factors. Among the specific accusations levelled were targeting UNP supporters for government benefits and services, use of public positions for private gain, increased use of thuggery against political opponents, politicisation of the police force and, finally, subverting Sri Lanka's tradition of fair elections in the December 1982 referendum. An examination of political leadership during the July 1977-July 1983 period would not be complete without examining whether corruption and disrespect for the rule of law were significantly greater than under previous administrations.

In Sri Lanka, political leaders of both major parties acknowledge that their supporters receive preferential treatment from government when they are in power. Distributing benefits had been a major function of government since independence and the 'spoils system' is an accepted fact of Sri Lanka's political life. As government's economic role expanded, there was commensurate expansion in jobs and benefits that could be distributed to political supporters. One explanation of poor economic performance during the 1970-1977 period was that political loyalty often took priority over competence when hiring state sector managers. Under J.R. Jayewardene's government, development funds were controlled by influential cabinet members and flowed disproportionately to their districts. Benefits from village level rural development projects, such as Prime Minister Premadasa's 'Housing a Nation Program, typically went to individuals with UNP ties.[112] Loss of patronage was one reason top ministers opposed giving District Development Councils real power so strongly.

Political patronage had always opened the door to government jobs. In a society where unemployment rates for the young often exceeded 20 per cent, this was one reason political campaigns were so hard fought. Two UNP innovations linked political power and jobs even more overtly. First was the *Job Bank Scheme* for unemployed persons who were socially and economically underprivileged.[113] When President Jayewardene inaugurated this in 1978, he described it as an impartial system intended to eliminate past abuses, including political patronage. However those who sought Job Bank application forms discovered they were only available from members of parliament, with the lion's share being given to UNP members.[114] The political patronage practice known as the 'chit system' was also refined. For a number of years it had been common practice for MPs to provide chits (recommendations) to supporters seeking government jobs; normally a chit was required for employment, but at least a thin facade of impartiality had been maintained. The UNP government was to first to formalise this practice by authorising each of its MPs to make 1,000 appointments at the lower levels (peons, hospital workers, chauffeurs, etc.).[115] Even the upper ranks of the civil service were by now completely politicised. Not only recruitment, but specific postings were controlled by political appointees. Civil servants who refused political requests could anticipate demotion and banishment to 'outstation' assignments. Political intervention, even in relatively routine administrative processes, become a common practice. Some members of the judiciary still retained their independence, but only by standing firm against political pressures to which they were subjected.[116]

The pervasiveness of outright corruption – use of government positions for personal financial gain – is more difficult to document. Huge expenditures on development and large contracts to be let offered greater opportunities for corruption. Sri Lanka's first generation of political leaders after independence had included many independently wealthy men, but this was much less true in 1977. Some young men were now choosing politics as a career not only to exercise power but to accumulate capital.[117] Civil servants, whose salaries had been eroded by inflation and who saw the widening gap between their standard of living and those working in the private sector, also had strong motivations to step over the line. Some public officials, both elected and career 'indulged in conspicuous consumption far beyond their means.'[118] Others were accused of underworld ties.[119] No accusations of personal corruption were ever levelled against President Jayewardene, but the belief that he winked at corrupt practices of close associates was widespread. He did little to dispel this belief.[120]

Use of intimidation and violence by government-allied thugs was an even more serious problem. Respected Sinhalese anthropologist, Gananath Obeyesekere, documents thuggish activities during J.R. Jayewardene's early years in power in a compelling essay, 'The Origins and Institutionalisation of Political Violence'. Attacks on anti-government groups and meetings are the primary incidents reported, but he also describes assaults on opposition politicians and even a demonstration against Supreme Court justices who had rendered a decision government leaders did not like. Reportedly, UNP National

Workers Organisation (JSS) members were key participants in many of these attacks and demonstrations. Gangs with ties to individual ministers also played a role in some.[121] In Obeyesekere's view, these incidents exhibited a pattern that suggested government involvement at high levels.[122]Most disturbing was how frequently the police failed to come when called, stood idly by while attacks and demonstrations were in progress and in some cases appeared to be on the side of the perpetrators. This seemed to send a message to potentially lawless elements that violence would be tolerated, perhaps even encouraged, so long as government opponents were targeted. The message to police constables of lower rank was the same.[123] Many Sri Lankans now believed the law would not be enforced even-handedly. Widespread violations of election laws, thuggery and voter fraud during the referendum campaign and on polling day reinforced this view.

Government opponents, too, came to rely more on violent tactics, though for different reasons. In their case, pessimism rather than truculence was the motivation. Following the UNP's referendum victory, demoralised government opponents easily could conclude that Sri Lanka was moving irrevocably toward a one-party state, the model operating in several Southeast Asian nations that J.R. Jayewardene admired.[124] His government had created a strong presidency, manipulated the constitution to serve political goals, deprived the leading opposition leader of her civic rights and finally orchestrated a highly suspect procedure to secure an additional six years of unfettered power. Many wondered if there would be another truly free election Sri Lanka or if opposition parties would be in a sufficiently strong position to contest it. This prospect of endless years 'in the wilderness' loomed at a time when the government was, as we have seen, expanding political patronage and when charges of corruption were given wide credence.[125] In the past those who saw themselves shut out from the benefits government provided could hope that the next election would change things. This had been the pattern since independence. Now it appeared that traditional political processes might no longer be sufficient to change political leaders, policies, and the recipients of government largess.

16
The Open Economy –
Promises and Performance

In 1977, the potentially adverse social and political consequences of structural adjustment were less well understood than today. Just as Sri Lankan socialists believed central planning would allocate resources more efficiently and fairly, UNP reformers believed open economy policies would simultaneously promote economic expansion and well-being of the poor. In Sri Lanka, as in many other developing nations, these expectations proved false.

After six years of scarcities, stagnant incomes and high unemployment, Sri Lankans seemed ready for the economic reforms that J.R. Jayewardene's campaign had promised. But this did not mean universal support for the more painful aspects of structural adjustment. Inefficient state enterprises targeted for competition or privatisation provided employment. Food, transport and health care subsidies that were running the economy into the ground benefited many. A complex intermingling of the public and private sector, resulting from years of government interventions was not easy to unravel.[1] Entitlement programs were compatible with Buddhist Karmic law, which emphasises sharing as a source of merit in subsequent lives. Reforms emphasising individualism and entrepreneurship were viewed by some as threats to Sri Lanka's traditional values.[2]

A central theme of the government's first budget message – that a just and free society required a just and free economy – was intended to respond to this concern. J.R. Jayewardene's government promised capitalism with a Buddhist face. Broad goals differed little from previous messages: economic growth, revitalisation of industry and agriculture, new employment opportunities for youth and an improved balance of payments.[3] However, the proposed strategy for attaining these goals was fundamentally different. Between 1958 and 1977 most government planners viewed free markets as impediments to rational development. Now, policy documents and government propaganda emphasised how market mechanisms would be the key to attaining development goals.[4]

Promises and programs

Specific reforms were designed to open Sri Lanka's economy to global trade, stimulate investment, allow private enterprises to compete with state-controlled ones and supplant bureaucratic distribution mechanisms with free markets. The state monopoly on imports was reduced to a few key commodities and most other import controls were eliminated.[5] To make credit more readily available, state-owned banks were directed to expand branch banking in rural areas. Foreign banks were encouraged to compete in Sri Lanka. Fourteen new foreign banks commenced operations between 1979 and 1982. The government increased funds to existing development finance institutions and founded a new National Development Bank of Sri Lanka.[6] It eliminated the dual exchange rate and allowed the value of the rupee to float. Duties on some basic consumer goods—rice, wheat, full-cream milk, pharmaceuticals and fish—were reduced to zero. Both personal and corporate income taxes were reduced and the tax structure was simplified. Restrictions on foreign employment were lifted and a growing number of Sri Lankans began to seek positions in the Middle East.[7] To make domestic labour markets more attractive to investors, the government cracked down on labour unrest.

UNP leaders did not believe that regulatory reforms and liberalised credit would be sufficient to catalyse economic growth. Massive publicly funded capital expenditures on agriculture, industry, housing and infrastructure were also projected. These were intended to eliminate infrastructure bottlenecks that had stifled productivity and discouraged foreign investment. Planners theorised that government capital investments would increase productivity and stimulate consumption, thus increasing private-sector profitability. Increased profitability would complement incentives that had been put in place to attract investment.[8] Thus they saw no contradiction between the open economy philosophy and a larger government role in capital formation.

Grants of foreign aid and loans from foreign donors were the only feasible sources for the massive funding this strategy required. Donors required plans to justify expenditures, so policy makers who had campaigned against centralised economic planning had to frame detailed planning documents of their own. Sri Lanka's new *Public Investment Program* included a macroeconomic planning model, sectional development strategies and projected allocations for individual projects over a five year period.[9]

Three lead projects, Mahaweli irrigation and power generation, free trade zones and housing construction, were given top priority.[10] To ensure that economic development remained at centre stage and to improve co-ordination, President Jayewardene gave the Ministry of Plan Implementation increased powers and retained the portfolio himself. A new and more powerful Ministry of Finance and Planning was created by combining ministries that had previously divided these functions. Development Secretaries were named in all of the ministries concerned with development. These men met weekly to co-ordinate the work of their ministries, target key policy issues and make recommendations to the cabinet.[11] These changes confirmed development as the government's top priority.

The Accelerated Mahaweli Development Project

The massive 'accelerated' Mahaweli River hydroelectric and irrigation project came to symbolise both strengths and shortcomings of the UNP government's development strategy. Strengths were the ability to mobilise resources and expertise for initiatives that produced quick, highly visible results. Shortcomings were waste, neglect of longer-term social impacts, failure to deliver promised benefits to poor Sri Lankans and heightening of ethnic tensions.

We already encountered the Mahaweli river development scheme in chapters 9 and 12. Jayewardene's government inherited a master plan that projected completion of irrigation, hydroelectric, land development and resettlement projects over a 30 year time frame. Increased employment, self-sufficiency in rice and a more highly industrialised economy were among the multiple benefits envisioned.[12] Gamini Dissanayake, named to head up the project, was one of his most energetic and trusted Cabinet members.

Both Dissanayake and the President soon came to view the incremental development strategy set forth in the master plan's 30-year timetable as an impediment to their larger vision – making Sri Lanka Asia's next free market success story within their six-year term in office. 'Why not begin construction of the major dams and reservoirs all at once, rather than building them one at a time?' they queried engineers and planners at the project's headquarters. 'Why not begin tshe construction of irrigation works and the infrastructure for settlement schemes simultaneously rather than waiting for dams and reservoirs to be completed first?' At a pivotal meeting with senior project staff, Jayewardene is reported to have asked each participant: 'Can't you do this in six years? Why 30 years?' 'If you give us the money and equipment,' the staff members replied, 'we have the ability to do it.'[13]

Once convinced that 'accelerating' the project's timetable from 30 to six years was feasible, Jayewardene and Dissanayake moved quickly to marshal the political support and financial backing that would be needed to implement their plans. Cabinet approval was secured quickly for the accelerated timetable and for new organisations that would reflect Mahaweli's top priority.[14]

Though some World Bank and donor governments expressed reservations, Dissanayake and Finance Minister Ronnie de Mel, with personal help from the President, were highly successful in raising foreign capital. A combination of factors made the Mahaweli project an attractive prospect. Sri Lanka was already known as a development 'success story' and in 1978, was seen as a resilient democracy that had rejected socialism, moved toward closer ties with the West and voluntarily initiated free market reforms. Mahaweli was shrewdly marketed as a concrete, highly visible 'landmark' that would be the centrepiece of new successes. During the five-year period between 1978 and 1985, Sri Lanka would receive nearly 20 billion rupees (roughly one billion US dollars) in aid and loans for Mahaweli.[15] By the end of 1979, construction of two dams, as well as other works, was already in progress. In 1982, work on damming the last of the four major reservoirs commenced.[16] Mahaweli became one of the largest development projects in the world.

To what degree did the project achieve its ambitious goals and to what degree was it a development success? From an engineering standpoint, the strategy of building four large dams simultaneously was at least a qualified success. In August 1986, eight years after President Jayewardene's momentous decision, waters of all four reservoirs had been impounded, four of the five dams had been commissioned and two hydropower-generating facilities were in full operation. By 1988 all four were operational, though some nagging technical problems remained. Some analysts estimated that by the early 1990s, Sri Lanka had recovered the project's full costs in energy savings alone.[17] Benefits from industrial development, made possible by the availability of plentiful hydropower, added to the positive side of the ledger. In contributing to another project goal, self-sufficiency in rice production, Mahaweli is also counted a success. As the 1980s ended, Sri Lanka was meeting about 90 per cent of its domestic needs for rice, contrasted with 40 per cent in the 1950s. About 30 per cent of the island's irrigated lands were now supplied by the Mahaweli project. Mahaweli proponents maintain that given availability of foreign assistance, Sri Lanka could hardly afford not to undertake the project.

Though Mahaweli greatly strengthened Sri Lanka's agricultural and industrial infrastructure in a short period of time, there were major criticisms. Most common was that the government simply tried to do too much too fast, producing a broad spectrum of adverse impacts. Constructing four dams simultaneously meant that managerial talent was stretched to the limit, co-ordination sometimes broke down, and there was little opportunity to learn from experience.[18]

Meeting targets of an accelerated timetable also required capital-intensive methods and large numbers of expatriate workers. This inflated costs and caused the project to fall far short of optimistic projections for employment generation.[19] Sri Lankan professionals and local residents resented the influx of highly paid (and sometimes culturally insensitive) expatriates who were viewed as taking jobs that rightfully belonged to Sri Lankans. Massive inflows of foreign funds and lucrative contracts let without competitive bidding, coupled with weak accountability mechanisms, created obvious opportunities for favouritism, kickbacks and other corrupt practices. Further inflows of foreign funds created inflationary pressures that made it difficult for Finance Minister de Mel to keep the economy from overheating. Inflation, fiscal indiscipline and cost overruns escalated rupee expenditures on Mahaweli by more than 300 per cent over 1978 estimates.[20]

The high priority given to building physical infrastructure was not matched by attention to creating a strong social infrastructure in the newly settled areas. The need to build strong communities was particularly urgent because new settlers came from diverse regions and backgrounds (even though virtually all were Sinhalese). Strong farmer organisations were important for the co-ordination necessary to efficiently manage irrigated land. Initially, a commitment to building grass-roots-level participatory farmers organisations had been part of the Mahaweli plan, but the strong push to complete irrigation works quickly, predispositions of top managers and political considerations soon eroded this commitment.

Administrative regions within the project region were faced with the same problems of centralised administration controlled by bureaucrats clinging tenaciously to power that plagued local-level development throughout Sri Lanka. To cite one example, lack of co-ordination between agricultural extension staff and water management staff meant that farmers could be directed to plant rice without any assurance that sufficient irrigation water would be available.

Often, there was no single individual to whom they could turn to resolve such problems.[21] An emphasis on high technology farming and the type of assistance government agencies provided favoured the better educated more entrepreneurial farmers.[22] The gap between rich and poor soon widened in the settlement areas, increasing the potential for social unrest among people whose community ties were still very weak.

How Mahaweli development priorities and settlement schemes helped escalate ethnic tensions has already been outlined. Tamils viewed development priorities favouring Sinhalese majority regions as one more example of preferential treatment given to the majority community. They viewed settlement schemes (called 'colonisation schemes' by Tamils) as a calculated attack by Sinhalese politicians on Tamil numerical dominance in the 'traditional homelands.' Ethnic tensions created by the Mahaweli project had national implications, as we have already seen, and also heightened tensions in the Eastern Province. President Jayewardene anticipated that distribution of benefits from successful economic development would help mute ethnic and class tensions. In the case of Mahaweli, political considerations shaped a development strategy that heightened tensions before benefits could be realised.

Agricultural policies and programs

While the accelerated Mahaweli Project was given top priority, J.R. Jayewardene's government could not ignore the depressed state of Sri Lanka's agricultural sector outside of the Mahaweli region. In the all-important rice producing sector, Jayewardene's government inherited productivity problems, alienated farmers and a marketing-distribution system in need of fundamental overhaul. Longer-term problems of a traditional smallholder agricultural sector that had frustrated reformers for decades remained: primitive technologies, high risks for producers, bureaucratically encumbered land tenures, widespread poverty and the persistence of semi-feudal social-economic relations.[23] Sri Lanka's tea, rubber and coconut plantations, on which the nation still depended for foreign exchange, were in dire need of recapitalisation after nearly a decade of deferred maintenance and replantings. Complex, overstaffed bureaucracies needed streamlining by new management teams that would give productivity priority over politics.

Since the UNP, too, had its cadre of loyalists who anticipated government posts as a fruit of victory, privatisation and reform in agriculture would not be an easy task. In fact, reforms faced many of the same obstacles that impeded attempts to strengthen farmer organisations in the Mahaweli region and to grant local governments greater autonomy throughout the island. It was easy to make policy pronouncements and propose ambitious plans in Colombo. Implementation was another matter.

The UNP's strategy combined new market-friendly initiatives with more traditional farmer assistance programs. To lure investors, tax incentives were established for those willing to put funds into agriculture and agribusiness. Emphasis was given to non-traditional exports, livestock, fisheries, processed dairy products and sugar processing. Assistance programs for individual farmers included the expansion of rural credit, largely unsuccessful attempts to expand crop insurance coverage and new price incentives for shifting land to the production of subsidiary food crops.[24] The government expanded grants to increase productivity through more intensive fertilisation and use of improved seed strains. It encouraged diversified production schemes, including fruits and vegetables for export, and traditional handicrafts.

Agricultural reforms achieved their greatest successes in rice production. Between 1977 and 1983, annual output rose by nearly 50 per cent, from 1.68 to 2.48 million metric tons. Surprisingly, this increase occurred before the government's massive investments in land development and irrigation had a significant impact. Sri Lanka's farmers responded to improved market conditions by making more effective use of fertiliser and improved seed varieties that government extension services encouraged. The gradual reduction in the value of government price supports had little impact. Creating a competitive market and replacing the rice ration with food stamps for the needy had significantly reduced the government's role. In 1985, the once all-powerful Paddy Marketing Board purchased only four per cent of total rice production.[25] Sri Lanka was at last on the road toward achieving the goal that had eluded every post-independence government prior to 1977: self-sufficiency in rice.

The three major plantation crops remained a top priority. In 1977, overseas sales from the plantation sector provided nearly 75 per cent of export income, with tea alone comprising more than 50 per cent of the total. Ensuring that the industrial sector contributed more to export earnings was a major goal of the UNP's open economy program. In the interim, however, it was important to restore the plantations to health. Here, too, government initiatives to reverse recent downward trends experienced problems. Attempts to recapitalise the plantations and improve their efficiency were complicated by volatile export markets, the resistance of plantation smallholders to change, an ongoing need to divert foreign exchange earnings to other priorities and political resistance to unravelling a complex web of plantation sector bureaucracies.

As a result of United Front land confiscations, public officials directly managed more than two thirds of tea production, about a third of rubber production and about 10 per cent of coconut production. The remainder was in smallholdings that had fallen below the 1972 Land Reform Act's 50-acre threshold. According to his biographers, President Jayewardene had initially planned to reduce political influence over plantation agriculture by privatising management responsibilities, while retaining state ownership. A number of agencies that had formerly owned estates seemed receptive, but top UNP politicians who would have lost power under this plan opposed it fiercely and ultimately prevailed.[26]

For the most part, government reorganisations and new programs failed to reverse declining trends, though there were modest improvements in maintenance and replantings. Sri Lanka's smallholder producers and bureaucratically encumbered plantations found it increasingly difficult to respond to stiff international competition. The volume of tea and rubber production remained at or below 1977 levels, though coconut production rose in response to strong domestic demand. Stagnant production and the inability to reduce production costs meant that plantation sector foreign exchange earnings were highly sensitive to fluctuations in world market prices. Thus, inflation adjusted earnings from tea increased by nearly 70 per cent in the boom year of 1978, but dropped back to 1977 levels in 1981. In the 'bust' years of 1982 and 1983 earnings from tea were 29 per cent and 20 per cent below 1977 levels. Earnings from the plantation sector as a whole increased by 80 per cent in 1978, but also fell significantly below 1977 levels in 1982 and 1983. By the end of President Jayewardene's second term in 1988, inflation adjusted export earnings from the plantation sector were less than 80 per cent of their 1977 levels.[27]

Housing and urban development

Prime Minister Premadasa's housing and urban development programs represented the government's second largest capital investment. Adjusting for inflation, nearly three billion rupees, about one-fourth of Mahaweli expenditures, were spent during President Jayewardene's first term. In housing and urban development the government's primary role was direct intervention, rather than stimulating the private sector. Indeed, the program's rhetoric and philosophy were similar in many respects to initiatives that had been proposed by United Front leaders after their 1970 victory. Primary responsibility for housing construction was given to the newly created National Housing Development Authority. The agency's six programs included subsidised construction of new houses, upgrading of 'slums and shanties', low-cost construction loans and 'Aided Self-Help Rural Housing.' Private sector firms were offered incentives to participate. The program catalysed a construction boom, seriously straining the island's supply and distribution system for building materials.

Aided Self-Help Rural Housing, which was combined with a program of 'Village Awakening' (*Gam Udawa*) proved to be by far the most productive and cost effective. National Housing Development Authority staff members, often with Premadasa's direct involvement, selected villages to receive building supplies and technical assistance. The villagers themselves did most of the housing construction. In addition to housing construction, funds were provided for village infrastructure, including tubewells, public buildings and in some instances, electrification. Larger villages might be given a clock tower, said to symbolise the Prime Minister's strivings to make punctuality a norm in Sri Lankan culture. The philosophy of *Sarvodaya Shramadana*, a movement founded upon Buddhist principles of moral regeneration and community building through shared labour and self help, influenced the program.[28] Village Awakening's philosophy harked back to an idealised view of rural life in the era of the great Sinhalese kings as 'virtuous, co-operative and free from exploitation and discrimination.'[29]

Paradoxically, Premadasa's housing and urban development programs, which were peripheral to the open economy policy, came closest to achieving their goals during the UNP's first term. In contrast to Mahaweli, housing construction required neither technological sophistication, nor imported materials, nor foreign expertise. The energetic Prime Minister skilfully mobilised resources from outside his own ministry and from the private sector. He recognised quickly the cost effectiveness of self-help construction programs and shifted priorities in that direction. Despite funding cutbacks beginning in 1981, more than 50,000 new houses had been completed by December 1982, with many more under construction. By the end of 1984, data from the Local Government Ministry showed that the 'impossible' 100,000 house target had not only been attained, but surpassed. The programs were politically cost effective as well. Prime Minister Premadasa developed a formidable political base in rural Sri

Lanka and *Gam Udawa* villages, distributed throughout the Sinhalese majority areas of the island, came to symbolise a tangible government commitment to the rural poor.

There were also shortcomings, however, as an in-depth study of a single *Gam Udawa* village, Kukulewa,[30] by anthropologist James Brow emphasises. The problems of political favouritism he identifies resemble those that complicated grass-roots participation schemes in newly opened Mahaweli Areas. The Kukulewa programs' principal beneficiaries were village leaders affiliated with the UNP and their supporters: All of the 60 newly constructed houses were given to them. The unintended though foreseeable social impact was the polarisation of the village into bitter, resentful pro-and anti-UNP factions. Since the housing program, like most government programs, was used to reward loyal political supporters, there is good reason to believe that the pattern seen in Kukulewa was repeated in many *Gam Udawa* villages.

The Urban Development Authority was responsible for Prime Minister Premadasa's urban revitalisation program, with its combined goals of urban renewal and economic development. Economic growth would be stimulated, planners argued, by targeting major urban commercial areas for revitalisation. Using an integrated approach that combined urban renewal with housing construction, Premadasa hoped to ensure that poor families displaced by projects would improve their standard of living rather than becoming homeless. He had used this approach successfully in his highly urbanised Colombo Central constituency as an up-and-coming UNP politician.

Some projects did conform to the Authority's original concept. These included the refurbishing of Colombo's Central City Market, plus city-centre renewals in Galle, Jaffna, Kandy and some other regional centres. Often these were combined with slum and shanty upgrading.[31] However, by far the most ambitious project had little to do with either centre city revitalisation or economic development. This was the creation of a new governmental complex at Kotte, on the site of the fifteenth century capital city of Sri Jayewardanapura, about seven miles from Colombo. Included were governmental offices, plus residential zones, parks, gardens, a sports stadium, a 1,001-bed hospital, and other amenities. The project's showpiece was a spectacular parliamentary complex designed by Sri Lanka's premier architect, Geoffrey Bawa. The Parliament's setting, on an island in the midst of a small lake, was not only picturesque but also secure from public demonstrations that had sometimes engulfed the old Parliament building. More than one-third of the funds allocated for housing and urban development during President Jayewardene's first term were spent on this project, which was both praised for its physical beauty and questioned because of its high cost. One critic observed: 'Do we really need a five star Parliament?'[32]

Investment promotion and industrial development

While Mahaweli development, housing and urban revitalisation consumed the largest shares of government capital spending, investment promotion and industrialisation emphasising export-oriented industries were the heart of President Jayewardene's economic philosophy. His goal was to transform entrenched attitudes that viewed Sri Lanka's capitalist entrepreneurs as enemies of the people and repatriation of profits from foreign investments as a form of imperialism.[33]

Confidence boosting measures were needed first to reassure would-be investors, both domestic and foreign, that their assets would be protected, that their activities would be relatively free from regulation and that reasonable rates of return would be permitted. The removal of price controls on most manufactured products sold locally was among the first initiatives. Public sector investment in new industrial ventures was slowed or halted. Both individual and corporate tax rates were reduced. Publicly traded companies were exempted from capital gains taxes. To attract investment in export-oriented industries, the government offered tax concessions, security guarantees for investments, exemption from some export duties and relaxed foreign exchange controls. New Foreign Currency Banking Units were authorised to offer 'offshore' bank accounts to non-residents and some foreign concerns.[34]

Many of these policies were brought together in the newly established Greater Colombo Economic Commission, which was given authority to create Export Processing Zones in a 160 square mile area between Colombo and the international airport. The Commission's export promotion program was designated as a top priority 'lead project.' They planned to begin by attracting garment firms that would employ unskilled labour. Concurrently, improvements in zone infrastructures would attract electronic assembly plants and other 'high tech' factories.[35] Promotions touted Sri Lanka's labour force as docile, highly educated and willing to work for some of the lowest wages in South Asia.[36]

How successful were the new incentive schemes in luring private investors? Disinvestment of foreign capital during the United Front years made improvement in this area easier. Foreign sources averaged about 27 per cent of private capital formation between 1978 and 1982, rising to a high point of 46 per cent in 1980 and 1982. The bulk of these contributions, however, were in the form of loans rather than direct investment. Foreign direct investment comprised only 30 per cent of total foreign contributions and only eight per cent of private capital spending. Thus, most foreign investors chose to hedge their bets on Sri Lanka's industrial development. With many attractive opportunities available for their funds, they were awaiting solid evidence that President Jayewardene's open economy policies would deliver promised results.

During Jayewardene's first term, the industrial sector achieved mixed results. Between 1977 and 1981, the value of industrial output grew by nearly 80 per cent, but deteriorating terms of trade produced a 35 per cent decline in 1982 and a further decline in 1983. Capacity utilisation, which had hovered around 50 per cent during the United Front years, rose to about 75 per cent. Data on value added, however, which takes into account an increased dependence in imported raw materials, reveals that these indicators of a strengthened industrial sector were somewhat illusory.[37] Value added as a per cent of total industrial output (a very rough measure of productivity and efficiency) declined by nearly 20 per cent during the first five years of the open economy program. Thus, while there was considerably more activity in the industrial sector, the economic viability of many industries was still suspect.

Nowhere was this truer than in the massive state sector, a United Front legacy that proved resistant to reform. In 1977, the 26 State Corporations represented more that 60 per cent of Sri Lanka's industrial output, ranging from petroleum products and fertiliser to ayurvedic drugs and coconut whiskey (Arrack). Political control over Post and Telecommunications, the Ceylon Government Railways, and the Sri Lanka Transport Board (busses) was more direct and intrusive. A few state-run businesses were profitable, but most required both capital and operating subsidies. Wider availability of imported goods after 1977 made shortcomings in management and product quality more apparent.[38]

UNP pre-election promises to sell off state industries to private investors were blocked by political resistance, especially from Minister of Industries and Scientific Affairs Cyril Mathew.[39] Instead, the more modest goal of making state industries commercially viable, while gradually eliminating government subsidies, was set. Progress in attaining this goal was incremental at best, impacted as much by international market forces as by domestic policies. Between

1977 and 1982, state corporation employment dropped from about 75,000 to about 65,000 workers, but overall the corporations lost more than 500 million rupees in 1982, by far the worst record posted since President Jayewardene assumed office.[40] Despite these losses, however, government subsidies to state industries were reduced by about 75 per cent.

The telecommunications monopoly, directly administered by a government ministry, exemplified a state-sector enterprise that failed to achieve commercial viability during the first five years of open economy policies.[41] Scarce and unreliable telephone service continued to be an impediment to doing business efficiently in Sri Lanka.[42] In 1977, Sri Lanka had only about 45,000 telephone lines, with more than 21,000 potential customers waiting for service. By 1982, the number of installed lines had increased by more than 50 per cent, however more than 28,000 customers waited for service. International telex connections had increased from a scant 182 in 1977 to 853, but 250 applicants were on the waiting list. With demand exceeding supply so greatly, political connections, more often than not, played a key role in securing telephone and telex connections. Sri Lanka Telecomm posted a loss of more than 22,500,000 rupees in 1982.

International trade and finance

Accelerating demand for telex connections was just one manifestation of an economy that was becoming more outward looking, as the Jayewardene government dismantled the United Front import-substitution industrialisation policies. Export promotion, trade liberalisation and currency reforms were intended to spur economic growth by linking Sri Lanka more closely with an expanding, diversifying global economy.[43] As in other areas, implementation of these policies produced mixed results. This was due to tensions between long and short-term objectives, constraints on change imposed by political realities, fluctuations in international markets and political leaders' inability to fully control (or even predict) economic behaviour.

As we have seen, President Jayewardene's new government immediately showed its commitment to reform by reducing tariffs on 'essential goods'– rice, wheat flour and drugs – to zero. Import quotas, and the licensing bureaucracies responsible for enforcing them, were eliminated. However, the new policies fell far short of 'free trade,' since providing local industries with 'reasonable protection' competed with liberalisation as a policy objective. The result was a complex scheme of six tariff categories in which many rates remained unchanged from the United Front era. Duties on raw materials and some technologies ranged from five to 25 per cent, while imports of goods in other categories still faced charges of 50 per cent or more.[44] A Presidential Tariff Review Commission[45] was given power to adjust rates in response to specific requests for protection or liberalisation. This added additional complexity, while offering opportunities for political intervention.

Open economy policies achieved their greatest success in expanding industrial exports, which increased in value by nearly 250 per cent between 1977 and 1982. Overall, the percentage of Sri Lanka's exports represented by industrial products rose from 14 to an astonishing 40 per cent. For the first time, industrial exports surpassed tea in revenues. Unfortunately, the major contributors to this growth were overseas sales of textiles and petro-chemical fertilisers, both relatively low value-added products that depended heavily on imported materials.

On the negative side of the balance sheet, Sri Lanka's international financial position was buffeted by highly unfavourable trends in international markets. Two years after President Jayewardene assumed office, the price of imported petroleum more than tripled its 1977 value and a bushel of wheat more than doubled in price. Between 1978 and 1981, the cost of imported rice fluctuated between 160 and 200 per cent of its 1977 level. While international market prices of tea, rubber and coconuts also rose, until dropping in 1982, these increases were insufficient to compensate for the higher costs of goods that Sri Lanka needed to buy.

The aggregate impact of international market price fluctuations was a precipitous 45 per cent deterioration in Sri Lanka's terms of trade between 1977 and 1982. By 1982, the island nation's economy needed to sell almost twice as many export products in order to receive the same volume of imports purchased in 1977. But rising demand for foodstuffs, construction materials, petroleum products and consumer goods, coupled with rising prices had ballooned Sri Lanka's import bill to nearly four times its 1977 value. Sri Lanka was able to cover only half of its import bill with revenues from exports. In 1977 Sri Lanka had a positive trade balance of more than 10 per cent. External assets, the reserves of foreign exchange available to purchase imports, had shown healthy growth in 1978 and 1979, but then fell by more than 40 per cent in a single year. At the end of 1980, Sri Lanka's foreign reserves covered less than 11 weeks of imports.

Things would have been worse were it not for the additional foreign exchange provided by remittances from Sri Lankans working abroad, tourism and foreign aid. Nearly half of Sri Lanka's foreign currency earnings came from these sources between 1978 and 1982.[46] Sri Lanka's current account deficit averaged only about 55 per cent of its merchandise trade deficit between 1978 and 1982; prior to 1978 the current account deficit had often exceeded the trade deficit.[47]

The Jayewardene administration's liberalised emigration policies, coupled with labour shortages in booming Middle East and Southeast Asian economies, made possible the transfer of economically significant funds from temporarily employed workers to their families in Sri Lanka. Emigration for employment abroad grew from an insignificant number in 1976 to about 60,000 workers. The majority were female domestic workers and male unskilled labourers, however about 20 per cent were skilled craftsmen and nearly 10 per cent were professionals. Thus, open economy emigration policies contributed negatively to a skilled labour shortage that caused bottlenecks and inflated costs in the Mahaweli project. On the other hand, many emigrant workers would not have found any employment in Sri Lanka. By accepting positions abroad, they became an economic asset to their families and the nation, rather than a liability. By 1983, exchange earnings from foreign employment were greater than grants of foreign aid and exceeded earnings from exports of coconuts, rubber and gemstones combined. They were only slightly less than revenues from the sale of tea. Labour had become one of Sri Lanka's major exports.

Tourism, long an interest of J.R. Jayewardene, was another growing source of foreign exchange. Local and foreign investments increased the number of resort quality rooms available from about 4,500 to about 7,500 between 1977 and 1982. Travel to Sri Lanka was marketed more aggressively and the quality of tourist services improved. The island's beaches and historical sites became popular destinations, especially for Western Europeans. Tourist arrivals grew from about 153,000 to more than 400,000, while 'official' earnings from this sector increased by more than 300 per cent.[48] Tourism also became a major source of employment, adding more than 32,000 jobs to the economy.[49] Negative aspects of this picture included the high costs of imported goods necessary to maintain quality service, repatriation of profits from foreign investments[50] and occupancy rates averaging less than 55 per cent. Critics of the tourist trade pointed to the cultural insensitivity of many visitors along with rising levels of prostitution and venereal disease, especially in southwestern coastal resort areas. A growing gap in remuneration between tourist related businesses and government jobs fuelled resentment, made worse by the fact that knowledge of English was a prerequisite for the best paying jobs. But despite problems and resentments, promoting tourism continued to be a high priority and tourist hotels continued to attract foreign investors, with optimists predicting that arrivals would reach one million or more by the decade's end.

Foreign aid, the other major contributor to offsetting Sri Lanka's current account deficit has already been discussed in conjunction with the accelerated Mahaweli Development project and other capital spending. During President Jayewardene's first term in office, Sri Lanka received more foreign assistance per-capita than any other Global South country.[51] Project assistance, commodity loans and commodity assistance were given by the World Bank, the Asian Development Bank, the European Economic Community, the International Monetary Fund, the International Fund for Agricultural Development and numerous bilateral donors. More than 22 nations and organisations formed the Sri Lanka Aid group, which met periodically to co-ordinate funding efforts. Surprisingly, India was a member and loaned more than 300 million rupees for commodity purchases. The most generous bilateral donor was the United Kingdom, which provided nearly 4 billion rupees, entirely in the form of grants. Japan, the second largest bilateral donor, rewarded President Jayewardene for his landmark address at the San Francisco Peace Conference with about 3 billion rupees of assistance, about 25 per cent in grants. Not only did foreign aid make Sri Lanka's lead projects possible, it helped compensate for Sri Lanka's widening trade deficit and cushioned some of the worst hardships of structural adjustment.[52]

Sri Lanka's status as a favoured recipient of foreign assistance also had negative aspects. Between 1977 and 1982, funds were so plentiful that they could not be fully utilised according to agreed upon timetables.[53] The bottlenecks created by limited managerial talent and infrastructure in connection with the Mahaweli project extended to other areas as well. Massive infusions of funds inflated prices throughout the economy, but especially in the construction industry. There was also less pressure to use funds efficiently and hold contractors accountable for performance. As we have seen, many contracts were let without competitive bidding. Charges of corruption in projects supported by foreign assistance multiplied, further eroding the government's already tarnished reputation. The government became increasingly dependent on foreign funds for shorter-term budget needs as well as capital improvements. Like other forms of dependence, reliance on assistance, once established, was difficult to give up. As dependence increased, Sri Lanka's budgets became more beholden to prescriptions imposed by foreign donors.[54] To receive additional aid, the government was forced to cut politically popular social programs, such as food stamps and housing construction.

Most severe in its long-term implications was Sri Lanka's rising burden of foreign debt. In 1976, Sirimavo Bandaranaike's last full year in office, Sri Lanka's foreign debt was about 5 billion rupees ($US 590 million). By the end of 1982, it had increased to more than 35 billion rupees ($US 1.7 billion). Adjusted for inflation, Sri Lanka's obligations to foreign lenders had increased by nearly 150 per cent in less than seven years. Even more worrisome, the rate of indebtedness was increasing faster than income from imports or GNP as a whole.[55] Borrowing to capitalise infrastructure development projects was predicated on the assumption that such projects would catalyse a larger, more robust, more export-oriented economy, making the repayment of large loans possible. But the slump in economic growth, beginning in 1980, placed this assumption in doubt.

Government finance

The government's emphasis on capital investment meant that while reforms reduced bureaucratic economic controls, the government's overall economic role increased. Political commitments to simultaneously complete numerous major projects caused spending to balloon. In 1978 expenditures grew from 8.8 billion to 17.6 billion rupees, by far the largest budget increase since independence.[56] During Sirimavo Bandaranaike's second term, government spending averaged 31 per cent of gross national product. For 1978-82, it jumped to 39 per cent. In 1980, 43 per cent of all economic activity was government spending.

While spending grew, revenues lagged behind, creating a succession of increasingly severe deficits. In 1978, the first full year of open economy policies, deficit spending[57] jumped by more than 200 per cent, from 22 per cent to 36 per cent of expenditures. Since UNP policies emphasised massive investments to jump-start the economy and nearly two-thirds of the deficit was covered by foreign loans, this was not initially a matter of great concern. However, in subsequent years the problem grew worse, with current as well as capital expenditures contributing to deficits and domestic borrowing bearing an increasing share of the burden.[58]

Heavy borrowing combined with scarcities created by multiple development projects catalysed an unprecedented inflationary spiral.[59] Between 1977 and 1982, the rupee lost nearly two-thirds of its value and its exchange value on international markets dropped from about nine to more than 20 rupees per dollar. President Jayewardene's collegial, personalised governance style also contributed to high deficits.[60] An inter-ministerial committee of budget secretaries had been formed to warn the cabinet of budget overruns and recommend fiscal discipline, but recommendations were frequently ignored. The President preferred to work on budgets with individual cabinet members, making ad-hoc decisions in which political priorities often outweighed fiscal ones. It was not until 1980, when both spending and the deficit soared to new record highs, that stabilisation measures began to receive serious attention.[61] Modest tax increases and budget cuts produced some relief, but in 1981 the deteriorating trade balance began to drag both government revenues and the economy as a whole downward. In 1982, the deficit rose again.

Though the UNP government failed to bring spending or deficits under control, it did succeed in shifting priorities from short-term benefits to investment, something economists had long recommended. While overall government spending rose by 80 per cent, capital expenditures more than doubled. To achieve this, traditionally privileged areas received only modest increases, remained stagnant or were even cut.

Replacing food subsidies with food stamps produced the greatest budget savings, as well as substantial foreign exchange savings. Since stamps were denominated in rupees, rather than specific measures of rice and other commodities, the government was able to effect further savings by keeping increases in food stamp allocations to well below the level of inflation. These measures reduced the real value of food subsidy expenditures from nearly 2 billion rupees in 1978 to a scant 37 million in 1982. In this area, Jayewardene achieved a goal that had eluded him since he was a young cabinet minister in Dudley Senanayake's first government.

Spending on 'Social Services' for health and education remained stagnant in the face of rising demand.[62] Over its term, the UNP government allocated slightly more per year than its predecessor to this area, however the 1982 downturn pushed real values of social spending below 1977 levels. Another casualty was Sri Lanka's defence establishment, which saw its allocation fall from 2.5 per cent of government expenditures in 1977 to 1.4 per cent in 1982. The real value of the 1982 defence budget was 15 per cent below the relatively meagre allocation it had received in 1977. Thus, as the armed services faced increased demands to quell the ethnic unrest in the north they were given fewer resources to accomplish the task. While defence budgets shrank, spending on 'Civil Administration,' grew by 65 per cent and subsidies to Sri Lanka's notoriously unprofitable rail and bus transport services more than doubled.[63] These numbers suggest that military leaders had little political clout in the Jayewardene government.

The Jayewardene government's effort to shift spending priorities exhibits a mixed record. It was most successful in targeting newly available funds to new economic development priorities, but had difficulty slowing the momentum of spending when funds became scarcer. Where domestic and governmental constituencies lacked clout, it was able to hold spending below inflation and even impose cuts. But despite chronically rising deficits, the politically well endowed transport sector, public service sector and some state corporations successfully resisted budget cutting.

The task of keeping budgets in balance would have been easier if government receipts had not lagged so far behind spending. But in attempting to strengthen its revenue base, J.R. Jayewardene's government faced a conundrum. More than two-thirds of its income came from 'Taxes on Production and Expenditure'– import and export duties plus a general sales tax and a variety of other sales and turnover taxes. Such taxes targeted large, accessible revenue streams and were relatively easy to collect[64] but had two serious shortcomings. First, high production and expenditure tax rates tended to slow expansion in growth-promoting sectors that other open economy policies favoured. Import taxes raised prices of consumer goods and industrial materials. Export taxes raised prices of goods sold abroad and reduced exporters' profits. Sales taxes cut into demand; turnover taxes increased production costs. Sri Lanka's government was attempting to lure investors with tax concessions, but every concession reduced revenues and, at least in the short run, swelled the deficit. Thus, setting tax rates involved a difficult balancing act characterised by great uncertainty.

A second shortcoming of production and expenditure taxes, sensitivity to price-volatile international markets, complicated this balancing act still further.

As we have seen, Sri Lanka's import earnings were highly dependent on world market prices for tea, rubber and coconut. The profitability of its industrial sector and health of its economy, were increasingly dependent on world market prices for petroleum, industrial raw materials and intermediate products. When the terms of trade deteriorated, as they did precipitously between 1979 and 1982, the impact on tax revenues was severe. Sri Lanka's government experienced a six per cent decline in the real value of its revenues between 1980 and 1981 and an additional 19 per cent decline in 1982. Were it not for more than 3.3 billion rupees in foreign-aid grants, the real value of tax receipts would have been lower in 1982 than in 1977.

Faced with similar circumstances in November 1971, as readers will recall, Prime Minister Bandaranaike's government had pushed an austerity program through Parliament that deferred many United Front campaign pledges. In 1981 and 1982, Jayewardene rejected both austerity and tax increases. Instead, he opted for deficit financing, hoping that an election victory and continued adherence to open economy policies would be followed by better times ahead.

Deficit financing, however, was not a long-term solution to Sri Lanka's fiscal problems. By 1982, borrowing to cover three years of record deficits began to push Sri Lanka's public debt toward unsustainable levels. Adjusted for inflation, pubic debt grew from about 25 billion rupees in 1977 to 31.6 billion in 1982. This rate of growth was no higher than under the United Front, which also relied heavily on deficit financing. But two changes made things much worse. First, the percentage of debt held by foreign creditors nearly doubled, comprising 44 per cent of the total in 1982. Since massive capital development projects were financed with foreign loans, this was not surprising.

Second, in 1980, Sri Lanka's government also began covering more short-term obligations with foreign loans. Large foreign debts, especially those owed to commercial lenders, created yet another vicious cycle for the nation's beleaguered financial planners to address. Inflation of the rupee and the resultant deflation of its value against foreign currencies meant that the rupee value of foreign debts increased. As we have seen, Central Bank monetisation of domestic debt, coupled with large inflows of foreign funds, made it impossible to bring inflation under control. Reliance on foreign loans also placed Sri Lanka at the mercy of fluctuations in international interest rates. Steps taken by the U.S. Federal Reserve Board to bring inflation of the dollar under control contributed to a dramatic rise in those rates between 1977 and 1982.[65]

In combination, these factors pushed spending on debt service from eight per cent of government expenditures in 1978 to 14 per cent in 1982. By 1982, Sri Lanka's government was spending more on debt service than on all of its social and economic support programs. Even more worrisome, the percentage of government revenues that needed to be set aside for debt service had more than doubled from 11 per cent 1978 to 24 per cent in 1982. Debt service now comprised nearly 38 per cent of the annual budget deficit. If adverse trends continued, Sri Lanka would soon be faced with the prospect of taking out new foreign-currency loans simply to make payments on existing debts.

Appraisal

J.R. Jayewardene's government quickly demonstrated its ability to raise foreign funds, shift priorities from consumption to investment and implement modest regulatory reforms. But this did not guarantee that public sector projects would meet targeted goals nor that Sri Lanka's private sector would become more productive and competitive. Like its predecessors, the UNP leadership achieved its greatest successes in areas over which the government could exercise direct control – constructing houses, government buildings, dams, power plants and irrigation works. Where success required participation from domestic entrepreneurs and foreign private investors, achievements were more modest. Nor was Jayewardene very successful in overcoming entrenched political opposition to reforms in the plantations, state-controlled enterprises and state corporations.

Despite its high priority and massive expenditures, the Mahaweli project was somewhat slow off the mark. The project's major contribution to invigorating the economy was plentiful, cheap hydroelectric power. Prior to 1983, however, Mahaweli contributed nothing to Sri Lanka's electric power supply and power shortages continued to hamper industrial development. The high priority given to Mahaweli, and to Prime Minister Premadasa's public-sector development projects, meant slighting other shortcomings in Sri Lanka's infrastructure that deterred investors and created bottlenecks in the industrial sector.

By liberalising trade and increasing government spending J.R. Jayewardene's government succeeded in unleashing an economic boom during 1978, 1979 and 1980, years when all things seemed possible. As 1981 drew to a close, however, short-term economic portents were less favourable. A combination of rising government debts, high inflation, worsening trade deficits and stagnating economic performance began to impact ordinary Sri Lankans, and made cutbacks in popular programs inevitable. Moreover, as we shall see in the next section, benefits from the boom years were distributed unequally. The UNP leaders' plan to turn the economy around within a single electoral cycle and diffuse benefits throughout the society had proved unrealistic, though they were still optimistic about the longer-term future. That voters might punish them for transient shortcomings, giving a revitalised opposition the power to impede or even roll-back open economy policies, was a matter of deep concern._

Performance: delivering benefits to Sri Lanka's people

Never had a change in ruling party produced such a visible economic transformation as the UNP's reform program initially delivered. Within weeks, previously barren store shelves were laden with imported goods.[66] Long queues for rice, wheat, milk and other essentials disappeared as new marketing and distribution systems took hold. Infusions of capital, plus availability of imported raw materials caused a surge in industrial production. In 1978, Sri Lanka's real gross national product grew by an astonishing 25 per cent (Figure 16.1).

Whether or not growth could be sustained and its fruits widely shared were questions yet to be answered. Economic and administrative reforms helped produce the spurt of growth, but the release of pent-up consumer demand after years of austerity also played a role. Consumer goods were now more widely available, but priced beyond the reach of many. Open economy reforms weakened government social safety nets, placing the poor at greater risk. Investment incentives, along with reduced tax burdens on high incomes, began to widen the gap between rich and poor.

Economic growth, wages and income distribution

For most Sri Lankans, tangible benefits from the economic boom that transformed Sri Lanka's commercial climate in urban areas were short lived. UNP leaders touted high growth rates as proof that reforms were succeeding, but after 1978 much of this growth was fuelled by inflation. Prices rose nine per cent in 1978, 20 per cent in 1980 and a staggering 38 per cent in 1982. Adjusted for inflation, annual GNP growth averaged a respectable five per cent between 1979 and 1981, but a 16 per cent decline in 1982 erased those gains.[67]

Benefits from strong economic performance were no longer eroded by population growth, but residual problems from high growth rates of earlier years remained. Population densities in the agriculturally productive Western and Southern Provinces were among the highest in the world, making migra-

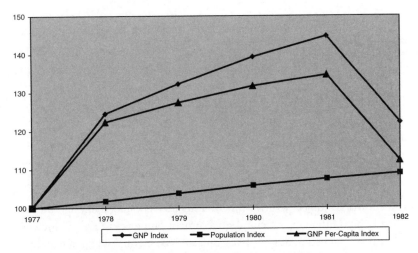

Figure 16.1 Trends in Population, GNP and GNP Per-Capita

tion to Colombo and to the newly opened Mahaweli lands an attractive option. Among the migrants – virtually all Sinhalese – were a very high proportion of mobile, newly literate young men who had completed some secondary schooling and felt frustrated by limited economic opportunities at home.[68] Often, they blamed politicians and Tamils for their plight.

Migration produced a higher than average male-female ratio in some parts of the island. The ratio averaged 103 for all Sri Lanka, but was 109 in urban areas and 113 in Colombo. In rural areas drained by the Mahaweli, this ratio ranged from 112 to 129. In some urban areas of northwestern Polonnaruwa district, bordering the Tamil-majority Eastern Province, the ratio of men to women was nearly two to one.[69] This demographic profile was fuel for social unrest, easily inflamed by bad economic conditions, perceived inequities and chauvinistic political rhetoric.

During the boom years of 1977-1980, economic conditions were more good than bad. Most sectors of the society appeared to benefit from growth. Real wages rose across the board, with the greatest increases – about 50 per cent in three years – for salaried agricultural workers. Well-to-do farmers produced rice and tobacco for local markets, successfully capitalising on new government incentive programs. Members of a new entrepreneurial class – private tractor owners, traders, small shopkeepers, transport agents and other middlemen – profited from the more open commercial environment.[70] Industrial and commercial workers also achieved modest gains, averaging about 10 per cent, and could still count themselves better off in 1980 than when the UNP had assumed power.[71] Government employees initially received big increases that outpaced inflation, but this changed after the 1980 budget cuts. By 1982 inflation had reduced their purchasing power to 1977 levels or less. Schoolteachers fared even worse: wage increases given in 1978 and 1979 barely kept pace with inflation. By the end of 1980, their purchasing power had already dropped 15 per cent below 1977 levels.[72]

Real incomes of many workers declined steeply in 1981 due to a slowdown in growth and then a decline in real GNP. In 1982, wages under direct government control or subject to government influence rebounded, though they still lagged behind inflation. Central government employees received increases of nearly 30 per cent. Wages of teachers and agricultural workers rose by 25 and 18 per cent. This reflected the time-honoured practice of providing steep pre-election increases, in order to influence results at the polls. Industrial and commercial sector wages grew by only seven per cent, however, while service sector wages remained stagnant. On average, prices rose more than 20 per cent in 1981 and more than 38 per cent in 1982.

Deteriorating terms of trade and ballooning government budgets widened the gap between inflation and wage increases, despite policy makers' best efforts. Cost of living raises were necessary to maintain political support but could only be financed by government borrowing. Borrowing fuelled inflation, which soon erased any real benefits from higher wages. Wage increases helped secure pro-UNP majorities in the fall of 1982, but this strategy was not sustainable. The inexorable outstripping of wage increases by inflation was particularly hard on middle class government employees in urban areas who experienced erosion of status as well as purchasing power in the open economy era. High wages in new commercial enterprises were not uniform, but some were highly visible, especially in the booming tourist sector. Hotel doormen, restaurant waiters and tour guides could earn more than department heads, university professors and senior police officers.[73]

Sri Lankan workers who lacked permanent formal employment fared worst of all.[74] They included landless agricultural workers outside the estate sector, small landholders who relied exclusively on family labour, self employed craftsmen, those making a living from fishing or animal husbandry, small 'cottage industry' workers and casual labourers.[75] Men and women in these categories were most vulnerable to economic downturns. They were last to be hired and first to be laid off. They lacked strong labour union representation that had helped tea-estate workers share the benefits of growth. Many of the economically marginalised lived in rural areas, but the more mobile among them, especially young men, were recent migrants to urban centres. In Colombo and other cities, they swelled the ranks of a frustrated lumpenproletariat whose members could not afford the tempting luxury goods newly displayed around them.[76]

Government Consumer Finances Surveys[77] documented a widening income gap between rich and poor. For the survey periods 1973-78/79 and 1978/79-81/82, only the top decile of the population increased their share of total income received. All others lost ground. In 1973, incomes of Sri Lanka's top-decile earners were 17 times greater than incomes of their counterparts in the lowest decile. By 1981/82, this ratio had more than doubled.[78]

The widening gap between the rich and the middle class was equally noteworthy. In 1973, the top decile of income earners received less then twice the income of those immediately below them on the income ladder. By 1981/82, their share had more than tripled.[79] This widening gap becomes apparent if one takes the share of fifth decile income recipients as a rough surrogate for the 'middle class.' In 1973, the income share of Sri Lanka's wealthiest was about four times as large as their 'middle class' counterparts. Less than 10 years later, in 1981/82, the size of their share had grown to nearly eight times that of the 'middle class.' Belying visions of a dharmista society, egalitarian norms of the 1960s and 1970s were now supplanted by a social Darwinist ethic that conferred merit on the fleetest in a new race for economic gain. One social critic pointed to 'lower middle class pauperisation' as a potentially more deadly problem that the nation's ethnic divisions.[80]

Lower middle class pauperisation was accompanied by an increase in the number of Sri Lankans living below the threshold of absolute poverty, though the extent of the increase is a matter of debate. Samarasinghe reports an increase in the number of 'ultra poor' from less than 20 per cent of the population in 1977-78 to about 25 per cent in 1981-82. He cites government and official sources, which describe more than 30 per cent of Sri Lanka's school children as 'chronically undernourished' and more than 12 per cent as 'acutely undernourished.'[81] Tambiah concludes that the poorest workers and those 'partly to fully

unemployed' saw their living standards worsen after 1977.[82] Lakshman's review
of nine separate studies reaches broadly similar conclusions about increasing
poverty levels, but notes that different definitions of poverty and measurement
schemes were used to support both optimistic and pessimistic assessments of
open economy policies. [83]

What did it mean to be 'poor' in Sri Lanka during this period of economic
and social transformation? A detailed, graphic picture emerges from investigations of Colombo sociologist, Nandasena Ratnapala. Ratnapala obtained a
self-definition of what it meant for family members to be living just above the
poverty line from respondents in nine geographically dispersed village communities:[84]

- They should have three meals a day (according to them a light meal
  in the morning and two heavy meals, necessarily rice at noon and for
  dinner) to keep them out of hunger.
- Three pieces of clothing for each member of the family.
- About two acres of paddy land and once acre of dry land with water
  or such other resources of employment to ensure a minimum of 500
  rupees per month.
- Presence of some savings (say 500 rupees) to be used in an emergency
  (to keep them out of debt).
- A house that shelters them from sun and rain.

Only a small fraction of the inhabitants in the nine villages had access to all
these necessities on a reliable basis. More 90 per cent or more of the residents
were illiterate and most had no marketable skill. Many of their houses lacked
a bed or a chair to sit on. More than 80 per cent of lactating mothers failed to
receive even one nutritious meal per-day. Average life expectancy for men was
about 52 years. Women lived a little longer.[85] 'The style of life in these villages,'
he concluded, 'is punctuated not by leisure or festivals or celebrations, holidays,
gatherings of friends, outings, parties, etc. but by the incessant struggle to eke
out an existence.'[86]

Poor people's struggle to eke out an existence was further complicated
by subsidy cuts, another facet of open economy reforms. Cuts did not occur across the board. For example, rail and bus transportation continued to
be heavily subsidised, money-losing government enterprises.[87] Wheat con-

tinued to be imported by the government and sold at below world-market prices. However, inflation-adjusted allocations to social services, health and education dropped between five and 10 per cent.[88]

Elimination of the rice ration, long a goal of J.R. Jayewardene, was the most radical subsidy reduction. Starting in 1978, more than one-third of the population saw their rice rations cancelled. In the following year, a food stamp program was implemented, replacing the rice ration entirely. Initially, it appeared that the new food stamp allocations might actually make poor people better off. Stamps were supposed to provide the same basket of goods the food subsidy program had provided, and in fact their initial market value was estimated at 112 per cent of the subsidised food. Food stamps, however, were not indexed to market prices of staple foods, which were soon pushed upward by inflation. Increasing the value of food stamps required political action, which only came grudgingly. Between 1979 and 1982, government expenditures on meeting poor Sri Lankans' food needs dropped from 13.9 per cent of the budget to 4.6 per cent. By 1982, food stamps supplied poor families with only about half as much rice as in 1979.[89]

The impact on nutrition levels was predictable. A 1983 study by Harvard University's Institute of International Development reported that rising market prices for rice and wheat 'tended to reduce the caloric intake of the lowest groups substantially compared to their historical levels.'[90] According to another study, estimated calorie consumption of the lowest income decile fell from 1,335 in 1978/79 to 1,181 in 1981/82. In 1970, when a full ration of rice was available to all those in need, poor families were consuming more than 2,000 calories per-capita. Poor families were also required to spend more of their discretionary income on food. In 1972, according to one estimate, 44 per cent of their food needs were being met by government subsidies. By 1982, this figure had dropped to 20 per cent.[91]

Unemployment and job creation

Open economy reforms were more successful in creating jobs than helping poor people. When the UNP government assumed office, a rising unemployment rate surpassing 25 per cent was one of the nation's most pressing problems. Under Prime Minister Bandaranaike's government, despite creation of new public sector positions, the nation had experienced a net job loss.[92] More than 1.2 million Sri Lankans seeking regular work were unable to find it. Adding to the problem, reforms motivated increasing numbers of women to seek employment, pushing labour force growth to an all time high.[93] By 1982, however, total unemployment had dropped to near 18 per cent and perhaps even lower.[94] If we accept the most conservative estimates, Sri Lanka's economy created at least 650,000 and probably more than 700,000 new jobs during J.R. Jayewardene's first term.

Creating more than half a million jobs in five years was a major achievement, but an 18 per cent unemployment rate was still very troublesome. Nearly one million Sri Lankans who wanted to work could not find any employment. An even larger number were either underemployed or doing work they felt was beneath them. Much of this unemployment and underemployment was structural. It stemmed from a long-standing mismatch between skills that a modernising economy needed and those provided by workers seeking employment.[95] Further, Sinhala-only education excluded many applicants from internationally oriented and tourist-sector positions that required English. Thus, in a new economic climate, language policies intended to break down class barriers wound up reinforcing the privileged position of elite government-school and fee-paying private school graduates.[96]

Paradoxically, manpower planners were forced to grapple simultaneously with problems of high unemployment and shortages of technically trained workers that created growth-impeding economic bottlenecks. A shortage of technically trained teachers, especially teachers who could instruct in Sinhala, made it difficult to provide classes for students who sought technical skills.[97] Often, teachers and education bureaucrats resisted curriculum reforms that would better match education and job opportunities. Not surprisingly, more than 75 per cent of those unemployed were 25 years old or less. Most had completed at least some primary education. A fairly large number had either 'O Level' or even 'A Level' qualifications.

Some years later, following a second Sinhalese youth insurrection that nearly overthrew the government,[98] a Presidential Commission on Youth strongly indicted the mismatch between employment opportunities and the education being provided to the most volatile segment of the society. 'The majority of secondary school leavers,' the Commissioners concluded, 'find very little opportunities (sic.) for self-employment as the education imparted to them in our school system does not equip them with the basic knowledge and the skills required for gainful, employment.' The report continued:

University students themselves are deeply frustrated, especially those who graduate in the liberal arts and humanities. ... [Unemployed university students] are both articulate and consequently, in the very nature of things likely to lead rebellion and organise unrest against a system which holds out minimal hope for greater social mobility.[99]

Thus, one of the great success-stories of open economy reforms, job creation, still left many young Sri Lankans unemployed, disillusioned and disaffected. UNP leaders were aware of these concerns, but as the economy turned downward and deficits ballooned, their options for responding effectively became increasingly circumscribed.

Ethnic disparities in income and employment

Chapter 12 described economist S.W.R. de A. Samarasinghe's attempt to sort out contending Sinhalese and Tamil claims of ethnically-based employment discrimination and income disparity.[100] He found kernels of truth in simplistic perceptions of discrimination on both sides, embedded in a more complex reality. In the state sector, Tamils had steadily lost ground to Sinhalese, but retained a disproportionate share of highly visible administrative, professional and technical positions. Low country Sinhalese, on average, received higher incomes than Tamils, but Tamils did better than Kandyan Sinhalese.

UNP open economy reforms did little to change these patterns which, Samarasinghe reminds us, were based as much on political as ethnic ties. Since both major political parties were Sinhalese-dominated, normal operation of the political spoils system tended to favour Sinhalese aspirants to government posts. J.R. Jayewardene expressed greater sympathy for Tamil aspirations than his predecessor, but was also attuned to perceptions and needs of his support-base in the Sinhalese community. Widely shared economic growth, he continued to believe, was a far better way to mute ethnic tensions than affirmative action programs.

As the private sector assumed an increasing role in Sri Lanka's economy, ethnically based hiring practices in private companies became a matter of public concern and political discussion. In a survey of 50 companies Samarasinghe attempted to throw light on these practices. Among more than 10,000 employees of these companies, he found that Sinhalese were somewhat over represented, while Tamils were somewhat under represented. Also, there was a clear relationship between ethnic identities of owners and employees.[101] There is some evidence that Tamil businessmen benefited disproportionately from a more open economic environment, because administration of complex commercial licensing procedures under the previous government had favoured Sinhalese. Whatever the realities, it is clear that some Sinhalese businessmen felt they had lost out as a result of open economy policies, and resented the gains of Tamil competitors. These resentful Sinhalese businessmen had their counterparts among Jaffna vegetable farmers who, as trade restrictions were relaxed, saw profits wiped out by cheap food imports from India.

Whether open economy reforms objectively helped reduce discrimination and distributed benefits more equitably across ethnic groups may never be satisfactorily resolved. In an ethnically conflicted society, however, it is perceptions of relative deprivation, rather than abstractions crafted by economists that matter. In both Sinhalese and Tamil communities, potentially disruptive elements *believed* they had been disadvantaged by open economy reforms. These elements viewed members of the 'other' ethnic group and Jayewardene's government as legitimate targets for their resentments.

Health care services

The UNP philosophy of combining government-managed systems with private sector initiatives extended to health care. Here, the government had pledged 'to restore the high standards of health and disease prevention that had existed earlier.' Planning documents defined improved preventive and primary care as major goals for the government-run health-care system. The private sector was given an increased role in providing curative care.

Changes were far reaching. Rules limiting establishment of private health care facilities were relaxed, and fiscal incentives encouraged the construction and management of private facilities. Beds for fee-paying patients were given priority in the new modern government hospital, built with Japanese funds, near the Kotte governmental complex.[102] Despite fierce opposition from Sri Lanka's medical establishment and left-leaning student organisations, permission was given to establish a private medical college for fee-paying students. Perhaps the most radical reform was authorising government doctors to set up clinics where fee-paying patients received treatment 'outside of normal working hours.'[103]

While improved care was touted as an outcome of health care reforms, reforms were also part of the government's across-the-board strategy to reduce spending on social entitlements. Thus, while there was an 80 per cent increase in overall government spending during President Jayewardene's first term, allocations to health care remained nearly stagnant. When stringent spending cuts were imposed in 1982, government health care had no powerful politician to speak up[104] and took a severe hit. Adjusted for inflation, 1982 spending was nearly 20 per cent below 1977.

Budget cuts, heavier patient loads and replacement of experienced doctors with a somewhat smaller number of inexperienced ones, produced an overall degradation in the quality of service, with the impact bearing most heavily on the poor and in rural areas. Like other open economy reforms, government-mandated changes in health care moved away from egalitarian norms that had long guided social-service delivery in Sri Lanka. Establishing the fee-for-service system made it possible for doctors to increase their incomes, reducing pressures to migrate somewhat, but also reduced the quality of care given to public patients.[105] Attracting good doctors to rural areas, never an easy task, became even more difficult. In contrast to Colombo and a few other cities, 'outstation' assignments provided no opportunities to build lucrative private practices that made the difference between a comfortable living and financial stringency. A two-tier health care system, with higher quality service given to those could afford to pay, became the norm. The political spillover from this two-tier system reinforced and perpetuated it. Wealthy, politically influential Sri Lankans were less and less likely to experience the health care available to lower class and poor citizens. Thus, health care system deficiencies were not a top political priority. Inexperienced physicians, deteriorating facilities and long waits for service were primarily matters of concern for those whose political voices were weak.

Although open economy reforms impacted health care services to the poor adversely, positive trends in overall public health indicators continued during J.R. Jayewardene's first term. Mortality rates fell by 18 per cent, infant mortality rates by 24 per cent and maternal mortality rates by a remarkable 40 per cent. These rates of improvement, which helped maintain Sri Lanka's reputation as a development 'success story,' were almost identical those achieved under Mrs. Bandaranaike's government. Samarasinghe interprets this as evidence that government programs emphasising public health, preventive care and immunisation were succeeding.[106] Another possible interpretation is that continued favourable trends in public health statistics were due more to effective programs implemented by previous administrations. Whatever the explanation,

Sri Lanka's continued improvements provided ammunition for proponents of the new two-tier system and budgets that gave health care lower priority. These views continued to shape policy in Jayewardene's government.

Primary and secondary education

A *de facto* two tier system already existed in primary and secondary education – top quality schools for wealthy, politically influential Sri Lankans, inferior ones for most ordinary citizens, but the government made no attempt to extend open economy principles to the nation's schools.[107] But a combination of increased demand for services and inflation-eroded budgets produced outcomes similar to those in health care.

Undoing Mrs. Bandaranaike's education reforms was the government's first priority. Students were now required to enter school at five, rather than six years of age. At the other end of the educational pipeline, General Certificate of Education (GCE) 'Ordinary' and 'Advanced' level examinations were reinstated. To meet these examination standards, years of post-kindergarten education were increased from 11 to 12.[108] This two-year boost in education requirements contributed to an enrolment surge of more than 500,000 students (21 per cent) in 1978.

A new program to provide free textbooks for all students in grades 1 through 10 targeted Sri Lanka's poorest students. Lack of sufficient income to buy textbooks had been identified as a major contributor to high dropout rates among poor children[109] and it was hoped that government supplied texts would help remedy the problem. Between 1980, when the program was initiated, and 1982, the government distributed 31.1 million texts costing nearly 192 million rupees. This new obligation represented more than four per cent of current expenditures on education.[110]

It would appear that J.R. Jayewardene's government began its term with a commitment to expand both educational services and funding for education. Inflation and competing budgetary pressures, however, soon vitiated the latter commitment. Thus, while inflation-adjusted education expenditures rose by 11 per cent between 1977 and 1980, they dropped by 14 per cent between 1980 and 1982 to a level below 1977. The severity of these budget shortfalls becomes more evident when the government's increased obligations are taken into account. Between 1977 and 1982, expenditures per teacher declined 17 per cent while expenditures per student fell by nearly one-third. After five years of UNP rule, Sri Lanka's pre-university education system was still among the developing world's best, but long-standing calls for reforms evoked little response from teachers and administrators who saw their facilities deteriorating, their workloads increasing and the purchasing power of their wages eroding simultaneously.

The disconnect between school curricula and marketplace needs, a primary area in need of reform, has already been identified as a major contributor to unemployment. Sri Lanka's expanding and diversifying economy required professionally trained managers and a more technically proficient workforce. Student demand for training in science and commerce far exceeded available offerings, but low teacher salaries and inadequate facilities impeded reforms. The Youth Commission Report, cited earlier, pointed to a 'dramatically diminishing status of teachers as badly paid and often poorly trained public servants, with little opportunity for career advancement' as a serious problem. Overcentralisation, excessive bureaucratisation and lack of continuity between successive ministers were identified as further impediments to reform.[111]

Widely differing school quality levels meant that poor children, especially those living in outlying areas, had little opportunity to improve their station through Sri Lanka's highly competitive educational system. For every 100 students who enrolled in kindergarten, only 51 would take the 'O' level examinations, only 24 would enrol in 'A' level courses and only two would gain university admission. To enrol in advanced courses, not only did students need to pass nationally standardised examinations, but the requisite schools also needed to be available. In Colombo's educational district,[112] more than 66 per cent of the schools offered advanced level courses and nearly 18 per cent offered training in science. By contrast, less that 12 per cent of rural Vavuniya district schools offered advanced training and only three percent provided science training.

A 1983 survey by the Ministry of Education concluded that: 'Equalisation of educational opportunity has continued to be a guiding principle, but the education system has not been able to provide even basic facilities such as blackboards, sanitation and water supply to about 20 per cent of the schools.' 'Inadequate funding of the system as a whole and an imbalance in the allocation of resources between the prestigious schools and the rest of the system' were identified as the principal causes of this problem.[113] Primary and secondary education, then, was yet another area where large numbers of Sri Lankans experienced deterioration in the quality of services they were receiving after five years of Jayewardene's open economy policies.

Higher education

UNP higher education policies were a different matter. In this politically vola-tile area, reforms and organisational changes were combined with budget increases for staff benefits, library resources, support services and equipment. A massive capital-spending program created three new university campuses and added new facilities to the existing ones. New continuing and technical education programs provided opportunities for students who were not admitted to traditional universi-ties or were unable to pursue a full-time program of study in residence.

Jayewardene's first higher education priority, as noted earlier, was to replace the communally divisive 'media-wise standardisation' university admissions policy with a merit-based scheme, designed to offer something to each interest-ed party. Tamil applicants were once again given the opportunity to compete with Sinhalese for places on the basis of their GCE 'A' level scores, irrespective of the language in which they were examined. Less-advantaged Sinhalese and Muslim applicants benefited from a complex scheme of district quotas that could be adjusted to political realities and by an increase in the absolute number of places available.[114]

Other priorities, set forth in a new Universities Act,[115] reversed United Front higher education reforms and established a more flexible system that could respond to the needs of Sri Lanka's expanding open economy. Quasi-in-dependent universities were re-established, replacing the bureaucratically cum-bersome University of Ceylon. The newly created University Grants Commis-sion was given overall management and fiduciary responsibilities for these in-stitutions. Commission members, appointed by the President, were supposed to be at least somewhat insulated from the political and communal imperatives that motivated ministry officials. Power of the Higher Education Minister to intervene in day-to-day university management was explicitly delimited. Fac-ulty autonomy and the autonomy of Vice Chancellors over educational policies were strengthened.[116] To provide a basis for longer-term planning, both an external review of the nation's higher education policies and an internal review by Higher Education Ministry planners were undertaken.

While these reforms could be initiated quickly, UNP leaders knew that tinkering with admissions quotas, redrawing organisation charts and commis-sioning planning documents would not resolve two fundamental problems that had made higher education a catalyst for political discontent among Sri Lanka's youth. One was the declining percentage of qualified applicants who could reasonably hope to gain university admission.[117] The second was the mismatch between educational qualifications of most Sri Lankan university graduates and the employment needs of Sri Lanka's economy.

Attacking the first problem was easier for a government that had made capital investment the centrepiece of its development policies. Annual spending for new university facilities increased nearly tenfold over 1977 levels. New institutions were founded in rural areas and facilities were expanded at the flagship campuses of Peradeniya and Colombo Universities. Other campuses received new teaching hospitals, laboratory facilities and residence halls.[118] The number of Sri Lanka's technical institutes, which provided specialised education below the university level, increased to 26.[119] An Open University, founded in 1980, provided continuing education for adult and other non-traditional students.

Reforming curricula to meet the needs of a more privatised, globalised, technologically sophisticated economy posed more difficult problems. The need for reform was well known. Indeed providing job-oriented higher education had been the centrepiece of the United Front's flawed higher education innovations. A 1979 manpower study warned about shortages of engineers, science graduates, doctors and commerce graduates.[120] Applications for these specialisations far exceeded the supply of university spaces. But universities were resistant to change, and ill prepared to compete with the private sector for qualified faculty who could teach technical subjects. Five years after the UNP took power, science graduates grew by nearly 10 per cent and commerce graduates by about half that much. The percentage of engineering graduates declined, however, and those receiving degrees in arts and oriental studies still comprised nearly half the total, as they had in 1977.

What prospects awaited these young men and women? A detailed review of university education and graduate employment in Sri Lanka, completed in 1983, included an extensive survey of graduates' job-market expectations and experiences.[121] Study results reinforced widely held views about the greater marketability of professional and science degrees. Among those unable to find permanent employment, more than 90 per cent had majored in an arts field. Typically, arts graduates also had to wait far longer to find jobs, often three years or more. Jobs they did land were frequently minor administrative or clerical posts that did not require a university degree at all. A survey of employers helped to explain this disparity. Their perception was that professional, science and engineering curricula met high standards and were relevant to future employment. Employers of arts graduates, however, complained of poor preparation as well as a mismatch between examination standards and job requirements.[122]

Less-advantaged students who gained admission were more likely to meet the lower standards required for concentration in arts or oriental studies. They, too, embarked on their careers as university students with high expectations, but those careers were more likely to end in frustration and disillusionment. Open economy rhetoric touted opportunities that an expanding private sector would provide, but the security of government employment in an administrative post not requiring specialised skills remained the goal of many. For recruitment to these posts, political ties were often far more important than a strong academic record.

Despite slowness of curricular reforms, UNP higher education policy would definitely qualify as a success story. President Jayewardene's personal involvement, a more politically nuanced admissions policy, sustained budget increases and administrative decentralisation restored a sense of normalcy and optimism at Sri Lanka's universities, following the turbulent United Front years.[123] Spaces in universities were still limited, relative to demand, but the Open University, external degree programs and expanded technical training courses provided an expanded menu of options for those who failed to gain admission to traditional programs. Serious unresolved problems – admissions pressures, student dissatisfaction with some curricula, shortages of qualified faculty in some technical areas, employability of arts graduates – remained. The uneven quality of secondary education, which limited the higher education opportunities of poor Sri Lankans, was a long-standing unresolved problem of the educational system as a whole. As Jayewardene's first term drew to a close, however, a talented group of senior university administrators, with the support of some top UNP leaders, seemed committed to addressing these problems. There was no reason to believe that the upward trajectory set during the previous five years could not continue.

The impact of open economy polices during J.R. Jayewardene's first term: a people's eye view

J.R. Jayewardene's open economy reforms were an early, partial experiment with 'structural adjustment' policies that were aggressively promoted by international lending agencies in the 1980s. The adjective 'partial' is appropriate for the Sri Lankan case because more conventional adjustment policies –

privatisation, currency reform, export promotion, entitlement cutbacks–were combined with massive publicly-funded investment projects and pledges to supplant the Darwinian ethic of free market economic competition with the gentler norms of a *dharmista* (righteous) society.

In 1977, the potentially adverse social and political consequences of structural adjustment were less well understood than today. Just as Sri Lankan socialists believed central planning would allocate resources more efficiently and fairly, UNP reformers believed open economy policies would simultaneously promote economic expansion and well-being of the poor. In Sri Lanka, as in many other developing nations, these expectations proved false.

While most income groups benefited from the initial spurt of growth during 1977-1979, many saw these initial gains eroded by inflation and by 1982 were actually worse off economically than they had been when the UNP assumed power. As wage earners lost ground, the gap between the highest income groups and all other sectors of society widened. The term 'middle class pauperisation' was first heard during the open economy era. The quality of government health care and of schools to which poor and middle class Sri Lankans looked to deteriorated. Those at the bottom of the income ladder, who bore the brunt of food subsidy cuts, fared worst of all.

Conventional wisdom holds that Sri Lankans as a whole viewed their lives as better during the UNP's first term than under the preceding government. Jayewardene's 1982 presidential election victory appears to confirm this. Bleak years of scarcity and economic privation under the United Front created lasting memories. Nearly 14 years would pass before they faded sufficiently for an SLFP-dominated coalition to win a narrow victory over a decimated UNP.

Sri Lanka's open economy reforms and their consequences have been described in considerable detail because when a president or prime minister's grand designs are implemented, 'the devil is in the detail.' The unpredictability and complexity of development trajectories provides a compelling reason for political leaders to keep communication channels open between themselves and those impacted by development programs. Such channels can provide them with the 'bad news' they need to know in order to remediate problems before they get out of hand. A competent, relatively independent bureaucracy can maintain open communication channels. So can the institutions of a robust democracy – strong opposition political parties, independent media organisations, human rights guarantees that protect dissent and free elections.

In J.R. Jayewardene's Sri Lanka, none of these channels functioned effectively. A once independent civil service was now fully politicised. It was a moderately effective instrument for implementing the President's will, but not for informing him when things were going wrong. Nor were democratic institutions robust. We saw in chapter 15 that President Jayewardene, who could discourse eloquently on democratic principles, chose the flawed referendum to move Sri Lanka closer to the one-party state model he seemed to favour. In chapter 17 we will see how he worked assiduously and effectively to emasculate opposition parties and other dissenting voices in the political middle. Chapter 18 describes how repressive measures directed against government opponents became increasingly severe. Those suffering from development failures increasingly viewed militant tactics as the most viable option for communicating to the government. Militant organisations, however, do not seek remediation. Their *raison d'être* is revolutionary transformation. Their feedback is rarely helpful to political leaders.

17
Political Identities, Attitudes and Organisations in the Open Economy Era

The story of opposition movements during this period is about how the Sri Lanka Freedom Party, the Tamil United Liberation Front, the Marxist parties, their labour union allies and independent civil society organisations in both the Sinhalese and Tamil communities all lost credibility. UNP leaders achieved this by skilfully using political assets and state power, while capitalising on opposition leadership shortcomings. But the way these triumphs were achieved exacted costs.

Four political trends in the open economy era's promising early years would pivotally impact Sri Lanka's future: intensifying communal polarisation, rising Tamil militancy, JVP resurgence and declining respect for the rule of law. Gifted with the wisdom of hindsight, we know that J.R. Jayewardene's first term coincided with a mutually reinforcing radicalisation of Sinhalese and Tamil political cultures.[1] Mainstream politicians, as well as militant activists, were complicit in this process. Extra-legal violence became, increasingly, an accepted political tactic. Those victimised by violence could not count on an increasingly politicised police force to uphold the rule of law. Declining respect for the rule of law legitimised more primordial forces in Sri Lankan society, increasing the probability that violent tactics would be used to achieve economic as well as political goals.

As we have seen, radicalisation began during the United Front's seven years in power. Inflammatory rhetoric, long used by Prime Minister Bandaranaike's Marxist allies, became more commonplace in mainstream political discourse. United Front orators pictured government policies, Sinhalese-Buddhist community priorities and Sri Lankan national interests as one and the same. Opponents were denounced as 'enemies of the (Sinhalese) people' or even 'traitors.' Tarring opponents with this brush made encroachments on political rights and use of police for political purposes more justifiable, if not strictly legal. Making wholesale changes in constitutional 'rules of the game' to further a communal-political agenda and hold on to power was another trend ushered in by the United Front government.

J.R. Jayewardene would later justify aggressive tactics as an appropriate riposte to United Front misdeeds. He was a far more skilful tactician than his predecessor.[2] The new constitution and subseqent amendments concentrated power in the Executive Presidency. The Special Presidential Commission neutralised Mrs. Bandaranaike, whom he saw as his most formidable political opponent. When needed, National Workers' Organisation (JSS) cadres could be assembled quickly to intimidate political opponents. The 1982 referendum victory doubled the length of time the UNP could exercise constitutionally sanctioned power, virtually unimpeded. In the early months of 1983, a Sri Lankan version of Malaysia's or Singapore's one-party government seemed within the President's reach.

This chapter describes how J.R. Jayewardene's success in discomfiting moderate opponents had unanticipated side effects that would, in time, threaten his Presidency. During a period when economic turbulence was contributing to social disruption, losers in political and economic competition perceived that traditional options for redressing grievances and reversing their fortunes were being closed off. Young citizens saw the SLFP, Marxist parties and moderate Tamil parties as less satisfying sources of political identity. That these parties would return to power, or exert leverage over the UNP leaders who held power, seemed improbable. Frustration levels resulting from economic disruption, uncertain identities and perceived political impotence rose, and unpunished attacks on government opponents appeared to legitimise violent tactics. For those who would not, or could not, support the UNP, the agendas of militant movements claiming that violence was the only path to political power seemed increasingly attractive. As militant movements gained popular support, some moderate leaders came to view them as temporary allies with whom they might collaborate to break the UNP's seeming stranglehold on power.

How ordinary Sri Lankans viewed government and politics

Electoral politics had long been linked to the government's role in distributing material benefits. United Front policies had strengthened this linkage by increasing the range of benefits provided and by giving pro-government MPs a much larger role in determining who would and would not receive them. After 1977, massive infusions of funds to support government initiated development projects meant that employment opportunities associated with publicly funded activities expanded still further. We have seen how the *Job Bank Scheme* and refinements of the 'chit system' channelled most of these opportunities to UNP supporters.

A revealing picture of how this system worked in one rural area has been provided by anthropologist Jonathan Spencer in his ethnographic study of 'Tenna,' a Sinhalese village of 197 households located in eastern Ratnapura District.[3] 'State-peasant relations,' Spencer writes, 'can be described in material terms: the state distributes, the peasant consumes. The resultant material interests explain why politics are so important – because everyone is heavily dependent on the state.'[4] Between 1963 and 1983, the number of government employees living in Tenna had grown from one to 23 and 'virtually every village resident benefited from some government program – subsidised rice and other foodstuffs, government agricultural development projects and programs, casual labour contracts for road and irrigation work.'[5]

How Sri Lanka's political spoils system functioned to provide both material benefits and status to supporters of the winning side became apparent in Tenna following Jayewardene's 1977 electoral victory.

After election, the local UNP officer was appointed cultivation officer for the surrounding area, despite limited farming experience. His wife's younger brother (and a political ally) became a schoolteacher; his wife's sisters and his own siblings all had government jobs. A relative who did not have a government job was involved in gem and timber dealing; both activities were on the fringe of legality and required protection from local officials. A review of life histories of the local elites of both parties revealed that the 'spoils of politics' had been pivotal in making them better off in the first place. Then their elite status reinforced their political standing.[6]

While political identities and affiliations often reflected material benefits received, this was only one facet of a more complex reality. For some families, ties to the UNP, SLFP, TULF or a Marxist party were matters of long standing tradition, akin almost to religious conviction. The pendulum swings of political power that set Sri Lanka apart from so many developing nations depended not only on voters who responded to changes in the political-economic climate, but also on core constituencies of fierce loyalists who would stick with their party, no matter what.

Thus, political affiliations could fulfil psychic as well as material needs. The thirteen years following Mrs. Bandaranaike's 1970 electoral landslide were often turbulent, politically, economically and socially.[7] Faced with instability and change, political and communal symbols provided many with some enduring basis for identity, social worth and meaning. Rhetorical appeals during this period, by moderate and militant leaders alike, often responded to this need for meaningful psychic anchors that could hold firm against the forces of turbulence and change. J.R. Jayewardene's *dharmista society* vision and the often-invoked Buddhist-Sinhalese vision of a society 'focused on the temple, tank and rice field'[8] were noteworthy examples. Such appeals did offer symbols that provided meaning, but could also have a pathological side. If revealed as hollow – the *dharmista society* again provides an example – resulting disillusionment could further intensify frustrations and breed cynicism. These feelings could impel the disillusioned toward more radical ideologies and more violent responses against real and imagined enemies. The temptation to use tactics that capitalised on these feelings proved irresistible to some political leaders including, at times, President Jayewardene.

Anti-democratic tendencies within Sri Lanka's political parties

The UNP rebirth under J.R. Jayewardene, and its triumph in the 1977 parliamentary elections, appeared to reaffirm conventional wisdom about the responsiveness of Sri Lanka's democratic institutions. Following its 1970 defeat and the death of Dudley Senanayake, the party had elevated a new leader and revitalised its organisation. It had recruited new blood, survived repressive measures and reversed its fortunes decisively. Marxist parties, espousing a revolutionary socialist ideology, were rejected overwhelmingly by voters. The small number of seats won by Sirimavo Bandaranaike's SLFP was mostly an artefact of single-member-district representation. SLFP supporters still comprised nearly a third of the electorate, providing it with a solid base for reversing its fortunes in a future contest. But if a viable, responsive democracy was now well established, the growth of militant movements and intensification of political violence during the open economy era is puzzling. What made it so difficult for those holding dissenting views to express them peacefully?

Our discussion of President Jayewardene's leadership style and the impact of his economic policies have already provided pieces of the puzzle. The governance philosophy and internal organisation of the major parties (and other parties as well) provide others. Parallels between Sri Lanka's political culture, circa 1978, and principles of liberal democracy need to be drawn with caution. Ethnographic studies of village-level party competition emphasise the low levels of tolerance for dissenting views.[9] Intolerance often characterised national-level competition, as well. According to anthropologist Michael Roberts, the democratic tradition of listening to opposing party members and seeing them prosper, without resorting to undemocratic means, was weak in Sri Lanka.[10]

Dissent within parties was even less welcomed. K.M. de Silva, who generally views Sri Lanka's democratic institutions quite favourably, highlights this problem. 'One of the crucial weaknesses of the Sri Lankan party system,' he observes, 'has been the reluctance if not refusal of the leadership to accept dissent as a necessary factor in the life of a political party.' Furthermore, 'Sri Lanka's leader-oriented political parties have generally responded to dissident opinion by seeking to drive the principal dissenters into the political wilderness.' De Silva concludes that: 'In most instances they have succeeded in doing so.'[11] Jayewardene's constitutional reforms further strengthened party leaders' authority by strengthening their control over candidate selection and giving them greater authority to punish dissidents.[12] One might have thought that political competition between disciplined, broad-based parties would be more 'democratic' than the older system of competition between loose coalitions of notables. However, this was not necessarily the case.

The UNP

Once J.R. Jayewardene assumed office, his revitalised UNP organisation became an arm of government power as well as an instrument for perpetuating itself in office. As we have seen, the spoils system was an accepted political reality in Sri Lanka. UNP loyalists were rewarded with official positions, patronage posts to distribute and preferential consideration for government contracts. The President's ill-fated District Development Councils provided an opportunity to name 25 UNP Parliamentarians to newly created positions as 'District Minister,' with appropriate staff and perquisites. Indeed, nearly two-thirds of the UNP parliamentary group had some sort of government appointment from the Executive President.[13] Party leaders were given positions where they could use party machinery to support government policies or weaken opponents. After winning re-election, President Jayewardene reinforced his authority still further by securing undated letters of resignation from the entire 168-member UNP parliamentary group.[14]

Both traditions and structures reinforced the leader's power, but Jayewardene's UNP was not a monolith. The UNP had shed the reputation of the 'Uncle Nephew Party' by recruiting some of Sri Lanka's most able young political leaders into its ranks. Some of these leaders had their own power bases, sought meaningful responsibilities and saw themselves as possible future presidents of Sri Lanka.[15] Giving them authority and discretion kept them within the ranks of government supporters while President Jayewardene retained the balance of power. He was comfortable delegating some authority to senior ministers, enabling him to focus his energies on top priority goals. Directly flouting the President's policies could evoke a sacking,[16] but he was willing to tolerate a fair amount of disputation among close associates, not only in cabinet and high level party meetings but even in public.

The UNP thus provided a broad ideological umbrella under which proponents of diverse views on economic and communal issues could fit with a degree of comfort. Caste and religious differences, too, were accommodated, even within the top leadership ranks. The free market views of Ronnie de Mel and the President himself found themselves a seat at the same cabinet table with those of the more left-leaning Premadasa. President Jayewardene recruited the Indian Tamil leader Thondaman to his cabinet (though he did not join the UNP), but tolerated the chauvinist diatribes of Cyril Mathew. Jayewardene could be personally caste conscious in social settings, but he put caste consciousness aside to elevate Premadasa to the posts of deputy party leader and Prime Minister. The President believed that, if possible, it was better to tolerate diverse and even strident views than to abandon their proponents to the opposition. The UNP was intended to provide a structure that would embody a broad national consensus on economic, social and communal issues while marginalising the SLFP, its former coalition partners and the TULF for the foreseeable future. To further this goal, President Jayewardene used his strengthened party organisation, along with his considerable political skills, to divide and demoralise the UNP's political opponents.

The SLFP

The SLFP, already weakened by the 1977 electoral landslide, was an inviting target. In contrast to the UNP, Sirimavo Bandaranaike's party was unable to use defeat as an opportunity to revitalise its leadership, reinvigorate its organisation and frame innovative new policies. Instead, defeat highlighted fundamental defects in the party's structure that had been less evident when an SLFP-dominated coalition held power or faced a relatively weak UNP government. It became apparent that the party had been overly dependent on its erstwhile Marxist allies for policy direction, leadership and organisational muscle. Even more problematic was the tradition of reserving top leadership posts for members of the Bandaranaike family.

In chapters 11 and 12, we saw that Marxist party leaders, despite limited parliamentary strength, held key posts in Prime Minister Bandaranaike's cabinet and were responsible for shaping economic policy. Especially in major urban areas, Marxist parties contributed organising skills and the capacity to mobilise coalition supporters. Thug-squads, used to intimidate opponents and protect supporters, were drawn disproportionately from Marxist party ranks. After 1977, these resources were lost to the SLFP. What remained was a party which 'had no mobilisation capability, limited high-level political talent, a relatively parochial perspective and no very distinctive political agenda beyond Sinhalese Buddhist revivalism.'[17]

Bandaranaike family dominance was the principal cause of these shortcomings and the principal impediment to remedying them. There had never been an SLFP party structure independent of the Bandaranaikes.[18] Their exclusivist leadership role partly reflected a 'politics of deference,'[19] characteristic of Sri Lankan and other South Asian political cultures, but it was carried to extremes. In the words of one critic, the founding family was like 'a massive banyan tree in whose shade no other trees may grow.'[20]

The problems family dominance created were particularly evident following parliamentary ratification of the Special Presidential Commission recommendation that deprived Mrs. Bandaranaike and Felix Dias Bandaranaike of their civic rights. Though legally barred from politics, the former Prime Minister made it clear that she had no intention of resigning her post as party leader. Her son Anura supported a faction that called for new leadership. For more than a year, Sri Lankan newspapers described comic-opera squabbles between members of the Bandaranaike family, spilling over into highly visible public litigation, about who would control the party's physical assets and symbols.[21]

Factional squabbling placed the SLFP in an extremely difficult position to contest the October 1982 presidential election. Initially, it appeared that contesting factions might name separate candidates, but they eventually settled on a single nominee, the former Minister of Agriculture and Lands, Hector Kobbekaduwa.

Kobbekaduwa's campaign faced seemingly insurmountable obstacles – a faction-ridden party, a formidable UNP opponent, the decision of some Marxist parties to name competing candidates and lukewarm support from a party rival's faction. The 39 per cent of the popular vote he won said as much about the resiliency of the SLFP's core supporters as about his strength as a candidate. The subsequent campaign against the referendum was led by Mrs. Bandaranaike herself, now firmly in control of the party machinery. The 45 per cent 'no' vote, in the face of a government-supported campaign to win at almost any cost, provided further evidence that an opposition party, organisationally revitalised and offering voters appealing programs, would have a chance against the UNP. In 1982, however, the prospects that the SLFP would strengthen its organisation, recruit new leaders and propose meaningful alternatives to open economy policies seemed slim.

The Marxist parties

Despite organisational strengths and intellectually gifted leaders,[22] political prospects of Mrs. Bandaranaike's erstwhile coalition partners, the Equal Society (LSSP) and Communist parties, seemed even less promising. Their uncompromising Marxist ideology was increasingly out of tune with the majority of Sri Lankan voters. 1977 Parliamentary Election losses, their worst showing since independence, evoked soul searching and leadership changes. However, both parties adopted more radical stances on economic issues, not less.

Factionalism further reduced their chances of success at the polls. Since 1956, no-contest agreements with the SLFP had been essential for most Marxist party candidates to win seats. In 1977, as we have seen, LSSP and Communist Party candidates not only contested against SLFP candidates but sometimes even against each other. At political rallies and in campaign tracts, Marxist leaders were as likely to attack other Marxist candidates as those of the UNP. Left-leaning Sri Lankans were now more likely to vote for JVP candidates, but an alliance between the JVP and old line Marxist parties was out of the question. Neither faction had forgotten how the JVP's 1971 rebellion threatened Marxist-inspired economic reforms and then was brutally repressed by Mrs. Bandaranaike's government, supported by her Marxist coalition partners.[23]

The Communist Party returned to coalition politics in the 1982 presidential campaign, supporting SLFP candidate, Hector Kobbekaduwa. The LSSP, however, continued on the self-destructive path of factionalism and divisive independent candidacies. Despite the party's poor showing in 1977 and subsequent local elections, leader Colvin R. de Silva declared for the Presidency. A second LSSP leader, Vasudeva Nanayakkara, became the candidate of a competing faction that called itself the New Equal Society Party (*Nava Sama Samaja Party*.)[24] These symbolic candidacies accomplished little except to further reduce the credibility of their parties in the eyes of Sri Lankan voters, while contributing to J.R. Jayewardene's margin of victory. De Silva received less than one per cent of the popular vote. Nanayakkara's total was less than one-quarter of one per-cent.[25] Voters who might once have supported the LSSP contributed to JVP candidate Rohana Wijeweera's vote total of more than six per cent. If Marxist ideas were once again to make inroads into the political mainstream, it appeared their source might be the uniquely Sri Lankan amalgam of Marxism and Buddhism that had germinated in rural Matara District villages, rather than imports from the USSR.

The JVP experiments with democracy

JVP leader Rohana Wijeweera emerged from prison convinced that his party should embark on a 'democratic phase.'[26] Overcoming dissent from some politburo members, he began creating a network of district secretaries, formed student organisations in the universities and organised a series of well-attended public meetings featuring himself as the lead speaker. Physically unimposing and with a somewhat squeaky voice, the JVP leader could nonetheless deliver the impassioned Sinhala orations that many Sri Lankans loved. After years of incarceration, he welcomed public adulation and may actually have believed that the JVP could gain sufficient mass support to supplant Sirimavo Bandaranaike's faltering SLFP as a credible political alternative to the UNP. Strong organisation turned out large crowds at his rallies. Party loyalists would travel from event to another, enthusiastically cheering the same speech three or four times in a single day.[27]

Formal participation in the political process began with the 1979 local elections, when the JVP, though failing to gain certification as an 'official' political party, nominated candidates who contested unsuccessfully for a number of posts.[28] Limited success in the 1981 District Development Council elections marked the party's emergence as a credible – though still uncertified – competitor for mainstream support. A last minute decision by the SLFP, LSSP and Communist Party not to participate benefited JVP candidates who contested in eight provinces and gained at least one seat in six provinces. Partly based on the strength of these results, Sri Lanka's Elections Commissioner finally accorded the JVP 'Official Recognition' as a political party in July 1982.

Wijeweera was sufficiently encouraged to continue the JVP's 'democratic phase.' He formally declared for the Executive Presidency in September 1982, and began waging a vigorous campaign. His beret, 'Gueverra-esque' beard and inflammatory rhetoric continued to be trademarks, but the JVP leader had by now acquired some trappings of respectability. A marriage had been arranged with Chitrangani Fernando, the teen-age daughter of an upper-middle class

Moratuwa family. He often travelled in a new Ford Laser automobile, complete
with chauffeur. Wijeweera hoped that a combination of radical and more conventional appeals would persuade newly enfranchised youthful voters to 'send
…old politicians home.'[29]

As noted earlier, Wijeweera's presidential election vote total placed him
third, far outdistancing other Marxist candidates. But JVP propaganda had
predicted an outright victory or that the party would, at least, emerge as Sri Lanka's main opposition party. JVP historian C.A. Chandraprema described the
result as 'a fiasco,' noting that young supporters who had joined in anticipation
of a quick victory 'began to leave the party in droves.'[30] Despite these setbacks,
JVP leaders still did not abandon 'the democratic phase.' They campaigned
with other opposition parties against J.R. Jayewardene's referendum. Five JVP
candidates contested the May 1983 by-elections, but failed to win a single seat.
JVP sympathisers did, however, win control over several university student organisations, where they would retain a solid core of support even after the party
was proscribed.[31]

Party leaders did not know it, but the 1983 May Day rallies would be the last
time the JVP was publicly visible as a democratic party for many years. Photographs show uniformed ranks of 'Red Guards' and 'Woman's Wing' members
carrying red flags and marching in military formations. Incongruously, there is
also a large formation of young Buddhist Priests in their saffron robes, members of the JVP's *Bikkhu* (Buddhist Priest) Front.[32] A less disciplined cadre of
young boys and girls, members of the JVP Students' Group, marched in their
white school uniforms, obviously enjoying the parade.[33] It is reported that
President Jayewardene noted with concern the military formations and reports
that the JVP was once again advocating violence. In late July, he accused the
party of complicity in devastating ethnic rioting that had erupted earlier in the
month (to be discussed below). Newly enacted emergency regulations were
used to proscribe the JVP, along with two other Marxist parties, and to 'suspend
all political activities by them with immediate effect.'[34] The JVP's experiment
with democracy had lasted five years and eight months. Now it became, once
again, an underground militant movement.

Perhaps the term 'once *again*' should be used advisedly since the JVP had
continued to recruit and train clandestinely a core group of revolutionary cadres throughout the 'democratic phase.' Most were drawn from advanced levels
of secondary schools and from universities. A one-week 'basic camp' and a

two-week 'advanced camp' provided indoctrination programs similar to those that had preceded the 1971 revolution, except that there was no weapons training. Wijeweera's *Five Lectures*, somewhat modified, still served as the basis for a course that emphasised discipline and physical deprivation. Rigorous conditions were intended to prepare future revolutionaries for the hardships of life as a guerrilla under combat conditions. Even as Wijeweera touted JVP democratic programs at election rallies, recruits were learning from his *Fifth Lecture* that a peaceful transition to socialism would be impossible.[35] When President Jayewardene's proscription seemed to validate this, the JVP was not wholly unprepared to go underground and begin planning for a violent revolution.

How Sri Lanka's economic, social and political climate spawned youthful militants

JVP recruiters found a receptive audience among Sri Lanka's youth, more than 20 per cent of whom were unemployed. Young men, especially, are naturally predisposed to radical activism and this segment of society was benefiting little from open economy reforms. Earlier, I described the problem of a mismatch between education and employment. This, however, was only one among many grievances that Youth Commissioners presented in the *Report of the Presidential Commission on Youth*. Some were long standing – a youthful rebellion had, after all, greeted Sirimavo Bandaranaike's United Front government – but many were created or exacerbated by open economy reforms and other Jayewardene policies.

Class and caste discrimination had always been a problem in Sri Lankan society, but the Darwinian values associated with free market economics seemed to make discrimination more visible and the barriers between classes more difficult to surmount. High wages and availability of luxury imported goods for the few bred what poor youths saw as 'rampant consumerism and unrestrained ostentation' of a small privileged class.[36] In the past, stable families had often provided a social and moral anchor during periods of social change, but the new economic structure was also eroding family stability. Women who once stayed at home now sought jobs to supplement family income. In the Export Processing Zones, which epitomised open economy policies, employment opportunities were much greater for women than for men. Both men and women were taking jobs in the Middle East. Long separations and two-job households contributed to a growing number of separations and divorces. A disproportionate number of youthful militants, Commission statistics suggested, came from broken homes.[37]

Official Language policies, once instituted to break down class barriers, now seemed to be reinforcing them. Members of the urban elite were viewed as hypocrites who promoted *swabasha* (indigenous language) education for the masses, but made sure that their own children were proficient in English. The term *Kaduwa* (sword) was used as a metaphor by monolingual Sinhala speakers to describe how proficient English-speakers could always 'cut down' those who lacked this skill. Preferential treatment in the job market for English-speakers made things worse; now the most prestigious and lucrative jobs were those linked to the international economy in some way. Whether the position was financial analyst in an international bank, secretary to an Export Processing Zone manager or bellman at a five-star hotel, a degree of English proficiency was *required*. Some youth felt there was a conspiracy to deny them the English training that would provide good jobs and social mobility.[38]

An educated but monolingual Sinhala speaker who sought government employment (English was not required for public-sector jobs) might find that doors were closed because of bribery or political favouritism. From the standpoint of those excluded, President Jayewardene's job bank and 'chit' schemes were seen as ways of keeping worthy applicants from jobs they deserved. This was particularly disillusioning for youths who had secured a prized spot at one of Sri Lanka's universities, but then been forced to take one of the less professionally relevant 'arts' degrees taught in Sinhala.

Frustration about government hiring practices was only one element in an overall syndrome of disillusionment with political processes and institutions that seemed to fall far short of democratic ideals. The *dharmista* government promised by J.R. Jayewardene was seen as corrupt. Students were called upon to celebrate '50 years of universal franchise' in the year that a flawed and constitutionally suspect referendum postponed parliamentary elections for five years.[39] Centralised controls had reduced the power and responsiveness of local government institutions. People saw judicial processes eroded by successive states of emergency, cumbersome procedures and costly legal expenses. Youths believed that 'justice' would either be 'delayed, not rendered, or inaccessible.'[40]

Thus, in the socially turbulent climate created by J.R. Jayewardene's open economy reforms and other policies, many young Sri Lankans saw the cards as irrevocably stacked against them. They believed that no matter how hard they worked, their nation's social, cultural and political order would conspire to deny them opportunities they sought and to which they felt entitled. If they sought redress for perceived injustices, established institutions offered them no place to turn.[41] Frustrated, and seeing a bleak future looming, only a small minority of young Sri Lankans actually joined the JVP. Others sought alternative outlets for their frustrations. But many sympathised with the party's social vision and revolutionary agenda.

Militant Buddhism

JVP doctrine, as we have seen, simultaneously embraced Buddhism and revolutionary violence. Moreover, the JVP was not alone in using Buddhist principles to justify violence, especially directed against Tamils. Some find this paradoxical,[42] but many scholars reject characterisations of Buddhism as distinctively non-violent. 'The condemnation of violence in Christianity,' writes Ananda Wickremeratne, 'is equally emphatic and categorical.' 'Buddhists are aware,' he continues, 'that violence, anger, ill-will, jealousy, hatred… are part of being human. Thus, they are not surprised when such conduct is present in Sri Lanka, or elsewhere.'[43]

What circumstances called for morally justified acts of violence? In the socially turbulent 1970s and 1980s a growing number of priests and lay Buddhists were attracted to schools of thought emphasising Sinhalese racial purity and the exclusion of 'alien' elements from the isle of Lanka. These schools, too, could point to historical and mythological antecedents. It is said that before Sri Lanka could be established as a unique haven for propagating his doctrines, The Buddha found it necessary to expel the *Yakkas*, 'a terrifying demonic race who occupied the island in vast numbers.' Since *Yakkas* were not viewed as fit subjects for conversion to the *Sasana* (Buddhist dispensation), expulsion was the only option.[44] Dealing with large groups who reject the premises of Theravada Buddhism has remained an ongoing dilemma in Sri Lankan history.

Buddhist exclusionism's role in rationalising anti-Tamil violence has been emphasised by anthropologist Stanley J. Tambiah in two controversial books, *Sri Lanka: Ethnic Fratricide and the Dismantling of Democracy* and especially *Buddhism Betrayed?*.[45] He points to the 'emergence of new components in Buddhism as a nationalist religion and a populist dogma with racial claims.' These proved appealing to poor Sinhalese in urban areas whose lives had been disrupted by economic and political change.[46]

The writings of some Buddhist monks, Tambiah argues, were particularly influential in shaping these views. Further, some played political roles in militant organisations and participated in violent agitations. This participation reflected not only chauvinist leanings, but also the appeal of causes that promised redress for the sufferings of poor and marginalised Sri Lankans. Saffron robed young men who marched in the JVP's May Day parade may have been deviants from the Buddhist mainstream, a view emphasised by other scholars, but they represented influential strands of thought and action in Sri Lanka of the early 1980s.

Militant Buddhist doctrines, then, offered Sinhalese – especially Sinhalese youth – a locus of identity, a frame of reference and a rationale for action in a rapidly changing social-economic environment. While elevation of Sinhalese-Buddhist identity did not necessarily imply denigration of Tamils, Sri Lanka's unique setting and history made this almost inevitable. On the island of Lanka, 'Sinhalese unity' strongly implied inferior status, if not outright exclusion, for non-Sinhalese. When non-Sinhalese were seen to have privileged status, when they demanded equal rights and – worst of all – when they used violent tactics, militant Buddhism characterised these circumstances as threats to a rightful (and righteous) social order. Administering a cathartic of violent counter-action could be seen as a logical, necessary, morally justifiable response.

How the Liberation Tigers of Tamil Eelam came to dominate Jaffna politics

By 1977, many Sinhalese viewed 'Tamils' as collectively threatening the ideal of a unified Sinhalese-Buddhist dominated Sri Lanka. When mainstream Tamil politicians labelled their party the *Tamil United Liberation Front*, called for an independent Tamil Eelam and spoke of 'secret plans,' Sinhalese fears were reinforced. Racist political oratory by Sinhalese politicians and articles in the Sinhala language media contributed to these fears. Growing numbers of Sinhalese, including security force cadres, now viewed Tamils through a prism of negative racial stereotypes. Refining these stereotypes to characterise 'Tamils' as pro-Eelamist militants, active militant sympathisers or at least passive acceptors of a militant stance, was not a radical shift. Actions of both Tamil militants and mainstream Tamil politicians encouraged this shift.

The realities of Tamil society were, of course, more nuanced than Sinhalese stereotypes. Amirthalingam and other TULF leaders represented one body of opinion, the old order, with its rigid caste distinctions. Independence for Tamil Eelam was now part of their rhetoric, but practically, they still favoured accommodations with Jayewardene's government that would grant Tamil majority regions more cultural, linguistic and political autonomy. A second body of Tamil opinion regarded the UNP more sceptically, but still believed that non-violent methods such as strikes, protest marches and demonstrations, in conjunction with democratic elections, could effect change. Proponents were found within the Jaffna University – students and faculty – and within organisations comprising a nascent civil society in Sri Lanka's northeast – human rights committees, refugee and self-help organisations, businessmen's groups and professional societies. A third body of opinion, unalterably committed to an independent Tamil Eelam, most closely approximated Sinhalese fears. Proponents were young men who were militant group members or sympathisers. Most believed that force and violence were the only means by which to attain their goals. Further, they believed that *all* Tamils, no matter where they lived and whether they sympathised or not, were *de facto* foot soldiers in the independence movement.[47]

In 1977, proponents of militant Eelamist views were a tiny minority, fragmented into small groups with imposing titles, but limited resources. They seemed to devote as much time to squabbling with one another as to occasional high visibility robberies, attacks and assassinations that were headlined in Sinhalese newspapers. Five years later, the balance of influence had shifted to the militants. Many who supported accommodation or spoke out against violence had been killed, silenced, converted or had chosen exile. Those who remained lived in peril of their lives. The Liberation Tigers of Tamil Eelam, led by Supremo Velupillai Prabakharan, had become the dominant militant group. 'We are not on top,' Sri Lanka's Army Chief told a British journalist in spring, 1983. 'The initiative is with the terrorists. They choose the time and place. We can only be reactive.'[48]

Prabakharan himself deserves much credit for providing the leadership skills and building the organisation that achieved this transformation. He was maturing into one of the worlds most feared and effective guerrilla leaders. Personal qualities that contributed to this – single-mindedness, self-discipline and personal courage – were described earlier. Friends who worked with him during this period also recall an almost obsessive concern with personal security. He had disciplined himself to withstand torture if it came to that, but had vowed never to be captured by Sri Lankan government forces. He always carried a revolver, placing it under his pillow when he slept, and insisted that compatriots do the same. Assassination was a constant fear: he would never meet with strangers who had not been thoroughly checked out by supporters.

Patient planning and meticulous attention to detail characterised all his operations. In contrast to JVP leader Wijeweera, Prabakharan never sought personal visibility, preferring to remain an elusive figure in the background. Clint Eastwood and The Phantom, a comic strip character who could become invisible, were his role models.[49]

Strongest of all was his belief that a successful outcome to the Eelam struggle would require discipline, unwavering commitment, loyalty and a long-term violent struggle. Preferring action, he had little use for the lengthy ideological debates in which the Jaffna academic community engaged. 'You (arm chair) intellectuals are afraid of blood,' he contemptuously ended one discussion. 'No struggle will take place without killings... You people live in comfort and try to prove me wrong. So what should I do? Take cyanide and die?'[50]

By 1977, outlines of the distinctive guerrilla organisation that would sustain a 20-plus year civil war against Sri Lanka's army and fight an Indian 'Peace Keeping Force' to a standstill had begun to take shape. Self-supporting farms and training camps were established in remote jungle areas of Vavuniya and Mullaittivu districts. Screening of prospective recruits was rigorous. In the camps, they had to endure a probationary period during which they helped grow vegetables, received some training and were assigned tasks to test their loyalty.[51] Full members of the organisation pledged loyalty to the LTTE constitution, which had been drafted by Prabakharan. This document called for armed struggle to establish a casteless society and promised that LTTE would dissolve once an independent Tamil Eelam had been established. Adherence to a strict disciplinary code was required. Love relationships, sex, alcohol and even cigarettes were prohibited. Organisational loyalty and obedience to orders were to take precedence over family ties. Cadres were organised in small cells, whose only links to one another were through an executive committee, ranging in size from five to nine members.[52] Many wore checked shirts hanging over short pants or sarongs and all carried cyanide capsules, worn on a lanyard around their necks.

Prabakharan's self-discipline and organisational skills set him apart from other militant leaders, but in 1977 it was by no means certain that he would emerge as the LTTE's number one. Attracting able lieutenants who were loyal and personally courageous helped him to survive both challenges from rivals and counter-terror operations mounted by Sri Lanka's security forces.[53]

We have already learned something of another early LTTE leader, Uma Maheswaren, whom Prabakharan tried to gun down in Madras City's Pondi Bazaar. His story is important both because he later headed another important militant group, the People's Liberation Organisation of Tamil Eelam (PLOTE), and because it illustrates another Prabakharan trait, an unwavering commitment to eliminate Eelamist leaders who opposed him. Maheswaren, who had served as the TULF Colombo chapter secretary, was the only LTTE inner core member who was a visible public figure and one of the few who had not been one of Prabakharan's close personal friends.[54] Initially, the two men were close, but allegations of a Maheswaren love affair with an LTTE sympathiser, violating his oath to the organisation, ruptured the relationship. Other disagreements soon followed. In 1979, LTTE Central Committee members bowed to pressure from Prabakharan and expelled Maheswaren. Despite this, an angry Prabakharan resigned from the LTTE over the affair – he felt the response to his rival's alleged derelictions had been too lenient. He was quickly reinstated as the undisputed number one. Maheswaren joined PLOTE as deputy director and soon became its leader. Before long, PLOTE and LTTE cadres were punctuating attacks against Sri Lankan government institutions with internecine strikes against one another.[55]

Though the militants had achieved visibility and some notable successes, it was hard to be optimistic about the course of that struggle as 1982 dawned. In June 1981, a tightening police dragnet forced Prabakharan to flee in a rented boat to Madras, with a few close lieutenants. Soon afterwards PLOTE leader Maheswaren too, fled to Madras. There, he faced the continuing wrath of Prabakharan. The Pondi Bazaar shoot-out was the LTTE leader's second attempt to murder his rival, face-to-face, since he had arrived in India.[56] Prabakharan's incarceration and subsequent house arrest in Madurai was the only time, during his long career as a militant leader, that he was in police custody.

M.R. Narayan Swamy describes this period of enforced inactivity as a fruitful 'time for introspection and for reading and preparing for the years to come.'[57] The leftist Tamil politician P. Nedumaran befriended Prabakharan and became his host in Tamil Nadu.[58] Prabakharan studied the writings of other guerrilla leaders extensively, even having one of Che Guevera's books translated from Spanish into Tamil so that he could read it. He began identifying and networking with sympathetic Indian politicians and army officers. Safe houses, also used to train Sri Lankan Tamil youths in guerrilla tactics, were established in several towns. Nedumaran's influence with police gave Prabakharan some flexibility to move about and make contacts. When the LTTE leader slipped back to Jaffna, after seven months of 'house' arrest, it was with his host's permission.

Prabakharan's return revitalised the LTTE, which began the series of attacks directed at government officials, the security forces, PLOTE and other Tamil opponents, described earlier. By now, J.R. Jayewardene's referendum had been overwhelmingly rejected in Tamil majority districts. When TULF leader Amirthalingam announced that TULF candidates would contest local government elections announced by the UNP government, the Tigers circulated open letters throughout Jaffna, urging a boycott. LTTE bullets and bombs felled police officers and constables, soldiers, rival group members and even a TULF Parliamentarian who had criticised the Tigers. On election day, almost 90 per cent of registered voters in the Northern Province stayed home. The year before, nearly 80 per cent had turned out for the District Development Council elections

The LTTE was clearly Jaffna's dominant political force by July 1983, but whether the ensuing militarisation of Tamil society could have been avoided, had the riots not intervened, is debated. *The Broken Palmyra*'s authors are among those who assert that an alternative path was still open. The TULF had clearly been discredited but sympathy for 'our boys,' was not widespread, they maintain.

The five years following J.R. Jayewardene's election victory was a period when militant groups, especially the LTTE, began to define what it meant to be a *Tamil* and to repress alternative views. Sinhalese provocations, especially security force provocations, played a major role in their ascendancy, but centrist Tamil community leaders – Amirthalingam in particular – were also complicit. Their inept negotiations with J.R. Jayewardene's government, along with equivocal stances on human rights and non-violence, helped cede leadership to Prabakharan. The Tamil Tiger leader, in turn, was both politically shrewd and able to project an image of the quintessential anti-politician. He did not vacillate. Both his long-term goal – an independent Tamil Eelam – and strategy for attaining it were clear. At his command was a resilient force, whose members had no reservations about using violence. The LTTE was small in the summer of 1983, but its members were loyal, disciplined and effective. When opportunity presented itself, Prabakharan was the Tamil leader who was best prepared to seize the moment.

Marginalisation of the TULF and weakening of Tamil civil society

Appapillai Amirthalingam, too, had a moment of opportunity, but he failed to seize it. His opportunity to solidify a role as unrivalled leader came in the months following TULF victories in the 1977 parliamentary elections. Calls for an independent Tamil Eelam and allusions to a 'secret plan' for attaining it helped Amirthalingam mobilise overwhelming pro-TULF support in Tamil majority constituencies. Like Sinhalese parties, the TULF's structure was hierarchical, according the party leader virtually unfettered power. As officially designated Leader of the Opposition (the first Tamil ever to hold that post) Amirthalingam had central government resources at his disposal, international visibility and access to top officials, including the President. International support from the Tamil diaspora, some governments and sympathetic non-governmental organisations seemed to provide additional resources for pressuring President Jayewardene. Tamil militant leaders, for the most part, were beholden to him. He sometimes used them as unacknowledged TULF enforcers much as UNP, SLFP and Marxist leaders used their thuggish allies.

Having assumed the mantle of Sri Lanka's most powerful Tamil politician and used a highly volatile issue to mobilise popular support, Amirthalingam needed to deliver on at least some promises to retain his constituents' confidence. His position eerily resembled that of another eloquent Sri Lankan politician – S.W.R.D. Bandaranaike – who had mobilised Sinhalese communal sentiments with promises of 'Sinhala only in twenty-four hours.' We learned that once in power, Bandaranaike expected his aroused supporters to accept a less rapid and less encompassing trajectory of political change, which many were reluctant to do.

Amirthalingam faced a similar dilemma. He had raised the aspirations of his community without a clear strategy for realising them. His speechmaking and political deal-making skills were typical of Sri Lankan political leaders. Deal making, Amirthalingam hoped, would produce at least some of the promised results. J.R. Jayewardene appeared to be the man with whom the deal could be cut. Publicly, the President had promised to redress long-standing minority grievances. Privately, in pre-election meetings, he had assured Tamil leaders that his promises were serious. But as we have already seen, President Jayewardene's agenda and ordering of priorities were very different than Amirthalingam's. Moreover, he was a far more skilful negotiator.

Tamils in the north and east had many grievances, but devolution of power was the pivotal issue. On this issue, a chasm separated Tamil pro-independence factions and the UNP's core Sinhalese constituencies. Extracting concessions from Jayewardene that would at least partially meet Tamil aspirations for autonomy was Amirthalingam's challenge. Eelamist rhetoric notwithstanding, he saw some power-sharing arrangement between Colombo and regional governments as the most practical scenario. Reluctantly, he decided that President Jayewardene's scheme for District Development Councils was at least a point where the devolution process could begin. Processes of negotiating to establish Councils, electing Council representatives, appointing officials, formally devolving power and allocating resources, came to be viewed by many Tamils as tests of Amirthalingam's ability to influence the President.

The torturous, convoluted pace at which these processes unfolded has already been described. Councils were not finally established until President Jayewardene had won a second term and orchestrated his referendum victory. Even then, the mechanism was so flawed and controversial that a commission had been formed to see how Councils could be made more effective.[59] The commission's *Interim Report* had yet to be acted upon when the riots of July 1983 effectively ended the District Development Council experiment.

J.R. Jayewardene's detractors argue that discrediting Amirthalingam was a consideration in his stage management of the District Development Council process. Others disagree. Whatever his motivations, there can be no argument about the outcome. Having committed himself to political deal making, Amirthalingam found himself negotiating from a position of weakness. His strategy of tacitly supporting militants, while arguing in Colombo that Sinhalese concessions were necessary to control them, proved counterproductive on both fronts. Militant leaders and the Tamil public believed that Amirthalingam accepted violence as a tactic. Jayewardene, on the other hand, viewed violent attacks as threats against the integrity of the Sri Lankan state that required a resolute, forceful response, whatever the cost. As security force sanctions intensified, and District Development Council negotiations stagnated, Amirthalingam saw his options narrow and his power wane. Still exercising the perquisites of power in Colombo, he continued to hope that further negotiations and concessions might produce a breakthrough. But as he moved toward it, the deal he sought receded ever further toward the horizon. For editors of Jaffna's *Saturday Review*, who still spoke with an independent voice in December 1982, the TULF's passive stance toward the referendum symbolised its leader's final emasculation by President Jayewardene. They wrote:

> To many, it would seem unbelievable that the TULF, under a once combative leader like Amirthalingam, should sit back and allow things to drift, waiting for the promised jam [patronage and concessions from President Jayewardene]. ...Although not very evident at the time, the TULF's inactivity during the referendum had cut it adrift from its political base. The Jaffna voter had shown that he had a mind of his own by registering a 91.3% vote against the government's proposal.
>
> President Jayewardene could now afford to treat the Tamils and their representatives with contempt. As far as his immediate ambitions were concerned, he had the Tamils in his pocket, as he did his party's MPs. The Tamils were now subject to his whims and his irresponsibility. He was not going to give them jam. He was going to give them cake in the sense in which Marie Antoinette meant it, when the Parisians asked for bread.[60]

In retrospect, J.R. Jayewardene's strategy seems less astute than it may have appeared to contemporaries. We now know that his most dangerous enemy by far was Velupillai Prabakharan, not Amirthalingam. A strong, well-led Tamil political party, committed to democracy, even if opposed to the UNP, could have served as a counterweight to the LTTE. Instead, Amirthalingam's failures helped create a political vacuum in Tamil majority regions, which Prabakharan was best able to fill.

Government policies also weakened another potential counterweight in the Tamil community: non-governmental organisations and movements that, in the 1970s, comprised an emerging civil society. Like the TULF and militants, these groups rejected government policies and favoured greater Tamil autonomy. However, they opposed both business-as-usual Colombo politics and political violence. While some had an overtly political mission, others saw themselves as 'non-political' (though remaining free of political involvement was difficult in Sri Lanka).

A concern with refugees, who had been displaced by rioting Sinhalese and ignored by government officials, provided one rationale for creating non-governmental organisations. Fighting government abuses of human rights provided another. A leading refugee organisation was *Gandhiyam*, co-founded by a successful London physician. Using funds raised locally and from international organisations, *Gandhiyam* established self-help agricultural projects, schools and day care centres for displaced families who had settled near Vavuniya. The Tamil Refugees Rehabilitation Organisation (TRRO), co-founded by a successful corporate attorney, implemented similar projects in other areas of the north and placed particular emphasis on involving members of the Tamil diaspora in their work.[61] University of Jaffna students became actively involved in relief work after a cyclone devastated the Eastern Province. Discrimination against Tamil victims was so blatant that it became an issue in Parliament. Rather than waiting for officials to act, students raised needed supplies through house-to-house canvassing, then collaborated with social service and relief organisations to distribute them to victims. University faculty and students also engaged in political protests, speaking out and demonstrating against Prevention of Terrorism Act detentions, election law abuses linked to the referendum and abuses of power by the security forces. While some sympathised with militant groups, many strongly opposed their use of violent tactics.[62]

Protests against the Prevention of Terrorism Act and other abuses of power were not limited to the Tamil Community. This was, in fact, one of a few issues where at least some Tamils and Sinhalese found common cause. Two island-wide organisations, the Movement for Inter Racial Justice and Equality (MIRJE) and the Civil Rights Movement provided focal points for those who opposed both the Jayewardene government's internal security policies and militant violence.[63] MIRJE members were active in anti-government demonstrations and often worked with refugee organisations such as Ghandhiyam and TRRO. Because some priests affiliated with MIRJE had left-wing political leanings the organisation was viewed with suspicion by embattled security force officers and by UNP conservatives, including the President.

The Civil Rights Movement was founded in 1971 to respond to human rights abuses by government forces during the JVP rebellion. It was in the vanguard of opposition to the 1982 referendum, stating publicly that postponing elections 'threatened the very basis of democratic parliamentary government founded on periodic elections of the people's representatives.'[64] Civil Rights Movement leaders repeatedly protested against civil rights abuses and police misconduct. Grants of emergency powers to the security forces, they warned,

...will create again the excesses of 1971 when similar power resulted in deaths under torture, indiscriminate killings and execution without trial by security forces, which usurp functions
of courts in determining who is a terrorist and who is not and
leading to the slaughter of many never established to have been
involved in insurgent activities.[65]

Police and army frustration over rising numbers of terrorist attacks
and their inability to capture perpetrators motivated a campaign against all
spokespersons for human rights and Tamil autonomy. Armed with emergency powers freeing them from legal accountability for their actions, soldiers and police constables targeted leaders of Tamil civil society – university
faculty, intellectuals, student leaders and heads of non-governmental organisations. Despite threats from militant groups, these men (and a few women)
had remained proponents of non-violent political change strategies. They
were willing to speak out publicly against human rights abuses perpetrated
by both sides, militants as well as the security forces. Thus, they were ideal
targets – visible, outspoken and vulnerable. By targeting these individuals
and their organisations, Sri Lanka's army and police became unwitting allies
of Prabakharan in a campaign against the most credible political alternative
to the LTTE.

A final act in the Jayewardene government's assault on Tamil civil society
was silencing its leading publication. Despite militant threats and security force
pressures, Jaffna's *Saturday Review* had continued to speak with a humane and
relatively uncensored voice in the south as well as the north. *Review* articles
had spoken out against internecine warfare between militant groups and political assassinations. But others had criticised security force excesses, such as the
burning of Gandhiyam farms, the arrest and torture of priests and beatings of
schoolgirl demonstrators. This was too much for the government. Early in July,
officials sealed the *Review's* presses. In an article for the unpublished 2 July 1983
issue, columnist Gamini Navaratne had penned the following lines: 'If I have
my own way, I will send most of the present politicians to the moon. That is
where they really belong.'[66]

Forging a strategic alliance: how Indian Tamils entered Sri Lanka's political mainstream

It seems paradoxical that a period in which militant separatism came to dominate Sri Lanka Tamil politics was also one in which the Indian Tamil community entered the political mainstream. J.R. Jayewardene's new constitution regularised the status of Indian Tamil citizens by abolishing the 'citizen by registration category.' Remaining 'stateless' plantation workers were accorded most 'fundamental rights' and Tamil plantation residents received voting rights in local government elections. Ceylon Workers' Congress (CWC) leader Savumiamoorthy Thondaman joined the government as a cabinet minister in September 1978. He used his position to leverage wage gains for plantation workers and a long-sought government take-over of the 'Estate School' system.[67] How was it that Thondaman secured significant advances for his community, during a time of rising anti-Tamil sentiment among many Sinhalese, while Amirthalingam failed to move forward with his agenda? To unravel this puzzle we must see how Indian Tamil political demands and leadership strategies differed from those of their counterparts in the north.

In 1977, Tamil plantation workers still ranked at the bottom of Sri Lankan society, politically, economically and socially. Many remained disenfranchised or stateless. Working conditions were harsh. Living conditions were crowded and primitive. Illiteracy was widespread, especially among women. Health care and educational services lagged far beyond the norm.[68] Caste conscious Sri Lanka Tamils were as likely to discriminate against plantation Tamils as were Sinhalese. As we have seen, up-country parliamentary 'representatives,' kept in place by a rigged electoral formula, were Sinhalese-Buddhist nationalists. Plantation workers' goals – citizenship parity, educational opportunity, full voting rights and resolution of the long-festering 'stateless' issue – were far more modest than the TULF's separatist agenda, which Thondaman had disavowed explicitly.

The Indian Tamil community was both more cohesive and more passive, thus more receptive to strong leadership than Amirthalingam's Jaffna-based constituency. There were no divisive caste differences, no articulate university intellectuals, no independent publications like the *Saturday Review*, no rebellious militant groups. Other unions vied for plantation workers' loyalty, but did not seriously threaten CWC's dominance. Thondaman's political clout, ratified by his election to Parliament in 1977, extended beyond the well-organised CWC rank-and-file. Often he referred to plantation workers as 'my people' implying – accurately – they could be mobilised at his command and would accept his judgements as *Thalaivar* (leader) Thondaman.[69] His ability to cut deals with J.R. Jayewardene and function as a cabinet member was not limited by strong dissenting voices or potential threats to his leadership.

Thus Thondaman was positioned to implement a pragmatic, gradualist political strategy that fit well with J.R. Jayewardene's predispositions, avoided confrontations and produced tangible, if limited, benefits for his constituents.[70] As a cabinet minister, Thondaman chose the role of mediator between the Sri Lanka Tamil and Sinhalese communities, while seeking to maintain credibility with both.[71] While his efforts to find common ground between Jayewardene's government and Sri Lanka Tamils in the northeast failed, he largely kept his own community free from entanglement in the escalating conflict. Often J.R. Jayewardene rejected or ignored Thondaman's advice on communal issues, evoking dismissive comments about his influence from Tamil scholars such as A. J. Wilson.[72] But the President accepted Thondaman as a colleague in a way that he could never accept Amirthalingam. Thondaman's grasp of parliamentary culture, political pragmatism and ability to keep promises were qualities J. R. Jayewardene could relate to and respect. This helped Thondaman to move forward on his agendas and protect his vulnerable community.

Emergence of the National Workers Organisation as Sri Lanka's strongest labour organisation

Sri Lanka's system of close ties between labour unions and political parties was, as we have seen, costly to both old-line Marxist unions and workers they represented. Workers lost out because union leaders were subservient to United Front government ministers responsible for implementing austerity programs. Until 1975, when the United Front coalition fractured, rank-and-file pressures to fight inflation with strikes for higher wages were resisted. Politically motivated strikes that were authorised, beginning in 1975, had no short-term economic objectives and were costly to union members. Both passivity and costly political activism weakened ties between Marxist union leaders and members. An alternative now open to working men and women was the pro-UNP National Workers Organisation (*Jatika Sevaka Sangamaya* – JSS).

We saw in chapter 13 how J.R. Jayewardene's political craftsmanship created this improbable mutant of Sri Lanka's labour union structure – a workers' organisation, devoid of pro-labour ideological underpinnings, affiliated with the nation's most pro-business political party. Despite its questionable rationale, however, the JSS membership rolls began to swell with new labour force members and with Marxist union defectors seeking a union willing to take strong stands against government-affiliated employers on economic issues. One might have predicted, then, that Jayewardene's election victory would prove costly to the JSS in the same way that the United Front's victory had weakened its competitors. Labour peace was a centrepiece of the new government's pro-investment economic programs. Naming Industries Minister Cyril Matthew as JSS head further emphasised the degree to which union activities would be linked to government policies. But instead of returning to marginal status, the JSS grew to be arguably Sri Lanka's most powerful labour organisation under the UNP government. How did this transpire?

Anthropologist Gananath Obeyesekere described the JSS's growth and distinctive role during Jayewardene's first term.[73] Urban UNP leaders, he writes, used the union's structure to organise cadres beholden to them through patronage and personal loyalty. These men, often members of the urban *lumpenproletariat*, were given preferential access to public sector jobs. Militant Sinhalese-Buddhist nationalism, articulated in the writings of Cyril Mathew and other proponents, provided a source of identity and justification for union-sanctioned activism. When Marxist unions tried to demonstrate their strength through a series of disruptive strikes,[74] JSS members not only opposed the strikes, but also supported government countermeasures by serving as strike breakers. When the strikes proved ineffective, this further weakened the older unions' credibility. As the JSS grew in strength, organisers began using intimidation to recruit reluctant prospective members, using well-organised gangs of thugs to back up their threats.

Thuggery had always been a facet of trade union activity in Sri Lanka. Indeed, President Jayewardene told me that one of his reasons for organising the JSS in the first place was to constitute a force that could respond to thuggish attacks organised by Marxist unions. With the UNP in power, however, Obeyesekere argues that a threshold was crossed. Thuggery became 'less particularised' than previously. JSS cadres now 'wielded enough power to transfer and intimidate even high government officials.'[75] They targeted government opponents more directly and were supported with public resources more overtly than previously. When victims sought police assistance, political pressure enabled their attackers to escape prosecution.

Even the principled Dudley Senanayake sometimes winked at thuggery and most successful Sri Lankan politicians occasionally used such tactics. But in the climate of disillusionment that followed J.R. Jayewardene's referendum victory, some government supporters began to voice concerns about JSS attacks. In January 1983, the Government Medical Officers Association, itself a fairly militant union organisation, petitioned government officials for protection from union thugs, which it alleged had infiltrated the lower ranks of hospital staffs. Surprisingly, an editorial in the government-owned *Daily News* supported the officers' plea. 'One thing is clear enough,' the editors wrote, 'no state, no government, no party that condemns [militant] methods can condone equally outrageous behaviour in any institution under its control... It is futile to denounce thuggery on the one hand and resort to it or let it go unpunished on the other.'[76]

By 1983, President Jayewardene had clearly achieved the goal that he envisioned when founding the JSS. The power of Marxist unions, long a thorn in the side of both UNP and SLFP governments, had been eviscerated. Sri Lanka's strongest labour organisation was now a more or less pliable arm of his government that could be mobilised to support free market economic policies and silence opponents. How the functioning of this new institution, over time, would impact Sri Lanka's social fabric and still-fragile democratic institutions was a question that remained to be answered.

J.R. Jayewardene's tactical triumphs in retrospect

Consolidation of JSS power was a final tactical triumph over traditional UNP opponents achieved by Jayewardene during his first term in office. We have seen that the story of opposition movements during this period is about how the SLFP, the TULF, the Marxist parties, their labour union allies and independent civil society organisations in both the Sinhalese and Tamil communities all lost credibility. UNP leaders achieved this by skilfully using political assets and state power, while capitalising on opposition leadership shortcomings. But the way these triumphs were achieved exacted costs. Emasculation of legitimate opposition groups, further politicisation of the security forces, repressive measures and electoral manipulations disillusioned many. Both class and communal relations were more polarised in 1983 than 1977. Polarisation and disillusionment with 'legitimate' politics contributed to a climate in which violent scapegoating and organised militancy became more probable.

Sri Lanka's security forces were responsible for maintaining public order, neutralising militant forces and quelling militant violence. UNP political tactics, however, added complexities and contradictions to their roles. Sometimes, police officers and soldiers were tasked to prevent and quell violent outbreaks. In other circumstances, when government opponents were targets, their mission might be to stand by passively, facilitate violent attacks or even participate actively in the violence. Thus, our discussion of state-sanctioned violence in the following chapter must address two questions. First, how the did the UNP government attempt to balance its use of state-sanctioned violence as a political tactic with its responsibility to maintain public order in the face of intensifying militant pressures? Second, how did Sri Lanka's police officers, soldiers and sailors cope with the complex, sometimes conflicting demands that this created?

18

How State-Sanctioned Violence Clouded Political Feedback

With the wisdom of hindsight, we can see how miscalculations by the President and his advisors contributed to policy failures that adversely impacted the public mood and increased the potential for conflict escalation. A predisposition toward repressing dissent and electoral feedback increased the probability that there would be miscalculations and that their consequences would continue uncorrected.

J.R. Jayewardene saw himself as a democrat, not an autocrat.[1] He also saw himself as a national leader with a mission that would require wide-ranging authority: transforming Sri Lanka's moribund but entrenched command economy. Like many strong leaders, political goals and Sri Lanka's 'national interest' were inextricably linked in his mind.

The President could speak and write eloquently of his personal commitment to non-violence, but he believed that a head of government must put aside personal beliefs and use whatever force was needed when national security and public order were threatened.[2] Communal riots, politically inspired robberies, assassinations, bombings and attacks against the security forces were seen as unambiguous threats to national security and public order. Responding forcefully to these threats seemed imperative.

Anti-terrorist legislation was a principal tool. It authorised police officers and soldiers to not only to fight back when attacked but also to anticipate and neutralise 'potential threats.' Practically, this meant that, at times, relatively untrained young men arrogated *de facto* authority to act as accuser, arresting officer, interrogator, judge, jury and even executioner. 'Emergency regulations' freed them from legal accountability for their actions.

In the climate created by militant attacks and anti-terrorist legislation, it was tempting for UNP leaders and supporters to cross over the line, taking advantage of immunities that emergency regulations granted to clamp down on political opponents who were not necessarily violent. Sirimavo Bandaranaike's adherents had been unable to resist this temptation. J.R. Jayewardene's

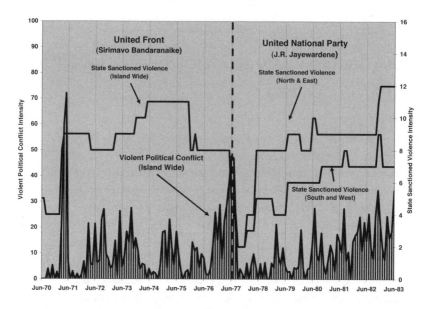

Figure 18.1 State-Sanctioned Violence and Violent Conflict 1970 – 1983

would succumb as well, first targeting opponents of open economy reforms and then, during pre-referendum campaigning, proponents of *any* change in government.

State-sanctioned violence patterns

Figure 18.1 shows an overall topology of violent conflict and state-sanctioned violence, covering the period from June 1970 through June 1983. The format is similar to that shown in previous chapters with one exception. Beginning in August 1977 when J.R. Jayewardene assumed power, state-sanctioned violence has been disaggregated between Sinhalese majority regions (southwest) and Tamil majority regions (northwest).[3] I chose to disaggregate because after 1977 the national security situation in Sinhalese and Tamil majority regions differed so markedly.

In the southwest, UNP state-sanctioned violence policies were fairly similar to those of Sirimavo Bandaranaike's United Front government. Internal security measures – such as the suspension of constitutional guarantees and censorship – were tightened in response to civil unrest, but then exploited for

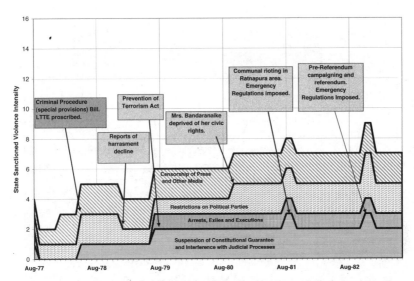

Figure 18.2 State-Sanctioned Violence Pattterns, Southwest Region

political advantage. Police officers were the principal enforcers. Police indifference or even active support sometimes facilitated attacks against political opponents by pro-government thugs.

In the northeast, as we have seen, the security forces faced intensifying attacks from Tamil militants to which they responded with increasingly strong measures. Police attempts to maintain order and fight militants were supported by growing numbers of soldiers – for a time, civil administration was supplanted by a military governor. Arrests and detentions were more frequent. Thus, our topology shows intensifying levels of state-sanctioned violence throughout the island, but significantly higher levels in Tamil majority than in Sinhalese majority regions. Under President Jayewardene, use of state-sanctioned violence in the southwest was somewhat less intense than under his predecessor. By December of 1982 in the northeast, state-sanctioned violence had reached levels never before seen in Sri Lanka.

Figure 18.2 gives a more detailed breakdown of patterns in the southwest, showing, as in previous chapters, the four components of our state-sanctioned violence index – *suspension of constitutional guarantees, arrests, exiles and executions, censorship of the press and other media,* and *restrictions on political parties.* Increasing index scores reflected passage of anti-terrorist legislation and other restrictions

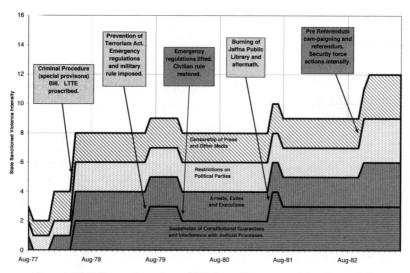

Figure 18.3 State-Sanctioned Violence Patterns, Northeast Region

on political opposition, forceful actions by the security forces that such legislation encouraged, organised campaigns of pro-government thuggery, events
surrounding the tarnished referendum and effective (albeit largely informal)
measures restricting free expression in Sri Lanka's print media.

Patterns in the northeast (Figure 18.3) map escalating restrictions on fundamental rights, harassment of opposition groups (non-militant as well as militant) and detentions of alleged militant supporters.

Two anti-terrorist laws, the *Criminal Procedures (Special Provisions) Bill* and the
Prevention of Terrorism Act sanctioned progressively more severe measures against
those seen to be enemies of the Sri Lankan state. Each was justified as a necessary response to militant violence, but very broad powers and immunities given
to the security forces opened the door to possible abuses, both inadvertent
detentions of innocent civilians and repressive measures against government
opponents who were not militants. A third piece of legislation, *The Presidential
Commission of Inquiry (Special Provisions) Bill* targeted Sri Lanka's principal opposition leaders, Sirimavo Bandaranaike and Felix Dias Bandaranaike.

Some may wonder if the last entry on this list is not inappropriately lumped
with two anti-terrorist laws that suspended constitutionally mandated rights
of all Sri Lankan citizens. I have included it because President Jayewardene's

motivations for creating the Commission appear to have been not only political but anti-democratic.[4] The Commission legislation required a constitutional amendment and provided for retroactive prosecution of offences that had not been crimes when they were committed. Commissioners, appointed by President Jayewardene himself, were given broad discretion in defining rules of evidence. Punishment was to be imposed by a Parliament in which the UNP commanded an overwhelming majority.[5] Duff and McCamant's volume, from which the state-sanctioned violence index is drawn, has this to say about *Restrictions on Political Parties:*

> Opposition political parties...provide the most explicit threat to the monopoly of rule by the incumbent regime... The temptation is great, then, for the leaders in power to prevent the formation and activity of some or all opposing political parties. When larger groups of political organisations are suppressed or simply harassed, the free play between opposition and government in no longer possible. The regime can be seen, then, to be using coercion not just to maintain the democratic system, but to maintain itself in power.[6]

Anti-terrorist legislation, too, provided J.R. Jayewardene's government with opportunities to use coercion 'not just to maintain the democratic system, but to maintain itself in power.' The Criminal Procedures (Special Provisions) Bill along with a companion piece of legislation, the *Proscribing of the Liberation Tigers of Tamil Eelam and Similar Organisations Bill,* were enacted in May 1978. They responded to two widely publicised incidents in which Tamil Militants killed a total of five police officers.[7] The President was given broad discretionary powers to ban organisations that, in his opinion, advocated violence and were either directly or indirectly concerned with or engaged in unlawful activity. There was no provision for appeal. Protesting a ban, once it had been published, could itself be defined as criminal conduct as could publishing of any material, without government permission, relating to a proscribed organisation. Also defined as criminal was 'exciting or attempting to excite disaffection, inciting change otherwise than by lawful means or promoting hostility between classes.' Suspects could be detained for a year without trial and without bail. They could be sentenced to long jail terms and forfeit of all their property.[8]

The Prevention of Terrorism Act (Temporary Provisions) Bill, enacted in July 1979,[9] further expanded government powers to deal with 'unlawful' opposition. Government spokespersons likened it to legislation passed in Britain directed against Irish Republican Army terrorism,[10] but critics said it was more like the 1967 Terrorism Act enacted by South Africa's white minority government.[11] In brief, the act freed security force members from legal accountability for their actions when dealing with suspected terrorists, and stripped suspects of most fundamental rights that had been spelled out in the 1978 Constitution.

Human rights groups warned that this legislation would likely lead to the detention of innocent people and the widespread use of torture in interrogations. Police and soldiers could now arrest anyone at any time simply by stating that 'reasonable grounds' existed to suspect them of terrorist links. There was no requirement that suspects be informed of the charges against them, or even that there be any charges. They could be held incommunicado, in unregistered locations, without access to legal counsel or even close family members for virtually indefinite periods. Prevention of Terrorism Act provisions also made arbitrary killings and disappearances more probable. Police were shielded from civil and criminal prosecution for alleged misdeeds carried out under the act. When emergency regulations were in force, as they increasingly were during this period, the security forces were given even greater latitude to arrest, detain, torture and kill.[12]

That existence of anti-terrorism legislation and regulations empowering police and soldiers to use violent force more indiscriminately is easy to document. Determining the degree to which such legislation contributed to increased 'arrests, exiles and executions,' and to 'restrictions on [opposition] political parties,' is more difficult. Governments are never keen to have information on repressive acts publicised. Newspapers may be censored and local human rights organisations threatened. International monitoring and human rights organisations may be given limited access or none at all. Victims are often dead, intimidated or without venues for publicising their experiences.

All of these obstacles to documenting state-sanctioned violence were present in Sri Lanka, but to a lesser degree than in many nations tipping towards authoritarianism. Decades-long traditions of free speech, free elections, parliamentary debates, strikes and demonstrations were not so easy to suppress, as Sirimavo Bandaranaike's government had already discovered. J.R. Jayewardene's commitment to democratic principles, though qualified by other commitments, was more than a façade. Moreover, when seeking foreign aid and investments, officials knew it was important to have Sri Lanka present a democratic face to the world.

In responding to international concerns about anti-terrorist legislation, discriminatory practices against Tamils and security force excesses, government spokespersons had to contend with the Tamil diaspora's vociferous publicity machine, which was often more effective than their own. This made it difficult for officials to refuse access to groups like the International Commission of Jurists, Amnesty International and Asia Watch. Relatively strong traditions of academic freedom encouraged university professors to speak out, to publish internationally, and to participate in groups like the Civil Rights Movement, the Committee for Rational Development and the Jaffna Teachers for Human Rights. Several Sri Lankan expatriates were world class scholars who still wrote about Sri Lanka and maintained close ties with local communities.[13] Thus, while many – possibly the majority – of anti-democratic actions by security forces were unpublicised, a significant number did see the light of day. International human rights representatives, local activists and scholars spoke with opposition leaders, interviewed family members of victims, ferreted out documentation and published the results of these investigations. From these materials, a relatively clear picture emerges of how J.R. Jayewardene's security establishment was used to solidify the government's hold on power and respond to militant violence.[14]

In the southwest, maintaining industrial peace and reinforcing the image of a government that 'enjoys unprecedented popular support' were top priorities.[15] Between 1978 and 1980 there were several incidents in which police intervened to help break strikes and peaceful demonstrations by opposition labour unions.[16] Though anti-terrorist laws had been designed to help fight Tamil militancy in the northeast, they also could be used to suppress opposition in the southwest. Police suppressed a poster campaign criticising the government because it was 'inciting change by other than lawful means and promoting hostility between classes.'[17] Arrests of more than 30 political and labour union leaders who participated in anti-government demonstrations during the summer of 1980 were justified by Prevention of Terrorism Act provisions. Three became 'disappearance' victims.[18]

A pattern of increased tension between Sri Lanka's relatively independent Supreme Court and the security forces emerged in 1982. In one incident, a police officer seized leaflets being distributed by a Buddhist priest to members of a patriotic organisation of Buddhist and Christian clergy. Supreme Court justices ruled that the priest's fundamental rights had been violated and directed the offending officer to pay damages and court costs. In a second incident, several women were arrested as police broke up a demonstration against nu-clearisation of the U.S. Navy's Diego Garcia base. One was assaulted at the police station and filed suit. Again, the Supreme Court found in favour of the plaintiff, this time ordering the government to pay compensation. Both incidents became topics of cabinet-level discussion. Officers involved in both cases were promoted by cabinet directive, and the government paid the obliga-tions of the one who had been judged personally liable. 'Public officers,' an official explanation stated, 'should do their jobs without fear of consequences from adverse court decisions.' Soon after rendering the second decision, the three justices involved were greeted outside their homes by obscenity chanting thugs who arrived in government-owned busses. Calls for police protection received no response.[19]

The theme of collusion between police and pro-government thugs will be revisited shortly, but incidents in the northeast, where soldiers and police offic-ers were more aggressively involved in maintaining order and muting anti-gov-ernment sentiments, need to be described first. They fall into three categories: disruption of political gatherings, reprisals and detentions.

Security officers'[20] roles in disrupting political gatherings were more or less similar in the northeast and southwest. Disruptions were selective, focusing on events that appeared to challenge state authority, while normal political cam-paigning and some other gatherings were often allowed to proceed unimpeded. After May 1982, all demonstrations were banned, but this did not necessarily prevent Tamil citizens from trying to organise peaceful protests. In one widely reported incident, 'hundreds of girls, women, children and men' organised a fast and parade at St. Anthony's Church, near Vavuniya, to protest against the Prevention of Terrorism Act. When demonstrators passed through the church gates, they were baton charged and beaten by steel helmeted riot police. Fleeing demonstrators who sought refuge in the church were subjected to tear gassing and further beatings before the police withdrew.[21]

Maintaining order and protecting politicians to allow political campaigning and normal political meetings to be held were the responsibilities of the po-lice and army. This complicates the task of assessing their roles in controlling demonstrators. Lack of proficiency in Tamil, limited training, low morale and militant disruptive tactics were near insuperable obstacles to carrying out these responsibilities effectively. The dangers security officers faced were real. Between August 1977 and June 1983, 31 police constables and soldiers lost their lives in 19 terrorist attacks.[22] Many more were injured or narrowly escaped injury. Young Sinhalese men assigned to northeast regions resented risking their lives to protect unco-operative Tamil citizens who seemed to be constantly criticising and harassing them.[23] These resentments, of course, played into the hands of militant leaders.

Nothing alienated northeast residents more from their putative protectors than reprisals. In a typical scenario, LTTE or PLOTE cadres would carry out a successful guerrilla attack, perhaps killing one or two security officers. The perpetrators would quickly melt into the landscape. Tamil civilians who might have witnessed the incident would respond to inquiries with protestations of ignorance or silence. Whatever their sentiments, these beleaguered men, women and children knew that giving evidence against a militant hit squad was akin to signing their own death warrants. Angered by the loss of their comrades and frustrated by this wall of silence, police and soldiers would conclude that the civilians were militant sympathisers at least and probably collaborators as well. The next step was for these men, with or without the connivance of their commanders, to strike back indiscriminately at civilians and their property. In the worst cases, security forces would 'go on a rampage' of burnings, lootings, beatings and killings. Thus, paradoxically, young Sinhalese security officers became unwitting allies of their militant tormentors by helping to discredit Sri Lanka's central government, both with Tamil civilians and internationally.

While major reprisals captured public attention, they were just the tip of the iceberg. More stressful for ordinary citizens were smaller scale reprisals that could be exacted by security officers either in response to provocations or, seemingly, at random. Many went unreported, but a few attracted the attention of news media and international human rights organisations. In addition to harassing the refugee organisation *Gandhiyam* by closing down its offices and by detaining and torturing its leaders, the security forces targeted the refugees themselves, most of whom had sought protection in camps after earlier violent incidents. Between March and June 1983, security officers set upon a number of refugee settlements, burning houses, destroying crops, driving families from the land and beating those who resisted.[24] Families in a multiracial area of

Trincomalee faced an even more devastating form of intimidation, apparently intended to remove them from their homes permanently. Reportedly, security force officers colluded with Sinhalese thugs to orchestrate a series of nighttime raids against Tamil family homes during curfew hours. The thugs, allowed to roam freely during curfew, smashed into Tamil homes and beat up the residents, or set the homes afire with families inside. When the victims tried to flee, waiting security officers administered further beatings and even shot some to death as 'curfew breakers.'[25]

Reprisals could be devastating to victims, but they occurred out in the open and thus were difficult to conceal. Detentions were another matter entirely. As we have seen, increasingly broad anti-terrorist laws and emergency regulations gave security officers a protective shield of immunities behind which they could deal with suspects (and others who opposed them) as they saw fit. As terrorist attacks and security force counter-terrorist measures escalated, the number of detainees grew. Sometimes arrests occurred at protest demonstrations. Or they targeted young men in the environs of an attack who might have seemed suspicious to a police constable. Sometimes, the pounding of batons and fists on the door of their home awakened suspects in the early morning darkness. Individuals detained in this way might have been fingered for arrest by police informants, or identified by other detainees in interrogations. Torture was often used to extract information and 'confessions.'[26] Political or commercial rivals might try to eliminate a competitor by identifying them to police as a 'terrorist.' Speaking out against a reprisal or arrest, or simply seeking information about a detainee, could itself lead to arrest and detention. Once arrested, a suspect could disappear for long periods, with officials denying any knowledge of his whereabouts. Release might come after weeks or months of detention, with no explanation given, or a body might be discovered for relatives to mourn and bury. Sometimes detainees simply 'disappeared.'

Government spokespersons could defend anti-terrorist legislation and security force excesses as regrettable, but understandable responses to terrorist threats. Another form of state-sanctioned violence, orchestrated attacks by thugs against government opponents, was more difficult to justify. Typically, these incidents were either ignored by government spokespersons or described as random events for which the government had no responsibility. Publications of human rights organisations and reputable independent scholars presented a different picture.[27]

In earlier chapters, I discussed a number of specific incidents, along with the UNP labour union's distinctive role in them. Thuggery was a long entrenched feature of Sri Lanka's political and commercial cultures, but use of the National Worker's Organisation (JSS) as a centrally co-ordinated, albeit unacknowledged, arm of Sri Lanka's state-sanctioned violence establishment, was new.[28] This gave UNP leaders greater flexibility in dealing with political opponents – labour unions, activist student groups, opposition politicians, human rights advocates and uncooperative jurist – whose exercise of their democratic rights might be legal, but inconvenient.

Strategies and tactics used by pro-government thugs during this period differed from the years prior to 1977 in at least three respects. First, pro-government thugs made it a priority to infiltrate some businesses under the guise of being labour organisers or employees. Once situated, they were in a position to intimidate both managers and fellow workers who might be unsympathetic to government policies or politicians. The reluctance of police to intervene strengthened their position.[29]

Second, pro-government thugs could take advantage of government intelligence sources and transport. Reports of attacks against anti-government strikes and demonstrations note that gangs often arrived in government-owned busses. They were well organised. Sometimes one or more UNP parliamentarians accompanied them. Thugs knew about demonstrators' plans and were able to single out key leaders for more intense harassment.[30]

Close collaboration between pro-government thugs and security officers was a third distinctive trait during this period. Sometimes, thugs and security officers actively co-operated in attacks. More commonly, police stood by passively while thugs beat up government opponents or, as when the three uncooperative Supreme Court Justices were harassed, simply failed to respond to pleas for help.

Orchestrating thuggery and using the security forces against political opponents were made easier for the government by significant constraints on media freedom. I have assigned an index value of '2', denoting 'longer term restrictions on publication of some kinds of political information [and] banning of Communist or other minority presses' to virtually all of this period. The immediate period of pre-referendum campaigning and in the northeast, the entire period after November 1982, receives a value of 3, denoting 'censorship of all political news.'

By and large, President Jayewardene did not resort to the heavy-handed censorship of his predecessor,[31] but neither did he move to restore the relatively vibrant free press of the pre-1970s. The Lake House Group, Sri Lanka's largest publisher, remained under government control and functioned as a UNP 'house organ.'[32] Shortly after assuming power, UNP government intervention rescued The Times of Ceylon Ltd., Sri Lanka's second largest newspaper group, from bankruptcy. Inevitably, financial control was followed by editorial control. By 1978, government-owned newspapers controlled 75 per cent of the English language market, 77 per cent of the Sinhala language market and 55 per cent of the Tamil language market. Critics charged that 'government control of the newspapers has led to inexcusable abuse of political power and restriction in the supply of information to the public.'[33]

When it came to important stories on sensitive matters, the line not to be crossed was generally well known. Government leaders could exert indirect pressures short of censorship on independent publications. Advertising revenues could begin drying up, shipments of newsprint could be slowed and distribution channels for offending issues could be disrupted. Editors of ostensibly independent publications would think twice before publishing critical materials or exposing malfeasance.

If indirect pressures were not enough, editors knew officials had broad authority, soon strengthened by anti-terrorist legislation, to restrict publication of offending materials and punish those who crossed over the line. Sri Lanka's 1978 constitution made freedom of expression a protected right, but gave political leaders powers to restrict that freedom 'in the interests of racial and religious harmony or in relation to parliamentary privilege, contempt of court, defamation, or incitement to an offence.'[34] Passage of anti-terrorist legislation in 1978 and 1979 gave public officials virtually unfettered power to limit the dissemination of unfavourable news, if they chose to use it.

Publication of some critical news stories in the mainstream press, survival of some fringe news organs and the absence of formal censorship mechanisms gave UNP spokespersons grounds for claiming that press freedom was greater under J.R. Jayewardene's government than under its predecessor. A dispassionate comparison of the two regimes would probably support this claim. But if press censorship was less heavy handed, it was still pervasive. News coverage overwhelmingly favoured the government. When writing about sensitive matters, editors of opposition publications had ample reason to fear reprisals.

On rare occasions, reprisals included sealed presses and padlocked offices. The conclusion that news organs faced 'serious long-term restrictions on the publication of some kinds of political information' during J.R. Jayewardene's first term is amply justified.

Use of state-sanctioned violence to retain political power reached a crescendo during pre-referendum campaigning and on the day of voting. The escalation shown in Figures 18.2 and 18.3 denotes the imposition of emergency regulations, more severe restrictions on political opposition (including arrests of opposition leaders) and the silencing of Jaffna's independent *Saturday Review*, which had circulated throughout the island. In the southwest, use of forceful measures against government opponents declined after the UNP's referendum victory. There was no corresponding decline in the northeast, however, as conflict between Tamil militants and the security forces continued to escalate.

Earlier, I described the 'no holds barred' campaign tactics used to increase the probability of victory. Most were not new, but critics say that intimidation, arrests of opposition figures, illegal campaigning and impersonation of voters reached levels never before seen in Sri Lanka. Referendum polling was neither free, nor fair, but the government's power to influence the result had its limits. Campaigning for a 'No' vote was permitted. Two privately owned newspapers covered the positions of both sides. Some time was made available on state-owned media for opposition leaders to state their case. In the end, nearly half of those who voted rejected the government's proposal. Without the widespread use of state-sanctioned violence, J.R. Jayewardene's bid to guarantee himself a compliant parliament for six more years might well have lost.

The security forces

Sri Lanka's police and military establishments bore increasingly heavy burdens during the August 1977-July 1983 period. Escalating attacks by Tamil militants meant that security officers detailed to the northeast faced a hostile environment where their lives seemed always to be at risk. Elsewhere, growing communal tensions, periodic civil disturbances and the stresses of a more complex social-political order complicated police responsibilities. Anti-terrorist legislation, as we have seen, gave young men who wore the uniforms of Sri Lanka's police and army broad discretion to use force against their fellow citizens. I have recounted a number of instances where this discretion was abused; where discipline broke down; where police actions or inaction served partisan political goals.

Policies and trends of this period culminated in the catastrophic communal riots of late July 1983, which propelled Sri Lankan society into a state of violent and seemingly irresolvable communal conflict. This was a prototypical example of conflict escalation caused by state-sanctioned violence ineffectiveness. By failing to maintain public order and in some instances actively abetting rioters, police and soldiers played a key role – perhaps the pivotal role – in allowing riots to spiral out of control.

What factors contributed most to this breakdown? Examining individual security officers' lives and working conditions is a good place to begin. Who were these young men who, in a time of crisis, abandoned discipline and chose not to carry out their duties? What were the circumstances of their lives? For the police force, Nandasena Ratnapala's ethnographic study, *The Police of Sri Lanka*, provides some answers.[35] No comparable study exists for the army, but one can draw conclusions from several more general works that do address its organisation, role and effectiveness as an anti-terrorist force.

Three themes emerge most clearly from Ratnapala's work. The first, emphasised by many other studies as well, is the degree to which all phases of police life – recruitment, assignments, promotions and enforcement – had become politicised. The second, which has received less attention, is the degree to which the inflation-eroded salaries of police officers added economic stresses to the normal day-to-day stresses of police work and increased the likelihood of corruption. The third, receiving the least attention of all, is the degree to which many police officers, even in southwest areas, felt alienated from the communities in which they served.

The transition from a politically neutral police force to a politicised force began long before J.R. Jayewardene became president. As in other areas, however, the UNP government's efforts to exercise political influence over the police were more organised and effective than those of its predecessors. One critic notes that 'by December 1982, it had become evident that it simply did not pay to enforce the law against ruling politicians, their thugs and supporters.'[36]

From reading police officers' accounts, one does not get the impression that most political interventions came from the highest levels of government. More commonly interventions came from members of parliament and local political bosses, with only tacit approval from cabinet ministers and the President. The chit system, described earlier, applied to police recruitment as well as other areas of government employment, making officers beholden to the MPs who had secured their appointment. Most officers believed that promotions and transfers depended more on political influence than effective performance of duty. On a day-to-day basis, 'political interference' had little to do with matters of high policy and much more to do with maintaining influence networks of local bosses.[37]

More nationally significant was the police force's role in supporting the government's pre-referendum 'Yes' campaign, by failing to enforce election laws and not responding to pleas from opposition supporters who were being threatened and intimidated by pro-government thugs. In one typical incident, an LSSP poll watcher was driven from his post by a mob and sought police assistance at nearby station. The officer in charge expressed sympathy, but said he would be 'transferred to Jaffna' if he intervened. He advised the watcher to look out for his own safety.[38]

This story provides evidence that the practice of transferring politically unreliable officers and those with discipline problems to Tamil majority areas continued under the UNP. Thus, personnel problems that plagued the force as a whole – low morale, indiscipline, lack of respect for human rights – were more pronounced in the northeast where, in addition, the challenges of policing were severe and ties to the community were rare. Moreover, as we have seen, anti-terrorism laws insulated officers from accountability for human rights violations. That Tamil citizens were often scapegoats for the frustrations this climate created is hardly surprising.[39]

Economic hardship, the second major theme in Ratnapala's description of police officers' daily lives, was a problem most mid- and low-level public servants faced during the open economy era. By 1982, wages had been severely eroded by inflation. Police officers and their families were worse off economically than they had been in 1977. Among 100 married constables interviewed by Ratnapala and his researchers, 87 were in debt. Most lived in rented accommodations with very modest furnishings. For many, providing basic necessities – nutritious food, clothing and school uniforms – was a struggle.[40] When transferred to northeast areas, it was often impossible for the men to bring wives and children along, adding to the unattractiveness of those assignments.[41]

Low wages made bribery and corruption almost inevitable, though some officers remained honest. In many areas police developed symbiotic relationships with local gangs who controlled illicit trading, loan sharking and the production of bootleg spirits. Resisting bribes was made more difficult by the fact that gangs often had ties to local politicians, who used them as enforcers at political rallies and on polling days. 'When I joined the Police Service,' one officer told Ratnapala, 'I was full of expectations. I risked my life during the insurgency. But instead I was given a transfer on account of the machinations of a superior officer.' He attributed subsequent career setbacks at least partly to his refusal of bribes. 'My colleagues who took bribes are very rich now,' he concluded. 'They laugh at me. 'What have you got in return for your honesty?' they ask.'

Police alienation from their communities, Ratnapala's third theme, appears to have been a long-standing phenomenon in Sri Lanka, resulting from a combination of economic pressures, transient assignments and accepted norms within the police force. Alienation was more pronounced at lower ranks than higher, where officers' powers and status made it easier for them to forge ties with influential community members. Some officers said that they were simply too exhausted to think of community activities. Others said they wanted to be respected, even feared in the community and friendships would get in the way. Finally officers worried about becoming too visible to local political bosses. Officers were concerned that community work 'would inevitably antagonise local politicians.' 'We would then be transferred,' they continued. 'So why create trouble. Just be where you are and then no trouble for you.' The sum total of these attitudes, Ratnapala concludes, caused officers to erect a 'barrier of 'restricted isolation around themselves' which was reinforced by police training, law and tradition.[42] Often, police feelings of alienation were reciprocated by community members. A common expectation was that interactions with officers would be characterised by 'callous, partial, cruel uncivil or uncultured behavior.'[43]

Many similar problems faced Sri Lanka's soldiers, who became increasingly responsible for maintaining order and fighting terrorists in the north. As we have seen, plans to modernise the armed forces fell victim to budget cutting following victory over the JVP. Funding levels were first increased by the Jayewardene government, but failed to keep up with inflation after 1981. In 1982, the real value of defence spending was no higher than it had been in 1970, the year prior to the JVP rebellion. Moreover, the military was shortchanged relative to other government priorities like Mahaweli development and housing. As the army was asked to assume increasingly burdensome responsibilities in the northeast, functioning almost as an army of occupation in some areas, defence spending fell from 2.5 per cent of government expenditures in 1977 to 1.4 per cent in 1982.

Inflation's effects on military effectiveness can be especially pernicious, because they are mostly hidden from politicians. Since there was no reduction in the size of Sri Lanka's 11,000-man army, there were fewer funds, per-capita, to go around. This was reflected in inflation-eroded wages and in reduced spending on training, maintenance, facilities and weapons modernisation. To cope with a shortage of platoon-level officers, the cadet-training course was reduced in length from 90 to 56 weeks. The Army had only 33 tanks and armored vehicles at its disposal, plus some light trucks, so transport was always a problem. Troops travelled on foot or used government busses and minibuses, which were particularly vulnerable to landmines. Under Mrs. Bandaranaike's government, army weapons had been modernised with purchases from the USSR, China and Yugoslavia. J.R. Jayewardene's government turned more to the United States and other western nations for its purchases, which created logistical problems.

The problems budget shortfalls created were more visible at the unit level than in Colombo. When equipment broke down, spare parts were unavailable. When supplies came late and officers showed their inexperience, morale suffered. It was easy to attribute problems to corruption or incompetence of politically connected senior officers. Sometimes the suspicions of the lower ranks were well founded. Like prospective police constables, most recruits owed their appointment to a political 'chit.' Military service was not viewed as a particularly attractive form of employment, but applicants regarded any job as better than none in employment-starved Sri Lanka. Most came from rural areas, where educational opportunities were limited. By now, virtually all army personnel were Sinhalese. Like their counterparts in the police, they did not welcome assignments that involved fighting terrorists in Tamil majority regions.

Soldiers' limited military training provided little preparation for the circumstances they would encounter in Jaffna. More than a decade would pass before even the most sophisticated armed forces began to develop useful doctrines for counter-terrorism and 'peacekeeping' operations. Soldiers felt isolated in an alien land where they could not speak the language and where attacks could come at any time and from any quarter. Journalist Sinha Ratnatunga has described the nearly impossible position they faced:

> The soldier serving in the north was under tremendous strain. He could not walk into a tavern in Jaffna during off duty hours. If he wanted to bathe in the sea, he had to be guarded by colleagues. Men and women feared to talk to them (sic.) because of reprisals... The soldier was not permitted to act, but only to react to a terrorist attack.... In short, the Armed Forces were the pariahs or outcasts of society.[44]

David Selbourne reported that 'the Tigers seem better disciplined and less frightened than their political and military opponents.' Their numbers and confidence appeared to be growing. Tiger spokespersons told him they had little respect for the police or army and felt that Tamil civilians were largely behind them.[45]

President Jayewardene, a man without personal military experience, had little grasp of his army's limitations. Much later, I asked him whether he was concerned that the challenges of pacifying the northeast might be too great for his undermanned and under-resourced security forces. 'I was Sri Lanka's President,' he responded, and 'it was my responsibility to maintain order throughout the island. These were the forces at my disposal and so I ordered them to carry out the task.' A.J. Wilson gained a similar impression from a conversation in December 1983. 'One factor that failed to strike President Jayewardene,' Wilson reported, 'was that he had no army to speak of. It could be armed and trained, but had no will to fight a war.'[46]

Political feedback – a clouded message

Democratically elected politicians often justify their policies as 'the people's will.'[47] J.R. Jayewardene's UNP won more than 51 per cent of the votes and 140 of 168 seats in the 1977 general election. In three elections held during 1981 and 1982, the UNP prevailed by even larger margins. We have seen that the 1977 general election victory was taken as a mandate for far-reaching economic, political and social changes. Many viewed the subsequent victories as affirmations of these changes.

The realities were more complex. Both the 1970 and 1977 general elections had pitted pro-government parties against unified oppositions offering contrasting political-economic philosophies. In 1981 and 1982, opposition forces

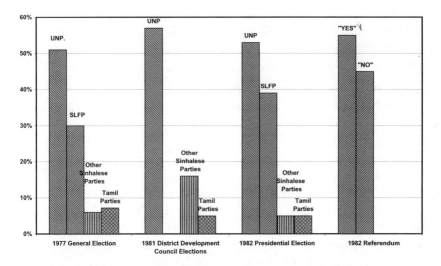

Figure 18.4 Support for Major Parties in Island Wide Elections 1977-1982

were divided and alternatives to the status quo less clear, raising questions about the message that large pro-UNP vote totals conveyed. Many circumstances surrounding the 1981 and 1982 elections have already been described. An examination of voting patterns will complete the picture.

Figure 18.4 shows major results and trends for the 1977 general election, 1981 District Development Council elections, October 1982 presidential election and December 1982 referendum. In each election, the UNP (or pro-UNP position) won with more than 50 per cent of the popular votes. Prior to 1977, no Sri Lankan political party had ever won with an absolute majority. Upon closer scrutiny, however, the endorsement of the UNP reflected in these results seems less overwhelming.

Distinguishing between vote totals in *Sinhalese majority districts* and *Tamil majority districts*,[48] helps document J.R. Jayewardene's inability to bridge Sri Lanka's ethnic divide. By 1977, intensifying cleavages had made ethnicity an overriding determinant of voting behavior. Electoral results documented this polarisation of political attitudes on ethnically divisive issues. For Sri Lanka Tamils living in the Northern and Eastern Provinces, comprising about 12 per cent of the national electorate, political rights for 'Tamil homelands' became increasingly the lens through which all political choices were viewed. Sinhalese and

Muslim voters gave greater weight to traditional political and economic issues, but resisted proposals to devolve power. Politicians could always tap into ethnoreligous wells of emotion that underlay this resistance. As in the past, seeking compromises on issues dividing the two communities was politically perilous.

Results in Sinhalese majority districts

Figure 18.5 shows results for the Sinhalese majority districts. In two of the three elections following implementation of open economy reforms, the UNP bettered its 1977 percentage, winning 70 per cent of the votes in contested District Development Council constituencies and 58 per cent in the referendum. J.R. Jayewardene's presidential election total was 54 per cent.

As a barometer of support for UNP policies and for President Jayewardene himself, the District Development Council results are the least meaningful. For the most part, Sinhalese were either indifferent or opposed to this experiment in devolution. Opposition from militant Buddhists, both activist priests and lay persons, was particularly vociferous. Sirimavo Bandaranaike, soon to be sequestered from active politics, led her tiny cohort out of Parliament before the vote on District Development Councils. An SLFP election boycott meant that candidates from Sri Lanka's strongest opposition party did not contest. Among the remaining opposition parties, Rohana Wijeweera's JVP had the most popular support but had not won designation as a legal political party. Thus, its candidates could only appear on the ballot as 'independents.' The JVP and other Marxist parties were only able to field candidates in 11 of the 18 Sinhalese districts, where they received only 30 per cent of the vote. J.R. Jayewardene achieved his goal of an overwhelming victory – the UNP won 110 of 130 seats in Sinhalese districts – but with an unusually low turnout of only 50 per cent in the contested elections. Thus District Development Councils, to the degree they functioned at all in Sinhalese districts, were simply one more manifestation of UNP power. As a mechanism for expressing a range of public opinion on political-economic issues at the local level, they offered little.

J.R. Jayewardene's 54 per cent to 40 per cent presidential election triumph over Kobbekaduwa in Sinhalese districts is a more meaningful barometer of pro-UNP sentiment. An 84 per cent turnout reflected continued voter confidence in the electoral process. Jayewardene carried all 18 Sinhalese districts, winning 16 by absolute majorities. As we have seen, the President had crafted the most favourable climate possible for his reelection bid. A constitutional amendment, ratified by the compliant UNP parliamentary majority, advanced

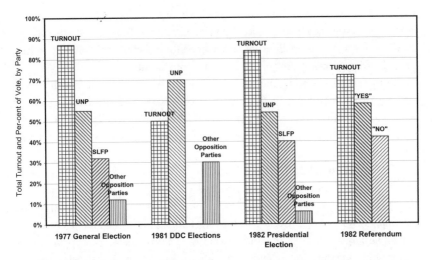

Figure 18.5 Results and Voter Turnout in Sinhalese Majority Districts

the polling date by a year, muting a possible backlash from deteriorating economic conditions.[49] Austerity measures recommended by international donors were postponed until after voters had rendered their verdict. The strongest SLFP candidate, Sirimavo Bandaranaike, was banned from contesting or campaigning. Hector Kobbekaduwa, a belatedly chosen stand-in, was less well known, and his campaign received only lukewarm support from the SLFP's centrist faction. Amirthalingam chose not to contest, using the TULF's unwillingness to recognise the 1978 constitution as his rationale.[50] Kumar Ponnambalam, who ran as the Tamil Congress candidate, had far less support in the Tamil community.

Even without these advantages, however, Jayewardene probably would have won decisively. What the faction-ridden SLFP offered in its manifesto was a return to failed economic policies that had been decisively rejected by the electorate. Kobbekaduwa also promised pro-labour policies, but was opposed by Marxist parties that still had strong ties to powerful unions.[51] Promises to revoke anti-terrorist legislation were viewed sceptically. Many recalled Mrs. Bandaranaike's anti-terrorist measures, following the JVP rebellion, as even more draconian that those of the UNP. A co-ordinated campaign team of highly effective Sinhala orators hammered the SLFP candidate in well-orchestrated rallies that repeatedly reminded voters of United Front shortcomings and UNP achievements. As campaigning drew to a close, even the cautious Jayewardene was 'confident of a solid victory.'[52] A combination of shrewd political tactics, opposition disarray and successful policies had guaranteed him overwhelming support among the majority community.

Support for extending the life of Parliament by six years was another matter. Regularly scheduled Parliamentary elections were an unbroken tradition in Sri Lanka, dating back to the colonial era. President Jayewardene's rationale for the referendum scheme was greeted with scepticism and cynicism, even by UNP supporters.

Official returns record that 58 per cent of voters supported the government's proposal, but the electoral process was marred by illegal campaigning, intimidation, arrest of opposition leaders, voter impersonation and ballot box stuffing. A 14 per cent decline in turnout from the presidential election provides a tangible index of voter disillusionment. The real level of support in the majority community for extending the life of Parliament is difficult to assess, but two things are clear. First, President Jayewardene came to view a referendum victory as essential to the success of his political-economic program. The success of that program, he believed, would guarantee Sri Lanka's economic health and political future for the foreseeable future. Second, top UNP leaders had grave doubts about the outcome of a fairly contested election. Negative reaction to the proposal was widespread, and opposition forces had not been so unified since 1970. Even some UNP supporters spoke out against canceling parliamentary elections. Belief that the referendum marked a critical fork in Sri Lanka's developmental path, coupled with the fear that voters might make a wrong choice, were used by UNP leaders to rationalise the extreme measures employed to secure a victory.

Results in Tamil majority districts

Voting trends in Tamil districts are an almost mirror image of their Sinhalese counterparts. They show the failure of J.R. Jayewardene's more conciliatory policies to win over Tamils, but also that there was at least some hope for their success at the time District Development Council elections were held (Figure 18.6). Results for Jaffna district alone show the same patterns, but with much stronger evidence of alienation from the UNP.[53]

What is most striking about the Tamil district electoral results is not that opposition to the UNP was strong, but that a significant number of Tamils still exhibited confidence that democratic processes could help address their con-

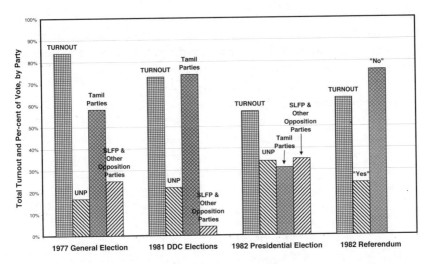

Figure 18.6 Results and Voter Turnout in Tamil Majority Districts.

cerns. Voter turnout exceeded 70 per cent in District Development Council elections. In the referendum, when voters faced a combination of draconian emergency regulations and pro-government intimidation, turnout exceeded 60 per cent and an overwhelming majority voted 'No.' In a presidential election where there was no candidate who remotely spoke for the Tamil community, more than 55 per cent of voters queued up at polling stations in the north and east, mostly to express their disapproval of J.R. Jayewardene and the UNP. The significance of these high voter turnouts stands out when compared to the U.S., where a 50 per cent turnout even for presidential elections is now widely accepted as the norm.

These data reinforce other evidence that the Liberation Tigers were not yet the dominant force they later became. Killing and intimidating individual candidates was now within their power, but calls for election boycotts failed to keep large numbers of voters away from the polls. Even in Jaffna, the Tiger's home base, turnout was 68 per cent for postponed District Development Council elections and 59 per cent for the referendum. Only in the presidential election did less than half of Jaffna's voters go to the polls.

Five months later, however, only 10 per cent of registered voters in the Northern Province turned out for local government elections. By this time, voting made little difference. In most constituencies, only the TULF candidates stood for office. UNP and Tamil Congress candidates, themselves Sri Lanka Tamils, had either been killed or intimidated into withdrawing by threats of violence. In a Vavuniya campaign address before a crowd of 1,500, not long before the election, Amirthalingam reportedly said that 'he was proud of the acts of Tamil youths fighting for liberation.'[54]

How were these election results perceived from President J.R. Jayewardene's Colombo vantage point? The President saw himself as a peacemaker – the only Sri Lankan leader with the power and political skills to bridge the island's widening communal divide. His strategy sought a middle ground between Sinhalese and Tamil extremists, hoping that rising levels of economic prosperity would maintain his high levels of popular support and would mute their disruptive potential. Despite the power conferred by the 1977 landslide, recent political history emphasised the risk of this strategy. Every predecessor who had tried to respond to Tamil demands by devolving power, as District Development Councils proposed to do, had both failed and paid a political price. Militants, in the President's eyes, were a small group of mostly lower class young men whose terrorist acts and extremist demands were rejected by mainstream Tamil opinion. The anti-terrorist measures imposed on the north were intended not only to maintain the central government's authority but also to protect Tamils, who were almost invariably the targets of militant actions.

We know that most Sri Lanka Tamils in the north and east saw matters differently and communicated this to the President with a succession of electoral humiliations. In Jaffna, the UNP won only seven per cent of the votes in the District Development Council elections and only nine per cent in the referendum. In the presidential election, Jayewardene came in third, losing not only to Tamil Congress candidate Kumar Ponnambalam, but also to the SLFP candidate, Hector Kobbekaduwa. As we have seen, the President continued to press forward with his devolution plan, but it would have been hard for him not to view the Tamil community as an adversary and the Tamil majority districts as politically hostile territory. Perhaps he came to view Tamil grievances as a problem to be contained, rather than solved, while he focused on other priorities.

UNP governance before the 1983 riots: reflections

It would be difficult to imagine a stronger political resume than the one J.R. Jayewardene brought to Sri Lanka's top leadership post in 1977. He had held major posts in every UNP government and served as leader of the opposition.

Though respected as an international figure, he was deeply rooted in Sinhalese and cultural traditions. He had transformed the UNP from the 'Uncle-Nephew Party' into Sri Lanka's most formidable political machine, attracting able young deputies with diverse political backgrounds in the process. He was willing to surround himself with able, strong-minded men, tolerate dissenting views and delegate authority. His pledge to devolve power and his reputation as a moderate on communal issues made him the preferred Sinhalese candidate of most moderate Tamil leaders. His legendary political skills were widely respected – and feared. By the end of President Jayewardene's first term, however, open economy reforms had fallen short of expectations, a once popular regime had resorted to repressive measures to remain in power, communal divisions had widened, and Tamil militant groups challenged the writ of the government in the north. How did this happen?

As we have seen, the UNP government's first three years in office were marked by positive accomplishments on many fronts, but two years later its prospects were uncertain. A general election reversal, in 1983, that would undo open economy reforms, seemed possible. From the UNP leaders' vantage point, this justified a constitutional amendment to advance the date of the Presidential election, and following President Jayewardene's victory, the controversial referendum to extend the life of Parliament for six more years. The repressive measures used to guarantee a referendum victory leave little doubt that UNP leaders believed they might lose a free and fair election. In the northeast, even repressive measures could not prevent an increasingly alienated Tamil community from registering their opposition to the President and his policies.

With the wisdom of hindsight, we can see how miscalculations by the President and his advisors contributed to policy failures that adversely impacted the public mood and increased the potential for conflict escalation. A predisposition toward repressing dissent and electoral feedback increased the probability that there would be miscalculations and that their consequences would continue uncorrected. First, they overestimated the degree to which government policies could revitalise the private sector and underestimated the power of entrenched interests within the UNP to resist free-market reforms in the state sector. Like its predecessors, President Jayewardene's government achieved its greatest successes in areas over which the government could exercise direct control – constructing dams, power plants, irrigation works, houses and government buildings. Where success required participation from domestic entrepreneurs and foreign private investors, achievements were more modest. Inefficiencies in the plantation, transport and telecommunications sectors continued to drain government resources and impede economic growth.

Miscalculations contributed to an overoptimistic view about the speed with which Sri Lanka's economy could generate self-sustaining growth and improve poor people's well-being . Overoptimism was reinforced by the economic boom of 1978-80, years when the government's ability to deliver on this promises seemed assured. Neither government ministers nor Sri Lankan citizens were prepared for the combination of external shocks, inflation and stagnation that forced cutbacks in popular programs and adversely impacted the well-being of the middle class as well as the poor.

There was also a more fundamental miscalculation about the degree to which the benefits of open economy reforms would be shared equally throughout the society. Achieving the massive capitalisation and restructuring J.R. Jayewardene had promised could not be accomplished without pain and social dislocation. It proved impossible to control or fully cushion the impact of inflationary pressures produced by a volatile juxtaposition of generous foreign aid, high government deficits and adverse shifts in Sri Lanka's terms of trade. The turbulent economic and social climate that reforms produced created new opportunities, but preponderantly for economically advantaged, socially privileged and politically connected Sri Lankans. Belying President Jayewardene's campaign pledges, social norms were becoming more Darwinian than *dharmista*.

Thus, President Jayewardene's fundamental belief that economic reforms would contribute to social and political stability proved to be false. The privations that became ever more visible in 1981 and 1982 were a direct consequence of open economy policies. These differed in three respects from those of earlier years, with profound implications for the volatility of Sri Lankan society. First, privations followed hard upon a three-year boom when nearly everyone appeared to be getting better off. Suffering under the UNP soured a climate of good times and heightened expectations. Second, privations were unequally shared, to a much greater degree. Especially in commercialising urban areas, the disparities between rich and poor were gaudily displayed for all to see. Under the United Front virtually everyone – poor and well-to-do alike – queued for basic foodstuffs at sparsely provisioned government outlets. Now the poorest

Sri Lankans could see that foodstuffs were plentiful, but they had no money to buy them. Third, declining living standards, a widening gap between classes and displays of unaffordable opulence were coincident in urban areas with an invasion of material goods, cultural artifacts and tourists that offended many Sri Lankans deeply. Additionally, the corruption of some top UNP officials and pro-government businessmen made things worse.

In a turbulent social-economic climate, those experiencing relative deprivation and lack of control over their circumstances are likely to seek scapegoats. Ethnic minorities are prime targets for scapegoating. Irresponsible politicians will stoke the rage of the deprived to enhance their own power. Pre-election campaigning is a particularly accessible forum for showcasing this tactic. Sri Lanka, as we have seen, had two political campaigns, within three months at the end of 1982. Inevitably these campaigns heightened the degree to which Sinhalese and Tamil community members viewed each other through a prism of negative ethnic stereotypes. Ending the electoral cycle does not necessarily dissipate the hostile feelings that campaigning has aroused, especially in a climate of continued deprivation where campaign promises are unfulfilled. All of these factors were present in Sri Lanka's major urban centres as J.R. Jayewardene's UNP government began its second term. Thus President Jayewardene's hope that open economy reforms would narrow communal divisions also proved to be ill founded. Instead the juxtaposition of Tamil militancy and Sinhalese resentments, fuelled by economic volatility, uncertainty and deprivation, had created circumstances where provocations initiated by members of one community or the other could easily catalyze an explosion.

With militancy gaining strength in the north and Sinhalese resentments rising in the south, maintenance of public order depended, increasingly, on the effectiveness of the security forces. Management and use of the security forces proved to be one of the UNP leaders' most serious areas of miscalculation. Security officers in all services were by this time overwhelmingly Sinhalese, with implications for their performance of duty in both the north and the south. Sinhalese security offices detailed to the north would have been ill prepared to carry out their duties under the best of circumstances. By 1977, Tamil citizens viewed security officers as an army of occupation, and the distance between security forces and citizens was also enforced by militant threats. The escalation of violence that occurred – of provocations and retaliations – was predictable. In the south, 'maintaining public order' might mean protecting Tamil citizens from rioters who were, themselves, reacting to Tamil militant provocations in the north. But the security officers, like other Sinhalese, were subjected to ethno-nationalist rhetoric from politicians who characterised 'Tamils' as collectively responsible for militant violence. Faced with a decision whether or not to risk injury or death protecting Tamil citizens against Sinhalese attackers, the choice was not an easy one.

UNP political tactics added further complexities and potential contradictions to security officers' roles, quite apart from communal issues. Sometimes police constables and soldiers were asked to prevent and quell violent outbreaks. In other circumstances, when government opponents were targets, their mission might be to stand by and passively facilitate violent attacks or even participate actively in the violence. In high stress situations, where quick action was necessary, guidelines were unclear and commanders were not present, security officers might understandably be reluctant to become involved.

There was also the matter of providing the security forces with adequate resources – funds for wages, training, facilities and equipment. We have already seen how budget cuts created problems for the security forces during the United Front government's final years. Initially, UNP leaders tried to remedy these shortfalls, but the impact of initial budget increases was quickly eroded by inflation. By 1983, the military and police forces were worse off, in real terms, than they had been in 1977.

One need not fully agree with A.J. Wilson's bleak appraisal – that President Jayewardene 'had no army to speak of'– to acknowledge that Sri Lanka's security forces might be ineffective or counterproductive in fighting militants and quelling civil disorders provoked by communally related incidents. J.R. Jayewardene's opaqueness on this point, in my view, is one of the most puzzling aspects of his presidency. When responding to moderate dissenting views in the Tamil community and to extremist political rhetoric on both sides of the political divide, UNP leaders would have been well advised to take the limited capabilities of their security forces into account.

My comments on President Jayewardene's management of relations with India need not be repeated, but Indo-Lanka relations must certainly be included in a listing of his miscalculations. Whether more cordial relations between the two heads of government – J.R. Jayewardene and Indira Gandhi – would have served as some counterweight to the political and geostrategic considerations that motivated India's support for Tamil militants can only be matter of speculation. However, the conclusion that in this sensitive arena, the President's political judgement was clouded by his personal feelings is difficult to escape.

Finally, and perhaps most important, there is the degree to which President Jayewardene underestimated the degree to which differences between Sinhalese and Tamil communities – differences which his open economy policies, resistance to devolving power, and electoral strategy intensified – could escalate into civil war. This civil war would become, after 1984, not only the defining event of his Presidency but of Sri Lanka's entire post-independence history.

19
Protracted Civil War Begins

Having successfully 'climbed to the top of the greasy pole,' this visionary, gifted and sophisticated political leader, J.R. Jayewardene, was the wrong man for his time. His tactical successes helped insulate him from 'bad news' about development failures and security force ineffectiveness that might, conceivably, have saved his Presidency. Protracted civil war, rather than an economic miracle and a stable multi-ethnic society became the legacy of his second term.

Chapter five described how the ineffective use of state-sanctioned violence can contribute to conflict escalation by heightening feelings of deprivation, deepening ethnic identities and solidifying militant movements. When security force cadres are underfunded, under equipped and inexperienced, their capabilities to carry out complex assignments will be limited. When political functions have repeatedly superseded professional ones, military and police personnel may be unwilling to take risks and make difficult judgements that complex assignments require. When ethno-nationalist rhetoric has polarised a society, cadres serving in ethnically homogeneous forces may come to equate 'the nation' with their ethnic kin. Members of other ethnic groups, regardless of citizenship, can then be seen as beings of a different species and as 'the enemy.' Security officers who have internalised this point of view are unlikely to function effectively in ethnically volatile circumstances.

Fighting militants in alien territory and controlling riotous mobs in densely populated, multi-ethnic urban settings are among the most challenging and complex assignments that young men and women who have chosen to wear their country's uniforms can be called upon to face. In July 1983, Sri Lanka's soldiers, sailors and police officers fighting militants in Jaffna and Colombo faced the most severe outbreak of mob violence in the island's history. Both the short- and long-term consequences were, as we already know, tragic.

Turning point – the July 1983 riots

The precarious circumstances faced by military and police forces tasked to maintain public order on the Jaffna peninsula have already been described. On the night of 23 July, a near-inevitable scenario unfolded. The reconnaissance mission of Sri Lankan Army patrol 'Four Four Bravo', close to Jaffna University, was halted by a land mine explosion and fusillade of automatic weapons fire. Tamil Tiger Supremo Velupillai Prabakharan orchestrated and personally led the carefully planned ambush.[1] Thirteen of the 15 Sinhalese soldiers assigned to the mission were killed. They had reported for duty in Jaffna only the previous day.

Police and soldiers had been killed in the north before 23 July, but this was the largest number of fatalities by far in a single action. (In ensuing years, civil strife would claim more than 60,000 lives, the majority of them Sinhalese.) Army retribution was swift. Ceylon Light Infantry troops decamped from their barracks and quickly killed 39 Tamil civilians who had the misfortune to encounter them, injuring many more. Discipline was only restored when Sri Lanka's army commander personally intervened.

Maintaining army discipline and public order in Colombo were the uppermost concerns in the minds of President Jayewardene and his advisors as they considered how to honour the fallen Sinhalese men and whether or not to return their remains to grieving families.[2] Officials hoped to keep funerals from becoming disruptive political demonstrations, directed against the government and Tamil citizens, which could get out of hand. Their plan was to hold a dignified ceremony at a funeral home, with senior government officials participating, and then bury the soldiers immediately in Colombo's central cemetery.[3]

A series of not atypical delays, miscommunications and bureaucratic missteps transformed this optimistic scenario into a disaster.[4] Shipment of the bodies from Jaffna was delayed for many hours. By the time they did arrive, it was too late for the funeral to go forward and it was cancelled. In the interim, however, a large crowd had gathered at the cemetery. It included not only mourners, but also individuals living in the crowded surrounding neighbourhoods with nothing to do on a hot Sunday night. As hours wore on, with little or no reliable information available about what was happening, the crowd's anger grew. About 10:00 PM it erupted into violence. Not all of the violence was random: Gangs of young men armed with petrol bombs led the rioters in targeting nearby Tamil shops and homes. Soon many were in flames with inhabitants driven into the streets and in some cases beaten by the mobs.[5]

The events of that fateful Sunday evening precipitated a week of rioting. It ebbed and flowed through Colombo's business and residential districts and spread to neighbouring regions, including the plantation districts. Most victims were Tamil families who had lived and worked peaceably along side Sinhalese neighbours for decades and had little sympathy for the Eelamist agenda of Jaffna militants. An extensive literature describes the gruesome experiences faced by many members of this bewildered minority – homes and businesses destroyed, relatives and friends beaten, shot or in some cases burned alive in homes and vehicles. Women were raped or forced to exhibit themselves naked before jeering crowds. Gangs of Sinhalese prisoners beat Tamil detainees to death in Colombo's maximum-security prison while guards and soldiers stood by. Not all Sinhalese were rioters. Many risked their lives and homes to protect Tamil friends and neighbours from the mobs.[6]

While much of the violence was random, many incidents appeared to be orchestrated. Numerous first-person reports described gangs of young men, armed with petrol bombs as well as voting rolls, able to target Tamil families and Tamil-owned properties and businesses precisely for destruction. With some exceptions, Sri Lankan military and police forces did little to restore order or protect Tamil citizens. Soldiers in particular were seen to be encouraging the rioters or even actively participating in mayhem.

As the week unfolded, graphic accounts of these events began appearing in international news reports. News reporters gathered in Colombo, photographing the destruction and seeking interviews with victims and government officials. By the time the violence subsided on 31 July, at least 60,000 Tamils had become refugees. Later, the number swelled to more than 100,000, including a substantial number that fled to India. Sri Lanka's international reputation was transformed from paradise to pariah in the space of a week.

The government's role in these events, and that of President Jayewardene in particular, have been endlessly debated. Were government officials complicit in organising the attacks against Tamils? Had the President intended to 'teach Tamils a lesson' using pro-government thugs, only to lose control of events he had helped to precipitate? Were Sinhalese businessmen, along with their political allies, the principal instigators and were their motives primarily commercial, rather than communal?

The bare facts regarding the President's role and roles of his key advisors appear to be these. During the first three days, top officials had little control over events. They made serious attempts to re-establish discipline among the security forces based in Colombo and were deeply concerned about their inability to do so. They lacked effective crisis management mechanisms. President Jayewardene's often repeated justification for delaying the imposition of a curfew was that the troops would not follow his orders. He delayed an address to the nation until 27 July because he believed that few would pay attention to an address given earlier. Some advisors and perhaps the President himself appear to have taken seriously the possibility that the government might be overthrown by rebellious troops, who would intervene militarily to 'restore order' and then assume political power.[7] That many officers harboured Sinhalese-nationalist sentiments was well known.

This may partially explain the President's stance when he did address the nation. A proposed sixth amendment to Sri Lanka's Constitution, which banned political parties advocating separatism, was the centrepiece of his address.[8] Further, it mandated that no person could practice a profession in Sri Lanka 'without taking an oath of allegiance to the sovereignty and unitary status of the state.'[9] President Jayewardene stated that he introduced the amendment 'to appease the natural desire and request of the Sinhala people.'[10] The message to Sri Lanka's Tamil citizens seemed clear: J.R. Jayewardene viewed the riots as a justifiable response to Tamil separatism and militancy. Those who trod that path in the future would have only themselves to blame for harsh treatment. Neither the President nor his close cabinet colleagues publicly expressed sympathy to the thousands of Tamil citizens,[11] many of them 1982 UNP voters, who had lost homes, businesses, friends and relatives, at the hands of their Sinhalese fellow citizens.[12]

With violence subsiding and security force discipline reasserting itself, UNP leaders reached another decision. They began explaining the riots as part of a left-wing plot to overthrow the government, possibly with Soviet complicity. Three Marxist parties, including the recently legitimised JVP, were proscribed. Some leaders were arrested, while others, including the JVP's Rohana Wijeweera, went underground. Few regard the government's theory as credible, but it did deflect some western reporters from describing the riots as a Sinhalese pogrom directed against Tamils.[13] During the 'Evil Empire' era (Ronald Reagan was the U.S. President in 1983) Marxist conspiracy explanations of unrest in developing nations were popular, especially in the United States and Britain.

Tamil youth respond and militancy becomes institutionalised

The impact of the riots on Tamil youth seems hardly to have entered into government leaders' calculations. Prior to July 1983, many young Tamil men sympathised with the idea of Eelam, but most were sceptical about the prospects for armed struggle. As we have seen, even the leading militant groups were small hit-and-run operations lacking secure bases, reliable arms supplies and solid funding. The successful, draconian response of Sri Lanka's army to the JVP rebellion, with the assistance of India and other foreign powers, was still recent history.

Photographs of the rioting and personal accounts of Colombo relatives, friends and refugees transformed these sceptical attitudes. Moreover, whatever the truth was about the complicity of senior UNP officials, most Tamils *believed* there was complicity.[14] One militant recruiter reported that:

> The Mentality of the youth underwent a sea change when they saw these people from Colombo. Until then, I had found it difficult to bring people into the [Tamil militant] movement. From then on, there was such a rush for joining our struggle that I found it difficult to control the crowds.[15]

While riots provided the recruits needed to transform Sri Lanka's militant groups, India provided the resources. At least three considerations motivated India's government toward greater involvement in the Eelam struggle. First, leaders of India's intelligence establishment, the Department of Defence 'Research and Analysis Wing' (RAW), had been increasingly concerned with the strategic implications of J.R. Jayewardene's more pro-Western foreign and economic policies.[16] Second, Tamil Nadu state politics remained a concern for Prime Minister Indira Gandhi's government. She continued to need political support in Parliament from at least one of the state's two leading political parties. Following the riots, the two party leaders, both former movie idols, vied to outdo one another in their vociferous public support for Sri Lanka's Tamils.[17] Finally, there was the personal antipathy between the two leaders that has already been described. Mrs. Gandhi moved on two fronts – diplomatic and clandestine – to capitalise on the opportunity created by events in Sri Lanka.

On the political front, she constituted herself as a mediator between Sri Lanka's government and the respective groups that claimed to speak for the island's Tamil citizens. The announced goal of this initiative was to negotiate a political middle ground that would provide some satisfaction to all parties and resolve the conflict peaceably.

On the clandestine front, Mrs. Gandhi authorised RAW operatives to establish secret training camps for Tamil youth in a mountainous area of Uttar Pradesh state. Interestingly, training was provided separately for the five militant groups that were supported and they had litttle contact with one another.[18] RAW's strategy was to maintain control by preventing any one group from becoming dominant – a strategy that eventually failed. For the better part of four years, young men crossed from Jaffna to Tamil Nadu and were transported to the camps, where they underwent three to six months of military training. Indian army officers were primarily responsible for the training.[19] Additional camps were established Tamil Nadu, under auspices of individual groups, but with tacit support from the state government. Here, the instructors were graduates of the RAW training and retired army officers whom the groups hired.[20]

India also armed the militant forces fighting in Sri Lanka, although captured weapons from the Sri Lankan army were a second important source of supply. Beginning in 1984, Indian military planes provided regular shipments to Tamil Nadu. From there, weapons were moved to militant camps along the coast, and then smuggled into Sri Lanka.[21] This practice continued until India intervened directly in mid-1987. Throughout this period, Indian government officials and diplomats resolutely denied that their country was either training or arming Tamil militants.

By 1986, militant forces included about 15,000 men who had undergone training in India. While rivalries and internecine battles prevented the several militant groups from forming a united front, their combined strength was comparable to Sri Lanka's army.[22] In 1984, when these new recruits began to have an impact, the conflict between Sri Lanka's government and the militants changed qualitatively. Conflict resolution options available to J.R. Jayewardene's government in 1978 or even 1982 were now foreclosed.

Violent conflict patterns

Our fever chart for the 1977-1988 period shows this qualitative change clearly (Figure 19.1). Prior to 1985, fever chart topologies never show violence intensity levels higher than 75. The highest level, also involving widespread militant incidents, was produced by the JVP insurrection of 1972. Between mid-1985 and the end of J.R. Jayewardene's second term, there is only one month with levels below 100. In 1988, scores exceeding 500 are recorded for several months.[23]

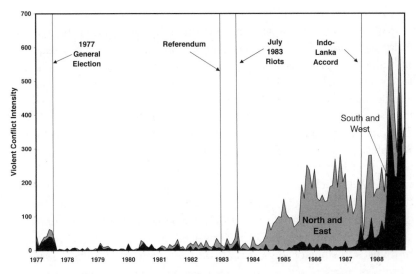

19.1 Violent Conflict Intensity January 1977 – December 1988

Figure 19.1 also distinguishes between conflict incidents occurring in Sinhalese (the southwest) and Tamil (the northeast) majority regions. Until mid-1987, when the Indo-Lanka Accord authorised Indian army troops to take up peacekeeping duties in Sri Lanka, the preponderance of violent conflict occurred in the northeast. Indian intervention produced spillover effects in the southwest. Not only did the IPKF not pacify the Tamil majority regions, it motivated Sinhalese youth to join the ranks of a resurgent JVP, which began an insurrection intended to topple the Jayewardene government. Chapter 1 described the deterioration of public security from JVP attacks and urban terrorism. As 1988 drew to close, violent conflict in Sinhalese majority regions had become the predominant concern of Sri Lanka's embattled government.

Most descriptions of how civil war infected Sri Lanka focus on a few landmark incidents. These are presented as milestones, chronologically demarcating an unfolding scenario of escalating conflict. Describing landmark incidents is a useful place to begin, but they represent only a tiny fraction of more than 5,000 reported violent conflict incidents that occurred between June 1983 and December 1988. We need to supplement this discussion of landmarks with observations based on the hundreds of conflict incident descriptions that underlie numbers graphed in fever charts. These descriptions make possible a more nuanced and contextually rich presentation of this escalating conflict scenario.

The Tamil militants' war

An observer who was ignorant of events in India might have thought normalcy had returned to Sri Lanka in the months that followed the riots. An ambush of a Jaffna-based army convoy in April 1984 dispelled this illusion. The following day, militants in Jaffna torched a school for Sinhalese children and the Sinhalese-owned Matara bakery, widely patronised by Jaffna residents for years. Journalist Sinha Ratnatunga states that militants intended this to symbolise a final breaking of links with the south.[24] In November, militants killed nearly 80 Sinhalese civilians confined in a government detention camp. The detainees were, of course, defenceless and even their guards were unarmed. By the end of 1984, Jaffna had become a war zone. Army troops, rolling through the streets in their vehicles and manning sand-bagged sentry posts, controlled the city in daylight. At night, life came to a halt and the militants were in control.[25]

An LTTE massacre of Sinhalese civilians at the ancient capital and popular tourist site, Anuradhapura, was the landmark incident of 1985. The LTTE hit squad leader's account of this was given in Chapter 4. Arriving in a stolen bus, militants gunned down civilians waiting in the Anuradhapura bus station. They moved on to a nearby Buddhist shrine where they shot to death priests, nuns, pilgrims and tourists, including women and children.[26] A total of 146 died in the carnage.[27] The incident demonstrated that Sinhalese civilians were no longer safe in their own heartland. Sri Lanka's army together with a newly created cadre of paramilitary police, the Special Task Force (STF), responded with reprisal killings throughout the island. In one reported incident, 40 young Tamil men were taken to a secluded area, ordered to dig their own graves and then shot.[28] A pattern of successful guerrilla attacks and reprisal killings of Tamil civilians continued in 1986.

Unproductive truces, used by Tamil militants to rebuild their strength, were another pattern. The first began in July and ended in September 1985.[29] Sri Lanka's army detachments ceased offensive operations and remained in their encampments. This stand down was intended to provide a favourable climate for Indian-brokered negotiations between Sri Lankan government officials and militant representatives in Bhutan's capital, Thimpu. But while talks proceeded, LTTE cadres laid land mines and erected barriers on roads leading from the encampments, severely limiting the Army's mobility. When the truce and talks ended unproductively, LTTE hit squads were in a much stronger position to attack Sinhalese civilians. By decimating rival groups, they established themselves as the dominant Tamil force.[30]

In the north, this dominance was asserted forcefully on 30 April 1986, with an LTTE-initiated 'night of the long knives' against its rival, the Tamil Eelam Liberation Organisation (TELO). TELO had gained notoriety and recruits with a series of spectacular bombings and raids, but its members lacked discipline, exploited civilians and were given to ostentatious displays. Prabakharan could not tolerate the beatings of two LTTE members and the killing of a third. Near midnight on 30 April, disciplined LTTE hit squads moved against 24 TELO camps simultaneously, killing many of their rivals as they lay sleeping. Mopping up operations over the next three days killed most survivors of the first attack, including many who tried to surrender.

Jaffna camps of a second rival group, the Eelam Peoples Revolutionary Liberation Front (EPRLF) were attacked in December, but members were treated more leniently than their erstwhile TELO counterparts. It retained strength in the east and some support in India.[31] LTTE leaders began issuing public statements arrogating to their organisation sole authority to represent the Tamil people. In early January 1987, Velupillai Prabakharan crossed the straits to take personal command of the liberation struggle, ending nearly four years of exile in India.[32] By now, the Liberation Tigers were Jaffna's *de facto* rulers.

President Jayewardene continued to hope that his security forces, directed by a new 'Ministry of National Security,' could produce a military victory. 'I expect them to end guerrilla violence by the end of the year,' he stated in the summer of 1986.[33] In 1987, however, the President learned that India's leaders would not allow their clients to lose. The year began with a promising military campaign, halted by a truce declared in response to Indian pressure.[34] The LTTE ended this truce dramatically, by massacring of 130 bus passengers in the Eastern Province and then bombing Colombo's central bus stand, killing more than 100 and injuring more than 200.[35]

Sri Lanka's armed forces responded with 'Operation Liberation,' a surprisingly successful offensive intended to cut off smuggling routes from India and ultimately wrest control of Jaffna from the Liberation Tigers. By now, Sri Lanka's government had escalated the level of conflict by acquiring a small air force, which it used effectively against militant forces, though with heavy civilian casualties.[36] When it appeared that the offensive might achieve its goals, India intervened directly. First, a flotilla of 20 fishing boats was dispatched from Tamil Nadu to provide 'humanitarian assistance' to the Jaffna citizens.

Sri Lankan navy patrol boats turned back the flotilla, but it was clear that a sustained military response to India's intervention would be impossible. Rajiv Gandhi's government drove this point home the next day by sending transport planes, protected by Mirage fighter jets, to airdrop supplies to Jaffna. If President Jayewardene hoped that western powers, with which his government had close ties, would intervene to restrain India he was to be disappointed. While not formally approving of India's actions, they signalled clearly that they would not become involved.[37] Sri Lankan officials then gave formal permission for additional shipments to Jaffna. Acknowledging the inevitable, President Jayewardene's representatives began to seek an agreement that India would ratify and that Sinhalese public opinion would accept.[38]

The Indo-Lanka Accord, signed by Prime Minister Rajiv Gandhi and President Jayewardene on 29 June, met the first criterion but not the second. In brief, it provided for a turnover of arms by the LTTE, increased autonomy for Tamils in a temporarily merged Northeastern Province that united Tamil majority areas in a single political unit and the temporary introduction of Indian troops into Sri Lanka to enforce peace in the northeast. Sri Lanka also made foreign policy concessions to India in an annexure.[39]

We have seen that political parties out of power in Sri Lanka typically use government concessions to Tamil aspirations as a vehicle for mobilising and arousing their followers. In June 1987, Mrs. Bandaranaike and other SLFP leaders made common cause with militant nationalist groups, including the proscribed JVP. Concessions and the acceptance of Indian troops on Sri Lankan soil were characterised as betrayals of the Sinhala people. Protests, many of them violent, erupted throughout the south. Colombo was particularly hard hit. Smoke from burning barriers and buildings provided a backdrop for the official signing of the accord.[40] More than 500 Ceylon Transport Board busses were burned. The value of property destroyed by mob violence ran to millions of dollars.[41] As Indian troops moved into Jaffna, the Sri Lankan troops they replaced were transported south to secure the capital.[42]

For Tamils in the northeast, the accord signalled one of those brief, hopeful respites that have periodically tantalised Sri Lanka.[43] Travel between north and south became possible once again. Aid officials and non-governmental organisations flowed into war torn zones and began planning reconstruction projects.[44] Senior LTTE leaders began socialising with Indian Army officers and several even got married. But Prabakharan had acceded to the accord under duress.[45] He had never really accepted it or abandoned the goal of an independent Eelam. The LTTE was supposed to turn over all their arms within five days, but they held many back and the Indians did not press them to comply. With only 5,000 Indian troops on the ground, intelligence was limited and they were in no position to enforce the accord effectively.

In September and October, relations between the LTTE and the Indian peacekeepers unravelled, while Sinhalese suspicions of Indian *bona fides* grew. Prabakharan's forces attacked rival groups in the east, killing more than 150. Uncertain of their mission, IPKF did nothing to intervene. The head of the LTTE's political wing, Tileepan, staged a 'fast to the death' in support of new political demands that appeared to be a pretext for breaking off the accord. When he did in fact die, the LTTE orchestrated massive public demonstrations against the Indians, whom Jaffna's citizens had not long before welcomed as liberators.[46] Not all Jaffna citizens supported the LTTE. Many yearned for peace and were willing to accept a negotiated political settlement short of Eelam, but few were willing to speak out against the LTTE publicly. Of those who did speak out, few survived.[47]

The landmark date customarily cited as signalling an irrevocable breakdown of the accord is 4 October 1987. Seventeen LTTE leaders were captured by Sri Lanka's navy while attempting to smuggle arms into Jaffna, in violation of the accord. Inexplicably, they were able to receive smuggled cyanide capsules and 12 committed suicide while awaiting transport to Colombo.[48] The LTTE responded with a ferocious attack that killed more than 200 Sinhalese. Many of these ill-fated men and women had recently travelled to the northeast, hoping to build bridges between the two communities. Not surprisingly each side blamed the other for the renewed hostilities. Three days after the killings, India's leaders in Delhi, overruling the recommendations of their Jaffna field commander, decided to crush the Tigers with a military offensive. One reported estimate for the time needed to complete the task was 72 hours.[49] This estimate was optimistic. When India's troops finally completed their withdrawal, in March 1990, the Liberation Tigers remained a viable and feared military force. More than 1,200 Indian officers and men had died in the operation.

India's military operations provide yet another example of conflict escalation from ineffective state-sanctioned violence. After initial reverses, the IPKF was augmented by massive reinforcements, raising its strength to more than 50,000.[50] Liberation Tiger forces were driven from Jaffna in an assault backed by tanks and artillery that caused nearly 2,000 civilian deaths.[51] A semblance of civil administration was restored, but the Indian generals responsible for Jaffna Town and the peninsula as a whole reported that 90 per cent of the Tamil population or more were at least passive LTTE supporters.[52] Like their Sinhalese predecessors, many IPKF troops came to view ordinary Tamil citizens as 'the enemy' and to act accordingly.[53] Attempts to penetrate Prabakharan's jungle redoubts south of Jaffna never succeeded. Despite their superior forces, Indian incursions remained vulnerable to landmines, snipers and sabotage.[54]

In the east, IPKF troops were supported by militant groups that had opposed the LTTE and a population, including Muslims and Sinhalese, that was not anxious to become citizens of a Jaffna-dominated Eelam. Confrontations between IPKF troops and the LTTE were less frequent, but conditions were hardly better for ordinary citizens. Sinhalese and Muslim villages were targeted regularly for gruesome massacres that were reported in the Colombo newspapers.[55] IPKF troops were no more able to protect these villages than the Sri Lankan security forces had been. Increasingly news reports and some politicians criticised IPFK troops not only for ineffectiveness, but also for rapes and other atrocities.[56] Often, the criticisms were well founded. The IPKF phase of the war had become a classic confrontation between a powerful conventional army and a tenacious, highly motivated guerrilla force. So long as the militants remained viable, they would win. If the IPKF could not win, it would lose. The IPKF's circumstances become almost identical to those faced by the Sri Lankan army troops they supplanted – and whose advice they had spurned when they began their offensive[57].

The People's Liberation Front (JVP) war

Several militant groups claimed to speak for Tamils, but only one, the JVP, offered a militant agenda to Sinhalese. In contrast to Tamil militant groups, the JVP had no foreign sanctuaries, no supportive diaspora, no international propaganda arm and no hegemonic power to supply training and arms. As in 1970, Rohana Wijeweera's political program was a fuzzy, complex admixture of Sinhalese nationalist, Buddhist and Marxist rhetoric. But his goal was simple – to forcefully seize and exercise absolute power. Tactically, alliances with non-revolutionary opposition parties were possible, but these would be only temporary.

Wijeweera's strategy was to use propaganda, terror, sabotage and assassinations to eviscerate Sri Lanka's governmental, economic and security institutions. Massive institutional failures, he believed, would produce chaos, loss of legitimacy for the established order and a power vacuum. Chaotic circumstances would give JVP forces an opportunity to seize and consolidate power, using draconian, authoritarian measures. Sri Lanka's 'masses,' they believed, would welcome the insurgents as saviours.[58] Holdouts who opposed the new regime would simply be liquidated. In 1988 and 1989, it appeared this plan might succeed.

The July riots were pivotal for the JVP as well as Tamil militant groups. During J.R. Jayewardene's first term, as we have seen, the JVP followed a democratic agenda, while also maintaining a clandestine wing. It emerged as the largest vote-getter among the radical left and was certified as a legitimate political party by Sri Lanka's Commissioner of Elections. There can be no way of determining, for sure, whether JVP leaders would have continued with a democratic program had their party not been proscribed. That proscription both disillusioned and drove them underground is certain. Evidence that the JVP was complicit in the riots was flimsy and vehemently rejected by the party's leaders.[59] No credible source supports the government's contention, though at the height of the crisis, the fears of some UNP leaders that a leftist conspiracy contributed to the turmoil appear to be genuine.

The theory of Australian scholar Patricia Hyndman seems more plausible, though J.R. Jayewardene and his colleagues deny it.[60] Hyndman asserts that the JVP was regarded more as a political threat than a threat to national security. Initially, proscription may have been used to deflect criticism for the government and Sinhalese community, but it then became a pretext for disabling a potential opponent with a large following among Sri Lanka's youth.[61] Police arrests and detentions targeted not only top JVP leaders, but also individuals that may have expressed sympathy for JVP positions but had no official links to the party. UNP and SLFP activists used the proscription to target left-leaning opponents at the local level, by identifying them to the police as JVP sympathisers. The police – who themselves might be political allies of the activists – then arrested, detained and sometimes beat the victims, including men, women and even children.[62]

Proscription of the JVP provides yet another example of *conflict escalation from state-sanctioned violence ineffectiveness.* Covered by the umbrella of emergency regulations, the police made numerous arrests. They closed down JVP publications. They even prohibited the singing of some patriotic songs that had been popular features at JVP events. But Rohana Wijeweera and several key lieutenants escaped, and the JVP was not destroyed as an organisation. Disaffected youth who had supported the JVP when it was legitimate became prime recruits for JVP militant cells during the crackdown. Many felt they had no where else to turn.

The *conflict escalation from development failures feedback loop* also helped swell the ranks of the JVP. Through this loop, the impacts of escalating conflict instigated by Tamil militants and by the JVP intermingled and reinforced one another. During this period, the adverse economic impact of conflict in the northeast, reinforced by Tamil militant actions and bombings in Colombo, was crucial.[63] The carefully cultivated image of Sri Lanka as a human and economic success story with a docile, hard working work force could no longer be sustained. Foreign investors were quick to take note of Sri Lanka's deteriorating political circumstances and pariah image. Domestic investors, too, were now seeking opportunities outside of Sri Lanka for their capital. This was especially true of Tamil business leaders. Many of them had seen their homes burned and factories destroyed. Some had lost friends and relatives to the rage of Sinhalese mobs. Most believed that a conspiracy of their Sinhalese business rivals and government officials had been complicit in the rioting.

Paradoxically, it was non-elite Sinhalese youth, some who were rioters themselves, that were most victimised by the adverse economic consequences of the rioting. As investment dried up, the economy slowed and tourist arrivals plummeted, non-English speaking young men with limited education and no technical skills – this described most young men in Sri Lanka – were the first to lose jobs and the last to be employed. Youth unemployment rates, which had dropped in the late 1970s, crept upwards towards 20 per cent. The expectations created by UNP promises and visible manifestations of elite affluence remained, but opportunities seemed to be dwindling or simply not available. Many young men who wished to better themselves could see only three possible career paths: the police, the army or JVP forces. Often the first two options were foreclosed by lack of the right political connections. Thus, during the period between the riots and the signing of the Indo-Lanka Accord, the JVP was able to recruit and train a solid cadre of core supporters.[64]

When the accord was announced, six days before the actual signing, JVP forces were ready to spearhead disruptive demonstrations. They found natural allies in other anti-government groups that espoused a Sinhalese-Buddhist nationalist agenda and favoured direct action in opposition to the Accord.[65] While Mrs. Bandaranaike provided the initial leadership and legitimacy for demonstrations against the Accord, well-organised JVP activists were able to ensure they were maximally destructive and disruptive. The Accord, the riots that accompanied it and the anti-Accord backlash drew recruits to the JVP, much as the 1983 riots had motivated young men to become Tamil militants. Successful JVP attacks and propaganda further spurred recruitment. As conflict in the south and west escalated, many came to take the JVP seriously, with hope or trepidation, as a credible alternative to Sri Lanka's mainstream parties.

It is not easy to characterise the JVP's civil war in terms of identifiable landmarks. There were few major actions against the security forces, no spectacular bombings and no symbolic mass killings to rival the Anuradhapura massacre. Individual killings were often directed against mid-level officials, UNP supporters, their families, and others who failed to carry out JVP directives. These men, women and children had little or no security protection.

Some spectacular assassinations and assassination attempts were exceptions. In August 1977, top cabinet members, including the President, narrowly escaped death when grenades were tossed into a meeting of the UNP Parliamentary Group and exploded. In December, the UNP's president and three companions were killed on a Colombo street by a grenade lobbed into their car. In February, popular film star and politician Vijay Kumaratunga was shot to death by a motorcycle pylon rider in the driveway of his Colombo home. Kumaratunga, who had a wide popular following, had been advocating a more conciliatory approach to resolving the conflict with Tamil militants. In May, the UNP's general secretary was gunned down.[66]

Rohana Wijeweera also proved himself to be a masterful organiser of disruptive strikes and propaganda campaigns. The campaign that impelled J.R. Jayewardene's government to evacuate foreign tourists was described in the opening chapter of this book. It included closure of petrol stations so that busses could not be fuelled and forced 'strikes' by hotel employees so that tourist needs could not be met. Other campaigns, often announced with street posters or post-cards sent through Sri Lanka's still reliable mails, closed down government departments, halted trains, kept public busses off the road, disrupted electrical supplies and, on several memorable occasions, closed down economic activity and public business in the entire country. JVP activists gained control of student organisations in most universities and closed down

classes with threats against faculty and administrators. JVP threats were taken
seriously because they were often carried out. Vice chancellors and faculty
members were killed. Others were forced from office. Among those who
lived in Colombo (as my wife Emily and I did) in the fall of 1988, there was a
feeling that the JVP was an invisible but ubiquitous presence. We were never
sure where, when or how it would strike next.[67] The government vacillated
between conciliation and draconian measures: Neither was effective. It was, in
the words of J.R. Jayewardene's biographers, 'a time of turmoil.'[68]

The predominance of militancy in violent conflict escalation

This chapter has focused on the institutionalisation of militant groups,
the process by which such groups gained the recruits and resources necessary
to become viable, strong organisations. That is because escalating, persistent
violent conflict is invariably *organised* violent conflict. Militant groups are the
organisers.

The description of escalating violent conflict in earlier chapters showed the
increasing prevalence of 'militant incidents'– incidents in which militant groups
played a role.[69] During the first 22 years after Sri Lanka's independence, 'militant incidents' were so infrequent they do not show up as a separate category.
While there were thuggish attacks from time to time, organised militancy does
not appear as a phenomenon until the closing months of Dudley Senanayake's
'United Front' government. 'Communal incidents' (communally motivated
incidents), too, were relatively infrequent, though never absent. Following implementation of 'Sinhala only' language regulations, they began to increase in
frequency, but were still dwarfed by political strikes and demonstrations prior
to 1970.

Under Sirimavo Bandaranaike's United Front government, militant incidents became suddenly the most frequent category. The short-lived JVP rebellion of 1971 produced this change, of course. Militancy, however, did not
become institutionalised. There was an effective, if draconian 'immune system
response' by Sri Lanka's security forces, and the JVP temporarily faded from
view.

For reasons that have been discussed at length, J.R. Jayewardene's open
economy reforms and policies of communal reconciliation failed to produce
the outcomes envisioned. During his first term, militant incidents were once
again the most frequent and communal incidents rose to second place in frequency. But militancy still had not yet become institutionalised. As we have

seen, the riots of July 1983, the ineffective deployment of state-sanctioned violence and political tactics that emasculated the moderate centre helped produce this transformation in Tamil militant groups as well as the JVP. Circumstances surrounding the Indo-Lanka Accord completed the JVP's emergence as a fully institutionalised militant organisation.

The qualitative changes institutionalised militancy produced in Sri Lankan society have been described anecdotally. The despairing query chosen to open Chapter One – *How could we have come to this?* – says it all. A brief statistical description focusing on five years will complement this portrait.[70] The years are:

- 1978 – the first full year of open economy policies;
- 1982 – the last year of J.R. Jayewardene's first term; the year of the presidential election and referendum;
- 1985 – the first full year that leading Tamil militant groups (LTTE, EPRLF, PLOTE and TELO) were a major institutionalised presence in Sri Lanka;
- 1987 – the year of the Indo-Lanka Accord;
- 1988 – the first full year that the JVP was a major institutionalised presence in Sri Lanka as militant organisation.[71]

The bar graph depicted in Figure 19.2 compares the number of reported conflict incidents in three categories: *Total Incidents*, *Militant Incidents*, and *Mortality Incidents*. Mortality incidents are those in which one or more persons died. (Readers are reminded that it is relative orders of magnitude, not specific numbers that are important.)

The evidence that militancy caused the escalation of conflict intensity in Sri Lanka's civil wars is overwhelming. Between 1978 and 1988, the number of reported conflict incidents increased by *more than 100-fold.* The increase in militant incidents during the same period was *250-fold.* In 1978 and 1982, militant incidents comprised less than 40 per cent of total conflict incidents. In 1987 and 1988, militant events comprised more than 90 per cent of total conflict incidents. Contrasting 1987 and 1988 shows the increasing impact of the JVP on Sri Lanka's political life. Reported conflict incidents more than doubled as a result of JVP actions in the south and west. In fact, since the IPKF was having some success in reducing conflict in the north and east, the impact of the now-institutionalised JVP was even greater. The last bar on our graph

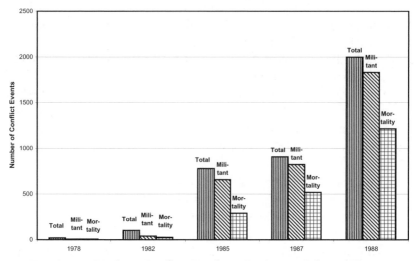

Figure 19.2 Violent Conflict Incidents Per Year – Selected Years

displays another important, tragic characteristic of militant incidents. In 1978 and 1982, less than one-third of conflict incidents involved deaths of one or more individuals. In 1987 and 1988, the number incidents involving deaths was more than 55 per cent of the total. A conflict dominated by militant groups is not only violent but deadly.

Sri Lanka's government responds – futile negotiations.

Sri Lanka Tamils comprise no more than about 12 per cent of the island's registered voters. Beginning with the landmark election of 1956, electoral/parliamentary politics was primarily politics of the Sinhalese majority. This was especially true during the terms of Prime Minister Sirimavo Bandaranaike's United Front government and President J.R. Jayewardene's UNP government, when those in power were able to amend the constitution at will.

In democracies, balancing the will of majorities against the rights of minorities always poses complicated challenges. Contests over political power and distribution of benefits in ethnically divided democracies complicate these challenges further, as Sri Lankans have discovered. The 1987 Indo-Lanka Accord was the latest of many failed attempts to simultaneously accommodate Sinhalese and Tamil norms, traditions, economic aspirations and political visions in a manner acceptable to both communities.[72] After 1983, well-organised forces serving as proxies for each community attempted to impose their particular communitarian vision by force of arms. Escalating conflict gave urgency to negotiations – they took place almost continuously, beginning in 1984 – but also made reaching a satisfactory resolution more difficult.

S.W.R.D. Bandaranaike's Official Language Act was the first use of majority power by a Sinhalese politician to impose an unacceptable communitarian vision on Sri Lankan Tamils.[73] As we have seen, this sparked an ongoing cycle of increasingly strident (and ultimately violent) confrontations and failed negotiations. Sinhalese nationalist factions and self-serving politicians of both major parties dominated earlier stages of this cycle, preventing an accommodation that would be broadly acceptable to Tamil community members. J.R. Jayewardene and Dudley Senanayake formed an improbable alliance with Sinhalese nationalists to scuttle the Bandaranaike-Chelvanayakam pact of 1957.[74] Sirimavo Bandaranaike used similar tactics to scuttle a less encompassing pact, negotiated by Dudley Senanayake and Chelvanayakam between 1965 and 1967. Mrs. Bandaranaike promised a sympathetic response to Tamil concerns in pre-election manoeuvring but reneged after the United Front's overwhelming 1970 general election victory. Her 'Republican Constitution' enshrined Sinhalese-Buddhist norms and preferential treatment for Sinhalese as Sri Lanka's law of the land. J.R. Jayewardene promised he would devolve power to District Development Councils, but dragged negotiations on for five years before finally implementing a 'half a loaf' devolution. As the cycle dragged on, moderate Tamil politicians were marginalised and militants grew stronger.[75] Very probably, this pattern would have repeated itself at a slow pace for a few more years had not the July 1983 riots intervened.

What distinguished the cycle between 1984 and 1987 was India's intervention on the Tamil side. This did not resolve the conflict, but successive negotiations in which Indian pressure on Sri Lanka's government mounted, produced a framework more sympathetic to Tamil aspirations than earlier accommodations proposed in Dudley Senanayake and J.R. Jayewardene's successive District Development Council schemes. In chapter 1, I quoted I. William Zartman's observation that 'mutually satisfactory, second best settlements are unattractive to parties playing for ultimate stakes.'[76] This may partially explain why participants on both sides continued to jockey for political and personal advantage, while losses from violence mounted. Recapitulating some high points of the negotiations will illustrate this.

First was the 'All Party Conference,' an unwieldy gathering that included not only representatives of all major Sri Lankan political parties but also many religious denominations. Moderate Tamil politicians represented that community's point of view but militants were excluded. The negotiating text was a product of discussions between President Jayewardene and Mrs. Gandhi's personal representative, a respected South Indian Tamil diplomat.[77] Basically, it proposed returning to the formula of the 1956 Bandaranaike-Chelvanayakam pact, granting substantial autonomy to Provincial Councils and limiting Sinhalese land settlements. A more controversial proposal, mooted by Tamil representatives, was to combine the predominantly Tamil Northern Province with the multi-ethnic Eastern Province into a single autonomous unit (in which Sri Lanka Tamils would be a substantial majority). The conference ended inconclusively in December. Reflecting the Tamil and Indian point of view, J.N. Dixit, India's influential Ambassador to Sri Lanka during this period, described President Jayewardene's strategy as an 'obfuscatory exercise' design to stall negotiations while he built up his military forces.[78]

The All Party Conference was followed by two rounds of 'Thimpu Talks,' held in Bhutan's capital during August and September 1985. In what he regarded as a significant concession, President Jayewardene agreed that Sri Lanka's delegation (headed by his younger brother, Harry) would officially recognise Tamil militant group representatives as parties to the negotiation. The discussions, facilitated by India's foreign secretary, were mostly fractious and unproductive, but did ultimately produce a document that became the basis for further discussion with Indian and Sri Lanka government representatives.[79]

As public negotiations sputtered, President Jayewardene and Prime Minister Rajiv Gandhi pursued alternative track negotiations in several venues and exchanged messages through personal representatives. Reportedly their relations were cordial despite the fact that India's government continued to arm Tamil Militants and Sri Lanka's continued to stall on meaningful concessions to its Tamil minority.[80] This track appears to have been the most productive in 1986, a year devoid of meetings that included all protagonists. Toward the end of the year, President Jayewardene and Prime Minister Gandhi caucused at the SAARC head of state meeting and made plans to moot an agreement, to be signed by both governments early in 1987.[81] India was pressuring both sides, but whether either side would have voluntarily agreed is problematic. Union of the two Tamil majority provinces, now included in the agreement, was strongly opposed by Sinhalese and Muslim minorities living in the east. As became clear at the time of the accord, Prabakharan was sceptical about any agreement with Sri Lanka's government short of an independent Eelam.

Basic provisions of the accord that was finally negotiated, in the crisis circumstances of July 1987, have already been discussed. This must be described as an imposed, rather than a negotiated settlement. Nevertheless, a basic framework was in place thanks to previous rounds of negotiations, especially the private dialogues between Sri Lanka's President and India's Prime Minister. Even at this late stage, influential members of President Jayewardene's cabinet distanced themselves from the agreement.

The provisions of the accord closely resembled the Bandaranaike-Chelvanayakam pact, against which J.R. Jayewardene had led successful protests in 1957. Thirty years later, almost to the day, he was being forced to accept essentially the same provisions. If provisions of a possible accommodation were the same, after 30 years, Sri Lanka was not. Violent political conflict had transformed the island nation.

Sri Lanka's government responds – state-sanctioned violence

An alternative to negotiation is force, a 'military solution.'[82] We have already viewed this option from a militant group vantage point. In this section we shift our vantage point to the government side, to state-sanctioned violence. Linkages between state-sanctioned violence, ineffectively applied, and rising conflict intensity have already been considered. However, readers should not infer that forceful application of state-sanctioned violence is never an appropriate response to conflict escalation. It is the effectiveness – or ineffectiveness – of security forces that is key.

Topologies of state-sanctioned violence intensity and violent conflict intensity in Sri Lanka's northeast and southwest provide de facto evidence of ineffectiveness (Figures 19.3 and 19.4). In both regions, 'Prevention of Terrorism' legislation gave security forces virtually unfettered powers to arrest, detain and kill. Opposition parties that deviated too far from the mainstream could be proscribed and their members arrested. Moderate opposition parties had greater latitude for action but could be victimised by pro-government thugs, with little legal recourse. Victims who protested too loudly had reason to fear draconian sanctions, which prevention of terrorism rules could be used to justify or conceal. Print and electronic media were under direct government control or subject to censorship. Despite these measures, violent conflict had

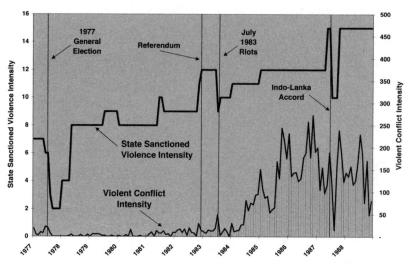

Figure 19.3 State-sanctioned violence and Violent Conflict – North and East

reached hitherto unimagined levels in Sri Lanka by 1988. Did the ineffective use of state-sanctioned violence, indeed, contribute to this scenario? An examination of the Sri Lankan and Indian forces unsuccessful efforts to bring militant violence under control provides some answers to this question.

State-sanctioned violence in the north and east

In the northeast as early as 1984, little remained of democratic governance, protected human rights or normal political discourse. When the IPKF blasted Prabakharan's most visible forces[83] out of Jaffna, military government replaced any vestige of civilian rule. Indian officers and men portrayed themselves as benevolent masters –'we have come to stay to protect innocent civilians' read a sign next to one IPKF sentry post"[84]– but left no doubt that their word was the law, without recourse.

In truth, neither the IPKF *Jawans*, nor Sri Lanka's Sinhalese soldiers who preceded them as Jaffna's putative rulers, cared much about protecting innocent civilians. More often, Jaffna's hapless Tamil residents (which included a large number of LTTE supporters) were objects of their rage and frustration. Rage and frustration were felt often by Sri Lankan soldiers because they so rarely succeeded in achieving their military objectives.

By now, Sri Lanka's army was able to do more than hold parades. Establishing the National Security Ministry placed the conduct of the war under an ambitious, no-nonsense cabinet minister who personally believed that a military solution was attainable. A respected senior general was recalled from retirement to serve as his chief of staff.[85] Military expenditures and troop strength more than doubled, and President Jayewardene's son organised an elite 'Special Task Force.' With the assistance of Israeli and British mercenaries, training and discipline improved.[86]

Initially, none of this was sufficient to produce the victories that were so necessary for Sinhalese public opinion and troop morale. As is typical in guerrilla warfare, the initiative lay with the militants, now well armed and trained by India. They knew the countryside, were supported by many civilians and could choose their targets. Throughout 1984 and 1985, a dreary pattern of failed engagements was repeated over and over again. Militants would mount a surprise attack on a police station, military base or other installation. The defenders would call for reinforcements, which would rush to the scene, only to be intercepted by blasts from carefully planted land mines. In the ensuing confusion, militants waiting in ambush would kill additional soldiers.[87] Sometimes, as with patrol 'Four Four Bravo,' the reinforcements would be wiped out or forced back before reaching their objective. If government forces did arrive in sufficient strength, their adversaries would melt into the jungle or the civilian population.

Unable to deal with these tactics, soldiers would retaliate by killing civilians at random in the vicinity of the attack and detaining larger numbers of youths who were tortured, beaten and sometimes killed while in custody. Increasingly 'death squad' tactics were used. Human rights organisations reported a number of instances in which armed men, dressed in civilian clothes, simply corralled groups of Tamil civilians and shot them.[88] (Militants were also killing Sinhalese civilians at random, as already noted).

There were also onerous military regulations that were intended to make life more difficult for militants but mostly impacted civilians. A coastal 'surveillance zone' was established to prevent smuggling. This had little impact on the flow of arms and newly trained recruits to Jaffna, but ruined the livelihoods of Tamil fisherfolk, many of whom fled to Tamil Nadu as refugees.[89] Later, the National Security Minister banned use of private cars, minibuses, motorbikes and even pedal bikes. Humorists joked that tricycles would be next.[90] These tactics did not 'win the hearts and minds' of Sri Lanka's Tamil citizens living in the northeast. Youthful recruits – women as well as men – continued to swell militant ranks. Many who were not active fighters supported militant groups covertly or at least passively.

In 1987, it appeared that reforms were bearing fruit. Many observers believe that 'Operation Liberation' would have achieved its military objectives.[91] Reportedly the ferocity and effectiveness of the attacks surprised LTTE forces. There were draconian measures against civilians: The advancing forces summarily shot men, women and children seeking shelter from the crossfire in trenches. Sometimes, soldiers directed them to take shelter in churches, schools and temples that were subsequently targeted by artillery shells.[92] Militants did not necessarily oppose atrocities against Tamil civilians, all whom were viewed as *de facto* supporters of Tamil Eelam. In fact, their tactics were sometimes designed to provoke Sri Lankan soldiers into atrocities. Atrocities generated international support for the Eelamist cause and helped motivate India's leaders to intervene. Despite Prabakharan's reservations about the accord, it is hardly surprising that civilians welcomed the first contingents of Indian 'peacekeepers' with garlands.

We have seen that this honeymoon period soon ended. By provoking the October offensive, the LTTE successfully manoeuvred the Indian peacekeepers into the role of oppressors. Some of the excesses committed by Indian soldiers during the assault on Jaffna, particularly the massacre of doctors, staff and patients in the Jaffna Hospital, were particularly gruesome.[93] As the war progressed, discipline improved, but most Indian soldiers, far from home and enmeshed in a complex guerrilla war, had little sympathy for the citizens they were supposed to be 'protecting.'

To understand this, it is important to understand the conflict from the vantage point of the Indian foot soldier, a perspective that Ranjan Hoole and his colleagues present effectively.[94] Most were from North India and often from very poor backgrounds. Very few spoke Tamil and their grasp of Sri Lanka's political situation was limited. If their mission had been explained at all, it was presented as protecting Tamils from Sinhalese oppressors. But to them, Jaffna Tamils did not seem 'oppressed.' There seemed to be a large prosperous middle class and living conditions for even the poorest were better than the villages from which they had come. When these people, instigated by the LTTE, began to insult and humiliate them, they found it hard to respond passively, as they were ordered to do. Moreover, the Indians seriously underestimated their adversaries, and suffered a number of embarrassing reverses, with high casualties.[95] This contributed to a climate that sometimes led soldiers to take out their frustrations on civilians in the heat of battle.

In contrast to Sri Lanka's leaders, however, the chiefs of India's defence establishment had reserves of overwhelming force at their disposal. They soon realised that they faced a resourceful, well-armed adversary and responded with a tenfold or more increase in the size of their forces. I can remember driving past Indian encampments on the road from Colombo to Jaffna and being impressed by the numbers of tanks and attack helicopters, and by the aura of toughness and discipline.[96] Liberation Tiger forces, unable to withstand the Indian onslaught, were forced back into their difficult-to-penetrate jungle hideouts.

After deliberating with close colleagues, Prabakharan decided to engage the IPKF in a protracted guerrilla war, which would be coupled with an aggressive propaganda campaign.[97] LTTE forces rarely defeated the Indians in combat but were able to sustain the war until Sri Lanka's political leadership changed and the Indian government's political will weakened. Sri Lanka became India's 'Viet Nam.' When the peacekeepers departed after J.R. Jayewardene had left office, the Northeastern Provincial Council government they had propped up soon suffered the same fate at the hands of LTTE forces that had earlier befallen the U.S. client state of South Viet Nam. India's attempts to combine mediation and a military solution had failed. The Liberation Tigers remained strong. The civil war continued.

State-sanctioned violence in the south and west

In the south and west, too, state-sanctioned violence reached a level after the disturbances of July 1987 never before seen in Sri Lanka, though conditions were less draconian than in the north. Here, government forces tried to fight the insidious attacks of a hidden enemy while maintaining a semblance of normal economic activity and democratic practice. The policy failed.

JVP militants were Sinhalese, which made the task of fighting them more difficult. JVP propaganda emphasised the same Sinhalese and Buddhist values that mainstream politicians sometimes used to mobilise support. JVP opposition to India's intervention was popular with many Sinhalese and was also supported by Sirimavo Bandaranaike's SLFP. JVP supporters were drawn from the same strata of society and regions as the lower ranks of the police and

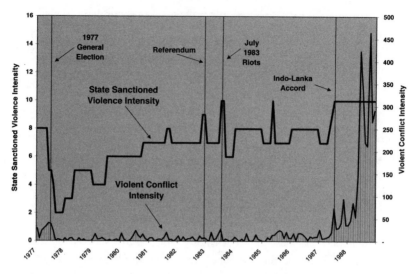

Figure 19.4 State-sanctioned violence – South and West

armed forces. Until JVP leaders embarked on a tactically disastrous campaign against security force members and their families, there was a real fear that the forces might be infiltrated. Like LTTE cadres, JVP cadres could melt into the civilian population. But in this case the population was Sinhalese and lived in the cities and villages of the south and west.

JVP leaders cleverly created a sham organisation that differentiated its political wing – called the JVP–from its military wing, which was labelled the Patriotic Peoples Movement (DJV).[98] In the summer of 1988, in fact, the government was hoaxed into lifting the proscription on the JVP, imposed in 1983, in order to pursue 'political negotiations.' The hoax was soon uncovered but the JVP retained its status as a quasi-legitimate political movement, even while its 'military wing' was threatening to topple the government.[99] This allowed J.R. Jayewardene's government to pursue a two-track strategy that combined security force actions with offers to negotiate.

Figure 19.4 provides graphic evidence that neither tactic produced results during the waning months of President Jayewardene's term. State-sanctioned violence and violent conflict intensity rose in tandem. The negotiation track simply provided opportunities for posturing and propaganda on the part of JVP leaders, who felt that victory was within their grasp. The security forces used emergency regulations to detain large numbers of Sinhalese men and women, but failed to make a dent in the JVP's effectiveness.[100] As in the north, these actions were as likely to breed new JVP supporters as to weaken the movement. Rising unemployment, produced by deteriorating economic conditions, also swelled the JVP's ranks. Police officers who had been victimised and in some cases corrupted by low pay and political interference under successive governments[101] were reluctant to put their lives at risk against a movement that seemed so effective in carrying out its threats. J.R. Jayewardene was not solely responsible for policies that limited the effectiveness of Sri Lanka's security forces against the JVP, but he helped shape those policies and he (along with many other Sri Lankans) paid the price.

J.R. Jayewardene's legacy

Before concluding this examination of J.R. Jayewardene's long term in office, it seems appropriate to return to the theme of presidential miscalculations, introduced in Chapter 18. My reflections, there, omitted a larger question that begs for attention: how could such an able political leader have miscalculated so badly? In a televised press conference, following the Indo-Lanka accord signing, J.R. Jayewardene's self appraisal was candid. Responding to a reporter's query about why he had not reached an agreement with Tamil leaders, earlier on, the President said, 'It is a lack of courage on my part, a lack of intelligence on my part, a lack of foresight on my part.'[102]

This public acknowledgment of responsibility is remarkable for a politician, but not satisfying. One seeks a deeper understanding. My own explanation of President Jayewardene's miscalculations draws a parallel with his predecessor. Describing Sirimavo Bandaranaike's failure to grasp the magnitude of Tamil alienation, I observed that political leaders give top priority to concerns that appear to threaten their power and the stability of their government. By mid-1979, when Jayewardene's government had outlawed the Liberation Tigers, passed the Prevention of Terrorism Act and instructed its Jaffna military commander to 'eliminate ...the menace of terrorism in all its forms' it would appear that the threat posed by Tamil militancy was taken seriously.

What was not grasped was that events in Jaffna, the seat of Tamil militancy could be more than a political side show, albeit an increasingly troublesome and frustrating one. President Jayewardene was a quintessential political realist. Sri Lanka's demographic realities seemed to make it obvious that concessions could not be made to Jaffna politicians that would cost him significant support

in Sinhalese majority regions.   Only 3 per-cent of Sri Lanka's voters lived in
Jaffna district, where calls for secession originated.   An additional 2 per-cent
lived in Batticaloa district, where opposition to the government was also becoming strong, though support for the Liberation Tigers was weak.   As late as
Spring, 1983, the highly visible militants numbered in the hundreds at most.   In
President Jayewardene's view, most Tamils living in the North were law abiding
men and women who opposed violence and were ambivalent about separatism.

Thus, for this experienced, pragmatic politician, the political main event
continued to be in the South.   His principal political adversaries continued to
be Sirimavo Bandaranaike, along with her allies in the Sri Lanka Freedom and
Marxist parties.   His goal was to keep these adversaries demoralised, maintain
his hard won base of Sinhalese political support and use the six year window
of opportunity provided by his presidential election and referendum victories
to effect an economic miracle in Sri Lanka.   Skilful politician that he was, Jayewardene hoped to offer palliatives that would keep Tamil separatism at bay, but
not cost him the support of Sinhalese nationalists.   By maintaining alliances
with nationalist extremists, giving them forums in party councils and Parliament where they could 'let off steam,' he hoped to control their most virulent
tendencies, while retaining their support for the United National Party.   Over
the six year life of his second government, Jayewardene believed that economic
prosperity, widely diffused throughout the population, would reduce the appeal
of Tamil separatism and the virulence of Sinhalese nationalism.

In crafting this very reasonable strategy, as we have seen, Jayewardene drew
upon unparalleled political skills and nearly five decades of experience in Sri
Lankan politics, but these skills and experience failed to provide lasting solutions to the problems he faced.   That is J.R. Jayewardene's and Sri Lanka's
tragedy.   Having successfully 'climbed to the top of the greasy pole,'[103] this
visionary, gifted and sophisticated political leader was the wrong man for his
time.   His tactical successes helped insulate him from 'bad news' about development failures and security force ineffectiveness that might, conceivably, have
saved his presidency.   Protracted civil war, rather than an economic miracle and
a stable multi-ethnic society became the legacy of his second term in office.

Part V

Diagnosis, Treatment and Prevention:
Why Deadly Conflict and Terrorism
are not only Predictable,
but Preventable

20

Costs and Benefits of Protracted Violent Conflict

Proposals for massive youth training programs or co-optation of militant groups may seem fanciful or prohibitively costly. A realistic cost-benefit analysis of the policies that were actually implemented might make them seem more attractive.

Protracted violent conflict is costly. When conflict breaks out or is threatened, 'national security' becomes political leaders' overriding concern. U.S. President George W. Bush's 'War on Terrorism' provides the most recent of many examples. Leaders reallocate resources to police and military forces, while other priorities diminish in importance. Militant forces, too, seek resources to sustain their activities. Bank robberies, extortion, drug trafficking and appeals for contributions from international sources are among the fund raising strategies used. Protracted conflict destroys productive capacity and infrastructure, which must then be rebuilt.[1] Capital flees to safer havens. International competitors take over markets. Businesses fail. Talented men and women are killed. The economy stagnates or declines. In worst case scenarios – Liberia, Somalia, Afghanistan, and Sierra Leone – national political and economic institutions cease to exist.

Protracted violent conflict does benefit some economically. This further complicates the already complex challenge of conflict resolution. The social-economic context of protracted conflict provides lucrative business opportunities, allowing protagonists and third parties to profit. Local warlords would lose control over resources – diamonds or oil for example – if conflicts were resolved. But despite the fact that there are some winners as well as many losers, the costs of protracted conflicts almost invariably outweigh the benefits by several orders of magnitude. To what degree is this taken into account by those whose decisions catalyse protracted violent conflict as part of a nation's development scenario? Sadly, such decisions are rarely – if ever – subjected to cost-benefit analysis.

Economic criteria weigh most heavily in development policy decisions. Political and military considerations weigh more heavily in security policy decisions. In fact, development policy and security policy decisions are most often made by different decision makers and in very different ways. To cite just one example, World Bank analysts were proscribed for years from taking 'political' considerations into account, even though their recommendations obviously had profound political consequences. Yet development policies almost always have profound political and security implications. This is especially true in ethnically diverse nations, where they will almost invariably advantage one group over another. Similarly, security policy decisions have profound economic implications, especially when they lead to protracted civil war.

Those who choose violence as a tactic or strategy often overestimate benefits and underestimate costs, however this is difficult to document. Decisions to use violence-prone strategies are often shrouded in secrecy. Sometimes, violence is used covertly. Insurgent groups are even less accessible than government security establishments. Unlike privatisation, redistribution, grass-roots empowerment, structural adjustment and meeting basic human needs, violence is rarely debated as a strategy of developmental change. Only ideologues and militants publicly advocate revolution and terrorism as social-change strategies. But governments often opt for repression, coercion or use of military force rather than alternatives such as negotiation, compromise, co-optation, resignation or surrender. When revolutionary violence, terrorism, coercion or repression is chosen, what costs and benefits should be weighed? Can the process of weighing the costs and benefits of violence-prone strategies be improved?

Sri Lankan economist S.W.R.D. Samarasinghe and I sought answers to these questions by documenting the economic costs of Sri Lanka's two civil wars during the July 1983-December 1988 period. We argued that political leaders and especially business community members might choose differently if economic costs of decisions that could potentially foment violent conflict and strengthen militant groups were measured accurately and taken into account realistically. The first part of this chapter summarises our analysis and cost estimates.[2]

Defining and measuring 'primary', 'secondary' and 'tertiary' costs of violent conflict

Costs of violent conflict can usefully be labelled *primary, secondary* or *tertiary. Primary (direct) costs* include the value of houses, commercial establishments, factories, government buildings, roads, irrigation systems and other infrastructure elements destroyed by violence. There are also expenses of ammunition expended, fuels consumed and weapons[3] lost, over and above normal training and maintenance, by protagonists. A third direct cost is lives lost and injuries sustained, though the economic cost of these is more difficult to quantify.

Secondary costs include funds expended to build up military, police and opposition forces in preparation for or in response to violent conflict.[4] Negative economic responses to violence or in anticipation of future violence also fall into this category. Loss of foreign and local investment and the flight of capital and educated citizens abroad are examples. Finally, there is lost production due to the destruction of infrastructure, disruption of work schedules, loss of trained manpower and loss of investment.

Tertiary costs are medium to long-term economic impacts resulting from the sense of instability and uncertainty that violent political conflict creates. Instability and uncertainty contribute subtly to losses of income, economic output and jobs over the long run. For example, protracted conflict may force a government to abandon or compromise a promising long-term economic development strategy such as privatisation or export promotion. It may deny a country the opportunity to join a regional economic group or to participate effectively in such a group.

Measuring physical destruction and estimating replacement costs is a relatively straightforward task, though data may be difficult to collect. In Sri Lanka, government ministries were required to compile such estimates for the Ministry of Rehabilitation and the World Bank. We took marginal direct costs of military actions into account as a component of increases in overall defence and 'public order and security' budgets. These data were readily available in Central Bank *Annual Reports*.[5]

Rough numerical estimates of deaths and injuries could be derived from the violent political conflict data base, complemented by other sources. In the end, however, we chose not to approximate an economic value for these, based on 'replacement costs' or some other scheme.[6] This was not because we devalued human lives, but because we tried to be realistic about how the value of human life enters into the calculus of security policy decisions. 'Human costs' are rhetorically acknowledged by political leaders, but seem rarely to carry weight with those who are deciding to use or not to use violence.[7] We decided that an analysis emphasising more readily quantified economic costs might provide a fresh, more widely accepted contribution to a long-standing problem.

Secondary costs cannot be measured directly. Ideally, a sophisticated model might have been used to make estimates but none was available. As a crude alternative, we made assumptions about economic growth and military budget scenarios that Sri Lanka might have experienced under peaceful conditions. Estimates of economic output (GDP) and military expenditures based on these scenarios were compared with reported productivity and military expenditures. Differences between assumed and reported scenarios were interpreted as a rough measure of secondary costs.

We used a similar approach to take tertiary costs into account, comparing economic output generated by a 'successful development' scenario with reported output. The scenario used for this estimate was more optimistic than that used to estimate secondary costs. This scenario must be viewed as more speculative than the 'peaceful' scenario described above, but both are consistent with optimistic descriptions of Sri Lanka's economic prospects published in early years of the 'open economy' experiment.

Primary costs' estimates

As noted above, our primary costs' estimates included only destruction of physical infrastructure. Destruction from the July 1983 riots was partly documented in the Sri Lanka government's *Master Plan for the Rehabilitation of Persons Displaced in the Disturbances of July 1983*[8]. According to the *Master Plan*, 122 factories and 2,300 other commercial buildings were destroyed. From other sources, we estimated the number of houses destroyed at about 20,000.[9] To measure total costs we used average cost per house and per commercial structure estimates developed by Sri Lanka's Ministry of Rehabilitation, working in conjunction with the World Bank. Although these estimates were compiled for the northeast, we judged them to be the best available per-unit approximations for the southwest as well. However some adjustments needed to be made in estimates of the distribution of different types of structures because of the more urban character of the 1983 violence. Based on these assumptions total housing losses were estimated at 784 million rupees and industrial structure losses at 169 million rupees for a total of 953 million (about $U.S. 29 million).[10]

Estimates of physical destruction in the northeast, for the period from 1983 through July 1987, were compiled by ministries of the Sri Lanka government in connection with a request for rehabilitation funding from the World Bank.[11] 69,400 houses were reported destroyed and 30,000 houses damaged. Approximately 11,300 commercial businesses were reported damaged of which 8,000 were completely destroyed. Heavy destruction of irrigation structures, roads and bridges, water supply systems, transport systems, power supply systems and public buildings was also reported. Total rehabilitation and reconstruction costs, which we regard as a conservative estimate of losses, were put at 23.5 billion rupees (about $U.S. 712 million).

No comparable estimates of physical destruction existed for the turbulent period from the signing of the Indo-Lanka Accord until the end of 1988. To provide an estimate of physical destruction costs, we assumed that a rough correlation existed between intensities of violence, as measured by our scale, and levels of physical destruction.[12] This provided a basis for extrapolating average monthly destruction costs using available data on destruction costs and violence levels for the 1983-87 period. For the two months of the Indian offensive against Jaffna (October - November 1987) we inflated costs by an additional 40 per cent.[13] Based on these assumptions, losses due to destruction of infrastructure during this later period were estimated as 12.7 billion rupees for the northeast and 9.2 billion rupees for the south. Summing these figures produced an overall primary cost estimate of somewhat less than 50 billion rupees (about $U.S. 1.4 billion). This is a conservative figure but a huge sum for a nation of Sri Lanka's size and level of development. To put it in perspective, the sum was roughly equivalent to some cost estimates for the 10-year Accelerated Mahaweli Development Program, Sri Lanka's largest ever development project.[14]

Secondary costs' estimates

Before presenting the macroeconomic analysis we used to estimate secondary costs, Samarasinghe and I provided a series of within-sector illustrations of conflict's pervasive detrimental economic impact. Only three—tourism, education, and employment—are presented here.[15] The Development—Deadly-Conflict System Model, shows this impact as a linkage between conflict intensity and economic performance.

Economic losses in the tourist sector were particularly damaging because of their impact on foreign exchange earnings. Between 1977 and 1982 tourist arrivals increased by more than 150 per cent to over 400,000. A least a 10 per cent annual growth rate was projected for the rest of the decade. The escalation of conflict, beginning with the July 1983 rioting, reversed this trend. In 1988, there were only 183,000 arrivals, less than half the 1982 figure. We estimated that conflict cost Sri Lanka more than 17 billion rupees during this period (more than $U.S. 500 million). This was roughly the amount of foreign aid that was disbursed in 1986.

Sri Lanka's educational system was long regarded as one of the most advanced in the Global South. Political conflict imposed costs on this system that were difficult to measure, but severe. All universities in the south were closed most of the time from 1987 through 1989.[16] In the fall of 1988, high school and even elementary school students became involved in political demonstrations and their schools closed as well, some for nearly a year. Closings meant that the supply of newly trained personnel virtually dried up in medicine, engineering and other fields requiring a college degree. University level students with means or the ability to win scholarships left the country in large numbers to study abroad.[17] Ongoing conflicts discouraged them from returning. University faculty, especially younger scholars with technical degrees, also emigrated in large numbers. The impact of this emigration is being felt now. A generation of senior professors are retiring and causing the quality of instruction, overall, to drop precipitously. Years of effort and substantial funding increases will be needed to reverse this.[18]

Violent conflict's impact on labour markets is more than economically damaging. Unemployed and underemployed youths are prime recruiting targets for militant groups. The *conflict escalation from development failures loop* represents this. Earlier, we saw that J.R. Jayewardene's government made substantial headway in job creation during the early years of open economy reforms: After July 1983, this changed. About 15,000 factory workers, 3,500 plantation workers and 10,000 self-employed persons lost their jobs immediately as a result of the riots. Tourist industry contraction cost at least 30,000 more. Even more important was the loss of new jobs that economic growth had been expected to create. Government figures in 1982 projected a job creation rate at or above 200,000 per year, reducing unemployment to about three per cent of the labour force. This goal would have been attainable if the manufacturing sector and some of the more labour intensive and high wage service sector industries such as tourism had grown rapidly. Increased output from the heavy investments in infrastructure, made in the late 1970s and early 1980s, was also expected to come on stream in the late 1980s and early 1990s. This would have created additional jobs. The actual scenario was, of course, very different. From 1983 the level of unemployment began to rise and around 1988 topped the one million mark, about 18 per cent of the labour force. Virtually all the ground that had been gained by open economy reforms was lost.

Overall, we chose to estimate the economic impact of violent conflict by comparing actual economic output (measured as GDP) with three scenarios that assumed more favourable conditions in differing degrees. The *optimistic growth scenario* assumed that peaceful conditions would have produced an additional one per cent increase in growth during 1983-85 and a continued six per cent growth rate thereafter. A growth rate of six per cent for 1983-85 was consistent with most estimates, but failed to factor in moderately poor harvests in 1986 and 1988 and a very poor harvest in 1987.[19] The *moderate growth scenario* took these poor harvests into account. The projected growth rate was reduced by 25 per cent of the difference between the actual growth rate and the optimistic projection in 1986 and 1988 and by 50 per cent of the difference in 1987. The *pessimistic growth scenario* assumed only a five per cent increase in growth under peaceful conditions and a 50 per cent impact of the bad harvests in all three years. We then estimated the economic impact of violent conflict on output (the secondary cost of violent conflict) during the 1983-1988 period by taking the difference between actual GDP per year and projected GDP per year for each scenario. The total cost estimates summed the differences for each year.

The results were as follows. Under the most optimistic assumptions about economic growth, the cost of violence due to losses in output may have been as much as 65 billion rupees (about $U.S. 2 billion). If one is more pessimistic than virtually all observers of Sri Lanka's economy, the cost may have been as little as 29.5 billion rupees ($U.S. 900 million). Costs based on the moderate scenario were 51 billion rupees (about $U.S. 1.5 billion). For further analysis, we used the estimate based on the moderate growth scenario, as I do in this chapter.

We also used a scenario approach to estimate the portion of expenditures for the armed forces and police that was attributable to violent political conflict. In real terms, government expenditure on defence and maintenance of public order rose from 1.54 billion rupees in 1982 to 7.6 billion rupees in 1988.[20] Part of this was an expenditure of about 3.3 billion rupees ($U.S. 100 billion) on imported armaments, an allocation of foreign exchange that Sri Lanka could ill afford given its balance of payments situation. Excluded from budgeted expenditures were private expenditures on security to guard homes, commercial establishments and factories as well as expenditures on security not reflected in the budgets for defence and maintenance of public order. Accounting for these expenditures would have increased the estimates presented below.

To estimate increased costs attributable to violent political conflict, I assumed that defence and public order spending would have remained at six per cent of current government expenditures during the period from 1983 through 1988.[21] The difference between actual expenditures for defence and public order and those projected by the scenario was about 21.8 billion rupees (about $U.S. 660 million).

A final secondary cost was India's expenditures on the IPKF.[22] 20 million rupees was the figure most frequently reported by the Sri Lankan and Indian press as the daily cost of supporting IPKF operations. The IPKF operated in Sri Lanka for about 150 days in 1987 and throughout 1988 (366 days, a leap year). At 20 million rupees per day, the cost of these operations was about 10,300 million rupees (about $U.S. 300 million).

Our estimated secondary costs then, were the macro economic impact of the conflict (51 billion rupees), the additional costs of expenditures on defence and public order (21.8 billion rupees) and the costs of the IPKF operations (10.3 billion rupees). The total estimate of secondary costs is 83.1 billion rupees (about $U.S. 2.5 billion).

Tertiary costs' estimates

Two tertiary costs were taken into account. First was the impact of violent conflict on the viability of the post-1977 export-oriented liberal economic strategy. Second was the impact of violent conflict on prospects for regional co-operation involving Sri Lanka.

The key to political acceptability of the open economy program was its ability to create new jobs and raise incomes, especially of lower income groups. As we have seen, from 1978 through 1982, economic growth averaged more than 10 per cent per year and unemployment was low. These positive developments created a climate of acceptance for more unpopular aspects of the program such as privatisation, price decontrol, and cuts in subsidies. Negative public reactions to the worsening income distribution that accompanied economic liberalisation were cushioned by an appreciable reduction in absolute poverty. As the economy slowed down, however, particularly after 1983, the trade-offs between growth and equity inherent in economic liberalisation came into sharp focus. Growing political opposition to the open economy program forced the government to defer privatisation of unprofitable state enterprises and even institute a new entitlement program.[23] Despite some implementation problems, the UNP's strategy of economic liberalisation, combined with industrial export development by a revitalised private sector, appeared to offer the best prospects for sustained economic growth. Adverse social and political fallout from protracted violent conflict jeopardised that strategy.

Protracted conflict also subverted the possibility of South Asian regional economic co-operation that could benefit Sri Lanka. The dispute between Sri Lanka and India made it more difficult for South Asian Association for Regional Co-operation (SAARC) members to develop a common economic program. Even apart from SAARC there were sound economic reasons for Sri Lanka to strengthen economic ties with India. But strained relations resulting from India's support for Tamil militants made Sri Lankans wary of too much future economic dependence on India, whatever the financial benefits might be.

As noted above, we also used a scenario approach to take tertiary costs into account. Our 'no tertiary costs' scenario used the moderate growth scenario as a base, adding assumptions about full implementation of the open economy program and high levels of regional economic co-operation during the 1980s. Since tertiary costs address longer-term impacts of conflict, we assumed no difference between the moderate growth and 'no tertiary costs' scenarios in 1983 and 1984. We assumed the growth rate would have been 0.5 per cent greater in 1985 and 1.0 per cent greater in 1986-88 than projected by the moderate growth scenario. Comparing the two scenarios and summing the annual differences produced a rupees 16.3 billion (about $U.S.500 million) estimate of tertiary costs.

Implications

Summing estimates for primary, secondary and tertiary costs provided an estimate of the total economic costs of violent conflict in Sri Lanka during the period from 1983 through 1988. The total was rupees 145.3 billion (about $U.S. 4.4 billion). As already noted, our estimate of 'total' costs was conservative, because some costs (for example private and unbudgeted costs of security) were not taken into account. Nonetheless, these costs were roughly equivalent to three Accelerated Mahaweli Development Projects, but produced few benefits.

Choices to implement violence-prone strategies made by government and anti-government leaders were at least proximate causes of the conflicts that generated these costs. If leaders 'had no choice' then assessing the costs of violent conflict remains an interesting academic exercise but has little practical relevance. This book's message, however, is that options other than those than leading to protracted violent conflict are often available and were available to policy makers in Sri Lanka.

There will be much more to say about this in chapter 21, which specifically answers the question posed in chapter 1 – 'how could we have come to this?' My smoking-good health metaphor, already introduced, highlights what is most essential. The problem facing policy makers in conflict prone circumstances resembles the relationship between smoking and good health. We know that heavy smokers place their health at risk though we cannot make precise predictions about the onset of lung cancer or the exact minute of death. Similarly we can point to policies that contribute to a climate in which protracted violent conflict is more probable but may not be able to predict the timing, intensity or duration of violent outbreaks.

Even so, policy makers must be convinced they have more attractive options than violence-prone strategies. Estimated costs of such strategies in one specific case have been described. To consider what alternative strategies might have been available, Samarasinghe and I considered illustrative opportunity costs of protracted violent conflict. We asked: To what alternative uses that might have helped prevent protracted violent conflict could the sum of 145 billion rupees have been put?[24]

Opportunity costs

145 billion rupees was a huge cost to be imposed on a small developing nation's fragile economy. It amounted to 70 per cent of Sri Lanka's 1988 GDP. It was three times as large as Sri Lanka's 1988 current government expenditures. It was, as noted earlier, roughly equivalent to the cost of three accelerated Mahaweli development projects.

Because we wanted to view opportunity costs from the vantage point of those actually recruited to militant movements it was necessary for us to distinguish between costs primarily attributable to the conflict in the northeast and those primarily attributable to the conflict in the southwest. This was relatively easy to do for physical destruction of infrastructure[25], but more difficult for other primary costs and for secondary and tertiary costs. To estimate these latter costs, we made assumptions about the relative economic impacts of the two insurrections. In 1983 and 1984, we assumed that the anti-Tamil riots had the greatest impact. Beginning at the end of 1984 and through the middle of 1987, we assumed that the preponderant impact was from the ethnic violence in the north and east. After mid-1987, we assumed that the contribution to secondary and tertiary costs was more evenly divided, with the southern conflict having a somewhat greater impact in 1988.[26] The costs of the IPKF were solely attributed to the northeastern conflict. Based on these assumptions, we attributed costs of about 96 billion rupees to the northeastern conflict and about 47 billion rupees to the southwestern conflict.

An average annual cost of violent conflict was calculated as one-sixth of the total cost. This was not intended to be an accurate estimate of yearly costs, which were certainly greater in later than earlier years. Average cost estimates were made to have a number that could be more meaningfully compared with annual budget estimates when discussing opportunity costs.

Young men between the ages 15 and 24 have been the principal actors in Sri Lanka's political conflicts (as they are, indeed, in most violent political conflicts.) For that reason, we focused on the costs of violence in relation to this segment of society more closely. In 1988, Sri Lanka's population included 1.75 million men in this age cohort of whom 220,000 were Sri Lanka Tamils (the source of most LTTE recruits) and 1.3 million were Sinhalese (the recruitment pool for the JVP).

We know that poor prospects for employment, underemployment and unemployment are prime factors creating a sense of deprivation. If an individual feels discriminated against because of race, language or religion, deprivation is more likely to produce frustration and anger. When a young man feels he has no future in the existing social economic order, the simplistic appeals of militant groups calling for ethnic solidarity, offering a romantic, adventurous life and promising a transformed social order become more attractive. He may become a recruit or at least a passive supporter. Sri Lanka's *Poverty Alleviation Through People-Based Development* (1988) described the psychological effects of unemployment vividly:

> Unemployment is the main cause for poverty. Unemployment causes psychological damage to the individual. He gets demoralised, frustrated and disillusioned when his efforts of finding a job are not realised. The family considers him a burden to the point of losing expectations about further support. He feels he is not wanted and insecure. This makes him a rebel within the family and a rebel against the society that provides him with no hope for the future. The position gets aggravated when the limited jobs available are not given on merit.

Unemployment statistics are only rough guesses in any Global South country: Sri Lanka is no exception. Official figures placed the unemployment rate at about 12 per cent in 1982 and at 18 per cent in 1988. Estimates for the 15-25 cohort were as high as 25 per cent in 1982 and 30 per cent in 1982. Using these pessimistic estimates, we have calculated the total number of unemployed young men as 407,000 1982 and 525,000 in 1988.[27]

Suppose, as an alternative to policies involving coercion or violence, the government had initiated an education, employment and/or training program, directed at improving the prospects of those youths potentially most at risk to become militant group members or supporters. Assume the funds available would have been the funds that we estimate were costs incurred due to violent conflict. The total funds available per year for this program would have been about 46,000 rupees ($U.S. 1,400), about four times Sri Lanka's annual GDP per-capita *for each unemployed young man*. The total funds available over the six-year period for *each unemployed young man* would have been about rupees 276,000 ($U.S. 8,400).[28]

Consider one final indicator of opportunity costs, which we shall call the *economic* impact per-militant. Estimates of the size of militant groups are even more hazardous than employment statistics. This is especially true in the case of the JVP. Nonetheless, the upper bounds of these estimates are typically about 20,000. Since larger estimates of group size produce more conservative cost-per-militant estimates, we have chosen 20,000 as the number to use as an estimate for the size of actively fighting Tamil militant groups and the JVP.[29] Given this assumption, the total and annual economic impact per-militant can be easily calculated. According to this scheme, *each Tamil militant* imposed economic costs on Sri Lankan society of about rupees 750,000 ($U.S. 23,000) per year during the 1983-1988 period, for an overall total of RS 4,500,000 ($U.S. 136,000). Each Sinhalese militant imposed costs of RS 405,000 per year ($U.S. 12,000 per year) for an overall total of $74,000 during the same period.

If one accepts these estimates in as reasonable orders of magnitude, they show the potential power of a relatively small number of militants to impose costs on a developing country. Moreover, the LTTE, at least, still exists as a powerful force in 2004, having imposed massive additional costs on Sri Lankan society in the intervening period.[30]

Measurement of the economic impact per-militant does not necessarily point to a program for militants analogous to the proposed program for the unemployed, but the magnitude of costs that militants can impose certainly raises the possibility of some co-optation options as an alternative to the costly and relatively ineffective coercive strategies that were chosen.

For example, what would have been the outcome if, following his landslide election victory in 1982, President Jayewardene had proposed a commission with militant leaders Prabakharan and Wijeweera as key members to examine problems of ethnic identity and youth unrest in Sri Lanka. Suppose the commission had been given discretionary funding that realistically took into account the costs that militant youth are able to impose upon a society. Alternatively, suppose JVP and LTTE members had been offered government or private sector funded four year scholarships at the foreign university of their choice or substantial grants to start businesses of their own.   Proposals   for massive youth training programs or co-optation of militant groups may seem fanciful or prohibitively costly. A realistic cost-benefit analysis of the policies that were actually implemented might make them seem more attractive.

Benefits of violent conflict?

When Samarasinghe and I first estimated the costs of violent conflict in Sri Lanka, we noted that Sri Lanka's civil wars – and other civil wars too – were not necessarily a negative sum game for all concerned. One possible explanation for the irresolvability of many civil wars, we suggested, was the psychic and economic benefits that protracted conflict provided to at least some protagonists. Members of militant groups, for example, might derive the same psychic satisfaction from a terrorist action as from a successful athletic competition, further enhanced by the aura of 'fighting for a just cause.' Militant leaders often benefited from revenues generated to sustain an ongoing conflict, for example from drug dealing, 'tax' levies and donations (some extorted) from diaspora communities.

The availability of foreign assistance might encourage governments to pursue coercive strategies because foreign donors seemed more responsive to requests for military assistance than development assistance. A government could use an ongoing conflict in a geographically remote region to coerce mainstream political opponents to become more accommodating. Security threats could also divert attention from intractable economic and social problems, providing a welcome diversion for a hard-pressed political leader. Powerful factions in the military might have vested interests in perpetuating the large budgets that an ongoing conflict required.[31]

A typical small-scale example was the Jaffna bus *mudalalis*[32] scheme. A Tamil friend, the former Jaffna University Vice Chancellor, explained this while we were waiting, late one night, for my wife to come home from Jaffna, by bus, for a brief period of leave. I remarked that the journey, which could take twelve hours or more, would be much less arduous when the trains ran once again. My friend said the bus *mudalalis* would be among those who would oppose this. These entrepreneurs arranged transport for Tamils to and from Jaffna in overcrowded busses for high fares. To obtain necessary permits they paid fees to government officials in Colombo. To ensure unimpeded passage, fees were also paid to police officials along the route who could make things difficult. (There was no mention of fees paid to Indian Army soldiers who manned roadblocks and inspected passengers at checkpoints in their area of jurisdiction.) LTTE tax collectors also received fees to ensure safe passage (along with the continued good health of bus *mudalalis* and drivers). Many benefited from the fares, which could be as much as 10 times higher than rail or bus passage in normal times.

Samarasinghe and I first presented our analysis before the proliferation of post-Cold War research on protracted civil war.[33] There were few other case studies from which we could seek supporting evidence and comparative insights, especially about the benefits of conflict. Now, this has changed.[34] Scholars have begun to recognise that some protagonists benefit from protracted civil wars and have an economic interest in perpetuating them.[35]

To situate our own observations in a broader context, I asked my doctoral student, Naren Kumarakulasingam, who had worked as a research assistant at the U.S. Institute of Peace, to prepare a short working paper[36] reviewing discussions in recently published literature of benefits deriving from protracted conflict.[37] Six major themes emerged from his survey:

Theme 1. Relatively low-level participants, including footsoldiers can benefit.

Followers as well as leaders are able to enrich themselves in the context that accompanies a protracted conflict. One of the most common ways of doing this has been through looting. Prospects for garnering loot have been even used as a recruitment incentive, especially in economically depressed areas. Stephen Ellis, in his research into the causes of Liberia's collapse into civil war, concluded that many youths who joined Charles Taylor's National Patriotic Front of Liberia did so in order to 'acquire properties and riches.'[38]

Theme 2. Conflicts can generate new profit networks within an economy.

In the case of Somalia, Daniel Compagnon showed that goods looted by armed groups were sold to businessmen, who then re-sold them either within or outside Somalia.[39] In some cases, this led businessmen to financially support armed Somali factions. Compagnon even noted a few extreme cases where spoils of war proved to be so attractive that businessmen became faction leaders in order to advance their interests.[40] Steven Ellis reported similar practices in Liberia.[41] The high incidence of routinised looting in many conflicts, along with targeted killings of businessmen and traders, suggest that once established, these profit networks themselves *generate* violence in order to guarantee a continued flow of profits.

Theme 3. Control over natural resources can be an important benefit of protracted conflict.

Populist rhetoric is often used to justify violence on both sides of a conflict, but control over lucrative natural resource stocks may provide the real motivation. In Sierra Leone, the war was prolonged because the government sought to enrich itself through illicit diamond mining and logging. On the other side, the Revolutionary United Front (RUF) fought to retain its control over diamond mining revenues. In Liberia, the desire to gain control over stocks of diamonds, gold, and iron ore precipitated fighting between different factions. That control of resource stocks can motivate and perpetuate conflict is not surprising, given the huge sums at stake. The UNITA faction in Angola is believed to have earned around $U.S. 500 million a year from the sale of diamonds. Similarly, the FARC earns an estimated $U.S. 450 million annually from the drug trade under its control in Colombia. Some might not characterise cocaine production as a 'natural resource' but the principle is the same. With a $450 million revenue stream at stake, FARC leaders may be less motivated to make peace.

Neighbouring countries to a conflict may also be beneficiaries. Musifiky Mwanasali notes that war in the Democratic Republic of Congo (DRC) enabled its neighbours to 'export' resources for which they had become conduits.[42] Precious minerals, timber, coffee, and elephant tusks that were looted in the DRC and subsequently 'exported' through the black market became major sources of foreign exchange.

Theme 4. Even non-combatants can benefit from protracted violent conflict.

Charles King noted that non-combatant populations in rebel-controlled areas may sometimes benefit from living there. Some militant groups do a better job of maintaining law and order and providing social services than the government. This may be especially true in remote areas populated by ethnic minorities that have been objects of government mandated discrimination.[43] He cited the establishment of a mini-state by the LTTE in the Jaffna Peninsula from 1990-1995 as one example, though many observers, including some Tamils might disagree.[44] Another example he provides is of FARC's ability to provide low-interest loans to peasants and farmers living in areas of Colombia that it controls.[45] This pattern is by no means universal, however. Ibrahim Abdullah and Patrick Muana report that while the RUF of Sierra Leone 'governed' civil enclaves, it provided no benefits to residents, while taxing and expropriating free labour from them.[46]

Theme 5. Humanitarian aid unwittingly fuels conflict and benefits combatants.

Mary Anderson's path breaking work, *Do No Harm* showed how humanitarian assistance often helped prolong conflict by transferring resources to war economies.[47] Simple theft was one of ways this occurred. She estimated that during the height of famine in Somalia in 1992, over 50 per cent of all food brought into Mogadishu port was either looted or hijacked.[48] Anderson also showed how combatants were able to sustain themselves with humanitarian aid by mixing with refugee populations. Rwandan Hutu refugee camps in Eastern Zaire provided a particularly telling case. Humanitarian assistance there helped sustain former soldiers of the Rwandan Army who had been involved in the 1994 genocide.[49]

Another contribution to the war economy was payment of 'taxes' to local militias, warlords, and factions for permission to do humanitarian work in areas under their control.[50] Humanitarian agencies sometimes even hired militia members for protection. In addition to protection, agencies needed housing and services, for which they were willing to pay prices far in excess of local rates. Local hires earned inflated salaries (though they were tiny in comparison with expatriate salaries). Thus, the presence of humanitarian agencies created a class of beneficiaries whose well-being was tied to the war economy. As these beneficiaries knew well, the war economy would continue to function only so long as violent conflict continued.

Theme 6. Opposing leaders sometimes collude so they can both continue to benefit from the spoils of conflict.

Not surprisingly, then, there were instances of the collusion between warring party leaders to perpetuate conflicts simply so they could continue to benefit. For example, senior figures in the Angolan government's security forces sold weapons to UNITA.[51] Similarly, between 1993 and 1997, Khmer Rouge commanders, Thai military officers, and Cambodian government officials colluded in gem trading and illegal logging even though they were at war.[52]

In his research on the establishment of unrecognised, breakaway states in the former Soviet Union, Charles King noted the existence of mutually beneficial links between corrupt central governments and corrupt leaders in separatist regions.[53] Both Georgian and South Ossetian authorities 'taxed' and 'fined' goods that were traded between the two states despite the fact that Georgia still had not recognised Abkhazia's secession. Georgian police officials on the border with Abkhazia were reported to hold a monopoly on this trans-border trade.[54] The persistence of a high degree of collaboration between government troops and RUF forces in Sierra Leone has led Sierra Leonians to refer to the conflict as 'sell-game'–their term for a fixed football (soccer) game.[55]

Who wins and who loses?

A market system works best when participants are fully informed about cost/benefit ratios and must bear the costs as well as reap the benefits that result from their choices. The system labelled by Mary Anderson as 'the war economy' falls far short of this ideal. This helps explain why conflicts seem to drag on interminably, despite their costliness. While costs are disproportionately greater than benefits, costs and benefits are not borne equally. Benefits accrue to a small segment of the warring society, often those who were responsible for choosing violence-prone options and who are, as we have seen, responsible for perpetuating their use. But these segments – political, militant and sometimes business leaders – bear only a small fraction of the costs. Most costs are borne by relatively helpless men, women and children in the community at large who had little or no role in choosing between violence-prone and non-violent options.

Once militant groups become institutionalised, violent conflict escalates and a war economy is in place, conflict resolution may be impossible in the short term. Thus cost-benefit analysis of violence-prone strategies provides yet another strong argument for conflict avoidance. Moreover, a realistic assessment of opportunity costs makes it clear that cost effective, non-violence-prone options are often available, if not always politically attractive. For example, resources might be invested in a remote or ethnically distinct region to promote harmony even though such spending might not be defensible on narrow cost-benefit criteria. Or, a given group or segment of society might be given special opportunities simply because of its members' potential to create disruption.

The political, institutional – even moral – issues that such proposals raise should not be minimised, but seeking alternatives to the status quo is essential. Government and opposition leaders in developing nations, along with interested third parties, must assess more realistically the costs of violence-prone policies. They must implement development strategies that are less violent, costly and tragic. Two concluding chapters develop these themes more fully.

21

How it Came to This –
Learning from Sri Lanka's Civil Wars

When development policies fail, the seeds of militancy are down. Escalating deadly conflict and terrorism provide evidence that these seeds have been fertilised and are beginning to flourish.

Chapter 1 posed four questions that bewildered residents of conflict-wracked nations often ask themselves:

* *How could we have come to this?*
* *What could we have done to prevent the conflict that has killed our family members and friends, devastated our lives, destroyed what was being so painstakingly developed?*
* *What can we learn and share from our experiences that may help others to avoid the path that we have trod?*
* *How can we share lessons from our experience most powerfully and effectively?*

This chapter and the one that follows provide answers.

The syndrome: why violent conflict and terrorism metastasised in Sri Lanka

Sri Lanka began life as an independent nation peacefully, with democratic institutions in place, with only infrequent outbreaks of violent conflict in its history and with good economic prospects. It ended the millennium with more than 60,000 dead, a divided society, a devastated economy and one of the world's most effective militant movements contesting the government's sovereignty over a third of the island. Protracted deadly conflict became the norm, beginning in 1984. A succession of 'fever charts' picture the pattern and magnitude of this transformation. How can this best be explained? As we have seen, the Development – Deadly-Conflict System Model, described at length in chapter 5, points to five symptoms that characterise escalating conflict and terrorism.

To recapitulate, the symptoms are:

1. Deteriorating economic performance
2. An increasing number of development failures
3. Rising levels of relative deprivation manifested in heightened ethnic identities and groups mobilised around these identities
4. Declining effectiveness in the application of state-sanctioned violence
5. Growing strength of militant movements

Chapter 2 showed how a spectrum of theories attributed importance to these symptoms as proximate causes of violent conflict escalation. Chapter 5 showed how symptoms and violent conflict were linked through two reinforcing feedback loops, *conflict escalation from development failures* and *conflict escalation from state-sanctioned violence ineffectiveness*. How did these symptoms manifest themselves in Sri Lanka?

With the exception of development failures, narratives and graphs presented in chapters 6 through 19 describe the manifestations quite clearly. *Economic performance* exhibited relatively steady growth, with only minor downturns for 22 years following independence. After 1970, boom and bust cycles, inflation, periods of stagnation, and a weakening of the government's financial position became increasingly evident. These changes were coincident with, though not necessarily direct causes of, heightened violent conflict levels. Escalating violent conflict following the 1983 riots had an increasingly severe economic impact during the remaining years of J.R. Jayewardene's term, an impact that continued. By the end of 1988, economic activity was at a virtual standstill. Political leaders who had once hoped to transform Sri Lanka into an 'Asian Tiger' were preoccupied with maintaining some semblance of government authority and clinging to power.

Deprivation levels are hard to measure directly, but there is ample evidence that ambitious development programs were highly touted and then failed to deliver on their promises. As programs faltered, groups whose solidarity depended on the ethnic identities of members became more numerous and influential. Mainstream groups became more ethnically militant. This included not only the Sri Lanka Freedom Party, responsible for introducing ethnic politics into the political mainstream, but also the United National and Marxist parties, which had initially advocated multicultural, secularist political agendas.

J.R. Jayewardene, ostensibly a liberal democrat, was responsible for founding the pro-Sinhalese National Workers' Organisation (JSS) and for appointing an outspoken Sinhalese nationalist, Cyril Mathew, to head it. The Federal Party became the Tamil United Liberation Front and an advocate of 'self determination' for the 'Tamil nation.' By 1988, armed militant groups dominated Tamil politics, with Prabakharan's Liberation Tigers in control of the agenda.

To document the declining effectiveness of state-sanctioned violence, one needs only examine fever charts that simultaneously display the 'disease' – levels of violent conflict intensity – and the 'cure' – levels of state-sanctioned violence. Occasionally, security force intervention and repressive measures brought violent conflict under control, but increased applications of state-sanctioned violence were more commonly coincident with conflict escalation. Often Sri Lanka's armed forces served as unwitting recruitment agents for the LTTE, the JVP and other militant groups by applying repressive tactics indiscriminately and responding to attacks with undisciplined broad-brush retaliations against mostly innocent civilians. In 1988 both violent conflict and state-sanctioned violence had reached their highest levels in the island's history.

The growing strength of militant movements is documented by data that shows the frequency of political conflict incidents, in different categories. Once again, the pattern is clear. Prior to 1970, incidents linked to militant movements played an inconsequential role in Sri Lanka's political scene (although militant labour unions were active). Beginning in 1970, they assumed increasing importance, first due to the JVP insurrection and then to the growing visibility of Tamil militants in the north and east. After 1983, conflict between militants and Sri Lanka's government became more and more all-encompassing. In the space of a decade, the number of violent conflict incidents increased at least twenty-fold and the overwhelming majority were militant.[1]

Development failures

The most important symptom and the most difficult to precisely measure, development failures, has been left until last. Why do I characterise this symptom as 'most important?' It is because orchestrating successful development trajectories and taking quick corrective action when a trajectory shows signs of failure are the most cost effective ways for countries to escape the syndrome of protracted deadly conflict and terrorism.

Chapters 1 and 3 gave reasons why this is so. Most developing country residents, indeed, most residents of all countries, share common aspirations.

They want to feel good about their lives, the circumstances in which they live and future prospects for themselves and their children. They seek a humane and peaceable society, characterised by material sufficiency, personal security and psychic fulfilment. They seek leaders and political institutions that will respond satisfactorily to their concerns and grievances. Development policies seek to fulfil these aspirations with strategies and programs that will improve residents' circumstances and sense of well-being.

All too often, development policies fail. They fail because politically in-flated rhetoric raises hopes and aspirations that cannot realistically be fulfilled. They fail because programs and strategies are grounded in political economic theories based more on ideology than fact. They fail because programs and strategies emphasise performance criteria that bear scant relationship to what people want and need. They fail because programs and strategies raise and than dash expectations by delivering short-term benefits that cannot be sustained. Development policies fail because political leaders fail to heed unmistakable feedback that things are going wrong and cling to power, using state-sanctioned violence, long after it is time to go. When development policies fail, the seeds of militancy are down. Escalating deadly conflict and terrorism provide evi-dence that these seeds have been fertilised and are beginning to flourish.

Development policy failures experienced in Sri Lanka illustrate this. They contributed to escalating deadly conflict between 1948 and 1988. They precipi-tated the symptoms described above. Listing and recapitulating these devel-opment failures provides a useful answer to the question 'how could we have come to this?'. How these failures might have been avoided is discussed in a concluding chapter.

The following are 10 development policy failures, which if avoided or cor-rected, could have prevented escalating deadly conflict and terrorism in Sri Lanka.

1. Unsustainable entitlement programs
2. Polarising political rhetoric and tactics
3. 'Winner take all' official language policies
4. Failure to devolve power – the 'outstation' mentality in implementing Sri Lanka's development strategies and programs
5. Half hearted reforms of secondary and higher education, coupled with discriminatory university admissions policies targeting Tamil youth
6. Perpetuation of government-controlled economic management schemes long after their economic inefficacy had been demonstrated

7. The over-ambitious and over-politicised economic reform policies of J.R. Jayewardene
8. Inadequate funding, Sinhalisation and politicisation of the security forces
9. Use of repressive measures to secure the United National Party's parliamentary majority for an additional term in 1982
10. The attempt to restore order in the north and east (especially in volatile Jaffna province) with military forces that were clearly incapable of achieving that goal.

Narratives describing each failed policy have been given in earlier chapters. A brief recapitulation here emphasises important points.

Unsustainable entitlement programs

During Sri Lanka's first 22 years of independence, successive governments provided residents with a mix of entitlement programs that included subsidised food and transportation, free medical care, free education and a variety of agricultural subsidies and insurance programs. Residents came to take entitlements for granted and political leaders vied with one another to promise more. Meanwhile, Sri Lanka's economy failed to diversify and its position *vis à vis* the international economy became increasingly vulnerable to external shocks. Leaders who called attention to this vulnerability and proposed remedial measures, most notably J.R. Jayewardene, were attacked by political opponents and then punished by voters. After 1970, when the international economic environment became more competitive and more volatile, neither United Front nor United National Party governments could avoid cutbacks. When out of power each party blamed the other.

The unsustainability of entitlement programs need not have become a political issue, since both parties faced the same problems, caused by structural weaknesses in Sri Lanka's economy. Paradoxically, the party in power was more disadvantaged by this problem. The absence of a democratic discourse emphasising sustainability as a national goal magnified the sense of deprivation that cutbacks in entitlements created.

Polarising political rhetoric and tactics

Primordial violence, rooted in nationalist and ethnic identities, is latent in most societies. Whether or not it becomes manifest will be determined, in large degree, by the legitimacy of ethno-nationalist political rhetoric in mainstream political discourse. The example of World War II Nazi Germany taught

Europeans this lesson, and 'hate speech' is now widely condemned, despite resurgent right-wing nationalist movements in several countries. Some Asian nations, most notably Singapore, have recognised the potentially corrosive influence of ethno-nationalist political rhetoric and legislated against it.[2]

Post-1956 Sri Lanka provides an object lesson in the corrosiveness of such rhetoric and tactics that often accompany it. S.W.R.D. Bandaranaike's calls for 'Sinhala only' were intended to mobilise political support, but were also intended to serve an important development goal. In 1956, members of Sri Lanka's Sinhala-speaking majority community were second-class citizens in their own country. Public education was inferior or unavailable. Opportunities for public employment were limited. Thus Bandaranaike's appeals struck a responsive chord among individuals who previously felt they had little voice. Sinhalese-nationalist rhetoric became a staple of both mainstream parties, especially when they were out of power. Voices of extremist fringes, too, gained additional legitimacy.

Polarising rhetoric and tactics are corrosive because they invariably provoke counter-polarisation, leading to an escalating divisive cycle on both sides of an ethnic divide. When Bandaranaike began his political movement, he apparently gave little thought to the impact that his new discourse would have on Tamils and on the civility of Sri Lanka's political culture. But outcomes of the cycle his rhetoric and tactics initiated were the July 1983 riots, the Liberation Tigers' emergence as a dominant political force, and protracted civil war.

'Winner take all' official language policies

After years of civil war, Sri Lanka finally adopted policies that made Tamil an official language and established English as an official 'link' language. Had Sirimavo Bandaranaike's newly elected government adopted such policies in 1960, it might have helped prevent those years of civil war. Once elected, S.W.R.D. Bandaranaike's language policies had been more accomodationist than his 'Sinhala only' campaign rhetoric implied. The Tamil Language (Special Provisions) Act, which he steered through Parliament in 1958, mandated the government to implement regulations providing for the 'reasonable use of Tamil.' In July 1960 general election campaigning, Sirimavo Bandaranaike pledged to implement official language policies in a manner that would respond sensitively to Tamil concerns.

Once elected, she reneged on these promises, implementing provisions requiring that Sinhala become the language of administration throughout the island (including Tamil regions) on January 1, 1961. Like many Colombo-orig-inated directives, this one was not fully implemented; however, many Tamil civil servants, including some with years of government service, were displaced from their jobs. Moreover, Mrs. Bandaranaike chose not to issue regulations providing for the reasonable use of Tamil at all, notwithstanding the law that required her to do so. They were issued only after Dudley Senanayake assumed office in 1965.

Even more pernicious, over the long run, were policies that required Sin-halese and Tamil students to be educated in their own medium (language). Es-sentially, Sinhalese students were discouraged from studying in Tamil or Eng-lish, even if they wished to do so. Tamil students, too, were discouraged from studying in languages other than their own. Thus, increasingly, students who attended the same schools in multiethnic areas became less and less familiar with the culture of their schoolmates and less and less able to communicate with them easily.

Another consequence of Mrs. Bandaranaike's policies was the dismantling of excellent English language courses of instruction that existed in some urban areas, although not in rural areas. Increasingly, Sri Lankans who could afford it chose to educate their children in English-medium international schools or to hire private tutors. Thus English remained a 'sword' that divided the island along class lines. After 1977, when leaders attempted to link Sri Lanka more closely with the international economy, their revitalisation plans were impeded by a generation of indigenous language educated men and women who lacked necessary language skills to participate effectively. This, too, contributed to feelings of relative deprivation.

Centralisation of power in Colombo – the 'outstation' mentality in implementing Sri Lanka's development strategies and programs

We have seen how a succession of attempts to devolve power either failed or were only implemented half-heartedly. Even under the United Front lead-ers, with their commitment to central planning, there were proposals that rec-ognised the importance of granting local authorities some role in development programs. Narratives in several chapters emphasised that resistance to devolv-ing power stemmed as much from the Colombo-centric attitudes of politicians and bureaucrats as from ideological commitments to a unitary state. Where devolution proposals were intended to cede autonomy to Tamil majority re-gions, these two points of view reinforced one another.

Denigration of 'outstation' regions is a common legacy of colonial regimes, which centralised authority in the capital city and structured a dependent economy to supply commodities and raw materials to the 'mother country.' Rural, peripheral areas were invariably short-changed when it came to economic development, educational opportunities, and government services. These patterns were perpetuated after independence. Sri Lanka implemented a number of rural development programs, but most bogged down in politics and bureaucracy.[3] The accelerated Mahaweli Development Project specifically targeted rural areas but the opportunities it provided so blatantly favoured UNP supporters that it probably created as much discontent in rural areas as it remedied. Newly educated youth, seeking to enter the workforce in rural areas, invariably experienced the greatest frustrations. Bad economic times had a particularly severe impact on these young men and women, creating a climate where, in the south, the JVP became strong. In the northeast, discriminatory policies based on ethnicity added to volatile attitudes created by adverse economic circumstances and obviously second-class government services.

Half hearted reforms of secondary and higher education, coupled with discriminatory university admissions policies, targeting Tamil youth.

Since young men and women (especially young men) are the primary participants in militant movements, the success or failure of education programs in providing economic opportunities play key roles in determining whether or not militant movements grow strong. In Sri Lanka, the mismatch between economic needs and the education secondary schools and universities provided was an ongoing problem and remains a problem to this day.

Sri Lankans value education. Even in remote areas, travellers will see crowds of boys and girls and also young men and women, typically clad in white uniforms, walking to school each day. Between 1956 and 1966, S.W.R.D. and Sirimavo Bandaranaike's populist governments implemented policies that swelled primary, secondary and university enrolments ten-fold. Most of these new students were educated in Sinhala and in non-technical 'arts' subjects, which were the only curricula that rapidly expanding schools and universities could offer to their new clientele. New graduates, even those with coveted university degrees, learned that their studies did not guarantee employment in a competitive labour market where most good jobs required technical or professional training. This was disillusioning.

Successive governments recognised the problem and implemented some reforms, but failed to give the matter sufficient priority. Dudley Senanayake's government created technical training institutes and 'practical farms.' United Front leaders mandated radical secondary education reforms, and experimented with 'job-oriented curricula' at the university level. J.R. Jayewardene's government reversed these reforms, which had been gutted by budget cuts in any case. UNP leaders invested massively in university facilities, but short-changed primary and secondary education. Despite the bottlenecks created by an inadequately trained labour force and a restive youthful population that was disproportionately unemployed, no government made education a top budgetary or political priority. This made it easier for entrenched conservatives in the educational establishment to resist needed changes. Thus Sri Lanka's education policies became a textbook example of how to alienate the most volatile segment of the island's population.

The United Front government's tinkering with university admissions procedures may have been the most alienating of all. Readers will recall from chapter 11 that 'media-wise standardisation' adjusted the scores of Sinhalese applicants to make them more competitive with Tamils. 'District quotas' gave applicants from 'disadvantaged' (Kandyan Sinhalese and Muslim) districts preferential treatment. Since Tamils were disproportionately represented in universities, and especially in technical and professional fields, the reforms could be seen as allocating a scarce resource more fairly.[4] At the time United Front leaders were more concerned with placating potential JVP recruits than potential Tamil militants. But the policy came to symbolise racist government polices among a segment of the Tamil community that could provide militant groups not only with willing recruits but also effective leaders.

Perpetuation of government controlled economic management schemes long after their economic inefficacy had been demonstrated

As stated in chapter 12, I do not fault Sirimavo Bandaranaike's United Front for nationalising many basic industries and for creating regulatory incentives that favoured import substitution industrialisation. In 1970, the ideologically driven policies of Marxist coalition members were still accepted by many experts as a potentially viable economic development strategy for poor nations. A key goal of such policies – weighting social goals more equally with profitability – remains desirable, if difficult to attain.

United Front leaders' error was to cling tenaciously to their experiment long after it became obvious it was not working. It did not take long for the shortcomings of state managed industries to become apparent – use of political and ethnic criteria to hire senior managers, inappropriate use of capital-intensive technologies, regulatory regimes that mandated inefficient uses of scarce foreign exchange, and politically-mandated pricing policies that guaranteed unprofitability. Even policy makers who were blind to the causes of poor economic performance could not miss the evidence – stagnating economic output, low capacity utilisation, rising unemployment, government revenue shortfalls and scarcities of basic goods.

The failed policies had destabilising social consequences. Faced with budget shortfalls, leaders were forced to make cuts in social programs that had been the centrepiece of the United Front's campaign manifesto. The adverse impacts of cutbacks in education have already been described. Economies imposed on the security forces weakened morale and efficiency. Additional tasks, such as the control of 'domestic smuggling' stretched police and army resources to the breaking point. Program cutbacks made by a government with such strong Sinhalese leanings in an environment of scarcity were viewed as discriminatory by Tamils even when this may not have been the case.

It is by no means certain that Sirimavo Bandaranaike had the vision and power to orchestrate fundamental economic policy changes in mid-term. The unimaginative 1977 SLFP campaign manifesto suggests this was not the case. But overlong adherence to *dirigiste* policies widened ethnic divisions in Sri Lankan society and made the implementation of economic reform programs, when it did occur, more difficult.

The over ambitious and over politicised economic reform policies of J.R. Jayewardene

Simultaneously faulting Sirimavo Bandaranaike's government for Marxist policies and J.R. Jayewardene's government for open economy reforms may seem inconsistent, but these contrasting polices were development failures•for different reasons. The United Front's program was flawed in conception. The UNP's open economy programs were flawed in implementation. I label these programs too ambitious because J.R. Jayewardene's promise of rapid growth, combined with social justice, could not be fulfilled. Unfulfilled promises and unmet expectations are prime sources of relative deprivation. The programs were too political because UNP supporters were so blatantly targeted for preferential treatment. This was particularly disheartening for opposition party supporters, as it became apparent that President Jayewardene's goal was to entrench the UNP in power for an extended period of *de facto* one party government.

Problems encountered by the Mahaweli Development Project, described in chapter 16, were typical of those encountered elsewhere. Managerial talent was stretched to the limit. Large numbers of expatriate workers were recruited, inflating costs and intensifying social tensions. Massive inflows of foreign aid, mostly loans, fuelled inflation and created opportunities for corruption. Pressures to produce quick results overwhelmed procedures that were set up to account for expenditures and maintain cost effectiveness. Priority was given to creating physical infrastructure. Little attention was given to compensating for the social dislocations that massive construction projects and settlement programs created.

As we have seen, inflation and the social consequences of inflation became a pervasive problem, especially when the economic downturn, beginning in 1981, started taking its toll. The gap between rich Sri Lankans and others widened. 'Middle class pauperisation' became a commonly discussed problem. Privations imposed on the poor were particularly severe because open economy reforms had gutted the subsidy programs and entitlements that once sustained them. Feelings of deprivation were heightened by the sudden downturn following three years of good times, by feelings that traditional values were being eroded and by ostentatious displays of luxuries that most could not afford. The widespread belief that many politicians were corrupt made things worse. This mix of disappointments and discontents, especially among urban dwelling youth, created a receptive audience for polarising rhetoric and a climate in which violent outbreaks were not only possible, but probable.

Inadequate funding, Sinhalisation and politicisation of the security forces

Why include the security forces in a discussion of *development* failures? First, personal physical security of individual country residents is an intrinsically important element of successful development. Second, countries must be relatively peaceful and stable for social and economic development agendas to succeed. Security forces are supposed to be guarantors of physical security, political stability and peace,

A country's police, army, air force and navy are political leaders' instruments of state-sanctioned violence, which may be used to maintain public order, and for other purposes as well. Development practitioners rarely pay heed to the security forces, except to criticise, but this must change. When, as in Sri Lanka, security forces catalyse conflict escalation rather than intervening to restore order, development agendas suffer. Security force ineffectiveness thus clearly qualifies as a *development* failure.

Whether or not forces are effective depends both on their intrinsic capabilities and the missions they are assigned. Dudley Senanayake's modest forces, for example, maintained public order quite successfully during his 'middle path' regime. Two decades later, inaction and collusion by a larger, better-equipped force helped precipitate the devastating July 1983 riots. Sinhalisation, politicisation and under-funding became more serious problems because of increasingly heavy burdens that police and military personnel were asked to bear.

Inadequate funding had the most pervasive impact, especially on police officers in lower ranks. Why a succession of Sri Lankan leaders chose to pay these first-line security officers no more than a bare living wage and to skimp on basic logistical support would make an interesting topic for further investigation. Low pay eroded morale, and spawned corruption, though many officers continued to function with professionalism and integrity under difficult circumstances. Low morale and corruption poisoned police-community relations, which most experts view as a crucial ingredient of good policing. In times of crisis, police officers were less likely to put their lives on the line and ordinary residents were more likely to view them as oppressors than protectors. As demands on the police increased, deficiencies traceable to inadequate funding became more apparent.

Interjecting political considerations into police work, which became pervasive after 1970, further complicated police officers' lives and sapped their morale. Political considerations became key determinants of promotions and choice assignments. Those who offended powerful politicians would be banished to 'outstations' or to Jaffna as punishment. During election campaigns, police complicity in thuggish attacks on government opponents, either by 'standing aside' or even active intervention, became an all-too-common practice. The reluctance of police officers to intervene in July 1983 when it appeared that marauding gangs might have been unleashed by powerful UNP politicians is not difficult to understand.

Sinhalisation affected the military services as well as the police force. Its impact appears to have been greatest on the army. As we have seen, this process began in 1961 when Mrs. Bandaranaike first replaced a Tamil regimental commander with a Sinhalese officer, her relative, before dispatching troops to Jaffna. Within few years both the army and police were almost entirely Sinhalese. The message this practice communicated to both Sinhalese and Tamil citizens was obvious. There is no evidence that potentially negative consequences of Sinhalisation were fully debated.

These consequences were amply demonstrated when Sinhalese soldiers and police officers were the only forces available to enforce discriminatory policies, fight militants in Tamil majority regions, and protect Tamil citizens where they were a minority. As we have seen, many security force personnel seemed to view Tamil Sri Lankan citizens, in Colombo as well as the north and east, as 'the enemy.' In July 1983, when senior officers ordered soldiers to prevent Sinhalese mobs from butchering Tamil civilians and destroying their property, many refused and some actually joined the mobs. In July 1987, when Prime Minister Rajiv Gandhi reviewed a military honour guard, after signing the Indo-Lanka Accord, one of its members, a Sinhalese, broke ranks and nearly killed him.

Use of state-sanctioned violence to secure the United National Party's parliamentary majority for an additional term in 1982.

UNP leaders had it right when, with J.R. Jayewardene's support, they drafted the 1978 constitution's electoral reforms. As chapter 15 noted, their proportional representation scheme was designed to sharpen the fidelity of feedback from democratic elections and prevent politically expedient constitutional amendments. Sri Lanka would be more stable, they reasoned, if its constitution was grounded in a broad national consensus and not captive to the pendulum swings of political fortune that general elections based on single member districts could sometimes produce (and had produced in 1970 and 1977).

After four years as Executive President, however, J.R. Jayewardene had become addicted to the pliant support of legislation and routine affirmation of constitutional amendments that a three-fourths UNP majority provided. More important, he was deeply committed to the vision of a transformed Sri Lanka that had been economically revitalised by open economy reforms and the accelerated Mahaweli Development Project. Opposing points of view were no longer regarded, if they ever had been, as communicating useful information about development failures and areas of national dissensus. Instead they were viewed as misguided or even pernicious impediments to policies that would benefit all Sri Lankans, narrow the ethnic divide, and secure the President's legacy, if only they could be carried forward for a few more years without interruption.

This thinking spawned the December 1982 Referendum on which J.R. Jayewardene chose to gamble the legitimacy and future of his presidency. As chapter 18 reported, UNP leaders chose to go for a certain win, making maximum use of state-sanctioned violence and ignoring democratic niceties for the most part. The government won its inevitable referendum victory, but in fact the gamble failed and had little chance of succeeding.

This was because in 1982, Sri Lanka's stability was already threatened by three development failures that have been discussed above. Economic reform polices had weakened the government's financial position, made the economy more vulnerable to external shocks, corroded Sri Lanka's social fabric, widened the class divisions and heightened economic tensions. Security forces – weakened by inadequate funding, Sinhalisation, politicisation and humiliations by militants – were ill equipped to cope with outbreaks that might be precipitated in a volatile social climate. Foot dragging on devolution of power, the product of Colombo-centrism and ethnic polarisation, had, along with security force ineffectiveness, strengthened the influence of Tamil militants and weakened the influence of Tamil moderates.

J.R. Jayewardene abetted these destabilising trends with a transparently undemocratic strategy that undermined the legitimacy of his government and eroded respect for the law. A climate of disillusionment with governmental institutions contributed to the catastrophe that soon followed as well as its tragic dénouement. The referendum was designed to guarantee the President five more years of unfettered power to realise his vision, but that power soon became a poisoned chalice.

The attempt to restore order in the northeast (especially in volatile Jaffna Province) with military forces that were clearly incapable of attaining that goal

In 1977, as already noted, Sri Lanka's army was, essentially 100 per cent Sinhalese. Preponderantly, soldiers came from rural areas and had only basic education. Training was limited and there was almost no training in the complexities of counter-insurgency and counter-terrorism. Transport was primitive. Modern weapons were scarce and those that were available were a hodgepodge of Soviet bloc and Western imports. Junior officers were inexperienced. Some senior officers owed their rank to professional distinction, but many others had been promoted because of their political reliability. J.R. Jayewardene, like his predecessors, did not make military readiness a matter of high priority during his first term. I have already identified inattention to the capabilities of Sri Lanka's army as a development failure, while acknowledging that some development scholars might disagree.

The development failure highlighted in this section is different. Faced with a growing number of attacks by Tamil militants, President Jayewardene's goal – necessarily – was to restore order and respect for the rule of law in the northeast. Had he and his close advisors been fully informed about the capabilities of Sri Lanka's military forces, they would have known that using those forces to pacify the northeast was simply not a viable option. The unfolding scenario of conflict escalation from state-sanctioned violence ineffectiveness was all the more tragic because it was predictable and inevitable. Had UNP leaders correctly judged that force was not an option, given the cabilities of police and military contingents available to them, they would have been compelled to look more closely alternative options, however politically unpalatable, and to choose from among them.

The concluding chapter of *Paradise Poisoned* considers such options.

22
Preventing Deadly Conflict and Terrorism: Ten Imperatives

Given what we know about linkages between deadly conflict, terrorism and development, were there ways of expending $300 billion or more, prior to September 11, that could have prevented the formation of a strong resilient al Qa'eda; that could have prevented the World Trade Centre Bombings; that could have forestalled the need to invade Afghanistan and Iraq? Sri Lanka's civil wars could teach us that the answer is yes.

In 1993, Arun Gandhi, the grandson of Mohandas K. Gandhi, invited me to contribute to a volume, entitled *World Without Violence*, memorialising the 125th anniversary of the Mahatma's birth.[1] Motivation for the project, he told contributors, was rooted in a life-changing sojourn at his grandfather's ashram when he was a very young man. Through relatively simple words and examples, Gandhi tried to share some fundamental ideas with his young grandson. The causes of violence in society were not complicated, Gandhi maintained, and could be traced to 'eight blunders':[2]

1. Wealth without work
2. Pleasure without conscience
3. Knowledge without character
4. Commerce without morality
5. Science without humanity
6. Worship without sacrifice
7. Politics without principle
8. Rights without responsibilities

The 'eight blunders' became the organising concept for Arun Gandhi's commemorative volume. Each contributor was invited to use one 'blunder' as a theme around which to organise an essay on a *World Without Violence*. I chose 'politics without principle' and drew two lessons from Sri Lanka's experience.

First was that *practising politics without principle, even in pursuit of principled goals, is likely to push a society toward violent conflict.* Ethnically diverse societies are particularly susceptible to this pathology. The second lesson was that *processes of democratic political campaigning and elections pose nearly irresistible temptations to practice politics without principle.* The more worthy the aspirant, the stronger the belief that his or her leadership is needed to deal with crises or achieve worthy goals, the more irresistible will be the temptation to compromise the principle of *satya* (truthful or moral conduct) and commit the seventh blunder.

The illustrative examples I chose focused on the development failure of polarising political rhetoric and tactics, described in chapter 21. S.W.R.D. Bandaranaike's 1956 general election campaign used racist appeals, in which he did not personally believe, to mobilise support for his People's United Front. Not long afterwards, as readers will recall, J.R. Jayewardene and Dudley Senanayake used similarly expedient tactics to defeat a carefully crafted compromise plan for devolving power to Tamils, the Bandaranaike-Chelvanayakam pact.

The overarching message embodied in Mahatma Gandhi's enumeration of blunders and my enumeration of development failures is the same. **We know more than enough to choose policies that will help prevent protracted deadly conflict – and to not choose policies that will cause protracted deadly conflict.** I have used the following metaphor in previous chapters, but it cannot be repeated too often: **The situation is analogous to our knowledge about the relationship between cigarette smoking and lung cancer. We know that smoking is a principal cause of lung cancer, though there are other causes. We know that refraining from smoking is the best way of avoiding lung cancer, though some abstainers may still contract the disease.**

The 10 development failures enumerated in chapter 21 correspond to 'smoking' in the metaphor. They have been drawn from Sri Lanka's experiences specifically, but can easily be generalised to other developing countries. The smoker's body corresponds to a country that the 'development – deadly -conflict system' model represents. Protracted deadly conflict is the cancer that consumes and may destroy it.

But what is the equivalent to the cancer avoidance strategy, 'refrain from smoking?' A medical practitioner would not simply advocate abstinence. He or she might recommend regular exercise, a healthy diet and a regimen of antioxidants. The prescriptions of an ayurvedic physician, taking the body as a whole system into account, would include much more. Thus 'avoid development failures' is an insufficient prophylactic for protracted deadly conflict. More proactive remedies are needed.

10 imperatives for preventing deadly conflict and terrorism.

Ten imperatives for preventing deadly conflict and terrorism follow. They summarise what I have learned from studying – and from time to time experiencing – Sri Lanka's civil wars for more than seventeen years. Their relevance extends well beyond Sri Lanka – to Kosovo, Kashmir, Palestine, the Sudan, Afghanistan and now, in particular, to Iraq. They are relevant not only to conflict prevention, but to post conflict stabilisation. Most seem simple and obvious, but that does not make them less useful.

1. Maintaining public order and preventing social turbulence from escalating into protracted deadly conflict are prerequisite to the success of all other development policies.

Public order is *intrinsically* beneficial, apart from its contribution to other development goals. Advocates of radical change by radical methods typically fail to recognise or acknowledge this. Providing for the physical security of residents is a fundamental responsibility of government. As with most pathologies, it is the poor who suffer most when a government fails in this responsibility. When public order breaks down, both political leaders and residents become preoccupied with survival and other development goals are threatened. Sir Lanka's experience, post-1983, makes this clear.

Public order may not mean tranquillity. A degree of social turbulence, characterised by some conflict incidents, characterises all developing countries. But low levels of conflict should be the norm and signs of escalation should evoke a firm response. A balance must be struck that tolerates acceptable levels of dissent, while reining in destabilising violence. Many countries have achieved this balance. The balance point may differ from culture to culture.

There is a clear distinction between public order and repression, though political leaders often use 'public order' to falsely justify repression. Public order means that the physical security of all citizens is guaranteed equally. When a government is repressive, the physical security of government opponents is at risk.

2. Polarising political rhetoric and tactics must be forgone, however tempting their short-term benefits may seem. Like mustard gas, which had to be abandoned as a weapon in World War I, this strategy has a tendency to 'blow back' upon the user.[3]

Political leaders are accountable for the discourses they legitimise. Polarising rhetoric, such as that which S.W.R.D. Bandaranaike introduced into Sri Lanka's political mainstream, is one of the most pernicious. Such rhetoric, and the tactics that accompany it, threaten public order by energising primordial destabilising forces that are present in every society. Ethno-nationalist rhetoric invariably provokes counter polarisation. Among the recent conflicts to which polarising rhetoric and tactics have contributed are those in Rwanda, the former Yugoslavia, and Israel/Palestine. There are few, if any, instances in which short-term gains reaped by political leaders from polarising rhetoric and tactics have not been overwhelmed by costs and tragic consequences. The partition riots on the Indian subcontinent may have been the most costly and tragic of all. Their costs are still being borne by citizens of India, Pakistan and Bangladesh. Gandhi foresaw the tragedy, but could not avert it, nor his own assassination at the hands of militant Hindu terrorists.

3. Meeting the needs and aspirations of fighting age young men should be the first priority of national development polices and of programs funded by international donors.

Conflict escalates into protracted civil war when effective leaders form militant groups, recruit followers, mobilise resources and become strong. Alienated, unemployed young men with 'nothing to lose' are naturally drawn to militancy. Such young men, when properly organised, have real power to disrupt complex societies, using terrorist and guerrilla tactics. Once such groups have been formed, no security force, however skilled, can completely prevent their depredations. In Sri Lanka, the Liberation Tigers have successfully resisted attempts to impose a 'military solution' for more than 20 years. Israel may be the most security-conscious country in the world, with one of the most skilled, professional security forces, but it has been unable to defend against suicide bombings by Palestinian youth. The armed might of the U.S. military forces, plus the FBI, CIA, local police and airport security officers, failed to prevent the World Trade Centre Bombings. Though badly mauled in Afghanistan, *al Qa'eda* remains a viable and feared organisation, able to impose severe costs. Militants have been able to seriously challenge U.S. hegemony in Iraq. These cases represent a small subset of those where militant groups have successfully carried out terrorist attacks, escalated violent conflicts and sustained protracted deadly conflicts.

By far the most cost-effective way to deal with the threat posed by militant groups is to prevent them from growing strong in the first place. The most cost-effective way to prevent them from growing strong is to give young men in a society, especially the most able young men, something to live for. What most young men want is not mysterious. Sri Lanka's *Report of the Presidential Commission on Youth*, discussed in chapter 17, described their concerns and needs quite clearly. They want opportunities to engage their physical energy and idealism. They want a decent education that prepares them for the work force. They want job opportunities and fair recruitment practices. They want to be led by politicians who are honest and keep their promises. They want opportunities to marry, raise a family and provide a good life for their children. These wants are universal, not exceptional.

In two respects, however, young men are distinguished from other cohorts in society. First, they tend to be preponderantly disadvantaged. To cite just one example, unemployment figures are invariably highest for this cohort, reaching 50 per cent or more in many developing countries. Second, members of this cohort are more likely to believe that they have the power to change their circumstances. Moreover, they are more willing to take risks and make sacrifices, including their lives, to effect change. That the segment of society with the greatest power to disrupt should also be among the most disadvantaged seems paradoxical. The potential consequences of failing to change this are perilous.

4. **Developing countries should have internal security forces (police and paramilitary) that are generously funded, professional, apolitical and trained to meet the complex challenges of maintaining public order in a changing society.**

This imperative emphasises the importance of a highly paid, professional police force, including a paramilitary element, as a successful development prerequisite. I note an important distinction between police and military forces. Police and soldiers both wear uniforms and may carry guns, but their training and functions are quite different. Effective police officers are members of the communities in which they serve. They carry out their duties for the most part functioning as individuals. They should speak the same language and share the same cultural values as community members. Where a community is ethnically and culturally diverse, police forces should reflect that diversity. Police officers should be viewed as fair and impartial guardians of the rule of law. Community members should see them as allies, not oppressors. Police professionals who are respected as community members will be able to intervene effectively to prevent and control violent outbreaks, and their presence in communities will contribute to a climate in which violent outbreaks are less likely to occur. The role of a police officer should be highly valued and highly respected in a society. It is the responsibility of political leaders to create a discourse and provide resources that affirm this. Few developing countries even remotely approximate these norms and many industrialised nations fall short, as well.

To carry out their role effectively, police officers must be trained to meet the complex challenges they are likely to encounter in a developing country that can be socially volatile. They must have the logistical support that they need to function effectively. They must be adequately compensated so that they can provide decent lives for their family, educate their children, and hold up their heads proudly among community members. Promotions and positions of responsibility should reward exemplary performance of duty, not political pliability.[4]

Nandasena Ratnapala's research and Senior DIG Merril Gunaratne's recounting of personal experiences describe how far Sri Lanka's police forces departed from this ideal.[5] Low pay, inadequate budgets, and political interference made it difficult for even the most dedicated officers to carry out their duties professionally. A succession of political leaders created a climate in which many Sri Lankans viewed police officers as oppressors and in which police officers feared the consequences of taking decisive action in crisis situations. Officers in many developing countries face far worse circumstances. Since police officers are invariably in the front lines when escalating conflict and terrorism challenge governments, the low priority given to effective policing is puzzling. This needs to be corrected.

I have said little about the military, whose role has been so visible in Sri Lanka's civil wars. My view is that military forces have relatively little role to play in preventing or controlling deadly conflict. Countries that face no serious external military threats should emulate Costa Rica: they should have no military forces.[6] Military personnel are not trained for internal policing duties and do not function effectively in that role. Soldiers are not members of the communities they serve, but instead mostly live apart from them. They are trained to function in groups, not as individuals. They are trained to view the 'opposition forces' with which they are dealing as enemies, not fellow community members. They are trained to use violent force as a principal tool in carrying out their duties, not as a last resort.[7] When the government of a developing country has to call out the army against its own citizens, the battle to prevent conflict escalation in a cost-effective way has already been lost. Sri Lanka had no real need for an army or air force, other than for ceremonial purposes. A coast guard rather than a navy would have sufficed. Military budgets could have been spent far more productively on the police.

5. Development policies that meet human beings' common aspirations – to feel good about their lives, the circumstances in which they live and future prospects for themselves and their children – will contribute most effectively to keeping violent conflict and terrorism within acceptable bounds.

Since this principle was developed so fully in chapter 3, a brief summary of what I said there will be sufficient. People share fundamental needs and aspirations. They are capable of expressing them politically. They will be more predisposed to violence and militancy when they feel disheartened about the circumstances of their lives and future prospects for themselves and their children. The performance measures used to design and evaluate most development policies have been chosen for reasons other than intrinsic merit of the worldview they promote. Imposition, from above, of development policies framed by those performance measures is likely to evoke feelings of hostility and alienation. The development failures linked to both United Front and United National Party economic polices after 1970 are explained, at least in part, by these problems,

Obviously development policies cannot meet the aspirations of all country residents all of the time. Many policies will necessarily benefit some, while disadvantaging others. But when this occurs, compensation for those who lose out should be part of the package. Politicians who assume that the disadvantaged will simply 'sit back and take it' for extended periods of time, do so at their peril.

After 1956, a succession of Sri Lankan political leaders implemented policies that relatively disadvantaged the island's Tamil minority on multiple fronts simultaneously – linguistic, cultural, political, educational and economic. I use the word 'relatively' to avoid arguing about whether these policies were 'unfair' or simply legitimate remedies for historical deprivations previously visited on the Sinhalese. Practically, it does not matter whether broad-spectrum discriminatory policies were 'right' in some intrinsic moral sense. What matters is that protracted deadly conflict was their predictable, highly probable outcome. Both Sinhalese and Tamils have suffered from Sri Lanka's civil wars Development policies that acknowledged the 'losers' feelings of deprivation and compensated them would have been far more cost-effective.

6. Those who frame development policies should seek a middle path between capitalism's efficient, but Darwinian precepts, and socialism's egalitarian, but stultifying precepts.

One of my favourite parables caricatures petrol filling stations in different nations of the world. A driver in Japan is served by five crisply appointed attendants who clean her windscreen, fill the tank and then stop traffic so she can return to the highway. Petrol costs $6.00 per gallon. In France the price is also $6.00 per gallon. Five attendants are employed to service customers, but service is slow and less crisp than in Japan. One attendant is on extended sick leave and two are on vacation. On the other hand, motorists can pause for a glass of wine and croissant at an attractive café adjoining the station. In the United States, the price is $1.50 per gallon, self-service only. A lone cashier sits in a bullet-proof kiosk to receive payment from those who do not have credit cards. The other attendant is an armed security guard who stands by to protect customers from the homeless panhandlers who stand on the station's periphery. In the former Soviet Union (the parable is a bit dated) the price of petrol was only $.50 per gallon. Seven attendants, all government employees, worked at the station. They stood by indifferently as customers drove up – and there was no petrol for sale.

Which 'development model' is best? Development practice tends to oscillate between ideologically driven extremes, even though some middle path is clearly preferable. With the 'end of the Cold War', U.S.-style capitalism has emerged triumphant. American leaders are now using their nation's geopolitical clout to promote free market capitalism as the only viable economic model. American ideologues also equate American-style capitalism and 'democracy,' though a variety of economic models are clearly compatible with democratic institutions. America has achieved a remarkable trajectory of sustained economic growth and, on many dimensions, it remains a 'land of opportunity. But like America's petrol station in my parable, capitalism American-style has its shortcomings. America's economic boom years have widened the gap between rich and poor, while many government services have deteriorated. Millions lack basic health care and homelessness is a problem in most urban centres, not only for adults, but also for hundreds of thousands of children.[8] Clearly other economic-political models, including those of Iceland, Sweden, Singapore, Canada, the European Union, and Japan can also provide useful lessons to developing nations. That American 'efficiency' and 'competitiveness' may threaten some of these models in a global economy does not diminish their intrinsic value as possible models of 'successful development.'

What design strategy is most likely to produce appropriate middle path policies for a given nation? Here are two guidelines.

First, represent diverse points of view at the table when development policies are being designed and take them seriously. The voices of lawyers, economists and successful businessmen predominated when Sri Lanka's development policies were being designed and implemented. Absent were anthropologists, police officers, ecologists, social workers, systems analysts, homemakers and rural farmers. This pattern characterises the design of most development policies and, most egregiously, policies crafted by the world's premier development institution, the World Bank. For those who question this, World Bank Chief Economist Joseph Stiglitz's description of 'The Washington Consensus' bears repeating: *The success of the Washington Consensus as an intellectual doctrine rests on its simplicity: its policy recommendations could be administered by economists using little more than simple accounting frameworks. A few economic indicators – inflation, money supply growth, interest rates, and budget and trade deficits – could serve as the basis for a set of policy recommendations.* [9] A simple requirement that every economist on World Bank task forces and planning teams be balanced by an anthropologist and a full-time homemaker (with childcare provided) would, in itself, have a significant, beneficial impact.

Second, build self-correcting feedback mechanisms, representing the views of those most impacted, into the development policy implementation process. The importance of feedback was emphasised throughout my elaboration of the 'development – deadly-conflict system model.' Feedback provides political leaders with the 'bad news' that scenarios are not unfolding as anticipated. Timely receipt of bad news by those willing to listen can motivate remedial action before it is too late. Useful feedback mechanisms will differ from project to project. The many 'fever charts' and codifications of conflict events given in this book provide one example of potentially useful feedback. Nutritional impact studies that documented the impact of UNP food subsidy cuts, described in chapter 16, provide another.

7. Good governance and democratisation must be part of the 'successful development' mix. Most important are governance institutions that are open to 'bad news' and self-correcting.

If accessibility and responsiveness to 'bad news' are prerequisites for successful development, democracy is the best way to build this into a country's political process. Democratic institutions do not necessarily guarantee good policies or good leaders, but are more effective at 'learning' than authoritarian ones. They empower citizens to learn about the ingredients of effective policy through a process of communication, competition, trial and error. They provide mechanisms for getting rid of bad leaders. Self-corrective mechanisms are necessary because mistakes are inevitable and will occur at all levels. Democracy itself is learned behaviour. A succession of democratic leadership transitions makes it more probable that the next transition will be democratic.[10]

Sri Lanka, despite its tribulations, illustrates the value of resilient democratic institutions, especially elections.[11] They have clearly functioned as an error correction mechanism when the ship of the state appeared to be drifting badly off course. Sirimavo Bandanaraike's manipulation of the electoral rules was widely condemned. Even J.R. Jayewardene's supporters believe the 1982 referendum undermined the legitimacy of his government and contributed to the tragedy of July 1983. Subsequent Sri Lankan governments have tried to rule autocratically, but acquiesced more or less peacefully to holding scheduled elections and to results that removed them from power. UNP leaders allowed Chandrika Kumaratunga to become *de facto* head of government when her People's Alliance won a parliamentary majority in 1994. President Kumaratunga did the same, ceding power (albeit reluctantly) to UNP leader Ranil Wickremasinghe when her party was trounced by the UNP in December 2001. In early 2004, the two Sri Lankan leaders were jockeying for power once again, using a variety of political tactics, but neither was overtly challenging the legitimacy of Sri Lanka's democratic practices.

The elements of good governance – managerial competence, accountability, predictability and transparency – were once viewed as distinct from successful development and democratisation. Now there is wide acceptance of the view that good governance may be essential for effective development and will help sustain democratic institutions as well.[12] That resilient democratic institutions may foster good governance over the long run seems probable – good governance is relatively common in industrialised democracies – but there is no evidence that they do so in the short run. In Sri Lanka, the probability that elections would be held and that those in power would be turned from office does not appear to have seriously limited corrupt and absolutist practices by at least some office-holders. Sri Lanka's 'spoils system,' a product of democracy, politicised both the police and military services.

In 1998, Kristine Herrmann and I speculated about the degree to which international pressure, which developed nations and multilaterals have tried to exercise from time to time, could promote democratisation. I see little reason to alter the conclusion we reached then:

> ...International pressure may catalyse a democratic transition, but its impact on the quality of political life will be more limited. ...International pressure cannot ensure that governments will be more stable, that politicians will not squabble, that campaigns will not be divisive or that political competition will not bring out the worst as well as the best in a nation's people. Since even democracies of long standing exhibit such traits, this is hardly surprising. The learning process through which democratic institutions are rooted takes time, may never be 'completed', and is likely to be turbulent.[13]

The issue of 'international pressure' motivates a brief concluding comment on the role of the United States since the 'war on terrorism' has become the top foreign policy priority of its leaders. The U.S. role is important because political leaders in developing nations are more likely to be influenced by what U.S. leaders do, when those actions differ from America's principles of democracy, freedom, and transparency. Prior to 1990, the United States supported a number of vile regimes and movements because their leaders were Cold War allies.[14] Between 1990 and September 2001, the U.S. leaders were more or less consistent in their support for democratisation and democratic regimes. The decision to embrace General Pervez Musharraf's military dictatorship in Pakistan, in return for Musharraf's support of the U.S. war on terrorism, represented a return to Cold War style alliances.[15] Overt and covert alliances with other dictators, especially in states of the former Soviet Union bordering Afghanistan, have followed. Judging whether or not these alliances serve U.S. national interests is beyond the scope of this book. Pointing out that such alliances are unlikely to promote or help sustain democratisation in developing countries is not.

8. Multinational corporations, businesses and businessmen's organisations[16] should play a more active role in supporting successful development policies.

Stable, successful development is good for business. Protracted deadly conflict is bad for business. When protracted deadly conflict breaks out, multinationals can move their operations elsewhere, but not without costs. Local businessmen may see the work of a lifetime obliterated in a matter of months. Sri Lankan businessmen who are my personal friends have experienced this. Increasingly, the private sector is a major source of government revenue in developing countries. Absent these revenues, governments could not function. Business people are uniquely positioned to take a long-term view and to promote imperatives like those presented here. In fact, their time horizons must be longer than the election-driven time horizons of many politicians. The life of a hotel, factory or other capital investment often amortises over a decade or more, the lifetime of several governments. Political risk analysts take a similarly long-term view when advising clients about investments in developing countries.

That business community members would have both the motivation and power to intervene on behalf of policies that promote stable sustainable development seems obvious. However, in Sri Lanka at least, they rarely do so, even when counterproductive behaviour by political leaders puts their livelihood at risk. The principal justifications I have heard for non-intervention – that businessmen fear politicians' power and are uncertain what specifically to recommend – seem unconvincing.

My recommendation that business community members become more involved is less fully elaborated than other points because I do not fully understand the obstacles to involvement in Sri Lanka, let alone in other developing countries. This is a subject I intend to explore more fully. Still, the evidence that businessmen and their organisations could become more politically involved, and that that such involvement would be in their self-interest, seems compelling.

9. Successful development requires a long-term view. Giving sufficient weight to the long-term requires institutional mechanisms and discourses that extend beyond the next election and term in office of political leaders presently in power.

Foreshortened time horizons of those planning and implementing development policies cause many development failures. I have heard the argument that human beings are inherently short-sighted, but on a personal level this is not the case. A concern for the well-being of the future generations in a family seems even more deeply rooted in developing nations like Sri Lanka than in the United States. I am often impressed by the sacrifices, on behalf of their children, of my Sri Lankan friends and of those from many nations who are recent immigrants to the United States.

The probabilities are small that I will live much beyond 2020, or if do, that my life in that time frame will make much difference. God willing, my children will be living productive lives in 2040 and their children in 2060. We do care about our children and grandchildren as individuals. We try to give them moral anchors and to educate them. We may try to amass estates to provide for their security. But neither in the developed nor the developing world do we frame development polices as if we cared about them. This widespread myopia has helped to foster conditions in which the seeds of militancy flourish. September 11, 2001 is just the latest wake up call.

Readers knowing something of my background will detect that I am now injecting views learned while conducting pioneering 'global modelling' research in the 1970s, under the Club of Rome's auspices.[17] Like the experiences of astronauts who first viewed the earth from outer space, this work taught those of us who engaged in it to broaden our geographic and temporal horizons. In numerous speeches and publications, my global modelling colleagues and I have urged political leaders and development practitioners to do the same.

How does one *institutionalise* a concern for grandchildren in development decision-making? My best effort to do so came 20 years ago, when I was employed as a consultant by U.S. President Jimmy Carter's staff to prepare follow up recommendations to the *Global 2000 Report to the President*. Global 2000 was the U.S. government's most ambitious attempt to project future trends and use the information to frame current policies.

Since my recommendations were written for President Carter and his staff, they focused on how the U.S. government could improve its 'foresight' capability.[18] I recommended institutional changes to give the long-term future additional political clout. I proposed that a special assistant for foresight be named to the President's staff, that an 'Ombudsman for Grandchildren' be designated and given a visible, high status position, and that an 'Institute for Foresight' be created with funding and stature comparative to the National Institutes of Health.

President Carter did not win re-election in 1980. President Ronald Reagan's conservative administration succeeded Carter's and quickly disavowed Global 2000. His staff did not seek out my services as consultant, and President Reagan did not appoint an Ombudsman for Grandchildren, nor has any subsequent president.[19] Grandchildren did reappear, however, in the Brundtland Commission's widely quoted definition of sustainable development.[20] There are few instances where grandchildren's perspectives have yet been institutionalised, but many opportunities to do so.

10. There must be realistic, rigorous, opportunity-costs analyses of military options, versus *equivalent expenditures* for non-military options, before proceeding down the slippery slope of 'military solutions' to complex development problems.

Political leaders often say they 'had no choice', when implementing policies such as the U.S. invasion of Iraq. This is rarely true. Multiple choices are almost always available. The longer the time horizon, the greater the range of choices. Chapter 20 provided an estimate of funds that might have been expended on non-violent options in Sri Lanka, like providing economically relevant non-discriminatory educational opportunities for Sri Lanka's youth. Rarely, if ever, are military options contrasted with *equivalent expenditures* for non-military ones. Development professionals sometimes joke that development assistance budgets are denominated in millions, while military budgets are denominated in billions, but the joke is not funny.

Mahatma Gandhi identified eight blunders that lead to violence. He deeply understood the causes of violent conflict and terrorism in human society. British, Muslim and his own Congress Party leaders failed to heed his warnings or follow his imperatives. Their decisions, words and actions catalysed the partition riots. In addition to the initial carnage and economic devastation visited on one of the world's poorest regions, partition has – so far – spawned three full-scale wars, a protracted insurgency and a nuclear arms race.

Paradise Poisoned has identified ten development failures that spawned violent conflict and terrorism in Sri Lanka. It proposes a conflict prevention strategy, summarised here in ten imperatives. Gandhi's prescience is beyond my reach, but I have learned from Sri Lanka's civil wars that outbreaks of protracted, deadly conflict and terrorism are predictable and preventable.

If deadly conflict and terrorism are preventable, are there sufficient resources for the task? An analysis that focuses on opportunity costs provides a compelling affirmative answer. For Sri Lanka, this was given in chapter 20.

But being an American, I need not look to Sri Lanka for an answer to this question. There are lessons to be learned closer to home. Consider, from the vantage point of opportunity costs, the World Trade Centre bombing of September 11, 2001 and its consequences. Consider the subsequent expenditures in the U.S. on 'homeland security.' Consider the expenditures, so far, on the invasion of Afghanistan, the invasion of Iraq and subsequent military operations in those nations.

Following the model of cost estimates for Sri Lanka's civil wars, I could estimate primary secondary and tertiary costs of these conflicts, but some of this work has already been done by others. A very conservative order-of-magnitude cost estimate, *so far,* would fall in the range of 300 to 500 billion US dollars.[21]

In June 2002, an Associated Press news article assessed opportunity costs for the Iraq invasion and occupation, based solely on funds appropriated so far by the U.S. government, $119.4 billion *at that time.* This sum, the article reported, would provide 748,495 four year scholarships to Harvard University and 2,806,506 scholarships to an average U.S. state university. It would provide each resident of Iraq with $4,776, a sum roughly equivalent to eight times Iraq's per-capita income in 2003.[22]

Given what we know about linkages between deadly conflict, terrorism, and development, were there ways of expending $300 billion or more, prior to September 11, that could have prevented the formation of a strong resilient al Qa'eda; that could have prevented the World Trade Centre Bombings; that could have forestalled the need to invade Afghanistan and Iraq? Sri Lanka's civil wars could teach us that the answer is yes.

Notes

Prologue Notes

[1] See Tuchman (1984: 357).

[2] I use a gendered term here simply because men predominate to such a great degree in businesses and business organisations in developing countries. I do not endorse this, but I do acknowledge it.

[3] See The Hunger Project (1985).

[4] See Carnegie Commission on Preventing Deadly Conflict (1997).

[5] Ibid: chapter 4.

[6] Ibid: 9.

Chapter One Notes

[1] I mean by *deadly civil conflict* a violent conflict 'involving geographically contiguous people concerned about possibly having to live with one another in the same political unit after the conflict' (Licklider 1993: 9). I sometimes use civil war or violent conflict as synonyms. In the case of Sri Lanka, it is particularly important to use such terms rather than the more popular 'ethnic conflict' because the nation has faced two civil wars. The less publicised one, an insurrection by Sinhalese youth under the banner of the *Janatha Vimukti Peramuna* (JVP; People's Liberation Front) was almost exclusively a conflict between protagonists of the *same* ethnic group, the majority Sinhalese.

[2] A number of military aircraft were also destroyed.

[3] Personal communication from Burcu Akan. The seminar, organised by the Institute for Defense Analysis and the U.S. Institute of Peace, presented a computer simulation of economic reconstruction in a hypothetical war-torn society.

[4] See *Measuring the Condition of the World's Poor* (Morris 1979).

[5] See for example *Ethnic Groups in Conflict* (Horowitz 1985), *Ethnic Conflict and Political Development* (Enloe 1986), and *The State, Religion, and Ethnic Politics: Afghanistan, Iran, and Pakistan* (Banuazizi and Weiner 1990).

[6] I called attention to this in a 1987 article noting that 'The relationship between development and internal security is left to politicians and sequestered within the confines of military, police and intelligence organisations.' (Richardson 1987b: 652).

[7] See Carnegie Commission on Preventing Deadly Conflict (1997: 11).

[8] Roy Licklider (1993: 5-6) reminds us that civil wars were a pervasive phenomenon of the post World War II period, even though most scholars paid less attention to them than

to interstate wars. For example, he quotes Jimmy Carter's observation that of the 116 wars since World War II, all but the Iraqi invasion of Kuwait were civil wars, and Saddam Hussein would even disagree about that exceptional case.

[9] See especially the first two chapters of the Carnegie Commission report (1997).

[10] See United Nations High Commission for Refugees (1999).

[11] See Zartman (1993: 20). The author is among the world's leading experts on negotiation, founded the journal *International Negotiation*, and has also won great regard as an Africa scholar.

[12] Ibid: 21-24.

[13] A brief insurrection organised by Sinhalese JVP militants did occur in 1971.

[14] See Zartman (1993: 24).

[15] This point is made in Skocpol's classic *States and Social Revolutions* (1979) and in a more recent collection of essays by Skocpol and her students, *Social Revolutions in the Modern World* (1994).

[16] See chapter 4 in the Carnegie Commission report (1997).

[17] Ibid: 69.

[18] Ibid.

[19] 'Sustainable development' is a development scenario that leads to a sustainable society. The term was popularised by the World Commission on Environment and Development (1987), chaired by Norwegian Prime Minister Gro Harlem Brundtland. The "Brundtland Commission Report" defined sustainable development as 'development that meets the needs of the present without compromising the ability of future generations to meet their own needs.' See Weaver et al. (1997: 34). The definition of a sustainable society that I like comes from Donella Meadows, et al.: 'A sustainable society is one that can persist over generations, one that is far seeing enough, flexible enough and wise enough not to undermine either its physical or its social systems of support.' (1992: 209) While the term 'successful' is really redundant, writers sometimes use it as an alternative to or in conjunction with 'sustainable' development, as I have chosen to do here.

[20] See the Carnegie Commission (1997: 69).

[21] See UNDP (2001: 10, Table 1.2.). The Human Development Index is discussed more fully in chapter 3 of this book.

[22] Cornia (1999), quoted in UNDP (2001: 17).

[23] See 'Why Inequality Matters,' (UNDP 2001: 17, Box 1.2).

[24] See 'Flows of Aid from DAC Member Countries' (UNDP 2001: 190, Table 14). Greece was admitted to membership in the Development Assistance Committee in 1999, increasing total DAC membership to 22 states. The comparative statistics here, however, come from the 21 countries represented in the group in 1990. Luxembourg tied with the United States for the smallest per-centage of its GNP allocated to development assistance in 1990 (.21 per-cent), but rose to fourth place with a contribution of .66 per cent in 1999.

[25] See the Carnegie Commission (1997: 5).

[26] Ibid: 5.

[27] Ibid: 9, emphasis added.

[28] This is the conclusion of a working paper prepared for the Commission by Alexander E. George and Jane E. Holt (1997), quoted in Carnegie Commission (1997: 43).

[29] See Carnegie Commission (1997: 44, Box. 3.1). Studies that provide the basis for the list of indicators are Esty, et al. (1995) and Baker and Ausnik (1996). I have made one editorial change, for purposes of clarification, in the first bulleted item.

[30] Brinton (1965: 16-17).

[31] I use this phrase because the left-leaning Sri Lanka Freedom Party (SLFP) always headed coalition governments that included one or more Marxist parties. The more conservative United National Party (UNP) sometimes formed coalitions with Tamil parties and others – for example, in the case of Dudley Senanayake's 'National Government' that held power from 1965 through 1970.

[32] This approach is somewhat similar to the 'events data' analysis popularised by the late Edward Azar and others. See for example *The Management of Protracted Social Conflict: Theory and Cases* (Azar 1990).

[33] This definition and elaboration is taken, with some editing, from the coding manual I developed for my research in Sri Lanka. Data collection was mostly completed in 1988.

[34] Members of all Sri Lanka's major ethnic groups – Sinhalese, Tamils, Muslims and Burghers – numbered among the team members. One member was a relatively recent migrant from India.

[35] See Sorokin (1937: 383-408).

[36] See Greater Colombo Economic Commission (1986).

[37] See J.G. Anderson, et al. (1985: 12). The British name, Ceylon, came from the Portuguese, who ruled the island briefly.

[38] Many sources provide basic information on Sri Lanka's geography. This brief summary is primarily based on Anthonis (1985), K.M. de Silva (1986) and Singer (1989).

[39] See Karunatilake (1987: 43, 272).

[40] Ibid: 43, 44.

[41] See Moore (1985: xiii).

[42] See Singer (1989: 3). Originally, the plantations were mostly owned by English and Scotch proprietors, though some Sri Lankans also had large holdings. Most were nationalised in early 1970s. A program to return them to private management was initiated in 1994.

[43] See K.M. de Silva (1986: 9).

[44] Singer (1989: 4).

[45] *Caste and Family in the Politics of the Sinhalese* (Jiggins 1979) is often cited as the definitive work on this subject, though it has been criticised by some Sri Lankans and some anthropologists specialising in Sri Lanka.

[46] See K.M. de Silva (1986:19-22) and Weeramunda and J.G. Anderson (1985: 75-76).

[47] Typically cabinets have one or two minority members and several powerful Sinhalese castes will be represented.

[48] Before visiting Sri Lanka, Emily and I were told, *sotto voce,* that Premadasa, then Prime Minister, would never become President because he was lower caste. He proved these predictions wrong, but nevertheless would suffer many snubs, even from *Goyigama* members of his own party, the UNP.

[49] Sirimavo Bandaranaike became Prime Minister once again in 1994 when her daughter, Chandrika Bandaranaike Kumaratunga became Executive President in 1994. At that time, however, the office had greatly reduced power.

[50] *Theravada,* the School of Elders, is a conservative Buddhist sect that emphasises the role of priests in attaining enlightenment. Laypersons are mandated to lead meritorious lives, but in general cannot expect to become enlightened in their lifetime as a layperson. Their role is to support members of the priesthood (*Sangha*) in following the path given by the Buddha. See Carrithers (1982) for a brief overview. A fuller discussion of Buddhism's role in Sri Lanka will be found in later chapters. Virtually all Sri Lankan Buddhists follow Theravada doctrines.

[51] K.M. de Silva (1986: 361-368). Sinhalese see themselves as a minority in view of the 55 million Tamils who live in the southern Indian state of Tamil Nadu.

[52] Singer (1989: 4).

[53] K.M. de Silva (1986: 368).

[54] Ibid: 11.

[55] This brief summary is based on K.M. de Silva (1986: 11-16) and (1985b: 37-40).

[56] Singer (1989: 5). By the time of the July 1983 riots the Colombo Tamil population numbered around 500,000.

[57] This brief discussion of caste among the Sri Lanka Tamils is based mostly on Weeramunda and J.G. Anderson (1985: 81-82) and K.M. de Silva (1986: 22, 219-220) as well as numerous personal conversations.

[58] The term 'Indian Tamils' is rejected by some whose views I respect, most notably my colleague and friend, linguist Arjuna Parakrama. They argue for 'Tamils of Indian origin,' 'plantation Tamils' or more complex characterisations. I am aware of these concerns, but have opted to continue with 'Indian Tamil' as a non-cumbersome label that appears widely in published literature and is still used in popular discourse -- including the discourse of many Sri Lankans who describe themselves as 'Indian Tamils.'

[59] Most were low caste, but a small number of high caste Indian Tamils came to Sri Lanka as labour recruiters and organisers. Later, some of these men became plantation

owners and influential leaders in the Indian Tamil political party, the Ceylon Workers' Congress (CWC).

[60] This brief discussion of the Indian Tamils is based largely on K.M. de Silva (1986: 18-19), G.H. Peiris (1991), Moore (1985: 30-49), and Singer (1989: 4).

[61] K.M. de Silva (1986: 156-57).

[62] Ibid: 221-225 and G.H. Peiris (1991).

[63] This results partly because both men and women earn wages, which occurs less commonly in other rural areas. The intensive hand labour of tea picking has become a job almost exclusively for women.

[64] For example, see K.M. de Silva (1986: 318-321).

[65] Ibid: 115-123 and Weeramunda and J.G. Anderson (1985: 87).

[66] Ibid: 227-235.

[67] K.M. de Silva (1986: 414). Statistics are drawn from the 1981 Census published by the Department of Census and Statistics, Government of Sri Lanka.

[68] New language policies initiated after 1956 *required* that Sinhalese students be educated in Sinhala and Tamil students in Tamil.

[69] Yasmine Gooneratne describes the experience of one such couple, migrants to Australia, in her novel, *A Change of Skies* (1991). Her book *Relative Merits: A Personal Memoir of the Bandaranaike Family of Sri Lanka* (1986) is an elegantly crafted chronicling of elite life in Sri Lanka, using the experience of Sri Lanka's most politically powerful family as a lens. Professor Gooneratne, a niece of the late Prime Minister, Sirimavo Bandaranaike, has mostly lived in Australia for many years but retains close ties with Sri Lanka.

[70] Advanced-level or 'A level' examinations, which mark the completion of secondary school, also serve as university entrance examinations.

[71] Speaking of a Tiger leader, one man told me, 'He was nothing. He used to be a peon, hanging around my father's front porch, waiting to run errands.'

[72] The Hunger Project (1985: 390).

[73] American University's School of International Service had helped to found a graduate international relations program, affiliated with the department, in 1986. I became the third and final exchange professor from AU to teach in the program as part of this collaboration.

[74] This is excerpted from my paper 'Ordinary Living in the Midst of Civil War: Notes to Family and Friends', published in an edited volume by Tissa Jayatilaka (2002).

[75] At that time, trains did not run to Jaffna, where the Liberation Tigers of Tamil Eelam controlled and administered the city.

[76] Some weeks before the agreement was signed, the Sri Lankan armed forces had launched a major offensive against Tamil rebels in the North. The Indian government, which had funded and trained some rebel groups, responded with a 'humanitarian' air drop of supplies to the rebels. The cargo planes were protected by fighter aircraft of the

Indian Air Force. This convinced Jayewardene, most observers believe, that some sort of accommodation with the Indians would be necessary.

[77] In 1971 radical Sinhalese youth nearly toppled the recently elected government of Prime Minister Sirimavo Bandaranaike.

[78] During this period, *The Island* enjoyed a relative degree of editorial independence, while *The Daily News* operated under government control.

[79] See Tuchman (1984).

[80] This practice prevailed during a recent visit to Sri Lanka, as well.

[81] Sri Lanka's international airport is now named after assassinated Prime Minister S.W.R.D. Bandaranaike, also the father of the current President, Chandrika Bandaranaike Kumaratunga.

[82] This material comes from an article entitled 'Body Blow to Southern Tourism' in *The Lanka Guardian* (November 15, 1988: 6) as well as other newspaper and personal accounts.

[83] See Mervyn de Silva's 'Fear is the Key' article in the same issue of *The Lanka Guardian* (Ibid: 1-6). *The Lanka Guardian* was a left-leaning bi-weekly publication of political commentary and opinion, one of Sri Lanka's truly independent journalistic voices during this period. It ceased publication in 2000, following editor de Silva's death.

Chapter Two Notes

[1] K.M. de Silva (1986) presents this point of view and cites a number of relevant sources. His richly textured historical perspective displays more nuance than this brief conjecture.

[2] Concerns over the unfulfilled aspirations of young women and especially young men feature prominently (with voluminous supporting detail) in the *Report of the Presidential Commission on Youth* (Sri Lanka Government, 1990). The report takes an eclectic position on the causes of these concerns.

[3] Snodgrass (1966) was one of the first to point to structural weaknesses in the Sri Lankan economy as a potential source of social instability. Lakshman (1997a) provides a recent edited volume that includes a number of useful contributions and an extensive bibliography. Abeyratne (1998), S.W.R. de A. Samarasinghe and Coughlin, eds. (1991) and Scott (1989) also make useful contributions.

[4] Abeyratne (1998: chapter 3) provides a concise description of Marxist and neo-Marxist accounts of this period, along with an extensive bibliography.

[5] I develop this argument later in this volume and in previous writings. My point of view also emphasises leadership failures, however. Scholars often cite Gunasinghe (1984) as a seminal statement of this point of view.

[6] Proponents of this argument contrast Sri Lanka's experience with that of more economically successful 'Asian Tigers,' such as Hong Kong, Taiwan, South Korea and

Singapore. They contend that these countries achieved both rapid economic growth and political stability because relatively non-democratic governments could maintain consistently free-market economic policies long enough for economic growth to gain momentum. This point of view was offered in justification of a legally suspect strategy for extending the life of Parliament under J.R. Jayewardene (Athulathmudali, 1984). In addition, this argument reflects the views held by the leader of perhaps the most successful 'Asian Tiger' economy, Singapore's Lee Kuan Yew (Josey, 1980: especially chapter 10), who strongly influenced Jayewardene.

[7] Moore (1992) presents a clear, succinct statement of this point of view. Two compilations that address the issue of democratic breakdowns and governance failures from varied perspectives are Manor (1984) and K.M. de Silva, ed. (1993a). Hoole et al. (1992) is a powerful statement from a Sri Lanka Tamil perspective.

[8] As the wording of this conjecture suggests, many proponents tend to link together the erosion of democracy and leadership failure. Works cited in note 7 are also relevant here. K.M. de Silva (1999b) is highly critical of Mrs. Bandaranaike's leadership, but views J.R. Jayewardene more favourably (K.M. de Silva and Wriggins 1988, 1994).

[9] The Hunger Project (1985) illustrates this approach.

[10] A few among many important works comprising this voluminous literature are Glazer and Moynihan (1975), Horowitz (1985), de Vos and Romanucci-Ross (1995), and Tambiah (1996). Samuel Huntington's widely cited -- and criticised – *Clash of Civilisations* (1996) has reawakened popular consciousness of this outlook.

[11] Skocpol (1994), which includes some co-authored articles and articles by her students, provides an excellent survey of the corpus of her work on the relationship between state structures and social revolutions.

[12] In chapter 3, I examine more fully 'unresolved questions' about the relationship between governance and development.

[13] The Committee on Comparative Politics of the Social Science Research Council played a particularly important role in catalysing research that produced this literature, to which many of its members contributed. Gabriel A. Almond, himself a major figure in this activity, provides a useful retrospective in 'The Development of Political Development' (1987).

[14] An early marker of this trend was Lynne Reinner Publishers' massive four-volume series, *Democracy in Developing Nations*, edited by Larry Diamond, Seymour Martin Lipset, and Juan Linz (1988 et seq.).

[15] Thomas Carothers' *Aiding Democracy Abroad: The Learning Curve* (1999) provides a comprehensive, meticulously researched survey of this history from a US perspective.

[16] See Carnegie Commission (1997: 151).

[17] The second or 'Marxist' theory reflects Karl Marx's deterministic view of how world history unfolds. All of the other contenders reflect more conventional social science theory, falling generally within the positivist or behavioural traditions, though they have been influenced by different disciplines – psychology, sociology and economics, primarily.

[18] For the Sri Lankan case, details for many of these proximate causes appear in the *Report of the Presidential Commission on Youth* (1990), as noted above.

[19] See for example Ted R. Gurr's *Why Men Rebel* (1970) and Charles Tilly *From Mobilisation to Revolution* (1978).

[20] See for example Harold R. Kerbo (1982: 646), and David Snyder and Charles Tilly (1972).

[21] See for example Ernest Duff et al. in *Violence and Repression in Latin America: A Quantitative and Historical Analysis* (1976), David Pion Berlin, 'Political Repression and Economic Doctrines: The Case of Argentina (1983), and Rudolf J. Rummel (1985).

[22] A recent text by Ted Gurr and Barbara Harff (1994) exemplifies this more eclectic, synthetic approach.

[23] Horowitz (1985) remains one of the most compelling statements of this view. Burcu Akan-Ellis' unpublished doctoral dissertation (2000) provides a more recent statement, focusing on the Turkish Diaspora in Macedonia, which includes a thorough review of recent literature.

[24] I have omitted Marxist theories' dialectical explanations from this discussion because of their differing position regarding proximate causes.

[25] This work is described in Richardson (1987a, 1987b, and 1991).

[26] Representative works from a voluminous literature include Forrester (1961, 1969, 1975), D.H. Meadows et al. (1972, 1992), and D.L. Meadows, et al. (1974). Sterman (2000) provides the most comprehensive survey of the field and its methodology.

[27] See Sterman (2000: chapter 4).

[28] Ibid: chapters 4 and 21.

[29] A number of the essays in Forrester (1975) emphasise this.

[30] More commonly, social scientists either compare a small number of cases, selected to highlight theoretically interesting similarities and differences, or they compare a very large number of cases, seeking to uncover statistically meaningful relationships.

Chapter Three Notes

[1] American University's School of International Service first established a Master of Arts program in International Development in 1982. Later, a Master of Science in Development Management degree was added. About 40 students receive degrees each year.

[2] Auroville is a 'city in the making' inspired by the vision of the Indian spiritual visionary, Sri Aurobindo and founded in 1968 by his 'spiritual collaborator,' known as 'The Mother.' The city is located on South India's Coromandel coast, near Pondicherry. Community members aim to become 'the first realisation of human unity,' based on Aurobindo's

teachings, 'where men of all countries would be at home.' Information (including the above quotations) is available at the Aurovillle website: <http://www.auroville.org/vision/background.htm>.

[3] See Zurcher (1984: 198-199) and Heinemann (1984: 222-223).

[4] See Wright (1958). *Islandia* was located on the 'Karian continent' in the South Pacific. Its economy was primarily agricultural, with families owning and living on the same farms for generations. Preservation of family ties and traditions were strong norms. In some ways, Islandian society resembles the Amish of the Eastern United States, though the Islandians accepted technology and higher education to a greater degree.

[5] Bellamy's work has appeared in many editions, most recently in *Looking Backward 2000-1887* (1995), edited with an introduction by Daniel H. Borus.

[6] I am indebted to Robert Fritz for introducing me to this approach in a workshop organised by the Massachusetts-based consulting firm Innovation Associates.

[7] For example, see Bennis (1989), Nanus (1992), and Senge (1990). The quotation comes from D.H. Meadows, et al. (1992: 224-225).

[8] See D.H. Meadows, et al. (1992).

[9] Ibid: 225-226.

[10] See <http://www.worldbank.org>, accessed December 1, 2001.

[11] See <http://www.undp.org/info/discover/mission.html>, accessed December 1, 2001.

[12] See <http://www.china.org.cn/e-china/development/introduction.htm>, accessed December 1, 2001.

[13] See J. Weaver, et al. (1997: chapter 3).

[14] See Griffin (1989).

[15] This is a fundamental principle in the applications-oriented disciplines of Operations Research and Systems Engineering. For example, see Simon (1981: especially chapters 1 and 5). There are significant implications for international development practice, explored very briefly here, that have received surprisingly little attention.

[16] See UNDP (1990). Then-UNDP Director William H. Draper III retained Mahbub ul-Haq – a former Pakistani cabinet minister and charismatic international development scholar/practitioner – as a Special Assistant for the purpose of producing this landmark first report. Interestingly, ul-Haq had previously served as the World Bank's Director of Policy Planning.

[17] See World Bank (2000: 274). I have abridged the definition slightly.

[18] See J. Weaver, et al. (1997: chapter 1, note 3)

[19] Sir Richard Stone is regarded by many as the father of national income accounting, and he received the 1984 Nobel Prize in Economics for this work. See Stone and Stone (1962).

[20] For example, see Kuznets (1965 and 1971).

[21] This critique of GNP-based performance measures mostly summarises Morris (1979: 7 -14).

[22] Several publications reporting on this work are summarised in Morris (1979: 114, note 77).

[23] Some of this story is told in the foreword of Morris (1979); however it is also based on my own personal experience. Jim Grant was a colleague in the U.S. Association for the Club of Rome at the time we were working on two projects together. Grant introduced me to Dr. Morris, who was on leave from the Jackson School of International Studies at the University of Washington.

[24] See Morris (1979: 21). A composite index typically uses some mathematical manipulations to aggregate incommensurable numerical indicators – such as literacy, life expectancy and infant mortality – into a single number. I briefly discuss below how the PQLI does this.

[25] See Morris (1979: 30). Literacy is measured as percentage of a country's population fifteen years or older with basic reading skills. Infant mortality is the number of infant deaths, per-thousand prior to age one. To avoid overlap with infant mortality, life expectancy is measured at year one (Ibid: 42-3).

[26] For example the lower bound, i.e. worst value of infant mortality was set at 229 and the upper bound or best value was set at 7. Values of the worst scoring country, Gabon (228), and the best scoring country, Sweden (8) provided the basis for this. Thus, Nigeria's infant mortality rate of 180 gave it an index value of 22. The United States' value of 16 gave it an index value of 96.

[27] Morris (1979: 61, 63).

[28] See Ibid: 61.

[29] These conclusions are presented in chapter 6 of Ibid, titled 'What Does the PQLI Show?'

[30] Morris returned to academic pursuits, though he continued to write and speak about the PQLI. John Sewell – who replaced James Grant as President of the Overseas Development Council – directed the organisation's priorities towards other agendas. In the 1990s, the ODC found it increasingly difficult to secure funding for its work, and it ceased operations on December 31, 2000.

[31] See UNDP (1990: 104-105), McGranihan et al. (1985), and OECD (1976).

[32] I participated in both relatively unsuccessful (Richardson and Forgette 1976 and 1979) and relatively successful (The Hunger Project 1985) efforts to craft development performance indices and can speak to these challenges from personal experience.

[33] Mendez (2001) tells this story briefly.

[34] This observation stems from personal experience. I had a collegial relationship with Jim Grant before he moved to UNICEF. I knew ul-Haq less well, but had the opportunity to hear him speak and interact with him personally on several occasions.

[35] See UNDP (1990: iii).

[36] See Ibid: 9.

[37] GNP per-capita figures for each nation were first adjusted to reflect cross-national differences in purchasing power of incomes equal in dollar value, using wealthier nations as a frame of reference. For example, this 'purchasing power parity' (PPP) adjustment corrects India's per-capita GNP upward to take into account that maintaining a decent standard of living in Chandigarh or Madras proves considerably less costly than maintaining the same standard of living in Tokyo or Geneva. Instead of using this value, however, the logarithm was used, considerably reducing values for wealthier countries. HDI designers argued that logged values would take the diminishing marginal utility of income into account – the fact that wealthy income-earners derived fewer benefits from increased increments of income than would poor and middle class earners. A disadvantage of this elegant scheme was that probably few consumers of the HDI understood, or do understand, it fully.

[38] See UNDP (1990: 13).

[39] For those interested in the details, the scheme can be simply illustrated by the best-case and worst-case indices for literacy deprivation, i.e. Japan and Somalia. Japan's 100 per cent rate of literacy was set as the 'best case' and Somalia's 12 per cent as the 'worst case.' The denominator of all indices for literacy deprivation was 88, i.e. Japan's best-case rate minus Somalia's worst-case rate. For Somalia, the numerator was 88, the best-case rate minus Somalia's literacy. For Japan, however, the numerator was zero, the best-case rate of 100 minus Japan's literacy. These calculations yielded a literacy deprivation index of zero – the theoretical minimum literacy deprivation – for Japan, and one – the theoretical maximum literacy deprivation – for Somalia.

[40] The rankings in this paragraph come from UNDP (1990: 130).

[41] The one Middle Eastern country classified with a high level of human development, Kuwait (#42), was invaded by Iraq (#54) in August 1990. Kuwait was liberated by a United States-led multinational coalition in March 1991.

[42] These exceptions were Bhutan (#118) and Nepal (#113). Among Sub-Saharan African countries, only South Africa (#62) was ranked in the 'medium human development' category.

[43] See UNDP (1990: 3).

[44] See World Bank (2000: 1). Three other 'lessons' followed: (1) Macroeconomic stability is an essential prerequisite for achieving the growth needed for development; (2) no one policy will trigger development, so a comprehensive approach is needed; and (3) institutions matter. Sustained development should be rooted in processes that are socially inclusive and responsive to changing circumstances.

[45] Williamson (1990) is usually cited as the author that coined this term.

[46] See Stiglitz (1998: 5).

[47] There are many examples of numerical indices in addition to GNP and GNP per-capita that people accept and understand in popular discourse. These include the Dow Jones Industrial Average and other stock indices, the consumer price index, the wind-chill factor, baseball batting averages, the air quality index ('code red' for dangerous ozone-concentration levels), and the logarithmic 'Richter Scale' for measuring earthquake intensity. Sailors heed a similar 'sea state' scale that measures the severity of waves produced by storms. Environmental scientists have recognised to a much greater degree than development scholar/practitioners the importance of indices that communicate effectively. The ideas of William A. Thomas, who led the Environmental Indices Group at Oak Ridge National Laboratory, exerted a particular influence in shaping my own thinking on this subject.

[48] I describe in my book *Partners in Development* (1969: especially chapters 2 and 3) how the philosophy and institutional structures of the Marshall Plan came to dominate foreign assistance in the United States.

[49] An Austrian colleague has told me that not long after World War II, in a time of great hardship, Viennese citizens had the opportunity to choose the city's first 'development' priority: Restoration of the State Opera House won the vote overwhelmingly.

[50] The early paragraphs of the *Human Development Report 1990*, which introduce the concept of 'human development,' are particularly revealing. Human development is defined, most broadly, as creation of an 'environment for people to enjoy long, healthy and creative lives.' Authorities cited to justify and elaborate this idea include Aristotle, Immanuel Kant, 'early leaders of quantification in economics' and 'the leading political economists.' The views of anthropologists and grass-roots activists who have lived with poor people and tried to understand what they want out of life – Oscar Lewis (1959; 1961) would be just one example – are not mentioned.

[51] My use of the term 'resident' rather than 'citizen' is not casual. The circumstances of development clearly affect citizens and non-citizens alike. The perceptions and attitudes of both enter into dynamics that determine the degree to which a country's society is conflict-ridden or tranquil.

[52] See J. Weaver et al. (1997) and Seligson and Passe-Smith, eds. (1998), for example.

[53] See Sterman (2000: 6).

[54] This policy was implemented in 1979, though the Chinese government had a strong prior commitment to family planning. For a brief synopsis of the policy from the perspective of an opposition, see the Life Coalition International website (accessed December 1, 2001): <http://www.forerunner.com/lci/X0004_Population_Control_C.html>.

[55] This was the subject of D.H. Meadows' 1988 essay considering 'Quality of Life' measurement.

[56] For basic primers, see *Whose Reality Counts: Putting the First Last* (Chambers 1997), *Encountering Development: The Making and Unmaking of the Third World* (Escobar 1995),

Empowerment: The Politics of Alternative Development (Friedman 1992), and *Getting to the 21ˢᵗ Century: Voluntary Action and the Global Agenda* (Korten 1999).

[57] See Sen's *Development as Freedom* (1999).

[58] For example see Diener and Suh (1999), Diener (1994), Frey and Stutzer (2002) and Helliwell (2002).

[59] Among many publications supporting this point of view, the Sri Lankan Government's *Report of the Presidential Commission on Youth* (1990) is, because of the extensive testimony taken from youth, one of the most compelling.

Chapter Four Notes

[1] For a brief description of the 1915 riots, see K.M. de Silva (1986: 60-64).

[2] Our luncheon took place, as I recall, in 1992.

[3] See Kemeny's *A Philosopher Looks at Science* (1959: chapter 8).

[4] A common experiment illustrates this. The subject places one hand in a bowl of hot water, then places the other in a bowl of water at room temperature. The water in the second bowl feels 'cold'. Now the subject places one hand in a bowl of cold water and the other in a bowl of room temperature water. The water in the second bowl feels 'hot.'

[5] Thomas S. Kuhn's classic work on *The Structure of Scientific Revolutions* (1962) describes this process.

[6] See Kemeny (1959), chapters 1 and 3. There have been extensive philosophical debates about the form and usefulness of operational definitions, but these need not concern us here.

[7] At the time I was making decisions about a violent political conflict index, Banks (1975), Taylor and Jodice (1986) and the database supporting Ted R. Gurr's 'Civil Violence Index' (1968) were among the most widely cited data sources. Among works that examined the problem of defining and measuring 'political violence,' variously defined, were Gurr and Ruttenberg (1969), Gurr and Duvall (1973), Hibbs (1973), Lichbach and Gurr (1979), Tilly (1978) and E. Muller (1980 and 1985). In addition, several scholars – for example Rummel (1963) and Feierabend and Feierabend (1966) had used factor analysis to reduce observable single components of violence to a smaller number of underlying dimensions.

[8] The approach is somewhat similar to the use of 'events data' to measure hostility-friendliness between nations, pioneered by the late Edward Azar (1986 and 1993). See also Azar and Ben-Dak (1975).

[9] Twelve Sri Lankans assisted me in collecting, recording, and coding the data. Because universities were on strike, a number of very talented students were available. As indicated in my notes for chapter 1, although I did not specifically seek ethnic diversity when hiring assistants, members of the Sinhalese, Tamil, Muslim and Burgher communities were all represented. One team member was of Indian descent.

[10] A copy of the Sri Lankan Political Conflict Data Base is available at the International Centre for Ethnic Studies, Kandy. A copy has also been provided to the National Archives of Sri Lanka, Colombo, however I am uncertain of its availability. It should be available on the internet by the time this book is released. Contact the author at jrich@american. edu for details. Data was collected from the newspaper files of the National Archives, the Peradeniya University Library, and the International Centre for Ethnic Studies, Kandy.

[11] 'Sri Lanka: Now Terror in the South.' *Asia Week*, January 22, 1988: 12.

[12] This is the translation of a report on the Anuradhapura massacre of May 14, 1985 from LTTE files quoted in R. Gunaratna (1987: 42-44).

[13] Over time the instructions were refined and revised, based on our experiences working with the data. This description is the final product.

[14] Kacheries are multi-purpose government offices.

[15] SLTB is the Sri Lanka Transport Board, the government agency that runs buses and trains.

[16] If in doubt, I included the event.

[17] *Satyagraha* is the name for the non-violent demonstrations popularised by the Indian nationalist leader, Mahatma Gandhi.

[18] Sorokin (1937: 383).

[19] See Buckle's *History of Civilisation in England* (1861), Spengler's *The Decline of the West* (1929), and Toynbee's *A Study of History* (1935).

[20] See Sorokin (1937: 384-85).

[21] In my previous work with the index, events were coded on a yearly basis. Sorokin, whose work covered a much longer time horizon, coded events only once, so the duration code assumed greater significance.

[22] Sorokin uses the concept 'intensity' to describe this dimension. I prefer to use intensity to describe what the magnitude of the index measures overall. Thus it seems clearer to label this dimension as 'severity.'

[23] I also scored the 'hartals' or general strikes imposed by militant groups -- the LTTE in the north and the JVP in the South -- as 4 because the prime movers of such events were a group less than 5,000, even though many more people were affected.

[24] The geometric mean is the fourth root of the product of the 4 individual scores.

[25] Consider two different sets of values for a four-dimension index. The first has values of 1, 1, 1, 97; total = 100. The second has values of 25, 25, 25, 25; total = 100. The arithmetic mean of both sets would be 25. The geometric mean of the second set would be 25. But the geometric mean of the first would be just slightly larger than 3, while the mean of the second would still be 25.

[26] See Duff et al. (1976: 24-42): The authors use the terms *repression* and *official violence* interchangeably for what I call state-sanctioned violence.

[27] Ibid: 31.

[28] Ibid: 32.

[29] Ibid: 33.

[30] Ibid: 36.

[31] See K.M. de Silva (1986: 340).

[32] Duff et al. (1976: 38).

[33] More recently, several independent television stations have been permitted to broadcast and there is some access to CNN in major markets. Television is now widely available, with at least some coverage even in most rural areas.

Chapter Five Notes

[1] The 2000 online edition of the *Oxford English Dictionary*, accessed January 12, 2001 from http://dictionary.oed.com), defines 'mahout' as '[i]n South Asia: an elephant driver.' The root of the term is the Sanskrit *mahamatra*, meaning 'high official, elephant keeper,' and the Hindi *mahaut* or *mahavat*. The plural is 'mahouts.'

[2] Namboodiri's *Practical Elephant Management: A Handbook for Mahouts* (1998) is a complex encyclopaedic document that covers, among other topics, elephant evolutionary history, physiology, diseases, psychology, sensitive points, sensitive regions, inauspicious signs and auspicious signs. This 'book knowledge' moreover represents only a portion of the mahout's knowledge about his animal.

[3] Two mahouts comprise a team, the less experienced 'ground mahout,' who walks alongside the animal with a prod, and the more experienced 'neck mahout' who, as his title suggests, rides astride.

[4] One might even draw an analogy between heads of government and the 'neck mahout,' while security officials and technocrats would correspond more to the 'ground mahout.'

[5] This view of decision making reflects my own work applying control theoretic concepts to social systems (Richardson and Pelsoci 1972; Richardson 1974) but also draws upon the Carnegie School of organisation theory that dates from Herbert Simon's classic, *Administrative Behaviour* (1945). For a contemporary statement by a leading systems analyst, see Sterman (2000: 597-660).

[6] Chapter 3 described the superiority of democracies as error-correction mechanisms.

[7] Chapter 2 touched briefly upon this concept.

[8] Nancy Roberts et al. (1982: 11-86) provides a clear, non-technical description of causal loops and causal loop diagramming, with numerous examples. Sterman (2000: 135-229)

provides a more technically elegant description, along with numerous examples. The labels 'reinforcing' and 'counteracting,' replacing the more widely used, but often confusing 'positive' and 'negative' labels for feedback loops come from Sterman (2000).

[9] See Sterman (2000: 13).

[10] The strengths and limitations of 'mental models' in comparison with computer models are discussed in D. H. Meadows et al. (1992: 9-12).

[11] See Forrester (1975: 220).

[12] See Forrester (1969: 110-111); Sterman (2000: 5-14).

[13] See Sterman (2000: 10)

[14] This theme is developed in my paper, 'Systems Engineering and Political Science: Toward Symbiosis' (1974).

[15] Most readers will find it easy to visualise biological organisms and space stations as complex systems, but visualising a city in this way may be more difficult. Mesarovic and Reisman (1972) and Forrester (1969) provide good illustrations. The latter work uses the System Dynamics methodology, discussed more fully below.

[16] A flight simulator became the basis for the first widely used general-purpose computer, designed by Forrester; see Redmond and Smith (1980).

[17] Forrester's own collected papers (1975) provide the best recapitulation of the System Dynamics outlook's early history, and of the philosophy that still guides most practitioners. D. H. Meadows and Robinson (1985: chapter 2) provides a concise description of the approach's basic principles. The most complete and up to date treatment is Sterman (2000).

[18] See Forrester (1975: 215).

[19] I touched upon this point in chapter 2 when I emphasised the importance of context in system dynamics modelling.

[20] By 'robustness,' I mean the ability of the economy to respond to shocks – such as the oil price shocks of the 1970s or the terrorist strikes of September 11, 2001 – without seriously degrading output and efficiency.

[21] In most countries, however, parties have a core of die-hard supporters who maintain their allegiance, no matter what.

[22] Because elections confer a degree of legitimacy, voters often go to the polls in authoritarian regimes as well, but such elections communicate little in the way of feedback.

[23] Non-democratic systems may partially mimic some democratic practices; however, 'election results' communicate little or no useful information.

[24] Such manipulations are accepted practices not only in Global South nations, but also in developed nations such as the United States. The term 'gerrymandering,' the redrawing of legislative boundaries for political advantage, owes its origins to the redistricting shenanigans of the U.S. state of Massachusetts Governor Elbridge Gerry in 1812. One

of the irregular districts Gerry created had the shape of a salamander. 'You should call it a Gerrymander,' one wag supposedly commented, and the term became part of political vocabularies.

[25] In December 2001 Congressional testimony, U.S. Attorney General John Ashcroft seemed to imply that those who questioned new security procedures established by the Department of Justice were giving aid and comfort to America's enemies.

[26] See Azar (1990: 1-17).

[27] The circumstances surrounding Hong Kong, the fourth 'Asian Tiger,' seem less generalisable.

[28] 'State security forces' is used broadly to include any agents of repression – for example party apparatchiks and paramilitaries – used by the government.

[29] During the 1970s, I had the opportunity to work with a number of Soviet bloc scientists, economists and engineers, who were resident scholars or temporary visitors at the Vienna-based International Institute for Applied Systems Analysis (IIASA). One of the striking differences between their work and that of Western sciences was the range of basic economic data that was viewed as politically sensitive. This included most national accounts, government budget and human development data, and much ecological data as well. Not only did this make policy modelling difficult, it must also have made it extraordinarily difficult for Soviet leaders to obtain accurate information on which to base their decisions.

[30] The work of Theda Skocpol and her students (1994) show why violent revolutions are almost always succeeded by more repressive regimes than those overthrown.

[31] This definition was accessed December 12, 2001 from the *Oxford English Dictionary Online* (<http://dictionary.oed.com>).

[32] One of my lasting impressions from several hours of interviews with Sri Lanka's late President came from his response when I questioned the advisability of sending poorly-trained, ill-equipped Sinhala-speaking military detachments to 'restore order' in the Tamil-speaking North. 'I was the President,' Jayewardene responded. 'The security of the state was threatened. This was the army that I had, so I sent them.'

[33] Pandora, the 'all-giving' became the first woman in Greek mythology. She opened the box in which Zeus had placed 'all manner of misery and evil.' In some versions, 'hope' remained in the box. See 'Pandora' in the Encyclopædia Britannica Online, accessed December 12, 2001 at http://www.search.eb.com.

Chapter Six Notes

[1] Of course before August 1947 India and Pakistan, plus a collection of princely states, were 'crown jewels' of the British Empire. The rioting that followed partition became one of the first 'ethnic conflicts' of the post-war era and, in terms of innocent lives lost, one of the most tragic. The British Raj, though it had redeeming features, was an elitist, racist

dictatorship over a subject people, characterised by little feedback from ruled to rulers. Many share complicity for the partition riots, but decades of imperial rule set the stage.

[2] See *Ceylon Daily News*, September 20, 1948: 3 and *Times of Ceylon*, July 4, 1949: 10. The two events in Kurunegala district were reported nearly a year later, when the UNP cadre was convicted in court of killing the Communist Party supporter. The political motive for the killing was established in the proceedings.

[3] The composite score is the geometric mean of the four scores for each event. A more detailed description of scoring procedures appears in chapter 4.

[4] For purposes of easy comparison, this and subsequent charts describing individual periods up to 1984 will be scaled in the range from zero to 100.

[5] See *Ceylon Daily News*, July 1, 1954: 1.

[6] A residual 'miscellaneous' category, comprising about 8 per cent of the total events, has been excluded.

[7] See K.M. de Silva (1981: 131, ff. and 1986: 449, ff.). The document, known as the 'Minister's Draft Constitution,' was prepared by a working committee of the Ceylon National Congress under the leadership of J.R. Jayewardene and J.A.L. Cooray.

[8] See Hulugalle (2000), especially chapter 20. Jennings was Vice Chancellor of Peradeniya University, then regarded as one of the finest institutions of higher education in Asia. According to his biographer, Senanayake's role in the drafting was minimised by some because he lacked formal education. However Richards asserts that he was the prime mover, though he relied on others for counsel.

[9] See K.M. de Silva (1986: 131). One half of the Senate members were named by the House, the remainder by the Governor General. To protect minorities, provision was made for up to six additional House members to be nominated by the head of state 'where he considers that any important interest was not adequately represented.'

[10] See Hulugalle (2000); K.M. de Silva (1986: chapter 9); K.M. de Silva and Wriggins (1988: chapter 14); K.M. de Silva (1981: 490); and Manor (1989: 161, ff.).

[11] See K.M. de Silva (1986: 152-154). The First Delimitation Commission established 86 single member constituencies, three constituencies returning two members and one, Colombo Central, returning three members.

[12] See Ibid: 130. The provision is found in section 29(2) of the Soulbury Constitution.

[13] See K.M. de Silva (1986: 155). *The Ceylon Citizenship Act No. 18 of 1948* restricted the status of a national Sri Lankan to those who could claim it by descent or registration. Procedures for claiming citizenship were defined in *The Indian and Pakistani Residents (Citizenship) Act No. 3 of 1949. The Ceylon (Parliamentary Elections) Amendment Act (No. 48 of 1949)* removed voters of Indian origin from the electoral rolls.

[14] The influential role of the Bandaranaike family in Sri Lankan life is sensitively told in Yasmine Gooneratne's autobiographical retrospective, *Relative Merits: A Personal Memoir of the Bandaranaike Family of Sri Lanka* (1986).

[15] See Manor (1989: 168).

[16] See Manor (1989: 199, ff.).

[17] See K.M. de Silva (1986: 157) and Manor (1989: 204).

[18] See Wriggins (1960: 250). D.S. Senanayake's failing health was known to close confidants as early as January. This initiated a series of meetings to plan for the succession and to ensure the designation of his son as Prime Minister.

[19] The flamboyant Sir John Kotelawala, who later succeeded Dudley Senanayake as Prime Minister, was the other candidate.

[20] See K.M. de Silva (1986: 156, ff.); K.M. de Silva and Wriggins (1988: 18); and Manor (1989: 209, ff.).

[21] See Manor (1989: 215). Detailed election statistics are found in G.P.S.H. de Silva, *A Statistical Survey of Elections to the Legislatures of Sri Lanka, 1911-1977* (1979). Dr. de Silva's meticulously compiled volume was an invaluable resource throughout the writing of this book.

[22] See Manor (1989: 220). Most noteworthy was a massive demonstration on Galle Face Green, across from the Parliament Building, led by S.W.R.D. Bandaranaike himself. The demonstration is said to have drawn over 200,000 people, up to that time one of the largest crowds ever assembled on the island.

[23] See Manor (1989: 221). Sri Lanka's Marxist parties orchestrated the general strike -- see below. The major work stoppage occurred on August 12 and some activity continued for several days. Bandaranaike, who tried to present himself as a moderate, did not endorse the *hartal*. However he certainly benefited from it politically.

[24] Sir John's autobiography (1956) tells his side of the story.

[25] See K.M. de Silva (1956: 73). Sinhalese communal groups – Sinhalese school teachers, Ayurvedic or traditional physicians, Sinhalese writers and peasants – federated in a new organisation, the *Pancha Maha Bala Mandalaya*, to promote Sinhala as the sole official language and state support for the Buddhist religion.

[26] See K.M. de Silva (1986: 173).

[27] See K.M. de Silva and Wriggins (1988: 302).

[28] See K.M. de Silva (1986: 174, ff).

[29] See Manor (1989: 243).

[30] See Wriggins (1960: 130). Some argued that the Marxist leaders, many trained at the London School of Economics, 'were the only ones who really understood economics.' In the next administration, some of these men would be given the opportunity to put their theories of economic development into practice.

[31] See Moore (1985: 45-48).

[32] See Karunatilake (1987: 139, ff).

[33] See Moore (1985: 50, ff.) and Karunatilake (1987: 61).

[34] See K.M. de Silva and Wriggins (1988: 216). Unfortunately, this system continued to emphasise 'liberal arts, skills of clerkship and white collar employment.'

[35] See Karunatilake (1987: 206).

[36] See Snodgrass (1966: 84). Deaths per thousand in the population dropped from 19.7 during the period from 1940-44 to 11.6 for the 1950-54 period. Mosquito eradication, an emphasis on public health, and the wide availability of primary health care services throughout the island all contributed to this change.

[37] See Karunatilake (1987: 140). Despite the UNP commitment to private sector industrial development, fledgling industries in areas of great need were first established as government departments. In 1954, legislation was passed to convert these industries to semi-public corporations, but this was resisted by politicians and not fully implemented prior to the general election.

[38] See Snodgrass (1966: 200, ff.) and Karunatilake (1987: 35-41).

[39] Jayewardene lost his Finance portfolio, though he was given a new position in the Cabinet as Agriculture Minister. The experience made a lifetime impression on him.

[40] See K.M. de Silva (1986b: 77, ff.). Senanayake's opposition to making Sinhala the nation's official language – proposed by J.R. Jayewardene as early as 1943 – reflected Senanayake's view that Sri Lanka needed a 'linking' language to maintain communication between the nation's majority Sinhalese and minority Tamil/Tamil-speaking Muslim communities.

[41] Peebles (1982) provides an invaluable compilation through about 1980. More recent data is available from reports published by Sri Lanka's Central Bank.

[42] To facilitate comparisons, the three trajectory measures have all been indexed, with 1948 as the base year. The index values of economic data are also adjusted for inflation.

[43] See C.R. de Silva (1977). In 1955, 2,061 students sat for the university entrance examinations; and of these, 658 or 32 per cent gained admission.

[44] W. Howard Wriggins' classic study, *Ceylon: Dilemmas of a New Nation* (1960) and Marshall Singer's study of Sri Lanka's 'emerging elite' (1964) were among the works that presented a more nuanced view. Both appeared after the pivotal 1956 general election, however.

[45] On the UNP's founding and organisation, see K.M. de Silva (1986: 155, ff.), Wriggins (1960: 106, ff.), A.J. Wilson (1974: 130, ff.); and Manor (1989: 168, ff.).

[46] See Wriggins (1960: 113). In the post colonial period of UNP Cabinets, no more than three of the 11-12 Sinhalese posts were given to men of non-*Goyagama* castes.

[47] See Ibid: 113-116. The author notes that '[a]ccording to the party's constitution, the working committee was elected by the executive committee, a larger body composed of 25 members elected at the annual conference by the party's MPs, and by members representing each electoral association or party branch. Over a thousand delegates, (in theory) sent by the different party branches attended the annual conference each year. Its decision making power was small. In only one instance has a real disagreement been aired

at the annual conference.' See also K.M. de Silva and Wriggins (1988) and Manor (1989: 204, ff.).

[48] See Wriggins (1960: 106, ff.) and Manor (1989: 177). In the 1947 election, several seats were contested by multiple candidates identifying themselves as UNP supporters.

[49] See Wriggins (1960: 106-108).

[50] See Ibid: 124, ff. and Wilson (1974). Among the most outstanding of this group were N.M. Perera, Colvin R. de Silva, Leslie Goonewardene and Dr. S.A. Wickremasinghe. The *doyen* of the movement, Philip Gunewardena, had studied first at the University of Wisconsin, but then visited England in 1928 where he became acquainted with leaders of the British Communist Party.

[51] Among the larger factions contesting elections during this period were the Bolshevik Leninist Party of India; the Bolshevik Samasamaja Party or 'Bolshevik Equal Society Party;' the Communist Party, allied with Moscow; the Labor Party; the Lanka Sama Samaja Party or 'Ceylon Equal Society Party;' the United Left Front; and the Viplavakari or Revolutionary Lanka Sama Samaja Party. Of these, the Trotskyist LSSP has commanded the largest support among Sri Lankan voters. Wriggins (1960: 151, ff.) provides the best discussion of these factions that is generally available.

[52] See, for example, Ibid: 132, ff. N.M. Perera served as a popular and effective mayor of Colombo in the 1950s and strongly influenced the young Ranasinghe Premadasa, who later became Sri Lanka's President. Colvin R. de Silva, an 'old boy' of Colombo's prestigious Royal College, was a respected lawyer and orator. Communist Party leader Pieter Keuneman, a former President of the Oxford Union, also became an effective speaker at mass rallies in urban areas as well as in Parliamentary debates.

[53] An exception was Tamil plantation workers, who lost their citizenship and voting rights in 1949.

[54] See Wriggins (1960: 132, 142).

[55] See especially K.M. de Silva (1986: 161, ff.).

[56] The LSSP contested 39 seats in the 1952 general election at its high point. It contested 28 and 21 seats, respectively, in the 1947 and 1956 general elections. In 1956, LSSP leaders negotiated a no-contest with S.W.R.D. Bandaranaike's MEP coalition.

[57] See Manor (1989: 118).

[58] Ibid: 128 and K.M. de Silva (1986: 65).

[59] Manor (1989: 129) quotes Bandaranaike's speeches published in the *Ceylon Daily News* of November 18, 23, and 25, 1937 and May, 1938.

[60] Ibid: 191, ff. and Wriggins (1960: 120-21).

[61] Ibid: 122-23 and Manor (1989: 227, ff.).

[62] Ibid: 227-239.

[63] See K.M. de Silva (1986: 161, ff.). Manor (1960: 127) states that the first politician approached by the revivalists to lead their movement was Dudley Senanyake, regarded as

a more authentic Buddhist and a more trustworthy advocate of the rural Sinhalese. Only when Senanyake refused did revivalists turn to Bandaranaike.

[64] Ibid: 208, ff.

[65] See Wriggins (1960: 337).

[66] 'Ayurvedic medicine is the oldest comprehensive system of medicine and served as the basis for many that followed. Like Chinese medicine, it combines natural therapies with a highly personalised, holistic approach to the treatment of disease. It treats the whole person, addressing body, mind, and spirit.' Quoted from the Platelet Disorder Support Association website <http://www.itppeople.com/ayurvedi.htm>, accessed December 18, 2001.

[67] See Wriggins (1960: 339-341).

[68] Ibid: 347. As noted, '[t]he high priests of the largest sect on the island called upon their members to refrain from political campaigning and to remain neutral during the election. They were joined by the acting head of the Ramayana sect in the low-country and by the principals of the most important *bhikkhu* training colleges.'

[69] Among these was Mapitagama Buddharakkita, the chief *bhikkhu* of the Kelanaya temple, who later would be implicated in S.W.R.D. Bandaranaike's assassination.

[70] See K.M. de Silva (1986: 174-75) and Wriggins (1960: 344).

[71] Ibid: 347.

[72] K.M. de Silva (1986: 208-10) discusses the divergent political traditions represented by these two Tamil leaders.

[73] See Wilson (1988: 71, ff.). A complete listing of Cabinet members until 1978 appears in G.P.S.H. de Silva (1979: 307, ff.). Ponnambalam became one of two Tamil members in Senanyake's cabinet. The second was the independent MP, C. Sittampalam.

[74] See Wilson (1988: 76). For a view of these events from an Indian Tamil perspective, see Sabaratnam (1990). Wilson is harshly critical of Ponnambalam's role during this period and praises the integrity of his father in law, Chelvanayakam. Both Wriggins (1960) and K.M. de Silva (1981, 1986) view Ponnambalam's role more positively.

[75] See K.M. de Silva (1986: 198). The claim that the Eastern Province, in which Tamils were a minority, was part of a 'traditional homeland' was anathema to most Sinhalese.

[76] See Wriggins (1960: 146).

[77] Kearney (1971) provides an excellent survey of Sri Lanka's trade-union movement from the time of independence through about 1970. V.K. Jayawardena (1972) discusses historical antecedents of trade unionism in Sri Lanka.

[78] A detailed breakdown of the composition of Sri Lanka's labour force during this period appears in Snodgrass (1966: 322). Peebles (1982: 102-103) provides a useful series on the estate labour force.

[79] Kearney (1971: 16) reports trade-union membership figures based on compulsory annual reports to the Commissioner of Labour. The numbers reported here round-

off those figures. The growth in trade unionism was fostered in part by government regulations and programs intended to help wage earners, including wages boards for setting minimum wages and industrial courts with the power to require compulsory arbitration of some labour disputes.

[80] For discussions of the C.W.C., see Sabaratnam (1990), Kearney (1971: 120, ff.), Wriggins (1960: 154-55), and Wilson (1974: 165-66).

[81] On the Marxist Unions, see particularly Kearney (1971), chapters 5 and 6.

[82] Ibid: chapter 6.

[83] For example, unions played a major role in organising support for the successful *hartal* of August 1953, which led to the resignation of Prime Minister Dudley Senanyake. See Manor (1989: 220, ff.).

[84] Sir John Kotelewala was one UNP leader apparently willing to resort to extra-legal violence. For example, with regard to the 1954 visit of the Queen of England to Sri Lanka, Kotelewala later wrote, 'Marxist elements tried to prevent the visit. ...One of their leaders came to me shortly before the event and asked for an assurance that those who demonstrated against the visit with black flags and in other ways would not be taken to police stations. I told him I had given instructions that they should be taken, not to police stations, but hospitals.' See Kotelewala (1956: 112), quoted in K.M. de Silva and Wriggins (1988: 287).

[85] The criterion is 'extremist' groups with less than ten per cent of adult population as a following are not allowed to run candidates and legally organise political parties. As noted, this is probably stretching the point, though a politically mobilised Indian Tamil population was seen an 'extremist' threat by D.S. Senanayake's government.

[86] See Wilson (1974: 273). By 1947, 5,380 men had entered service. Twenty years later, the number had doubled to 11,323.

[87] This resulted partly from the British policy of recruiting security-force officers from minority groups, but more from the fact that members of these groups were far more likely to speak fluent English than the average Sinhalese-Buddhist. The ethnic composition of the security forces became a political issue for the SLFP and its supporters.

[88] See Wriggins (1960: 150, ff.) and Nyrop (1971: 468, ff.).

[89] Manor (1989: 224) notes that Sir John Kotelawala used labourers from his graphite mines as a private force to intimidate opponents throughout his political career. Many incidents of political conflict involved squads of 'goondas' or 'thugs,' especially during political meetings and campaigns.

[90] During World War II, Trincomalee served as a major naval base for the British Fleet. Later, it became a major petroleum storage area. Tamil nationalists envision it as a prosperous free port which could compete with Colombo, Singapore and Hong Kong.

[91] See K.M. de Silva (1986: 210-216; 1987). The picture is further complicated by the fact that Tamil is the primary language of many of the region's Muslims, although they do not consider themselves 'Tamil.'

[92] The UNP won 38 per cent of the vote total in 1947 and increased its vote share to 41 per cent in 1952.

[93] In later years, they would contest and win some seats.

Chapter Seven Notes

[1] 'National dress' for men includes a white sarong and high-necked long sleeved shirt, worn untucked. Some of my Sri Lankan friends call this attire 'politician's dress.'

[2] See Manor (1989: 255). Like many other promises, the Government could not fulfill this commitment. The Governor General, UNP stalwart Sir Oliver Goonetilleke, could not read Sinhala well enough to give a speech in it, even with a text in Roman letters rather than Sinhala script.

[3] Ibid.

[4] Biographer James Manor (1989) offers a more complex view, rendering Bandaranaike as well-intentioned but weak, expedient and politically unskilled.

[5] A discussion of the pact follows later in this chapter.

[6] Even if Bandaranaike had not fallen to an assassin, it would have become necessary to hold general elections in 1960.

[7] I scale the UNP numbers to account for a term of office that ran approximately 14 months shorter.

[8] In chapters 4 and 6, I have already emphasised the elements of judgement involved in identifying, scaling and categorising conflict incidents. I introduce another simplification here by including in this compilation incidents occurring during Dudley Senanayake's 'interregnum government' of approximately four months.

[9] Later in this chapter, I provide a more-detailed consideration of Federal Party leaders and policies.

[10] For example, Piyadasa (1984: especially chapter 4) argues from a Marxist perspective that Bandaranaike also used communalism to divert attention from the basically elitist composition of Sri Lankan politics and society, including the SLFP.

[11] This view of Bandaranaike differs from Manor (1989), but agrees with interviews I have conducted of both supporters and critics of the late Prime Minister.

[12] Manor uses the term 'Arbiter' to describe the years of Bandaranaike's Prime Ministership (1989: 254-318).

[13] Ibid: 259.

[14] Ibid: 261.

[15] Attributed to M. Sivasthaparam of the Tamil Congress; see Ponnambalam (1983: 101).

[16] See Manor (1989: 267, ff.), K.M. de Silva (1986: 181-184), and Ponnambalam (1983: 107-114).

[17] Manor (1989: 269-270).

[18] Ibid: 269.

[19] See Vittachi (1958) and Manor (1989: 287, ff.). Eravur town, where the first incident occurred, and Polonnaruwa town, where the violence first spread, both lie on the rail line from Batticaloa to Colombo.

[20] Not all the burnings and lootings had communal motivations. In this and subsequent riots, communal strife sometimes provided cover for gaining an advantage over business rivals.

[21] According to K.M. de Silva (1986: 196) the term *Sasana* 'was one of infinite flexibility, encompassing as it did the institutions, property, including monastic lands and the rights, obligations, duties and privileges of the bhikkhus...It had something to satisfy everybody: advocates of institutional reform could regard it as a mandate for modernisation; adherents of the *status quo* were encouraged to believe there was no inherent incompatibility between their interests and those of the reformers. The task ...was the unenviable one of reconciling these obviously conflicting interests.'

[22] Drawn from Section 29(c); See K.M. de Silva (1986: 197).

[23] See Manor (1989: 321).

[24] See G.P.S.H. de Silva (1979: 67-69) and Wilson (1974: 190). In the 151 constituencies, 146 MPs came from 140-single member constituencies, four two-member constituencies, and one three-member constituency. The Government retained the practice of appointing six Members of Parliament to represent minority interests. The Joint Parliamentary Select Committee on Constitutional Reform, which proposed the constitutional amendment, made other recommendations, but the acrimony over official language policy and decentralisation of power diverted attention from broader reform issues.

[25] Ibid: 230.

[26] See Manor (1989: 263-4). Conservatives became frustrated by the Prime Minister's equivocation on social policies they favoured, including prohibition of the sales of alcohol; banning of gambling and horse racing; and major funding for programs to encourage Sinhalese culture.

[27] See K.M. de Silva (1981: 524). C.P. de Silva, Minister of Lands and Land Development, H.W. de Silva, Minister of Industries and Fisheries and Philip R. Goonewardene, Minister of Agriculture and Food, had the Prime Minister's respect for their 'intellectual ability, their administrative skills, their sense of priorities and purposeful approach, and above all their integrity.' Because the SLFP had just recently organised, attracting large numbers of political outsiders, Bandaranaike had difficulty finding competent ministers from among the ranks of his supporters to fill cabinet posts.

[28] This discussion draws largely from the two principal works on Sri Lanka's foreign policy, Kodikara (1982) and Nissanka (1984). K.M. de Silva (1981: 521) argues that

Bandaranaike has received more credit than his due for changes in foreign policy, when these adjustments mainly reflected changes in Sri Lanka's political life and its external political environment.

[29] See Wilson (1974: 297). Bandaranaike could demonstrate flexibility and avoid confrontation, however. He arranged for a 'generous financial settlement' when the military installations at Katunayake and Trincomalee transferred to Sri Lankan control in 1957 at the conclusion of the Mutual Defence Agreement with Britain. 'Never mind Sir,' he said to Sir Oliver Goonetilleke, who protested over the size of the settlement, adding that 'they have been very good friends of Sri Lanka and will continue to be so.'

[30] See Manor (1989: 316). Sonarama had conspired with a bitter personal enemy of Bandaranaike, the Venerable Mapitagama Buddharakkita, High Priest of Kelaniya Temple. Many believe that the Prime Minister's opposition to one of Buddharakkita's commercial ventures factored into the plot.

[31] Ibid: 315-316. Bandaranaike's statement appeared in the *Ceylon Daily News* on September 26, 1959.

[32] Seneviratne (1975: 179).

[33] Ibid: chapters 1-6. Located in the southernmost part of the old Kandyan Kingdom, Sabaragamuwa is one of Sri Lanka's most remote and sparsely populated provinces.

[34] Ibid: 43.

[35] Ibid: 65-66. Ms. Seneviratne's biography provides an official, or at least approved, version of the Prime Minister's life. One searches in vain for a critical word about either Mrs. Bandaranaike or her husband. However the book proves useful – apart from its presentation of personal detail – for its clear picture of how Mrs. Bandaranaike might want to see her life conveyed for public consumption. Interestingly in this regard, the reader notes that descriptions of Mrs. Bandaranaike's concern for Sri Lanka's 'common people' seem to refer only to the Sinhalese, with no mention of the minority Tamils, even though Tamil tea plantation workers comprised a substantial fraction of the old Kandyan kingdom's population. One must presume that problems involving Sri Lanka Tamils of the north and east and the Indian Tamil plantation workers sometimes merited discussion in the Ratwatte household of her youth, and even in the secluded precincts of St. Bridget's.

[36] See K.M. de Silva (1981: 525). After the delimitation of 1959, the Kandyans – with 26 per cent of the island's population – controlled 42 per cent of the elected parliamentary seats.

[37] Seneviratne (1975: 81) quotes Malini Wijeratne's *The Marriage Customs of Ceylon: Times Annual.* Wijeratne notes that '[a] husband...should treat his wife with respectful attention, his language to her should be courteous and affectionate, he should not illicitly consort with other women, should cause her to be honoured by others, and furnish with suitable ornaments and apparel.'

[38] Manor (1989: 323) quotes the following recollection from *The Sun* (Colombo, September 7, 1978) noting that while possibly overblown, 'by most accounts it accurately

captures the relationship between the premier and his wife, as well as his ebullient insensitivity:'

> One day he [Bandaranaike] noticed that there was a delay in the tea being served and his stentorian voice rose above the murmur of voices: 'Sirima'.
>
> A coy figure appeared at the doorway and asked: 'Why?'
>
> Mr. Bandaranaike said: 'What about the tea?'
>
> A while later, tea was served. But Mr. Bandaranaike, the shrewd observer that he was, noticed something wrong and once again the stentorian voice rose: 'Sirima'.
>
> A shy figure appeared at the door again. 'These gentlemen', he explained, 'drink tea with sugar. For the sugar to get into the cup, there must be some instrument. You have not put a spoon in the sugar bowl.'
>
> And the dutiful wife went to fetch a spoon and Mr. Bandaranaike quipped: 'We have to think for them too.'

[39] See Seneviratne (1975: 175). 'He even went to the extent of negotiating with strikers, a method I am implacably opposed to and would never permit,' Mrs. Bandaranaike later told her biographer, adding that '[a]t times, his kindness was taken for weakness by designing people who tried to exploit him.'

[40] Unlike her husband, Mrs. Bandaranaike did not relish the hours of political discussion with all comers. Instead, she took advice primarily from a small group of family members, especially her brothers and nephew. According to de K.M. de Silva and Wriggins (1994: 74-75), 'It was as if she had built a moat between herself and her cabinet colleagues, her MPs and political associates alike, and left the drawbridge in charge of her family. Unfortunately, the family members who were her close advisers, like Mrs. Bandaranaike herself, had little practical political experience and no experience or training in the all-important area of economics.'

[41] See K.M. de Silva (1986). The *Tamil Language (Special Provisions) Act*, which S.W.R.D. Bandaranaike had steered through Parliament after the 1958 riots, called for the Prime Minister to promulgate specific regulations to give it effect. Mrs. Bandaranaike would not promulgate such regulations, delaying implementation of the Act's provisions until 1966, during the term of her successor Dudley Senanayake.

[42] See Horowitz (1980: 113): 'The resentment among artillery officers and men at this decision was keen. A sit-down strike at the railway station was narrowly averted when [the commanding officer] personally appealed to his unit to move out without him.'

[43] See Kearney (1967: 113-114).

[44] For a discussion of secondary-school nationalisation, see K.M. de Silva (1986: 200-02) and (1981: 527-28).

[45] See Wilson (1974: 144).

[46] Details of the coup appear in *Dawasa*, (January 29, 1962), and Somasundaram (1992).

[47] In a book based on extensive interviews (1980), Horowitz discusses the motives of the conspirators in detail. 'They were mostly Christians,' he notes, 'and their ideology was in some ways conservative, but they were above all, cosmopolitans, men who believed that the increasing use of segmental affiliations to judge people was part – although only part – of what was deeply wrong with Mrs. Bandaranaike's government.'

[48] See K.M. de Silva (1981: 529) and Wilson (1974: 144).

[49] In deference to Buddhist sensibilities about gambling, the government outlawed the highly popular sport of horse racing in 1964. However, this symbolic gesture had little effect in a nation of inveterate gamblers.

[50] See Kodikara (1982: 34-35); K.M. de Silva (1986: 222-25): Dudley Senanayake first proposed the basic formula – distinguishing three categories of Indian Tamils – to Pandit Nehru at a 1953 conference of Commonwealth Prime Ministers in London.

[51] See Nissanka (1984: 69-71).

[52] See K.M. de Silva (1981: 532-33).

[53] Ibid: 532. A U.S. foreign-assistance amendment, authored by Senator Bourke Hickenlooper (R-Iowa) required termination of aid to countries that nationalised the assets of American companies without compensation.

[54] K.M. de Silva emphasises continuity in Sri Lanka's foreign policy. Nissanka (1984) and especially Kodikara (1982) place greater emphasis on the differences between the Bandaranaikes' foreign policy and that of predecessor UNP governments.

[55] *Dawasa* (May 25, 1962: 1).

[56] For an account of the fall of Mrs. Bandaranaike's government and the general election of 1965, see Wilson (1974: 137, ff.).

[57] See Seneviratne (1975: 195).

[58] Karunatilake (1987: 140). The government set forth these broad goals in a *Ten Year Economic Plan*, published by the newly-created National Planning Commission (1959b).

[59] In 1957, the *Annual Report of the Director of Industries* published for the first time the Government's views on the division of economic management between the public and private sector; see especially pages 32-34 and Snodgrass (1966: 175). They intended this as a blueprint for the soon-to-be-proposed nationalisation program. The *Report* designated most heavy industries, including iron, steel, cement, chemicals and fertilisers as 'areas reserved to government production.' The plan also specified a second list of 23 lighter industries, including textiles, tires, glassware and paper as 'areas open to government corporations, mixed corporations or private corporations.' The policy listed another 82 industries, mostly producing light consumer goods, as 'reserved to private enterprise;' nevertheless, the *Report* envisioned a far more extensive degree of regulation even in these segments.

[60] See K.M. De Silva (1981: 522).

[61] See Karunatilake (1987: 63). In 1956, prevailing wisdom perceived Sri Lanka as more economically advantaged than the 'Newly Industrialising Countries (NICs)' of the 1970s, South Korea, Taiwan, Singapore and Hong Kong.

[62] Moore (1985: 56, ff.) provides a detailed discussion of the Act.

[63] See Ibid. for an extended discussion of the failure of the Paddy Lands Act, as well as other efforts intended to improve the lot of the rural poor in Sri Lanka. Government ineffectiveness in enforcing the act did not go entirely unnoticed. For example, on September 30, 1961, the Sinhala daily *Dawasa* reported on a 'fast unto death' at Horagolla's S.W.R.D. Bandaranaike Monument, declared by the Ceylon Administrative Secretaries Association to protest the slow pace of implementing some Paddy Lands Act Provisions.

[64] See K.M. de Silva (1981: 522). According to de Silva, significant wage increases were granted, without corresponding increases in productivity.

[65] See K.M. de Silva and Wriggins (1994: 91-92).

[66] See government reports on *The State of the Economy* (especially 1957-59) as well as Karunatilake (1987: 140-42) and Wilson (1974: 142).

[67] See K.M. de Silva and Wriggins (1994: 91).

[68] This measure became implemented through the *People's Bank Act No. 29 of 1961*. The government established offices of the People's Bank in small towns that had previously lacked banking facilities. Subsequently, accusations surfaced that the Bank made loans for political purposes that often went unpaid.

[69] This assessment comes from K.M. de Silva and Wriggins (1994: 91).

[70] See Snodgrass (1966: 202). Philip Gunawardene, a Marxist serving as Minister of Agriculture, had announced a plan for the full-scale nationalisation of the plantations shortly after coming to power, but the Prime Minister later agreed to a ten-year moratorium on nationalisation.

[71] See *Papers by Visiting Economists* (1959a).

[72] I hasten to add that these pressures characterise most economic decision-making involving governments, not only in the states of the Global South, but also in modern industrialised nations.

[73] See Karunatilake (1987: 63).

[74] Snodgrass (1966: 174 and Table A-70) provides a detailed appraisal of the first four years of the government's industrialisation policy. He concludes that 'state industrial corporations had performed disappointingly in terms of output, employment and import competitiveness and had been an expensive experiment in government economic initiative.'

[75] While absenteeism and indiscipline in the labour force posed problems throughout Sri Lanka, as workers with a predominantly rural background adapted to the regimentation of an industrial society, these issues became particular problems in state-owned corporations. According to one report cited in Kearney (1971: 31), approximately 15 per cent of all organised labourers in Sri Lanka did not report to work on any given day. For the state

corporations and engineering industry, the average daily rate of absenteeism ran around 30 per cent!

[76] See Figure 7-3 in this chapter: Sri Lanka's population grew by more than 25 per cent between 1956 and 1965.

[77] See K.M. de Silva and Wriggins (1994: 73). These authors find Felix Dias Bandaranaike the most brilliant, the most powerful and the most arrogant member of the Cabinet. He was trained as an attorney, but he had no background in business, finance or economics.

[78] This occurred partly because of a further deterioration in terms of trade and in partly because of selective relaxation of some import controls in deference to an upcoming election year.

[79] For an extensive discussion of this transition in policymaking, see Snodgrass (1966: 193-200).

[80] Ibid: 194-95. Recall from chapter 6 that cancellation of the food subsidy in 1953 had precipitated violent riots and the fall of Dudley Senanayake's government. The subsidy returned at the increased level of 2 measures or 4 pounds per week for everyone, charging a nominal price of about 50 cents – about 14 cents US – for each ration. The price fell to 25 cents under S.W.R.D. Bandaranaike's government.

[81] In an exception, the Sri Lanka Transport Board – the nationalised bus company – ran profitably between 1962 and 1966, after incurring losses for four years after nationalisation: See Karunatilake (1987: 209-10).

[82] That these capital investments failed to produce sustainable growth in most Communist states because of corruption and bad management should not obscure the fact that Communist governments did make substantial investments.

[83] Data calculated from Peebles (1982: Table III.4 at 244).

[84] See Snodgrass (1966:187-93), Karunatilake (1987: 292-312) and successive Central Bank annual reports on *The State of the Economy* covering this period. Among other new levies, the government introduced a tax on net wealth other than immovable properties outside of Sri Lanka; a gift tax; new estate duties; a new land tax; a business names registration tax; a company share capital tax; an income tax surcharge and a variety of sales taxes.

[85] Data calculated from Peebles (1982: Table III.4 at 244).

[86] See Snodgrass (1966:199 and Table A-67). Financing methods included borrowing from the Central Bank, 'administrative borrowing' from government trust funds, and drawing from government cash balances and reserves.

[87] Data calculated from Peebles (1982: Table XIII.5 at 247). In the 1955-56 budget year, interest payments accounted for about 2 per cent of expenditures.

[88] Unless otherwise specified, the demographic data presented here come from the tabulations provided in Ibid: 25-38).

[89] Calculated from Ibid: 27-28. These data measure the rural-urban distribution of population across political jurisdictions rather than across demographic groups; as a result, they offer limited utility. Moore (1985: Chapter 4) provides a nuanced and useful discussion of the urban rural distinction in Sri Lanka and its distinctive character. All authorities agree that the rural character of Sri Lankan society helps to make Sri Lanka unique. While part of this rural character stems from a strong rural ethic in Sri Lankan society, one could also point to the effectiveness of government programs in providing at least some services to rural areas.

[90] For an explanation, see Snodgrass (1966: 221, ff.). After 1961, the declining availability of goods, increasingly draconian controls, and Marxist rhetoric from some ministers aroused fears that the government might confiscate bank holdings. In response, many individuals began to hoard increasing amounts of currency, thus reducing the money supply. The more well-informed, knowing the government could also manipulate the currency, purchased real property.

[91] See Peebles (1982: 97). In 1956, urban workers earned wages amounting to less than twice the wages of agricultural workers.

[92] Nevertheless, Karunatilake (1987: 213) notes that government consumer-finance surveys tend to understate consumption, due not only to memory lapses among respondents, but also due to rural householders' frequent inability to quantify their purchases accurately. Moreover, since a great many workers in the rural and plantation sectors did not pay taxes, they tended to avoid disclosing either their incomes or consumption expenditures.

[93] Calculations based on data from the Central Bank's 1973 *Consumer Finances and Socio Economic Survey.* 60. Reprinted in Peebles (1982: Table VI.8).

[94] For a sustained discussion of the problems of estimating unemployment, see Karunatilake, (1987: chapter 10) and Peebles (1982: chapter 6).

[95] Karunatilake (1987: 264, 267). The *Census of Population - 1953* estimated the size of the labour force at 2,993,000 persons, while the *Census of Population - 1963* estimated a labour force of 3,464,000 persons, an increase of 471,000. Using somewhat different definitions, the *Labour Force Survey - 1968* estimated a labour force of 4,150,000 persons.

[96] Data from Peebles (1982: 98), expressed in round numbers. The author notes that in their best year, 1952, employment exchanges succeeded in placing about 15 per cent of registered applicants. The number of placements declined in almost every subsequent year. He notes that some of the registrants already had jobs, but sought better ones. Nevertheless, many of the unemployed, especially in rural areas, never registered at all.

[97] See Karunatilake (1987: 197).

[98] These calculations are based on data found in Peebles (1982: Table III.7). The number of doctors increased from 984 to 1,494, while the number of nurses increased from 2,305 to 3,642. The total number of health-care personnel other than doctors increased from 8,727 to 11,879.

[99] The association of Ayurvedic physicians comprised about 10,000 members in 1957. See Wriggins (1960: 154, ff.).

[100] Western-trained doctors belonging to Sri Lanka's powerful Government Medical Officers Association (GMOA) have tried to limit the role of traditional medicine. As recently as 1993, they opposed a government-supported plan to offer courses in Western medicine to students learning ayurveda at the Institute of Traditional Medicine. GMOA members passed a resolution that would expel any Sri Lankan doctors who participated in traditional-medicine programs, thus effectively denying them the right to practice medicine in Sri Lanka. To keep program alive, the government had to hire retired physicians from India to teach at the Institute.

[101] This discussion mainly draws from Karunatilake (1987: 210-11).

[102] Sri Lanka's democratic system also helped the rural poor, although Moore (1985) points out that they did not use their political leverage to full advantage. After the disenfranchisement of the Indian Tamils, populations in rural districts, especially Kandyan rural districts, found themselves significantly overrepresented in Parliament.

[103] These rounded estimates are based on data found in Peebles (1982: Chapter 5, Tables V.2, V.3 and V.4).

[104] See C.R. de Silva (1977: 412).

[105] As noted above, the tea estates numbered among the few major sectors of the Sri Lankan economy that remained under private, foreign management. Typically, each estate maintained a small, one-room school staffed by a single teacher, intended to provide rudimentary education to the estate workers' children. In 1961, about 1,200 teachers in the estate-school system served 80,000 pupils, resulting in a teacher-student ratio of 1:67. This compares with a teacher-student ratio for the nation as a whole of 1:32.

[106] Peebles (1982: 78) notes, however, that there were no laws compelling attendance, and attrition was severe in some areas.

[107] The Sinhala language, with its unique alphabet, is used only in Sri Lanka, leading to only a small demand for Sinhala texts. Further, virtually all Sri Lankan scholars up to this time had received their educations in English, and so generally published their work in that language. Because of the large number of Tamil-speakers in India, texts in Tamil were more widely availabile.

[108] See C.R. de Silva (1977: 416). Up to 1973, students who had completed eight years of education tracked into one of three 'streams,' or fields of concentration. 'Arts' students wrote a first basic (GCE Ordinary Level) examination on History, Civics and Geography. 'Science' students prepared for examinations in Physics and Chemistry. Those in the 'Commerce' track took accounts, shorthand and typing. The government also made some attempt to offer 'practical' subjects such as needlework, woodworking, metalwork and ceramics.

[109] The best of these, then and now, include Royal College in Colombo's Cinnamon Gardens, which graduated most of Sri Lanka's Prime Ministers, St. Thomas College in the Colombo Suburb of Mount Lavinia and Trinity College in Kandy. Ladies College and St.

Bridget's Convent – Mrs. Bandaranaike's *alma mater* – stood among the best of the women's schools.

[110] See Karunatilake (1987: 201-02) and Nyrop et al. (1971: 156-57). Both the *Vidyodaya Pirivena* at Nugegoda and the *Vidyalankara Pirivena* at Kelaniya, lay in towns near Colombo.

Chapter Eight Notes

[1] Singer (1964: 145).

[2] On political parties, see particularly Wriggins (1960:147, ff.) and Wilson (1974: ff.). Kearney (1971: 42, ff.) provides the most comprehensive discussion of Sri Lanka's labour unions during this period.

[3] Mrs. S.W.R.D. Bandaranaike held the top leadership post in the SLFP from 1960 until her death in 2001). Pieter Keunemann became the Communist Party leader before independence and held the post for decades. J.R. Jayewardene succeeded to the top UNP leadership post in 1973, upon the death of Dudley Senanayake, and held that position until his retirement in 1988.

[4] See Kearney (1971: 52-53).

[5] Ibid: 13-14 cites a 1964 'Readership Survey' conducted by the Market Research Department of Lever Brothers (Ceylon) Limited for the Audit Bureau of Circulations. Among the estate workers, only 18 per cent of the men and 3 per cent of the women described themselves as newspaper readers. 37 per cent of the men and 15 per cent of the women sometimes listened to the radio.

[6] *Ceylon Year Book, 1967*: 297-298; quoted in Kearney (1971: 13).

[7] In addition, about 75 per cent of the island's total population earned their living within an 80 mile radius of Colombo during this period, although rural areas were disproportionately represented in Parliament. See Wilson (1974: 129, ff.).

[8] K.M. de Silva and Wriggins (1994: 3-4) characterise the Bandaranaike-Obeyesekere family as 'a leader of the traditional elite that had worked closely with the British during the colonial period… and one of the most reactionary of Sri Lanka families.' For a more nuanced view, see Y. Gooneratne (1986).

[9] For example, see Manor (1989: 319, ff.) and K.M. de Silva and Wriggins (1994: 59, ff.). Biographer James Manor writes (p. 320) that 'the assassination has obscured the wasted opportunities of his premiership by distracting attention from the disintegration of the political experiment that he had undertaken as Prime Minister. His murder and the legend that grew up around him thereafter did more to revive the fortunes of that experiment than could anything that he might have done had he survived.'

[10] Woodward (1969: 194-95) writes that 'the SLFP has not yet become, either ideologically or organisationally, a fully cohesive unit, and its career has therefore been

characterised by a search for an ideological position that is acceptable to its many notables and electorally profitable in respect to the wide social base it seeks to mobilise.'

[11] See K.M. de Silva and Wriggins (1994: 82).

[12] See K.M. de Silva (1986: 202).

[13] See K.M. de Silva and Wriggins (1994: 2).

[14] See Woodward (1969: 187). The author quotes from the 'Report of the Special Committee of the United National Party.' *Ceylon Observer*, July 28, 1956.

[15] See K.M. de Silva and Wriggins (1994: 102). The new constitution broadened the party's representational base, but did not really make it more democratic. Policy-making power was still vested in a small working committee. In fact, under the new constitution, members of the working committee were appointed by the party leader, rather than being appointed, as previously. However as a practical matter this made little difference.

[16] See B. Weerakoon (1992: 22-23). Premadasa had served as a member of the Colombo Municipal Council, representing St. Sebastian Ward, and then as the City's Deputy Mayor. He later became Sri Lanka's Prime Minister and second Executive President, before dying at the hands of an assassin in 1993.

[17] Tolerance within the UNP had its limits. Despite path-breaking achievements, Premadasa never won full social acceptance from J.R. Jayewardene or his close *goyagama* associates.

[18] K.M. de Silva (1986: 209) writes this of the Federal Party leader: 'Chelvanayakam ...was an eminent lawyer, but was unique in being a Christian, not a Hindu unlike all the main Tamil political figures... A victim of Parkinson's disease, Chelvanayakam could hardly speak above a whisper, but yet in a superb triumph of character over these two major drawbacks - in religion and physical condition - he achieved an eminence in Tamil politics... In the asceticism of his lifestyle and his frail physical appearance he was the delight alike of the political cartoonist and the political image-maker. For the latter, he was a gift from the gods, an uncanny representation of all that one needed to portray the ideal leader of an ethnic group proclaiming itself an oppressed minority.'

[19] See Wilson (1988: 105). A.J. Wilson, a respected Tamil scholar who held the founding Chair of Political Science at Sri Lanka's Peradeniya University and subsequently migrated to Canada, was the son-in-law of Federal Party leader, S.J.V. Chelvanayakam.

[20] See Woodward (1969: 231).

[21] See K.M. de Silva (1986: 230-31).

[22] This discussion of Federal Party tactics draws from Wilson (1988: 105, ff.).

[23] See Wriggins (1960: 154) and Kearney (1971: 16-17). Figures submitted by trade unions as compulsory reports to the Commissioner of Labour showed an increase in membership from 261,681 in 1956 to 1,215,654 in 1965.

[24] Ibid: 17. Kearney quotes a governmental *Administration Report of the Commissioner of Labour* (1958: 181).

[25] Kearney (1971: 37). For example, public-sector employees were prohibited from striking for the purpose of 'overawing or influencing the government' in areas unrelated to their work. Sympathy strikes were also prohibited. However public-sector employee participation in political and sympathy strikes was 'frequent and conspicuous.' The first action to enforce these prohibitions did not occur until 1966 under Dudley Senanayake's UNP-dominated 'National Government.'

[26] Ibid: 39.

[27] See K.M. de Silva (1986: 221-226) and Sabaratnam, (1990: chapters 5-6). Recall that fear of left-wing sentiments from a unionised Indian Tamil work force had motivated D.S. Senanayake's government to disenfranchise most of the estate workers. The politically astute Thondaman recognised that militancy on the part of his union – especially if perceived as 'political' or if carried to extremes – could evoke punitive government reprisals, which would be supported by most Sinhalese.

[28] These included the Ceylon Trade Union Federation (Communist Party), the Ceylon Federation of Labour (LSSP), Government Workers Trade Union Federation (LSSP) and the Central Council of Ceylon Trade Unions (VLSSP - An offshoot of the LSSP). See Kearney (1971: 77, ff.).

[29] Ibid: 177.

[30] This was classified as 'suspension of constitutional guarantees for the entire country.' Proscription of the Federal Party, detention of its leaders and press censorship under the emergency regulations were taken into account by increasing the index values for 'restrictions on political parties;' for 'arrests, exiles and executions;' and for 'censorship of the press.'

[31] See the discussion earlier in this chapter. Order was restored by June 3, some 13 days after Governor General Goonetileke declared the state of emergency.

[32] Index values in each category were reduced by one point. Constitutional guarantees remained at 2 because of the government's language policy, and press censorship remained at 2 because of continued reports of censorship. 'Arrests and executions' and 'proscription of opposition political parties' received values of 1.

[33] See *Times of Ceylon*, August 3 and August 8, 1960 and *Ceylon Daily News*, August 6, 1960.

[34] Following the seizure of *Time* magazine, *The New York Times* ran a series of articles about press censorship in Sri Lanka. The government's press policy is also described in Abeynaike and Amaratunga, eds. (1965). The latter volume, published by the same Lake House Group principally targeted in government attacks, can hardly be regarded as an official source.

[35] See *Ceylon Daily News*, December 22 and 27, 1960.

[36] This population included the Sri Lankan Tamils who dominated the Federal Party, the Indian Tamil plantation workers, and a number of Tamil-speaking Muslims, mostly living in

the Eastern Province. Together, Tamil-speakers comprised a little less that 20 per cent of Sri Lanka's population.

[37] See *New York Times*, October 3, 1960.

[38] For this period prior to the April 17 State of Emergency, I increased the score for 'suspension of constitutional guarantees' to 2, reflecting the government's language policy, but did not further increase the value of any sub-index for state sanctioned violence policy to take schools policy into account. I might have possibly classified the schools policy as political harassment, since the government viewed most Christians as UNP supporters; however, I chose not to do so.

[39] See *Ceylon Daily News*, April 4, 1961.

[40] Ibid, May 7, 1962.

[41] Ibid, July 14 and August 9, 1962. The offending volume was M.S.F. de Silva's *Ceylon and World History*. A revision of the book, with the offending chapter deleted, was later published.

[42] See *Ceylon Daily News*, August 11, 1962.

[43] Ibid, December 17, 1964.

[44] Ibid, October 31, 1962.

[45] Ibid, May 29, 1962. According to the article, imposition of censorship was in response to a report on China that embarrassed the Chinese government.

[46] Ibid, October 18, 1962.

[47] Ibid, May 11, 1962.

[48] Ibid, April 17, 1962.

[49] Ibid, May 22, 1962. The by-elections in question occurred in Anuradhapura, Muttur and Welimada districts.

[50] See *Times of Ceylon*, July 23, 1962.

[51] See *Ceylon Daily News*, October 11, 1962.

[52] Ibid, February 21, 1963.

[53] Ibid, March 16, 1963.

[54] Ibid, October 19, 1963.

[55] Ibid, November 16, 1964.

[56] Ibid, March 20, 1964. In April, the government reduced the amount of foreign exchange allowed newspaper publishers for the purchase of newsprint. Although Sri Lanka was facing exchange problems at the time, this was interpreted by many as another approach by the government to censor and harass newspapers.

[57] See Horowitz (1980: 158).

[58] See Peebles (1982: 266, Table XIV.2).

[59] See Jupp (1978: 246-248).

[60] See Vittachi (1958: 42, ff.).

[61] See Horowitz (1980), especially chapter 8.

[62] This discussion draws to some degree on Jupp (1978), but even more from interviews with politicians and retired senior officers of the police and army.

[63] Ibid: 244, ff.

[64] See Horowitz (1980: 68, ff.).

[65] Ibid: 212.

[66] See Ibid: 68 and K.M. de Silva (1986: 268-271).

[67] This certainly describes the view held by biographer James Manor (1989) and historian K.M. de Silva (1981, 1986).

[68] See Wilson (1974: 144-45). Dahanayake belonged to the SLFP's right wing.

[69] When referring to "the leading Marxist parties" I mean, in general, the Trotskyist Sri Lanka Equal Society Party (LSSP), lead by Philip Goonewardene, N.M. Perera and Colvin R. de Silva and the 'Moscow Wing' of the Communist Party, lead by Pieter Keuneman and S.A. Wickremasinghe. This broad labelling, of course, does little justice to the bewildering complexity of Sri Lanka's Marxist politics, only some of which has been described above.

[70] See the election manifestos of the LSSP and the Communist Party, "Moscow Wing" (CP) as reported in the Government's *Parliaments of Sri Lanka, 1960* (1961). By contrast, communal issues and especially the personalities of its leaders were the centrepieces of SLFP election manifestos and campaigns. The party's 'middle' ground of 'democratic socialism' was defined in rather vague terms and was left, as a practical matter, for Marxist-oriented cabinet members and planners to implement.

[71] Ibid: 227. The LSSP fielded 110 candidates, of whom only 10 won seats and 52 lost deposits. The Communist Party fielded 53 candidates; only 3 won seats and 38 lost deposits. Philip Goonewardene's MEP fielded 89 candidates, winning 10 seats.

[72] In this quality, I believe only J.R. Jayewardene and Ranasinghe Premadasa could match Mrs. Bandaranaike among Sri Lanka's post independence politicians, and only Premadasa combined a grasp of power with the ability to mobilise the masses. In organisational ability and the intricacies of political in-fighting, Jayewardene was superior to both.

Chapter Nine Notes

[1] As noted in earlier chapters, information on outbreaks comes from the *Violent Political Conflict Data Base* (Richardson 1990) unless otherwise noted.

[2] Only the campaign season preceding the March 22, 1965 general election was more violent.

[3] Two persons were reported killed in a post-election clash between supporters of rival parties in the small Central Province village of Unantenna.

[4] To achieve comparability, the number of events under S.W.R.D. and Mrs. Bandaranaike's terms in office were reduced by a factor of 62/108 to take into account the fact that Dudley Senanayake's term in office was shorter – 62 months vs. 108 months. As in previous cases, this adjustment serves to draw qualitative distinctions, not precise numerical ones.

[5] Upon assuming office, Mrs. Bandaranaike quickly replaced this Tamil officer with a Sinhalese DIG.

[6] Readers may recall that Gopallawa was not only Mrs. Bandaranaike's appointee, but her uncle. When his term expired, Dudley Senanayake reappointed him to the Governor General's post.

[7] See K.M. de Silva and Wriggins (1994: 145). A key consideration in the complex negotiations to name a new Prime Minister was the constitutional provision for the appointment of six members of Parliament 'to represent minority interests.' The person designated by the Governor General to form the government was given the right to appoint the minority Members and naturally chose them from the ranks of supporters.

[8] Ibid: 143-45. The authors provide a detailed description of the events surrounding Dudley Senanayake's accession to power. Once it became clear than Gopallawa would ask him to lead the government, Senanayake enlisted the support of Colombo Mayor V.A. Sugathadasa, who mobilised his own gangs of supporters to ensure the Prime Minister-designate safe passage to Queen's House. Sugathadasa became Minister of Nationalised Services in the new government and is now memorialised by Colombo's largest municipal stadium.

[9] Ibid: 145.

[10] See Jupp (1978: 61).

[11] Much of this discussion draws on K.M. de Silva and Wriggins (1988, 1994), but also includes a number of interviews. This study presents a somewhat more favourable view of Dudley Senanayake than that offered by J.R. Jayewardene's biographers. A similar view emerges from Chanaka Amaratunga (1994), then leader of Sri Lanka's small Liberal Party. 'The greatness of Dudley Senanayake,' Amaratunga writes, 'lay not in his being four times Prime Minister ... but in being Dudley Senanayake, a liberal democrat whose faith in personal freedom could not be questioned and whose honour stood higher than the gaudiest bauble of power.'

[12] See K.M de Silva and Wriggins (1994: 146). 'Ministers of State' are traditionally subordinate to cabinet ministers in Sri Lanka. Jayewardene also served as Parliamentary Secretary to the Ministry of Defence and External Affairs, a position held previously by Mrs. Bandaranaike's most powerful deputy, Felix Dias Bandaranaike. Senanayake, like virtually all Sri Lankan Prime Ministers, retained direct control over the ministries of Defence and External Affairs.

[13] See K.M. de Silva (1986: 203, 271) and K.M. de Silva and Wriggins (1994: 155). The men accused of leading the coup were the army commander – and relative of Mrs. Bandaranaike – Major General Richard Udagama; N.Q. Dias, who had served Mrs. Bandaranaike's government as Permanent Secretary to the Ministry of Defence and External Affairs; and a politically active Buddhist Priest, the Venerable Hepitagedera Gnanasinha. All eventually won acquittal. Those convicted were all junior and non commissioned officers.

[14] Ibid: 172.

[15] Ibid: 152.

[16] See Ponnambalam (1983: 145). According to the author, this contradicted Senanayake's pledge to Chelvanayakam that 'a Tamil-speaking person should be allowed to transact business in Tamil throughout the island.'

[17] See Wilson (1974: 51).

[18] I discuss the fate of the Bandaranaike-Chelvanayakam negotiations and the way that controversy over the pact contributed to polarisation of Sinhalese-Tamil relations in Sri Lanka in chapter 10.

[19] See K.M. de Silva and Wriggins (1994: 166).

[20] See Ponnambalam (1983: 146).

[21] For reasons already discussed, giving up power to Tamil-dominated local governments was a sensitive issue among the Sinhalese. Proposing such devolutions had proven a fatal flaw in the Bandaranaike-Chelvanayakam pact. Senanayake's government hoped to avoid this pitfall by specifying that District councils would *function under the control and direction of the central government* (K.M. de Silva 1986: 191, quoting the Government's 'Throne' speech of 1966) and making the Councils coordinating bodies with no powers other than those already held by local governments (Ponnambalam 1983: 146). In *Managing Ethnic Conflict in a Multiethnic Society* (1986), K.M. de Silva argues that understanding the devolution of power issue is central to understanding communal relations in Sri Lanka.

[22] See Ibid: 191 and K.M. de Silva and Wriggins (1994: 178).

[23] See K.M. de Silva (1986: 193, 233-235) and K.M. de Silva and Wriggins (1994: 178).

[24] See Wilson (1988: 126; 1974: 51) and K.M. de Silva and Wriggins (1994: 179). In an interesting footnote to these events, Ranasinghe Premadasa followed Murugusan Tiruchelvam as Minister of Local Government after the Tamil Cabinet member resigned. From this ministry, Premadasa began to build the power base that would win him Sri Lanka's Executive Presidency in December 1988.

[25] See Wilson (1974: 51; 1988: 127) and Ponnambalam (1983: 146). In a November speech given at Batticaloa and reported in the Sinhalese newspaper *Dawasa* (November 6, 1968: 1) Chelvanayakam vowed that the Federal Party would 'fight on until an independent Tamil State is established after uniting the Ceylon citizens and Indian Tamils resident in Ceylon.'

[26] I discuss these negotiations in chapter 8.

[27] See K.M. de Silva (1986: 225).

[28] See Ibid, K.M. de Silva and Wriggins (1994: 179-80), and Sabaratnam (1990: 86-95). Mrs. Bandaranaike also proposed to limit the granting of Sri Lankan citizenship to Indian Tamils allowed to remain in Sri Lanka according to the rate of repatriation by those returning to India. Four Sri Lankan citizenship grants would be given for every seven plantation workers who returned. This proposal did not appear in the National Government's legislation, the 'Indo-Ceylon (Implementation) Bill,' and efforts by the opposition to add it failed.

[29] K.M. de Silva (1986: 224-25) discusses Thondaman's successful strategy and contrasts it with the more confrontational approach adopted by the Federal Party leaders. This demonstrated, he concludes 'that the linguistic nationalism of the Tamils had its own limits and could not bring all Tamils together within the Sri Lanka polity.'

[30] See Jupp (1978: 61, ff.).

[31] Ibid: 175.

[32] See Ponnambalam (1983: 145) and K.M. de Silva and Wriggins (1994: 166).

[33] See Kodikara (1982: 117-18, 206), Nissanka (1984: 154), and Wilson (1974: 295).

[34] Nissanka (1984: 154) quotes this April 1965 address by Senanayake.

[35] See Kodikara (1982: 123, 126) and K.M. de Silva and Wriggins (1994: 164).

[36] See K.M. de Silva and Wriggins (1994: 167), Nissanka (1984: 276, ff.), and Kodikara (1982: 214). Among other conditions, the World Bank required reductions in food subsidies, greater opportunity for private initiative in both domestic and international investment, more careful screening of public investment proposals; increased domestic production, and reductions in current-account and balance of payments deficits.

[37] Ibid: 123. Sri Lanka agreed to pay a sum of 55 million rupees (about $US 5.5 million) to the companies over a period of five years.

[38] Ibid. See also K.M. de Silva and Wriggins (1994: 150-51).

[39] See Kodikara (1982: 46-47).

[40] See Nissanka (1984: 154).

[41] See Kodikara (1982: 75, 118, ff.).

[42] See K.M. de Silva and Wriggins (1994: 181) and Kodikara (1982: 122-23, 187).

[43] None of the three Sri Lankan leaders most often praised for acumen in foreign affairs – S.W.R.D. Bandaranaike, Sirimavo Bandaranaike, or J.R. Jayewardene – achieved comparable results.

[44] See Jupp (1978: 166-67) and K.M. de Silva and Wriggins (1994: 183).

[45] Ibid: 186, ff. Despite their differences, Senanayake and Jayewardene did work together in the 1970 campaign, but not with the same kind of effective teamwork that had contributed to their 1965 victory.

[46] Ibid: 150-51.

[47] See chapter 5.

[48] See Karunatilake (1987: 64).

[49] See Balakrishnan (1977: 207) and *The State of the Economy* (1965), quoting the government's 1965-66 budget.

[50] Karunatilake (1987: 73, ff.).

[51] Ibid: 66, ff. and Moore (1985: especially chapters 4 and 5). These initiatives included the Paddy Lands Act, a Guaranteed Price Scheme for rice, crop-insurance services, agricultural extension services, agricultural credit schemes, and subsidy programs for seed and fertiliser. Karunatilake, basically a sympathetic observer of SLFP governments, notes that the policies had not achieved their objectives because of ineffective policy decisions and legislation, 'poor administrative organisation' and 'inadequate coordination by responsible agencies.'

[52] See K.M. de Silva and Wriggins (1994: 173).

[53] This is based on data from Peebles (1982: 122-23 and 130-31).

[54] See K.M. de Silva and Wriggins (1994: 173) and Karunatilake (1987: 67).

[55] See the *Mahaweli, Ganga Irrigation and Hydro Power Survey* conducted by the United Nations Development Program, Food and Agriculture Organisation, and Government (1969). Much of this background on the Mahaweli Project emerges from an unpublished study, *The Mahaweli Development Report*, prepared by Andrew Dailey (1990), then a senior at Swarthmore College. At present, Muller and Hettige, eds. (1995) is probably the most comprehensive study of the project widely avaialable.

[56] The Mahaweli flows out of the mountains above the ancient capital of Kandy through the flatlands of the Dry Zone and into the Indian Ocean at Trincomalee. It runs 206 miles, drains more than 15 per cent of Sri Lanka's land, and carries more than 20 per cent of the total runoff borne by the island's rivers. The Mahaweli's hydrodynamic characteristics make it virtually ideal for a gravity-based irrigation system.

[57] Dailey (1990: 2) quotes the *Culavamsa* 68: 6-16.

[58] See Nicholas (1955: 66-67). King Parakramabahu I reportedly constructed or restored 165 dams, 3,910 canals, 163 major reservoirs and 2,376 minor reservoirs. In fact, Sinhalese interest in irrigation long predated the era of Parakramabahu I. The first diversion of a major Sri Lankan river for irrigation purposes, namely the Amban River in the Mahaweli system, occurred in about AD 65.

[59] See K.M. de Silva and Wriggins (1994: 174).

[60] See Dailey (1990: Appendix II, 2).

[61] See Karunatilake (1987: 64) and the Government's *State of the Economy* (1966 and 1967).

[62] See K.M. de Silva and Wriggins (1994: 168). As noted in chapter 7 and in Manor

(1989), most Sri Lankans trained in economics had passed through the left-leaning curriculum which prevailed at the London School of Economics at mid-century.

[63] Discussion of Shenoy's proposals and response to them comes from K.M. de Silva and Wriggins (1994: 168-71).

[64] See Ibid: 164, Note 1. Initially, only the Prime Minister, Minister of State, and Minister of Finance sat on the panel, with the respected and influential international economist Gamini Corea serving as secretary to the subcommittee. Interestingly, the group did not include the Minister of Trade and Commerce.

[65] Gunawardena also served as Minister of Fisheries.

[66] See K.M. de Silva and Wriggins (1994: 176).

[67] See Karunatilake (1987: 111).

[68] While the new policies may have contributed to an improvement in investor confidence, it is also probable that some investors, fearing another shift in the political climate, took the opportunity to disinvest from Sri Lanka under conditions relatively favourable for doing so.

[69] See Naylor (1966).

[70] See Karunatilake (1987: 234-6). The Ceylon Government Railroad (CGR) ran as a government department with capital and annual operating subsidies provided by the treasury as 'loans' which were never paid back. Between 1953 and 1971, there were no fare increases. The Sri Lanka (Ceylon) Transport Board, which managed public busses, actually showed a profit from 1953 through 1967. However its work force, which was dispersed throughout the island, became a prime target for political appointments by members of Parliament. Between 1958 and 1971, the ratio of employees to busses increased from 4.7 to 8.2 and, unsurprisingly, the Transport Board began to require government subsidies to continue in operations.

[71] See Balakrishnan (1977: 199).

[72] See Karunatilake (1987: 149). During this period, state investments in industry (in current prices) rose from rupees 483 million to rupees 1,200 million.

[73] In 1963, there were 14 state industrial corporations engaged in production. By the end of 1967,the number of state corporations had risen to 21.

[74] See Karunatilake (1987: 149) and Balakrishnan (1977: 199, 202).

[75] Data from Peebles (1982: 351, Table VIII.8).

[76] Data from Ibid: 189, Table XI.5.

[77] Data from Ibid: 216, Table XII.8.

[78] Data from Ibid: 251-52, Table XIII.7).

[79] Mrs. Bandaranaike's government received 117 million rupees during its five year term while Senanayake's government received 159 million, rupees an increase of 35 per cent. However, as noted above, the government devalued the rupee in 1967 from 4.78 to

5.93, and later 5.96 to the dollar. Thus, this assistance cost foreign donors less, and had a lesser value on international markets. Denominated in constant 1965 $US, the difference between grants received by Senanayake's government and that of Mrs. Bandaranaike amounted to $US 3 million, an increase of only about 16 per cent.

[80] See Karunatilake (1987: 351).

[81] See Jupp (1978: 360).

[82] Because the costs of the food subsidy could fluctuate from year to year, depending on weather and market conditions, one must measure both changes in *total expenditure for the life of an administration* and *annual spending*.

[83] Data on government expenditures from Peebles (1982: Table XIII.5). Percentage calculations are based on data deflated to 1965 constant rupees.

[84] Data from Ibid: 251, Table XIII.7. Percentage calculations based on data deflated to 1965 constant rupees.

[85] The government ran budget surpluses during the last two years of Sir John Kotelawala's administration and a deficit of less than 5 per cent of GDP in 1956. In 1965, the budget deficit amounted to 30 per cent of GDP.

[86] Nelson et al. (1989) provides a good overview of both the political and economic dimensions of structural adjustment.

[87] When government reforms are imposed rapidly, often under pressure from international lending agencies, analysts sometimes refer to the remedy as 'shock therapy.'

[88] See the Government's *State of the Economy* (1967-1970). In 1967, wages for government employees went up for the first time in nearly a decade, in part to compensate for the currency devaluation. Increases amounted to 10.8 per cent for clerical and technical employees, 20.9 per cent for minor employees, and 10.4 per cent for school teachers. Additional 'pre-election' wage increases occurred for teachers and many government employees in 1969 and 1970.

[89] Data from Peebles (1982: 107, Table VI.7), denominated in current rupees and adjusted to 1965 base values for the purpose of these estimates according to above-described procedures. 'Agriculture' includes cultivation and processing of tea and rubber, along with coconut growing. It does not include wages in the rice-growing paddy sectors. For the most part, rice growers operated as small entrepreneurs, with incomes just slightly above subsistence levels.

[90] Pre-election wage increases, intended to win votes for the government in power, are a time-honoured tradition in Sri Lanka. Details of public-sector wage increases – which benefited certain clerical, technical and 'minor' employees – appear in the Central Bank reports on the *State of the Economy*. Data from the 1967, 1969 and 1970 reports contributed to preparation of this section.

[91] I compiled the figures presented in the discussion that follows using data from Karunatilake (1987: chapter 10) and Peebles (1982: chapter 6). Although the statistics mostly derive from government surveys, readers should remember to view them as

approximations. As noted above, I do find these statistics useful as indicators of broad trends: If anything, they understate the severity of Sri Lanka's unemployment problems.

[92] The discussion that follows relies upon figures from the 1953, 1963 and 1968 *State of the Economy* reports.

[93] Since published unemployment statistics in developing nations invariably understate the severity of the problem, one may assume that the actual rate of unemployment levels ran higher, and perhaps substantially so.

[94] Employment increased at an annual rate of three per cent from 1963-68, in contrast to a .7 per cent rate of increase during the 1953-63 period. The government did not generate comparable figures for 1969-70, but I would assume an even faster rate of job creation during those two years of very rapid economic growth.

[95] Peebles (1982: 54, ff., Table III.6 and III.7). From 1965 to 1970, the number of doctors grew from 1,494 to 1,932, nurses from 3,642 to 5,542, and hospital beds from 33,802 to 37,753.

[96] See The Hunger Project (1985: 17, note 12).

[97] Some University courses in science and engineering, especially graduate-level courses, were the principal exceptions.

[98] The influential Iriyagolle and been an early member of S.W.R.D. Bandaranaike's Great Sinhalese League (*Sinhala Maha Sabha*) and a strong supporter of the slain Prime Minister.

[99] See K.M de Silva (1986: 202).

[100] See C.R. de Silva (1977: 430).

[101] See Peebles (1982: 89, Table V.4), Nyrop, et al. (1971: 153, 158), and C.R. de Silva (1977: 24). In a total cadre of about 90,500 teachers, the number with university degrees rose from 6,735 in 1965 to 7,441, an increase of about 10 per cent. The number of uncertified teachers – i.e. those who had failed even to pass a government qualifying examination – dropped from 28,639 to 13,450, a decrease of more than 50 per cent.

[102] At that time, most of the Government's top leaders had graduated from one of these elite schools, which no doubt contributed to the preferential treatment they received.

[103] See C.R. de Silva (1977: 427-28). The Council consisted of a Chairman and eight other members appointed by the Governor General on recommendation of the Prime Minister, plus representatives from the Ministry of Education and the Vice Chancellors of Sri Lanka's four universities.

[104] In the UK and Commonwealth Nations, universities' chief executive officers carry the title of 'Vice Chancellor.' In Sri Lanka, the Head of State – now the President – served as the 'Chancellor' of all universities, but had little direct involvement.

[105] See C.R. de Silva (1977: 422-23).

[106] The statistics supporting this discussion come from Ibid: 423, Table 8.

[107] Ibid: 430.

Chapter Ten Notes

[1] See Jupp (1978: 46, ff.). The author, then a Professor at York University, first visited Sri Lanka in 1956 and studied the country for more than 20 years before publication of his book.

[2] Ibid: 49. The families were Senanayake-Jayewardene-Wijewardene-Kotelawala, Bandaranaike-Ratwatte-Obeyesekere, Maithrapala-Senanayake, and Rajapakse.

[3] Ranasinghe Premadasa, who came from low-caste origins and a poor family in the south with no political connections, would break this mould by becoming Sri Lanka's Executive President in 1988. He was assassinated in 1993.

[4] In 1988, the pre-independence political leaders Colvin R. de Silva (LSSP), Pieter Keuneman (Communist) and J.R. Jayewardene (UNP) remained active politically, though Jayewardene retired at the end of that year. Mrs. Bandaranaike, a relatively late arrival, seriously contemplated a run for Sri Lanka's Executive Presidency in the 1994 general election.

[5] Residents in the Western Province, in the vicinity of Colombo, plus the Kandyan dominated north central and central highlands provinces comprised 60 per cent of Sri Lanka's registered voters and elected 61 per cent of Parliament members in 1970.

[6] See Wilson (1975: 141). The Associated Newspapers of Ceylon (Lake House Group) published five daily newspapers – two Sinhala, two English and one Tamil – with a combined circulation of 273,893, and four weekly papers – one Sinhala, two English and one Tamil – with a combined circulation of 479,126. The *Times Group* published three dailies – one Sinhala, two English – with a combined circulation of 83,853, and two weeklies – one Sinhala and one English – with a combined circulation of 162,706.

[7] Ibid: 141, 152, ff. Wilson reports an 'estimated' circulation of 6800 for the *Sun*, 58,600 for *Dawasa* and 12,100 for the Tamil Daily, *Dinapathy*. No circulation figures were readily available for the Sinhala and Tamil weekly papers.

[8] Ibid: 157. *Aththa's* circulation ran from 40,000-50,000. *Janadina* reached between 20,000 and 30,000 readers.

[9] See Jupp (1978: 163).

[10] Ibid: 113. Political rallies of several hours' duration, combining entertainment, education, religious observance and political speech-making, remain a tradition in Sri Lanka to this day. The late President Ranasinghe Premadasa was a master of this genre.

[11] Ibid.

[12] Ibid: 94. This figure does not include the estate workers or members of numerous minor and splinter parties. The UNP claimed a membership of about 120,000, the SLFP claimed about 60,000 members and the LSSP about 25,000. According to Jupp, the ratio of party members to votes compared reasonably to party organisations in many European nations.

[13] Ibid: 95. Symbols of the major parties included the SLFP's Hand, the UNP's Elephant, the LSSP's Key, the Communist Party's Star, and the Federal Party's House. The major party symbols also represented important aspects of Sri Lankan culture, the Elephant for warrior King Dutugemunu, who defeated the Tamils, and the Hand for the Buddha.

[14] This discussion derives primarily from Jupp (1978: 109, ff.). However, similar observations also appear in Calvin Woodward's study of Sri Lanka's party system (1979), although this latter work does not include the formation of the United Front or the 1970 General Election. A.J. Wilson's detailed study of the 1970 election campaign (1975) and his more general study of Sri Lankan politics (1974) also examined party organisation.

[15] See previous note as well as K.M. de Silva and Wriggins (1994: 184, ff.).

[16] See Wilson (1974: 137) and K.M. de Silva and Wriggins (1994: 187-88).

[17] In a notable exception, young Gamini Dissanayake successfully contested the tea planting Nuwara Eliya district in 1970, and later became one of the most influential members of J.R. Jayewardene's cabinet.

[18] See K.M. de Silva and Wriggins (1994: 187).

[19] See Jupp (1978: 62, 126).

[20] Ibid: 147-51 and K.M. de Silva and Wriggins (1994: 146, 166).

[21] See Jupp (1978: 155-56). Mahamud was rewarded with the education ministry in Mrs. Bandaranaike's Cabinet following the United Front's election victory and held that position throughout her administration.

[22] See Ibid: 109, 125. In chapter 8, we saw how opposition from feudal landowners made working with the Marxist parties difficult for S.W.R.D. Bandaranaike and created obstacles to his reform programs.

[23] Communist Party leader Pieter Keuneman held this 'safe' seat..

[24] See Jupp (1978: 95, 105, 106). Matara was the home district of party leader, Dr. S.A. Wickremasinghe. S.W.R. de A. Samarasinghe's compilation of election results in *Universal Franchise 1931-1981* (1981: 208, ff.) provides a useful picture of the three parties' areas of strength.

[25] See Wilson (1974: 147).

[26] Ibid: According to Wilson, unity of purpose among opposition parliamentarians created the appearance of a 'parallel government.'

[27] Recall that historically, Sri Lanka's Marxist parties had opposed this agenda and had been strong supporters of minority rights.

[28] See Wilson (1975: 40).

[29] Descriptions of the 'Common Program' appear in K.M. de Silva and Wriggins (1994: 187, ff.), Wilson (1974: 147, ff.), and Wilson (1975: 95, ff.).

[30] Ibid: 131-2 and Jupp (1978: 71-72, 125). However, militant communalism quickly reasserted itself following the United Front's overwhelming victory.

[31] See Chandraprema (1989: 97, ff.), who describes the deteriorating economic conditions in the south during this period, owing to population pressures and a stagnant economy. Between 1962 and 1973, the average size of land holding dropped from 2.07 to 1.73 acres in Galle and from 2.44 acres to 2.06 acres in Matara. Of those employed in agriculture, 48.7 per cent in Galle and 44.3 per cent in Matara were classified as agricultural labourers. The comparable figures for Colombo and Jaffna were 22 per cent and 15 per cent respectively. Although Sri Lanka enjoys plentiful rainfall, the absence of ground water complicated intensive cultivation, such as that practiced in the Jaffna peninsula. See also Jupp (1978: 299).

[32] Ibid: 153 and Wilson (1974: 192).

[33] See R. Gunaratna (1990: 1). Wilson (1974: 162) places the founding of the People's Liberation Front in 1964, but this organisation was not directly linked to Wijeweera's, although it shared some objectives.

[34] See Chandraprema (1989: 93, ff.).

[35] See R. Gunaratna (1990: 1) and Chandraprema (1991: 21). Wijeweera's father was injured in brawl between Communist and UNP supporters and remained bedridden for the rest of his life.

[36] Interestingly, the Communist Party (Peking Wing) was led during this period by a Tamil, N.S. Shanmugathasan.

[37] Wilson (1974: 162-63).

[38] Ibid: 163. Sri Lankans have told me they feared that Pol Pot's Kampuchea would also serve as a model for a Wijeweera-led government.

[39] See Jupp (1978: 297-300).

[40] See R. Gunaratna (1990: 6-7) and Wilson (1974: 162).

[41] See Jupp (1978: 300).

[42] No work regarding the rise of militancy among Tamil youth that I have consulted gives any attention to this phenomenon prior to 1970, the beginning of Mrs. Bandaranaike's second administration. For example, see Piyadasa (1984: chapters 3 and 4) and Ponnambalam (1983: chapters 4 and 5).

[43] Friends living in Colombo told me they regularly visited black-market emporia on the Northwest coast to purchase 'duty free' Indian goods during this period.

[44] Kearney (1971: 109) draws the figure of 3,000 from the Ceylon Teachers Union 1965-66 *Annual Report of the General Secretary* .

[45] Several powerful unions not allied with the opposition parties chose not to strike.

[46] Kearney (1971: 108-11, 139, 147-52).

[47] Ibid: 146-147.

[48] In fairness to Mrs. Bandaranaike, readers should remember that most newspapers still supported the UNP and would probably incline toward not publishing material that criticised Dudley Senanayake's National Government.

[49] Previous periods when the index for state-sanctioned violence dropped to a level of two included March 1960 - July 1960, August 1955 - May 1956, and October 1953 - February 1954. As noted in chapter 7, values as low as 1 were recorded in the first years following independence.

[50] See Wilson (1975: 36).

[51] The government's vigorous response during the early months of emergency rule may have been due in part to J.R. Jayewardene, who held the reins of power in Colombo during the Prime Minister's extended overseas trip to the United States and England.

[52] Kearney (1973: 198).

[53] See Nyrop et al. (1971: 449). 22 suspects came to trial in January 1968, and charges against 10 were dropped during the course of the trial. The remainder won acquittal in January, 1970 by a unanimous jury verdict.

[54] *New York Times*, January 28, 1968.

[55] *Ceylon Daily News*, May 3, 1969. The *News* reported that 15 arrests were made, but this may have understated the actual number.

[56] See Jupp (1978: 311) and the Colombo *Daily Mirror*, February 28, 1970. Wijeweera told a rally of his followers at Colombo's Hyde Park, 'We will strike when we are provoked to do so by the armed forces, which are now trying to accuse us of a conspiracy, but we are not conspirators... [W]e caution the government not to send us underground. The revolution will commence on the day that our group is banned, as we would have no alternative but to retaliate.'

[57] Ibid: 317.

[58] The most detailed discussions appear in Nyrop et al. (1971) and Ross and Savada (1990), each of which devote a chapter to national security questions and discuss the army and police as institutions. J.R. Jayewardene's biographer, K.M. de Silva, devotes a chapter of his recent work on *Problems of Governance in Sri Lanka* (1993a) to national security, but Dudley Senanayake's administration receives only once sentence in this account.

[59] See K.M. de Silva and Wriggins (1994: 156) and especially K.M. de Silva (1986: 203, 271).

[60] See Jupp (1978: 245).

[61] See K.M. de Silva (1993b: 347).

[62] Ibid: 357.

[63] Nyrop et al. (1971: 452). According to Nyrop, the Commission report was issued in the late 1960s, but not widely available until early 1970. I was unable to obtain a copy.

[64] Ibid: 455, ff. A new structure of competitive examinations and screening boards became the basis for selecting recruits. The government moved the police training academy from Kalutara on the Southern Coast to Colombo, and redesigned its curriculum.

[65] Ibid: 454, ff. quotes an *Administration Report of the Inspector General of Police for the Financial Year 1966-67*. The report noted that the police had deployed about 3,000 men in Colombo for crowd control during the five-day celebration of Buddhist New Year (*Vesak*) in April 1967. At that time, the minimum authorised strength for Colombo district was 2,600 and the actual strength was below that level.

[66] *Dawasa*, June 6, 1968.

[67] Nyrop et al. (1971: 468).

[68] The army was called out to support the police in the December 1966 Tamil Language demonstrations, in the student strikes of February 1969, and in the Colombo/Trincomalee port strikes that began in December 1969.

[69] These figures come from Nyrop et al. (1971: 468). Substantially fewer of these boats and aircraft were operational at any given time.

[70] The phrase comes from Bjorkman (1985). See also Jupp (1978: 241) and K.M. de Silva (1993b: 347, ff.).

[71] Unless otherwise noted, election results in this section appear in a database compiled by the author using the following sources: S.W.R. de A. Samarasinghe (1981: 218-21), Wilson (1975: chapter 9), and G.P.S.H. de Silva (1979), plus compilations of electoral data from post election reports of the *Ceylon Daily News*, *The Times of Ceylon*, and *The Sun*, all in English, and *Dawasa*, in Sinhala.

[72] Description of the United Front campaign strategy derives primarily from Wilson (1974: 147, ff. and 1975: 95, ff.).

[73] Ibid: 40.

[74] Wilson (1975: 104) quotes *Ceylon Daily News*, May 18, 1970.

[75] A discussion of the UNP's campaign appears in Wilson (1975: 85, ff.) and K.M. de Silva and Wriggins (1994: 186, ff).

[76] Ibid: 105 quotes *Ceylon Daily News*, May 25, 1970.

[77] The Federal Party Candidates defeated Tamil Congress parliamentarians in Ponnambalam's Jaffna constituency, coastal Uduppidi and rural Vavuniya. The Tamil Congress won in the coastal constituency of Vadukkodai, and two rural constituencies, Mannar and Kilinochchi. Jaffna, Mannar and Vavuniya were the only Northern Province constituencies with a less than 80 per cent Tamil majority.

[78] The Federal Party's share of the popular vote in the Eastern Province dropped from 24 to 19 per cent. The Tamil Congress did not contest.

[79] Another indication of declining Muslim support for the Federal Party came from the defeat of the Party's candidate in the Northern Province Constituency of Mannar, with a population identified as 59 per cent Muslim.

Chapter Eleven Notes

[1] Readers will recall from chapter 10 than JVP refers to the Sinhalese words for 'JVP,' *Janatha Vimukti Peramuna*. Writers commonly use these initials when writing about the movement, and I will do so from time to time.

[2] See K.M. de Silva (1998a: especially chapters 2-6) and K.M de Silva and Wriggins (1994: especially chapter 19).

[3] Later, I will discuss the other common remembrance of these times, namely long waits in line for food and other necessities.

[4] Quoted in R. Gunaratna (1990: 85). Wijesekera's official title was 'President of the Patriotic Students Front of the JVP.'

[5] See Chandraprema (1991: 44).

[6] Ibid: 49. Chandraprema, a JVP insider who provided Sri Lankans with the first clear picture of the movement in a 1990 series of newspaper articles, notes that Wijeweera's strength as a speaker could also prove a weakness. He could become completely carried away by the sight of a crowd and make intemperate, provocative statements.

[7] See R. Gunaratna (1990: 86).

[8] Ibid: 94-95.

[9] See Chandraprema (1991: 93). The author argues that Sri Lankans would have experienced what the Kampucheans went through under Pol Pot in 1972-1975 had the revolution succeeded. The gruesome events of the second JVP insurrection, which reached its peak in 1989, give some credence to this view.

[10] In addition, more than 100 demonstrators staged a protest at the American Embassy in Colombo. While such protests occurred fairly frequently, some demonstrators did throw home made bombs at the Embassy during this protest.

[11] See my *Violent Political Conflict Data Base* (1990: 36). The strikes occurred in the villages of Esalamulla, near Dedigama, on March 10, and Kondagala, near Nelundeniya, on March 11. Six youths died and a greater number suffered injuries in the two explosions.

[12] The arrest took place in remote Ampara district, on the southeastern part of the island.

[13] See R. Gunaratna (1990: 90) and Chandraprema (1991: 31). Chandraprema describes the conditions at Fort Hemmenheil as 'near inhuman.' After the Jaffna Chief Magistrate had to be called to investigate the death of a prisoner, conditions improved somewhat.

[14] Chandraprema (Ibid) reports that the decision was taken on April 2 at a meeting of JVP factions held in the *Sangharamaya*, or Buddhist priests' residence, of Vidyodaya University.

[15] On factionalism within the JVP, see Ibid: 33, ff. The strongest arguments about the ineffectiveness and disorganisation of the central JVP leadership comes from Alexander

(1981: 125, ff.), who bases his conclusions on extensive anthropological field research, focusing on former rebels and peasants in the most affected areas. He concludes that 'the insurrection did not pose an objective military threat to the Sri Lankan government and the apparent successes were the direct result of government panic.' The most widely cited source on the insurrection, Supreme Court Justice A.C. Alles' *Insurgency 1971* (1977), pictures the JVP as more effective and better organised.

[16] R. Gunaratna (1990: 103) reports that at the rebellion's height, JVP guerrillas controlled 35 police areas and 50 'chief towns.' The government abandoned a number of other police stations.

[17] On this point, see Alexander (1981: 125, ff.), K.M. de Silva and Wriggins (1994: 213-14), and Jupp (1978: 315).

[18] See R. Gunaratna (1990: 108-09).

[19] Alexander (1981: 128) reports: 'Many of those killed had not participated in armed attacks; in the immediate area of my field work, they included three fishermen laying nets after curfew, some prominent supporters of opposition political parties and two black market liquor traders who were shot by the police and left to die at the police station.'

[20] Ibid: 130. Use of informing to settle scores also became a pattern in later insurrections, as we shall see.

[21] This event was originally reported by the Criminal Justice Commission and in Alles (1977: chapter 28). It has also appeared in many other accounts of the insurrection. This quotation comes from R. Gunaratna (1990: 99).

[22] Ibid: 115. See also Alexander (1981: 130) and Jupp (1978: 19-20).

[23] Not only did lower caste status limit educational and employment opportunities, but members of lower castes could not even worship in some Hindu Temples.

[24] The Tamil United Front originated in May 1972 at a meeting in Trincomalee. The event that brought the three Tamil parties together was ratification of Sri Lanka's 'Republican Constitution.' I discuss both the constitution and the new coalition later in this chapter.

[25] For widely differing accounts of this event, see K.M. de Silva (1986: 272, ff.) and Ponnambalam (1983: 181, ff.).

[26] Later in this chapter, I provide a more detailed biographical sketch of Prabakharan.

[27] As note in previous chapters, I calculate this according to the formula:

$$\text{Scaled Events}_{Sen} = \text{Events}_{Sen} * \text{Months in Office}_{Ban} / \text{Months in Office}_{Sen}$$

[28] I made this estimate by reading the descriptions of each political conflict event involving deaths during the period from March 23 through July 20 and counting the number of deaths reported. Where the number reported was 'several' as it was in the case of two events – one extending over several months – I assumed that as many as 20 people may have died. Some personal accounts characterise the number of dead as probably fewer than 20 in both instances.

[29] This comes from conversations with army and naval officers involved in putting down the JVP rebellion.

[30] The discussion of Sirimavo Bandaranaike's personal and political style draws heavily on interviews with both UNP and SLFP politicians, as well as other individuals personally acquainted with the Prime Minister. See also Jupp (1978: 294, ff.), Wilson (1975: 181, ff.), Oberst (1985: 75, ff.), Seneviratne (1975: 171, ff.), K.M. de Silva and Wriggins (1994: especially chapters 11 and 13-16) and other sources dealing with Mrs. Bandaranaike's first term in office, cited in chapter 7.

[31] Bandaranaike's position as Parliamentary opposition leader had also marked a post-war first for a woman.

[32] See K.M. de Silva and Wriggins (1994: 111, 202). Other alleged participants among top-level politicians included former Prime Minister Sir John Kotelawala and Governor General Sir Oliver Goonetilleke. Some of the coup plotters made the allegations, and subsequently saw them presented to Parliament by Felix Dias Bandaranaike. The coup is described in more detail by K.M. de Silva and Wriggins (1994: 107, ff.). As already noted, political scientist Donald R. Horowitz has written an entire book on the coup (1980) although he does not offer a judgment about the UNP leaders' complicity.

[33] See K.M. de Silva and Wriggins (1994: 202): A Parliamentary select committee investigated Mrs. Bandaranaike following charges that she had personally benefited while in office from a commercial transaction between the government and an insurance company. The panel cleared her of the charges. While the government later charged her brother with bribery, the investigation eventually 'collapsed.'

[34] A discussion of the political roles played by Mrs. Bandaranaike's children during this period appears in Ibid: 290-295.

[35] Chandrika Bandaranaike later married Vijaya Kumaratunga, a popular film star, and with her husband formed the *Sri Lanka Majana Pakshaya*, a political party advocating stronger socialist measures than the SLFP. In 1993, she rejoined the SLFP and won election as Prime Minister of the Western Province. In 1994, following defeat of the United Party in parliamentary elections, she was named Prime Minister of Sri Lanka. In 1995, she won election as Sri Lanka's fourth Executive President.

[36] Mrs. Bandaranaike also retained personal control over the Foreign Ministry.

[37] See K.M. de Silva (1986: 253). Traditional Roman Catholic support for the UNP suffered several defections in the 1970 General Election.

[38] See Jupp (1978: 151). Buddhist 'Full Moon Poya Days' remained a national holiday devoted to Buddhist observances, during which no business took place and most commercial establishments could serve no alcohol.

[39] See Wilson (1975: 190).

[40] K.M. de Silva and Wriggins (1994: 208) and Jupp (1978: 286) offer somewhat different perspectives on these changes. In the former study, the authors find 'that [the changes] had a debilitating effect on administrative efficiency, with over-enthusiastic and politically influential amateurs interfering with the working of institutions and undermining the

morale of the higher bureaucracy.' Jupp observes 'that the logic of the move...was precisely that such alien notions as an insulated judiciary and public service should be abandoned and that groups and classes previously excluded from these areas of government should be free to enter them. The colonial Platonism which had inspired the Soulbury Constitution,' he continues, 'was replaced by a cruder but more politically realistic assertion of majority domination.'

[41] See K.M. de Silva (1986: 271). The JVP insurrection raised questions about this assumption, as we have seen.

[42] See Jupp (1978: 261-68), Ponnambalam (1983: 161), and K.M. de Silva and Wriggins (1994: 20).

[43] See Jupp (1978: 277).

[44] See Kearney (1979: 450), Little (1994: 75), and K.M. de Silva and Wriggins (1994: 206-207). I discuss the substance of the Constitution in greater detail below. For additional details on the procedures of the Constituent Assembly as well as the substance of the final document, see Cooray (1973).

[45] See Jupp (1978: 252-53). The Commission legislation, spearheaded by Felix Dias Bandaranaike, resembled that passed by an SLFP-dominated Parliament as a way of dealing with the 1962 coup plotters. Britain's Privy Council had overturned the 1962 law as 'a legislative plan *ex post facto*' to secure the conviction and enhance the punishment of ... particular individuals.'

[46] See Jupp (1978: 252, 256). The Commission procedure was used to try alleged currency speculators, including one of Sri Lanka's leading businessmen. Later, the former Governor General, Sir Oliver Goonetilleke, then living in England, underwent trial *in absentia* by a Commission, receiving a sentence of four years' imprisonment.

[47] See Ibid: 28, 233, ff. A more detailed discussion of local government reforms occurs later in this chapter.

[48] See Obeyesekere (1974: 384).

[49] This judgement follows discussions with a number of Sri Lankans – mostly UNP supporters – adversely impacted by land reform, limits on housing and the wealth tax.

[50] Provisions of the then-unreplaced Soulbury Constitution allowed this.

[51] Many large Colombo mansions, formerly owned privately, now function as embassies, resource libraries for foreign governments, headquarters of non-governmental organisations, or government offices. The elegant Victorian structure now named 'College House,' which serves as administrative headquarters for Colombo University, had previously served as a family home. Some large holdings, including the Ward Place home of J.R. Jayewardene and the Bandaranaike family compound on Rosemead Place, have remained in private hands.

[52] See Jupp (1978: 251) and Wilson (1975: 185).

[53] See the Government's Land Reform Act No. 1 of 1972 as well as Karunatilake (1987: 75, 222) and K.M. de Silva, ed. (1977: 233-34, 251-52). A more detailed discussion of the

Act appears in the section of this chapter dealing with development goals and economic policies.

[54] Karunatilake (1987: 223).

[55] Writing about this period, Wilson (1975: 185) notes that '[the better-off layers of Ceylonese Society] comprise not more than some 50,000 individuals and are not worth flogging. But the Government gains some benefit from the fact that the exercise gives much satisfaction to the poorer sections of the community.'

[56] This brief discussion of the Government's austerity program and public reaction to it derives from K.M. de Silva and Wriggins (1994: 214-217). See also Karunatilake (1987: 316-18).

[57] Quoted in K.M. de Silva and Wriggins (1994: 215).

[58] Ibid: 217-18. The authors report that United Front 'backbench' members staged an unusual revolt against the budget proposals. Senior ministers met with them for six hours before introduction of the budget to address their concerns. Later, backbenchers demanded reconsideration of the austerity measures and succeeded in scaling-back some of them.

[59] Rice becomes the centrepiece of Sinhalese New Year's celebrations, which emphasise the Buddhist practice of almsgiving. On the main streets of towns and villages, groups will organise to cook and distribute free meals, typically rice and curry and a type of rice pudding, to all who pass.

[60] The Central Bank *Reviews of the Economy* for 1973 and 1974 examine these problems in depth, while K.M. de Silva and Wriggins (1994: 271-72) and Karunatilake (1987: 319-20) summarise these issues.

[61] Descriptions of government food policies during this period occur in many sources, including K.M. de Silva and Wriggins (1994: 272-73). However, my description here of government policies and Sri Lankans' reaction to them synthesises numerous stories told to me by Sri Lankan friends and acquaintances.

[62] See Jupp (1978: 272). By contrast, establishment of the Soulbury Constitution as fundamental law had been 'hereby ordered by his Majesty by and with the advice of His Privy Council.'

[63] See Wilson (1975: 272-75).

[64] For example, see Cooray (1973), K.M. de Silva (1985a and 1986), and Jupp (1978).

[65] See Uyangoda (1994: 53).

[66] Jupp (1978: 272) quotes Section 2 of the 1972 *Constitution of Sri Lanka*.

[67] Readers will recall that a power-sharing arrangement was first surfaced in the abortive Bandaranaike-Chelvanayakam pact, which Sinhalese-Buddhist pressure forced Prime Minister S.W.R.D. Bandaranaike to repudiate.

[68] Specifically, the Constitution referred to the Official Language Act. No. 33 of 1956 and the Tamil Language (Special Provisions) Act of 1958, passed by S.W.R.D. Bandaranaike's government. I discuss this legislation in chapter 8, below.

[69] See Jupp (1978: 273-74).

[70] I offer this view as my own, though it concurs with the argument in Jupp (1978: 273), and, implicitly, with many other scholars who tend to give more attention to language, economic opportunity – including access to education – and devolution of power as issues dividing the Sinhalese and Tamil communities. David Little's book, *Sri Lanka: The Invention of Enmity* (1994) presents a contrasting view.

[71] Ibid: 276. The demands that Buddhism become the State Religion and Sri Lanka carry the title of Buddhist Socialist Republic are attributed to Hema Basanayake, a spokesperson for the Council of All-Ceylon Sinhala Societies. The demand to limit the Presidency to Buddhists came from the All-Ceylon Buddhist Congress.

[72] See Kearney (1979: 450). After ratification of the new Constitution, Prime Minister Bandaranaike traveled to Kandy's 'Temple of the Tooth,' (*Dalada Maligawa)* one of the most sacred Buddhist shrines on the island. With Buddhist priests in attendance and the public watching she invoked the blessings of the Sacred Tooth Relic, reputedly a tooth of the Buddha, on the document.

[73] See K.M. de Silva and Wriggins (1994: 219). The authors view adoption of the new constitution as ushering in 'a deeply significant, indeed historical, shift in the balance of power within the Constitution which remains unchanged to the present day.'

[74] See Jupp (1978: 285). Under the previous constitution, judicial appointments had come from an Independent Judicial Service Commission. The Sri Lankan Bar strongly opposed abolition of the Commission. Eventually, the government compromised by allowing establishment of Advisory and Disciplinary Boards, which gave legal professionals some control over their own affairs.

[75] See Wilson (1975: 281). Members of a 'Constitutional Court,' established to provide judicial review, had their seats as Cabinet appointments, eligible for replacement when governments change and issuing decisions reversible by a two-thirds majority of the National Assembly. Wilson notes that the Constitutional Court could exercise considerable power over a government with only a small Parliamentary majority.

[76] See Jupp (1978: 286-87).

[77] More accurately, this amounted to the maximum time which could elapse between general elections. The Assembly's term could run shorter if the government lost a vote of confidence, or if the Prime Minister requested a general election before the end of the government's term in office.

[78] K.M. de Silva and Wriggins (1994: 220), whose work often reflects the viewpoint of their biographical subject J.R. Jayewardene, describe this as 'a cynical and unprincipled stratagem, unprecedented in the annals of democracy.'

[79] Ibid: 251-52. The authors' account of events surrounding Dudley Senanayake's death results from interviews with J.R. Jayewardene, supplemented by newspaper accounts.

[80] I discuss these measures more fully later in this chapter, in the section addressing 'State-sanctioned violence.'

[81] See Jupp (1978: 367-68).

[82] The government's budget proposals for 1975 recommended these measures.

[83] For a description of the coalition's break up, see K.M. de Silva and Wriggins (1994: 295-311).

[84] Readers will recall that this coalition, comprising the Federal Party, Tamil Congress and Ceylon Workers Congress, had formed in 1972. They adopted the name *Tamil United Liberation Front* in 1976. I will discuss this in greater detail below. The words 'Liberation Front' were used by many revolutionary movements, especially Marxist revolutionary movements, throughout the developing world.

[85] Roughly translated, 'Sri Lanka' means 'the resplendent land' in Sinhala.

[86] Readers will recall that the Kandyan Kingdom did not formally accede to British rule until 1815, and the Kandyans were not fully subjugated until 1818. British rule did not become secure until the 1830s, when Governor Sir Edward Barnes completed a road system into the Kandyan regions that made guerrilla resisitance more difficult.

[87] These themes play a prominent role in the writings of the respected Sinhalese Buddhist revivalist, Anagarika Dharmapala. For example, see Schwartz (1979: 5) and Kumari Jayawardene (1984: 181).

[88] According to Jupp (1978: 127) 'The SLFP's 'nationalism'...wanted Sinhala hegemony to be exercised through the ballot box and through legislation which preserved the rights of minorities so long as they accepted that they *were* minorities.'

[89] Most Christians in the Sinhalese and Tamil communities are Roman Catholics. However, these groups also include small, but influential numbers of Anglican Christians.

[90] See Ponnambalam (1983: 180).

[91] Every author who writes about rising ethnic tensions during the United Front's years in power devotes at least some attention to divisions created by changes in university admissions policies. The discussion here stems primarily from K.M. de Silva (1986: 261-68) and Tambiah (1992: 66-68). Readers can find the most in-depth treatment of the university admissions issue in the writings of C.R. de Silva (1977, 1978, and 1979), whose less widely available publications are cited by most other authors.

[92] See Jayawardene (1984: 118). Tracts such as a 1970 pamphlet titled 'Ancient Enemy of the Sinhalese' *(Sinhalayage Adist Hatura)*, reinforced the perception of discrimination.

[93] See K.M. de Silva (1986: 264).

[94] Ibid: 265. Though Tamils constituted only about 11 percent of Sri Lanka's population, they accounted for 30 percent of secondary-school science students.

[95] Ibid and Tambiah (1992: 66). The share of total places granted to Tamils in science-based programs fell from 35.3 percent in 1970 to 20.9 per cent in 1974 and 19 per cent in 1975.

[96] When questioned about this later, Mrs. Bandaranaike said she regarded the education of her children as a personal matter.

[97] See K.M. de Silva (1986: 268). In 1976, the share of total places in science programs awarded to Tamils rose to 25 percent.

[98] See Ponnambalam (1983: 174).

[99] See K.M. de Silva and Wriggins (1994: 221). The complete text of the resolution reads as follows: 'The constitution had completely failed to met the legitimate aspirations of the Tamil-speaking people by refusing to grant constitutional status to the Tamil language in the fields of education, administration and justice, and thereby reduces them to the position of second-class citizens in their own country.'

[100] See Swami (1994: 31).

[101] See K.M. de Silva (1986: 259) and Ponnambalam (1983: 185). The resolution described the Tamils as 'a nation distinct and apart from the Sinhalese and their constitution announces to the world that the Republican Constitution of 1972 has made the Tamils a slave nation ruled by the new colonial masters, the Sinhalese.'

[102] T. Sabaratnam (1990: 113), Thondaman's biographer, reports that he met Chelvanayakam in Colombo after the Pannakam meetings. When questioned about the Vaddukoddai Resolutions, Chelvanayakam explained that he personally opposed a separate state, but had subscribed to the demand for an independent Eelam as a bargaining position that he hoped would lead to a federal system for Sri Lanka. 'Without Indian support we will never be able to attain Eelam,' Chelvanayakam said. 'We are going to ask for Eelam to make the Sinhala people agree to an autonomous Tamil region.'

[103] Ibid: 108-09.

[104] High-country Ceylon Tea is known in the trade as 'champagne tea' because of low acidity and superb flavour.

[105] Several visits to Sri Lanka's tea country and conversations with present and former plantation managers contributed to this discussion.

[106] For example, see Sabaratnam (1990: 109-11). Readers will recall that in Sri Lanka, labour unions often affiliate with political parties. Typically, several competing unions organise in a given industry, and this proved true in the tea industry during this period. The Lanka Estate Workers Union (LEWU), for example affiliated with the SLFP. The most powerful union, however, was the independent Ceylon Workers Congress.

[107] For a description of labour relations on the plantations during this period, see Ibid (99-111).

[108] Ibid: 103. During her entire term in office Prime Minister Bandaranaike did not meet once with Indian Tamil leader Savumiamoorthy Thondaman on Sri Lankan soil, Thondaman reported in a 1977 press interview. Their occasional meetings in international venues were cordial.

[109] See Kodikara (1982: 35-37) and K.M. de Silva (1986: 276).

[110] As noted above, Savumiamoorthy Thondaman had distanced the Ceylon Workers' Congress from the Vaddukodai resolution, with its demand for an independent Tamil Eelam, although the Indian Tamil party maintained a nominal affiliation with the Tamil

United Liberation Front (TULF). When J.R. Jayewardene became Sri Lanka's first Executive President in 1978, he invited Thondaman to join his cabinet as Minister of Rural Industries Development. Thondaman remained an influential member of UNP governments throughout the 1980s and early 1990s.

[111] This account derives largely from K.M. de Silva (1986: 227-35, 282). A description of the Puttalam conflict appears in the *Political Conflict Data Base* Richardson (1990). Election statistics for Mahmud's Batticaloa constituency are reported in G.P.S.H. de Silva (1979: 133-34).

[112] Ibid: 133. Batticaloa elected two representatives to the National Assembly, one of the few constituencies allocated more than one. The candidate elected to the second seat, a Muslim affiliated with the UNP, received 25,345 votes. Mahmud received 21,275 votes in his first run for elective office. He had previously served as an appointed member of Parliament. The Republican Constitution eliminated appointed members, as we have seen, but allowed those appointed to the House of Representatives following the 1970 election to serve out the remainder of their terms in the National Assembly.

[113] See the tabulations of UN voting in Nissanka (1984: 199-215). Although support for the US on controversial issues improved from a surprisingly low level under Dudley Senanayake, Sri Lanka still voted with the U.S.S.R. almost 3 times as often as with the US.

[114] The account of this initiative derives primarily based from lengthy discussions found in the two major studies of Sri Lankan foreign policy, Kodikara (1982: 136-46) and Nissanka (1984: 216-47). It also benefited from lengthy discussions with my colleague and friend, the late Professor Kodikara. Keerawella's more recent account (1989) covers basically the same ground, but with a greater emphasis on perspectives from academic writings in the field of international relations.

[115] Details of votes on the successive resolutions appear in Nissanka (1984: 223, ff.). No votes were ever reported in opposition to the resolutions – states opposed to Sri Lanka's initiative abstained.

[116] See Ibid: 238, note 35. Sri Lanka's Permanent Representative to the United Nations, Shirley Amerasinghe, admitted as much in a report to his government that was quoted in the June 30, 1975 edition of the *Ceylon Daily News*.

[117] K.M. de Silva and Wriggins (1994: 316-17).

[118] Under the strong Executive Presidency system put in place by Sri Lanka's 1978 Constitution, the Prime Minister still served as the Government's leader in Parliament, but with greatly diminished powers. The President was both head of state and head of government. Mrs. Bandaranaike had run for the office of Executive President against Ranasinghe Premadasa in 1988, but lost.

[119] Kodikara (1982) emphasises this strongly. I will return to the topic later.

[120] Selection resulted from vigorous lobbying on the part of the Prime Minister and Felix Dias Bandaranaike, who had been disappointed when their efforts to bring the Fourth Summit to Colombo proved unsuccessful.

[121] See Nissanka (1984: 318). At time, Sri Lanka's entire foreign service numbered only 71 officers.

[122] According to Nissanka (1984: 318), there were no flaws in protocol, traffic arrangements, receptions or security measures.

[123] Interestingly, the debate over these questions was carried out by party leaders before voters in rural Mulkirigala constituency, located in the Southern Province's Hambantota district, where a by election was held on August 27, 1976. See reports in the *Ceylon Daily News* for August 27 and 28, 1976. The SLFP candidate, Lakshman Rajapakse, retained the seat with larger popular vote total, but a slightly smaller margin of victory than in 1970.

[124] See Nissanka (1984: 322-23).

[125] See Ibid: 23. The government carried out a 'tremendous propaganda campaign' emphasising the potential benefits that would flow from the summit.

[126] See K.M. de Silva (1986: 283).

[127] Kodikara (1982: 144) quotes from the Department of Information's *Non Alignment – A Deliberate Choice* (N.d.: 18).

[128] The four Asian Tigers are Taiwan, South Korea, Hong Kong and Singapore. While these countries embraced free-market economics, the state also played a major economic management role in Singapore, Taiwan and South Korea.

[129] Nissanka (1984: 321-22), who writes sympathetically about many of Sirimavo Bandaranaike's accomplishments, offers a somewhat similar appraisal in the conclusion of his major survey of Sri Lankan foreign policy: 'It appears then,' he states, 'that the administration of Mrs. Bandaranaike concerned itself too greatly with foreign affairs to the detriment of home administration; and consequently its own image in the eyes of the electorate. It is a truism that one of the most important objectives of the foreign policy of any country should be to bring about stability in the government of the ruling party. In this respect, both Mrs. Bandaranaike and Mrs. Gandhi...have failed.'

Chapter Twelve Notes

[1] Jupp (1978: 182) presents the overall rationale for the government's economic planning, along with Columbage and Karunaratne (1986: 207-10). See also Wilson (1974: 184), Moore (1990a: 33), and K.M. de Silva and Wriggins (1994: 208-10).

[2] See Wiles (1962) for a thorough treatment of Marxist economic theory and development planning models that were influential during this period. Griffin (1989), especially chapters 7 and 8, provides a more recent discussion, including a brief case study of Sri Lanka.

[3] Details of the Five-Year Plan appear in Karunatilake (1987: 316, ff).

[4] The study, *Switching on to Growth* appeared in April 1972, and marked the first in an independently published series titled *Guides to Growth*. While scholars cite Jiggins' work (1972) often, I have seen no references to subsequent works in the series.

[5] See Ibid (1972: 5).

[6] Ibid: 17. The author describes public corporations as 'welfare states within the welfare state. ...They are areas of political patronage and intervention, not creators of a new managerial class.'

[7] Ibid. Examples of hidden subsidies included free telephones and calls allowed to senior officials for private use, free cars and petrol (gasoline), free rail transit and subsidised government housing and comprehensive health care for both officials and their families.

[8] See the Government's *Review of the Economy 1979*, various tables.

[9] See Peebles (1982: 100).

[10] These included the Estates (Control and Transfer) Act No. 2 of 1972, the State Agricultural Corporations Act No. 11 of 1972, the Agricultural Lands Law No. 42 of 1973, and amendments to the Land Acquisition Law of 1950.

[11] This complied with the mandate of the Land Reform (Amendment) Law No. 39 of 1975.

[12] The best treatment of these problems appears in British political economist Mick Moore's meticulously researched volume, *The State and Peasant Politics in Sri Lanka* (1985).

[13] Nevertheless, Mick Moore (1985: 99) argues that 1971 did not mark the first time that managers faced the temptation to make the Guaranteed Pricing Scheme 'an arm of the Food Commissioner oriented to procuring as much rice as cheaply as possible to feed the ration scheme.'

[14] See Chandrapala (1986: 253, Table 28).

[15] Ibid.

[16] Ibid: 250. The new system emerged from the Agricultural Insurance Law of 1973.

[17] See Karunatilake (1973: 73). According to the author, government policy was traditionally based on the assumption that the plantation sector should provide development resources for other sectors.

[18] This proceeded under the authority of the Estates (Control and Transfer) Act No. 2 of 1972, the State Agricultural Corporations Act No. 11 of 1972, and the Land Reform (Amendment) Act No. 39 of 1975.

[19] See *Review of the Economy 1979*, Table 14.

[20] See Chandrapala (1986: 244-45). Responsibility for the plantations was divided among three organisations, the Upcountry Estates Development Board (USAWASAMA), the Janatha (People's) Estate Development Board, both under the Agriculture Ministry and the State Plantations Corporation, under the Ministry of Plantation Industries. USAWASAMA was disbanded in 1977, following accusations of political interference, inefficiency and corruption, and its functions were divided between the other two organisations.

[21] See Karunatilake (1973: 87-90) and Chandrapala (1986: 244, ff.). These conclusions are generally borne out by government-generated statistics.

[22] See Jupp (1978: 251), Wilson (1975: 185); and Karunatilake (1973: 184, 187, ff.). This latter provision gave United Front leaders the opportunity to nationalise concerns owned

by political opponents and to threaten nationalisation as a political sanction. One of the first sectors nationalised was the graphite mining industry, which had provided two of the most influential UNP families — the Senanayakes and the Kotelawalas — with their fortunes.

[23] See Columbage and Karunaratne (1986: 209).

[24] Discussions of these measures appear in K.M. de Silva and Wriggins (1994: 208, ff.), Colombage and Karunaratne (1986: 208, ff.), Wilson (1975: 185), and Jupp (1978: 251).

[25] See the 'Statistical Appendix' to *Review of the Economy 1979*, Table 7.

[26] K.M. de Silva and Wriggins (1994: 210) emphasise this point.

[27] Failure to meet plan targets and other economic problems figured consistently in the *Review[s] of the Economy* and *Annual Reports* published by Sri Lanka's Central Bank. In contrast to many developing nations, especially those strongly committed to Marxist economics, reports indicate little attempt to manipulate data in order to portray the government in a more favourable light in Sri Lanka. This made it easier for both government leaders and others to gauge the effectiveness of economic policies and for the former to move away from the redistributive policies and rigid controls of the early 1970s.

[28] We have seen how this debate even split the Prime Minister's own family, with Felix Dias Bandaranaike and Anura Bandaranaike supporting more moderate policies, while Sunethra Bandaranaike Rupasingha and Chandrika Bandaranaike favoured more doctrinaire Marxist approaches to economic management.

[29] See Colombage and Karunaratne (1986: 209) and Vidanpathirana (1986: 166-68).

[30] Data from Peebles (1982: 337) and the 'Statistical Appendix' to *Review of the Economy 1979*, Table 7 (deflated values calculated by the author). In constant 1970 rupees, gross domestic capital formation in the private sector amounted to 8,249 million rupees for 1971-77; in public corporations, 2,720 million rupees and in government and public enterprises, 5,778 million rupees.

[31] See Wilson (1974: 184).

[32] See Vidanpathirana (1986: 168-69). A government White Paper issued in 1972 stated that only investments that conformed with the Five-Year Plan would be considered. In addition, the Ministry of Planning had to certify that the investments would produce 'adequate yields' according to cost-benefit criteria, for permits to be granted.

[33] See Karunatilake (1987: 148). The new policies included guaranteed security of investments, guaranteed repatriation of profits, and guaranteed repatriation of capital on liquidation, reduced taxes and rebates for some development projects.

[34] See K.M. de Silva and Wriggins (1994: 283). The zones were proposed for Katunayake, in the vicinity of Sri Lanka's international airport, and the seaport of Trincomalee. The Katunayake zone was later established under J.R. Jayewardene's government.

[35] Data on this expansion is provided in Karunatilake (1987: 144, ff.) and Vidanpathirana (1986: 175-80).

[36] Central Bank *Annual Reports* and *Review[s] of the Economy* enumerate the various state sector enterprises and provide information on their performance.

[37] See Karunatilake (1987: 160). These were defined as 'operational objectives' of public enterprises.

[38] Ibid: 151. These requirements were set forth in the Finance Act No. 38 of 1971 that dealt with 'Financial Control of Public Corporations.'

[39] For example, see Vidanpathirana (1986: 186-87). The shortcomings described come through clearly in the Central Bank's own *Annual Reports* and *Review[s] of the Economy*. The 1977 *Review*, for example, notes that in a generally good economic year, the output of public-sector industries declined by three per cent 'despite preferential treatment in a government controlled market.' Value-added in manufacturing rose by only one per cent, 'displaying the inherent weaknesses of a heavily protected and controlled import-substitution industrial complex that has emerged in Sri Lanka.' K.M. de Silva and Wriggins (1994: 208) report that return on investment in the state's manufacturing, trading and service ventures in the early 1970s ran as low as one per cent 'an index of the maladministration and gross inefficiency that characterised most of them.'

[40] See Jupp (1978: 24042). Prior to the election, a SLFP Member of Parliament related to the Prime Minister emphasised the importance of political loyalty in appointing public officials: 'Some government servants are hand in glove with the UNP and are working against others who are not UNPers,' she observed. 'Note them well, even if they are transferred from your areas. We know how to deal with them. Taking revenge is evil, but we have to do it since the UNP has taught us to take revenge.'(*Ceylon Observer*, January 15, 1969).

[41] See Jiggins (1972: 17).

[42] See Wilson (1975: 185). The author notes that the wealth tax and income ceiling also motivated some Sri Lankans with movable assets or marketable skills to consider opportunities abroad.

[43] This discussion of Sri Lanka's industrial development strategy and its consequences draws heavily on the analysis presented in Bhargava (1987: 131-35). The same issues receive a more general treatment in other sources, including Karunatilake (1987: 144, ff.); K.M. de Silva and Wriggins (1994: 208-11); and Vidanpathirana (1986: 177, ff.).

[44] See Bhargava (1987: 131).

[45] Vidanpathirana (1986: 177-78) describes this problem.

[46] This average figure comes from Ibid: 177. Capacity utilisation estimates for major industries and for the economy as a whole come from the Central Bank's annual *Review of the Economy* publications.

[47] Karunatilake (1987: 150-51) discusses the problems of pricing policy.

[48] Since the Central Bank controlled Sri Lanka's currency, 'loans' from the Central Bank to the government had an effect roughly equivalent to paying government bills by simply printing additional currency.

[49] Data supporting the following analysis comes from the economic database compiled for this volume and in the tables printed in the 'Statistical Appendix' to *Review of the Economy 1979*: 65-78. A detailed analysis of Sirimavo Bandaranaike's economic policies, supported by econometric modelling, appears in Bhargava (1987: chapters 3-5).

[50] According to Central Bank indices, the total volume from international sales of all three major export crops trended downward, running markedly lower in 1977 than in 1970.

[51] This amounted to a remarkable 67 per cent increase over 1970 levels.

[52] For other assessments of the United Front Government's trade policies, see Nissanka (1984: 311), Bhargava (1987: 71-72), and Ross and Savada (1990: 158-59). Nissanka's assessment that 'Mrs. Bandaranaike's regime was able to show remarkable success in promoting Sri Lanka's foreign trade' makes the most favourable judgment, but lacks extensive documentation.

[53] See *Review of the Economy 1977*. Under the United Front Government, Sri Lanka had an officially fixed exchange rate, pegged to currencies of nations which traded extensively with Sri Lanka. Under this system, the 'official' rupee was valued about $0.16 (or 7 rupees per dollar) in 1970, and had dropped to $0.115 (or 8.72 rupees per dollar) in 1977. The rupee, however, traded at much lower values on international markets. This explains why businessmen coveted the Foreign Exchange Entitlement certificates that allowed them to purchase international currencies at the cheaper official rate. As part of its open-economy policy, J.R. Jayewardene's government devalued the rupee at the end of 1977 to nearly its market value, and then allowed more or less free trade in rupees, resulting in a new value of $0.062 (or 15.9 rupees per dollar).

[54] These data come from the compilation of foreign-assistance receipts provided in Karunatilake (1987: 360). Similar – though more detailed – information appears in the annual *Review[s] of the Economy* from this period.

[55] Readers will recall from Part 2 of this chapter that the Conference Hall was a 'gift of the Chinese people' to Sri Lanka. Interestingly, at the time during which Sri Lanka received major aid flows from China, reports indicated that China had a smaller per- capita gross national product than Sri Lanka's.

[56] For example, see Karunatilake (1987: 357) and Wilson (1975: 180). Nissanka (1984: 262, ff.), whose work includes a detailed comparative compilation of foreign-aid receipts, provides a more accurate picture in my assessment.

[57] In 1970 constant rupees, total and annual receipts of foreign-aid loans under Dudley Senanayake ran, respectively, 1,011 million rupees and 202 million rupees. Grant receipts amounted, respectively, to 148 million rupees and 30 million rupees. Under Sirimavo Bandaranaike's government, comparable loans ran to 1,928 million rupees and 275 million rupees respectively, while comparable grants ran to 646 million and 92 million rupees respectively. Expressed in US dollars, the gap between the two governments narrows somewhat because of the rupee's depreciation relative to the dollar, but the record of Sirimavo Bandaranaike's government was still better than that of Dudley Senanayake's.

[58] The analysis in this section draws on data from the Central Bank *Review[s] of the Economy* and *Annual Reports* for 1970 through 1977 and from Peebles (1982: chapter 13). I make extensive use of data provided in the 'Statistical Appendix' to *Review of the Economy*

1979, which provides complete and corrected time series for the period 1970-77. Previous years use estimated values for data in later years.

[59] However, inflation did reduce the real value of public debt. Taking inflation into account, public debt increased by 50 per cent, compared with 23 per cent under Dudley Senanayake.

[60] Data from Peebles (1982: chapter 18), *Review of the Economy 1979*, and Moore (1990a: 9).

[61] Based on data from Peebles (1982: 107, Table VI.7). Previously, I emphasised that one should interpret these aggregate indices cautiously. However, it is unlikely that they show Sri Lanka's poor wage earners as better off than their actual standard of living. Many 'casual labourers' who worked by the day, along with women, and underage workers received wages less that the *minimum day rate*.

[62] The index rose by 8.7 per cent in 1977. For the years 1971 though 1977, the average annual increase ran to .65 per cent. According to a convention described earlier, for years in which a change in government occurred, I normally attribute all changes in the economy to the policies of the government that began the year in power. In this instance, it seems probable that wages may have risen after implementation of J.R. Jayewardene's 'open-economy' policy. Thus the picture of wages shown by the data may present Sirimavo Bandaranaike's government in a more favourable light than justified.

[63] See 'Statistical Appendix' to *Review of the Economy 1979*, Table 64. Wage performance improved slightly under Dudley Senanayake's government, but the disparity proved less than one might have anticipated from the disparity in per-capita GNP.

[64] See Karunatilake (1987: 197-98). Children born in Sri Lanka qualified for a ration book after their first birthday. This made them eligible for free and subsidised rice as well as other rationed commodities.

[65] Income distributions by decile appeared in *Consumer Finances and Socio Economic Surveys* for 1953, 1963, 1973, 1978/79, 1981/82, and 1986/87. Survey data on income distribution comes from Karunatilake (1987: 227, Table 8.10).

[66] Ibid.

[67] See I. Coomaraswamy (1986: 287). The Five-Year Plan set a job-creation target of 810,000, broken out as follows: agriculture – 300,000; industry – 165,000; construction – 60,000, and services – 285,000. Actual job creation in every one of these sectors fell short of targeted levels.

[68] See *Review of the Economy 1979*: 91, Table 5.6.

[69] According to the *Review of the Economy 1979*, the government employed 217,817 people in 1970 and 328,663 in 1971. By 1977, the government employed 422,647 men and women.

[70] Some public corporations in Sri Lanka carried the title of a 'Board,' including the National Milk Board and the Ceylon Transport Board (national bus company) .

[71] See 'Statistical Appendix' to *Review of the Economy 1979*: Table 56. For example, a big jump, from 259,184 employees in 1975 to 541,044 employees in 1976, was due mostly to the fact that foreign-owned tea plantations became para-statal institutions.

[72] The experience of the Ceylon Transport Board, under both Dudley Senanayake's and Sirimavo Bandaranaike's administrations, illustrates this. Shortly after nationalisation of the bus services, the Board employed 4.67 people for each bus in service. This figure had increased to 6.93 employees per bus in 1965 and to 8.21 employees per bus in 1970-71. A further increase to 12.30 occurred in 1974, followed by a decrease to 8.81 in 1977.

[73] Studies which address the unemployment problem during this period include Tambiah (1986: 56-57), Karunatilake (1987: 155, ff.), S.W.R. de A. Samarasinghe (1988a); Shastri (1990), Philipupillai and Wilson (1983), and Gunatilleke (1983). Many other books and articles point to unemployment as a serious problem during this period, without providing details.

[74] Sri Lanka's success in introducing vernacular education and the neglect of English teaching contributed to unemployment because many jobs in industry, commerce and tourism required English; see Gunatilleke (1983: 54). Paradoxically, a reform intended to reduce the advantaged position of Sri Lanka's English-speaking elite actually improved their position over the growing number of Sri Lankans who could only speak Sinhala. Many Tamils, even those with relatively modest incomes, also maintained some fluency in English.

[75] Gunatilleke (1983: 41) cites an estimate that in 1971 as many as 62 per cent of the unemployed may have come from the 15-24 age group.

[76] See Karunatilake (1987: 281-82).

[77] Philipupillai and Wilson (1983: 183) report that paradoxically, the Sri Lankan economy faced shortages of technically trained professionals. Out-migration, particularly of technically qualified Tamils, worsened this problem. Between May 1971 and June 1974, for example, 588 doctors and 275 scientists numbered among 1,705 migrants. Oberst (1985: 65) calls attention to a different problem, namely the unwillingness of young people seeking white-collar jobs to accept employment as manual labourers. This sometimes created labour shortages, especially in cases of demand for large numbers of workers, such as construction projects.

[78] Indian Tamil plantation workers, against whom both Sinhalese and Sri Lanka Tamils discriminated, show up as the only clearly disadvantaged group in S.W.R. de A. Samarasinghe's study (1988b: 16-17). Between 1963 and 1973, their median income dropped from 72 per cent to 50 per cent of the all-island level. The 1981-82 survey reports Indian Tamil median income at 55 per cent of the all-island level. The median income of Indian Tamil *families*, however, could exceed that of their rural Sinhalese counterparts. Typically husbands, wives and older children all had jobs and received wages. Women did most tea picking. Unemployment in the estate areas ran lower than anyplace else on the island, only about 6 per cent.

[79] Shastri (1990).

[80] Ibid: 72. Jaffna's annual population growth rate averaged 1.9 per cent, compared with 1.7 per cent island-wide. Population density increased by 4.1 per cent annually, contrasting with 1.2 per cent increases in Colombo and Galle.

[81] Ibid: 71. In 1975, almost 90 per cent of Sri Lanka's industries had located in the Western Province. The Northern and Eastern Provinces, the next most-industrialised, accounted respectively for 6 per cent and 2 per cent.

[82] Ibid. Pesalai Oil Prospecting on Mannar Island, where Sinhalese accounted for only three per cent of population, employed 120 Sinhalese and 80 others from the Tamil and Muslim groups. Trincomalee's Prima Flour Mill, located in a district with Sinhalese comprising about 23 per cent of population, numbered 379 Sinhalese among its 451 employees. I found district ethnic concentrations in G.P.S.H. de Silva (1979).

[83] See the 'Statistical Appendix' to *Review of the Economy 1979*: Table 16. Across the island, chili production rose from 7,400 metric tons in 1971 to a peak of 31,300 metric tons in 1977. Red onion production rose from 42,300 metric tons in 1971 to a peak of 78,300 metric tons in 1976. Research did not yield a district-to-district breakdown of minor crop production for this period.

[84] Shastri (1990: 71) and Sri Lankan acquaintances with whom I have discussed the question, take this view.

[85] However, according to a study conducted by Priyani Soysa, Professor of Pediatrics at Peradeniya University, 6.6 per cent of pre school children in Sri Lanka were acutely undernourished and 34 per cent suffered from chronic undernourishment. Despite the decline in infant mortality statistics at the national level, three districts had infant mortality rates exceeding 70 per thousand, and three more had rates of more than 60 per thousand. This information appears in the March 1977 issue of *Vidurava* and is quoted in Piyadasa (1984: 39). *Vidurava* is the Bulletin of the National Science Council of Sri Lanka.

[86] Mortality rates fell by one per cent, compared with nine per cent under Dudley Senanayake. Maternal mortality rates fell by 17 per cent, compared with 50 per cent under Senanayake. Infant mortality rates dropped by 12 per cent, compared with a 9 per cent drop under Senanayake.

[87] Data from 'Statistical Appendix' to *Review of the Economy 1979*: Table 93.

[88] Data comes from Peebles (1982: Tables III.6 and III.7). However, the number of physicians employed by the Ministry of Health did increase by ten per cent.

[89] See K.M. de Silva and Wriggins (1994: 215).

[90] During this period, 139 new hospitals opened. However, all this construction added fewer than 4,000 beds to Sri Lanka's total stock.

[91] No discussions of this period which I have seen even mention that the United Front government cut back on health care spending or gave it lower priority than previous administrations.

[92] The Minister, W.P.G. Aryadasa, represented Haputale Constituency in Uva Province's Badulla District, to the South and East of Colombo. Ariyadasa first won election to Parliament in 1956 as a member of S.W.R.D. Bandaranaike's People's United Front Coalition. He had held no cabinet post prior to 1970.

[93] See C.R. de Silva (1977: 427).

⁹⁴ Both Wijetunga (1983: 120-21) and C.R. de Silva (1977: 428-29) describe these changes. 'Rationalisation' attempted to use resources more efficiently by reducing duplicative programs at the several campuses. Most campuses either gained or lost faculties, with the Kelaniya and Sri Jayawardenapura campuses, the former Vidyodaya and Vidylankara Buddhist seminaries, emerging as the big losers. The process had far to go when the single-university structure was abolished in 1977.

⁹⁵ See Bastiampillai (1983: 149-77).

⁹⁶ See the Government's *Five-Year Plan 1972-1976*: 109-11.

⁹⁷ This is drawn from statistics provided in Wijetunga (1983: 138).

⁹⁸ While overall admissions policies discriminated against Tamil youth, funding of the newly created Jaffna Campus proved relatively generous. According to government statistics compiled by Wijetunga for 1975-77 (1983: 130), the Jaffna Campus ranked first in expenditure per student and had the most favourable student-ratio of all Sri Lankan institutions, including the nation's most prestigious university at Peradeniya.

⁹⁹ Moore (1990a) highlights Snodgrass' analysis.

¹⁰⁰ Along with other critics cited earlier, economist H.N.S. Karunatilake (1987: 150) takes this point of view. Significantly, he generally displays sympathy for Sirimavo Bandaranaike's policies.

Chapter Thirteen Notes

¹ On these points, see Wilson (1975: 189, ff.).

² See Oberst (1985). The author interviewed 101 legislators who served in at least one of the two parliaments. His sample reflected a cross section of parties -- 32 UNP, 35 SLFP, 16 Tamil, 12 Marxist, 2 independents -- and regions, with rural legislators somewhat over represented. To reduce Colombo-centric bias, Oberst conducted many of his lengthy interviews, some lasting more than 3 hours, in the Members' home districts.

³ Ibid: 61. He reports that ministers with sufficient resources would set up a temporary office, staffed by three or four clerks. Constituents would line up for hours outside the door. A police officer would often stand by to keep the crowd under control. As constituents entered the office, usually in groups of 10 or 20, they would wait in line to see the Minister. Conversations might run as short as a minute and typically not three or four minutes.

⁴ Ibid: 25.

⁵ In a borderline case, the Communist Party (Peking Wing) publicly advocated violence and revolution, but did not follow through in any serious way.

⁶ Respondents of Oberst (1985: 39-40) characterised interest groups as mostly 'unorganised and weak.' Concentration of policy-making in a few ministries, as well as

the tradition of using extended family networks to wield influence, numbered among the factors cited as limiting their power.

[7] This proved particularly true of the LSSP leadership, as A.J. Wilson (1975: 193-94) makes clear.

[8] Dr. Colvin R. de Silva gave an interview entitled '35 years of the LSSP: Overthrowing Capitalism Our New Challenge' to the *Ceylon Observer Magazine Edition* on December 20, 1970. Quoted in Wilson (1975: 192-93).

[9] See V. Karalasingham, 'An LSSP Viewpoint: What Should be Today's Slogans?' in the *Ceylon Daily News*, September 2, 1970. Quoted in Wilson (1975: 193).

[10] Ministers may have also recalled the example of LSSP founder Philip Gunawardena, who had died in 1973. Gunawardena played a key role in S.W.R.D. Bandaranaike's cabinet, then jumped to the UNP where, as readers will recall, he served as Minister of Industry. Despite years as one of Sri Lanka's leading political figures, he could not hold his seat in the 1970 General Election.

[11] Even prior to the 1977 debacle, James Jupp (1978: 330) observes that 'Ceylonese Marxists have consistently failed to understand or even adequately describe their own society.'

[12] Much of this account draws from the second volume of K.M. de Silva and Wriggins' biography of J.R. Jayewardene (1994). As noted previously, the authors had access to previously unpublished materials. The biography is a valuable resource for any student of Sri Lankan politics though some feel the authors treated their subject too gently.

[13] See Ibid: 191-192, ff. Since Senanayake had won re-election, the request surprised Jayewardene, according to his biographers. Customarily, a party president holding a seat in Parliament would lead that party, and if the party had the largest share of seats in the minority, would serve as leader of the opposition.

[14] See Ibid: 240-41. Not even Jayewardene's biographers know the reconciliation's details. Senanayake's apology and admission that the attempt to expel Jayewardene had been 'a serious error in judgement' apparently played an important part of the process.

[15] Ibid: 258-259.

[16] Ibid: 267-269. The first appointee, Anandatissa de Alwis, had held high-level government positions and then served as managing director of two different advertising firms.

[17] For a description of this struggle, see Ibid: chapters 14 and 15.

[18] Ibid: chapter 16.

[19] For details of the proposed reforms, see Colombage and Karunaratne (1986: 213-15) and Karunatilake (1987: 379-81).

[20] A description of the discussions leading up to this decision appears in K.M. de Silva and Wriggins (1994: 307-08).

[21] See Ponnambalam (1983: 191).

[22] See K.M. de Silva and Wriggins (1994: 308-09) and Ponnambalam (1983: 193).

[23] Reflecting on this appeal, K.M. de Silva and Wriggins (1994: 309) find that 'whatever its utility in tapping a vein of morality in the electorate, the appeal to morality was tantamount to placing a series of hostages to posterity. Nothing was more certain than a gap between promise and fulfilment, between aspiration and realisation, when he and his party would rule the country and make the difficult and often unpalatable choices that governments have to make.'

[24] See *Buddhist Essays*, a compilation of J.R. Jayewardene's writings first published in 1942. The quotations here come from the fifth edition. The Buddhist scholar and former Sri Lankan Ambassador in Washington, Dr. Ananda Guruge, edited the volume, published by Sri Lanka's government press in 1982. The former President presented me with a copy of this book as we sat over drinks in the memorabilia-filled study of his Colombo home after a lengthy interview. Four long conversations with President Jayewardene stand out among the many memorable personal experiences I had writing this book.

[25] See J.R. Jayewardene (1982: 66-67).

[26] See Obeyesekere (1974). At the time of the article's publication Obeyesekere -- one of Sri Lanka's most distinguished scholars -- held a chair in Anthropology at the University of California, San Diego. He later joined the Department of Anthropology at Princeton University.

[27] Among 'suspected insurgents' taken into custody, police arrested 44.1 per cent, while 55.9 per cent surrendered voluntarily, in response to an appeal from the Prime Minister. After suspects came under government control, authorities incarcerated them in rehabilitation camps, where 'carefully selected senior government officials' interviewed them. The author received this information from an anonymous source, then followed up the data analysis with field research in Sri Lanka.

[28] See Obeyesekere (1974: 371, Table IV). James Jupp (1978: 298) and others have argued that anti-*goyigama* feeling contributed to the insurrection.

[29] See Obeyesekere (1974: 376). At the time, 8,081 suspected insurgents attended village 'primary' schools, while an additional 652 attended village 'high school.' Jupp (1978: 300) notes that teachers played a particularly influential role in certain areas, and that in some cases, groups of students led by their teachers became JVP units.

[30] Obeyesekere (1974: 375-76) argues that parents and children had radically different views of their life situation. Parents, by and large, had reconciled themselves to their lowly economic position. Higher aspirations, coupled with realisation of their tenuousness, lay at the root of their sons' frustrations.

[31] Moore (1990a) notes that in many developing nations during the 1960s and 70s, governments promoted the idea that educated youth had a 'legitimate claim' to a state-sector job. This view had a high degree of currency in Sri Lanka, despite the fact that widespread accessibility to education made the proportion of 'educated youths' seeking jobs a much greater share of population than in other developing countries.

[32] See Obeyesekere (1974: 373, Table V).

[33] See Chandraprema (1989: 99-100).

[34] See Alexander (1981: 119-21).

[35] Both Obeyesekere (1974) and Alexander (1981: 116) report this. The latter notes that by that time, employment in any government department or nationalised industry required a letter from a government MP.

[36] So concludes Obeyesekere (1974: 382).

[37] Both Jupp (1978: 303, ff.) and Chandraprema (1989: 94, ff.) both discuss the movement's ideology. According to Singer (1990: 418), the average JVP cadre hardly knew more about Marx than about how to fight a modern army. Wijeweera, however, certainly had better information, thanks to his father's Communist affiliations, his Moscow studies and his early work with N.S. Shanmugathasan's Maoist faction.

[38] For a description, see Chandreprema (1989).

[39] Alexander (1981) makes the case for the sceptics most strongly.

[40] See especially R. Gunaratna (1990: 86-87) and Chandraprema (1991: 27-38).

[41] Most notably, he lacked physical courage and skill with weapons – he may not have even known how to fire a pistol. In this respect, he differed greatly from his Tamil counterpart, Velupillai Prabakharan.

[42] R. Gunaratna (1990: 126, ff.) discusses a number of splinter groups that functioned during Wijeweera's years in prison.

[43] This brief demographic overview omits the Indian Tamil population, located primarily in the tea growing central highlands. As noted earlier, Indian Tamil leaders adopted a more accommodating political strategy, rarely becoming involved in militancy or Eelamist agitations.

[44] This figure is also found in chapter 1, figure 1.3.

[45] This account of the early activism of Tamil youth draws primarily from an unpublished paper by the Tamil journalist, D.B.S. Jeyaraj (1987: especially chapter 12).

[46] See Swamy (1994: 24).

[47] For a discussion of these policies, see Section 2 of this chapter. The pivotal impact of changes in university admissions policies on Jaffna youth is one point on which most Sri Lankan scholars agree. For example, see K.M. de Silva (1986: 262), Hoole et al. (1990: 16), Swamy (1994: 26-27), and Tambiah (1992: 66-68).

[48] See Jeyaraj (1987: 16).

[49] See Hoole et al. (1990: 16) and Jeyaraj (1987: 13).

[50] Swamy (1994: 27).

[51] This brief account of Bangladesh's independence draws primarily from Nissanka (1984: 167-77). For the reaction of Tamil youth, see Hoole et al. (1990: 16), Jeyaraj (1987: 13), and Swamy (1994: 27-28).

[52] Both geopolitical considerations and the practical problems of dealing with several million refugees fleeing to West Bengal motivated Indira Gandhi's government to support the Bangladesh independence movement.

[53] Readers will recall that in contrast to her support of Bangladesh's independence, no other national leader had responded more quickly than Indira Gandhi to Prime Minister Bandaranaike's calls for assistance in putting down the JVP rebellion. In fact, the Indian Navy had participated in a quarantine of Sri Lanka.

[54] For a discussion of these plans, see Hoole et al. (1990) and Shastri (1990: 73-74). According to Hoole and his associates, the Peradeniya students used Bangladesh explicitly as a model. They planned for limited militant action, followed by a unilateral declaration of independence. Following this declaration, they hoped the Indian Army would intervene, defeat Sri Lanka's army and force the Sri Lankan government to recognise the new nation.

[55] Shastri (1990: 74-75) points out two other problems with the Tamil plan. First, the river heads and reservoirs providing irrigation sources for the new state lay outside its borders. Second, despite their importance to the independence scheme, businessmen and professionals — especially those living outside the North and East — felt ambivalent at best about it.

[56] See Swamy (1994: 24-25).

[57] See Hoole et al. (1990: 17). Most Sinhalese political parties had commonly used 'enforcers' or thugs for years.

[58] Ibid.

[59] See Michael Roberts (1982) for a discussion of the *Karava* (fishing caste) community among Sri Lanka's low-country Sinhalese. Interestingly, Rohana Wijeweera and several other top People's Liberation Front (JVP) leaders also belonged to this caste.

[60] See Swamy (1994: 24-25) and Jeyaraj (1987: Appendix 2). Like many Tamil militants, both these men later took aliases, by which they have become best known. Nadaraja Thangavelu became 'Thangadurai' and Selvaraja Yogachandran became 'Kuttimani.' Thangadurai and Kuttimani went to prison as part of a government crackdown in 1983. Both died when Sinhalese prisoners, possibly with police complicity, rioted and massacred Tamil prisoners in Colombo's Welikada prison.

[61] India's government euphemistically titled their equivalent of the US Central Intelligence the 'Research and Analysis Wing' of the Department of Defence. I discuss their support of Tamil militant groups in subsequent chapters.

[62] Swamy devotes one chapter of his volume *Tigers of Lanka* (1994: 40-92) entirely to Prabakharan, adding greatly to generally available knowledge about this enigmatic leader. Additional sources include Jeyaraj (1987), R. Gunaratna (1987), and Mary Anne Weaver (1988), although the latter contains several inaccuracies.

[63] These vignettes of Prabakharan's early life come from Swamy (1994: 50-51) and are based on extensive interviews conducted by the author over a 42-month period in both India and Sri Lanka. Prabakharan's admiration of Clint Eastwood comes from Mary Anne Weaver (1988: 41-42).

[64] See Swamy (1994: 52-53).

[65] Ibid: 59 and note 6 to chapter 4. According to one LTTE member interviewed by the author, Prabakharan got the idea for the insignia from a matchbox.

[66] Prabakharan is personally abstemious; he does not smoke and drinks no alcohol, coffee or tea. LTTE policy expected recruits to follow the same regime, and to remain celibate so that love affairs would not compromise their loyalty to the organisation. The Tigers practice a severe form of discipline, which could include the death penalty for those who broke the rules or deserted. Unlike other guerrilla leaders, Prabakharan did not shirk from carrying out executions personally. He has killed a number of men and women who opposed him or who became singled out as 'traitors' to the movement.

[67] See Jeyaraj (1987: Appendix 2), Ali (1993: 225), and Swamy (1994: 30, 97-98).

[68] See Ali (1993: 225) and Swamy (1994: 30).

[69] See Jeyaraj (1987: Appendix 2) and Swamy (1994: 98-100).

[70] See M. Roberts (1994: 15).

[71] Anthropologist Michael Roberts (1994: 14) suggests that as early as 1972 or 1973, militant organisations 'had discovered the power of polarity.' They reached the conclusion that 'the generations of Tamil leaders based in Colombo had let their nationality down, that the requirements had to be wrested by force, that the Tamils residing in Colombo could no longer be allowed to serve as a hostage to fortune, indeed that Tamils down south could be written off, if need be.' This philosophy, coupled with the examples of young 'martyrs,' made the new organisations 'an empowered force.'

[72] As noted in chapter 9, vicious factional fighting took place between Tamil militant groups in the 1980s. This was precipitated largely by Prabakharan's implacable drive to establish LTTE dominance and to exterminate those who opposed him.

[73] Both Hoole et al. (1990: 17) and Arasaratnam (1979: 518) emphasise this.

[74] K.M. de Silva (1986: 268) views the mid-1970s as pivotal years in the emergence of Tamil militancy. He attaches significance to the initial targeting of Tamil supporters of the government, rather than Sinhalese or security force members.

[75] See Jupp (1978: 141). Interestingly, Chelvanayakam like many Tamils, was Christian.

[76] See Wilson (1988: 86).

[77] See Ibid: 88-90 for a useful discussion of these issues. After adoption of the Vaddukoddai resolution, Amirthalingam and some TULF members accompanying him were arrested for distributing pamphlets at a public meeting. Indictments for sedition followed. In a special 'trial at bar' before Supreme Court Justices, they were represented by virtually all the Tamil barristers practising in Colombo, and won acquittal.

[78] TULF Election Manifesto, quoted in Ponnambalam (1983: 192). Emphasis added.

[79] Jupp (1978: 368) concludes that despite the TULF's formal commitment to separatism, 'the TULF was, for the most part, simply the cautious and constitutional Federal Party, goaded by its younger supporters into a more militant posture.'

[80] When M. Tiruchelvam, a leading TULF member and former cabinet minister who had not attended the Pannakam meeting, first saw the Vaddukoddai Resolution he contacted Amirthalingam and asked, 'What is the meaning of this?' Amirthalingam replied that the resolution was adopted in response to pressure from the youth and that when the time comes to negotiate with the government, a compromise could be reached. See Hoole et al. (1990: 19).

[81] Jeyaraj (1987: 16) notes that many youths who canvassed for the TULF during the 1977 campaign defected to militant groups after the election because they viewed Amirthalingam's stances on communal issues as 'collaborating' with the government.

[82] For example, three electoral districts in the heart of the tea country, Maskeliya, Kotmale and Haputale, had Indian Tamil population shares of 60, 53 and 57 per cent, respectively. Following the 1970 general election, Sinhalese members of the SLFP, P.G. Ariatilake, J.D. Weerasekera and W.P.G. Ariyadasa, 'represented' all of these districts.

[83] Following the 1970 general election, the Executive Committee of the CWC asked the Ceylon Estate Owners Federation for a guaranteed monthly wage of 90 rupees for 25 days of work. See Sabaratnam (1990: 100). Translated into US currency, this meant a daily wage of about 60 cents for 12 hours of backbreaking work. Employers replied that paying this wage would destroy Sri Lankan tea's competitiveness on international markets.

[84] See Jupp (1978: 176-77) and Sabaratnam (1990: 102). The four unions included the Lanka Estate Workers' Union, affiliated with the LSSP; the United Plantation Workers' Union, affiliated with the Communist Party; the Sri Lanka Estate Workers' Union, affiliated with the SLFP; and the Democratic Workers Congress, an independent union. Like Thondaman's CWC, the Democratic Workers' Congress had belonged to the Ceylon Indian Congress. Sirimavo Bandaranaike appointed the DWC's leader, A. Aziz, to a seat in Parliament.

[85] For a discussion of the collaboration between the three parties, see Sabaratnam (1990: 105, ff.) and K.M. de Silva (1986: 257-61).

[86] Sabaratnam discusses the development of this relationship (1990: 114-16), as do K.M. de Silva and Wriggins (1994: 330-31) and K.M. de Silva (1986: 318-19).

[87] K.M. de Silva (1986:259).

[88] In an exception to this pattern of affiliation, the Ceylon National Teacher's Union had links to the SLFP. For the definitive study of Sri Lanka's labour movement, see Kearney (1971).

[89] A very extreme case occurred in the plantation sector, where Democratic Worker's Congress leader A. Aziz campaigned actively against a labour agreement that would have shortened hours and improved working conditions for tea pickers.

[90] See the 'Statistical Appendix' to *Review of the Economy 1979*: Table 59.

[91] Of course, some strikes did occur. For example, 6,500 Ceylon Bank Employees' Union members struck for four months during the Fall of 1972. Readers will recall that politically motivated strikes also included economic demands, though their principle, and sometimes sole, motivation lay in politics.

[92] My discussion of the JSS draws upon K.M. de Silva and Wriggins (1994: 269-71), as well as personal interviews.

[93] See Obeyesekere (1984b: 160, ff.). I will explore this theme more fully in the chapter that follows.

[94] See Moore (1990a) and Jupp (1978: 177).

[95] See Obeyesekere (1984b: 161).

[96] See 'State of Emergency: Statement by the Prime Minister on March 16, 1971' in the parliamentary debates registry: *Hansard*, Volume 93 (18), 2210-2211.

[97] See H.A.I. Goonetileke (1976: 86). Mark Rosenblum of the Associated Press, who departed Sri Lanka on April 19, became the first of several foreign correspondents expelled for 'infringing the regulations on reporting.'

[98] Both Jupp (1978: 318) and Wilson (1974: 186) report this incident. Publication in Britain's newspapers further damaged the reputation of a government already hurt by Sirimavo Bandaranaike's leftward tilt, but had little impact in Sri Lanka's detention camps.

[99] See Civil Rights Movement of Sri Lanka (1979a: 8-10, 15-17).

[100] For the period following this legislation, I have increased the 'press censorship' score from 2 to 3. This scoring denotes censorship of all political news, with the maintenance in private hands of at least some decisions concerning news selection.

[101] At that time, R. S. Perera, an SLFP stalwart who represented Kelaniya district, near Colombo, served as Minister of Information. Though colleagues did not regard Perera as a cabinet heavyweight, they did know of the Prime Minister's sensitivities to press coverage. Both the Prime Minister and Felix Dias Bandaranaike involved themselves personally in some censorship decisions.

[102] See Wilson (1975: 188). Nationalisation of Lake House proceeded under the Associated Newspapers of Ceylon (Special Provisions) Act. Under this law, Sri Lanka's government became the majority stockholder in Lake House and had representation on the Board of Directors through a Public Trustee. The first Public Trustee was Prime Minister Bandaranaike's brother.

[103] K.M. de Silva and Wriggins (1994: 265) write that the views of Prime Minister Bandaranaike's daughter Sunethra and her then-husband, Kumar Rupasingha, had particular influence in the final decision to nationalise Lake House.

[104] Beginning in May 1974, I increase the index for press censorship from 3 to 4, denoting that the 'government directs what news shall be published' and 'all other news is excluded.'

[105] In this 1973 by-election, Dudley Senanayake's nephew Ruckman made his political debut. Jayewardene later expelled him from the party, as noted previously. The SLFP also ran a newcomer to politics: Dharmasiri Alwis Senanayake had a name intended to appeal to Dedigama voters.

[106] Accounts of the Dedigama by-election come from K.M. de Silva and Wriggins (1994: 263-65), who based their description on interviews with J.R. Jayewardene and with workers who participated actively in the campaign.

[107] See G.P.S.H. de Silva (1979: 154-155). Ruckman Senanayake's victory margin, in a constituency comprising over 80 per cent Kandyan Sinhalese, amounted to 4,508 votes. With 42,675 votes polled, more than 91 per cent of those eligible turned-out.

[108] I used this incident as the basis for increasing the 'Restrictions on Political Parties' index from 1 to 2, denoting circumstances where 'all but small extremist groups are allowed to form political parties, but groups with large followings are harassed by restrictions on meetings and acts against leaders.'

[109] For a description of the events at Attanagalla, see K.M. de Silva and Wriggins (1994: 274-75). R. Premadasa formally protested use of the security forces at Attanagalla in Parliament on December 10. His statement and the response from Prime Minister Bandaranaike appear in the *Hansard* for December 10, 1973. A subsequent speech about Attanagalla by J.R. Jayewardene appears in the December 14, 1973 *Hansard*.

[110] A report by Amnesty International, following a January 1976 visit to Sri Lanka, included numerous reports of assault and torture by arresting officers and interrogators.

[111] See K.M. de Silva (1986: 282). The Prime Minister's statement appears in *Hansard*, Volume 28, 467-9.

[112] See Jupp (1978: 246).

[113] Sinhalese officers invariably replaced retiring Tamil officers. The key role played by loyal Tamil officers in putting down the JVP rebellion did nothing to change this pattern in later years.

[114] See K.M. de Silva (1986: 271).

[115] Many accounts of this period have focused attention on the police's inability to provide relatives with information about their loved ones, or their needing lengthy spans of time to do so. In some cases, police probably did deliberately attempt to conceal information. However, one should not underestimate the difficulty of maintaining accurate records in rural areas under stressful conditions. This issue later included other complications because of communication problems between different elements of the police and, after they became involved, between military and police forces.

[116] See Alexander (1981: 129).

[117] See Civil Rights Movement of Sri Lanka (1979b: 79).

[118] Data from Peebles (1982: 247-249, Table XIII.5).

[119] See Ross and Savada (1991: 239-42). Air Force capabilities improved thanks to jet fighters from Britain and fighter bombers from the USSR. The Navy received fast attack patrol boats from China.

[120] K.M. de Silva, ed. (1993a) also notes that spending flagged, especially after 1974.

[121] Statistics provided in Peebles (1982: Table XIV.2) report the total size of the police force as 10,557 in 1968, 13,412 in 1976, and 16,360 in 1976.

[122] Data on 'Total Crimes' from Peebles (1982: 268, Table XIV.3) and 'Prison Receptions' from Ibid: 277, Table XIV.8. The tables compare observations taken between 1966-70 and 1971-76. These data do not include individuals arrested and detained under emergency regulations. Unfortunately, the police data that is provided in Peebles' volume ends in 1976. Interestingly, traffic accidents marked one of the few public-safety statistics that did not increase during this period. Presumably, this reflected low automobile imports and gasoline shortages due to scarcity of foreign exchange.

[123] This account of police community relations draws on K.M. de Silva (1986: 269-70 and 1993b: 358-60) as well as Burger (1987: especially 827). My own interviews with senior police officers and with Tamils living in Jaffna during this period confirm these sources.

[124] With characteristic elegance, K.M. de Silva (1986: 270) observes that 'a force perceived as an army of occupation was driven by the inexorable logic of their ambiguous position in Jaffna into behaving like one.'

[125] See K.M. de Silva and Wriggins (1994: 323). In multi-member districts, each major party traditionally ran fewer candidates than the number of seats available, thus concentrating the votes of supporters for one or two candidates.

[126] See G.P.S.H. de Silva (1979: 124-25). The Prime Minister won in Attanagalla by a margin of 10,663 votes where in 1970 she had secured a margin of 21,273 votes. The Minister of Irrigation, Power and Highways, Maithrapala Senanayake, squeaked through in the overwhelmingly Kandyan Sinhalese district of Medawachchiya by just 366 votes. He had represented the district since independence, and had won by more than 9,500 votes in 1970.

[127] Ibid: 163. See also K.M. de Silva and Wriggins (1994: 323). Dompe constituency covered about half of the original Attanagalla constituency, from which S.W.R.D. Bandaranaike had first won election in 1947. The remaining half of the constituency, represented by Sirimavo Bandaranaike, had retained the name Attanagalla. In 1970, Felix Dias Bandaranaike had won by 23,373 votes, with 77.5 per cent of the total cast. He had represented Dompe since its creation in the 1960 delimitation of electoral districts.

[128] Surprise losers included all three of the United Front cabinet ministers mentioned earlier, N.M. Pererra, Colvin R. de Silva, and Pieter Keunemann.

[129] Readers will recall that Sri Lankans refer to secondary schools as 'colleges.'

[130] In a departure from past practice, Sri Lanka's government-controlled radio did not begin announcing official returns until after 1:30 AM.

[131] This account comes from K.M. de Silva and Wriggins (1994: 322-24). Following a tradition inherited from Great Britain, a new Prime Minister assumed office in Sri Lanka almost immediately after an election victory. According to his diary, Jayewardene took his oath from President William Gopallawa shortly before 10 AM on July 23. By 6:00 PM, newly named UNP cabinet ministers had also taken their oaths and gathered for their first meeting.

[132] For descriptions of the UNP campaign, see Dissanayake (1977: especially 120, ff.) and K.M. de Silva and Wriggins (1994: 319-22). The respective party manifestos appear in Abeynaike (1977).

[133] Dissanayake (1977: 124-25) notes that government spokespersons did little until the official launch of the SLFP Campaign on June 12, 1977, a bare six weeks before the election. Because SLFP candidates struggled to avert defeat in their home districts, the Prime Minister often had few co-speakers at her rallies, viewed as yet another sign of weakness.

[134] The manifesto stated that under a future SLFP regime, the government 'shall not permit foreign industrial enterprises to undermine our state cooperative and industrial undertakings.'

[135] This draws from the Tamil United Liberation Front Election Manifesto, quoted in Ponnambalam (1983).

Chapter Fourteen Notes

[1] See Ponnambalam (1983: 194-95). According to Ponnambalam, the rioters were 'Sinhalese thugs and hooligans, instigated by ...chauvinists.' K.M. de Silva (1986: 286) and K.M. de Silva and Wriggins (1994: 354) provide a more even-handed description of these events. De Silva and Wriggins note that Amirthalingam chose August 18, in the midst of the rioting, to introduce a Parliamentary resolution as an amendment to the government's policy statement, affirming the TULF commitment to a separate state.

[2] See Ibid: 348. The Commission was headed by M.C. Sansoni, a respected former Chief Justice of Sri Lanka's Supreme Court. Because Sansoni belonged to the minority Burgher community, both Tamil and Sinhalese leaders accepted him as a neutral observer.

[3] See Swamy (1994: 63). The Parliamentarian, M. Kanagaratnam was killed by Prabakharan and Uma Mareswaren, then still allies, on January 27.

[4] Additional details appear in the section below on 'State-sanctioned violence.'

[5] Ratnatunga (1988: 208-09) quotes the directive from President J.R. Jayewardene to Brigadier T.I. Weeratunge, dated July 12, 1979. The state of emergency was allowed to lapse on December 1979, but terrorism was by no means curbed.

[6] These include February, March, May, July, August, September, November and December.

[7] See K.M. de Silva and Wriggins (1994: 444, ff.). Premadasa is widely viewed as a strong Sinhalese nationalist, but this characterisation oversimplifies him. Colombo Central district, where Premadasa had grown up and which he now represented, numbered large communities of Muslims and Tamils among its residents. Premadasa was among the few Sinhalese politicians fluent in Tamil; he often delivered speeches in that language to Tamil audiences.

[8] These incidents occurred, respectively on March 16 and 25. Another police constable fell wounded in the bank robbery, which netted about 6.8 million rupees and a number of police firearms.

[9] The UNP organiser, M. Thiyagarajah, also stood as a DDC candidate in his own right.

[10] According to anthropologist S.J. Tambiah (1986: 20-21), 'this book burning by Sinhalese police has come to signify for many a living Tamil the apogean barbarity of Sinhalese vindictiveness that seeks physical as well as cultural obliteration.'

[11] The vote total for TULF candidates was 263,369 out of 315,999 votes polled.

[12] A contrasting view of the disturbances appears in K.M. de Silva and Wriggins (1994: 446-47), who downplay the rioting and state that the security forces were timely and effective in restoring order. The more widely-held view expressed here reflects descriptions found in the international and local press, in Tamil sources such as Tambiah (1986: 21-22) and Ponnambalam (1983: 209-11), and an unpublished report by a New York State University Law Professor, Virginia Leary (1981).

[13] Many viewed the referendum as the most corrupt national-level election since Sri Lanka's independence. I discuss the conduct of the referendum in greater detail, below.

[14] Sirimavo Bandaranaike had lost her civic rights through the action of a presidential commission, and could not seek elective office or campaign. She continued as SLFP party leader, but the party foundered because of squabbling between Anura Bandaranaike's centrist faction and the left-of-centre faction lead by Mrs. Bandaranaike's daughters.

[15] In an exception, nearly two weeks of rioting between Sinhalese and Muslims in the southern coastal city of Galle broke out on July 26, 1982 and spread to several neighbouring villages. Anthropologist George Scott (1989) argued that the principal causes of the rioting were economic, rather than the religious causes that several contemporary observers emphasised.

[16] This account of election disruptions appears in Ratnatunga (1988: 217-19) and from local press reports.

[17] See Wilson (1988: 171). Professor A. J. Wilson was the son-in-law of the respected TULF leader S.L.V. Chelvanayakam.

[18] Pro-Tamil tracts such as Ponnambalam (1983) and Piyadasa (1984) provide more detailed accounts of security force excesses, but these accounts are often difficult or impossible to corroborate from other sources.

[19] See K.M. de Silva and Wriggins (1994: 557).

[20] Sinhalese nationalist rhetoric was, as already noted, an important theme in Sirimavo Bandaranaike's second administration. However such rhetoric was also an important part of the political discourse of the more 'moderate' Jayewardene administration according to a number of authors: see Piyadasa (1984), Obeyesekere (1984a); Tambiah (1986); and Wilson (1988). Piyadasa alleges that Cyril Mathew's fiery rhetoric circulated widely among members of the armed forces during the Jayewardene administration's early years. For a widely-cited collection of Mathew's speeches, see *Diabolical Conspiracy* (1979).

[21] Right-of-centre UNP governments almost always had greater success in keeping the labour movement under control. Left-of-centre governments raised rarely-met expectations in political campaigns. When unions went out on strike, as we have seen, leftist government officials, often labour union officers themselves, proved reluctant to order workers back on the job or to follow-up back-to-work orders strongly.

Chapter Fifteen Notes

[1] Jayewardene lost his Kelaniya seat in S.W.R.D. Bandaranaike's 1956 landslide victory but regained it in the March 19, 1960 general election, following Bandaranaike's death. In the subsequent election, he moved to the relatively 'safe' Colombo South constituency, which he held for his remaining years in Parliament.

[2] See K.M. de Silva and Wriggins (1988: 72, ff.). Jayewardene's wife, Colombo heiress Elina Rupesinghe, brought far more than money to the marriage. Although personally retiring and not fond of the public side of a politician's life, she enjoyed great respect for her common sense, intelligence and loyalty to her husband. Interestingly, the match was arranged by Jayewardene's mother, Agnes.

[3] For example see Moore (1992: 71). Even Jayewardene's severe critics, including Mick Moore, do not question his personal honesty and incorruptibility. Nevertheless, these writers do make clear he was not aggressive in rooting out dishonesty and corruption among his close associates, as the discussion below makes clear.

[4] As reported in K.M. de Silva and Wriggins (1994: 183, ff.) and above, he became estranged from Dudley Senanayake and isolated within the cabinet in 1968 and played a much less influential role during the remainder of Senanayake's term.

[5] See Moore (1990b and 1992). Moore, a political economist affiliated with the Development Studies Program at the University of Sussex, has provided carefully crafted, insightful observations of Sri Lankan politics and society for nearly two decades.

[6] See Wilson (1988: 209-13). The author observes of Jayewardene, '[h]is gravest problem was that he did not have a single colleague whom he could trust and with whom he could freely discuss affairs of state.'

[7] Manor, ed. (1984: 28).

[8] In describing Jayewardene's first speech as Prime Minister from the Octagon, K.M. de Silva and Wriggins (1994: 328) characterise Jayewardene as a man with deep understanding of Sri Lanka's past, who sought to be 'what Sinhalese rulers in the past had endeavoured to be, one with the people.' However in most of their biography, they give greater emphasis to Jayewardene's ties to British traditions and practices than to his links with Sinhalese culture.

[9] Ibid: 327.

[10] See J.R. Jayewardene's *Buddhist Essays* (1982).

[11] The text of Jayewardene's speech and a description of his activities at the San Francisco Conference appear in K.M. de Silva and Wriggins (1988: chapter 17).

[12] In my own series of interviews with President Jayewardene, he returned to this theme repeatedly as we discussed controversial issues and events in his lengthy political career.

[13] Anthropologist Steven Kemper develops this theme in his piece, 'J.R. Jayewardene, Righteousness and *Realpolitik*' (1990), the source of the examples that follow.

[14] Ibid: 193. The author reports that in a toast to President Reagan during his 1984 state visit to the United States, Jayewardene announced that his favourite song was Frank Sinatra's 'My Way.' Sinatra himself also attended the dinner.

[15] D.S. Senanayake's first cabinet comprised only sixteen members, including the Prime Minister. 'Project Ministers' had task-oriented assignments that might fall within a single ministry, or include the jurisdictions of several. The establishment of District Development Councils in 1980 created openings for District Ministers. Since each 'minister' had staff support, subsidies for the purchase of vehicles, expense accounts and other perquisites, these became prized appointments, though the offices may have had a very limited degree of real power. According to K.M. de Silva and Wriggins (1994: 489-90) nearly three-fifths of the UNP parliamentary group eventually held some sort of 'ministerial' position.

[16] Biographers K.M. de Silva and Wriggins (1994) present the strongest case for the position that Jayewardene acted as a strong leader, for the most part dominating his ministers and fully controlling his government. However, even their biography describes instances where Jayewardene appeared to lose control, and/or faced public opposition from his Ministers. This proved especially true in the area of communal relations, as noted in the following discussion. Thoughtful Tamil scholars such as A.J. Wilson and Stanley Tambiah picture Jayewardene as contributing greatly to communal divisions because of his unwillingness, at critical junctures, to challenge extremist elements in his own party.

[17] Ibid: 377-78.

[18] See Zafrullah (1981: 12).

[19] See R. Gunaratna (1990: 138-42; quotations from J.R. Jayewardene on 141-42).

[20] See K.M. de Silva and Wriggins (1994: 362-63), M.L.H. Wickremeratne (1995: 26-34) and Jayantha Jayewardene (1995: 244-48). Jayewardene also asked a respected management consultant and political ally, M.G.P. Panditharatne, to head a project-coordinating committee. Panditharatne's dual role as Chairman of the ruling UNP gave the committee maximum political clout and emphasised its importance in the President's scheme of priorities.

[21] See B. Weerakoon (1992: 44-48); K.M. de Silva and Wriggins (1994: 460-62).

[22] See the Government's *Sri Lanka: Housing a Nation* (1980).

[23] The brief discussion that follows on Sri Lanka's 1978 Constitution draws primarily on more detailed discussions found in Zafrullah (1981), K.M. de Silva and Wriggins

(1994: especially 377-95), and R. Coomaraswamy (1993a and 1993b). Jain (1979) provided another useful resource.

[24] However, following two general elections in which the President's party lost control of Parliament in 1994 and 2001, the opposition-party prime ministers had received authority to name cabinet ministers and to function, essentially, as a prime minister on the Westminster Model.

[25] For a discussion of separation of powers, see H.M. Zafrullah, *Sri Lanka's Hybrid Presidential System and the Separation of Powers Doctrine* (1981). Zafrullah's volume also provides a useful and detailed general commentary on Sri Lanka's 1978 Constitution. Coomaraswamy (1993a: 138, ff.) makes similar points about the limitations of Sri Lanka's judicial-review procedures.

[26] See Zafrullah (1981: 44). Regulations were not subject to questioning or litigation in any court of law.

[27] Ibid: 64-65. The bill could not conflict with or propose to change the Constitution, however.

[28] Ibid and Coomaraswamy (1993a: 140-41) provide detailed discussions of the 1978 Constitution's referenda provisions.

[29] M.P. Jain, 'Sri Lanka's New Constitution.' Quoted in Zafrullah (1981:132).

[30] The detainees included President Jayewardene's nephew, who served as his personal secretary, in addition to his son. See K.M. de Silva and Wriggins (1994: 402).

[31] Ibid: 498.

[32] Zafrullah (1981: 96). An individual who suffered imposition of civic disabilities lost their right to vote, and could neither stand as a candidate, nor canvass on behalf of another candidate. Such persons also could not address political meetings.

[33] A discussion of this tradition appears in Ibid: 96-97 and the government's *Second Interim Report of the Special Presidential Commission of Inquiry* (1979b).

[34] This brief summary of events leading to the penalties imposed upon Sirimavo and Felix Dias Bandaranaike derives primarily from the much more extended discussion found in K.M. de Silva and Wriggins (1994: chapter 26).

[35] See Moore (1984: 63-64). Jayewardene expelled an MP from the UNP – and thus from Parliament – for publicly expressing opposition to government policies of communal reconciliation.

[36] Ibid: 425. The authors characterise constitutional reform, the open economy, district councils and new university admissions policies as the 'four pillars' of Jayewardene's communal reconciliation policy.

[37] His primary motivation in making this appointment probably lay in further weakening the SLFP, which had won the second largest number of popular votes and which he still regarded as his most serious political threat.

[38] See Wilson (1988: 141).

[39] This recapitulates a critique of Sri Lanka's open-economy policies developed more fully by the late Newton Gunasinghe (1984), a brilliant and outspoken sociologist from the University of Colombo. Economist S.W.R. de A. Samarasinghe, however, argues for cautious interpretation of Gunasinghe's findings, because available data does not provide convincing evidence of widespread economic deprivation.

[40] See Manor, ed. (1984: 16-17).

[41] See K.M. de Silva (1993d: 296).

[42] See Vamadevan (1996). The author, who directed Sri Lanka's Department of National Planning, provides a revealing discussion of practical issues relating to the use of language in public administration and communications between citizens and public officials.

[43] See Ponnambalam (1983: 197-98).

[44] See Kemper (1990: 200). The author notes that the Department of Buddhist Affairs, within the Ministry of Cultural Affairs had a central location and a large staff, while the corresponding Muslim and Hindu departments did not. Interestingly, the Hindu Affairs Department resided in the Ministry of Regional Development.

[45] When the Council of Sri Lanka Buddhist Societies, prior to the 1983 presidential election, asked that candidates pledge to make Sri Lanka a Buddhist Republic, he replied that Buddha did not preach only to one race and that *nirvana* can only be attained by individuals, not nations: See C.R. de Silva (1984: 41).

[46] See Kemper (1990: 201).

[47] A discussion of these developments appears in K.M. de Silva (1986: 306-11) and K.M. de Silva and Wriggins (1994: 425-30). The authors note that the government almost continually tinkered with university admissions formulas throughout the remainder of President Jayewardene's term in office.

[48] As noted above, the wet zone merits is name because it receives rainfall from both the Fall (Northeast) and Spring (Southwest) monsoons. Substantial amounts of rain facilitate both fall and spring plantings of rice, known as the *Maha* crop and the *Yala* crop, respectively. Only the Southwest monsoon waters the dry zone, and interference from towering mountains in the central highlands makes rainfall sparse in some areas.

[49] Population densities in the vicinity of Colombo run 2,500 per square km. in the vicinity of Colombo and in the range of 300 to 600 per square km. throughout most of the region.

[50] Shastri (1990: 64, ff.) develops this theme.

[51] See Moore (1985: 44-49, 167-201).

[52] Chapter 9 above discusses the Mahaweli Project's origins, and develops this theme.

[53] See Shastri (1990: 66). In 1962, the government separated the predominantly Sinhalese Ampara district from Batticaloa district, reducing the territory controlled by Batticaloa's Tamil majority. The subsequent abolition of provinces as an administrative

unit also reduced Tamil clout because Tamils, though geographically concentrated in Batticaloa and on the coast north of Trincomalee, had constituted the majority in the Eastern Province as a whole. Provinces became reconstituted as administrative units – and political units, too – in the Indo-Lanka Accord.

[54] Ibid: 65, Table 2.

[55] See M.L.H. Wickremeratne (1995: 39) for a discussion. The author formerly served as Director General of the Mahaweli Authority of Sri Lanka.

[56] See Samarasinghe (1988b: 23). Statistics noting the disproportionate amount of land received by Sinhalese also appear in Peebles (1990: 43) and M.L.H. Wickremeratne (1995: 39).

[57] Uyangoda (1994) provides a useful long-term perspective on this issue.

[58] The contrasting views appear in K.M. de Silva (1986: 313-18, 331-34) and Wilson (1988: 141-74). Both men offer an insider's perspective on the events they describe. De Silva was personally close to President Jayewardene and conducted numerous personal interviews with him in the course of preparing the two volume biography that he co-authored with Howard Wriggins. Wilson also knew President Jayewardene well and served as an intermediary between him and the TULF throughout many of the events recapitulated here. Both de Silva and Wilson have written on these matters elsewhere; however, I rely primarily on the accounts cited above for this brief discussion.

[59] The UNP election manifesto promised District Development Councils to spearhead a decentralisation of administration, making the people 'partners in the planning, organisation, and implementation of policy.' See K.M. de Silva (1986: 289).

[60] This occurred in July and has been discussed in Chapter 14, above.

[61] The story of the Commission from the moderate Tamil perspective appears in Wilson (1988: 143-60). Professor Wilson, who served as a Commissioner, also participated in a number of separate discussions with President Jayewardene regarding devolution of power. K.M. de Silva presents a somewhat different perspective in several of his works.

[62] See K.M. de Silva (1986: 315).

[63] The title of Wilson's book, *The Break-up of Sri Lanka* (1988) emphasises this.

[64] See K.M. de Silva (1986: 318).

[65] Analysts interpreted this as a protest vote since the SLFP candidate, Hector Kobbekaduwa, had a long history of opposition to Tamil interests.

[66] See K.M. de Silva (1986: 316).

[67] See Wilson (1988: 170) and Tambiah (1986: 29).

[68] See the *Interim Report of the Committee on Implementation of the Scheme of Development Councils* (1982).

[69] See K.M. de Silva (1986: 337).

[70] According to Wilson (1988: 171), Lalith Athulathmudali, who later served as Minister

of National Security, argued that the government could contain the violence with little effort and that government agents could recruit paid informants who would finger militants and militant supporters for the security forces.

[71] See Hoole, et al. (1990: 19-20). Surprisingly, the Jaffna Teachers for Human Rights, authors of *The Broken Palmyrah*, strongly criticise the Tamil United Liberation Front leaders.

[72] See Ratnatunga (1988: 211-13).

[73] See Hoole et al. (1990: 99). The Sansoni Commission report quoted Amirthalingam as saying to a Tamil police inspector testifying in court 'You are a Tamil; you are a Traitor.' See also Ratnatunga (1988: 213).

[74] See Piyadasa (1984: 101-03).

[75] See Ponnambalam (1983: 211).

[76] See Ratnatunga (1988: 275).

[77] Germany, with the Holocaust as part of recent national history, had a particularly tolerant refugee policy.

[78] Ratnatunga (1988: 284-95) provides a detailed country-by-country enumeration of these groups.

[79] Ibid: 275. The author accuses the UK demonstrators of hypocrisy, noting that in Sri Lanka, Jaffna Tamils like them treated the Indian Tamil plantation workers as outcasts.

[80] See K.M. de Silva and Wriggins (1994: 435).

[81] For example, see Ratnatunga (1988: 279-84).

[82] See K.M. de Silva and Wriggins (1994: 397, ff.).

[83] See Nissanka (1984: 345-46). Previously, the President had always retained the Foreign Affairs portfolio. This change provided a degree of distance between the Ministry and the President's office, while the President and other cabinet ministers remained personally involved. Foreign affairs were often on the agenda at weekly cabinet meetings. Though A.C.S. Hameed had almost no international experience when appointed foreign minister, his selection won approval in the Middle East, where previous UNP governments' ties with Israel had caused strains.

[84] As an expression of gratitude, the Japanese gave Sri Lanka a new hospital, located close to the new parliamentary complex at Sri Jayewardenapura. The hospital had 1001 beds, the President told me, with the extra bed especially designated for him. The President died in a private Colombo hospital, however.

[85] The British call the small island chain off Argentina's southern coast the Falkland Islands, while Argentines call it *las Islas Malvinas*. Argentina's military junta briefly captured the islands in 1982, but a British expeditionary force quickly routed the invaders.

[86] See K.M. de Silva and Wriggins (1994: 400-04).

[87] Ibid.: 411-13.

[88] Ibid: 416 and Kodikara (1982: 416-17).

[89] See 'A Brahmanic Framework of Power?,' *Economic and Political Weekly*, April 7, 1989 as quoted in K.M. de Silva (1993f: 385-86).

[90] This theme features prominently in Rohan Gunaratna's lengthy and extensively documented volume, *Indian Intervention in Sri Lanka: the Role of India's Intelligence Agencies* (1993).

[91] See Kodikara (1989b: 58 and 1991b: 26-27), R. Gunaratna (1993: 15-16), and K.M. de Silva and Wriggins (1994: 420-21). India had sufficient concerns about US designs on Sri Lanka to raise the matter with U.S. Ambassador Donald Toussant and his successor, James Spain. Both envoys assuaged Indian representatives' concerns.

[92] See Ratnatunga (1988: 81, 93).

[93] Under India's Constitution, the Prime Minister has broad powers to dismiss state governors and appoint interim successors.

[94] This recounting of the capture and release of the two men rests largely on a more detailed account in Swamy (1994: 72-79). See also K.M. de Silva and Wriggins (1994: 526-27).

[95] K.M. de Silva and Wriggins discuss the estrangement of the two leaders (Ibid: 413-17), but do not probe deeply into why President Jayewardene acted as he did, seeming to ignore geopolitical realities.

[96] Circumstances leading up to the decision to advance the Presidential election date, of course, receive ample coverage in many sources. Among those covering the same ground as here, but in greater detail, include Ibid: 515-30 and C.R. de Silva (1984: 35-37). Wiswa Warnapala and Hewagama (1983: 1-34) gives a contemporary Sri Lankan account. For a Tamil perspective on the same events, see Wilson (1988: 167-68).

[97] See C.R. de Silva (1984: 35-36) and K.M. de Silva and Wriggins (1994: 528-29). C.R. de Silva suggests that the successful strategy of French President Francois Mitterand – who dissolved Parliament shortly after winning a presidential election, and won a decisive majority in the ensuing election – also may have influenced UNP strategists' thinking.

[98] See K.M. de Silva and Wriggins (1994: 530). The authors say that J.R. Jayewardene set little store by astrological forecasts, but acknowledged that they belonged to the reality of Sri Lankan political life. In this instance, the auguries of astrologers who read the President's horoscope and predicted a victory turned out to be correct.

[99] Ibid: 539.

[100] Ibid: 542. J.R. Jayewardene's biographers – who view most of his career in a very positive light – strongly criticise his decision to call a referendum, as well as the subsequent conduct of the polls.

[101] Ibid: 540. The President offered this rationale in a November 2 speech to the UNP Parliamentary group and on numerous subsequent occasions, including my own interviews with him. According to 'Samarkone' (1984), a subsequent CID investigation into the alleged plot turned up little more than 'intra party squabbles' and nothing illegal, much less

a plot to assassinate anyone.

[102] See K.M. de Silva (1986: 355).

[103] See Athulathmudali (1984: 80-81).

[104] See Wilson (1988: 140).

[105] See the Government's *Report on the First Referendum in Sri Lanka* (1987c).

[106] See C.R. de Silva (1984: 48).

[107] See Civil Rights Movement of Sri Lanka (1983) as quoted in 'Samarkone' (1984: 113).

[108] In particular, see Manor, ed. (1984).

[109] See K.M. de Silva and Wriggins (1994: 551-54).

[110] See Obeyesekere (1984b: 170).

[111] See Spencer (1990b: 258).

[112] Anthropologist James Brow describes vividly how this occurred in one rural village, Kukelewa, in Anuradhapura District (1990: 129-42).

[113] See Philipupillai and Wilson (1983: 182).

[114] See K.M. de Silva (1993c: 92). In one of our interviews, I raised this concern about the Job Bank scheme benefiting only UNP friends and supporters with President Jayewardene. 'Of course I gave jobs to my friends and supporters,' the President replied, adding 'who would you have me give them to?'

[115] See Tambiah (1986: 84). Scoring for the chit system also appears in the *Report of the Presidential Commission on Youth* (1990).

[116] See Moore (1990b and 1992) as well as K.M. de Silva (1993c: 86, ff.).

[117] See Moore (1992: 71).

[118] See Wilson (1988: 140).

[119] See Piyadasa (1984: 96).

[120] According to K.M. de Silva and Wriggins (1994: 178), President Jayewardene 'was unable (or unwilling) to discipline those members of his Cabinet who were egregiously enriching themselves in office.'

[121] See Obeyesekere (1984b: especially 162-69). Additional documentation of government intimidation and repression follows later in this chapter.

[122] Ibid: 164.

[123] Obeyesekere reinforces this point by citing the government's response to Supreme Court decisions in two human rights cases (Ibid: 165). Police officers stood accused of unlawful activities in both cases and in both, the Court found against the government. Even after these decisions, however, the offending officers received promotions. In one instance, the promotion followed cabinet-level discussion over which President Jayewardene presided. Also, this officer's fine and indemnity for damages came from public – rather than his own private – funds, in violation of the Court's order.

[124] Malaysia and Singapore exemplified the one-party state model. The three 'Asian Tigers' other than Singapore, Taiwan, South Korea and Hong Kong, were also governed by authoritarian regimes.

[125] G.H Peiris (1993d: 266-67) reminds readers that despite open economy reforms, government still touched many lives directly. Approximately 25 per cent of the population still depended on government wages and about the same number lived on government land allotments. Roughly 40-45 per cent lived in houses either constructed directly by the government or with substantial government assistance.

Chapter Sixteen Notes

[1] M.P. Pieris (1997: 46).

[2] See Ratnapala (1989: 24) and Abeyesekere (1986: 291-292).

[3] See Alailima (1997: 155) and Columbage and Karunaratne (1986: 210).

[4] Liyanage (1997: 449-451).

[5] The monopoly on petroleum products was retained.

[6] Banking reforms are discussed in Hettiarachchi (1985: 143, ff.), Lal and Rajapathirana (1989: 48, ff.), and M.P. Pieris (1997: 48-54).

[7] General discussions of the UNP reform program are found in S.W.R. de A. Samarasinghe (1988c: 52-3), Lakshman (1997b: 8, ff.), and Lal and Rajapitarana (1989: 25-66). References are also seen in contributions to Rasaputra, et al., eds. (1986) and Lakshman, ed. (1997a).

[8] See Jayasundera (1986: 56-57, 67-70).

[9] Columbage and Karunaratne (1986: 211-215), L. Fernando (1997: 116, ff.), and Karunatilake (1987: 379, ff.). To maintain flexibility and adjust for fluctuations in individual markets, fixed targets were replaced by a 'rolling' scheme that would update the plan each year. The first comprehensive planning document was *Public Investment 1979-1984* (1979a).

[10] K.M. de Silva and Wriggins (1994: 455, ff.).

[11] See Columbage and Karunaratne (1986: 214) and L. Fernando (1997: 117).

[12] See K. Goonesekara (1995: 71) and M.L.H. Wickremeratne (1995:26).

[13] Jayewardene's thoughts about the project and the meeting with senior staff at the headquarters of the Mahaweli Development Board are described in K.M. de Silva and Wriggins (1994: 360-363).

[14] A week after announcing the accelerated program, President Jayewardene is reported to have said, 'I am going to stake the entire future of the UNP on the successful completion of the Mahaweli scheme' (Peebles 1990: 43).

[15] Karunatilake (1987: 375) reports 'Total Aid for Mahaweli Projects 1978-1985' as rupees 19,411.8 million. I have converted this to US dollars at the rate of 20 rupees to the dollar, which is roughly the exchange rate at the mid-point of this period.

[16] Although five dams — Victoria, Kotmale, Randengala, Rantembe and Maduru Oya — were constructed, there were only four major reservoirs. Rantembe Dam, not begun until 1987, was built to balance the daily discharge of Randingala, allowing it to provide full peak energy load. See Daily (1990: 12-13) and Karunatilake (1988: 132). Interestingly, though Mahaweli is widely viewed as a project that focuses on the dry zone, three of the initial project's dams, plus a dam and diversion tunnel constructed earlier, are located in Kandy District and a fourth is in Nuwara Eliya District. The Maduru Oya dam is in the northwestern part of Amparai district.

[17] See Daily (1990: 15) and Karunatilake (1988). T. Jogarantham (1995: 114) provides a more tempered assessment, noting that it is still too soon to fully weigh the project's economic costs and benefits.

[18] For examples see Daily (1990: 11, ff.) and Karunatilake (1987: 411).

[19] The total number of local jobs created at the peak of construction was only about 45,000 (Daily 1990: 13).

[20] See Karunatilake (1987: 413). Estimated total cost of the project in 1978 was rupees 11 billion (about $US 710 million). In 1985, with work on the Randengala-Rantembe site still unfinished, about 34 billion (about $US 1.3 billion) had already been spent.

[21] See Muller and Hettige, eds. (1995: 4-7) and Jayantha Jayewardene (1995: 250-252).

[22] Rajapakse (1995: 272-273).

[23] See Nakamura et al.(1997: 289, ff.) for a discussion of these problems.

[24] Among the major 'subsidiary food crops' are maize, manioc, onions, sesame (gingelly), green grahams, cowpeas and potatoes.

[25] This discussion of the rice-producing sector is largely from Chandrapala (1986: 270-271). Statistics are from Chandrapala and from the *Review of the Economy* for 1977 and 1987.

[26] K.M. de Silva and Wriggins (1994: 458).

[27] Data is drawn from Central Bank *Reviews of the Economy* and *Annual Reports* for years covering this period. For an overall appraisal of agricultural sector performance, see also Nakamura, et al. (1997: 288, ff.).

[28] Later, however, Premadasa had serious differences with *Sarvodaya Shramadana* organisers and attacked the movement.

[29] Brow (1990: 125-131). For a discussion of *Sarvodaya Shramadana* by the movement's founder, see A.T. Ariyaratne's *In Search of Development* (1982).

[30] Kukulewa is an isolated dry-zone rural village in Anuradhapura district.

[31] See Karunatilake (1987: 421-422).

[32] Wanigasundara (1985: 64).

[33] G.H. Peiris (1993c: 231) comments that industrial policy has never been centre stage in Sri Lankan politics, in contrast to welfare and agricultural policies. For this reason, new governments have been more willing to make radical policy changes in this arena, reflecting differences in their ideological stances.

[34] Rabushka (1981: 57).

[35] See K.M. de Silva and Wriggins (1994: 460) and Rabushka (1981: 57-58).

[36] See Vidanapathirana (1986: 188) as well as various promotional materials published by the Greater Colombo Economic Commission and the Foreign Investment Advisory Committee. One brochure characterised Sri Lankan workers as 'intelligent and trainable, eager and productive, available and inexpensive.'

[37] *Value added* measures the difference between the cost of inputs (raw materials and intermediate products) in an industry and revenues from the sale of finished products. For the 'boom' year of 1981, the value added contributed by Sri Lanka's industries exceeded 1977 levels by only 22 per cent. In the 'bust' year of 1982, value added fell below 1977 levels.

[38] Bhargava (1987: 163) reports that in 1984, the State Fertiliser Manufacturing Corporation operated at less than 40 per cent of capacity and required operating subsidies of 302 million rupees on a gross output of about 839 million rupees (in current rupees). The cost of the fertiliser produced was approximately twice that of comparable imports.

[39] See K.M. de Silva and Wriggins (1994: 458).

[40] In constant 1977 rupees, the losses were 198 million, compared with profits of 68 million in 1977 and 679 million in 1980. These numbers were greatly affected by the volatility of world petroleum prices, since the output of the Ceylon Petroleum Refining Corporation comprised more than 50 per cent of total state sector output.

[41] Additional exemplars are Sri Lanka's bus and rail transport systems, which were major sources of employment for UNP supporters.

[42] Nor had the problems been fully resolved in 1988, when I lived in Sri Lanka. The telephone pole outside our Colombo home, in one of the more prosperous areas of the city, contained a veritable spider web of connections, open to the elements. Not infrequently, an hour or more of persistent dialing was necessary to get through. Often, unreliable service forced businesses and individuals to send drivers across town with messages or to deliver them personally. By 2000, the widespread availability of cellular telephones (more than the efficiency of the landline telephone system) had begun to remedy this problem.

[43] While the initial impetus for structural adjustment came from within Sri Lanka, reflecting long standing concerns of President Jayewardene himself, the government was later subjected to pressures from foreign donors to speed up and 'rationalise' its policies. See Abeyratne (1997: 370-371).

[44] The Jayewardene government's new tariff structure is discussed in Savundranayagam (1986: 100, ff.) and Abeyratne (1997: 370, ff.).

[45] See Savundranayagam (1986: 100) and Lal and Rajapatirana (1989: 36). Before 1980, this organisation was known simply as the *Tariff Review Commission.*

[46] As measured by the difference between the merchandise trade deficit and the current account deficit.

[47] The *merchandise balance of trade* takes only imports and exports into account. The *current account balance* includes most cross-border financial transfers.

[48] Data is drawn from *Reviews of the Economy* and *Annual Reports* (1977-1989). In millions of current rupees, earnings rose from 363 million to 3.05 billion. Adjusted for inflation, the increase was from 363 million to about 1.2 billion.

[49] This figure includes both 'Direct' and 'Indirect' employment.

[50] G.H. Peiris (1993c: 247).

[51] K.M. de Silva and Wriggins (1994: 451). As introduced in chapter 3, the term 'Global South' refers to any part of the world where poor, less industrialised countries are found.

[52] See S.W.R. de A. Samarasinghe (1988c: 77).

[53] A rough indicator of this problem is the 'Utilisation Rate for Foreign Loans Contracted' which fell from 81 per cent in 1978 to 33, 27 and 20 per cent, respectively, in 1980, 81 and 82.

[54] Among the most severe critics of foreign aid dependence was economist H.N.S. Karunatilake (1987: chapters 13 and 14.) In 1989 Karunatilake was named Governor General of the Central Bank by President Jayewardene's successor, Ranasinghe Premadasa.

[55] As a percentage of GNP, foreign debt increased from 103 per cent in 1976 to 164 per cent in 1982. As a percentage of imports the increase was from 19 to 36 per cent.

[56] Adjusted for inflation, the increase was nearly 85 per cent.

[57] Unless otherwise specified, all rates of change from year to year are adjusted for inflation to make numbers more comparable.

[58] Borrowing from domestic sources to cover deficits increased from 38 per cent of total borrowing in 1978 to 70 per cent in 1980 and 66 per cent in 1982. As under previous administrations, the principal source of 'loans' to the government was Sri Lanka's Central Bank.

[59] During the United Front's seven years in power, the rupee depreciated in value by about 53 per cent.

[60] K.M. de Silva and Wriggins (1994: 468).

[61] Jayasundera (1986: 57-58).

[62] 'Social Services' is a category in the Central Bank's *Annual Reports* and *Reviews of the Economy.*

[63] In 1977 constant rupees, allocations to cover deficits in the Sri Lanka Transport Board and National Railways grew from 185 million in 1977 to 398 million in 1982 (the increase in current values was from 185 million to 1.18 billion). The deflated value of 1982 defence budget was 191 million rupees (486 million rupees in current values).

[64] By contrast, the more difficult to collect personal and corporate income taxes contributed 12 per cent of government revenues between 1978 and 1982.

[65] Deflationary policies became particularly severe after Ronald Reagan succeeded Jimmy Carter as US President. One standard indicator, the London Interbank Offer Rate on Special Drawing Right Deposits (LIBOR) rose from 6 per cent in 1979 to 16 per cent in 1981, before dropping to 13.7 per cent in 1982. Rates continued to remain relatively high through 1985. Data is drawn from the IMF's 1995 *International Financial Statistical Yearbook* and Altman (1981: 14, 37).

[66] For example, see C.R. de Silva (1984: 39). Between 1974 and 1977, Sri Lanka imported only 1,000 bicycles. 12,000 were imported in 1978, while in 1979 and 1980 bicycle imports were, respectively, 33,000 and 98,000.

[67] See Alailima (1997: 156) for a discussion of major trends in Sri Lanka's economy between 1980 and 1990.

[68] Tambiah (1986: 51).

[69] Ibid. The more detailed figures were Colombo District – urban: 113.6, rural: 112.4; Vavuniya District – urban: 124.5, rural: 111.1; Polonnaruwa District – urban: 142.4, rural: 112.4; and Anuradhapura District – urban: 127.0, rural: 102.2.

[70] See Bhargava (1987: 201).

[71] Data are based on Central Bank estimates for 'Government Employees' and 'Workers in Wages Boards Trades' as provided in *Annual Reports* and *Reviews of the Economy*. Lal and Rajapatirana (1989: 30, ff.), Lakshman (1997c: 175, ff.), and S.W.R. de A. Samarasinghe (1988c: 58, ff.) offer generally similar views regarding the impact on wages of Open Economy reforms. A somewhat more favourable assessment is offered by G.H. Peiris (1993d).

[72] Data on the rupee value of wages in different sectors is readily available, but the impact of inflation on wage-earners purchasing power is a matter on which assessments differ. Central Bank estimates of *real wages*, which I have used when they are available, provide the brightest picture. According to these estimates, several categories of employees realised modest net gains for the 1977-82 period, though most lost ground between 1980 and 1982. Independently comparing wage increases with rates of inflation, rather than using Central Bank real wages estimates, produces a less-bright picture. Between 1977 and 1982, prices rose by more than 250 per cent in Sri Lanka. Wage increases to government employees lagged price increases by more than 15 per cent. Increases to industrial/ commercial workers lagged by more than 20 per cent. Teachers' raises lagged by more than 25 per cent. Only agricultural workers, starting from a lower base, gained ground.

[73] Manor, ed. (1984: 15-16).

[98] Once again, this insurrection, which intensified in mid-1987, was organised by R. Wijeweera under the banner of the *Janatha Vimukti Peramuna* (People's Liberation Front). It will be discussed in greater detail below.

[99] See the *Report of the Presidential Commission on Youth* (1990: 30).

[100] His results are reported in S.W.R. de A. Samarasinghe (1988a and 1988b).

[101] Ibid (1988a).

[102] There had always been a small number of beds for fee-paying patients, but the practice was greatly expanded under the UNP government.

[103] These reforms are discussed in S.W.R. de A. Samarasinghe (1988c: 68-73).

[104] Minister of Health Gamini Jayasuriya, who represented Homagama constituency east of Colombo, was a respected senior UNP politician, but not a member of President Jayewardene's inner circle.

[105] See Alailima (1997: 164-165). The author's assessment is supported by a wealth of anecdotal information about the health care system that I have heard during numerous visits to Sri Lanka over many years.

[106] S.W.R. de A. Samarasinghe (1988c: 75-77).

[107] Fee paying 'International Schools' were permitted at the secondary level and a small number of wealthy Sri Lankans, who were preparing their sons and daughters for admission to US and British Universities, sent their children there. However elite government-funded secondary schools – Royal, St. Thomas, Trinity, Ladies, St. Bridget's and others – continued to offer top quality education and were often still chosen by parents who could afford to send their children anywhere.

[108] The system was similar to the one that Prime Minister Bandaranaike's reforms had supplanted in 1972. The school structure was Primary Level – Kindergarten and Grades 1-5; Middle School – Grades 6-8; Secondary School, First Cycle – Grades 9-10 and Secondary School, Second Cycle – Grades 11-12. 'O Level' examinations were administered upon completion of Grade 10 and determined eligibility for further secondary schooling. 'A Level' examinations, administered upon completion of Grade 12, also served as university entrance examinations.

[109] See Diyasena (1983: 98).

[110] Data from *Review of the Economy 1982*: 87-88.

[111] See the *Report of the Presidential Commission on Youth* (1990: 31-32).

[112] Sri Lanka was divided into 30 *Educational Districts* with somewhat different borders than the island's *Administrative Districts*.

[113] Alailima (1997: 164) quotes this 1983 Ministry of Education report.

[114] See Wijetunga (1983: 139-140) and Sanyal et al., eds. (1983: 131). 30 per cent of the places were allocated on the basis of 'island-wide merit.' 55 per cent of the places allocated on the basis of comparative scores within districts, with an additional 15 per cent reserved for applicants from 'underprivileged districts.'

[115] See *The Universities Act No. 16* of 1978.

[116] K.M. de Silva and G.H. Peiris, eds. (1995: 41-42). As noted above, President Jayewardene named himself as Sri Lanka's first Minister of Higher Education.

[117] Ibid: 292. Paradoxically, university admissions were a perennially contentious political issue because Sri Lankans valued university education so highly, but Sri Lanka ranked near the bottom of developing nations in higher education funding and opportunities.

[118] Wijetunga (1983: 122-125).

[119] See *Review of the Economy 1983*: 86-87. Polytechnical institutes, junior technical institutes and affiliated technical units offered full and part-time diploma and certificate courses in engineering, technical crafts, commerce and agriculture.

[120] In 1978, Sri Lanka's universities awarded nearly 1,300 degrees in arts and oriental studies, but less than 500 in science and only 268 in Engineering.

[121] See Sanyal et al., eds. (1983: chapters 7-11). Some 534 undergraduates of a total of 3,622 in their final year were surveyed (Sundar, et al. 1983). Meanwhile, a study of recent graduates surveyed 1,206 individuals who had completed their degrees between 1974 and 1979 (Ibid).

[122] Wijemanna and Bastiampillai (1983: 314-321).

[123] K.M. de Silva and G.H. Peiris, eds. (1995: 41-42). 'By 1980,' the authors note, 'the universities were operating on the basis of a calendar which fixed the dates for commencement and the end of the academic year and for examinations. Teaching programs were uninterrupted and for the first time in over a dozen years, the universities began to hold ceremonial convocations at which degrees were awarded.'

Chapter Seventeen Notes

[1] The increased frequencies of violent conflict events amply document this.

[2] For example see K.M. de Silva and Wriggins (1994: 497, ff.).

[3] Jonathan Spencer, *A Sinhala Village in a Time of Trouble: Politics and Change in Rural Sri Lanka* (1990b). The author chose the name 'Tenna' in the interest of 'ethnographic disguise.' The total population of this village in 1982 – the year of Spencer's study – numbered 926.

[4] Ibid: 228-29.

[5] Ibid: 216-17. In a similar vein, political economist Mick Moore writes that 'politics is about who will be employed by the Ceylon Transport Board as bus conductors.' (1985: 224).

[6] See Spencer (1990b: 212).

[7] Ibid. The author notes that in Tenna, the expanded role of the state contributed to

this turbulence. 'The state,' Spencer observes, 'has been many things in the history of Tenna; a capricious source of trouble, a growing source of wealth, an unpredictable ally in the pursuit of local disputes.'

[8] Tambiah (1992: xiv), Moore (1985: chapter 8), and many other sources discuss this dominant theme in Sinhalese culture. Both Tambiah and Moore emphasise the wide gap between this vision and the realities of rural life in Sri Lanka.

[9] For example, see Spencer (1990b), Brow (1990), and Tambiah (1986), as well as numerous ethnographic studies and commentaries on ethnographic studies.

[10] See M. Roberts (1982: 7). K.M. de Silva (1993g: 21) attributes this to 'deep-seeded hostility between the leaderships of the UNP and the SLFP, which seeps down to the level of the village and urban ward.' Also, he says that SLFP leaders, like their Marxist allies, view UNP leaders as 'representatives of the class enemy, to be kept out of power at all costs.'

[11] See K.M. de Silva, ed. (1993a: 404). The author subsequently notes (1993g: 26) that once in power, the position of incumbent party leaders became one 'taken for granted.' Only one leader, Sir John Kotelawala, had ever resigned following a general election loss.

[12] See R. Coomaraswamy (1993a: 139).

[13] See Wilson (1988: 134).

[14] See K.M. de Silva and Wriggins (1994: 545). His biographers write that the President wanted this tool to demonstrate to voters his willingness to summarily remove from office UNP parliamentarians who had become unpopular.

[15] This proved particularly true of the men sometimes referred to as the 'crown princes,' Prime Minister Ranasinghe Premadasa, Mahaweli Development Minister Gamini Dissanayake and Trade and Shipping Minister Lalith Athulathmudali.

[16] In 1984, for example, N.G.P. Panditharatne lost his positions as the UNP's National Chairman and head of the Mahaweli Development Board. Cyril Mathew suffered a similar fate.

[17] See Moore (1997: 1011).

[18] Ibid.

[19] See K.M. de Silva (1999b: 254). The author characterises the SLFP as a political instrument for the perpetuation of the Bandaranaike family and its influence.

[20] Ibid: 243.

[21] See K.M. de Silva and Wriggins (1994: 524-26). The authors describe the squabbling, which received coverage from international newspapers. 'What adds even greater irony to the family quarrel,' reported the *Daily Telegraph* (London) on August 26, 1981, 'is that son and daughter live on either side of their mother at No. 65 Rosemead Place, Anura at 65a and Chandrika at 63.'

[22] See Moore (1997: 1011-12).

[23] See Moore (1985: 235).

[24] See Wiswa Warnapala and Hewagama (1983: 21). Readers will recall that Colvin R. de Silva served as Minister of Plantation Industries and Constitutional Affairs in the United Front Government, until the LSSP withdrew from the United Front Coalition in February 1972. Vasudeva Nanayakkara had represented Kiriella, a rural Southern Province constituency near Ratnapura, in the 1970 Parliament.

[25] Though the LSSP had played a highly visible role in Sri Lankan politics, its reliable base of support never exceeded about 10 percent of the electorate. In 1952 – the party's most successful year at the polls – LSSP candidates won eleven percent of the popular vote and 9 of 41 seats contested. In 1970, as part of the United Front Coalition, they won 8.7 percent of the popular vote, but only 5 seats out of 153 that they contested: See S.W.R. de A. Samarasinghe (1981).

[26] The phrase comes from Chandraprema (1991: chapter 8).

[27] Ibid: 47-49. The author notes that at a funeral ceremony memorialising a JVP member, party colleagues inflated the apparent size of the procession by several times walking to the rear, after having paid their respects, to rejoin the line of mourners.

[28] See R. Gunaratna (1990: 143). Certification came from the Commissioner of Elections. Candidates of uncertified parties, however, could file nomination papers by posting a 350 rupee deposit.

[29] Ibid: 177.

[30] Ibid: 54. The author, widely regarded in Sri Lanka as providing the best 'insider view' of the JVP, uses the metaphor of a 'vast crowded hall' to describe the organisation during this period. He writes that '[p]eople keep on entering through one doorway while another stream continuously leaves through the other doorway. The hall always remains full, nevertheless.'

[31] See Ibid: 180-84 and the *Political Conflict Data Base* for February – June 1983 (Richardson 1990).

[32] See Tambiah (1992: 96). No Sinhalese party recruited monks more systematically than the JVP. After the JVP's banning, monks provided an excellent cover for JVP front organisations.

[33] Reproductions of these pictures appear in R. Gunaratna (1990: 174-75).

[34] See Ibid: 188-89. Sri Lanka's newspapers and electronic media announced the prescription on July 31, 1983.

[35] See Chandraprema (1991: 51-53). Wijeweera gave the *Fifth Lecture* the title 'The Path of the Revolution in Sri Lanka.' He used the repression of Chilean President Allende's elected government and Indonesia's powerful Communist party to illustrate his point.

[36] See the *Report of Presidential Commission on Youth* (1990: xvii).

[37] Ibid: 24.

[38] Ibid: 78, ff.

[39] Ibid: xvii.

[40] Ibid: 11.

[41] Ibid: xvii, 13, 18, 22.

[42] 'Frequently during my travels in the United States,' Tambiah (1992: 1) writes, 'friends and acquaintances ask me the discomfiting question, 'if Buddhism preaches non-violence, why is there so much political violence in Sri Lanka today?''

[43] See A. Wickremeratne (1995: 83-84).

[44] Ibid: 81-82. The Buddha did not kill the Yakkas, however. Instead, he caused a region of the Indian subcontinent, Giridipa, to temporarily attach itself to Sri Lanka and drove the alien race into it with 'scorching flames.' Once the expulsion had ended, Giridipa, along with its cargo of undesirables, became separated from Sri Lanka and reattached to India.

[45] See Tambiah (1986 and 1992). The government banned distribution of *Buddhism Betrayed?* in Sri Lanka. The author self-consciously modelled the book's title after *The Betrayal of Buddhism*, the 1956 report of the All Ceylon Buddhist Congress.

[46] See Tambiah (1986: 58-59).

[47] This discussion mostly draws upon Hoole et al. (1990), though many other sources address similar themes.

[48] See Swamy (1994: 83-84). Major General Tissa Weeratunga served as Chief of Staff at the time. In the summer of 1978, as already noted, President Jayewardene had dispatched Weeratunga to the north with a mandate to eliminate terrorism in all of its forms before the end of calendar yar 1979.

[49] See Ibid: 56-80. This characterisation of Prabakharan also draws on other sources that present a similar picture.

[50] See Ibid: 68.

[51] See Jeyaraj (1987: 5, Appendix 2), R. Gunaratna (1987: 19); and Swamy (1994: 58-59).

[52] See Jeyaraj (1987: 2, Appendix 1).

[53] Descriptions of Prabhakaran's associates appear in Swamy (1994: 58, ff.).

[54] As with many militant leaders – but not Vellupillai Prabhakaran – this man used 'Uma Maheswaran' as an alias. He began life as Kdirgamapillai Nallainathan, and had worked for several years as a land surveyor before turning to politics.

[55] For a discussion of the split between Prabhakaran and Maheswaran, see Swamy (1994: 66, ff.).

[56] Uma Maheswaran lived nine more years, but Prabhakaran had a long memory and rarely forgave those who crossed him. The PLOTE leader was shot to death in 1989 as he walked near his Colombo home.

[57] Ibid: 78-80.

[58] See Ibid: 77-79. Nedumaran, a former Congress (Indira) member, had founded the Tamil Nadu Kamaraj Congress. He made a political intervention instrumental in obtaining Prabhakaran's release from jail. The friendship has become a lasting one. In its June 4,

2000 number, India's weekly news magazine *The Week* described Nedumaran as 'perhaps the most ardent supporter of LTTE chief Vellupillai Prabhakaran.'

[59] See K.M. de Silva and Wriggins (1994: 552-54).

[60] See *Saturday Review* (December 18, 1983). Quoted in Hoole et al. (1990: 49).

[61] Ibid: 21-22.

[62] Ibid: 22, ff.

[63] Stirrat (1984: 203).

[64] Hoole et al (1990: 40). The statement went on to say that 'the move was in breach of Sri Lanka's obligations under the International Covenant of Civil and Political Rights.'

[65] See the telegram from CRM Secretary Desmond Fernando to President Jayewardene as reported in the *Saturday Review* (June 11, 1983) and quoted in Hoole et al. (1990: 60).

[66] Ibid: 61-62. The *Review* later resumed publication, with Navaratne as its editor. Mr. S. Sivanayagam, the editor during the period described here, sought exile in India shortly after July 1983.

[67] Earlier sections discuss these developments in more detail.

[68] See G.H. Peiris (1991) for detailed descriptions of the Indian Tamil community's economic status during this period.

[69] S.T. Sivanayagam chose the title *Thalaivar Thondaman* for his Tamil-language biography of the CWC leader.

[70] This theme receives considerable attention in K.M. de Silva's description of Thondaman's role in several works. For example, see de Silva's *Managing Ethnic Tensions in a Multiethnic Society* (1986: 318-21).

[71] See Sabaratnam (1990: 128).

[72] See Wilson (1988: 138).

[73] See Obeyesekere (1984b: especially 158-66).

[74] A description of these strikes and their rationale appears in K.M. de Silva and Wriggins (1994: 492-93).

[75] See Obeyesekere (1984b: 161).

[76] See the *Daily News* (January 4, 1983). Quoted in Obeyesekere (1984b: 166).

Chapter Eighteen Notes

[1] Biographers K.M. de Silva and Howard Wriggins, both highly regarded scholars, portray Jayewardene as a democrat, albeit with qualifications (1988 and 1994).

[2] President Jayewardene stressed this theme repeatedly in our conversations. He believed that his duty to maintain public order took precedence over his other Presidential responsibilities.

[3] I have discussed the complexities of Sri Lanka's ethnic topography extensively in previous chapters. Here, when I refer to data for 'Tamil majority regions,' I mean the Northern and Eastern Provinces. Data for 'Sinhalese majority regions' refers to the remaining provinces. I sometimes use 'northeast' as stylistic shorthand for the former and 'southwest' to refer to the latter. Generalisations that refer to broad regions, even in a small country such as Sri Lanka, gloss over details and nuances, many of which I have discussed elsewhere in this volume, but they remain qualitatively useful nonetheless.

[4] As noted above, even J.R. Jayewardene's generally sympathetic biographers acknowledge this. See their discussion of 'The Mrs. Bandaranaike Affair...' in K.M. de Silva and Wriggins (1994: 497, ff.).

[5] On the parliamentary debate, see Ibid: 510-13. UNP whips offered caucus members a 'free vote' on the former Prime Minister's punishment, but few felt inclined to vote against a recommendation unanimously approved by the Cabinet.

[6] See Duff and McCamant (1976: 35).

[7] See Amnesty International (1979: 188).

[8] See Civil Rights Movement (1979b: 120-21).

[9] The Act became a permanent law in 1982.

[10] See K.M. de Silva and Wriggins (1994: 436) and Hoole et al. (1990: 25). The passage refers to the British Prevention of Terrorism Act of 1974.

[11] See Leary (1981) as quoted in Tambiah (1986: 44).

[12] This synopsis draws primarily on Rubin's Asia Watch report (1987), but several other sources cover similar ground. These include Leary (1981), Sieghart (1984), Amnesty International (1983), Tambiah (1986), and Ponnambalam (1983).

[13] Gananath Obeyesekere, a critic of the Jayewardene government's authoritarian tendencies (1984a, 1984b) was Professor of Anthropology at Princeton University. Stanley J. Tambiah, author of *Sri Lanka: Ethnic Fratricide and the Dismantling of Democracy* (1986) was Professor of Anthropology at Harvard University and Curator of South Asian Ethnology at the Peabody Museum. We have already encountered S.L.V. Chelvanayakam's son in law, A. Jeyaratnam Wilson, who was Professor of Political Science at Canada's University of New Brunswick.

[14] In compiling the State-Sanctioned Violence Index, I chose to rely almost exclusively on publicly available published materials. I had ready access to virtually all of these materials in Sri Lanka.

[15] See the Government's Foreign Investment Advisory Committee report (1983d). This publication assured investors that Sri Lanka 'offers ...a politically stable regime ensuring the continuity of economic policy.' 'A characteristic feature of the Sri Lankan economy,'

it continued, is 'the high standard of labour relations maintained through legislation and practice.'

[16] See Piyadasa (1984: 55-56), Civil Rights Movement (1979b: 120), and Amnesty International (1979: 120).

[17] See Ibid.

[18] See Ibid (1981: 261). Officials denied arresting the three men or any knowledge of their whereabouts. However, those detained never returned to their families, nor did their bodies ever surface.

[19] For a description of these incidents, see Committee for Rational Development (1984: 81) and Obeyesekere (1984b: 165).

[20] I will sometimes use this term to refer generically to police officers, soldiers, sailors and air force members assigned security duties in the northeast.

[21] See Hoole et al. (1990: 45-46).

[22] Data from *Sri Lanka Violent Political Conflict Data Base* (Richardson 1990: 47-54).

[23] Of course, both the young security officers and their youthful Tamil contemporaries had acquired their educations at a time of *Swabasha* official language policy, which made meaningful communication between them virtually impossible. Inability to communicate solidified already formidable barriers to building mutual understanding.

[24] See Hoole et al. (1990: 54-55).

[25] Ibid: 61.

[26] According to Amnesty International (1980: 234), methods of torture included 'suspending people upside down by the toes while placing their head in a bag with suffocating fumes of burning chilies, prolonged and severe beatings, insertion of pins in the finger tips, the application of broken chilies and biting ants to sensitive parts of the body, and threats of execution.'

[27] I have already cited a number of such works, including Hoole et al. (1990), Piyadasa (1984), and Tambiah (1986), as well as publications by the Civil Rights Movement of Sri Lanka (1978, 1979a, 1979b, 1983), Committee for Rational Development (1984), Amnesty International (1979-1981, 1983), and contributions to Manor (1984).

[28] Qualitative escalation in the use of political thuggery during J.R. Jayewardene's first term becomes a principal theme of Gananath Obeyesekere's article, 'The Origins and Institutionalisation of Political Violence' (1984b).

[29] See Piyadasa (1984: 55-56), Committee on Rational Development (1984: 80-81), and Obeyesekere (1984b: 163-64).

[30] See Ibid. Obeyesekere takes particular note both of this pattern and the apparent cooperation between thugs and police officers described in the following paragraph.

[31] Mrs. Bandaranaike's government received an index value of '3' for much of its term in office.

[32] Direct government control over the Lake House Group had by then become an accepted fact of life. At a Colombo dinner party not long after arriving in Sri Lanka, I asked a senior manager about the exercise of government control: did a government official review material before publication? He responded that the government used a simpler mechanism. With regard to all political matters, a senior government official simply called each day and together, they decided together what to publish.

[33] See R. Coomaraswamy (1981: 72).

[34] Ibid: 74. 'Of all the fundamental rights,' Coomaraswamy notes, 'freedom of expression is saddled with the largest number of enumerated restrictions.'

[35] See Ratnapala (1988). This study uses a number of personal interviews with police constables conducted by the author and a team of researchers. Ratnapala supplements interview information with insights from hours of participant observation in the field.

[36] See 'Samarakone' (1984: 108).

[37] See Ratnapala (1988: 14).

[38] See 'Samarakone' (1984: note 96 at 117).

[39] See Schwartz (1979: 15). The London-based Minority Rights Group reports that notices inciting attacks on Tamils appeared in several Jaffna-area police barracks. The notices bore the official stamp of Jaffna's senior police officer.

[40] See Ratnapala (1988: 15-16).

[41] Ibid: 84. The author and his researchers conducted in-depth interviews and collected data on the lifestyles of 24 married officers assigned to two stations, one urban and one rural. Only eight reported that they lived with their families.

[42] These descriptions of police attitudes appear in Ibid: 80-85.

[43] Ibid: 58.

[44] See Ratnatunga (1988: 63).

[45] Ponnambalam (1983: 216-17) cites Bombay's *Illustrated Weekly of India* from October 17, 1982.

[46] See Wilson (1988: 177).

[47] In Sri Lanka, where political discourse still reflects the influence of Marxist rhetoric, even right-leaning politicians sometimes use the term 'the masses.'

[48] For the purposes of this analysis, I define *Tamil (majority) districts* as all districts in the Northern and Eastern Provinces, but I exclude the Eastern Province district of Ampara (Amparai), which is grouped with *Sinhalese (majority) districts*. Fitting Ampara into a scheme that differentiates only between Sinhalese and Tamil districts becomes problematic because its largest ethnic group is neither Sinhalese (36 per cent) nor Sri Lankan Tamil (20 per cent), but rather Tamil-speaking Sri Lankan (Ceylon) Moors (40 per cent). Separatist Tamil political leaders include Ampara within the 'traditional Tamil homelands' – see de K.M. de Silva (1994: 40-44 and 1998a: 209-14) – and periodically have included the Moors within a grouping they term the 'Tamil-speaking people.' The Moors – virtually all Muslim – have

nevertheless rejected separatism and have become the targets of militant attacks. Their voting patterns clearly place them within the mainstream of Sri Lankan politics, rather than among adherents of separatism. Thus, for the purpose of tracking the increased bifurcation of Sri Lanka's political culture under J.R. Jayewardene, grouping Ampara with the Sinhalese majority districts, despite its inclusion in the Eastern Province, makes sense.

[49] See K.M. de Silva and Wriggins (1994: 528-29).

[50] See Wilson (1988: 167-68). The author notes that both the President and Prime Minister met with Amirthalingam prior to the election to seek his support. Jaffna's *Saturday Review* later reported that they had promised the TULF leader a high post in a 'National Government' formed after Jayewardene's re-election and passage of the referendum extending the life of Parliament. See Hoole et al. (1990: 39).

[51] By 1982, moreover, the pro-UNP National Workers' organisation had probably become Sri Lanka's most powerful union.

[52] See K.M. de Silva and Wriggins (1994: 538).

[53] The number of registered voters in Jaffna comprises 55 per cent of all registered voters in Tamil districts. This Jaffna total weighs heavily in any aggregate total for all Tamil districts. If one graphed results for the other Tamil districts excluding Jaffna, Jaffna's distinctiveness would become even more pronounced.

[54] See Ratnatunga (1988: 218). The author describes the circumstances surrounding the local government elections at Ibid: 26-27, 217-19.

Chapter Nineteen Notes

[1] Ratnatunga (1988: 1-9) and Swamy (1994: 89-91) provide good descriptions of these events. A principal motivation for the attack was the recent killing of Prabakharan's close friend and deputy, Charles Anthony (alias Seelan). He was shot by a companion to escape capture by the security forces.

[2] Most families came from villages outside of the capital and had to journey to Colombo by train or bus.

[3] See Ratnatunga (1988: 7-10).

[4] 'Disaster' is the term chosen by K.M. de Silva and Wriggins for the chapter in their biography of J.R. Jayewardene that describes the riots (1994: 550-565).

[5] This description is primarily based on the detailed description of events in Ratnatunga (1988: 9-18).

[6] Among many sources I have consulted for descriptions of these events are K.M. de Silva and Wriggins (1994), Ratnatunga (1988), Swamy (1994), Gombrich and Obeyesekere (1984a), Meyer (1984), Spencer (1984), Wilson (1988), Hoole et al. (1990) and Hoole (2001). When writing about this and other controversial events in Sri Lanka, I have tried to consult a variety of Sinhalese, Tamil and Western sources across the political spectrum.

[7] See K.M. de Silva and Wriggins (1994: 563-564) as well as Ratnatunga (1988: 33).

[8] K.M. de Silva (1986: 340). Parliament passed the amendment in August. None of the TULF members agreed to take the oath and they forfeited their seats.

[9] Ratnatunga (1988: 31).

[10] Wilson (1988: 137). 'With that statement, according to many Ceylon Tamils,' Wilson writes, 'President Jayewardene forfeited whatever rights he had to lead the Tamil people, many of whom, with complete trust had voted for him at the election for an Executive President.'

[11] Government ministries did make an effort to provide safe havens for refugees in Colombo and also provided transport for some to travel to Jaffna. See Ratnatunga (1988: 56-62).

[12] K.M. de Silva and Wriggins explain President Jayewardene's behaviour at this time as a (rare) 'failure of nerve' (1994: 565).

[13] See Ratnatunga (1988: 42-43).

[14] Obeyesekere (1984b: 174).

[15] Swamy (1994: 95-97).

[16] R. Gunaratna (1993: 27-34).

[17] For example see Wriggins and de Silva (1994: 569-570).

[18] Swamy (1994: 110).

[19] Ibid: 110-111.

[20] See R. Gunaratna (1993: 48) and Swamy (1994: 111-112).

[21] Ibid: 111.

[22] See Ibid: 112 and R. Gunaratna (1993: 48). Any estimate of the precise number must of course be an approximation.

[23] Caveats regarding the significance (or insignificance) of single numerical values derived from the database bear repeating. No conclusions should be grounded on such values; the possibilities for error are too great. But order of magnitude changes in conflict intensity patterns, spanning time periods of months and years, do merit serious attention. Such changes are evident throughout the July 1983 – December 1988 period.

[24] Ratnatunga (1988: 235). Swamy (1994: 96) reports that before July 1983, Tamil militants rarely targeted Sinhalese civilians. The riots motivated them to 'do to the Sinhalese in the Northeast and wherever else possible what the Sinhalese had done to the Tamils.'

[25] Ibid: 197.

[26] K.M. de Silva (1986: 355).

[27] Rubin (1987: 48).

[28] Ibid: 147-148. This Asia Watch report cites an Amnesty International report entitled *Disappearances' in Sri Lanka.*

[29] Negotiations between protagonists to the conflict that accompanied this truce are described below.

[30] K.M. de Silva and Wriggins (1994: 618).

[31] LTTE moves against its rivals are described in Swamy (1994: 191-225) and Hoole et al. (1994: 78-91). The EPRLF was later recognised by Sri Lanka's government as a legitimate political party and briefly governed a united Northeastern Province, under Indian Army protection.

[32] See K.M. de Silva and Wriggins (1994: 625-626) and Swamy (1994: 223-224).

[33] Ibid: 169. The new ministry, created in 1994, was headed by one of the President's ablest cabinet colleagues, Lalith Athulathmudali.

[34] K.M. de Silva and Wriggins (1994: 629) and Swamy (1994: 228).

[35] See K.M. de Silva and Wriggins (1994: 629) and the *Daily News* from April 22, 1987.

[36] See K.M. de Silva and Wriggins (1994: 630), Hoole et al. (1990: 120-126), and Swamy (1994: 227). Swamy suggests that the Tigers had been weakened by the internecine strife of the previous year.

[37] K.M. de Silva and Wriggins (1994: 633).

[38] The events of June 1987 are described in numerous sources. Tyronne Fernando's short narrative, *100 Days in Sri Lanka* (1988), is a useful compilation from the perspective of Sri Lanka's government. J.N. Dixit, India's Ambassador to Colombo during this period, presents a lucidly written narrative from an Indian perspective in his *Assignment Colombo* (1998). Since Emily and I were visiting Colombo in June, we were able follow events personally. We ended our first visit to Sri Lanka shortly before the Indo-Lanka Accord was signed.

[39] Kodikara ed. (1989a) provides a series of essays on the Accord. The complete text of the Accord is also provided.

[40] Dixit provides a graphic description of this tense period (1998: 152-177).

[41] Rubin (1987: 148).

[42] See K.M. de Silva and Wriggins (1994: 643) and T. Fernando (1988: 77-78).

[43] As I wrote these words in June 2002, Sri Lanka was in the midst of yet another hopeful respite, this time with Norwegian mediators attempting to move protagonists from an uneasy truce to a political solution. Previous respites were initiated by Presidents Ranasinghe Premadasa (UNP) and Chandrika Bandaranaike Kumaratunga (SLFP) as they began new terms in office. In each instance the LTTE broke the truce and the government turned – unsuccessfully – to a military solution. In 2004, as I was completing final editing, a uneasy truce still held, but jockeying for power by Sinhalese political leaders was complicating the negotiation process.

[44] I personally met with the Vice Chancellor of Jaffna University to discuss an aid project that would revitalise the social science faculties at his institutions.

[45] See Swamy (1994: 243-254). Rajiv Gandhi imposed the settlement on the LTTE leader, who was held under virtual house arrest (protected by his own bodyguards) in a Delhi hotel during the negotiations. He returned to Jaffna on August 2 and gave a speech to a large crowd in which his reservations about the accord were clearly evident.

[46] K.M. de Silva and Wriggins (1994: 653) and Swamy (1994: 261).

[47] Hoole et al. (1990: 161).

[48] Dixit (1998: 189-214) argues that Sri Lanka's government, especially National Security Minister Lalith Athulathmudali, played a major role in mismanaging this incident and sabotaging the agreement.

[49] Swamy (1994: 268-270).

[50] Some estimates place the number as high as 100,000.

[51] See Hoole et al. (1990: 271) and Ratnatunga (1988: 381). In the former source, Jaffna residents themselves provided graphic descriptions of how citizens felt as their liberators turned against them. Ratnatunga notes that while Indian government spokespersons had expressed outrage when Sri Lankan forces had killed Tamil civilians, they remained silent when their own forces engaged in the same behaviour.

[52] Swamy (1994: 278, 283).

[53] Hoole et al. (1990: 358, ff.).

[54] Swamy (1994: 279-280).

[55] See K.M. de Silva and Wriggins (1994: 672). Politicians who had opposed the accord were the harshest critics.

[56] During the year I lived in Sri Lanka, this change in reporting on the IPKF was clearly evident.

[57] See Ratnatunga (1988: 379). He notes that the Indians turned down intelligence briefings and offers to assign knowledgeable Sri Lankan officers as liasons for information about local conditions.

[58] As noted in earlier chapters, the most useful sources on the JVP are R. Gunaratna (1990) and Chandraprema (1991). Gunaratna provides more detail on the events of the JVP insurgency. Chandraprema gives more attention to the thinking and activities of the JVP's top leadership. His book is based on a collection of 51 articles that appeared in one of Sri Lanka's independent English language newspapers, *The Island*, from February 5 to June 16, 1990. At the time they were viewed as a unique source of information on the JVP and were read very widely.

[59] Wijeweera did this publicly in a letter to President Jayewardene dated October 8, 1983. Copies were sent to the Prime Minister, the Chief Justice and other top Sri Lankan officials as well as heads of Amnesty International and other international organisations. For the text see R. Gunaratna (1990: 193-196).

[60] National Security Minister Lalith Athulathmudali was the visible, articulate spokesperson for the government's point of view; however, President Jayewardene affirmed the government's position unequivocally in one of our personal conversations.

[61] R. Gunaratna (1990: 199) quotes Hyndman's June 7, 1985 report to the LAWASIA Human Rights Standing Committee on Democracy in Peril in Sri Lanka.

[62] See R. Gunaratna (1990: 192-199). The author does not assert that police might be political allies of the activists. That is my assertion, based on sources such as Ratnapala (1988) and M. Gunaratne (2001).

[63] From mid-1987 until the defeat of the militant JVP in 1990, the chaos created by JVP forces in the south would help the Tamil militant cause.

[64] Estimating the size of militant groups is a haphazard business. This is especially true of the JVP during the period between 1983 and 1987 when they were underground and initiated few actions. Estimates place the number of active members at about 5,000 during the time the insurrection was at its height.

[65] See R. Gunaratna (1990: 233). Most influential among these was the Movement for the Protection of the Motherland (*Mavubima Surakeeme Ariyadeva* – MSV) organised by politically active Buddhist priests, including some who were JVP members.

[66] These incidents are described in K.M. de Silva and Wriggins (1994: 660, ff. and 672-673). R. Gunaratna (1990: 270-289) provides brief descriptions of these and many other events as well. The *Political Conflict Data Base* (Richardson 1990) lists and describes several hundred events instigated by JVP activists during this period.

[67] According to R. Gunaratna (1990), murders averaged more than 100 per day by December 1988.

[68] K.M. de Silva and Wriggins (1994: 710).

[69] Both incidents in which militant group members initiated the action and those in which they were attacked by security forces qualify as 'militant.'

[70] I focus on five years rather than spanning J.R. Jayewardene's two terms in office.

[71] I use this phrasing because the JVP was arguably a major institutionalised presence in Sri Lanka as a legitimate political party in 1982, when Rohana Wijeweera contested the presidential elections, up through the ill-conceived May Day celebrations of 1983.

[72] Since 1987 there have been (depending on how one counts) at least four additional attempts to reach an accommodation within a united Sri Lanka. A fifth is in progress in 2003.

[73] See chapter 7.

[74] See chapter 9.

[75] See chapters 15 and 17.

[76] See Zartman (1993: 24).

[77] See K.M. de Silva and Wriggins (1994: 569-572). The diplomat, G. Parathasarathy, had been a close confident of Mrs. Gandhi's father Jawaharlal Nehru.

[78] Dixit (1998: 23). Interestingly, K.M. de Silva and Wriggins (1994: 612) characterise Ambassador Dixit as 'one of the most masterful diplomats India has ever sent to Sri Lanka.'

[79] Contrasting views of these talks and their surrounding circumstances are given in K.M. de Silva and Wriggins (1994: 612-15), Swamy (1994: 32-40) and Dixit (1998: 30-40).

[80] Both K.M. de Silva and Wriggins (1994) and Dixit (1998) devote considerable attention to discussions between the two leaders, which J.R. Jayewardene's biographers present in a somewhat more favourable light than does the Indian Ambassador.

[81] K.M. de Silva and Wriggins (1994: 622-626).

[82] A third alternative – surrender, or simply acceding to your adversary's demands – is rarely considered by political leaders when they say 'we have no choice' but to continue fighting.

[83] Many IPKF members remained in the city, mingling with civilians who protected them, as a clandestine presence.

[84] Hoole et al. (1990: 403).

[85] The Minister was Lalith Athulathmudali, one of President Jayewardene's intimates. Cyril Ratnatunge was the General. He was named head of a newly created 'Joint Operations Command' with authority over Air Forces and Naval units as well as Army.

[86] K.M. de Silva and Wriggins (1994: 580-581, 598).

[87] See Swamy (1994: 138-149).

[88] Ibid: 137, 148-149.

[89] K.M. de Silva and Wriggins (1994: 585).

[90] Swamy (1994: 137).

[91] National Security Minister (at the time) Lalith Athulathmudali seemed absolutely convinced of this when I discussed the campaign with him in the summer of 1990.

[92] Hoole et al. (1990: 126).

[93] Swamy (1994: 275-276).

[94] Hoole et al. (1994: 169-170).

[95] Swamy (1994: 274-275).

[96] This was in the spring 1988.

[97] Swamy (1994: 276).

[98] *Deshapremi Janatha Vyaparya* in Sinhala. See R. Gunaratna (1990: 224-229) and Chandraprema (1991: 64-70). The DJV did exist as a separate organisation, but the notion that the two 'wings' had a degree of independence from one another and were pursuing separate agendas was illusory. Rohana Wijeweera controlled both directly.

[99] Chandraprema (1991: 214-218).

[100] This changed under J.R. Jayewardene's successor, President Ranasinghe Premadasa, but that is another story.

[101] Data and conclusions from two works that document this, Ratnapala (1988) and M. Gunaratne (2001), were presented in earlier chapters.

[102] K.M. de Silva and Wriggins (1994: 645).

[103] 'To the top of the greasy pole' is the subtitle of the chapter in which K.M. de Silva and Wriggins describe J.R. Jayewardene's 1977 election victory (1994: 319-328).

Chapter Twenty Notes

[1] Social infrastructures suffer the same fate and may take even longer to rebuild. Costs associated with social infrastructures prove difficult to quantify, however, and I will not examine them in this chapter.

[2] See Richardson and S.W.R. de A. Samarasinghe (1991). This article provides a much more detailed methodological description and documentation of cost estimates than is presented here.

[3] I use 'weapons' here as a generic term to apply to all machines of war – tanks, armored personnel vehicles, ships, aircraft and the like.

[4] These funds do produce some short-term economic benefits, but these come at a high cost compared to the more productive uses to which governments can put the funds.

[5] Thus, as a practical matter, we chose to combine primary and secondary military costs.

[6] In the United States, actuaries have developed sophisticated techniques for valuing deaths and injuries as part of damage claims from automobile accidents and medical malpractice, but these did not seem relevant to Sri Lanka or other developing nations.

[7] In support of this unquestionably controversial point, I offer the routine disregard of civilian casualties by militant groups and the Sri Lankan Army. A similar degree of disregard occurs in many other civil wars as well. The U.S. led coalition that invaded Iraq does not report civilian casualties, though leaders say the troops try to avoid them.

[8] The Government published this *Master Plan* in 1984.

[9] One source provided this information under condition of anonymity.

[10] Unless otherwise specified, I express all rupee and US dollar figures in 1988 constant values. Rupees convert to US dollars at the rate of rupees 33 = $US 1, approximating the rate of exchange at the end of 1988.

[11] At the time when the Government made these estimates, many hoped that the Indo-Lanka Accord would usher in a period of tranquillity that would make rehabilitation possible.

[12] I emphasise the word 'rough'. Earlier I warned about using conflict intensity numbers for any kind of statistical analysis. Since at this point we merely sought to generate order-

of-magnitude estimates, with reservations about their precision clearly stated, I judged the inferences made were appropriate.

[13] The Indian Peace Keeping Force (IPKF) used heavy artillery and aircraft in their offensive to dislodge the Tigers from Jaffna. The Tigers also made extensive use of explosives in the weeks of bitter house-to-house fighting.

[14] Readers will recall several discussions of the Mahaweli project in earlier chapters. I use vague language to characterise Mahaweli cost estimates, because the Government has issued several such estimates, and all have subsequently become subject to upward revision.

[15] For additional illustrations focusing on fisheries, social welfare, foreign private investment, foreign aid, and migration, see Richardson and S.W.R. de A. Samarasinghe (1991: 201-05).

[16] Re-openings occurred intermittently, and some graduate programs – including the program in which I taught – continued to offer courses. Paradoxically, the University of Jaffna stood alone as one that remained opened most of the time, perhaps because LTTE leaders valued education highly. The Tigers told students threatening strikes in no uncertain terms that they would not accept any closures of the University.

[17] For example, about 2,200 'Sri Lankan' students were enrolled in US colleges and universities in 1987. Today the number is certain to be much higher.

[18] A text edited by K.M. de Silva and G.H. Peiris (1995) provides an excellent survey of Sri Lanka's higher-education system by several senior academics and government officials involved in educational policy. In addition, the volume discusses the system's post-1983 travails.

[19] Agriculture still contributes about 25 per cent of GNP in Sri Lanka. About 40 per cent of the labour force have jobs in agriculture.

[20] We based our published analysis on an estimated 1988 expenditure of 6.3 billion rupees. As predicted, the government actually spent more. In 1987, the outlay amounted to 9.1 billion rupees. I recalculated the results to reflect this change, but it makes only an inconsequential difference.

[21] Since such outlays accounted for 0.58 per cent in 1981 and 0.49 per cent in 1982, we consider this scenario a generous estimate.

[22] We did not include India's expenditures on training and arming militant forces, described in chapter 19. In the case of the LTTE, of course, the arms and training increased LTTE effectiveness against the IPKF, making India's intervention far more costly than it would have proven otherwise.

[23] This program, which promised an allowance of rupees 2,500 per month for the poor, became a centrepiece of UNP candidate Ranasinghe Premadasa's successful presidential election campaign in December 1988.

[24] A more recent study by Arunatilake et al. (2001) estimated the costs of conflict in Sri Lanka from 1983-1996 to be equivalent to 1,135 billion rupees at 1996 prices ($U.S. 20.6 billion).

[25] In a further complication, the LTTE and particularly the TELO would from time to time initiate major actions in Colombo and other areas lying south of the Northeast Region. Since we only sought to develop order-of-magnitude estimates, we felt that approximations based on good judgement would suffice.

[26] This assumption reflected the relative violent conflict intensities in our 'fever charts' for the period, described in chapter 19.

[27] Among the groups of unemployed of these estimated sizes, we would expect to see approximately 55,000 and 66,000 Tamils, respectively.

[28] We calculated this amount assuming the larger figure of 525,000 unemployed. For more details, see Richardson and S.W.R. de A. Samarasinghe (1991: 214-15).

[29] For a detailed discussion and documentation of these numbers, see Ibid: 216.

[30] The JVP has now become a legitimate political party and had members in President Chandrika Kumaratunga's 'People's Alliance' government before the government's 2002 general election loss. When Kumaratunga regained power in 2004, the JVP was again part of her coalition.

[31] We base this discussion on a much longer analysis in Richardson and Samarasinghe (1991: 211-13).

[32] In Sinhala, *mudalali* denotes a small- or mid-level trader. While the term applies broadly – *mudal* means 'money' in Sinhala – one often sees it used to describe entrepreneurs whose business success depends in some degree on their political connections. In point of fact, this view of the word does not prove too limiting, because political connections play an important role in the success of most businesses – small and large – in Sri Lanka. For example, see Spencer (1990b: 51, et passim) and Brow (1978: 129-30).

[33] On this point, see Richardson and Wang (1993: 172-74, et passim).

[34] This is another facet of the growing interest in protracted deadly conflicts that I discussed in Part I of this book.

[35] For extended discussion of greed and grievance in civil wars, see Keen (2000), accompanying contributions to Berdel and Malone's edited volume (2000), and Collier and Hoeffler (2001). The latter report can be accessed at www.worldbank.org.

[36] See Kumarakulasingam (2002), he, himself, is a Sri Lanka Tamil.

[37] Most of the literature in this area is drawn from research projects by the World Bank and the International Peace Research Institute in Oslo (PRIO). These projects have yielded two main conferences to date: 'Economic Agendas in Civil Wars' held April 6, 1999 in Canada House, London and 'The Economics of Political Violence' held March 7, 2000 at the Centre for International Studies at Princeton University.

[38] See Ellis (1998: 162).

[39] See Compagnon (1998: 86).

[40] Ibid.

[41] See Ellis (1998: 162-64, note 3).

[42] See Mwanasali (2000).

[43] See King (1997: 39).

[44] For example see Hoole et al. (1990) and Hoole (2001), cited in previous chapters. Hoole and his colleagues in Teachers for Human Rights (Jaffna) have harshly criticised Sinhalese politicians in Sri Lanka's Government, but have also criticised the LTTE. As noted earlier, Dr. Rajani Thiranagama, one of Hoole's colleagues, paid with her life for steadfastly drawing attention to LTTE excesses.

[45] See King (1997: 38).

[46] See Abdullah and Muana (1998).

[47] See M. B. Anderson (1999).

[48] See Shearer (2000).

[49] Ibid: 193.

[50] According to Shearer, Liberia's Charles Taylor epitomises this tendency, charging an aid tax for relief brought into the areas under his control.

[51] See Gamba and Cornwell (2000: 166).

[52] See Berdal and Malone (2000: 5).

[53] See King (2001).

[54] Ibid.: 546.

[55] See Keen (2000: 37).

Chapter Twenty-One Notes

[1] Readers are warned once again that importance should not be attached to specific numerical values derived from the *Violent Political Conflict Data Base* (Richardson 1990). It is order-of-magnitude changes in patterns over fairly long-time periods that should be viewed as significant.

[2] Singapore's former Primer Minister, Lee Kuan Yew spoke eloquently and often about the dangers of 'communalism' and dealt sternly with those who attempted to use communalist appeals to gain political advantage in Singapore. For example, see Josey (1980: chapter 17).

[3] See Moore (1985).

[4] See chapter 11.

Chapter Twenty-Two Notes

[1] See Arun Gandhi (1994). The author directs the M.K. Gandhi Institute for Non-Violence. Readers can find the Institute's website at <http://www.gandhiinstitute.org>.

[2] On the last day of the event launching *World Without Violence*, Arun Gandhi gave participants a 'talisman from grandfather to grandson to you,' listing the eight blunders. I have kept this framed in my office, and have quoted the 'eight blunders' from it.

[3] Tuchman (1984: 357).

[4] I am particularly indebted to Deputy Inspector General Dinkar Gupta, an extraordinarily capable member of India's police forces, for deepening my understanding of police functions. Friends over the years from Sri Lankan and US police have also contributed, unknowingly, to this section.

[5] See Ratnapala (1988) and M. Gunaratne (2001), as well as my recapitulation of their views in chapters 13 and 18.

[6] Critics still debate the actual extent of Costa Rican demilitarisation, particularly during the 1980s, marked by significant US assistance for heightened 'public security' and intervention given the war and upheaval in neighbouring countries. R. Anderson (1998) concludes that Costa Rica's expanding public security apparatus has remained under police and non-partisan civilian control.

[7] My personal military experience is the primary source of these generalisations, but they are supported by input from many friends and acquaintances with military backgrounds.

[8] For comprehensive statistics on homelessness in American, see the website of the National Law Centre on Homelessness and Poverty, <http://www.nlchp.org>.

[9] See chapter 3.

[10] For further development of this theme, see Kusterer (1998) and Richardson and Herrmann (1998).

[11] K.M. de Silva discusses this issue extensively in 'Sri Lanka: Electoral Politics and the Resilience of Democracy' (1998b).

[12] An article from the June 13, 2002 issue of *The Economist*, subtitled 'Good Governance in Poor Countries Would End Hunger Faster Than Rich-World Aid,' suggests that this has become conventional wisdom. 'Always With Us' (*The Economist*, 363: 73-74) remains accessible at <http://www.economist.com/>.

[13] See Richardson and Herrmann (1998: 339).

[14] On this point, see Ibid: 323-24.

[15] Former Cold Warriors predominate among the foreign policy advisors close to US President George W. Bush.

[16] I use a gendered term here simply because men predominate to such a great degree in businesses and business organisations in developing countries. I do not endorse this, but I do acknowledge it.

[17] For example see D.H. Meadows, Richardson and Bruckmann (1982).

[18] See Richardson (1980).

[19] In a brief sequel, a personal friend of President Reagan read my book *Making it Happen: A Positive Guide to the Future* (1982) and asked me to provide a copy which he might give to the President at a Camp David weekend they would spend together. The book includes an excerpt from 'Towards Effective Foresight'. I kept hoping President Reagan might read some of the book and contact me with his impressions, but I never heard from him.

[20] See chapter 3.

[21] This estimate is based on figures from a variety of sources and news reports, including insurance cost estimates for the World Trade Centre Bombing and budget submissions of the US Defence Department and the US Department of State. For the Iraq war, a particularly useful source written before the US invasion is Nordhaus (2002).

[22] See 'Other Things Iraq War Funding Can Pay For' in the June 1, 2004 edition of the *Miami Herald*, accessible at <http://www.miami.com/mld/miamiherald/>.

Selected Bibliography

Abdullah, Ibrahim and Patrick Muana. 1998. 'The Revolutionary United Front of Sierra Leone: A Revolt of the Lumpenproletariat', In *African Guerrillas*, Edited by C. Clapham. Oxford: James Currey, 172-194.

Abeyesekere, Gamini. 1986. 'Social Development', In *Facets of Development in Independent Sri Lanka: Felicitation Volume to Commemorate the 10th Successive Budget of Hon. Ronnie de Mel, Minister of Finance and Planning*, Edited by W. Rasaputra, et al. Colombo: Ministry of Finance and Planning, 291-309.

Abeynaike, H.B.W., Ed. 1977. *The Ceylon Daily News Parliament of Sri Lanka,1977*. Colombo: Lake House.

Abeynaike, H.B.W. and H.P. Amaratunga, Eds. 1965. *The Ceylon Daily News Parliament of Ceylon, 1965*. Colombo: Lake House.

Abeyratne, Sirimal. 1997. 'Trade Strategy and Industrialization', In *Dilemmas of Development: Fifty Years of Economic Change in Sri Lanka*, Edited by W. D. Lakshman. Colombo: Sri Lanka Association of Economists, 341-385.

_____. 1998. *Economic Change and Political Conflict in Developing Countries: With Special Reference to Sri Lanka*. Amsterdam: VU University Press.

Ahluwalia, Montek, Nicholas Carter and Hollis Chenery. 1979. 'Growth and Poverty in Developing Countries'. *Journal of Development Economics* 6: 299-341.

Akan-Ellis, Burcu. 2000. 'Shadow Genealogies: Memory and Identity Among Urban Muslims in Macedonia'. Unpublished Doctoral Dissertation, School of International Service, American University, Washington DC.

Alailima, Patricia J. 1997. 'Social Policy in Sri Lanka', In *Dilemmas of Development: Fifty Years of Economic Change in Sri Lanka*, Edited by W. D. Lakshman. Colombo: Sri Lanka Association of Economists, 127-170.

Alexander, Paul. 1981. 'Shared Fantasies and Elite Politics:The Sri Lankan Insurrection of 1971'. *Mankind* 13 (2): 113-132.

Ali, S. Mahmud. 1993. *The Fearful State: Power People and Internal War in South Asia*. New Jersey: Zed Books.

All-Ceylon Buddhist Congress. 1956. *The Betrayal of Buddhism: An Abridged Version of the Buddhist Commission of Inquiry*. Balangoda: Dharmavijaya Press.

Alles, A.C. 1977. *Insurgency 1971*. 2nd ed. Colombo: The Colombo Apothecaries Co. Ltd.

Almond, Gabriel A. 1987. 'The Development of Political Development', In *Understanding Political Development: An Analytic Study*, Edited by M. Weiner, et al. Boston: Little Brown, 437-490.

Altman, Edward. 1981. *Financial Handbook*. 5th ed. New York: John Wiley and Sons.

Amaratunga, Chanaka. 1994. *The Failure of the Unitary State in Sri Lanka: A Consideration of Alternatives*. Colombo: Council for Liberal Democracy.

Amirthalingam, A. 1974. 'The Path to Our Destiny', In *The Silver Jubilee Souvenir.* Jaffna: Federal Party.

Amnesty International. 1979. *1979 Report.* New York: Amnesty International.

_____. 1980. *1980 Report.* New York: Amnesty International.

_____. 1981. *1981 Report.* New York: Amnesty International.

_____. 1983. *Report of an Amnesty International Mission to Sri Lanka: 31st January to 9th February 1982.* New York: Amnesty International.

Amunagama, Sarath. 1991. 'Buddhaputra and Bhumiputra?: Dilemmas of Modern Sinhala Buddhist Monks in Relation to Ethnic and Political Conflict". *Religion* 21: 115-39.

Anderson, John Gottberg and Ravidralal Anthonis, Eds. 1985. *Sri Lanka: Insight Guide for the Sophisticated Traveler.* Englewood Cliffs: Prentice Hall.

Anderson, Mary B. 1999. *Do No Harm: How Aid Can Support Peace - Or War.* Boulder: Lynne Reinner.

Anderson, Robert B. 1998. *The Competitive Effects of Political Homogeneity in International Relations: Social Identity Theory and Systemic Analysis.* ISA Working Paper. International Studies Association.

Anthonis, Ravindralal. 1985. 'Land of Tanks and Jungles', In *Sri Lanka: Insight Guide for the Sophisticated Traveler,* Edited by J. G. Anderson and R. Anthonis. Englewood Cliffs: Prentice Hall, 25-28.

Arasaratnam, S. 1979. 'Nationalism in Sri Lanka and the Tamils', In *Collective Identities, Nationalism and Protest in Modern Sri Lanka,* Edited by M. Roberts. Colombo: Marga Institute, 500-518.

Ariyaratne, A.T. 1982. *In Search of Development.* Moratuwa: Sarvodaya Shramadana.

Ariyaratne, Vinya. 2004. *The Deshodaya Pathway to Consensual Politics: Healing the Political Crisis and the Peace Process.* Ratmalana: Sarvodaya Shramadana Movement.

Arrow, Kenneth J. 1951. *Social Choice and Individual Values.* New York: John Wiley & Sons.

Arunatilake, Nisha, Sisira Jayasuriya and Saman Kelegama. 2001. 'The Economic Cost of War in Sri Lanka'. *World Development* 29 (9): 1483-1500.

Aryasinha, Ravinatha P. 1988. 'The Significance of the Ideology of Nationalism in Understanding the Political Process in Post Independence Sri Lanka'. Unpublished Paper.

Atapattu, Danny. 1997. 'Capital Formation and Its Financing', In *Dilemmas of Development: Fifty Years of Economic Change in Sri Lanka,* Edited by W. D. Lakshman. Colombo: Sri Lanka Association of Economists, 55-100.

Athukorala, Premachandra. 1997. 'Foreign Direct Investment and Manufacturing for Export', In *Dilemmas of Development: Fifty Years of Economic Change in Sri Lanka,* Edited by W. D. Lakshman. Colombo: Sri Lanka Association of Economists, 386-422.

Athulathmudali, Lalith. 1984. 'The Elections of 1982', In *Sri Lanka in Change and Crisis,* Edited by J. Manor. London: Croom Helm, 76-83.

_____. 1988. 'Conflict in Sri Lanka and Perceptions of the U.S. Role'. Address at the University of Maryland, College Park, July 17.

Austin, Dennis and Anirudha Gupta. 1988. 'Lions and Tigers: The Crisis in Sri Lanka'. *Conflict Studies* 211: 1-19.

Azar, Edward. 1990. *The Management of Protracted Social Conflict: Theory and Cases*. Hampshire: Dartmouth Publishing Co.

_____. 1993. *Conflict and Peace Data Bank (COPDAB)*. Computer File and Codebook. Ann Arbor: Inter-university Consortium for Political and Social Research.

Azar, Edward and Joseph D. Ben-Dak, Eds. 1975. *Theory and Practice of Events Research: Studies in Inter-Nation Actions and Interactions*. New York: Gordon and Breach Science Publishers.

Azar, Edward and John Burton. 1986. *International Conflict Resolution, Theory and Practice*. Boulder: Wheatsheaf.

Baker, Pauline H. and John A. Ausnik. 1996. 'State Collapse and Ethnic Violence: Toward a Predictive Model'. *Parameters* 26 (1): 19-36.

Balakrishnan, N. 1977. 'Industrial Policy and Development Since Independence', In *Sri Lanka: A Survey*, Edited by K. M. d. Silva. Honolulu: University of Hawaii Press, 192-212.

Bandaranaike Centre for International Studies. 1977. *Non Aligned Conference: Basic Documents 1976*. Colombo: Bandaranaike Centre for International Studies.

Banks, Arthur S., Ed. 1975. *A Political Handbook of the World: 1975*. New York: McGraw Hill.

Banuazizi, Ali and Myron Weiner. 1990. *The State, Religion, and Ethnic Politics: Afghanistan, Iran, and Pakistan*. Syracuse: Syracuse University Press.

Bastiampillai, Bertram. 1983. 'The Job-Oriented Courses of Study in the Universities of Sri Lanka', In *University Education and Graduate Employment in Sri Lanka*, Edited by B. C. Sanyal, et al. Paris and Colombo: UNESCO and the Marga Institute, 149-177.

Bastian, Sunil, Ed. 1994. *Devolution and Development in Sri Lanka*. Colombo and New Delhi: International Centre for Ethnic Studies (ICES) and Konark Publishers.

Bechert, Heinz. 1984. 'Buddhist Revival in East and West', In *The World of Buddhism: Buddhist Monks and Nuns in Society and Culture*, Edited by H. Bechert and R. Gombrich. London: Thames and Hudson, 273-288.

Bechert, Heinz and Richard Gombrich, Eds. 1984. *The World of Buddhism: Buddhist Monks and Nuns in Society and Culture*. London: Thames and Hudson.

Bell, David E. and Michael R. Reich. 1988. *Health, Nutrition and Economic Crises: Approaches to Policy in the Third World*. Dover: Auburn House.

Bellamy, Edward. 1995. *Looking Backward, 2000-1887*. Edited by D. Borus, *Bedford Book in History and Culture*. Boston: Bedford Books/ St. Martin's.

Bennis, Warren. 1989. *On Becoming a Leader*. Reading: Addison-Wesley Publishing Company.

Berdal, M. and David M. Malone. 2000. 'Introduction', In *Greed and Grievance: Economic Agendas in Civil Wars*, Edited by M. Berdal and D. M. Malone. Boulder: Lynne Rienner, 1-15.

Berlin, David Pion. 1983. 'Political Repression and Economic Doctrines: The Case of Argentina'. *Comparative Political Studies* 16 (1): 37-66.

Bhalla, Surjith. 1988. 'Is Sri Lanka an Exception: A Comparative Study of Living Standards', In *Rural Poverty in South Asia*, Edited by T. N. Srinivasan and P. K. Bardhan. New York: Columbia University Press, 89-117.

_____. 1988. 'Sri Lanka's Achievements: Fact and Fancy', In *Rural Poverty in South Asia*, Edited by T. N. Srinivasan and P. K. Bardhan. New York: Columbia University Press, 557-565.

Bhalla, Surjith and Paul Glewwe. 1986. 'Growth and Equity in Developing Countries: a Reinterpretation of the Sri Lankan Experience'. *World Bank Economic Review* 1 (1): 35-63.

Bhargava, Pradeep. 1987. *Political Economy of Sri Lanka*. New Delhi: Navrang.

Bjorkman, J.W. 1985. 'Health Policy and Politics in Sri Lanka'. *Asian Survey* 25 (5).

Brinton, Crane. 1965. *The Anatomy of a Revolution*. Revised and Expanded edition. New York: Prentice Hall - Vintage Books.

Brow, James. 1978. *Vedda Villages of Anuradhapura*. Seattle: University of Washington Press.

_____. 1990. 'Nationalist Rhetoric and Local Practice: The Fate of the Village Community in Kukulewa', In *Sri Lanka: History and Roots of the Conflict*, Edited by J. Spencer. London and New York: Routledge, 125-144.

Buckle, Henry T. 1861. *History of Civilization in England*. London: Parker, Son and Bourn.

Burger, Angela S. 1987. 'Policing a Communal Society: The Case of Sri Lanka'. *Asian Survey* 27: 822-833.

Carlyle, Thomas, Michael K. Goldberg, Joel J. Brattin and Mark Engel. 1993. *On Heroes, Hero-worship, and the Heroic in History*. Berkeley: University of California Press.

Carnegie Commission on Preventing Deadly Conflict. 1997. *Preventing Deadly Conflict*. New York: Carnegie Corporation of New York.

Carothers, Thomas. 1999. *Aiding Democracy Abroad: The Learning Curve*. Washington DC: The Brookings Institution.

Carrithers, Michael B. 1982. 'Hell Fire and Urinal Sores: An Essay on Buddhist Purity and Authority', In *Contributions to South Asian Studies*, Edited by G. Krishna. Delhi: Oxford University Press.

_____. 1984. 'They Will be Lords Upon the Island: Buddhism in Sri Lanka', In *The World of Buddhism: Buddhist Monks and Nuns in Society and Culture*, Edited by H. Bechert and R. Gombrich. London: Thames and Hudson, 133-146.

Chambers, Robert. 1997. *Whose Reality Counts? Putting the Last First.* London: ITDG Publishing.

Chandrapala, H.A. 1986. 'Performance in the Agricultural Sector', In *Facets of Development in Independent Sri Lanka: Felicitation Volume to Commemorate the 10th Successive Budget of Hon. Ronnie de Mel, Minister of Finance and Planning,* Edited by W. Rasaputra, et al. Colombo: Ministry of Finance and Planning, 219-276.

Chandraprema, Candauda A. 1989. *Ruhuna: A Study of the History, Society and Ideology of Southern Sri Lanka.* Nugegoda: Bharat Publishers.

_____. 1991. *Sri Lanka - The Years of Terror: The JVP Insurrection 1987-1989.* Colombo: Lake House.

Civil Rights Movement of Sri Lanka. 1978. *Statement on the Proscribing of the Liberation Tigers of Tamil Eelam and Similar Organizations Bill.* Colombo.

_____. 1979a. *Statement on the Criminal Procedure (Special Provisions) Law.* Colombo.

_____. 1979b. *Documents of the Civil Rights Movement of Sri Lanka, 1971-1978.* Colombo.

_____. 1983. *Communal Violence: July 1983.* Colombo.

Clapham, C., Ed. 1998. *African Guerrillas.* Oxford: James Currey.

Collier, Paul and Anke Hoeffler. 2001. *Greed and Grievance in Civil War.* Washington DC: Development Research Group, World Bank.

Colombage, S. and S.A. Karunaratne. 1986. 'Development Planning and Investment', In *Facets of Development in Independent Sri Lanka: Felicitation Volume to Commemorate the 10th Successive Budget of Hon. Ronnie de Mel, Minister of Finance and Planning,* Edited by W. Rasaputra, et al. Colombo: Ministry of Finance and Planning, 195-218.

Committee for Rational Development, Ed. 1984. *Sri Lanka: The Ethnic Conflict: Myths, Realities and Perspectives.* New Delhi: Navrang.

Compagnon, Daniel. 1998. 'Somali Armed Units: The Interplay of Political Entrepreneurship and Clan-based Factions', In *African Guerrillas,* Edited by C. Clapham. Oxford: James Currey, 73-90.

Cooke, Ratna S. 1986. 'Mahaweli Ten Years After: A Historical Perspective of Mahaweli Development'. Presented at Sri Lanka Association for the Advancement of Science (SLAAS) Symposium on Mahaweli. Colombo, November 6-9.

Coomaraswamy, Indrajit. 1986. 'Employment Policies', In *Facets of Development in Independent Sri Lanka: Felicitation Volume to Commemorate the 10th Successive Budget of Hon. Ronnie de Mel, Minister of Finance and Planning,* Edited by W. Rasaputra, et al. Colombo: Ministry of Finance and Planning, 277-290.

Coomaraswamy, Radhika. 1981. 'The Regulatory Framework for the Press in Sri Lanka'. *Marga Quarterly Journal* 6 (2).

_____. 1993a. 'The Constitution and Constitutional Reform', In *Sri Lanka: Problems of Governance,* Edited by K. M. de Silva. Colombo: International Centre for Ethnic Studies (ICES), 126-147.

_____. 1993b. 'Civil Liberties and Human Rights Perspective', In *In Sri Lanka: Problems of Governance*, Edited by K. M. de Silva. Colombo: International Centre for Ethnic Studies (ICES), 148-176.

_____. 1994. 'Devolution, the Law and Judicial Construction', In *Devolution and Development in Sri Lanka*, Edited by S. Bastian. Colombo and New Delhi: International Centre for Ethnic Studies (ICES) and Konark Publishers, 121-142.

Cooray, J.A.L. 1973. *Constitutional and Administrative Law of Sri Lanka*. Colombo: Hansa Publishers.

Cornia, Andrea G. 1999. *Liberalization, Globalization and Income Distribution*. Helsinki: United Nations University, World Institute for Development Economics Research (WIDER).

Dailey, Andrew. 1990. *Mahaweli Development Report*. Unpublished Paper.

Das, Veena. 1988. 'Communities, Riots, Survivors: The South Asian Experience'. Presented at The Punitham Tiruchelvam Memorial Lecture. Colombo, September 5.

de Silva, C.R. 1975. 'Weightage in University Admissions: Standardization and District Quotas in Sri Lanka 1970-75'. *Modern Ceylon Studies* 5 (2): 152-178.

_____. 1977. 'Education', In *Sri Lanka: A Survey*, Edited by K. M. de Silva. Honolulu: The University Press of Hawaii, 403-433.

_____. 1978. 'The Politics of University Admissions: A Review of Some Aspects of the Admissions in Sri Lanka, 1972-1978'. *The Sri Lanka Journal of Social Sciences* 1 (2): 85-123.

_____. 1979. 'The Impact of Nationalism on Education: The Schools Takeover (1961) and the University Crisis, 1970-1975', In *Collective Identities: Nationalism and Protest in Modern Sri Lanka*, Edited by M. Roberts. Colombo: Marga Institute, 474-499.

_____. 1984. 'Plebiscitary Democracy or Creeping Authoritarianism?: The Presidential Election and Referendum of 1982', In *Sri Lanka in Change and Crisis*, Edited by J. Manor. London: Croom Helm, 35-50.

de Silva, G.P.S.H. 1979. *A Statistical Survey of Elections to the Legislatures of Sri Lanka 1911-1977*. Colombo: Marga Institute.

de Silva, Jani. 1994. 'Centripetal Pressures and Regime Change in the Post-Colonial Sri Lankan State', In *Devolution and Development in Sri Lanka*, Edited by S. Bastian. Colombo and New Delhi: International Centre for Ethnic Studies (ICES) and Konark Publishers, 20-47.

de Silva, Kingsley M., Ed. 1977. *Sri Lanka: A Survey*. Honolulu: The University Press of Hawaii.

_____. 1981. *A History of Sri Lanka*. London, Berkeley and Los Angeles: G. Hurst & Co. and University of California Press.

_____. 1985a. 'A Tale of Three Constitutions: 1946-48, 1972 and 1978'. *Ceylon Journal of Historical and Social Studies* 7 (2): 1-17.

_____. 1985b. 'The Classical Era', In *Sri Lanka: Insight Guide for the Sophisticated Traveler*, Edited by J. G. Anderson and R. Anthonis. Englewood Cliffs: Prentice Hall, 35-41.

_____. 1985c. 'The Colonial Era', In *Sri Lanka: Insight Guide for the Sophisticated Traveler*, Edited by J. G. Anderson and R. Anthonis. Englewood Cliffs: Prentice Hall, 42-54.

_____. 1986. *Managing Ethnic Tensions in a Multiethnic Society*. Lanham: University Press of America.

_____, Ed. 1993a. *Sri Lanka: Problems of Governance*. Colombo: International Centre for Ethnic Studies (ICES).

_____. 1993b. 'The Police and the Armed Services', In *Sri Lanka: Problems of Governance*, Edited by K. M. de Silva. Colombo: International Centre for Ethnic Studies (ICES), 347-371.

_____. 1993c. 'The Bureaucracy', In *Sri Lanka: Problems of Governance*, Edited by K. M. de Silva. Colombo: International Centre for Ethnic Studies (ICES), 83-98.

_____. 1993d. 'The Politics of Language Policy', In *Sri Lanka: Problems of Governance*, Edited by K. M. de Silva. Colombo: International Centre for Ethnic Studies (ICES), 275-305.

_____. 1993e. 'Religion and the State', In *Sri Lanka: Problems of Governance*, Edited by K. M. de Silva. Colombo: International Centre for Ethnic Studies (ICES), 306-344.

_____. 1993f. 'Sri Lanka's Security and Strategies for Survival', In *Sri Lanka: Problems of Governance*, Edited by K. M. de Silva. Colombo: International Centre for Ethnic Studies (ICES), 372-395.

_____. 1993g. 'Problems of Governance: Politics and the Political System', In *Sri Lanka: Problems of Governance*, Edited by K. M. de Silva. Colombo: International Centre for Ethnic Studies (ICES), 3-41.

_____. 1994. *The 'Traditional Homelands' of the Tamils: Separatist Ideology in Sri Lanka: A Historical Appraisal*. Occasional Paper #4 (Republished). Kandy: International Centre for Ethnic Studies (ICES).

_____. 1998a. *Reaping the Whirlwind: Ethnic Conflict, Ethnic Politics in Sri Lanka*. New Delhi: Penguin Books.

_____. 1998b. 'Sri Lanka: Electoral Politics and the Resilience of Democracy', In *Democratisation in South Asia: The First Fifty Years*, Edited by J. M. J. Richardson and S. W. R. d. A. Samarasinghe. Nedimala - Dehiwala: Sridevi Printers, Ltd. and the International Centre for Ethnic Studies (ICES), 163-185.

_____. 1999a. 'Sri Lanka: Ethnic Conflict and the Search for a Durable Peace, 1978-1999'. *Ethnic Studies Report* 17 (2): 301-344.

_____. 1999b. 'Sri Lanka: The Bandaranaikes in the Island's Politics and Public Life'. *The Round Table* 350 (1): 241-280.

de Silva, Kingsley M. and G.H. Peiris, Eds. 1995. *The University System of Sri Lanka: Vision and Reality*. New Delhi and Kandy: Macmillan India Ltd. and International Centre for Ethnic Studies (ICES).

de Silva, Kingsley M. and W. Howard Wriggins. 1988. *J.R. Jayewardene of Sri Lanka: A Political Biography. Volume One: The First Fifty Years*. Honolulu: University of Hawaii Press.

_____. 1994. *J.R. Jayewardene of Sri Lanka: A Political Biography. Volume Two: From 1956 to His Retirement (1989)*. Honolulu: University of Hawaii Press.

de Vos, George and Lola Romanucci-Ross, Eds. 1995. *Ethnic Identity: Creation, Conflict, and Accomodation*. Walnut Creek: Altamira Press.

Dharmadasa, K.N.O. 1996. *National Language Policy in Sri Lanka 1956 to 1996: Three Studies in its Implementation*. Occasional Paper. Kandy: International Centre for Ethnic Studies (ICES).

Diamond, Larry, Seymour Martin Lipset and Juan Linz, Eds. 1989. *Democracy in Developing Countries*. Vol. 1-4. Boulder: Lynne Rienner Publishers.

Diener, Ed. 1994. 'Assessing Subjective Well-being: Progress and Opportunities'. *Social Indicators Research* 31: 103-157.

Diener, Ed and Eunkook Suh. 1999. 'International Well-Being', In *Hedonic Psychology: Scientific Perspectives on Enjoyment, Suffering and Well-Being*, Edited by D. Kahneman, et al. New York: Russell Sage.

Dissanayake, T.D.S.A. 1977. *J.R. Jayewardene of Sri Lanka*. Colombo: Swastika Press.

_____. 1983. *The Agony of Sri Lanka*. Colombo: Swastika Press.

Dixit, Jyotindra Nath. 1998. *Assignment Colombo*. Delhi: Konark.

Diyasena, W. 1983. 'The Formal School Education System of Sri Lanka', In *University Education and Graduate Employment in Sri Lanka*, Edited by B. C. Sanyal, et al. Paris and Colombo: UNESCO and the Marga Institute, 62-111.

Duff, Ernest A., John F. McCamant and Waltrand Q. Morales. 1976. *Violence and Repression in Latin America: A Quantitative and Historical Analysis*. New York: Free Press.

Dye, Thomas R. and Harmod Zeigler. 1993. *The Irony of Democracy: An Uncommon Introduction to American Politics*. 9th ed. Belmont: Wadsworth.

Edirisinghe, Neville. 1987. *The Food Stamp Scheme in Sri Lanka: Costs, Benefits and Options for Modification*. Washington DC: International Food Policy Research Institute.

Ellis, Stephen. 1998. 'Liberia's Warlord Insurgency', In *African Guerrillas*, Edited by C. Clapham. Oxford: James Currey, 155-171.

Enloe, Cynthia H. 1980. *Police, Military and Ethnicity: Foundations of State Power*. Brunswick: Transaction Books.

_____. 1986. *Ethnic Conflict and Political Development*. Lanham: University Press of America.

Escobar, Arturo. 1995. *Encountering Development: The Making and Unmaking of the Third World*. Princeton: Princeton University Press.

Esty, Daniel C., Jack Goldstone, Ted R. Gurr, Pamela T. Surko and Alan N. Unger. 1995. *Working Papers: State Failure Task Force Report*. McLean: Science Applications International Corporation.

Feierabend, Ivo K. and Rosalind L. Feierabend. 1966. 'Aggressive Behaviors Within Polities, 1948-1962'. *Journal of Conflict Resolution* 10: 249-271.

Fernando, Lloyd. 1997. 'Development Planning in Sri Lanka', In *Dilemmas of Development: Fifty Years of Economic Change in Sri Lanka*, Edited by W. D. Lakshman. Colombo: Sri Lanka Association of Economists, 101-126.

Fernando, Tyronne. 1988. *100 Days in Sri Lanka*. Colombo: Personally Published.

Forrester, J.W. 1961. *Industrial Dynamics*. Cambridge, MA: M.I.T. Press.

_____. 1969. *Urban Dynamics*. Cambridge, MA: M.I.T. Press.

_____. 1975. *Collected Papers of Jay W. Forrester*. Cambridge, MA: Wright-Allen Press.

Frey, Bruno and Alois Stutzer. 2002. *Happiness and Economics: How the Economy and Institutions Affect Well-Being*. Princeton and Oxford: Princeton University Press.

Friedman, John. 1992. *Empowerment: The Politics of Alternative Development*. Cambridge, MA: Blackwell.

Friedrich, Carl and Zbigniew Brzezinski. 1961. *Totalitarian Dictatorship and Autocracy*. New York: Praeger.

Gamba, Virginia and Richard Cornwell. 2000. 'Arms, Elites, and Resources in the Angolan Civil War', In *Greed and Grievance: Economic Agendas in Civil Wars*, Edited by M. Berdal and D. M. Malone. Boulder: Lynne Reinner Publishers, 157-172.

Gamburd, Michele Ruth. 2000. *The Kitchen Spoon's Handle: Transnationalism and Sri Lanka's Migrant Housmaids*. Ithaca: Cornell University Press.

Gandhi, Arun. 1994. *World Without Violence: Can Gandhi's Dream Become Reality?* New Delhi: Wiley Eastern Limited.

George, Alexander and Jane E. Holt. 1997. *The Warning Response Problem and Missed Opportunities in Preventative Diplomacy*. Working Paper. Washington DC: Carnegie Commission on Preventing Deadly Conflict.

Glazer, Nathan and Daniel Patrick Moynihan, Eds. 1975. *Ethnicity: Theory and Experience*. Cambridge, MA: Harvard University Press.

Gombrich, Richard F. 1971. *Precept and Practice*. Oxford: Clarenden Press.

_____. 1984. 'Introduction: The Buddhist Way', In *The World of Buddhism: Buddhist Monks and Nuns in Society and Culture*, Edited by H. Bechert and R. Gombrich. London: Thames and Hudson, 9-14.

_____. 1988. *Theravada Buddhism: A Social History from Ancient Benares to Modern Colombo*. London: Routledge and Kegan Paul.

Goonasekera, Kapila. 1995. 'The Technical Structure of Mahaweli: Limitations and Possibilities', In *The Blurring of a Vision: The Mahaweli*, Edited by H. P. Muller and S. T. Hettige. Ratmalana: Sarvodaya Publishing, 71-94.

Gooneratne, Tilak. 1995. *S.W.R.D. Bandaranaike, Prime Minister of Ceylon*. London: Third World Promoters, Inc.

Gooneratne, Yasmine. 1986. *Relative Merits: A Personal Memoir of the Bandaranaike Family of Sri Lanka*. London: G.C. Hurst.

_____. 1991. *A Change of Skies*. Sydney: Pan Macmillan.

Goonetileke, H.A.I. 1975. *The April 1971 Insurrection in Ceylon: A Bibliographical Commentary*. 2nd ed. Louvan: Centre de Recherches Socio-Religieuses, Universite de Louvai.

_____. 1976. *Images of Sri Lanka Through American Eyes: Travelers in Ceylon in the Nineteenth and Twentieth Centuries - A Select Anthology*. Colombo: US Information Service.

Greater Colombo Economic Commission. 1986. *Sri Lanka: Opportunity in Asia*. Promotional Brochure for Foreign Investors. Colombo.

_____. 1987a. *Labor Standards and Labor Relations in Sri Lanka's Export Processing Zones*. Promotional Brochure for Foreign Investors. Colombo.

_____. 1987b. *Projects Implemented Under the Purview of the Greater Colombo Economic Commission as of 1st January, 1987*. Promotional Brochure for Foreign Investors. Colombo.

Griffin, Keith. 1989. *Alternative Strategies for Economic Development*. New York: St. Martin's Press and OECD Development Centre.

Gunaratna, Malinga. 1988. *For a Sovereign State*. Ratmalana: Sarvodaya Publishing.

Gunaratna, Rohan. 1987. *War and Peace in Sri Lanka*. Kandy: Institute of Fundamental Studies.

_____. 1990. *Sri Lanka: A Lost Revolution?: The Inside Story of the JVP*. Kandy: Institute for Fundamental Studies.

_____. 1993. *Indian Intervention in Sri Lanka*. Colombo: South Asian Network for Conflict Research.

Gunaratne, Merril. 2001. *Dilemma of an Island*. Colombo: Vijitha Yapa Publications.

Gunasekera, H.M. 1977. 'Foreign Trade of Sri Lanka', In *Sri Lanka: A Survey*, Edited by K. M. de Silva. Honolulu: The University Press of Hawaii, 172-191.

Gunasinghe, Newton. 1984. 'The Open Economy and its Impact on Ethnic Relations in Sri Lanka', In *Sri Lanka: The Ethnic Conflict: Myths, Realities and Perspectives*, Edited by Committee for Rational Development. New Delhi: Navrang, 197-213.

Gunatilleke, Godfrey. 1983. 'University Education and Graduate Employment in Sri Lanka: The Social Economic Background', In *University Education and Graduate Employment in Sri Lanka*, Edited by B. C. Sanyal, et al. Paris and Colombo: UNESCO and the Marga Institute, 37-61.

Gunatilleke, Godfrey, Neelan Tiruchelvam and Radhika Coomaraswamy, Eds. 1983. *Ethical Dilemmas of Development in Asia*. Lexington: Lexington Books, D.C. Heath and Co.

Gunawardena, R.S. and M.D. Nelson. 1987. *Trade Activities in Kandy with Special Reference to Aspects of Ethnic Participation*. ICES Research Report. Kandy: International Centre for Ethnic Studies (ICES).

Gurr, Ted R. 1968. 'Psychological Factors in Civil Violence'. *World Politics* 20: 520-532.

_____. 1970. *Why Men Rebel.* Princeton: Princeton University Press.

Gurr, Ted R. and Barbara Harff. 1994. *Ethnic Conflict in World Politics.* Boulder: Westview Press.

Gurr, Ted R. and Mark Irving Lichbach. 1979. 'Forecasting Domestic Political Conflict', In *To Auger Well: Early Warning Indicators in World Politics*, Edited by J. D. Singer and M. Wallace. Beverly Hills: Sage Publications.

Gurr, Ted R. and Charles Ruttenberg. 1969. *Cross-national Studies of Civil Violence.* Washington DC: American University, Center for Research in Social Systems.

Halliday, F. 1971. 'The Ceylonese Insurrection'. *New Left Review* 69: 55-93.

Harvard Institute for International Development. 1983. *Final Report for Strengthening of the Developing Planning Project.* Submitted to the Deputy Director, Contracts and Procurement Branch, Technical Cooperation for Development (TCD). New York: United Nations.

Heinemann, Robert K. 1984. 'The World and the Other Power: Contrasting Paths to Deliverance in Japan', In *The World of Buddhism: Buddhist Monks and Nuns in Society and Culture*, Edited by H. Bechert and R. Gombrich. London: Thames and Hudson, 212-230.

Helliwell, John. 2002. *How's Life? Combining Individual and National Variables to Explain Subjective Well-Being.* Working Paper # 9065. Washington DC: National Bureau of Economic Research.

Hellman-Rajanayagam, D. 1986. 'The Tamil Tigers in Northern Sri Lanka: Origins, Factions, and Programmes'. *Internationales Asienforum* 17 (1/2): 63-85.

Hettiarachchi, W. 1985. 'Growth and Expansion of Banking', In *Facets of Development in Independent Sri Lanka: Felicitation Volume to Commemorate the 10th Successive Budget of Hon. Ronnie de Mel, Minister of Finance and Planning*, Edited by W. Rasaputra, et al. Colombo: Ministry of Finance and Planning, 133-164.

Hibbs, Douglas A., Jr. 1973. *Mass Political Violence: A Cross-National, Causal Analysis.* New York: Wiley.

Hicks, J.R. 1959. 'Reflections on the Economic Problems of Ceylon', In *Papers by Visiting Economists.* Colombo: Planning Secretariat, 7-22.

Hobsbawm, Eric. 1972. 'Some Reflections on Nationalism', In *Imagination and Precision in the Social Sciences*, Edited by T. J. Nossiter, et al. London: Faber, 385-406.

Hoole, Rajan. 2001. *The Arrogance of Power: Myths, Decadence, and Murder.* Colombo: University Teachers for Human Rights (Jaffna).

Hoole, Rajan, D. Somasundaram, K. Sritharan and R. Thiranagama. 1990. *The Broken Palmyra: The Tamil Crisis in Sri Lanka: An Inside Account.* Claremont: Sri Lanka Studies Institute.

Horowitz, Donald L. 1980. *Coup Theories and Officers' Motives: Sri Lanka in Comparative Perspective.* Princeton: Princeton University Press.

_____. 1985. *Ethnic Groups in Conflict*. Berkeley: University of California Press.

_____. 1989. *Incentives and Behavior in the Ethnic Politics of Sri Lanka and Malaysia*. Working Papers in Asian/Pacific Studies 89-01. Durham: Asian/Pacific Studies Institute, Duke University.

Hulugalle, H.A.J. 2000. *Don Stephen Senanayake: First Prime Minister of Sri Lanka*. 2nd ed. Colombo: Arjuna Hulugalle Dictionaries.

Huntington, Samuel P. 1996. *The Clash of Civilizations and the Remaking of World Order*. New York: Simon and Shuster.

International Labor Organization. 1974. *Matching Employment Opportunities and Expectations: A Program of Action for Ceylon*. Geneva: ILO.

International Monetary Fund. Various Years. *International Financial Statistical Yearbooks*. Washington DC.

Jain, M.P. 1979. 'Sri Lanka's New Constitution'. *Journal of Malaysian and Comparative Law* 6.

Jayamaha, Ranee. 1986. 'Changes in Monetary Policy', In *Facets of Development in Independent Sri Lanka: Felicitation Volume to Commemorate the 10th Successive Budget of Hon. Ronnie de Mel, Minister of Finance and Planning*, Edited by W. Rasaputra, et al. Colombo: Ministry of Finance and Planning, 109-132.

Jayasundera, P.B. 1986. 'Fiscal Policy in Sri Lanka Since Independence', In *Facets of Development in Independent Sri Lanka: Felicitation Volume to Commemorate the 10th Successive Budget of Hon. Ronnie de Mel, Minister of Finance and Planning*, Edited by W. Rasaputra, et al. Colombo: Ministry of Finance and Planning, 43-85.

Jayatilaka, Tissa, Ed. 2002. *Excursions and Explorations: Cultural Encounters Between Sri Lanka and the United States*. Colombo: United States-Sri Lanka Fulbright Commission.

Jayatilleka, Dayan. 1995. *Sri Lanka: The Travails of a Democracy, Unfinished War, Protracted Crisis*. New Delhi: International Centre for Ethnic Studies (ICES) and Vikas.

Jayawardene, Kumari. 1972. *The Rise of the Labour Movement in Ceylon*. Durham: Duke University Press.

_____. 1984. 'Ethnic Consciousness in Sri Lanka: Continuity and Change', In *Sri Lanka: The Ethnic Conflict: Myths, Realities and Perspectives*, Edited by Committee for Rational Development. New Delhi: Navrang, 115-173.

_____. 1985. *Ethnic and Class Conflicts in Sri Lanka: Some Aspects of Sinhala Buddhist Consciousness Over the Past 100 Years*. Dehiwala: Centre for Social Analysis.

Jayewardene, C. H. S. and H. Jayewardene. 1984. *Tea for Two: Ethnic Violence in Sri Lanka*. Ottawa: Crimcare.

Jayewardene, Jayantha. 1986. 'Some Aspects of Agricultural Production in Mahaweli Areas'. Presented at Sri Lanka Association for the Advancement of Science (SLAAS) Symposium on Mahaweli. Colombo, November 6-9.

_____. 1995. 'Management of the Accelerated Mahaweli Development Project', In *The Blurring of a Vision: The Mahaweli*, Edited by H. P. Muller and S. T. Hettige. Ratmalana: Sarvodaya Publishing, 224-268.

Jayewardene, J.R. 1982. *Buddhist Essays.* 5th ed. Colombo: Sri Lanka Government Press.

Jayewardene, J.R. 1986. 'Ex Tempore Remarks'. Presented at Second SAARC Summit. Bangalore, November 16.

Jeyaraj, D.B.S. 1987. 'An Overview of the Tamil Secessionist Movement of Sri Lanka (1976-1985)'. Presented at International Centre for Ethnic Studies (ICES) Conference on Ethnic Conflict. Colombo.

Jiggins, Janice. 1972. *Switching on to Growth.* Vol. 1, *Guides to Growth.* Colombo: T. Rajadurai.

_____. 1979. *Caste and Family in the Politics of the Sinhalese: 1947-1976.* Cambridge, UK: Cambridge University Press.

Jogarantham, T. 1995. 'The Accelerated Mahaweli Development Program: Its Implications for the Economy of Sri Lanka', In *The Blurring of a Vision: The Mahaweli,* Edited by H. P. Muller and S. T. Hettige. Ratmalana: Sarvodaya Publishing, 95-117.

Josey, Alex. 1980. *Lee Kuan Yew.* 2nd ed. Singapore: Times Books International.

Jubilee 2000/USA. 2003. *Jubilee 2000/USA: Part of a Worldwide Movement to Cancel the Crushing Debt of Impoverished Countries Before the New Millennium* 2000 [Cited October 5 2003]. Available: <http://www.j2000usa.org>.

Jupp, James. 1978. *Sri Lanka: Third World Democracy.* London: Frank Cass.

Kabir, Mohammed H. 1985. 'Crisis Management: A Case Study of Tamil Crisis in Sri Lanka'. *Regional Studies (Islamabad)* 4 (1): 83-103.

Kaldor, Nicholas. 1959. 'Observations on the Problem of Economic Development in Ceylon', In *Papers by Visiting Economists.* Colombo: Planning Secretariat, 23-34.

Kapferer, B. 1988. *Legends of People, Myths of State.* Washington DC and London: Smithsonian Institution Press.

Karunatilake, H.N.S. 1973. *Central Banking and Monetary Policy in Sri Lanka.* Colombo: Lake House Investments.

_____. 1987. *The Economy of Sri Lanka.* Colombo: Centre for Demographic and Socioeconomic Studies.

_____. 1988. *The Accelerated Mahaweli Program and its Impact.* Colombo: Centre for Demographic and Socio-Economic Studies.

Kearney, Robert N. 1967. *Communalism and Language in the Politics of Ceylon.* Durham: Duke University Press.

_____. 1971. *Trade Unions and Politics in Ceylon.* Berkeley: University of California Press.

_____. 1973. *The Politics of Ceylon (Sri Lanka).* Ithaca: Cornell University Press.

_____. 1979. 'Nationalism, Modernization and Political Mobilization in a Plural Society', In *Collective Identities, Nationalism and Protest in Modern Sri Lanka,* Edited by M. Roberts. Colombo: Marga Institute, 440-461.

_____. 1985. 'Ethnic Conflict and the Tamil Separatist Movement in Sri Lanka'. *Asian Survey* 25 (9): 898-917.

Kearney, Robert N. and Janice Jiggins. 1975. 'The Ceylon Insurrection of 1971'. *Journal of Commonwealth and Comparative Politics* 3: 40-63.

Kearney, Robert N. and Barbara D. Miller. 1983. 'The Spiral of Suicide and Social Change in Sri Lanka'. *Journal of Asian Studies* 44: 81-101.

Keen, David. 2000. 'Incentives and Disincentives for Violence', In *Greed and Grievance: Economic Agendas in Civil Wars*, Edited by M. Berdal and D. M. Malone. Boulder: Lynne Reinner Publishers, 19-42.

Keerawella, Gamini Bandara. 1989. *The Growth of Superpower Navy Rivalry in the Indian Ocean in and Sri Lankan Response.* Ottawa: National Library of Canada.

Kelegama, Saman. 1997. 'Privatisation: An Overview of the Process and Issues', In *Dilemmas of Development: Fifty Years of Economic Change in Sri Lanka*, Edited by W. D. Lakshman. Colombo: Sri Lanka Association of Economists, 456-496.

Kemeny, John. 1959. *A Philosopher Looks at Science.* Princeton: D. Van Nostrand.

Kemper, Steven. 1990. 'J.R. Jayewardene, Righteousness and Realpolitik', In *Sri Lanka: History and Roots of the Conflict*, Edited by J. Spencer. London and New York: Routledge, 187-204.

Kerbo, Harold R. 1982. 'Movements of 'Crisis' and Movements and Movements of 'Affluence': A Critique of Deprivation and Resource Mobilization Theories'. *Journal of Conflict Resolution* 26 (4).

King, Charles. 1997. *Ending Civil Wars.* Adelphi Paper #308. Oxford: Oxford University Press.

Kiribanda, B.M. 1997. 'Population and Employment', In *Dilemmas of Development: Fifty Years of Economic Change in Sri Lanka*, Edited by W. D. Lakshman. Colombo: Sri Lanka Association of Economists, 223-249.

Kodikara, Shelton U. 1982. *Foreign Policy of Sri Lanka: A Third World Perspective.* Delhi: Chanakya Publications.

_____, Ed. 1989a. *Indo-Sri Lanka Agreement of July 1987.* Colombo: International Relations Programme, University of Colombo.

_____. 1989b. 'The Indo-Sri Lanka Agreement of July 1987: Retrospect', In *Indo-Sri Lanka Agreement of July 1987*, Edited by S. U. Kodikara. Colombo: International Relations Programme, University of Colombo, 54-70.

_____, Ed. 1990. *South Asian Strategic Issues: Sri Lankan Perspectives.* New Delhi: Sage Publications.

_____, Ed. 1991a. *Dilemmas of Indo-Sri Lankan relations.* Colombo: Bandaranaike Centre for International Studies, S.W.R.D. Bandaranaike National Memorial Foundation.

_____. 1991b. 'Geostrategic Perspectives of Indo-Sri Lanka Relations', In *Dilemmas of Indo-Sri Lankan relations*, Edited by S. U. Kodikara. Colombo: Bandaranaike Centre for International Studies, S.W.R.D. Bandaranaike National Memorial Foundation, 5-32.

Korale, R.B.M. 1988. *A Statistical Overview of Employment and Unemployment Trends.* Colombo: Ministry of Finance and Planning.

Korten, David. 1999. *Getting to the 21st Century: Voluntary Action and the Global Agenda.* West Hartford: Kumarian Press.

Kotelawala, Sir John. 1956. *An Asian Prime Minister's Story.* London: G.G. Harrap.

Kuhn, Thomas. 1962. *The Structure of Scientific Revolutions.* Chicago: University of Chicago Press.

Kumarakulasingam, Naren. 2002. *Benefits of Conflict.* Unpublished Working Paper.

Kumarakulasingam, Naren and Burcu Akan. 1999. *Entangled Linkages: Development, Ethnicity and Political Violence.* Unpublished Working Paper.

Kusterer, Kenneth. 1998. 'On Democratisation: What is It? How is It Encouraged? How is Its Progress Measured?' In *Democratisation in South Asia: The First Fifty Years,* Edited by J. M. Richardson and S. W. R. d. A. Samarasinghe. Nedimala - Dehiwala: Sridevi Printers, Ltd. and the International Centre for Ethnic Studies (ICES), 27-42.

Kuznets, Simon. 1965. *Economic Growth and Structure: Selected Essays.* New York: Norton.

_____. 1971. *Economic Growth of Nations: Total Output and Production Structure.* Cambridge, MA: Belknap Press/ Harvard University Press.

Lakshman, W.D. 1986. 'State Policy in Sri Lanka and Its Economic Impact, 1970-85: Selected Themes with Special Reference to Distributive Implication of Policy'. *Upanathi* 1 (1): 5-36.

_____. 1993. 'The Gulf Crisis of 1990-91: Economic Impact and Policy Response in Sri Lanka', In *The Gulf Crisis and South Asia: Studies on the Economic Impact,* Edited by P. Wickramasekara. New Delhi: Asian Regional Team for Employment Promotion, United Nations Development Programme, 145-171.

_____, Ed. 1997a. *Dilemmas of Development: Fifty Years of Economic Change in Sri Lanka.* Colombo: Sri Lanka Association of Economists.

_____. 1997b. 'Dilemmas of Development: Introduction', In *Dilemmas of Development: Fifty Years of Economic Change in Sri Lanka,* Edited by W. D. Lakshman. Colombo: Sri Lanka Association of Economists, 1-27.

_____. 1997c. 'Income Distribution and Poverty', In *Dilemmas of Development: Fifty Years of Economic Change in Sri Lanka,* Edited by W. D. Lakshman. Colombo: Sri Lanka Association of Economists, 171-222.

Lal, Deepak and Sarath Rajapatirana. 1989. *Impediments to Trade Liberalization in Sri Lanka, Thames Essay No. 51.* London: Gower Publishing Co. for the Trade Policy Research Centre.

LaMotte, Etienne. 1984. 'The Buddha, His Teachings and His Sangha', In *The World of Buddhism: Buddhist Monks and Nuns in Society and Culture,* Edited by H. Bechert and R. Gombrich. London: Thames and Hudson, 41-58.

Lange, Oskar. 1959. 'The Tasks of Economic Planning in Ceylon', In *Papers by Visiting Economists.* Colombo: Planning Secretariat, 73-93.

Leary, Virginia. 1981. *Ethnic Conflict and Violence in Sri Lanka in July-August 1981 on Behalf of the International Commission of Jurists.* Colombo: Interbook, Inc.

Lee, E.L.H. 1977. 'Rural Poverty in Sri Lanka', In *Poverty and Landlessness in Rural Asia.* Geneva: International Labour Organization (ILO), 161-182.

Lee, James R. 1993. *Trade Information and Trade Development: Comparing Sri Lanka and Hong Kong.* Unpublished Paper.

Leitan, G. R. Tressie. 1990. *Political Integration Through Decentralization and Devolution of Power: The Sri Lankan Experience.* Colombo: Dept. of History and Political Science, University of Colombo.

_____. 1992. *Local Administration in Sri Lanka.* Unpublished Manuscript.

Lewis, Oscar. 1959. *Five Families: Mexican Case Studies in the Culture of Poverty.* New York: Basic Books.

_____. 1961. *The Children of Sanchez: Autobiography of a Mexican Family.* New York: Random House.

Licklider, Roy, Ed. 1993. *Stopping the Killing: How Civil Wars End.* New York and London: New York University Press.

Little, David. 1994. *Sri Lanka: The Invention of Enmity.* Washington DC: United States Institute of Peace (USIP) Press.

Liyanage, Sumanasiri. 1997. 'The State, State Capital and Capitalistic Development', In *Dilemmas of Development: Fifty Years of Economic Change in Sri Lanka,* Edited by W. D. Lakshman. Colombo: Sri Lanka Association of Economists, 423-455.

Loganathan, Ketheshwaran. 1996. *Sri Lanka: Lost Opportunities: Past Attempts at Resolving Ethnic Conflict, Studies in Conflict Formation & Resolution;.* Colombo: Centre for Policy Research and Analysis, Faculty of Law, University of Colombo.

Manor, James, Ed. 1984. *Sri Lanka in Change and Crisis.* London: Croom Helm.

_____. 1989. *The Expedient Utopian: Bandaranaike and Ceylon.* Cambridge, UK: Cambridge University Press.

Mathew, Cyril. 1979. *Diabolical Conspiracy.* Colombo: Karandeniye Vimalajoti.

_____. 1981. *Sinhala People: Awake, Arise and Safeguard Buddhism.* Colombo: Seruvila Pujanagara Samvardhana Samitiye Prakasanayaki.

McGranihan, Donald V. and Eduardo Pizarro. 1985. *Measurement and Analysis of Socioeconomic Development.* Geneva: UN Research Institute for Social Development (UNRISD).

Meadows, D.H. 1988. 'Quality of Life', In *Earth '88: Changing Geographic Perspectives.* Washington DC: National Geographic Society.

Meadows, D.H., D.L. Meadows, J. Randers and W.W. Behrens III. 1972. *The Limits to Growth: A Report for the Club of Rome's Project on the Predicament of Mankind.* Washington DC: Potomac Associates.

Meadows, D.H., D.L. Meadows and J. Randers. 1992. *Beyond the Limits: Confronting Global Collapse: Envisioning a Sustainable Future.* Post Mills: Chelsea Green.

Meadows, D. H., J.M. Richardson Jr. and Gerhart Bruckmann. 1982. *Groping in the Dark: The First Decade of Global Modeling.* Chichester: John Wiley and Sons.

Meadows, D. H. and J. Robinson. 1985. *The Electronic Oracle: Computer Models and Social Decisions*. Chichester: John Wiley & Sons.

Meadows, D.L., W.W. Behrens III, D.H. Meadows, Roger F. Naill, J. Randers and E.K.O. Zahn. 1974. *Dynamics of Growth in a Finite World*. Cambridge, MA: Wright Allen Press.

Mellor, J.W. and G.M. Desai. 1985. 'Agricultural Change and Rural Poverty: A Synthesis', In *Agricultural Change and Rural Poverty: Variations on a Theme by Dharm Narain*, Edited by J. W. Mellor and G. M. Desai. Baltimore: Johns Hopkins University Press.

Mendez, Ruben P. 2001. *United Nations Development Programme* Yale University, United Nations Studies, 2001 [Cited November 1 2001]. Available: <http://www.yale.edu/unsy/undphist.htm>.

Mendis, Patrick. 1992. *The Political Economy of Poverty Alleviation in Developing Countries: Is Sri Lanka Really an Exception?* Staff Paper P92-11. Minneapolis: University of Minnesota, Department of Agricultural and Applied Economics.

Merry, Douglas J., Ed. 1995. *Potential for Devolution of Management to Farmers' Organizations in an Hierarchical Management Agency: The Case of the Mahaweli Authority of Sri Lanka*. In *The Blurring of a Vision: The Mahaweli*. Edited by H. P. Muller and S. T. Hettige. Ratmalana: Sarvodaya Publishing.

Merton, Thomas. 1975. 'The Asian Journal of Thomas Merton', In *Images of Sri Lanka Through American Eyes: Travelers in Ceylon in the Nineteenth and Twentieth Centuries - A Select Anthology*, Edited by H. A. I. Goonetileke. Colombo: U.S. Information Service, 380-389.

Mesarovic, M.D. and Arnold Reisman. 1972. *Systems Approach and the City*. New York: American Elsevier.

Meyer, Eric. 1984. 'Seeking the Roots of the Tragedy', In *Sri Lanka in Change and Crisis*, Edited by J. Manor. London and Sydney: Croom Helm, 137-152.

Migdal, Joel S. 1988. *Strong Societies and Weak States*. Princeton: Princeton University Press.

Mittelman, James H. and Mustapha Kamal Pasha. 1997. *Out from Underdevelopment Revisited: Changing Global Structures and the Remaking of the Third World*. New York: St. Martin's Press.

Moore, Mick P. 1984. 'The 1982 Elections and the New Gaullist - Bonapartist State in Sri Lanka', In *Sri Lanka in Change and Crisis*, Edited by J. Manor. London: Croom Helm, 51-75.

_____. 1985. *The State and Peasant Politics in Sri Lanka*. Cambridge, UK: Cambridge University Press.

_____. 1990. *Economic Liberalisation, Growth and Poverty: Sri Lanka in Long Run Perspective*. IDS Discussion Paper #274. Sussex: Institute for Development Studies, University of Sussex.

_____. 1990. 'Sri Lanka: The Contradictions of the Social Democratic State', In *The Post-Colonial State in Asia: Dialectics of Politics and Culture*, Edited by S. K. Mitra. New York and London: Harvester/Wheatsheaf, 155-92.

_____. 1992. 'Retreat from Democracy in Sri Lanka'. *Journal of Commonwealth and Comparative Politics* 30 (1): 64-84.

_____. 1997. 'Leading the Left to the Right: Populist Coalitions and Economic Reform'. *World Development* 25 (7): 1009-1028.

Morris, Morris D. and Michelle B. McAlpine. 1982. *Measuring the Conditions of India's Poor*. New Delhi: Promilla.

Morris, Morris W. 1979. *Measuring the Condition of the World's Poor: The Physical Quality of Life Index*. New York: Pergamon Press for The Overseas Development Council.

Muller, Edward N. 1980. 'The Psychology of Political Protest and Violence', In *Handbook of Political Conflict*, Edited by T. R. Gurr. New York: Free Press, 69-99.

Muller, Edward N. 1985. 'Income Inequality, Regime Repressiveness and Political Violence'. *American Sociological Review* 50: 47-61.

Muller, H.P and S.T. Hettige, Eds. 1995. *The Blurring of a Vision: The Mahaweli*. Ratmalana: Sarvodaya Publishing.

Mwanasali, Musifiky. 2000. 'The View from Below', In *Greed and Grievance: Economic Agendas in Civil Wars*, Edited by M. Berdal and D. M. Malone. Boulder: Lynne Reinner Publishers, 137-153.

Nakamura, H., P. Ratnayake and S.M.P. Senananayake. 1997. 'Agricultural Development: Past Trends and Policies', In *Dilemmas of Development: Fifty Years of Economic Change in Sri Lanka*, Edited by W. D. Lakshman. Colombo: Sri Lanka Association of Economists, 250-292.

Namboodiri, Nibha, Ed. 1998. *Practical Elephant Management: A Handbook for Mahouts*. Peelamedu: Zoo Outreach Organisation-CBSG-India and the Elephant Welfare Association.

Nanus, Burt. 1992. *Visionary Leadership*. San Francisco: Jossey-Bass.

Naylor, G.W. 1966. *Report of the Reconnaissance Mission to Ceylon in Connection with State Industrial Corporations*. Colombo: Ministry of Planning and Economic Affairs.

Nelson, Joan M, et al. 1989. *Fragile Coalitions: The Politics of Economic Adjustment*. New Brunswick: Transaction Books.

Nicholas, C.W. 1955. 'The Irrigation Works of King Parakkamabahu I'. *The Ceylon Historical Journal* 4: 58-76.

Nissan, Elizabeth. 1984. 'Some Thoughts on Sinhalese Justifications for the Violence', In *Sri Lanka in Change and Crisis*, Edited by J. Manor. London: Croom Helm, 175-186.

Nissanka, H.S.S. 1984. *Sri Lanka's Foreign Policy: A Study in Non-Alignment*. New Delhi: Vikas Publishing House, Ltd.

Nordhaus, William D. 2002. 'The Economic Consequences of War with Iraq', In *War with Iraq: Costs, Consequences and Alternatives*, Edited by C. Kaysen, et al. Cambridge, MA: Committee on International Security Studies, American Academy of Arts and Sciences, 51-86.

Nyrop, Richard E., et al. 1971. *Area Handbook of Ceylon.* Washington DC: U.S. Government Printing Office for The American University, Foreign Area Studies Program.

Oberst, Robert C. 1985. *Legislatures and Representation in Sri Lanka: The Decentralization of Development Planning.* Boulder and London: Westview Press.

Obeyesekere, Gananath. 1974. 'Some Comments on the Social Backgrounds of the April 1971 Insurgency in Sri Lanka (Ceylon)'. *Journal of Asian Studies* 33 (3): 367-384.

_____. 1975. 'Sorcery, Premeditated Murder and the Canalization of Aggression in Sri Lanka'. *Ethnology* 14 (1): 1-23.

_____. 1984. 'Political Violence and the Future of Democracy in Sri Lanka', In *Sri Lanka: The Ethnic Conflict: Myths Realities and Perspectives,* Edited by Committee for Rational Development. New Delhi: Navrang, 70-94.

_____. 1984. 'The Origins and Institutionalization of Political Violence', In *Sri Lanka in Change and Crisis,* Edited by J. Manor. London: Croom Helm, 153-174.

Organization of Economic Cooperation and Development. 1976. *Measuring Social Well Being.* Paris: OECD.

Peebles, Patrick. 1982. *Sri Lanka: A Handbook of Historical Statistics.* Boston: G.K. Hall & Co.

_____. 1990. 'Colonization and Ethnic Conflict in the Dry Zone of Sri Lanka'. *Journal of Asian Studies* 49 (1): 30-55.

Peiris, G.H. 1989. *Reflections on Priorities of Settlement Development in the Dry Zone of Sri Lanka.* Working Paper. Colombo: Sri Lanka Foundation Institute, Four Decades of Independence Workshop.

_____. 1991. 'Changing Prospects of the Plantation Workers of Sri Lanka', In *Economic Dimensions of Ethnic Conflict,* Edited by S. W. R. d. A. Samarasinghe and R. Coughlin. London: St Martin's/ Pinter, 156-193.

_____. 1993a. 'Sri Lanka Problems of Governance: Government and Social Welfare', In *Sri Lanka: Problems of Governance,* Edited by K. M. d. Silva. Colombo: International Centre for Ethnic Studies (ICES), 192-218.

_____. 1993b. 'Sri Lanka Problems of Governance: Government Policy and Agriculture', In *Sri Lanka: Problems of Governance,* Edited by K. M. d. Silva. Colombo: International Centre for Ethnic Studies (ICES), 219-230.

_____. 1993c. 'Sri Lanka Problems of Governance: Government Intervention in Industrial Development', In *Sri Lanka: Problems of Governance,* Edited by K. M. de Silva. Colombo: International Centre for Ethnic Studies (ICES), 231-249.

_____. 1993d. 'Sri Lanka Problems of Governance: Economic Growth, Poverty and Political Unrest", In *Sri Lanka: Problems of Governance,* Edited by K. M. d. Silva. Colombo: International Centre for Ethnic Studies (ICES), 250-272.

Peiris, G.L. 1992. 'Reshaping our Country's Educational System: Some Perspectives'. Presented at Sri Lanka Association for the Advancement of Education. Colombo, July 25.

Pfaffenberger, Bryan. 1987. 'Sri Lanka in 1986? A Nation at Crossroads'. *Asian Survey* 27 (2): 155-162.

Philipupillai, Phillip and P. Wilson. 1983. 'The Graduate Employment Situation', In *University Education and Graduate Employment in Sri Lanka*, Edited by B. C. Sanyal, et al. Paris and Colombo: UNESCO and the Marga Institute, 178-195.

Pieris, M.P. 1997. 'Economic Growth and Structural - Institutional Change Since Independence', In *Dilemmas of Development: Fifty Years of Economic Change in Sri Lanka*, Edited by W. D. Lakshman. Colombo: Sri Lanka Association of Economists, 28-54.

Piyadasa, L. 1984. *Sri Lanka: The Holocaust and After*. London: Marram Books.

Ponnambalam, Satchi. 1983. *Sri Lanka: The National Question and the Tamil Liberation Struggle*. London: Zed Books.

Rabushka, Alvin T. 1981. 'Adam Smith in Sri Lanka'. *Policy Review* 18 (54): 54-62.

Rajapakse, Darshini Anna. 1995. 'Laws of Chaos: The Impact of Large-Scale Irrigation Systems on Inter and Intra Household Teneurial and Labour Relations', In *The Blurring of a Vision: The Mahaweli*, Edited by H. P. Muller and S. T. Hettige. Ratmalana: Sarvodaya Publishing, 270-300.

Rasaputra, Warnasena, W. M. Tilakaratna, S. T. G. Fernando and L. E. N. Fernando, Eds. 1986. *Facets of Development in Independent Sri Lanka: Felicitation Volume to Commemorate the 10th Successive Budget of Hon. Ronnie de Mel, Minister of Finance and Planning*. Colombo: Ministry of Finance and Planning.

Ratnapala, Nandasena. 1988. *The Police of Sri Lanka*. Chicago: Office of International Criminal Justice, University of Illinois at Chicago.

_____. 1989. *Rural Poverty in Sri Lanka*. Nugegoda: Deepanee.

Ratnatunga, Sinha. 1988. *The Politics of Terrorism: The Sri Lanka Experience*. Canberra: International Fellowship for Social and Economic Development.

_____. 1991. 'The Role of the Media in Indo-Sri Lankan Relations', In *Dilemmas of Indo-Sri Lankan Relations*, Edited by S. U. Kodikara. Colombo: Bandaranaike Centre for International Studies, S.W.R.D. Bandaranaike National Memorial Foundation, 201-227.

Redmond, Kent C. and Thomas M. Smith. 1980. *Project Whirlwind: The History of a Pioneer Computer*. Bedford: Digital Press.

Richardson, J.M. Jr. 1969. *Partners in Development*. East Lansing: Michigan State University Press.

_____. 1974. *Systems Engineering and Political Science: Toward Symbiosis*. Cleveland: Systems Research Center, Case Western Reserve University.

_____. 1980. *Towards Effective Foresight in the United States Government*. Unpublished Consultancy Report for the US Council on Environmental Quality.

_____, Ed. 1982. *Making It Happen: A Positive Guide to the Future*. Washington DC: US Association for the Club of Rome.

_____. 1987a. 'Explaining Political Violence: A Dynamic Modeling Approach', In *Contributions of Technology to International Conflict Resolution*, Edited by H. Chestnut and Y. Y. Haimes. London: Pergamon, 9-17.

_____. 1987b. 'Violence and Repression: Neglected Factors in Development Planning'. *Futures* 19 (6): 651-668.

_____. 1990. *Sri Lanka Political Conflict Data Base 1948-1988*. Unpublished Paper: Available from the Author.

_____. 1991. 'Understanding Violent Conflict in Sri Lanka: How Theory Can Help'. *Ethnic Studies Report*. 19 (1).

_____. 2002. 'Sri Lanka in 1988, Viewed Through American Eyes: Notes to Family and Friends', In *Excursions and Explorations: Cultural Encounters Between Sri Lanka and the United States*, Edited by T. Jayatilaka. Colombo: United States-Sri Lanka Fulbright Commission.

Richardson, J.M. Jr. and Eloise Forgette. 1976. 'Towards an Indicator System for the Relationship Between Population and Basic Human Needs'. Presented at Fourth International Institute for Applied Systems Analysis (IIASA) Symposium on Global Modeling. Laxenberg.

_____. 1979. 'The Satisfaction of Basic Needs Index: A Progress Report', In *Input-Output Approaches to Global Modeling: Proceedings of the Fifth ILASA Symposium on Global Modeling*, Edited by G. Bruckmann. London: Pergamon.

Richardson, J.M. Jr. and Kristine Herrmann. 1998. 'Democratisation in South Asia: Lessons and Prospects', In *Democratisation in South Asia: The First Fifty Years*, Edited by J. M. Richardson Jr. and S. W. R. d. A. Samarasinghe. Nedimala - Dehiwala: Sridevi Printers, Ltd. and the International Centre for Ethnic Studies (ICES), 305-344.

Richardson, J.M. Jr. and T. Pelsoci. 1972. 'A Multilevel Approach and the City: A Proposed Strategy for Research', In *Systems Approach and the City*, Edited by M. D. Mesarovic and A. Reisman. Amsterdam: North Holland, 97-129.

Richardson, J.M. Jr. and S.W.R. de A. Samarasinghe. 1991. 'Measuring the Economic Dimensions of Sri Lanka's Ethnic Conflict', In *Economic Dimensions of Ethnic Conflict*, Edited by S. W. R. d. A. Samarasinghe and R. Coughlin. London: St Martin's/ Pinter, 194-223.

Richardson, J.M. Jr. and Shinjnee Sen. 1997. 'Ethnic Conflict and Economic Development: A Policy Oriented Analysis'. *Ethnic Studies Report*. 15 (1).

Richardson, J.M. Jr. and Jianxin Wang. 1993. 'Ethnic Peace Accords and Ethnic Conflict Resolution: A Survey', In *Peace Accords and Ethnic Conflict*, Edited by K. M. de Silva and S. W. R. d. A. Samarasinghe. New York: St. Martin's Press.

Roberts, Michael. 1982. *Caste Conflict and Elite Formation: The Rise of A Karava Elite in Sri Lanka*. Colombo: Lake House.

_____. 1989. 'Tambiah or de Silva? Apocalypse or Accommodation? Two Contrasting Views of Sinhala-Tamil Relations in Sri Lanka'. *South Asia* 12: 67-83.

_____. 1994. *Exploring Confrontation: Sri Lanka - Politics, Culture and History*. Chur: Harwood Academic Publishers.

Roberts, Nancy, et al. 1982. *Introduction to Computer Simulation: The System Dynamics Approach.* Reading: Addison-Wesley.

Robinson, Joan. 1959. 'Economic Possibilities of Ceylon', In *Papers by Visiting Economists.* Colombo: Planning Secretariat, 35-72.

Rogers, J.D. 1987a. 'Social Mobility, Popular Ideology and Collective Violence in Modern Sri Lanka'. *Journal of Asian Studies* 46: 583-602.

_____. 1987b. *Crime, Justice and Society in Colonial Sri Lanka.* London: Curzon.

Ross, Lee Ann and Tilak Samaranayake. 1986. 'The Economic Impact of the Recent Ethnic Disturbances'. *Asian Survey* 26 (11): 1240-1255.

Ross, Russell R. and Andrea Matles-Savada. 1990. *Sri Lanka: A Country Study.* Washington DC: Library of Congress, Federal Research Division.

Rostow, W. W. 1960. *The Stages of Economic Growth, A Non-Communist Manifesto.* Cambridge, UK: Cambridge University Press.

Rubin, Barnett R. 1987. *Cycles of Violence: Human Rights in Sri Lanka Since the Indo-Sri Lanka Agreement.* Washington DC: Asia Watch.

Rummel, Rudolf J. 1963. *Dimensions of Conflict Behavior Within and Between Nations.* Evanston: Northwestern University.

_____. 1985. 'Libertarian Propositions on Violence Within and Between Nations: A Test Against Published Research Results'. *Journal of Conflict Resolution* 29 (2): 419-455.

Sabaratnam, T. 1990. *Out of Bondage: A Biography.* Colombo: Sri Lanka Indian Community Council.

'Samarakone, Priya' (Pseudonym). 1984. 'The Conduct of the Referendum', In *Sri Lanka in Change and Crisis*, Edited by J. Manor. London: Croom Helm, 84-117.

Samarasinghe, S.W.R. de A. 1981. 'Universal Franchise: Statistical Appendix', In *Universal Franchise: The Sri Lankan Experience 1931-1981*, Edited by K. M. de Silva. Colombo: Government Press, 198-236.

_____. 1988a. 'Economic Equity and Ethnic Conflict: A Case Study from Sri Lanka'. Presented at International Workshop on the Economic Dimensions of Ethnic Conflict. Kandy, July 13-15.

_____. 1988b. *Ethnic Conflict and Economic Development in Sri Lanka.* Unpublished Paper.

_____. 1988c. 'Sri Lanka: A Case Study from the Third World', In *Health, Nutrition and Economic Crises: Approaches to Policy in the Third World*, Edited by D. E. Bell and M. R. Reich. Dover: Auburn House, 39-79.

Samarasinghe, S.W.R. de A. and Reed Coughlin, Eds. 1991. *Economic Dimensions of Ethnic Conflict.* London: St Martin's/ Pinter.

Samarasinghe, Vidyamali. 1987. 'Ethno - Regionalism as a Basis for Geographical Separation in Sri Lanka'. Presented at International Workshop on Comparative Secessionist Movements. Colombo, July 1-3.

Samarasinghe, Vidyamali, et al. 1990. *Maternal Nutrition and Health Status of Indian Tamil Female Tea Plantation Workers in Sri Lanka*. Report #8. Washington DC: International Center for Research on Women.

Samarasinghe, Vidyamali and S.W.R. de A. Samarasinghe. 1993. *Historical Dictionary of Sri Lanka*. Metuchen and London: Scarecrow Press.

Sanyal, Bikas C., et al, Ed. 1983. *University Education and Graduate Employment in Sri Lanka*. Paris and Colombo: UNESCO and the Marga Institute.

Sanyal, Bikas C. 1983. 'Introduction', In *University Education and Graduate Employment in Sri Lanka*, Edited by B. C. Sanyal, et al. Paris and Colombo: UNESCO and the Marga Institute, 1-36.

Sanyal, Bikas C., W. Diyasena and Bertram Bastiampillai. 1983. 'Principal Findings and Implications for Planning', In *University Education and Graduate Employment in Sri Lanka*, Edited by B. C. Sanyal, et al. Paris and Colombo: UNESCO and the Marga Institute, 322-362.

Saravanamuttu, P. 1990. 'Instability in Sri Lanka'. *Survival* 32 (5): 455-468.

Sardeshpande, Lt. Gen. S.C. 1992. *Assignment Jaffna*. New Delhi: Lancer Publishers.

Savundranayagam, Terrence. 1986. 'Balance of Payments', In *Facets of Development in Independent Sri Lanka: Felicitation Volume to Commemorate the 10th Successive Budget of Hon. Ronnie de Mel, Minister of Finance and Planning*, Edited by W. Rasaputra, et al. Colombo: Ministry of Finance and Planning, 83-108.

Schalk, Peter. 1989. 'Unity and Sovereignty: Key Concepts of a Militant Buddhist Organization in the Present Conflict in Sri Lanka'. *Temenos* 24: 55-82.

Schwartz, Walter. 1979. *The Tamils of Sri Lanka*. Report #25. London: Minority Rights Group.

Scott, George M. 1989. 'The Economic Bases of Sinhalese-Muslim Ethno-Religious Conflicts in Twentieth Century Sri Lanka'. *Ethnic Studies Report* 7 (1): 21-35.

Scott, James C. 1972. 'Patron-Client Politics and Political Change in Southeast Asia'. *American Political Science Review* 66: 91-113.

Scudder, Thayer. 1995. 'Constraints to the Development of Settler Incomes and Production-Oriented Participatory Organizations in Large-Scale Government Sponsored Projects: The Mahaweli Case', In *The Blurring of a Vision: The Mahaweli*, Edited by H. P. Muller and S. T. Hettige. Ratmalana: Sarvodaya Publishing, 148-173.

Seligson, Michael T. and John T. Passé-Smith, Eds. 1998. *Development and Underdevelopment: The Political Economy of Global Inequality*. 2nd ed. Boulder: Lynne Reinner.

Sen, Amartya. 1999. *Development as Freedom*. New York: Anchor Books.

Sen Gupta, Bhababi, Ed. 1986. *Regional Cooperation and Development in South Asia*. Vol. 1-2. New Delhi: South Asian Publishers.

Seneviratne, Maureen. 1975. *Sirimavo Bandaranaike, the World's First Woman Prime Minister: A Biography*. Colombo: Hansa Publishers and Laklooms.

Senge, Peter M. 1990. *The Fifth Discipline: The Art and Practice of the Learning Organization*. New York: Doubleday/Currency.

Shastri, Amita. 1990. 'The Material Basis for Separatism: The Tamil Eelam Movement in Sri Lanka'. *Journal of Asian Studies* 49 (1): 56-77.

Shearer, David. 2000. 'Aiding or Abetting?: Humanitarian Aid and Its Economic Role in Civil War', In *Greed and Grievance: Economic Agendas in Civil Wars*, Edited by M. Berdal and D. M. Malone. Boulder: Lynne Reinner Publishers, 189-203.

Sieghart, Paul. 1984. *Sri Lanka: A Mounting Tragedy of Errors, Report of a Mission on Sri Lanka in January 1984 on Behalf of the International Commission on Jurists and its British Section, Justice*. Dorchester: Henry Ling, Ltd. and Dorset Press.

Simon, Herbert A. 1945. *Administrative Behavior*. New York: Macmillan.

_____. 1957. *Models of Man: Social and Rational. Mathematical Essays on Rational Human Behavior in Society Setting*. New York: Wiley.

_____. 1982. *Models of Bounded Rationality*. Cambridge, MA: MIT Press.

Simon, Julian L. 1981. *The Ultimate Resource*. Princeton: Princeton University Press.

Singer, Marshall R. 1964. *The Emerging Elite: A Study of Political Leadership in Ceylon*. Cambridge, MA: M. I. T. Press.

_____. 1989. *The Tamil-Sinhalese Ethnic Conflict in Sri Lanka: A Case Study in Efforts to Negotiate a Settlement, 1983-1988*. Case #416. Pew Program in Case Teaching and Writing in International Affairs.

_____. 1990. 'New Realities in Sri Lankan Politics'. *Asian Survey* 30 (4): 409-425.

Siriwardene, Reggie. 1989. 'Violence and Human Rights'. Presented at K. Kanthasamy Memorial Lecture. Colombo, June 19.

Sivanesan, C. 1985. *A Vision of Sri Lanka for the 21st Century*. Colombo: Self-Published.

Sivarajah, A. 1990. 'South Indian Cultural Nationalism and Separatism in Sri Lanka'. Presented at U.S. Institute of Peace (USIP) Conference. Washington DC, September 4-5.

_____. 1991. 'Indo Sri-Lanka Relations and Sri Lanka's Ethnic Crisis: The Tamil Nadu Factor', In *Dilemmas of Indo-Sri Lankan Relations*, Edited by S. U. Kodikara. Colombo: Bandaranaike Centre for International Studies, S.W.R.D. Bandaranaike National Memorial Foundation, 135-158.

Skocpol, Theda. 1979. *States and Social Revolutions: A Comparative Analysis of France, Russia and China*. Cambridge, UK: Cambridge University Press.

_____, Ed. 1994. *Social Revolutions in the Modern World*. Cambridge, UK: Cambridge University Press.

Snodgrass, Donald R. 1966. *Ceylon: An Export Economy in Transition*. Homewood: Richard D. Irwin.

Snyder, David and Charles Tilly. 1972. 'Hardship and Collective Violence in France, 1830 to 1960'. *American Sociological Review* 37.

Somasekaram, T., M.P. Perera, M.B.G. de Silva and H. Godellawatta, Eds. 1997. *Arjuna's Atlas of Sri Lanka*. Dehiwala: Arjuna Consulting Co. Ltd.

Sorbo, Gunnar M. 1987. *Sri Lanka Country Study and Norwegian Aid Review*. Bergen: Centre for Development Studies, University of Bergen.

Sorokin, Pitrim. 1937. *Social and Cultural Dynamics: Fluctuation of Social Relationships, War and Revolution*. Vol. 3. London: George Allen and Unwin Ltd.

South Asian Association for Regional Cooperation (SAARC). 1985. *Charter of the South Asian Association for Regional Cooperation*. New Delhi.

South Commission. 1990. *Challenge to the South*. New York: Oxford University Press.

Spaeth, Anthony. 1991. 'Inventing an Ethnic Rivalry: Sri Lanka's Civil War Has Political, Not Historical Roots'. *Harper's* (November): 67-78.

Spencer, Jonathan. 1984. 'Popular Perceptions of the Violence: A Provincial View', In *Sri Lanka in Change and Crisis*, Edited by J. Manor. London: Croom Helm, 187-195.

———, Ed. 1990a. *Sri Lanka: History and the Roots of Conflict*. London and New York: Routledge.

———. 1990b. *A Sinhala Village in a Time of Trouble: Politics and Change in Rural Sri Lanka*, Oxford University South Asian Studies Series. New Delhi: Oxford.

———. 1990c. 'Collective Violence and Everyday Practice in Sri Lanka'. *Modern Asian Studies* 24: 603-23.

Spengler, Oswald. 1929. *The Decline of the West*. Translated by C. F. Atkinson. New York: A.A. Knopf.

Sri Lankan Government. *From the island's 1948 independence until 1972, official reports referred to the 'Government of Ceylon'. For bibliographic consistency, however, all government reports are standardized here as 'Sri Lankan Government'.*

———. 1948. *Report of the Committee on the Organization, Staffing and Operation Methods of Government Departments*. Sessional Paper # 5. Colombo: Huxham Committee.

———. 1955. *Report of the Commission on Local Government*. Sessional Paper # 33. Colombo: Choksy Commission.

———. 1957. *Annual Report of the Director of Industries*. Colombo: Director of Industries.

———. 1958. *Administration Report of the Commissioner of Labour*. Colombo: Ministry of Labour.

———, Ed. 1959a. *Papers by Visiting Economists*. Colombo: Planning Secretariat.

———. 1959b. *Report of the Delimitation Commission*. Sessional Paper # 15. Colombo: Delimitation Commission.

———. 1961. *Parliaments of Sri Lanka, 1960*. Colombo: Lake House.

———. 1968. *Administration Report of the Inspector General of Police for the Financial Year 1966-67*. Colombo: Office of the Inspector General of Police.

_____. 1969. *Economic and Social Progress, 1965-1969: Budget Supplement*. Colombo: Ministry of Finance.

_____. 1971a. *The Economy of Ceylon: Trends and Prospects*. Colombo: Ministry of Finance.

_____. 1971b. *Five Year Plan: 1972-1976*. Colombo: Ministry of Planning and Employment.

_____. 1972. *Education in Sri Lanka: New Horizons*. Colombo: Ministry of Education.

_____. 1976. *Judgment of the Criminal Justice Commission: Insurgency*. Colombo: Criminal Justice Commission.

_____. 1979a. *Public Investment 1979-1984*. Colombo: National Planning Division, Ministry of Finance and Planning.

_____. 1979b. *Second Interim Report of the Special Presidential Commission of Inquiry*. Sessional Paper #6. Colombo.

_____. 1980. *Sri Lanka: Housing a Nation*. Colombo: Ministry of Local Government, Housing, Construction and Highways.

_____. 1982. *Interim Report of the Committee on Implementation of the Scheme of Development Councils*. Colombo.

_____. 1983a. *To Live in Dignity - Sri Lanka: Thirty-Five years of the Universal Declaration of Human Rights*. Washington DC: Embassy of Sri Lanka.

_____. 1983b. *Report of the Presidential Commission of Inquiry into the Incidents Which Took Place Within the Administrative District of Galle From 25 July, 1982*. Colombo: Commission of Inquiry.

_____. 1983c. *Sri Lanka Today: Who Wants a Separate State?* Overseas Information Series #9. Colombo: Department of Information, Ministry of State.

_____. 1983d. *Sri Lanka: Newest Growth Centre in Asia*. Colombo: Foreign Investment Advisory Committee.

_____. 1984. *Master Plan for the Rehabilitation of Persons Displaced in the Disturbances of July, 1983*. Colombo: Commissioner General of Essential Services.

_____. 1987a. *Indo-Sri Lanka Agreement to Establish Peace and Normalcy in Sri Lanka; Annexure to the Agreement; Letters of Mutual Understanding*. Colombo.

_____. 1987b. *Public Investment 1987-1991*. Colombo: National Planning Division, Ministry of Finance and Planning.

_____. 1987c. *Report on the First Referendum in Sri Lanka*. Sessional Paper # 2. Colombo.

_____. 1988a. *Poverty Alleviation Through People-Based Development: Final Report on An Action Programme*. Colombo: High Level Committee of Officials.

_____. 1988b. *Sri Lanka Socio-Economic Data, 1987*. Colombo: Statistics Department, Central Bank of Sri Lanka.

_____. 1990. *Report of the Presidential Commission on Youth*. Sessional Paper # I. Colombo: Presidential Commission on Youth.

____. 1992. *Sri Lanka: A Model for Physical Quality of Life of its People.* Colombo.

____. No Date Given. *Tamil Terrorists: A Record of Murder and Robbery.* Overseas Information Series #6. Colombo: Department of Information, Ministry of State.

____. No Date Given. *Non Alignment -- A Deliberate Choice: Text of Speeches by Mrs. Sirima R.D. Bandaranaike, Prime Minister of Sri Lanka.* Colombo: Government Department of Information.

____. Various Years. *Review of the Economy.* Colombo: Economics Department, Central Bank of Sri Lanka.

____. Various Years. *The State of the Economy.* Colombo: Economics Department, Central Bank of Sri Lanka.

____. Various Years. *Annual Reports.* Colombo: Economics Department, Central Bank of Sri Lanka.

____. Various Years. *Consumer Finances and Socio Economic Survey: Sri Lanka.* Colombo: Economics Department, Central Bank of Sri Lanka.

Srinivasan, T.N. and Pranab K. Bardhan, Eds. 1988. *Rural Poverty in South Asia.* New York: Columbia University Press.

Sterman, J.D. 2000. *Business Dynamics: Systems Thinking and Modeling for a Complex World.* Boston: Irwin McGraw Hill.

Stiglitz, Joseph. 1998. 'More Instruments and Broader Goals: Moving Toward the Post-Washington Consensus'. Presented at World Institute for Development Economics Research (WIDER) Annual Lecture. Helsinki, January 7.

Stirrat, R.L. 1984. 'The Riots and the Roman Catholic Church in Historical Perspective', In *Sri Lanka in Change and Crisis,* Edited by J. Manor. London: Croom Helm, 196-213.

Stone, Sir Richard and Lady Giovanna Stone. 1962. *National Income and Expenditure.* 6th ed. Chicago: Quadrangle Books.

Sundar, T.R. Shyam, Amali Philipupillai and P. Wilson. 1983. 'Survey Data Analysis - Undergraduates (Final Year)', In *University Education and Graduate Employment in Sri Lanka,* Edited by B. C. Sanyal, et al. Paris and Colombo: UNESCO and the Marga Institute, 196-244.

Swamy, Narayan. 1994. *Tigers of Lanka: From Boys to Guerrillas.* Delhi: Konark.

Tambiah, Stanley Jeyaraja. 1986. *Sri Lanka: Ethnic Fratricide and the Dismantling of Democracy.* Delhi: Oxford University Press.

____. 1989. 'Ethnic Conflict in the World Today'. *American Ethnologist* 16 (2): 335-349.

____. 1992. *Buddhism Betrayed?: Religion, Politics, and Violence in Sri Lanka.* Chicago: University of Chicago Press.

____. 1996. *Leveling Crowds: Ethnonationalist Conflicts and Collective Violence n South Asia.* Berkeley: University of California Press.

Taylor, Charles Lewis and David A. Jodice. 1986. World Handbook of Political and Social Indicators III: 1948-1982 2nd ICPSR (Computer File). Inter-university Consortium for Political and Social Research (Production and Distribution) and Virginia Polytechnic Institute and State University (Compilation), Ann Arbor.

The Hunger Project. 1985. *Ending Hunger: An Idea Whose Time Has Come.* New York: Praeger.

Tilly, Charles. 1978. *From Mobilization to Revolution.* New York: McGraw Hill.

Toynbee, Arnold J. 1935-1961. *A Study of History.* 2nd ed. Vol. 1-12. London: Oxford University Press.

Tuchman, B.W. 1984. *The March of Folly.* New York: Knopf.

United Nations Development Program (UNDP). 1990. *Human Development Report 1990.* New York: Oxford University Press.

_____. 2001. *Human Development Report 2001.* New York: Oxford University Press.

United Nations Development Program (UNDP), Food and Agriculture Organisation (FAO) and Sri Lankan Government. 1969. *Mahaweli, Ganga Irrigation and Hydro Power Survey: Ceylon.* Final Report, Volume 1. Colombo: Irrigation Department.

United Nations High Commission for Refugees (UNHCR). 2000. *Refugees and Others of Concern to UNHCR, 1999 Statistical Overview, Table I.1.* UNHCR, 2000 [Cited December 2000]. Available: <http://www.unhcr.ch/statist/99oview/tab101.pdf.>

University of Jaffna. 1987. *Faculty of Medicine Handbook 1986-1987.* Jaffna: University of Jaffna.

_____. 1988. *Faculty of Science Handbook 1987-1988.* Jaffna: University of Jaffna.

Uphoff, Norman, Milton J. Esman and Anirudh Krishna. 1998. *Reasons for Success: Learning from Instructive Experiences in Rural Development.* West Hartford: Kumarian Press.

US Council on Environmental Quality and US Department of State. 1980. *The Global 2000 Report to the President.* Volume 1. Washington DC.

Uyangoda, Jayadeva. 1994. 'The State and the Process of Devolution', In *Devolution and Development in Sri Lanka,* Edited by S. Bastian. Colombo and New Delhi: International Centre for Ethnic Studies (ICES) and Konark Publishers, 83-120.

Vamadevan, M. 1996. *National Language Policy in Sri Lanka.* Occasional Paper #6. Colombo: International Centre for Ethnic Studies (ICES).

Vidanapathirana, Upananda. 1986. 'Pattern of Industrialisation: Strategies and Responses', In *Facets of Development in Independent Sri Lanka: Felicitation Volume to Commemorate the 10th Successive Budget of Hon. Ronnie de Mel, Minister of Finance and Planning,* Edited by W. Rasaputra, et al. Colombo: Ministry of Finance and Planning, 165-193.

Vittachi, Tarzie. 1958. *Emergency '58: The Story of the Ceylon Race Riots.* London: Andre Deutsch.

Wade, Robert. 1990. *Governing the Market: Economic Theory and the Role of Government in East Asian Industrialization.* Princeton: Princeton University Press.

Wanigasundara, Mallika. 1985. 'Modern Sri Lanka: Economic and Political Success Stories of the 1980s', In *Sri Lanka: Insight Guide for the Sophisticated Traveler*, Edited by J. G. Anderson. Englewood Cliffs: Prentice Hall, 59-67.

Ward, Michael Don, Ed. 1985. *Theories, Models, and Simulations in International Relations: Essays in Honor of Harold Guetzkow*. Boulder: Westview Press.

Weaver, James H., Michael T. Rock and Kenneth Kusterer. 1997. *Achieving Broad-Based Sustainable Development: Governance, Environment and Growth with Equity*. West Hartford: Kumarian Press.

Weaver, Mary Anne. 1988. 'The Gods and the Stars'. *The New Yorker* (March 21): 39-83.

Weerakoon, Bradman. 1992. *Premadasa of Sri Lanka: A Political Biography*. New Delhi: Vikas.

Weerakoon, L.U. 1989. 'Water Management on the Mahaweli'. *Sri Lanka Economic Journal* 4 (2).

Weeramunda, A.J. and John Gottberg Anderson. 1985. 'Society and Religion', In *Sri Lanka: Insight Guide for the Sophisticated Traveler*, Edited by J. G. Anderson and R. Anthonis. Englewood Cliffs: Prentice Hall, 66-91.

Weerasekera, Y.M.W.B. 1996. 'Financial Outlay of the Mahaweli Project'. Presented at Sri Lanka Association for the Advancement of Science (SLAAS) Symposium on Mahaweli. Colombo, November 6-9.

Weiner, Myron, Samuel P. Huntington and Gabriel A. Almond. 1987. *Understanding Political Development: An Analytic Study*. Boston: Little Brown.

Wickremeratne, Ananda. 1995. *Buddhism and Ethnicity in Sri Lanka: A Historical Analysis*. New Delhi: Vikas and the International Centre for Ethnic Studies (ICES).

Wickremeratne, M.L.H. 1995. 'The Rationale of the Accelerated Mahaweli Programme', In *The Blurring of a Vision: The Mahaweli*, Edited by H. P. Muller and S. T. Hettige. Ratmalana: Sarvodaya Publishing, 24-70.

Wijemanna, E. L. and Bertram Bastiampillai. 1983. 'Employers Perception of the Employment Problems of Graduates', In *University Education and Graduate Employment in Sri Lanka*, Edited by B. C. Sanyal, et al. Paris and Colombo: UNESCO and the Marga Institute, 311-321.

Wijetunga, W. M. K. 1983. 'Development of University Education in Sri Lanka', In *University Education and Graduate Employment in Sri Lanka*, Edited by B. C. Sanyal, et al. Paris and Colombo: UNESCO and the Marga Institute, 112-148.

Wiles, Peter John de la Fosse. 1962. *The Political Economy of Communism*. Cambridge, MA: Harvard University Press.

Williamson, John. 1990. 'What Washington Means by Policy Reform', In *Latin American Adjustment: How Much Has Happened?*, Edited by J. Williamson. Washington DC: Institute for International Economics, 7-20.

Wilson, A. Jeyaratnam. 1974. *Politics in Sri Lanka*. London: Macmillan.

_____. 1975. Electoral Politics in an Emergent State: The Ceylon General Election of May 1970. London: Cambridge University Press.

_____. 1988. *The Break-up of Sri Lanka: the Sinhalese-Tamil Conflict.* Honolulu: University of Hawaii Press.

Wiswa Warnapala, W. A. and L. Dias Hewagama. 1983. *Recent Politics in Sri Lanka: The Presidential Election and the Referendum of 1982 - A Study of Electoral Practice and Behaviour in an Asian Democracy.* New Delhi: Navrang.

Woodward, Calvin. 1979. *The Growth of a Party System in Ceylon.* Providence: Brown University Press.

World Bank. 1991. *Managing Development: The Governance Dimension.* Washington DC: The World Bank.

_____. 1997. *World Development Report 1997: The State in a Changing World.* New York: Oxford University Press.

_____. 2000. *Entering the 21st Century: World Development Report 1999/2000.* New York: Oxford University Press.

World Commission on Environment and Development (Brundtland Commission). 1987. *Our Common Future.* Oxford: Oxford University Press.

Wriggins, W. Howard. 1960. *Ceylon: Dilemmas of a New Nation.* Princeton: Princeton University Press.

Wright, Austin Tappan. 1958. *Islandia.* New York: Rinehart.

Zafrullah, H. M. 1981. *Sri Lanka's Hybrid Presidential and Parliamentary System & the Separation of Powers Doctrine.* Kuala Lumpur: University of Malaya Press.

Zartman, I. William. 1993. 'The Unfinished Agenda: Negotiating Internal Conflicts', In *Stopping the Killing: How Civil Wars End,* Edited by R. Licklider. New York and London: New York University Press, 20-34.

Zurcher, Erik. 1984. 'Beyond the Jade Gate: Buddhism in China, Vietnam and Korea', In *The World of Buddhism: Buddhist Monks and Nuns in Society and Culture,* Edited by H. Bechert and R. Gombrich. London: Thames and Hudson, 193-211.

Index